Computer Vision and Applications

A Guide for Students and Practitioners

Computer Vision and Applications

A Guide for Students and Practitioners

Editors
Bernd Jähne

Interdisciplinary Center for Scientific Computing
University of Heidelberg, Heidelberg, Germany
and
Scripps Institution of Oceanography
University of California, San Diego

Horst Haußecker

Xerox Palo Alto Research Center

ACADEMIC PRESS

A Harcourt Science and
Technology Company

San Diego   San Francisco   New York   Boston
London   Sydney   Tokyo

This book is printed on acid-free paper. ∞
Copyright © 2000 by Academic Press.

ACADEMIC PRESS
A Harcourt Science and Technology Company
525 B Street, Suite 1900, San Diego, CA 92101-4495, USA
http://www.academicpress.com

Academic Press
24-28 Oval Road, London NW1 7DX, UK
http://www.hbuk.co.uk/ap/

Printed and bound by CPI Group (UK) Ltd, Croydon, CR0 4YY
Transferred to Digital Print 2011

Library of Congress Catalog Number: 99-68829

International Standard Book Number: 0-12-379777-2

Contents

II Signal Processing and Pattern Recognition

III Application Gallery

Preface

What this book is about

This book offers a fresh approach to computer vision. The whole vision process from image formation to measuring, recognition, or reacting is regarded as an integral process. Computer vision is understood as the host of techniques to acquire, process, analyze, and understand complex higher-dimensional data from our environment for scientific and technical exploration.

In this sense this book takes into account the interdisciplinary nature of computer vision with its links to virtually all natural sciences and attempts to bridge two important gaps. The first is between modern physical sciences and the many novel techniques to acquire images. The second is between basic research and applications. When a reader with a background in one of the fields related to computer vision feels he has learned something from one of the many other facets of computer vision, the book will have fulfilled its purpose.

This book comprises three parts. The first part, *Sensors and Imaging*, covers image formation and acquisition. The second part, *Signal Processing and Pattern Recognition*, focuses on processing of the spatial and spatiotemporal signals acquired by imaging sensors. The third part consists of an *Application Gallery*, which shows in a concise overview a wide range of application examples from both industry and science. This part illustrates how computer vision is integrated into a variety of systems and applications.

Computer Vision and Applications was designed as a concise edition of the three-volume handbook:

Handbook of Computer Vision and Applications
edited by B. Jähne, H. Haußecker, and P. Geißler
Vol 1: Sensors and Imaging;
Vol 2: Signal Processing and Pattern Recognition;
Vol 3: Systems and Applications
Academic Press, 1999

It condenses the content of the handbook into one single volume and contains a selection of shortened versions of the most important contributions of the full edition. Although it cannot detail every single technique, this book still covers the entire spectrum of computer vision ranging from the imaging process to high-end algorithms and applications. Students in particular can benefit from the concise overview of the field of computer vision. It is perfectly suited for sequential reading into the subject and it is complemented by the more detailed *Handbook of Computer Vision and Applications*. The reader will find references to the full edition of the handbook whenever applicable. In order to simplify notation we refer to supplementary information in the handbook by the abbreviations [CVA1, Chapter N], [CVA2, Chapter N], and [CVA3, Chapter N] for the Nth chapter in the first, second and third volume, respectively. Similarly, direct references to individual sections in the handbook are given by [CVA1, Section N], [CVA2, Section N], and [CVA3, Section N] for section number N.

Prerequisites

It is assumed that the reader is familiar with elementary mathematical concepts commonly used in computer vision and in many other areas of natural sciences and technical disciplines. This includes the basics of set theory, matrix algebra, differential and integral equations, complex numbers, Fourier transform, probability, random variables, and graph theory. Wherever possible, mathematical topics are described intuitively. In this respect it is very helpful that complex mathematical relations can often be visualized intuitively by images. For a more formal treatment of the corresponding subject including proofs, suitable references are given.

How to use this book

The book has been designed to cover the different needs of its readership. First, it is suitable for *sequential reading.* In this way the reader gets an up-to-date account of the state of computer vision. It is presented in a way that makes it accessible for readers with different backgrounds. Second, the reader can look up specific topics of interest. The individual chapters are written in a self-consistent way with extensive cross-referencing to other chapters of the book and external references. Additionally, a detailed glossary allows to easily access the most important topics independently of individual chapters. The CD that accompanies this book contains the complete text of the book in the Adobe Acrobat portable document file format (PDF). This format can be read on all major platforms. Free Acrobat™ Reader version 4.0

for all major computing platforms is included on the CDs. The texts are hyperlinked in multiple ways. Thus the reader can collect the information of interest with ease. Third, the reader can delve more deeply into a subject with the material on the CDs. They contain additional reference material, interactive software components, code examples, image material, and references to sources on the Internet. For more details see the readme file on the CDs.

Acknowledgments

Writing a book on computer vision with this breadth of topics is a major undertaking that can succeed only in a coordinated effort that involves many co-workers. Thus the editors would like to thank first all contributors who were willing to participate in this effort. Their cooperation with the constrained time schedule made it possible that this concise edition of the *Handbook of Computer Vision and Applications* could be published in such a short period following the release of the handbook in May 1999. The editors are deeply grateful for the dedicated and professional work of the staff at AEON Verlag & Studio who did most of the editorial work. We also express our sincere thanks to Academic Press for the opportunity to write this book and for all professional advice.

Last but not least, we encourage the reader to send us any hints on errors, omissions, typing errors, or any other shortcomings of the book. Actual information about the book can be found at the editors homepage http://klimt.iwr.uni-heidelberg.de.

Heidelberg, Germany, and Palo Alto, California
Bernd Jähne, Horst Haußecker

Contributors

Prof. Dr. John L. Barron
Dept. of Computer Science, Middlesex College
The University of Western Ontario, London, Ontario, N6A 5B7, Canada
barron@csd.uwo.ca

Horst A. Beyer
Imetric SA, Technopole, CH-2900 Porrentry, Switzerland
imetric@dial.eunet.ch, http://www.imetric.com

Dr. Harald Bornfleth
Institut für Angewandte Physik, Universität Heidelberg
Albert-Überle-Str. 3-5, D-69120 Heidelberg, Germany
Harald.Bornfleth@iwr.uni-heidelberg.de
http://www.aphys.uni-heidelberg.de/AG_Cremer/

David Cheng
Dept. of Computer Science, Middlesex College
The University of Western Ontario, London, Ontario, N6A 5B7, Canada
cheng@csd.uwo.ca

Prof. Dr. Christoph Cremer
Institut für Angewandte Physik, Universität Heidelberg
Albert-Überle-Str. 3-5, D-69120 Heidelberg, Germany
cremer@popeye.aphys2.uni-heidelberg.de
http://www.aphys.uni-heidelberg.de/AG_Cremer/

Tobias Dierig
Forschungsgruppe Bildverarbeitung, IWR, Universität Heidelberg
Im Neuenheimer Feld 368, D-69120 Heidelberg
Tobias Dierig@iwr.uni-heidelberg.de
http://klimt.iwr.uni-heidelberg.de

Stefan Dauwe
Botanisches Institut, Universität Heidelberg
Im Neuenheimer Feld 360, D-69120 Heidelberg, Germany

Peter U. Edelmann
Institut für Angewandte Physik, Universität Heidelberg
Albert-Überle-Str. 3-5, D-69120 Heidelberg, Germany
edelmann@popeye.aphys2.uni-heidelberg.de
http://www.aphys.uni-heidelberg.de/AG_Cremer/edelmann

Sven Eichkorn
Max-Planck-Institut für Kernphysik, Abteilung Atmosphärenphysik

Saupfercheckweg 1, D-69117 Heidelberg, Germany
Sven.Eichkorn@mpi-hd.mpg.de

Dirk Engelmann
Forschungsgruppe Bildverarbeitung, IWR, Universität Heidelberg
Im Neuenheimer Feld 368, D-69120 Heidelberg
Dirk.Engelmann@iwr.uni-heidelberg.de
http://klimt.iwr.uni-heidelberg.de/~dengel

Prof. Dr. Rainer H. A. Fink
II. Physiologisches Institut, Universität Heidelberg
Im Neuenheimer Feld 326, D-69120 Heidelberg, Germany
fink@novsrv1.piol.uni-heidelberg.de

Dr. Robert Frischholz
DCS AG, Wetterkreuz 19a, D-91058 Erlangen, Germany
frz@dcs.de, http://www.bioid.com

Christoph Garbe
Forschungsgruppe Bildverarbeitung, IWR, Universität Heidelberg
Im Neuenheimer Feld 368, D-69120 Heidelberg
Christoph.Garbe@iwr.uni-heidelberg.de
http://klimt.iwr.uni-heidelberg.de

Dr. Peter Geißler
ARRI, Abteilung TFE, Türkenstraße 95, D-80799 München
pgeiss@hotmail.com
http://klimt.iwr.uni-heidelberg.de

Dipl.-Ing. Robert Godding
AICON GmbH, Celler Straße 32, D-38114 Braunschweig, Germany
robert.godding@aicon.de, http://www.aicon.de

Matthias Graf
Institut für Kunststoffprüfung und Kunststoffkunde
(IKP), Pfaffenwaldring 32, D-70569 Stuttgart, Germany
graf@ikp.uni-stuttgart.de, Matthias.Graf@t-online.de
http://www.ikp.uni-stuttgart.de

Hermann Gröning
Forschungsgruppe Bildverarbeitung, IWR, Universität Heidelberg
Im Neuenheimer Feld 360, D-69120 Heidelberg, Germany
Hermann.Groening@iwr.uni-heidelberg.de
http://klimt.iwr.uni-heidelberg.de

David Hansel
FORWISS, Bayerisches Forschungszentrum für Wissensbasierte Systeme
Forschungsgruppe Kognitive Systeme, Orleansstr. 34, 81667 München
http://www.forwiss.de/

Prof. Dr. Gerd Häusler
Chair for Optics, Universität Erlangen-Nürnberg
Staudtstraße 7/B2, D-91056 Erlangen, Germany
haeusler@physik.uni-erlangen.de
http://www.physik.uni-erlangen.de/optik/haeusler

Dr. Horst Haußecker
  Xerox Palo Alto Research Center (PARC)
  3333 Coyote Hill Road, Palo Alto, CA 94304
  hhaussec@parc.xerox.com, http://www.parc.xerox.com

Dr. Frank Hering
  SAP AG, Neurottstraße 16, D-69190 Walldorf, Germany
  frank.hering@sap.com

Dipl.-Inform. Thorsten Hermes
  Center for Computing Technology, Image Processing Department
  University of Bremen, P.O. Box 33 0440, D-28334 Bremen, Germany
  hermes@tzi.org, http://www.tzi.org/~hermes

Prof. Dr. Otthein Herzog
  Center for Computing Technology, Image Processing Department
  University of Bremen, P.O. Box 33 0440, D-28334 Bremen, Germany
  herzog@tzi.org, http://www.tzi.org/~herzog

Dr. Joachim Hornegger
  Lehrstuhl für Mustererkennung (Informatik 5)
  Universität Erlangen-Nürnberg, Martensstraße 3, 91058 Erlangen, Germany
  hornegger@informatik.uni-erlangen.de
  http://www5.informatik.uni-erlangen.de

Prof. Dr. Bernd Jähne
  Forschungsgruppe Bildverarbeitung, IWR, Universität Heidelberg
  Im Neuenheimer Feld 368, D-69120 Heidelberg
  Bernd.Jaehne@iwr.uni-heidelberg.de
  http://klimt.iwr.uni-heidelberg.de

Dr. Paul Joe
  King City Radar Station, Atmospheric Environmental Services
  4905 Dufferin St., Toronto, Ontario M3H 5T4, Canada
  joep@aestor.dots.doe.ca

Stefan Karbacher
  Chair for Optics, Universität Erlangen-Nürnberg
  Staudtstraße 7/B2, D-91056 Erlangen, Germany
  sbk@physik.uni-erlangen.de, http://www.physik.uni-erlangen.de

Prof. Dr.-Ing. Reinhard Koch
  Institut für Informatik und Praktische Mathematik
  Christian-Albrechts-Universität Kiel, Olshausenstr. 40, D 24098 Kiel, Germany
  rk@is.informatik.uni-kiel.de

Bernd Kümmerlen
  Botanisches Institut, Universität Heidelberg
  Im Neuenheimer Feld 360, D-69120 Heidelberg, Germany

Dr. Carsten Leue
  Institut für Umweltphysik, Universität Heidelberg
  Im Neuenheimer Feld 229, D-69120 Heidelberg, Germany
  Carsten.Leue@iwr.uni-heidelberg.de

Ulrike Lode
  Institut für Umweltphysik, Universität Heidelberg

Im Neuenheimer Feld 229, D-69120 Heidelberg, Germany
http://klimt.iwr.uni-heidelberg.de

Prof. Dr.-Ing. Hans-Gerd Maas
Institute for Photogrammetry and Remote Sensing
Technical University Dresden, D-01062 Dresden, Germany
maas@rcs.urz.tu-dresden.de

Prof. Dr.-Ing. Reinhard Malz
Fachhochschule Esslingen, Fachbereich Informationstechnik
Flandernstr. 101, D-73732 Esslingen
reinhard.malz@fht-esslingen.de

Dr. Hanspeter A. Mallot
Max-Planck-Institut für biologische Kybernetik
Spemannstr. 38, 72076 Tübingen, Germany
Hanspeter.Mallot@tuebingen.mpg.de
http://www.kyb.tuebingen.mpg.de/bu/

Prof. Robert E. Mercer
Dept. of Computer Science, Middlesex College
The University of Western Ontario, London, Ontario, N6A 5B7, Canada
mercer@csd.uwo.ca

Dr. Anke Meyer-Bäse
Dept. of Electrical Engineering and Computer Science
University of Florida, 454 New Engineering Building 33, Center Drive
PO Box 116130, Gainesville, FL 32611-6130, U.S.
anke@alpha.ee.ufl.edu

Bernhard Minge
VITRONIC Dr.-Ing. Stein Bildverarbeitungssysteme GmbH
Hasengartenstrasse 14a, D-65189 Wiesbaden, Germany
bm@vitronic.de, http://www.vitronic.de

Dr. Olaf Munkelt
FORWISS, Bayerisches Forschungszentrum für Wissensbasierte Systeme
Forschungsgruppe Kognitive Systeme, Orleansstr. 34, 81667 München
munkelt@forwiss.de, http://www.forwiss.de/˜munkelt

Dr. Thomas Münsterer
VITRONIC Dr.-Ing. Stein Bildverarbeitungssysteme GmbH
Hasengartenstr. 14a, D-65189 Wiesbaden, Germany
Phone: +49-611-7152-38, tm@vitronic.de

Prof. Dr.-Ing. Heinrich Niemann
Lehrstuhl für Mustererkennung (Informatik 5)
Universität Erlangen-Nürnberg, Martensstraße 3, 91058 Erlangen, Germany
niemann@informatik.uni-erlangen.de
http://www5.informatik.uni-erlangen.de

Dr. Dietrich Paulus
Lehrstuhl für Mustererkennung (Informatik 5)
Universität Erlangen-Nürnberg, Martensstraße 3, 91058 Erlangen, Germany
paulus@informatik.uni-erlangen.de
http://www5.informatik.uni-erlangen.de

Dipl.-Math. Peter Plankensteiner
Intego Plankensteiner Wagner Gbr
Am Weichselgarten 7, D-91058 Erlangen
ppl@intego.de

Prof. Dr. Ulrich Platt
Institut für Umweltphysik, Universität Heidelberg
Im Neuenheimer Feld 229, D-69120 Heidelberg, Germany
pl@uphys1.uphys.uni-heidelberg.de
http://www.iup.uni-heidelberg.de/urmel/atmos.html

Dr. Marc Pollefeys
Katholieke Universiteit Leuven, ESAT-PSI/VISICS
Kardinaal Mercierlaan 94, B-3001 Heverlee, Belgium
Marc.Pollefeys@esat.kuleuven.ac.be
http://www.esat.kuleuven.ac.be/~pollefey/

Christof Ridder
FORWISS, Bayerisches Forschungszentrum für Wissensbasierte Systeme
Forschungsgruppe Kognitive Systeme, Orleansstr. 34, 81667 München
ridder@forwiss.de, http://www.forwiss.de/~ridder

Dr. Torsten Scheuermann
Fraunhofer USA, Headquarters
24 Frank Lloyd Wright Drive, Ann Arbor, MI 48106-0335, U.S.
tscheuermann@fraunhofer.org, http://www.fraunhofer.org

Uwe Schimpf
Forschungsgruppe Bildverarbeitung, IWR, Universität Heidelberg
Im Neuenheimer Feld 360, D-69120 Heidelberg, Germany
Uwe.Schimpf@iwr.uni-heidelberg.de
http://klimt.iwr.uni-heidelberg.de

Dr. Dominik Schmundt
Forschungsgruppe Bildverarbeitung, IWR, Universität Heidelberg
Im Neuenheimer Feld 360, D-69120 Heidelberg, Germany
Dominik.Schmundt@iwr.uni-heidelberg.de
http://klimt.iwr.uni-heidelberg.de/~dschmun/

Prof. Dr. Christoph Schnörr
Dept. of Math. & Computer Science, University of Mannheim
D-68131 Mannheim, Germany
schnoerr@ti.uni-mannheim.de, http://www.ti.uni-mannheim.de

Dr. Thomas Scholz
SAP AG, Neurottstraße 16, D-69190 Walldorf, Germany
thomas.scholz@sap.com

Dr. Ulrich Schurr
Botanisches Institut, Universität Heidelberg
Im Neuenheimer Feld 360, D-69120 Heidelberg, Germany
uschurr@botanik1.bot.uni-heidelberg.de
http://klimt.iwr.uni-heidelberg.de/PublicFG/index.html

Prof. Dr. Rudolf Schwarte
Institut für Nachrichtenverarbeitung (INV)
Universität-GH Siegen, Hölderlinstr. 3, D-57068 Siegen, Germany
schwarte@nv.et-inf.uni-siegen.de
http://www.nv.et-inf.uni-siegen.de/inv/inv.html

Prof. Dr. Peter Seitz
Centre Suisse d'Electronique et de Microtechnique SA (CSEM)
Badenerstrasse 569, CH-8048 Zurich, Switzerland
peter.seitz@csem.ch, http://www.csem.ch/

Prof. Dr. Pierre Soille
Silsoe Research Institute, Wrest Park
Silsoe, Bedfordshire, MK45 4HS, United Kingdom
Pierre.Soille@bbsrc.ac.uk, http://www.bbsrc.ac.uk/

Hagen Spies
Forschungsgruppe Bildverarbeitung, IWR, Universität Heidelberg
Im Neuenheimer Feld 368, D-69120 Heidelberg
Hagen.Spies@iwr.uni-heidelberg.de
http://klimt.iwr.uni-heidelberg.de

Dr.-Ing. Norbert Stein
VITRONIC Dr.-Ing. Stein Bildverarbeitungssysteme GmbH
Hasengartenstrasse 14a, D-65189 Wiesbaden, Germany
st@vitronic.de, http://www.vitronic.de

Michael Stöhr
Forschungsgruppe Bildverarbeitung, IWR, Universität Heidelberg
Im Neuenheimer Feld 368, D-69120 Heidelberg
Michael.Stoehr@iwr.uni-heidelberg.de
http://klimt.iwr.uni-heidelberg.de

Hamid R. Tizhoosh
Universität Magdeburg (IPE)
P.O. Box 4120, D-39016 Magdeburg, Germany
tizhoosh@ipe.et.uni-magdeburg.de
http://pmt05.et.uni-magdeburg.de/~hamid/

Dr. Dietmar Uttenweiler
II. Physiologisches Institut, Universität Heidelberg
Im Neuenheimer Feld 326, D-69120 Heidelberg, Germany
dietmar.uttenweiler@urz.uni-heidelberg.de

Prof. Dr. Luc Van Gool
Katholieke Universiteit Leuven, ESAT-PSI/VISICS
Kardinaal Mercierlaan 94, B-3001 Heverlee, Belgium
luc.vangool@esat.kuleuven.ac.be
http://www.esat.kuleuven.ac.be/psi/visics.html

Dr. Thomas Wagner
Intego Plankensteiner Wagner Gbr
Am Weichselgarten 7, D-91058 Erlangen
wag@intego.de

Dr. Joachim Weickert
Dept. of Math. & Computer Science, University of Mannheim
D-68131 Mannheim, Germany
Joachim.Weickert@ti.uni-mannheim.de
http://www.ti.uni-mannheim.de

Mark O. Wenig
Institut für Umweltphysik, Universität Heidelberg
Im Neuenheimer Feld 229, D-69120 Heidelberg, Germany
Mark.Wenig@iwr.uni-heidelberg.de
http://klimt.iwr.uni-heidelberg.de/~mwenig

Georg Wiora
DaimlerChrysler AG, Research and Development
Wilhelm-Runge-Str. 11, D-89081 Ulm, Germany
georg.wiora@DaimlerChrysler.com

Dr. Christian Wolf
Max-Planck Institut für Astronomie
Königstuhl 17, D-69117 Heidelberg
cwolf@mpia-hd.mpg.de
http://www.mpia-hd.mpg.de

1 Introduction

Bernd Jähne

Interdisziplinäres Zentrum für Wissenschaftliches Rechnen (IWR)
Universität Heidelberg, Germany

1.1 Components of a vision system

Computer vision is a complex subject. As such it is helpful to divide it into its various components or function modules. On this level, it is also much easier to compare a technical system with a biological system. In this sense, the basic common functionality of biological and machine vision includes the following components (see also Table 1.1):

Radiation source. If no radiation is emitted from the scene or the object of interest, nothing can be observed or processed. Thus appropriate illumination is necessary for objects that are themselves not radiant.

Camera. The "camera" collects the radiation received from the object in such a way that the radiation's origins can be pinpointed. In the simplest case this is just an optical lens. But it could also be a completely different system, for example, an imaging optical spectrometer, an x-ray tomograph, or a microwave dish.

Sensor. The sensor converts the received radiative flux density into a suitable signal for further processing. For an imaging system normally a 2-D array of sensors is required to capture the spatial distribution of the radiation. With an appropriate scanning system in some cases a single sensor or a row of sensors could be sufficient.

Computer Vision and Applications

Table 1.1: Function modules of human and machine vision

Task	Human vision	Machine vision
Visualization	Passive, mainly by reflection of light from opaque surfaces	Passive and active (controlled illumination) using electromagnetic, particulate, and acoustic radiation
Image formation	Refractive optical system	Various systems
Control of irradiance	Muscle-controlled pupil	Motorized apertures, filter wheels, tunable filters
Focusing	Muscle-controlled change of focal length	Autofocus systems based on various principles of distance measurements
Irradiance resolution	Logarithmic sensitivity	Linear sensitivity, quantization between 8- and 16-bits; logarithmic sensitivity
Tracking	Highly mobile eyeball	Scanner and robot-mounted cameras
Processing and analysis	Hierarchically organized massively parallel processing	Serial processing still dominant; parallel processing not in general use

Processing unit. It processes the incoming, generally higher-dimensional data, extracting suitable features that can be used to measure object properties and categorize them into classes. Another important component is a memory system to collect and store knowledge about the scene, including mechanisms to delete unimportant things.

Actors. Actors react to the result of the visual observation. They become an integral part of the vision system when the vision system is actively responding to the observation by, for example, *tracking* an object of interest or by using a vision-guided navigation (*active vision, perception action cycle*).

1.2 Imaging systems

Imaging systems cover all processes involved in the formation of an image from objects and the sensors that convert radiation into electric signals, and further into digital signals that can be processed by a computer. Generally the goal is to attain a signal from an object in such a form that we know where it is (geometry), and what it is or what properties it has.

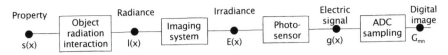

Figure 1.1: *Chain of steps linking an object property to the signal measured by an imaging system.*

It is important to note that the type of answer we receive from these two implicit questions depends on the purpose of the vision system. The answer could be of either a qualitative or a quantitative nature. For some applications it could be sufficient to obtain a qualitative answer like "there is a car on the left coming towards you." The "what" and "where" questions can thus cover the entire range from "there is something," a specification of the object in the form of a class, to a detailed quantitative description of various properties of the objects of interest.

The relation that links the object property to the signal measured by an imaging system is a complex chain of processes (Fig. 1.1). Interaction of the radiation with the object (possibly using an appropriate illumination system) causes the object to emit radiation. A portion (usually only a very small part) of the emitted radiative energy is collected by the optical system and perceived as an *irradiance* (radiative energy/area). A sensor (or rather an array of sensors) converts the received radiation into an electrical signal that is subsequently sampled and digitized to form a digital image as an array of digital numbers.

Only *direct imaging* systems provide a direct point-to-point correspondence between points of the objects in the 3-D world and at the image plane. *Indirect imaging* systems also give a spatially distributed irradiance but with no such one-to-one relation. Generation of an image requires reconstruction of the object from the perceived irradiance. Examples of such imaging techniques include radar imaging, various techniques for spectral imaging, acoustic imaging, tomographic imaging, and magnetic resonance imaging.

1.3 Signal processing for computer vision

One-dimensional *linear signal processing* and *system theory* is a standard topic in electrical engineering and is covered by many standard textbooks (e.g., [1, 2]). There is a clear trend that the classical signal processing community is moving into multidimensional signals, as indicated, for example, by the new annual international IEEE conference on image processing (ICIP). This can also be seen from some recently published handbooks on this subject. The digital signal processing handbook by Madisetti and Williams [3] includes several chapters that deal with image processing. Likewise the transforms and applications handbook by Poularikas [4] is not restricted to 1-D transforms.

There are, however, only a few monographs that treat signal processing specifically for computer vision and image processing. The monograph by Lim [5] deals with 2-D signal and image processing and tries to transfer the classical techniques for the analysis of time series to 2-D spatial data. Granlund and Knutsson [6] were the first to publish a monograph on signal processing for computer vision and elaborate on a number of novel ideas such as tensorial image processing and normalized convolution that did not have their origin in classical signal processing.

Time series are 1-D, signals in computer vision are of higher dimension. They are not restricted to digital images, that is, 2-D spatial signals (Chapter 8). *Volumetric sampling*, *image sequences*, and *hyperspectral imaging* all result in 3-D signals, a combination of any of these techniques in even higher-dimensional signals.

How much more complex does signal processing become with increasing dimension? First, there is the explosion in the number of data points. Already a medium resolution volumetric image with 512^3 voxels requires 128 MB if one voxel carries just one byte. Storage of even higher-dimensional data at comparable resolution is thus beyond the capabilities of today's computers.

Higher dimensional signals pose another problem. While we do not have difficulty in grasping 2-D data, it is already significantly more demanding to visualize 3-D data because the human visual system is built only to see surfaces in 3-D but not volumetric 3-D data. The more dimensions are processed, the more important it is that *computer graphics* and *computer vision* move closer together.

The elementary framework for lowlevel signal processing for computer vision is worked out in Chapters 8 and 9. Of central importance are neighborhood operations (Chapter 9), including fast algorithms for local averaging (Section 9.5), and accurate interpolation (Section 9.6).

1.4 Pattern recognition for computer vision

The basic goal of signal processing in computer vision is the extraction of "suitable *features*" for subsequent processing to recognize and classify objects. But what is a suitable feature? This is still less well defined than in other applications of signal processing. Certainly a mathematically well-defined description of local structure as discussed in Section 9.8 is an important basis. As signals processed in computer vision come from dynamical 3-D scenes, important features also include *motion* (Chapter 10) and various techniques to infer the depth in scenes including *stereo* (Section 11.2), shape from shading and photometric stereo, and depth from focus (Section 11.3).

There is little doubt that *nonlinear* techniques are crucial for feature extraction in computer vision. However, compared to linear filter techniques, these techniques are still in their infancy. There is also no single nonlinear technique but there are a host of such techniques often specifically adapted to a certain purpose [7]. In this volume, we give an overview of the various classes of nonlinear filter techniques (Section 9.4) and focus on a first-order tensor representation of of nonlinear filters by combination of linear convolution and nonlinear point operations (Chapter 9.8) and nonlinear diffusion filtering (Chapter 12).

In principle, *pattern classification* is nothing complex. Take some appropriate features and partition the feature space into classes. Why is it then so difficult for a computer vision system to recognize objects? The basic trouble is related to the fact that the dimensionality of the input space is so large. In principle, it would be possible to use the image itself as the input for a classification task, but no real-world classification technique—be it statistical, neuronal, or fuzzy—would be able to handle such high-dimensional feature spaces. Therefore, the need arises to extract features and to use them for classification.

Unfortunately, techniques for feature selection have very often been neglected in computer vision. They have not been developed to the same degree of sophistication as classification, where it is meanwhile well understood that the different techniques, especially statistical and neural techniques, can been considered under a unified view [8].

This book focuses in part on some more advanced feature-extraction techniques. An important role in this aspect is played by morphological operators (Chapter 14) because they manipulate the shape of objects in images. Fuzzy image processing (Chapter 16) contributes a tool to handle vague data and information.

Object recognition can be performed only if it is possible to represent the knowledge in an appropriate way. In simple cases the knowledge can just rest in simple models. Probabilistic modeling in computer vision is discussed in Chapter 15. In more complex cases this is not sufficient.

1.5 Performance evaluation of algorithms

A systematic evaluation of the algorithms for computer vision has been widely neglected. For a newcomer to computer vision with an engineering background or a general education in natural sciences this is a strange experience. It appears to him/her as if one would present results of measurements without giving error bars or even thinking about possible *statistical* and *systematic errors*.

What is the cause of this situation? On the one side, it is certainly true that some problems in computer vision are very hard and that it is even harder to perform a sophisticated error analysis. On the other hand, the computer vision community has ignored the fact to a large extent that any algorithm is only as good as its objective and solid evaluation and verification.

Fortunately, this misconception has been recognized in the meantime and there are serious efforts underway to establish generally accepted rules for the *performance analysis of computer vision algorithms* [9]. The three major criteria for the performance of computer vision algorithms are:

Successful solution of task. Any practitioner gives this a top priority. But also the designer of an algorithm should define precisely for which task it is suitable and what the limits are.

Accuracy. This includes an analysis of the statistical and systematic errors under carefully defined conditions (such as given *signal-to-noise ratio* (SNR), etc.).

Speed. Again this is an important criterion for the applicability of an algorithm.

There are different ways to evaluate algorithms according to the forementioned criteria. Ideally this should include three classes of studies:

Analytical studies. This is the mathematically most rigorous way to verify algorithms, check error propagation, and predict catastrophic failures.

Performance tests with computer generated images. These tests are useful as they can be carried out under carefully controlled conditions.

Performance tests with real-world images. This is the final test for practical applications.

Much of the material presented in this volume is written in the spirit of a careful and mathematically well-founded analysis of the methods that are described although the performance evaluation techniques are certainly more advanced in some areas than in others.

1.6 Classes of tasks

Applications of computer vision can be found today in almost every technical and scientific area. Thus it is not very helpful to list applications according to their field. In order to transfer experience from one application to another it is most useful to specify the problems that have to be solved and to categorize them into different classes.

Table 1.2: Classification of tasks for computer vision systems

Task	References
2-D & 3-D geometry, 6	
Position, distance	A26
Size, area	A12
Depth, 3-D optical metrology	11.2, A2, A4, A5, A6, A26
2-D form & 2-D shape	14, A13
3-D object shape	6, 7, A2, A4, A5, A6, A7
Radiometry-related, 2	
Reflectivity	2.5
Color	A2
Temperature	A15, A14
Fluorescence	A17, A18, A25, A26
Hyperspectral imaging	A22, A23, A24, A26
Motion, 10	
2-D motion field	10, A16, A17, A19, A20
3-D motion field	A19, A21
Spatial structure and texture	
Edges & lines	9.7
Local wave number; scale	8.9, 10.4, 12, 13
Local orientation	9.8, 13
Texture	9.8
High-level tasks	
Segmentation	13, 14, A12, A13
Object identification	A1, A12
Object classification	A1, A22, ??
Model- and knowledge-based recognition and retrieval	A1, A11, A12
3-D modeling	
3-D object recognition	A6, A10, A7
3-D object synthesis	A7
Tracking	A8, A9, A10, A19, A20

An attempt at such a classification is made in Table 1.2. The table categorizes both the tasks with respect to 2-D imaging and the analysis of dynamical 3-D scenes. The second column contains references to chapters dealing with the corresponding task.

1.7 References

[1] Oppenheim, A. V. and Schafer, R. W., (1989). *Discrete-Time Signal Processing. Prentice-Hall Signal Processing Series.* Englewood Cliffs, NJ: Prentice-Hall.

[2] Proakis, J. G. and Manolakis, D. G., (1992). *Digital Signal Processing. Principles, Algorithms, and Applications.* New York: McMillan.

[3] Madisetti, V. K. and Williams, D. B. (eds.), (1997). *The Digital Signal Processing Handbook.* Boca Raton, FL: CRC Press.

[4] Poularikas, A. D. (ed.), (1996). *The Transforms and Applications Handbook.* Boca Raton, FL: CRC Press.

[5] Lim, J. S., (1990). *Two-dimensional Signal and Image Processing.* Englewood Cliffs, NJ: Prentice-Hall.

[6] Granlund, G. H. and Knutsson, H., (1995). *Signal Processing for Computer Vision.* Norwell, MA: Kluwer Academic Publishers.

[7] Pitas, I. and Venetsanopoulos, A. N., (1990). *Nonlinear Digital Filters. Principles and Applications.* Norwell, MA: Kluwer Academic Publishers.

[8] Schürmann, J., (1996). *Pattern Classification, a Unified View of Statistical and Neural Approaches.* New York: John Wiley & Sons.

[9] Haralick, R. M., Klette, R., Stiehl, H.-S., and Viergever, M. (eds.), (1999). *Evaluation and Validation of Computer Vision Algorithms.* Boston: Kluwer.

Part I

Sensors and Imaging

2 Radiation and Illumination

Horst Haußecker

Xerox Palo Alto Research Center (PARC)

Computer Vision and Applications

2.1 Introduction

Visual perception of scenes depends on appropriate illumination to visualize objects. The human visual system is limited to a very narrow
portion of the spectrum of electromagnetic radiation, called *light*. In
some cases natural sources, such as solar radiation, moonlight, light-
ning flashes, or bioluminescence, provide sufficient ambient light to
navigate our environment. Because humankind was mainly restricted
to daylight, one of the first attempts was to invent an artificial light
source—fire (not only as a food preparation method).

Computer vision is not dependent upon visual radiation, fire, or
glowing objects to illuminate scenes. As soon as imaging detector systems became available other types of radiation were used to probe
scenes and objects of interest. Recent developments in imaging sensors cover almost the whole electromagnetic spectrum from x-rays to
radiowaves (Chapter 5). In standard computer vision applications illumination is frequently taken as given and optimized to illuminate objects evenly with high contrast. Such setups are appropriate for object
identification and geometric measurements. Radiation, however, can
also be used to visualize quantitatively physical properties of objects
by analyzing their interaction with radiation (Section 2.5).

Physical quantities such as penetration depth or surface reflectivity
are essential to probe the internal structures of objects, scene geometry, and surface-related properties. The properties of physical objects
therefore can be encoded not only in the geometrical distribution of
emitted radiation but also in the portion of radiation that is emitted,
scattered, absorbed or reflected, and finally reaches the imaging system. Most of these processes are sensitive to certain wavelengths and
additional information might be hidden in the spectral distribution of
radiation. Using different types of radiation allows taking images from
different depths or different object properties. As an example, infrared
radiation of between 3 and 5 μm is absorbed by human skin to a depth
of < 1 mm, while x-rays penetrate an entire body without major attenuation. Therefore, totally different properties of the human body (such
as skin temperature as well as skeletal structures) can be revealed for
medical diagnosis.

This chapter provides the fundamentals for a quantitative description of radiation emitted from sources, as well as the interaction of radiation with objects and matter. We will also show using a few selected
examples, how this knowledge can be used to design illumination setups for practical applications such that different physical properties
of objects are visualized. *Radiometry*, the measurement of radiation
properties by imaging systems, will be detailed in Chapter 4.

2.2 Fundamentals of electromagnetic radiation

2.2.1 Electromagnetic waves

Electromagnetic radiation consists of *electromagnetic waves* carrying energy and propagating through space. Electrical and magnetic fields are alternating with a temporal *frequency v* and a spatial *wavelength λ*. The metric units of v and λ are cycles per second (s^{-1}), and meter (m), respectively. The unit $1\,s^{-1}$ is also called one hertz (1 Hz). Wavelength and frequency of waves are related by the *speed of light c*:

$$c = v\lambda \tag{2.1}$$

The speed of light depends on the medium through which the electromagnetic wave is propagating. In vacuum, the speed of light has the value $2.9979 \times 10^8\,m\,s^{-1}$, which is one of the fundamental physical constants and constitutes the maximum possible speed of any object. The speed of light decreases as it penetrates matter, with slowdown being dependent upon the electromagnetic properties of the medium (see Section 2.5.2).

Photon energy. In addition to electromagnetic theory, radiation can be treated as a flow of particles, discrete packets of energy called *photons*. One photon travels at the speed of light c and carries the energy

$$e_p = hv = \frac{hc}{\lambda} \tag{2.2}$$

where $h = 6.626 \times 10^{-34}\,J\,s$ is Planck's constant. Therefore the energy content of radiation is quantized and can only be a multiple of hv for a certain frequency v. While the energy per photon is given by Eq. (2.2), the total energy of radiation is given by the number of photons. It was this quantization of radiation that gave birth to the theory of quantum mechanics at the beginning of the twentieth century.

The energy of a single photon is usually given in *electron volts* (1 eV $= 1.602 \times 10^{-19}$). One eV constitutes the energy of an electron being accelerated in an electrical field with a potential difference of one volt. Although photons do not carry electrical charge this unit is useful in radiometry, as electromagnetic radiation is usually detected by interaction of radiation with electrical charges in sensors (Chapter 5). In solid-state sensors, for example, the energy of absorbed photons is used to lift electrons from the valence band into the conduction band of a semiconductor. The bandgap energy E_g defines the minimum photon energy required for this process. As a rule of thumb the detector material is sensitive to radiation with energies $E_v > E_g$. As an example, *indium antimonide (InSb)* is a doped semiconductor with a bandgap of only 0.18 eV. It is sensitive to wavelengths below 6.9 μm (which can be

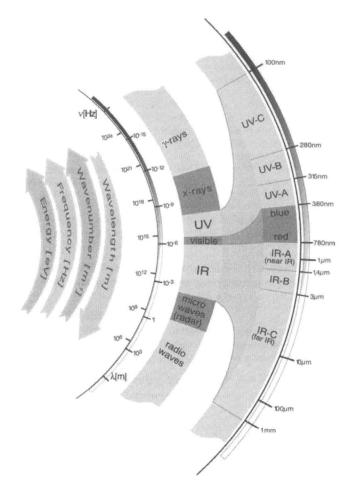

Figure 2.1: *Spectrum of electromagnetic radiation. (By Sven Mann, University of Heidelberg.)*

derived from Eq. (2.2)). *Silicon* (Si) has a bandgap of 1.1 eV and requires wavelengths below 1.1 μm to be detected. This shows why InSb can be used as detector material for infrared cameras in the 3-5 μm wavelength region, while silicon sensors are used for visible radiation. It also shows, however, that the sensitivity of standard silicon sensors extends beyond the visible range up to approximately 1 μm, which is often neglected in applications (Chapter 5).

Electromagnetic spectrum. Monochromatic radiation consists of only one frequency and wavelength. The distribution of radiation over the range of possible wavelengths is called *spectrum* or *spectral distribution*. Figure 2.1 shows the spectrum of electromagnetic radiation together with the standardized terminology[1] separating different parts. Electromagnetic radiation covers the whole range from very high energy cosmic rays with wavelengths in the order of 10^{-16} m ($\nu = 10^{24}$ Hz) to sound frequencies above wavelengths of 10^6 m ($\nu = 10^2$ Hz). Only a very narrow band of radiation between 380 and 780 nm is visible to the human eye.

Each portion of the electromagnetic spectrum obeys the same principal physical laws. Radiation of different wavelengths, however, appears to have different properties in terms of interaction with matter and detectability that can be used for wavelength selective detectors. For the last one hundred years detectors have been developed for radiation of almost any region of the electromagnetic spectrum. Recent developments in detector technology incorporate point sensors into integrated detector arrays, which allows setting up imaging radiometers instead of point measuring devices. Quantitative measurements of the spatial distribution of radiometric properties are now available for remote sensing at almost any wavelength.

2.2.2 Dispersion and attenuation

A mixture of radiation consisting of different wavelengths is subject to different speeds of light within the medium it is propagating. This fact is the basic reason for optical phenomena such as *refraction* and *dispersion*. While refraction changes the propagation direction of a beam of radiation passing the interface between two media with different optical properties, dispersion separates radiation of different wavelengths (Section 2.5.2).

2.2.3 Polarization of radiation

In electromagnetic theory, radiation is described as oscillating electric and magnetic fields, denoted by the electric field strength E and the magnetic field strength B, respectively. Both vector fields are given by the solution of a set of differential equations, referred to as *Maxwell's equations*.

In free space, that is, without electric sources and currents, a special solution is a *harmonic planar wave*, propagating linearly in space and time. As Maxwell's equations are linear equations, the superposition of two solutions also yields a solution. This fact is commonly referred to as the *superposition principle*. The superposition principle allows us to explain the phenomenon of *polarization*, another important property of electromagnetic radiation. In general, the 3-D orientation of vector E changes over time and mixtures of electromagnetic waves show

---

[1]International Commission on Illumination (Commission Internationale de l'Eclairage, CIE); http://www.cie.co.at/cie

a   *b*

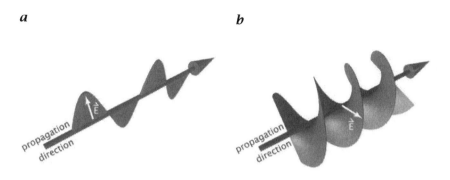

Figure 2.2: *Illustration of **a** linear and **b** circular polarization of electromagnetic radiation. (By C. Garbe, University of Heidelberg.)*

randomly distributed orientation directions of E. If, however, the electromagnetic field vector E is confined to a plane, the radiation is called *linearly polarized* (Fig. 2.2a).

If two linearly polarized electromagnetic waves are traveling in the same direction, the resulting electric field vector is given by $E = E_1 + E_2$. Depending on the phase shift Φ in the oscillations of E_1 and E_2, the net electric field vector E remains linearly polarized ($\Phi = 0$), or rotates around the propagation direction of the wave. For a phase shift of $\Phi = 90°$, the wave is called *circularly polarized* (Fig. 2.2b). The general case consists of *elliptical polarization*, that is, mixtures between both cases.

Due to polarization, radiation exhibits different properties in different directions, such as, for example, directional reflectivity or polarization dependent transmissivity.

2.2.4   Coherence of radiation

Mixtures of electromagnetic waves, which are emitted from conventional light sources, do not show any spatial and temporal relation. The phase shifts between the electric field vectors E and the corresponding orientations are randomly distributed. Such radiation is called *incoherent*.

Special types of light sources, mainly those operating by stimulated emission of radiation (e. g., lasers), emit radiation with a fixed systematic relationship between the phases of the electromagnetic field vectors, a property called *coherence*. Such radiation can be subject to constructive and destructive interference if it is superposed. As the electric field vectors can add up to high amplitudes, the local energy impact of coherent radiation is much more severe and can cause damage to delicate body tissue.

Figure 2.3: Definition of plane angle.

2.3   Radiometric quantities

2.3.1   Solid angle

In order to quantify the geometric spreading of radiation leaving a source, it is useful to recall the definition of solid angle. It extends the concept of plane angle into 3-D space. A *plane angle* θ is defined as the ratio of the arc length s on a circle to the radius r centered at the point of definition:

$$\theta = \frac{s}{r} \tag{2.3}$$

The arc length s can be considered as projection of an arbitrary line in the plane onto the circle (Fig. 2.3). Plane angles are measured in rad (radians). A plane angle θ quantifies the angular subtense of a line segment in the plane viewed from the point of definition. A circle has a circumference of $2\pi r$ and, therefore, subtends a plane angle of 2π rad.

A *solid angle* Ω is similarly defined as the ratio of an area A on the surface of a sphere to the square radius, as shown in Fig. 2.4:

$$\Omega = \frac{A}{r^2} \tag{2.4}$$

The area segment A can be considered as the projection of an arbitrarily shaped area in 3-D space onto the surface of a sphere. Solid angles are measured in sr (steradian). They quantify the areal subtense of a 2-D surface area in 3-D space viewed from the point of definition. A sphere subtends a surface area of $4\pi r^2$, which corresponds to a solid angle of 4π sr. Given a surface area A that is tilted under some angle θ between the surface normal and the line of sight the solid angle is reduced by a factor of $\cos\theta$:

$$\Omega = \frac{A}{r^2}\cos\theta \tag{2.5}$$

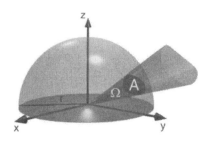

Figure 2.4: *Definition of solid angle. (By C. Garbe, University of Heidelberg.)*

Table 2.1: *Definitions of radiometric quantities (corresponding photometric quantities are defined in Table 2.2)*

Quantity	Symbol	Units	Definition
Radiant energy	Q	Ws	Total energy emitted by a source or received by a detector
Radiant flux	Φ	W	Total power emitted by a source or received by a detector
Radiant exitance	M	$W\,m^{-2}$	Power emitted per unit surface area
Irradiance	E	$W\,m^{-2}$	Power received at unit surface element
Radiant intensity	I	$W\,sr^{-1}$	Power leaving a point on a surface into unit solid angle
Radiance	L	$W\,m^{-2}\,sr^{-1}$	Power leaving unit projected surface area into unit solid angle

From the definition of angles as ratios of lengths or areas it follows that they have no physical unit. However, it is advisable always to use the artificial units rad and sr when referring to quantities related to angles to avoid confusion. Radiometric and photometric quantities also have to be defined carefully as their meaning cannot be inferred from physical units (Tables 2.1 and 2.2).

2.3.2 Conventions and overview

Measurements of radiometric and photometric quantities very often are subject to confusion related to terminology and units. Due to diverse historical developments and often inaccurate usage of names, radiometry is one of the least understood subjects in the field of op-

Table 2.2: *Definitions of photometric quantities (corresponding radiometric quantities are defined in Table 2.1)*

Quantity	Symbol	Units	Definition
Luminous energy	Q_v	lm s	Total luminous energy emitted by a source or received by a detector
Luminous flux	Φ_v	lm (lumen)	Total luminous power emitted by a source or received by a detector
Luminous exitance	M_v	lm m^{-2}	Luminous power emitted per unit surface area
Illuminance	E_v	lm m^{-2} = lx (lux)	Luminous power received at unit surface element
Luminous intensity	I_v	lumen sr^{-1} = cd (candela)	Luminous power leaving a point on a surface into unit solid angle
Luminance	L_v	lumen m^{-2} sr^{-1} = cd m^{-2}	Luminous power leaving unit projected surface area into unit solid angle

tics. However, it is not very difficult if some care is taken with regard to definitions of quantities related to angles and areas.

Despite confusion in the literature, there seems to be a trend towards standardization of units. (In pursuit of standardization we will use only SI units, in agreement with the International Commission on Illumination CIE. The CIE is the international authority defining terminology, standards, and basic concepts in radiometry and photometry. The radiometric and photometric terms and definitions are in compliance with the American National Standards Institute (ANSI) report RP-16, published in 1986. Further information on standards can be found at the web sites of CIE (http://www.cie.co.at/cie/) and ANSI (http://www.ansi.org), respectively.)

In this section, the fundamental quantities of radiometry will be defined. The transition to photometric quantities will be introduced by a generic Equation (2.27), which can be used to convert each of these radiometric quantities to its corresponding photometric counterpart.

We will start from the concept of radiative flux and derive the most important quantities necessary to define the geometric distribution of radiation emitted from or irradiated on surfaces. The six fundamental concepts relating the spatial distribution of energy in electromagnetic radiation are summarized in Table 2.1. The term "radiant" is only added to the names of those quantities that could be confused with the corresponding photometric quantity (see Table 2.2).

2.3.3 Definition of radiometric quantities

Radiant energy and radiant flux. Radiation carries energy that can be absorbed in matter heating up the absorber or interacting with electrical charges. *Radiant energy Q* is measured in units of Joule (1 J = 1 Ws). It quantifies the total energy emitted by a source or received by a detector.

Radiant flux Φ is defined as radiant energy per unit time interval

$$\Phi = \frac{dQ}{dt} \tag{2.6}$$

passing through or emitted from a surface. Radiant flux has the unit watts (W) and is also frequently called *radiant power*, which corresponds to its physical unit. Quantities describing the spatial and geometric distributions of radiative flux are introduced in the following sections.

The units for radiative energy, radiative flux, and all derived quantities listed in Table 2.1 are based on Joule as the fundamental unit. Instead of these *energy-derived* quantities an analogous set of *photon-derived* quantities can be defined based on the number of photons. Photon-derived quantities are denoted by the subscript p, while the energy-based quantities are written with a subscript e if necessary to distinguish between them. Without a subscript, all radiometric quantities are considered energy-derived. Given the radiant energy the number of photons can be computed from Eq. (2.2)

$$N_p = \frac{Q_e}{e_p} = \frac{\lambda}{hc} Q_e \tag{2.7}$$

With photon-based quantities the number of photons replaces the radiative energy. The set of photon-related quantities is useful if radiation is measured by detectors that correspond linearly to the number of absorbed photons (*photon detectors*) rather than to thermal energy stored in the detector material (*thermal detector*).

Photon flux Φ_p is defined as the number of photons per unit time interval

$$\Phi_p = \frac{dN_p}{dt} = \frac{\lambda}{hc} \frac{dQ_e}{dt} = \frac{\lambda}{hc} \Phi_e \tag{2.8}$$

Similarly, all other photon-related quantities can be computed from the corresponding energy-based quantities by dividing them by the energy of a single photon.

Because of the conversion from energy-derived to photon-derived quantities Eq. (2.7) depends on the wavelength of radiation. Spectral distributions of radiometric quantities will have different shapes for both sets of units.

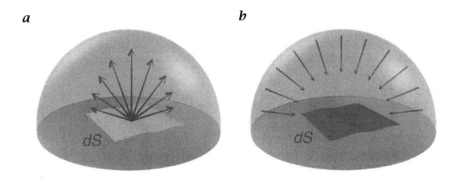

Figure 2.5: *Illustration of the radiometric quantities:* **a** *radiant exitance; and* **b** *irradiance. (By C. Garbe, University of Heidelberg.)*

Radiant exitance and irradiance. *Radiant exitance M* defines the radiative flux *emitted* per unit surface area

$$M = \frac{d\Phi}{dS} \tag{2.9}$$

of a specified surface. The flux leaving the surface is radiated into the whole hemisphere enclosing the surface element dS and has to be integrated over all angles to obtain M (Fig. 2.5a). The flux is, however, not radiated uniformly in angle. Radiant exitance is a function of position on the emitting surface, $M = M(\boldsymbol{x})$. Specification of the position on the surface can be omitted if the emitted flux Φ is equally distributed over an extended area S. In this case $M = \Phi/S$.

Irradiance E similarly defines the radiative flux *incident* on a certain point of a surface per unit surface element

$$E = \frac{d\Phi}{dS} \tag{2.10}$$

Again, incident radiation is integrated over all angles of the enclosing hemisphere (Fig. 2.5b). Radiant exitance characterizes an actively radiating source while irradiance characterizes a passive receiver surface. Both are measured in $W\,m^{-2}$ and cannot be distinguished by their units if not further specified.

Radiant intensity. *Radiant intensity I* describes the angular distribution of radiation emerging from a point in space. It is defined as radiant flux per unit solid angle

$$I = \frac{d\Phi}{d\Omega} \tag{2.11}$$

and measured in units of $W\,sr^{-1}$. Radiant intensity is a function of the direction of the beam of radiation, defined by the spherical coordinates

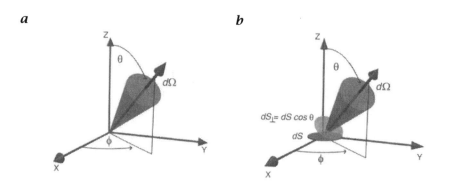

Figure 2.6: *Illustration of radiometric quantities:* **a** *radiant intensity; and* **b** *radiance. (By C. Garbe, University of Heidelberg.)*

θ and ϕ (Fig. 2.6). Intensity is usually used to specify radiation emitted from *point sources*, such as stars or sources that are much smaller than their distance from the detector, that is, $dx\,dy \ll r^2$. In order to use it for extended sources those sources have to be made up of an infinite number of infinitesimal areas. The radiant intensity in a given direction is the sum of the radiant flux contained in all rays emitted in that direction under a given solid angle by the entire source (see Eq. (2.18)).

The term intensity is frequently confused with irradiance or illuminance. It is, however, a precisely defined quantity in radiometric terminology and should only be used in this context to avoid confusion.

Radiance. *Radiance L* defines the amount of radiant flux per unit solid angle per unit projected area of the emitting source

$$L = \frac{d^2\Phi}{d\Omega\,dS_\perp} = \frac{d^2\Phi}{d\Omega\,dS\cos\theta} \tag{2.12}$$

where $dS_\perp = dS\cos\theta$ defines a surface element that is perpendicular to the direction of the radiated beam (Fig. 2.6b). The unit of radiance is $\mathrm{W\,m^{-2}\,sr^{-1}}$. Radiance combines the concepts of exitance and intensity, relating intensity in a certain direction to the area of the emitting surface. And conversely, it can be thought of as exitance of the projected area per unit solid angle.

Radiance is used to characterize an *extended source* that has an area comparable to the squared viewing distance. As radiance is a function of both position on the radiating surface as well as direction $L = L(\boldsymbol{x}, \theta, \phi)$, it is important always to specify the point in the surface and the emitting angles. It is the most versatile quantity in radiometry as all other radiometric quantities can be derived from the radiance integrating over solid angles or surface areas (Section 2.3.4).

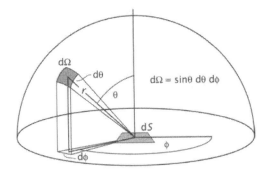

Figure 2.7: Illustration of spherical coordinates.

2.3.4 Relationship of radiometric quantities

Spatial distribution of exitance and irradiance. Solving Eq. (2.12) for $d\Phi/dS$ yields the fraction of exitance radiated under the specified direction into the solid angle $d\Omega$

$$dM(\boldsymbol{x}) = d\left(\frac{d\Phi}{dS}\right) = L(\boldsymbol{x},\theta,\phi)\cos\theta\,d\Omega \tag{2.13}$$

Given the radiance L of an emitting surface, the radiant exitance M can be derived by integrating over all solid angles of the hemispheric enclosure $\mathcal{H}$:

$$M(\boldsymbol{x}) = \int_{\mathcal{H}} L(\boldsymbol{x},\theta,\phi)\cos\theta\,d\Omega = \int_0^{2\pi}\int_0^{\pi/2} L(\boldsymbol{x},\theta,\phi)\cos\theta\sin\theta\,d\theta\,d\phi \tag{2.14}$$

In order to carry out the angular integration *spherical coordinates* have been used (Fig. 2.7), replacing the differential solid angle element $d\Omega$ by the two plane angle elements $d\theta$ and $d\phi$:

$$d\Omega = \sin\theta\,d\theta\,d\phi \tag{2.15}$$

Correspondingly, the irradiance E of a surface S can be derived from a given radiance by integrating over all solid angles of incident radiation:

$$E(\boldsymbol{x}) = \int_{\mathcal{H}} L(\boldsymbol{x},\theta,\phi)\cos\theta\,d\Omega = \int_0^{2\pi}\int_0^{\pi/2} L(\boldsymbol{x},\theta,\phi)\cos\theta\sin\theta\,d\theta\,d\phi \tag{2.16}$$

Angular distribution of intensity. Solving Eq. (2.12) for $d\Phi/d\Omega$ yields the fraction of intensity emitted from an infinitesimal surface element dS

$$dI = d\left(\frac{d\Phi}{d\Omega}\right) = L(\boldsymbol{x}, \theta, \phi) \cos\theta \, dS \tag{2.17}$$

Extending the point source concept of radiant intensity to extended sources, the intensity of a surface of finite area can be derived by integrating the radiance over the emitting surface area S:

$$I(\theta, \phi) = \int_S L(\boldsymbol{x}, \theta, \phi) \cos\theta \, dS \tag{2.18}$$

The infinitesimal surface area dS is given by $dS = ds_1 \, ds_2$, with the *generalized coordinates* $\boldsymbol{s} = [s_1, s_2]^T$ defining the position on the surface. For planar surfaces these coordinates can be replaced by *Cartesian coordinates* $\boldsymbol{x} = [x, y]^T$ in the plane of the surface.

Total radiant flux. Solving Eq. (2.12) for $d^2\Phi$ yields the fraction of radiant flux emitted from an infinitesimal surface element dS under the specified direction into the solid angle $d\Omega$

$$d^2\Phi = L(\boldsymbol{x}, \theta, \phi) \cos\theta \, dS \, d\Omega \tag{2.19}$$

The total flux emitted from the entire surface area S into the hemispherical enclosure $\mathcal{H}$ can be derived by integrating over both the surface area and the solid angle of the hemisphere

$$\Phi = \int_S \int_{\mathcal{H}} L(\boldsymbol{x}, \theta, \phi) \cos\theta \, d\Omega \, dS = \int_S \int_0^{2\pi} \int_0^{\pi/2} L(\boldsymbol{x}, \theta, \phi) \cos\theta \sin\theta \, d\theta \, d\phi \, dS$$
$$\tag{2.20}$$

Again, spherical coordinates have been used for $d\Omega$ and the surface element dS is given by $dS = ds_1 \, ds_2$, with the *generalized coordinates* $\boldsymbol{s} = [s_1, s_2]^T$. The flux emitted into a detector occupying only a fraction of the surrounding hemisphere can be derived from Eq. (2.20) by integrating over the solid angle Ω_D subtended by the detector area instead of the whole hemispheric enclosure $\mathcal{H}$.

Inverse square law. A common rule of thumb for the decrease of irradiance of a surface with distance of the emitting source is the *inverse square law*. Solving Eq. (2.11) for $d\Phi$ and dividing both sides by the area dS of the receiving surface, the irradiance of the surface is given by

$$E = \frac{d\Phi}{dS} = I \frac{d\Omega}{dS} \tag{2.21}$$

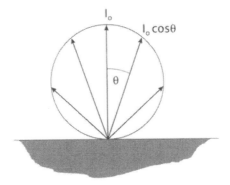

Figure 2.8: *Illustration of angular distribution of radiant intensity emitted from a Lambertian surface.*

For small surface elements dS perpendicular to the line between the point source and the surface at a distance r from the point source, the subtended solid angle $d\Omega$ can be written as $d\Omega = dS/r^2$. This yields the expression

$$E = \frac{I\,dS}{dS r^2} = \frac{I}{r^2} \qquad (2.22)$$

for the irradiance E at a distance r from a point source with radiant intensity I. This relation is an accurate and simple means of verifying the linearity of a detector. It is, however, only true for point sources. For extended sources the irradiance on the detector depends on the geometry of the emitting surface (Section 2.5).

Lambert's cosine law. Radiant intensity emitted from extended surfaces is usually not evenly distributed in angle. A very important relation for perfect emitters, or perfect receivers, is *Lambert's cosine law*. A surface is called *Lambertian* if its radiance is independent of view angle, that is, $L(\boldsymbol{x}, \theta, \phi) = L(\boldsymbol{x})$. The angular distribution of radiant intensity can be computed directly from Eq. (2.18):

$$I(\theta) = \cos\theta \int_S L(\boldsymbol{x})\,dS = I_0\cos\theta \qquad (2.23)$$

It is independent of angle ϕ and shows a cosine dependence on the angle of incidence θ as illustrated in Fig. 2.8. The exitance of a planar Lambertian surface is derived from Eq. (2.14), pulling L outside of the angular integrals

$$M(\boldsymbol{x}) = L(\boldsymbol{x}) \int_0^{2\pi}\int_0^{\pi/2} \cos\theta \sin\theta\,d\theta\,d\phi = \pi L(\boldsymbol{x}) \qquad (2.24)$$

The proportionality factor of π shows that the effect of Lambert's law is to yield only one-half the exitance, which might be expected for a surface radiating into 2π steradians. For point sources, radiating evenly into all directions with an intensity I, the proportionality factor would be 2π. Non-Lambertian surfaces would have proportionality constants smaller than π.

Another important consequence of Lambert's cosine law is the fact that Lambertian surfaces appear to have the same brightness under all view angles. This seems to be inconsistent with the cosine dependence of emitted intensity. To resolve this apparent contradiction, radiant power transfer from an extended source to a detector element with an area of finite size has to be investigated. This is the basic topic of *radiometry* and will be presented in detail in Chapter 4.

It is important to note that Lambert's cosine law only describes perfect radiators or perfect diffusers. It is not valid for real radiators in general. For small angles of incidence, however, Lambert's law holds for most surfaces. With increasing angles of incidence, deviations from the cosine relationship increase (Section 2.5.2).

2.3.5 Spectral distribution of radiation

So far *spectral distribution* of radiation has been neglected. Radiative flux is made up of radiation at a certain wavelength λ or mixtures of wavelengths, covering fractions of the electromagnetic spectrum with a certain wavelength distribution. Correspondingly, all derived radiometric quantities have certain spectral distributions. A prominent example for a spectral distribution is the spectral exitance of a blackbody given by Planck's distribution [CVA1, Chapter 2].

Let Q be any radiometric quantity. The subscript λ denotes the corresponding *spectral* quantity Q_λ concentrated at a specific wavelength within an infinitesimal wavelength interval $d\lambda$. Mathematically, Q_λ is defined as the derivative of Q with respect to wavelength λ:

$$Q_\lambda = \frac{dQ}{d\lambda} = \lim_{\Delta\lambda \to 0} \frac{\Delta Q}{\Delta\lambda} \qquad (2.25)$$

The unit of Q_λ is given by $[\cdot/m]$ with $[\cdot]$ denoting the unit of the quantity Q. Depending on the spectral range of radiation it sometimes is more convenient to express the wavelength dependence in units of $[\cdot/\mu m]$ ($1\,\mu m = 10^{-6}\,m$) or $[\cdot/nm]$ ($1\,nm = 10^{-9}\,m$). Integrated quantities over a specific wavelength range $[\lambda_1, \lambda_2]$ can be derived from spectral distributions by

$$Q_{\lambda_1}^{\lambda_2} = \int_{\lambda_1}^{\lambda_2} Q_\lambda \, d\lambda \qquad (2.26)$$

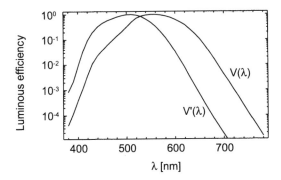

Figure 2.9: *Spectral luminous efficiency function of the "standard" light-adapted eye for photopic vision $V(\lambda)$ and scotopic vision $V'(\lambda)$, respectively.*

with $\lambda_1 = 0$ and $\lambda_2 = \infty$ as a special case. All definitions and relations derived in Sections 2.3.3 and 2.3.4 can be used for both spectral distributions of radiometric quantities and total quantities, integrated over the spectral distribution.

2.4 Fundamental concepts of photometry

Photometry relates radiometric quantities to the brightness sensation of the human eye. Historically, the naked eye was the first device to measure light, and visual perception remains important for designing illumination systems and computing the apparent brightness of sources and illuminated surfaces.

While radiometry deals with electromagnetic radiation of all wavelengths, photometry deals only with the visible portion of the electromagnetic spectrum. The human eye is sensitive to radiation between 380 and 780 nm and only radiation within this visible portion of the spectrum is called "light."

2.4.1 Spectral response of the human eye

Light is perceived by stimulating the retina after passing the preretinal optics of the eye. The retina consists of two different types of receptors: rods and cones. At high levels of irradiance the cones are used to detect light and to produce the sensation of colors (*photopic vision*). Rods are used mainly for night vision at low illumination levels (*scotopic vision*). Both types of receptors have different sensitivities to light at different wavelengths.

The response of the "standard" light-adapted eye is defined by the normalized *photopic spectral luminous efficiency function* $V(\lambda)$ (Fig. 2.9). It accounts for eye response variation as related to wavelength and shows the effectiveness of each wavelength in evoking a brightness sensation. Correspondingly, the *scotopic luminous efficiency function* $V'(\lambda)$ defines the spectral response of a dark-adapted human eye (Fig. 2.9). These curves were formally adopted as standards by the International Lighting Commission (CIE) in 1924 and 1951, respectively. Tabulated values can be found in [1, 2, 3, 4, 5]. Both curves are similar in shape. The peak of the relative spectral luminous efficiency curve for scotopic vision is shifted to 507 nm compared to the peak at 555 nm for photopic vision. The two efficiency functions can be thought of as the transfer function of a filter, which approximates the behavior of the human eye under good and bad lighting conditions, respectively.

As the response of the human eye to radiation depends on a variety of physiological parameters, differing for individual human observers, the spectral luminous efficiency function can correspond only to an average normalized observer. Additional uncertainty arises from the fact that at intermediate illumination levels both photopic and scotopic vision are involved. This range is called *mesopic vision.*

2.4.2 Definition of photometric quantities

In order to convert radiometric quantities to their photometric counterparts, absolute values of the spectral luminous efficiency function are needed instead of relative functions. The relative spectral luminous efficiency functions for photopic and scotopic vision are normalized to their peak values, which constitute the quantitative conversion factors. These values have been repeatedly revised and currently (since 1980) are assigned the values 683 lm W^{-1} (lumen/watt) at 555 nm for photopic vision, and 1754 lm W^{-1} at 507 nm for scotopic vision, respectively. The absolute values of the conversion factors are arbitrary numbers based on the definition of the unit *candela* (or international standard candle) as one of the seven base units of the metric system (SI) [6, 7].

The conversion from photometric to radiometric quantities reduces to one simple equation. Given the conversion factors for photopic and scotopic vision, any (energy-derived) radiometric quantity $Q_{e,\lambda}$ can be converted into its photometric counterpart Q_v by

$$Q_v = 683 \, \text{lm} \, \text{W}^{-1} \int_{380}^{780} Q_{e,\lambda} V(\lambda) \, d\lambda \qquad (2.27)$$

for photopic vision and

$$Q_v = 1754 \, \text{lm} \, \text{W}^{-1} \int_{380}^{780} Q_{e,\lambda} V'(\lambda) \, d\lambda \qquad (2.28)$$

for scotopic vision, respectively. From this definition it can be concluded that photometric quantities can be derived only from known spectral distributions of the corresponding radiometric quantities. For invisible sources emitting radiation below 380 nm or above 780 nm all photometric quantities are null.

Table 2.2 summarizes all basic photometric quantities together with their definition and units.

Luminous energy and luminous flux. The *luminous energy* can be thought of as the portion of radiant energy causing a visual sensation at the human retina. Radiant energy beyond the visible portion of the spectrum can also be absorbed by the retina, maybe causing severe damage to the tissue, but without being visible to the human eye.

The *luminous flux* defines the total luminous energy per unit time interval ("luminous power") emitted from a source or received by a detector. The units for luminous flux and luminous energy are lm (lumen) and lm s, respectively.

Luminous exitance and illuminance. Corresponding to radiant exitance and irradiance, the photometric quantities *luminous exitance* and *illuminance* define the luminous flux per unit surface area leaving a surface or incident on a surface, respectively. As with the radiometric quantities, they are integrated over the angular distribution of light. The units of both luminous exitance and illuminance are lm m^{-2} or lux.

Luminous intensity. *Luminous intensity* defines the total luminous flux emitted into unit solid angle under a specified direction. As with its radiometric counterpart, radiant intensity, it is used mainly to describe point sources and rays of light. Luminous intensity has the unit lm sr^{-1} or candela (cd). For a monochromatic radiation source with $I_\lambda = I_0 \, \delta(\lambda - 555\,\text{nm})$ and $I_0 = 1/683\,\text{W sr}^{-1}$, Eq. (2.27) yields $I_v = 1\,\text{cd}$ in correspondence to the definition of candela.

Luminance. *Luminance* describes the subjective perception of "brightness" because the output of a photometer is proportional to the luminance of the measured radiation (Chapter 4). It is defined as luminant flux per unit solid angle per unit projected surface area perpendicular to the specified direction, corresponding to radiance, its radiometric equivalent.

Luminance is the most versatile photometric quantity, as all other quantities can be derived by integrating the luminance over solid angles or surface areas. Luminance has the unit cd m^{-2}.

2.4.3 Luminous efficacy

Luminous efficacy is used to determine the effectiveness of radiative or electrical power in producing visible light. The term "efficacy" must not be confused with "efficiency." Efficiency is a dimensionless constant describing the ratio of some energy input to energy output. Luminous efficacy is not dimensionless and defines the fraction of luminous energy output able to stimulate the human visual system with respect to incoming radiation or electrical power. It is an important quantity for the design of illumination systems.

Radiation luminous efficacy. *Radiation luminous efficacy K_r is a mea-*sure of the effectiveness of incident radiation in stimulating the perception of light in the human eye. It is defined as the ratio of any photometric quantity Q_v to the radiometric counterpart Q_e integrated over the entire spectrum of electromagnetic radiation:

$$K_r = \frac{Q_v}{Q_e} \text{ [lm W}^{-1}], \quad \text{where} \quad Q_e = \int_0^\infty Q_{e,\lambda} \, d\lambda \qquad (2.29)$$

It is important to note that Eq. (2.29) can be evaluated for any radiometric quantity with the same result for K_r. Substituting Q_v in Eq. (2.29) by Eq. (2.27) and replacing $Q_{e,\lambda}$ by monochromatic radiation at 555 nm, that is, $Q_{e,\lambda} = Q_0 \delta(\lambda - 555 \text{ nm})$, K_r reaches the value 683 lm W^{-1}. It can be easily verified that this is the theoretical maximum luminous efficacy a beam can have. Any invisible radiation, such as infrared or ultraviolet radiation, has zero luminous efficacy.

Lighting system luminous efficacy. The *lighting system luminous efficacy K_s* of a light source is defined as the ratio of perceptible luminous flux Φ_v to the total power P_e supplied to the light source:

$$K_s = \frac{\Phi_v}{P_e} \text{ [lm W}^{-1}] \qquad (2.30)$$

With the *radiant efficiency* $\tilde{\eta} = \Phi_e/P_e$ defining the ratio of total radiative flux output of an illumination source to the supply power, Eq. (2.30) can be expressed by the radiation luminous efficacy, K_r:

$$K_s = \frac{\Phi_v}{\Phi_e} \frac{\Phi_e}{P_e} = K_r \tilde{\eta} \qquad (2.31)$$

Because the radiant efficiency of an illumination source is always smaller than 1, the lighting system luminous efficacy is always smaller than the radiation luminous efficacy. An extreme example is monochromatic laser light at a wavelength of 555 nm. Although K_r reaches the maximum value of 683 lm W^{-1}, K_s might be as low as 1 lm W^{-1} due to the low efficiency of laser radiation.

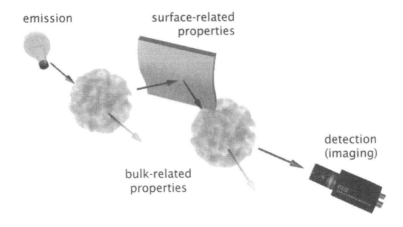

Figure 2.10: *Illustration of the radiometric chain of image formation. (By C. Garbe, University of Heidelberg.)*

2.5 Interaction of radiation with matter

Quantitative visualization in computer vision requires knowledge of both the physical properties of the objects of interest in terms of interaction with radiation as well as the optical properties of the imaging system. In addition to the performance of the detector, the performance and availability of optical components are essential factors for quality and computer vision system costs.

Physical quantities such as penetration depth or surface reflectivity are essential to probe the internal structures of objects, scene geometry, and surface-related properties. Physical object properties, therefore, not only can be encoded in the geometrical distribution of emitted radiation but also in the portion of radiation being emitted, scattered, absorbed, or reflected and finally reaching the imaging system.

Most of these processes are sensitive to certain wavelengths and additional information might be hidden in the spectral distribution of radiation. Using different types of radiation allows images from different depths or object properties to be attained.

Standard scenes usually contain more than one single object in a uniform enclosure. Radiation has to pass a series of events, called the *radiometric chain*, before it reaches the imaging system. Figure 2.10 illustrates how incident radiation is influenced by all objects and matter along the optical path. In this section, the basic mechanisms influencing the emission of radiation and its propagation in matter will be detailed.

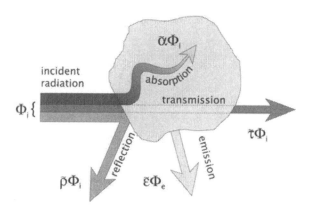

Figure 2.11: *Radiative flux,* Φ_i *incident on an object is partially reflected (fraction* $\tilde{\rho}$*) and absorbed (fraction* $\tilde{\alpha}$*). For nonopaque objects a fraction* $\tilde{\tau}$ *is passing the body. The radiative flux* $\tilde{\epsilon}\Phi_e$ *is emitted to maintain or reach thermodynamic equilibrium.*

2.5.1 Basic definitions and terminology

Definition of optical properties. Radiation incident on or passing through objects is subject to various processes changing the direction of propagation, attenuating or amplifying the radiant intensity, and changing the spectral distribution or polarization of radiation. Without going into the details of the complex physical processes governing the interaction of radiation with the molecular structure of objects, the macroscopic optical properties of objects are quantified by the following dimensionless quantities (Fig. 2.11):

Reflectivity *Reflectivity* or *reflectance* $\tilde{\rho}$ defines the ratio of the reflected radiative flux Φ_r to the incident radiative flux Φ_i,

$$\tilde{\rho} = \frac{\Phi_r}{\Phi_i} \tag{2.32}$$

Absorptivity *Absorptivity* or *absorptance* $\tilde{\alpha}$ defines the ratio of the absorbed radiative flux Φ_a to the incident radiative flux Φ_i,

$$\tilde{\alpha} = \frac{\Phi_a}{\Phi_i} \tag{2.33}$$

Transmissivity *Transmissivity* or *transmittance* $\tilde{\tau}$ defines the ratio of the radiative flux Φ_t transmitting the object to the incident radiative flux Φ_i,

$$\tilde{\tau} = \frac{\Phi_t}{\Phi_i} \tag{2.34}$$

Emissivity The forementioned quantities $\tilde{\rho}$, $\tilde{\alpha}$, and $\tilde{\tau}$ define the property of *passive* receivers in modifying incident radiative flux. The *emissivity* or *emittance* $\tilde{\epsilon}$ quantifies the performance of an *actively* radiating object compared to a blackbody, which provides the upper limit of the spectral exitance of a source. It is defined by the ratio of the exitances,

$$\tilde{\epsilon} = \frac{M_s(T)}{M_b(T)} \tag{2.35}$$

where M_s and M_b denote the exitance of the emitting source, and the exitance of the blackbody at the temperature T, respectively. A *blackbody* is defined as an ideal body absorbing all radiation incident on it regardless of wavelength or angle of incidence. No radiation is reflected from the surface or passing through the blackbody. Such a body is a perfect absorber. *Kirchhoff* demonstrated in 1860 that a good absorber is a good emitter and, consequently, a perfect absorber is a perfect emitter. A blackbody, therefore, would emit the maximum possible radiative flux that any body can radiate at a given kinetic temperature, unless it contains fluorescent or radioactive materials. As a blackbody has the maximum possible exitance of an object at the given temperature, $\tilde{\epsilon}$ is always smaller than 1.

Spectral and directional dependencies. All of the foregoing introduced quantities can have strong variations with direction, wavelength, and polarization state that have to be specified in order to measure the optical properties of an object. The emissivity of surfaces usually only slightly decreases for angles of up to 50° and rapidly falls off for angles larger than 60°; it approaches zero for 90° [8]. The reflectivity shows the inverse behavior.

To account for these dependencies, we define the spectral *directional* emissivity $\tilde{\epsilon}(\lambda, \theta, \phi)$ as ratio of the source spectral radiance $L_{\lambda,s}$ to the spectral radiance of a blackbody $L_{\lambda,b}$ at the same temperature T:

$$\tilde{\epsilon}(\lambda, \theta, \phi) = \frac{L_{\lambda,s}(\theta, \phi, T)}{L_{\lambda,b}(\theta, \phi, T)} \tag{2.36}$$

The spectral *hemispherical* emissivity $\tilde{\epsilon}(\lambda)$ is similarly given by the radiant exitance of the source and a blackbody at the same temperature, T:

$$\tilde{\epsilon}(\lambda) = \frac{M_{\lambda,s}(T)}{M_{\lambda,b}(T)} \tag{2.37}$$

Correspondingly, we can define the spectral directional reflectivity, the spectral directional absorptivity, and the spectral directional transmissivity as functions of direction and wavelength. In order to simplify notation, the symbols are restricted to $\tilde{\rho}$, $\tilde{\alpha}$, $\tilde{\tau}$ and $\tilde{\epsilon}$ without further indices. Spectral and/or directional dependencies will be indicated by the variables and are mentioned in the text.

Terminology conventions. Emission, transmission, reflection, and absorption of radiation either refer to surfaces and interfaces between objects or to the net effect of extended objects of finite thickness. In accordance with Siegel and Howell [9] and McCluney [3] we assign the suffix -ivity to surface-related (*intrinsic*) material properties and the suffix -ance to volume-related (*extrinsic*) object properties. To reduce the number of equations we exclusively use the symbols $\tilde{\epsilon}$, $\tilde{\alpha}$, $\tilde{\rho}$ and $\tilde{\tau}$ for both types. If not further specified, surface- and volume-related properties can be differentiated by the suffixes -ivity and -ance, respectively. More detailed definitions can be found in the *CIE International Lighting Vocabulary* [10].

Spectral selectivity. For most applications the spectral optical properties have to be related to the spectral sensitivity of the detector system or the spectral distribution of the radiation source. Let $\tilde{p}(\lambda)$ be any of the following material properties: $\tilde{\alpha}$, $\tilde{\rho}$, $\tilde{\tau}$, or $\tilde{\epsilon}$. The *spectral selective* optical properties $\tilde{p}_s$ can be defined by integrating the corresponding spectral optical property $\tilde{p}(\lambda)$ over the entire spectrum, weighted by a spectral window function $w(\lambda)$:

$$\tilde{p}_s = \frac{\displaystyle\int_0^\infty w(\lambda)\tilde{p}(\lambda)\,\mathrm{d}\lambda}{\displaystyle\int_0^\infty w(\lambda)\,\mathrm{d}\lambda} \tag{2.38}$$

Examples of spectral selective quantities include the *photopic luminous transmittance* or *reflectance* for $w(\lambda) = V(\lambda)$ (Section 2.4.1), the *solar transmittance*, *reflectance*, or *absorptance* for $w(\lambda) = E_{\lambda,s}$ (solar irradiance), and the *emittance* of an object at temperature T for $w(\lambda) = E_{\lambda,b}(T)$ (blackbody irradiance). The *total* quantities $\tilde{p}$ can be obtained by integrating $\tilde{p}(\lambda)$ over all wavelengths without weighting.

Kirchhoff's law. Consider a body that is in thermodynamic equilibrium with its surrounding environment. Conservation of energy requires $\Phi_i = \Phi_a + \Phi_r + \Phi_t$ and, therefore,

$$\tilde{\alpha} + \tilde{\rho} + \tilde{\tau} = 1 \tag{2.39}$$

In order to maintain equilibrium, the emitted flux must equal the absorbed flux at each wavelength and in each direction. Thus

$$\tilde{\alpha}(\lambda, \theta, \phi) = \tilde{\epsilon}(\lambda, \theta, \phi) \tag{2.40}$$

Table 2.3: *Basic (idealized) object and surface types*

Object	Properties	Description
Opaque body	$\tilde{\epsilon}(\lambda) + \tilde{\rho}(\lambda) = 1,$ $\tilde{\tau}(\lambda) = 0$	Cannot be penetrated by radiation. All exitant radiation is either reflected or emitted.
AR coating	$\tilde{\epsilon}(\lambda) + \tilde{\tau}(\lambda) = 1,$ $\tilde{\rho}(\lambda) = 0$	No radiation is reflected at the surface. All exitant radiation is transmitted or emitted.
Ideal window	$\tilde{\epsilon}(\lambda) = \tilde{\rho}(\lambda) = 0,$ $\tilde{\tau}(\lambda) = 1$	All radiation passes without attenuation. The temperature is not accessible by IR thermography because no thermal emission takes place.
Mirror	$\tilde{\epsilon}(\lambda) = \tilde{\tau}(\lambda) = 0,$ $\tilde{\rho}(\lambda) = 1$	All incident radiation is reflected. The temperature is not accessible by IR thermography because no thermal emission takes place.
Blackbody	$\tilde{\tau}(\lambda) = \tilde{\rho}(\lambda) = 0,$ $\tilde{\epsilon}(\lambda) = \tilde{\epsilon} = 1$	All incident radiation is absorbed. It has the maximum possible exitance of all objects.
Graybody	$\tilde{\epsilon}(\lambda) = \tilde{\epsilon} < 1,$ $\tilde{\rho}(\lambda) = 1 - \tilde{\epsilon},$ $\tilde{\tau}(\lambda) = 0$	Opaque object with wavelength independent emissivity. Same spectral radiance as a blackbody but reduced by the factor $\tilde{\epsilon}$.

This relation is known as *Kirchhoff's law* [11]. It also holds for the integrated quantities $\tilde{\epsilon}(\lambda)$ and $\tilde{\epsilon}$. Kirchoff's law does not hold for active optical effects shifting energy between wavelengths, such as fluorescence, or if thermodynamic equilibrium is not reached. Kirchhoff's law also does not apply generally for two different components of polarization [6, 12].

Table 2.3 summarizes basic idealized object and surface types in terms of the optical properties defined in this section. Real objects and surfaces can be considered a mixture of these types. Although the ideal cases usually do not exist for the entire spectrum, they can be realized for selective wavelengths. Surface coatings, such as, for example, antireflection (AR) coatings, can be technically produced with high precision for a narrow spectral region.

Figure 2.12 shows how radiometric measurements are influenced by the optical properties of objects. In order to measure the emitted flux Φ_1 (e. g., to estimate the temperature of the object), the remaining seven quantities $\tilde{\epsilon}_1$, $\tilde{\epsilon}_2$, $\tilde{\epsilon}_3$, $\tilde{\rho}_1$, $\tilde{\tau}_1$, Φ_2, and Φ_3 have to be known. Only for a blackbody is the total received flux the flux emitted from the object of interest.

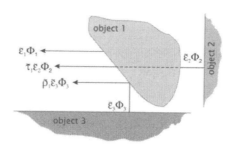

Figure 2.12: *Radiometric measurements of object 1 are biased by the radiation of the environment emitted from objects 2 and 3.*

Index of refraction. Solving the Maxwell equations for electromagnetic radiation in matter yields the *complex index of refraction, N:*

$$N(\lambda) = n(\lambda) + ik(\lambda) \tag{2.41}$$

with the real part n and the imaginary part k.

The real part n constitutes the well-known index of refraction of geometric optics (Section 2.5.2; Chapter 3). From the complex part k other important optical properties of materials, such as *reflection*, and *absorption* can be derived (Sections 2.5.2 and 2.5.3).

2.5.2   Properties related to interfaces and surfaces

In this section properties of interfaces between two different materials are detailed. In this context an interface is defined as a discontinuity in optical properties over a distance that is much smaller than the wavelength of the radiation.

Refraction. The real part $n(\lambda)$ of the complex index of refraction N Eq. (2.41) constitutes the index of refraction of geometric optics, that is, the ratio of the speed of light in a vacuum to the speed of light in a medium under consideration. It determines the change in the direction of propagation of radiation passing the interface of two materials with different dielectric properties. According to *Snell's law*, the angles of incidence θ_1 and refraction θ_2 are related by (Fig. 2.13)

$$\frac{\sin \theta_1}{\sin \theta_2} = \frac{n_2}{n_1} \tag{2.42}$$

where n_1 and n_2 are the indices of refraction of the two materials. It is the basis for transparent optical elements, such as lenses and prisms (Chapter 3). While prisms make use of the wavelength dependence of refraction to separate radiation of different wavelengths, lenses suffer from this effect (chromatic aberration).

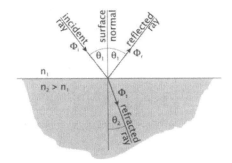

Figure 2.13: *Refraction and specular reflection at interfaces.*

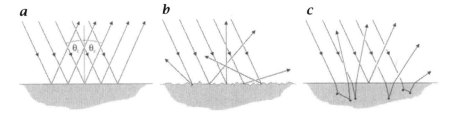

Figure 2.14: *a Specular; b diffuse; and c subsurface reflection at interfaces.*

Specular reflection. At smooth interfaces between two materials with different dielectric properties specular reflection occurs. The direction of incident ray, reflected ray, and the surface normal vector span the plane of incidence perpendicular to the surface of reflection (Fig. 2.13). The angles of incidence and reflection are equal (Fig. 2.14a).

The reflectivity $\tilde{\rho}$ of a surface is defined as the ratio between incident and reflected flux. It depends on the indices of refraction of the two materials, the angle of incidence, and the polarization of the radiation. The specular reflectivities of the polarization components parallel ($\parallel$) and perpendicular ($\perp$) to the plane of incidence are given by *Fresnel's equations* [13]:

$$\tilde{\rho}_{\parallel} = \frac{\tan^2(\theta_1 - \theta_2)}{\tan^2(\theta_1 + \theta_2)}, \quad \tilde{\rho}_{\perp} = \frac{\sin^2(\theta_1 - \theta_2)}{\sin^2(\theta_1 + \theta_2)}, \quad \text{and} \quad \tilde{\rho} = \frac{\tilde{\rho}_{\parallel} + \tilde{\rho}_{\perp}}{2} \quad (2.43)$$

where the total reflectivity for unpolarized radiation $\tilde{\rho}$ is the average (arithmetic mean) of the two polarization components. The angles θ_1 and θ_2 are the angles of incidence and refraction in the medium, which are related by Snell's law, Eq. (2.42). Figure 2.15 shows the angular dependence of Eq. (2.43) for the transition from *BK7* glass to air and vice versa.

From Fresnel's equations three important properties of specular reflection at object interfaces can be inferred (Fig. 2.15):

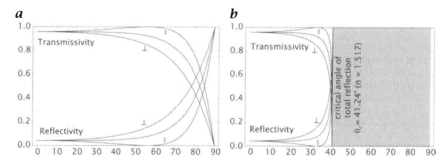

Figure 2.15: *Reflectivities and transmissivities vs angle of incidence for parallel (∥) and perpendicular (⊥) polarized light at the interface between air ($n_1 = 1.0$) and BK7 glass ($n_2 = 1.517$). **a** Transition air to glass. **b** Transition glass to air. The shaded area shows angles beyond the critical angle of total internal reflection.*

1. Parallel polarized light is not reflected at all at a certain angle, called the *polarizing* or *Brewster angle* θ_b. At this angle the reflected and refracted rays are perpendicular to each other [13]:

$$\theta_b = \arcsin \frac{1}{\sqrt{1 + n_1^2/n_2^2}} \qquad (2.44)$$

2. At the transition from the medium with higher refractive index to the medium with lower refractive index, there is a *critical angle* θ_c

$$\theta_c = \arcsin \frac{n_1}{n_2}, \quad \text{with} \quad n_1 < n_2 \qquad (2.45)$$

beyond which all light is reflected back into the medium of origin. At this angle Snell's law would produce an angle of refraction of 90°. The reflectivity is unity for all angles of incidence greater than θ_c, which is known as *total internal reflection* and used in light conductors and fiber optics.

3. At large (grazing) angles, object surfaces have a high reflectivity, independent from n. Therefore, objects usually deviate from an ideal Lambertian reflector for large angles of incidence.

At normal incidence ($\theta = 0$) there is no difference between perpendicular and parallel polarization and

$$\tilde{\rho} = \frac{(n_1 - n_2)^2}{(n_1 + n_2)^2} = \frac{(n-1)^2}{(n+1)^2}, \quad \text{with} \quad n = \frac{n_1}{n_2} \qquad (2.46)$$

Note that Eqs. (2.43) and (2.46) are only exact solutions for transparent dielectric objects (Section 2.5.3) with small imaginary parts k of

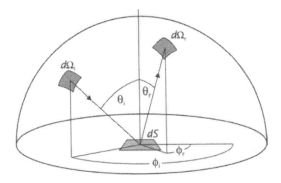

Figure 2.16: Illustration of the angles used in the definition of the bidirectional reflectivity distribution function (BRDF).

the complex refractive index N, Eq. (2.41): $k \ll 1$. For nonnegligible imaginary parts the normal reflectivity Eq. (2.46) has to be modified:

$$\tilde{\rho} = \frac{(n_1 - n_2)^2 + k^2}{(n_1 + n_2)^2 + k^2} \tag{2.47}$$

The wavelength dependence of the refractive index can change the spectral composition of radiation by reflection. Silver (Ag) has a high reflectivity above 0.9 over the entire visible spectrum. The reflectivity of Gold (Au) also lies above 0.9 for wavelengths beyond 600 nm, but shows a sudden decrease to 0.4 for wavelengths below 500 nm. This increased absorption of blue light compared to red light is responsible for the reddish appearance of gold surfaces in contrast to the white metallic glare of silver surfaces.

Diffuse reflection. Very few materials have pure specular surface reflectivity. Most surfaces show a mixture of matte and specular reflection. As soon as surface microroughness has the same scale as the wavelength of radiation, diffraction at the microstructures occurs. At larger scales, microfacets with randomly distributed slopes relative to the surface normal are reflecting incident light in various directions (Fig. 2.14b). Depending on the size and slope distribution of the microroughness, these surfaces have a great variety of reflectivity distributions ranging from isotropic (Lambertian) to strong forward reflection, where the main direction is still the angle of specular reflection. An excellent introduction into light scattering and surface roughness is provided by Bennet and Mattsson [14].

A mixture of specular and diffuse reflection can also be caused by subsurface scattering of radiation, which is no longer a pure surface-related property. Radiation penetrating a partially transparent object can be scattered at optical inhomogeneities (Section 2.5.3) and leave the object to cause diffuse reflection (Fig. 2.14c). Reflected light from below the surface is subject to bulk-related interactions of radiation with matter that can change the spectral composition of radiation before it is reemitted. For this reason, diffusely scattered light shows the colors of objects while highlights of specular reflections usually show the color of the incident light, which is white for ambient daylight.

In order to describe quantitatively the angular reflectivity distribution of arbitrary objects, the *bidirectional reflectivity distribution function* (BRDF), f, is used (Fig. 2.16). It is a function of the spherical angles of incidence (θ_i, ϕ_i) and reflection (θ_r, ϕ_r), and defines the ratio of reflected radiance L_r to the incident irradiance E_i of the reflecting surface [6]:

$$f(\theta_i, \phi_i, \theta_r, \phi_r) = \frac{L_r(\theta_r, \phi_r)}{E_i(\theta_i, \phi_i)} \tag{2.48}$$

This definition accounts for the fact that an optical system measures the radiance leaving a surface while distribution of incident radiation is quantified by the surface irradiance. The two extreme cases are specular and Lambertian surfaces. A purely specular surface has a nonzero value only for $\theta_i = \theta_r$ and $\phi_i = \phi_r$ so that $f = \tilde{\rho}\delta(\theta_i - \theta_r)\delta(\phi_i - \phi_r)$. A Lambertian surface has no dependence on angle, and a flat surface therefore has $f = \tilde{\rho}\pi^{-1}$. The hemispherical reflectivity in each case is $\tilde{\rho}$.

2.5.3 Bulk-related properties of objects

This section deals with the various processes influencing the propagation of radiation within optical materials. The basic processes are attenuation by absorption or scattering, changes in polarization, and frequency shifts. For active emitters, radiation emitted from partially transparent sources can originate from subsurface volumes, which changes the radiance compared to plain surface emission. The most important processes for practical applications are attenuation of radiation by absorption or scattering and luminescence. A more detailed treatment of bulk-related properties can be found in CVA1 [Chapter 3].

Attenuation of radiation.   Only a few optical materials have a transmissivity of unity, which allows radiation to penetrate without attenuation. The best example is ideal crystals with homogeneous regular grid structure. Most materials are either opaque or attenuate transmitted radiation to a certain degree. Let z be the direction of propagation along the optical path. Consider the medium being made up from a number of infinitesimal layers of thickness dz (Fig. 2.17). The fraction of radiance $dL_\lambda = L_\lambda(z) - L_\lambda(z + dz)$ removed within the layer will be

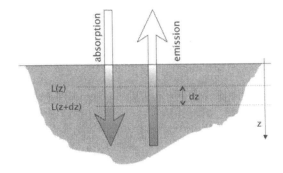

Figure 2.17: *Depth dependence of the volumetric absorption and emission of radiation.*

proportional to both the thickness dz and the radiance $L_\lambda(z)$ incident on the layer at z:

$$dL_\lambda(z) = -\kappa(\lambda, z)L_\lambda(z)\, dz \qquad (2.49)$$

with the *extinction coefficient* or *attenuation coefficient* κ of the material (in environmental sciences, κ is sometimes referred to as *turbidity*). The unit of κ is a reciprocal length, such as m^{-1}. Solving Eq. (2.49) for L and integrating over z yields:

$$L_\lambda(z) = L_\lambda(0)\exp\left(-\int_0^z \kappa(\lambda, z')\, dz'\right) \qquad (2.50)$$

If the medium shows homogeneous attenuation, that is, $\kappa(\lambda, z) = \kappa(\lambda)$, Eq. (2.50) reduces to

$$L_\lambda(z) = L_\lambda(0)\exp\left(-\kappa(\lambda)z\right) \qquad (2.51)$$

which is known as *Lambert Beer's* or *Bouguer's law* of attenuation. It has to be pointed out that Bouguer's law holds only for first-order (linear) processes, Eq. (2.49), where dL is proportional to L. This is true for a wide range of practical applications, but breaks down for very high intensities, such as laser radiation, or if multiscatter processes play a dominant role.

So far there has not been a discussion as to which processes are responsible for attenuation of radiation. The two basic processes are *absorption* and *scattering*. Separating the total amount dL of radiation that is lost into the parts dL_a (absorption) and dL_s (scattering), $dL = dL_a + dL_s$, the attenuation coefficient κ splits into the *absorption coefficient* α and the *scattering coefficient* β:

$$\kappa = -\frac{1}{L}\frac{dL}{dz} = -\frac{1}{L}\frac{dL_a}{dz} - \frac{1}{L}\frac{dL_s}{dz} = \alpha + \beta \qquad (2.52)$$

Both coefficients have the dimension of a reciprocal length (m^{-1}) and are intrinsic material properties.

In order to separate the effect of absorption and scattering on attenuation, both the transmitted as well as the scattered radiation in all directions has to be measured. For the transmitted beam, only the net effect of both processes can be measured if no further knowledge on the material properties is available.

The *transmittance*[2] of a layer of thickness z can be computed from Eq. (2.51) as

$$\tilde{\tau}(\lambda) = \frac{L_\lambda(z)}{L_\lambda(0)} = \exp(-\kappa(\lambda)z) \qquad (2.53)$$

Therefore, a layer of thickness $\kappa^{-1}(\lambda)$ has a transmittance of e^{-1}. This distance is called *penetration depth* of the radiation at the specific wavelength. A variety of materials do not exhibit scattering. In these cases $\kappa = \alpha$.

Another frequently used term (mainly in spectroscopy) is the *optical depth* $\tau(z_1, z_2)$ of a medium. It is defined as integral over the attenuation coefficient:

$$\tau(z_1, z_2) = \int_{z_1}^{z_2} \kappa(z)\, dz \qquad (2.54)$$

Taking the logarithm of the radiance, Lambert Beer's law (see Eq. (2.50)) reduces to a sum over the optical depths of all M layers of material:

$$\ln L_\lambda(z) - \ln L_\lambda(0) = \sum_{m=0}^{M} \tau(z_m, z_{m+1}) \qquad (2.55)$$

Again, for nonscattering media κ has to be replaced by α.

Absorption. The *absorption coefficient* α of a material can be computed from the imaginary part k of the complex index of refraction (Eq. (2.41)):

$$\alpha(\lambda) = \frac{4\pi k(\lambda)}{\lambda} \qquad (2.56)$$

Tabulated values of absorption coefficients for a variety of optical materials can be found in [6, 15, 16, 17].

The absorption coefficient of a medium is the basis for quantitative spectroscopy. With an imaging spectrometer, the distribution of

---

[2] As mentioned in Section 2.5.1, the *transmittance* of a layer of finite thickness must not be confused with the *transmissivity* of an interface.

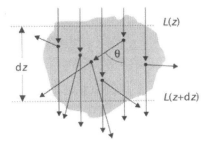

Figure 2.18: *Single and multiple scatter of radiation in materials with local inhomogeneities.*

a substance can be quantitatively measured, provided there is appropriate illumination (Section A23). The measured spectral absorption coefficient of a substance depends on the amount of material along the optical path and, therefore, is proportional to the concentration of the substance:

$$\alpha = \epsilon c \tag{2.57}$$

where c is the concentration in units mol l^{-1} and ϵ denotes the molar absorption coefficient with unit l mol^{-1} m^{-1}).

Scattering. Scatter of radiation is caused by variations of the refractive index as light passes through a material [16]. Causes include foreign particles or voids, gradual changes of composition, second phases at grain boundaries, and strains in the material. If radiation traverses a perfectly homogeneous medium, it is not scattered. Although any material medium has inhomogeneities as it consists of molecules, each of which can act as a scattering center, whether the scattering will be effective depends on the size and arrangement of these molecules. In a perfect crystal at zero temperature the molecules are arranged in a very regular way and the waves scattered by each molecule interfere in such a way as to cause no scattering at all but just a change in the velocity of propagation, given by the index of refraction (Section 2.5.2).

The net effect of scattering on incident radiation can be described in analogy to absorption Eq. (2.49) with the *scattering coefficient* $\beta(\lambda, z)$ defining the proportionality between incident radiance $L_\lambda(z)$ and the amount dL_λ removed by scattering along the layer of thickness dz (Fig. 2.18).

The basic assumption for applying Eq. (2.49) to scattering is that the effect of a volume containing M scattering particles is M times that scattered by a single particle. This simple proportionality to the number of particles holds only if the radiation to which each particle is exposed is essentially radiation of the initial beam. For high particle densities

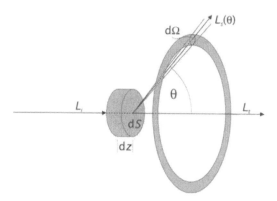

Figure 2.19: *Geometry for the definition of the volume scattering function f_{VSF}.*

and, correspondingly, high scattering coefficients, multiple scattering occurs (Fig. 2.18) and the simple proportionality does not exist. In this case the theory becomes very complex. A means of testing the proportionality is to measure the optical depth τ (Eq. (2.54)) of the sample. As a rule of thumb, single scattering prevails for $\tau < 0.1$. For $0.1 < \tau < 0.3$ a correction for double scatter may become necessary. For values of $\tau > 0.3$ the full complexity of multiple scattering becomes a factor [18]. Examples of multiple scatter media are white clouds. Although each droplet may be considered an independent scatterer, no direct solar radiation can penetrate the cloud. All droplets only diffuse light that has been scattered by other drops.

So far only the net attenuation of the transmitted beam due to scattering has been considered. A quantity accounting for the angular distribution of scattered radiation is the *spectral volume scattering function*, f_{VSF}:

$$f_{VSF}(\theta) = \frac{d^2 \Phi_s(\theta)}{E_i \, d\Omega \, dV} = \frac{d^2 L_s(\theta)}{L_i \, d\Omega \, dz} \tag{2.58}$$

where $dV = dS \, dz$ defines a volume element with a cross section of dS and an extension of dz along the optical path (Fig. 2.19). The indices i and s denote incident and scattered quantities, respectively. The volume scattering function considers scatter to depend only on the angle θ with axial symmetry and defines the fraction of incident radiance being scattered into a ring-shaped element of solid angle (Fig. 2.19).

From the volume scattering function, the total scattering coefficient β can be obtained by integrating f_{VSF} over a full spherical solid angle:

$$\beta(\lambda) = \int_0^{2\pi} \int_0^{\pi} f_{VSF}(\lambda, \theta) \, d\theta \, d\Phi = 2\pi \int_0^{\pi} \sin\theta \, f_{VSF}(\lambda, \theta) \, d\theta \tag{2.59}$$

Calculations of f_{VSF} require explicit solutions of Maxwell's equations in matter. A detailed theoretical derivation of scattering is given in [18].

Luminescence. *Luminescence* describes the emission of radiation from materials by radiative transition between an excited state and a lower state. In a complex molecule, a variety of possible transitions between states exist and not all are optically active. Some have longer lifetimes than others, leading to a delayed energy transfer. Two main cases of luminescence are classified by the time constant of the process:

1. *Fluorescence*, by definition, constitutes the emission of electromagnetic radiation, especially of visible light, stimulated in a substance by the absorption of incident radiation and persisting only as long as the stimulating radiation is continued. It has short lifetimes, that is, the radiative emission occurs within 1–200 ns after the excitation.

2. *Phosphorescence* defines a delayed luminescence, occurring milliseconds to minutes after the excitation. Prominent examples of such materials are watch displays or light switches that glow in the dark. The intensity decreases as the time from the last exposure to light increases.

There are a variety of physical and chemical processes leading to a transition between molecular states. A further classification of luminescence accounts for the processes that lead to excitation:

- *Photoluminescence*: Excitation by absorption of radiation (photons);
- *Electroluminescence*: Excitation by electric current (in solids and solutions) or electrical discharge (in gases);
- *Thermoluminescence*: Thermal *stimulation* of the emission of already excited states;
- *Radioluminescence*: Excitation by absorption of ionizing radiation or particle radiation;
- *Chemoluminescence*: Excitation by chemical reactions; and
- *Bioluminescence*: Chemoluminescence in living organisms; prominent examples include fireflies and marine organisms.

For practical usage in computer vision applications, we have to consider how luminescence can be used to visualize the processes or objects of interest. It is important to note that fluorescent intensity depends on both the concentration of the fluorescent material as well as on the mechanism that leads to excitation. Thus, fluorescence allows us to visualize *concentrations* and *processes quantitatively*.

The most straightforward application can be found in biology. Many biological processes are subject to low-level bioluminescence. Using appropriate cameras, such as amplified intensity cameras (Section 4), these processes can be directly visualized (Chapter A25, [CVA1, Chapter 12]). An application example is the imaging of Ca^{2+} concentration in muscle fibers, as will be outlined in CVA3 [Chapter 34].

Other biochemical applications make use of fluorescent markers. They use different types of fluorescent dyes to mark individual parts of chromosomes or gene sequences. The resulting image data are multispectral confocal microscopic images (Section A26, [CVA2, Chapter 41]) encoding different territories within the chromosomes).

Fluorescent dyes can also be used as tracers in fluid dynamics to visualize flow patterns. In combination with appropriate chemical tracers, the fluorescence intensity can be changed according to the relative concentration of the tracer. Some types of molecules, such as oxygen, are very efficient in deactivating excited states during collision without radiative transfer—a process referred to as *fluorescence quenching*. Thus, fluorescence is reduced proportional to the concentration of the quenching molecules. In addition to the flow field, a quantitative analysis of the fluorescence intensity within such images allows direct measurement of trace gas concentrations (Section A18).

2.6 Illumination techniques

In this chapter we turn to the question: How can radiation sources be used to visualize physical properties of objects? In order to set up an appropriate illumination system we have to consider the radiometric properties of the illumination sources, such as spectral characteristics, intensity distribution, radiant efficiency (Section 2.4.3), and luminous efficacy (Section 2.4.3). For practical applications we also have to carefully choose electrical properties, temporal characteristics, and package dimensions of the sources. A detailed overview of illumination sources including the relevant properties can be found in CVA1 [Chapter 6].

Single illumination sources alone are not the only way to illuminate a scene. There is a wealth of possibilities to arrange various sources geometrically, and eventually combine them with optical components to form an illumination setup that is suitable for different computer vision applications. In the following section we will show how this can be accomplished for some sample setups (Fig. 2.20). They are, however, only a small fraction of the almost unlimited possibilities to create problem-specific illumination setups. The importance of appropriate illumination setups cannot be overemphasized. In many cases, features of interest can be made visible by a certain geometrical arrangement or spectral characteristics of the illumination, rather than by trying to use expensive computer vision algorithms to solve the same task, sometimes in vain. Good image quality increases the performance and reliability of any computer vision algorithm.

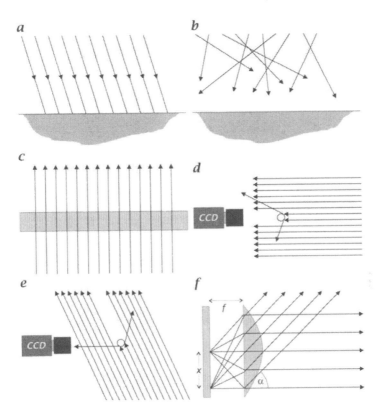

Figure 2.20: *Illustration of different illumination setups: **a** directed illumination; **b** diffuse illumination; **c** rear illumination; **d** light field illumination; **e** dark field illumination; **f** telecentric illumination.*

2.6.1 Directional illumination

Directional illumination or *specular illumination* denotes a setup in which parallel light or light from a point light source is used to illuminate the object (Fig. 2.20a). This is the most simple type of illumination, as the setup basically consists of a single light source at a certain distance.

For *matte (Lambertian) surfaces*, directional illumination produces an irradiance, which depends on the angle of incidence of the light upon the surface. Thus, it can be used to determine the inclination of surfaces with respect to the illumination direction. At the edges of objects, directional illumination casts shadows, and does not illuminate occluded parts of objects. If the camera is observing the scene under a different angle, these shadows are visible in the image and might be confused with object borders.

a   b

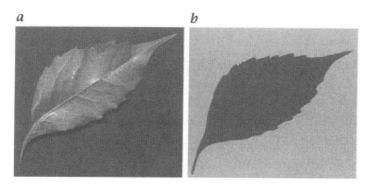

Figure 2.21: *Illustration of the difference between directed and rear illumination for a plant leaf.* **a** *Directed illumination.* **b** *Rear illumination.*

For *specular reflecting surfaces*, directional illumination is not the appropriate illumination. These surfaces will appear black for all points where the reflection condition is not met and show specular reflexes for the remaining points.

Most surfaces are mixtures of Lambertian surfaces with additional specular reflection. Thus, object surfaces show highlights that might be confused with surface structures or object edges. Furthermore, these regions might be overexposed and do not contain structural information. On the other hand, the position of specular highlights allows determination of the direction of the surface normal in these areas, as the exact reflection condition is fulfilled. This might be important information for 3-D reconstruction of the scene. Figure 2.21a shows an example of a plant leaf illuminated with directional illumination. The leaf shows highlights and a shadow is cast at the lower edge.

2.6.2 Diffuse illumination

A second type of front illumination is *diffuse illumination* (Fig. 2.20b). This illumination setup consists of an extended illumination source, which emits light under all directions. An optimal diffuse illumination creates an illuminance that is independent of the direction and impinges uniformly from the entire enclosing hemisphere. A good example of diffuse illumination is a completely overcast sky or heavy fog. Such an illumination is hard to realize in technical applications. Examples include extended diffusing plates or ring illuminations using LEDs or fiber optical illumination.

This type of illumination is well suited for both matte as well as specular surfaces. Although a diffuse illumination does not cast sharp shadows, thick edges of objects still partially block incident light. They appear as extended partially darkened regions, commonly referred to as *penumbra*.

2.6.3 Rear illumination

If only the geometrical outline of an opaque flat object is of interest, *rear illumination* is the common choice of illumination (Fig. 2.20c). Opaque objects appear as black objects without any structure. More interesting features can be obtained using rear illumination for semitransparent objects. For these types of objects, the transmitted radiation exhibits the entire spectrum of bulk-related interaction of radiation with matter, such as refraction, absorption, and scatter. Local inhomogeneities in the absorptivity show up as brightness patterns, integrated over the optical path of the radiation. Prominent examples of such images are x-ray images of medical applications. If the absorption is spectrally selective, the spectral content of the transmitted radiation carries additional information on the internal structure of objects.

Rear illumination can be set up with both directional as well as diffuse illumination. Figure 2.21b shows an example of a plant leaf illuminated by a diffuser screen behind the leaf. The background and the leaf show a well separated gray value distribution. The edge of the leaf is clearly visible. As the leaf is not totally opaque, it still shows fine structures, related to the more transparent water vessels.

2.6.4 Light and dark field illumination

Rear illumination can be considered to be a special case of *light field illumination*. Here a direct path exists from the light source to the camera, that is, the light source directly illuminates the sensor chip (Fig. 2.20d). As long as no object is present, the image appears bright. Any object in the light path diminishes the image irradiance by refraction, absorption, and scatter of light out of the illumination path. Thus, objects appear dark in front of a bright background. This type of illumination is commonly used to detect whether small objects (particles) are present in the volume between the illumination source and the camera (Section A13).

As opposed to light field illumination, *dark field illumination* inhibits a direct path between the light source and the camera (Fig. 2.20e). As long as no objects are present in the illumination path, the image appears dark. Objects in the illumination path become visible by scattering, reflecting, or refracting light into the camera. Thus, objects appear bright in front of a dark background. This type of illumination is as well used to detect small particles in the illumination path.

2.6.5 Telecentric illumination

Figure 2.20f illustrates the principal setup of a *telecentric illumination* system. It is used to convert the spatial radiance distribution of a light source into bundles of parallel rays that reflect the radiance (and spectral distribution) of a single point of the light source.

It principally consists of a large lens (often Fresnel lenses are used) which is placed at a distance of one focal length in front of an illumination source. A single point on the illumination source creates a bundle of parallel rays, leaving the lens into the direction of the line connecting the point and the center of the lens. The angle of the light bundle with the optical axis of the lens is given by the position on the focal plane using

$$\tan \alpha = \frac{x}{f} \tag{2.60}$$

where x is the distance between the intersection of the optical axis and the focal plane and f denotes the focal length of the lens. If the radiance of the light source is isotropic within the solid angle subtended by the lens, the intensity emitted by the lens is constant over the lens aperture. For a nonisotropic radiance distribution (non-Lambertian source), the spatial distribution of the intensity of the emitted bundle of rays reflects the angular distribution of the radiance.

Thus, a telecentric illumination converts the spatial radiance distribution of an extended illumination source into an angular radiance distribution and the angular radiance distribution of a single point into a spatial distribution over the cross section of the bundle of rays. It is the basic part of various types of illumination systems.

2.6.6 Pulsed and modulated illumination

Pulsed illumination can be used for a variety of purposes, such as increasing the performance of the illumination system, reducing blurring effects, and measuring time constants and distances, to mention only a few of them.

Some illumination sources (e. g., special lasers) can only be fired for a short time with a certain repetition rate. Others, such as LEDs, have a much higher light output if operated in pulsed mode. The pulsed-mode operation is especially useful for imaging applications. If LEDs are triggered on the frame sync of the camera signal, they can be pulsed with the frame rate of the camera. As the integration time of the camera only subtends a fraction of the time between two images, the LED output can be optimized by pulsed-mode operation. In order to operate the LED in pulsed mode, logical TTL-electronics can be used to generate an LED-pulse from the trigger signal of the camera. This signal can be used to switch the LED via transistors, as the TTL signal cannot be directly used for power switching of the LED. More detailed information about TTL electronics and interfaces driving optoelectronical components with TTL signals can be found in an excellent handbook on practical electronics by Horowitz and Hill [19].

Instead of synchronizing the pulsed illumination with the camera integration both can be intentionally separated. Using a grated camera, with an adjustable delay after the illumination pulse, radiation is received only from a certain depth range, corresponding to the run time of the backscattered signal.

Pulsed illumination can also be used to image fast processes that are either blurred by the integration time of the camera or need to be imaged twice during the time between two consecutive frames. In the first case, a short pulse within the integration time restricts the accumulated irradiance to this time interval, independent from the integration time of the camera. The second case is commonly used in high-speed particle imaging velocimetry. Here the momentary distribution of the particle concentration in a liquid is imaged twice per frame by a fast double pulse. From the autocorrelation function of the image, the displacement of the particle pattern within the time between the two pulses can be computed.

Another important application of pulsed signals is time-of-flight measurements to estimate the distance of the scattering surface (see Section 7.4). Such measurements are demanding with electromagnetic waves, as the signal travels with the speed of light and time delays are in the order of nanoseconds. For acoustic waves, however, it is much easier to apply. These waves need about 3 ms to travel the distance of 1 m in air, as opposed to 3 ns for electromagnetic waves. Many living species, such as bats and marine mammals, use acoustic signals to sense their 3-D environment in absolute darkness.

Instead of pulsing the illumination signal, it can also be *modulated* with a certain frequency. Examples can be found in scientific applications. Some processes that are visualized correspond with a certain time constant upon illumination with specific radiation. For example, active thermography uses infrared radiation to heat object surfaces and to observe temporal changes. Using a modulated thermal irradiance, the time constant of the processes related to the absorption and the internal transport of heat can be measured.

2.7 References

[1] Kaufman, J. E. (ed.), (1984). *IES Lighting Handbook—Reference Volume.* New York: Illuminating Engineering Society of North America.

[2] CIE, (1983). *The Basis of Physical Photometry.* Technical Report.

[3] McCluney, W. R., (1994). *Introduction to Radiometry and Photometry.* Boston: Artech House.

[4] Laurin Publishing, (1998). *The Photonics Design and Applications Handbook*, 44th edition. Pittsfield, MA: Laurin Publishing CO.

[5] Oriel Corporation, (1994). *Light Sources, Monochromators & Spectrographs, Detectors & Detection Systems, Fiber Optics*, Vol. II. Stratford, CT: Oriel Corporation.

[6] Wolfe, W. L. and Zissis, G. J. (eds.), (1989). *The Infrared Handbook*, 3rd edition. Michigan: The Infrared Information Analysis (IRIA) Center, Environmental Research Institute of Michigan.

[7] Walsh, J. W. T. (ed.), (1965). *Photometry*, 3rd edition. New York: Dover.

[8] Gaussorgues, G., (1994). *Infrared Thermography*. London: Chapmann & Hall.

[9] Siegel, R. and Howell, J. R. (eds.), (1981). *Thermal Radiation Heat Transfer*, 2nd edition. New York: McGraw-Hill Book, Co.

[10] CIE, (1987). *CIE International Lighting Vocabulary*. Technical Report.

[11] Kirchhoff, G., (1860). *Philosophical Magazine and Journal of Science*, **20(130)**.

[12] Nicodemus, F. E., (1965). Directional reflectance and emissivity of an opaque surface. *Applied Optics*, 4:767.

[13] Hecht, E. and Zajac, A., (1977). *Optics*, 2nd edition. Addison-Wesley World Student Series. Reading, MA: Addison-Wesley Publishing.

[14] Bennet, J. M. and Mattsson, L. (eds.), (1989). *Introduction to Surface Roughness and Scattering*. Washington, DC: Optical Society of America.

[15] Dereniak, E. L. and Boreman, G. D., (1996). *Infrared Detectors and Systems*. New York: John Wiley & Sons, Inc.

[16] Harris, D. C., (1994). *Infrared Window and Dome Materials*. Bellingham, WA: SPIE Optical Engineering Press.

[17] Bass, M., Van Stryland, E. W., Williams, D. R., and Wolfe, W. L. (eds.), (1995). *Handbook of Optics. Fundamentals, Techniques, and Design*, 2nd edition, Vol. 1. New York: McGraw-Hill.

[18] van de Hulst, H. C., (1981). *Light Scattering by Small Particles*. New York: Dover Publications.

[19] Horowitz, P. and Hill, W., (1998). *The Art of Electronics*. New York: Cambridge University Press.

3 Imaging Optics

Peter Geißler[1]

Interdisziplinäres Zentrum für Wissenschaftliches Rechnen (IWR)
Universität Heidelberg, Germany
[1]Now with ARRI, München, Germany

Computer Vision and Applications

3.1 Introduction

Computer vision and image processing always start with image acquisition, mostly done by illuminating the scene with natural or artificial
light in the visible range and capturing images with a photographic
lens. The importance of proper image acquisition is ignored in many
applications, at the expense of an increased effort in the processing
of the images. In addition to the fact that appropriate visualization
can enhance image quality in such a manner that image processing requires fewer processing steps, becomes much faster, or is even for the
first time possible, image degradations caused by unsuitable imaging
may seriously complicate image analysis or even be uncorrectable afterwards. Although most of today's camera lenses are of very good
quality, they are always optimized for a particular purpose and may
fail if used in other setups. In addition, in some applications an optics
setup from one or two simple lenses may provide better image quality than stock lenses because the setup can be optimized exactly for
that imaging problem. For these reasons, this chapter will provide the
reader with the essential concepts of optical imaging, focusing on the
geometric ray approximation, which will be sufficient for most applications other than microscopic imaging. Special emphasis is placed
on the description of nonparaxial optics (the main reason for image
distortions).

3.2 Basic concepts of geometric optics

Basic to geometric optics are light rays, which can be seen as an approximation of a parallel wavefront of zero cross section. Therefore, rays
are always perpendicular to the wavefront. In a homogeneous dielectric medium, a ray travels with the local speed of light c/n; c denotes
the vacuum light speed, and n is the refractive index of the dielectric
medium and depends on the medium and the wavelength. Of course,
rays represent an abstraction from wave optics that neglects diffraction
effects.

3.2.1 Reflection and refraction

Within a medium of constant index of refraction, a ray travels as a
straight line without any changes in its direction. A ray passing through
the boundary surface of two media that have different indices of refraction is bent by an angle described by the law of Snellius (Eq. (3.1)). It
relates the ratio of the incoming and outgoing deviation angles to the
ratio of the refractive indices.

$$n_1 \sin \alpha_1 = n_2 \sin \alpha_2 \qquad (3.1)$$

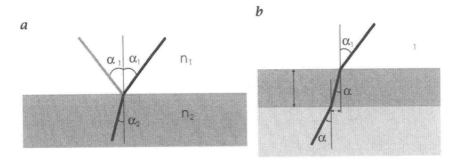

Figure 3.1: *a Snellius' law of refraction; b refraction at a three-media transition.*

Besides refraction into the adjacent medium, reflection of the incoming ray occurs. In this case the simple relation $\alpha_1 = \alpha_2$ applies.

It is useful in many cases to express both refraction and reflection as vector equations. We specify the direction of the incoming ray by the unit vector $\bar{r}$, the direction of the outgoing ray again by the unit vector $\bar{r}'$, and the vector normal to the surface dividing the two media by the unit vector $\bar{n}$. Then reflection can be written as

$$\bar{r}' = \bar{r} - 2(\bar{n}\bar{r})\bar{n} \qquad (3.2)$$

whereas refraction reads

$$\bar{r}' = \frac{1}{n_a/n_e}\bar{r} - \left[\frac{\bar{n}\bar{r}}{n_a/n_e} + \sqrt{1 - \frac{\left(1 + (\bar{n}\bar{r})^2\right)}{(n_a/n_e)^2}}\right]\bar{n} \qquad (3.3)$$

3.2.2 Multimedia refraction

Often not only does a single change of the refractive index have to be taken into account, but also a sequence of consecutive phase transitions. This is the case, for example, in any underwater optics, where a glass plate protects the optics from the aqueous medium. This situation is illustrated in Fig. 3.1b. Fortunately, Snellius' law remains valid between the media n_1 and n_3

$$\frac{\sin \alpha_1}{\sin \alpha_3} = \frac{\sin \alpha_1}{\sin \alpha_2}\frac{\sin \alpha_2}{\sin \alpha_3} = \frac{n_2}{n_1}\frac{n_3}{n_1} = \frac{n_3}{n_1} \qquad (3.4)$$

Because of the optical path length within the medium n_2, the ray is shifted in parallel by

$$d = D \tan \alpha_2 \qquad (3.5)$$

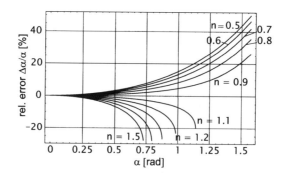

Figure 3.2: *Relative angular error of the paraxial approximation for various values of the ratio of refractive indices* $n = n_1/n_2$.

3.2.3 Paraxial optics

From the Taylor series of the trigonometric functions, their corresponding small angle approximation is found to be

$$\sin(\alpha) \approx \alpha \qquad \cos(\alpha) \approx 1 \qquad \tan(\alpha) \approx \alpha \qquad (3.6)$$

These rays form the *paraxial domain*, where the approximations in Eq. (3.6) can be applied with acceptable deviations. It is important to notice that there is no clear definition of the paraxial domain as its boundaries depend on the maximum error that is tolerated. Figure 3.2 shows the relative angular error of the paraxial approximation.

In paraxial approximation, Snellius simplifies to $n_1\alpha_1 = n_2\alpha_2$. Unless indicated otherwise, all calculations of geometric optics in this chapter are done using the paraxial approximation. Its power will be shown first in the description of lenses, from spherical lenses to the approximation of thin, paraxial lenses, which is sufficient in most cases. Deviations from the paraxial domain will be discussed with the lens aberrations in Section 3.5.

3.3 Lenses

All imaging optics use lenses as central imaging elements. Therefore it is important to examine the optical properties of these fundamental elements. We start with spherical lenses, which have only one kind of glass. Despite the fact that spherical lenses do not best approximate the ideal paraxial lens, they are the most common kind of lenses used. This is due to the fact that it is easier to manufacture spherical surfaces than it is to polish aspherical surfaces. Therefore, it is more economical in most cases to use systems of spherical surfaces and lenses in

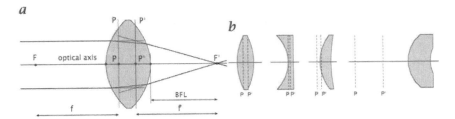

Figure 3.3: *a Fundamental terms of the paraxial description of lenses. b Position of principal planes for different lens types.*

order to correct lens aberrations than to use aspherical lenses. Nevertheless, new technologies in the pressing of plastic lenses have made the production of aspherical lenses inexpensive.

3.3.1 Definitions

Lenses can be described by means of a set of cardinal points and surfaces. This method also works for systems of lenses and other refracting surfaces, that is, it is commonly used to describe any optical system. The basic terms and definitions are as follows:

Optical Axis. The *optical axis* is the main axis of the optics, usually denoted as z-direction. For a typical system of centered and axial symmetric elements, it is the axis of symmetry of the optics. Usually it coincides with the main direction of light propagation. Points located on the optical axis and elements centered around it are called *on-axis*, otherwise denoted as *off-axis*. Mirrors can fold the linear axis into a set of piecewise linear sections.

Cardinal Planes. Refraction on the lens surfaces can be described by the concept of the *principal planes*, without having to take into account the exact radius of curvature. Extended towards the lens interior, the incoming and the outgoing rays intersect at a point on the *principal surface*. The projection of the intersection point onto the optical axis is called the corresponding *principal point*. In paraxial approximation the generally bent principal surface becomes flat, forming the *principal plane*. It is important to note that the principal planes are not necessarily located within the lens itself (Fig. 3.3b). This is often used to extend the optical length of compact telephoto lenses.

Focal Length. Within the paraxial domain, all incident rays entering parallel to the optical axis intersect at an on-axis point behind the lens, the *back focal point* (BFP) F'. Due to the reversibility of the ray paths, rays emerging from the *front focal point* (FFP) F run parallel to the axis

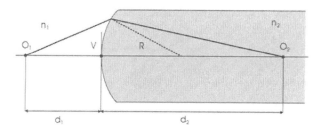

Figure 3.4: *Path of rays at a single spherical surface.*

after passing the lens. Rays emerging from off-axis points on the *focal plane* still form a parallel ray bundle, but are now nonparallel to the optical axis. The distance from the FFP to the front principal plane gives the *effective focal length* (EFL) of the lens. A change in refractive index from n_1 in front of the lens to n_2 behind the lens changes the back EFL f' to $n_2/n_1 f$. Therefore, the EFL in air is often referred to as the *focal length* of the lens. Additionally, the distances between the focal points and the lens vertices are called the *front focal length* (FFL) and *back focal length* (BFL), respectively; they equal each other only for symmetric lenses.

3.3.2 Spherical lenses

A spherical lens can be seen as two spherical surfaces with a medium of a constant index of refraction between them. To understand the behavior of these lenses, it is sufficient to analyze one of the surfaces. As illustrated in Fig. 3.4, a ray emerging from an on-axis object point O_1 intersects the optical axis at a point O_2 behind the spherical surface. Within the paraxial domain, all rays emerging from an object point intersect in one point in the image space. Thus, we say the object point is imaged onto its *optical conjugate* image point. The distances d_1 and d_2 of object and image points are correlated with the radius of curvature R of the surface and the indices of refraction n_1 and n_2 by *Abbe's invariant* Eq. (3.7).

$$\frac{n_2}{d_2} - \frac{n_1}{d_1} = \frac{n_2 - n_1}{R} \Rightarrow n_1 \left(\frac{1}{R} - \frac{1}{d_1} \right) = n_2 \left(\frac{1}{R} - \frac{1}{d_2} \right) \qquad (3.7)$$

A single surface separating regions of different refractive index is therefore sufficient to form an imaging optics, and can therefore be seen as the simplest possible lens. For every lens, focal length and principal planes can be used in order to describe paraxial properties. Setting either of the distances d_1 or d_2 to infinity yields both focal lengths

$$f_1 = R\frac{n_2}{n_2 - n_1} \qquad f_2 = -R\frac{n_1}{n_2 - n_1}$$

$$f_1 + f_2 = R \qquad n_1 f_1 = -n_2 f_2 \tag{3.8}$$

Both principal planes coincide at the location of the vertex V.

At present, a lens consists of two spherical surfaces, thereby enclosing the lens material. Using ray calculations similar to those for a single surface, without giving details of the calculations, the paraxial properties of the lens are obtained. We restrict ourselves to the commonly used case of a lens in air, thus the refractive indices of the surrounding medium become $n_1 = n_2 = 1$. With $D = V_1 V_2$ denoting the thickness of the lens, n_l its refractive index, and R_1 and R_2 the radii of curvature of its surfaces, the lens data calculates to

$$f = \frac{1}{n_l - 1}\frac{n_l R_1 R_2}{(n_l - 1)d + n_l(R_1 + R_2)} \tag{3.9}$$

$$v_1 = -\frac{R_2 D}{(n_l - 1)d + n_l(R_1 + R_2)} \tag{3.10}$$

$$v_2 = -\frac{R_1 D}{(n_l - 1)d + n_l(R_1 + R_2)} \tag{3.11}$$

$$h = D(1 - \frac{R_2 - R_1}{(n_l - 1)d + n_l(R_1 + R_2)}) \tag{3.12}$$

where $h = P_1 P_2$ denotes the distance between the principal planes, and $v_i = V_i P_i$ is the distance to the corresponding vertices. Because of the assumption of an identical refractive index on both sides of the lens, the front and back focal lengths of the lens coincide with the focal length f.

3.3.3 Aspherical lenses

Although they are the most popular lens type, spherical lenses are subject to certain limitations. For example, focusing of parallel ray bundles onto the focal point only works within the narrow paraxial domain. Nonspherically shaped surfaces allow lenses to be customized for specific purposes, for example, for optimal focusing, without the restriction to the paraxial domain. Typically, there are three types of aspherical surfaces:

Rotational symmetric surface. This type of surface is still rotationally symmetric to an axis, which usually coincides with the optical axis. Aspherical lenses are the most common type used for the correction of ray aberrations, which cannot be avoided. This type of surface can be

Table 3.1: *Conic surfaces*

Conic constant	Surface type
$K < -1$	Hyperboloid
$K = -1$	Paraboloid
$-1 < K < 0$	Ellipsoid
$K = 0$	Sphere
$K > 0$	Ellipsoid

described in terms of a curvature $C = 1/R$ and the *conic constant K*

$$z = \frac{Cx^2}{1 + \sqrt{1 - (K + 1)C^2x^2}} + \sum_{i=1}^{\infty} \alpha_{2i}x^{2i} \tag{3.13}$$

wherein the first term describes conic sections, and the second term higher-order deformations. As illustrated in Table 3.1, the conic constant controls the shape of the surface.

Aspherical lenses with conic surfaces are often used to extend ideal ray paths beyond the paraxial domain. These lenses do not satisfy the paraxial equations in any case, but have to be designed for the exact purpose for which they are intended. As an example, hyperbolic lenses can be designed for perfect focusing (Fig. 3.5a). If used for imaging with noninfinite distances, strong aberrations occur.

Toroidal lenses. Toroidal surfaces are spherical in two principal sections, which are perpendicular to each other. The radii of curvature differ between the two sections. The particular case of one of the curvatures is infinity, which results in *cylindrical lenses*. As an example of the use of toroidal lenses, two crossed cylindrical lenses of different focal length can be used to achieve different magnifications in sagittal and meridional sections. This *anamorphic imaging* is illustrated in Fig. 3.5b.

Freeform surfaces. Arbitrarily formed surfaces are used only for special applications and shall not be discussed herein.

3.3.4 Paraxial lenses

If the distance between the lens vertices (the lens thickness) can be neglected, the principal planes and the nodal planes converge onto a single plane, located at the lens position. Further restricting the rays to the paraxial domain, the lens can be described by a single parameter, its focal length. This is called the *thin paraxial lens*, which is used

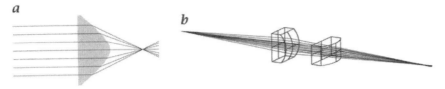

Figure 3.5: *a Perfect focusing outside the paraxial domain by an aspheric condensor lens. b Principle of anamorphic imaging.*

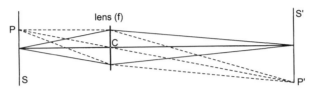

Figure 3.6: *Optical conjugates of a paraxial lens.*

widely in order to gain first-order approximations of the behavior of the optics. Above all, paraxial lens equations are most powerful in the first step of optics design, where its constraints can be established without the details of physical lenses. With a thin paraxial lens, all rays emerging from a point P intersect at its *conjugate point P'* behind the lens. Because all rays meet at exactly the same point, the lens is *aberration-free* (Fig. 3.6). Furthermore, because of the restriction to the paraxial domain, a plane S perpendicular to the optical axis is also imaged into a plane S'. In most optical systems several lenses are used to improve image quality. First, we introduce the extension of the thin paraxial lens toward the thick paraxial lens, where the lens thickness is taken into account. It can be shown that this lens can equivalently be seen as the combination of two thin paraxial lenses. This will lead to a general method to describe arbitrary paraxial systems by a single paraxial lens.

3.3.5 Thick lenses

If the thickness of a lens cannot be neglected, the concept of the paraxial lens has to be extended towards *thick paraxial lenses*. In this case, the two principal planes no longer converge to a single plane, but are separated by an equivalent distance, the *nodal space*. As a general rule, for lenses in air the nodal space is approximately one-third of the lens thickness [1]. As illustrated in Fig. 3.7a, rays can be constructed by elongation of the unrefracted ray towards the first principal plane P, traversing the ray parallel to the optical axis to the second principal plane, and continuing to the conjugate point P'. For geometric con-

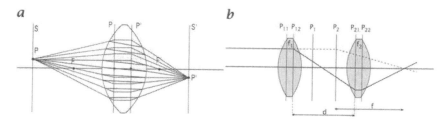

Figure 3.7: *a Ray paths for a thick paraxial lens. Dashed lines show the physical ray paths, solid lines show the virtual rays used for construction of ray paths; b a system of thick lenses and its equivalent thick lens.*

struction of ray paths, rays in between the principal planes are always parallel to the axis. As a consequence the nodal points coincide with the principal points.

3.3.6 Systems of lenses

A complex optical system consists of several thick lenses. A pair of thick lenses, described by the set of four principal planes and two focal points, can be converted into a new equivalent lens, with two principal planes and one focal length. Applying this recursively to the lens system, the complete setup can be condensed into one thick lens. Within the paraxial domain, this powerful approach facilitates dealing with optics of high complexity. Figure 3.7b illustrates the equivalent principal planes of the two-lens system; P_{11} and P_{12} are the principal planes of the first lens, and P_{21} and P_{22} are the principal planes of the second lens. The position p_i of the principal planes and the effective focal length of the equivalent system, provided the lenses are used in air (n=1), are given by

$$\frac{1}{f} = \frac{1}{f_1} + \frac{1}{f_2} - \frac{d}{f_1 f_2} \qquad p = \overline{P_1 P_2} = -\frac{f d^2}{f_1 f_2} \qquad (3.14)$$

$$p_1 = \overline{P_{11} P_1} = \frac{f d}{f_2} \qquad p_2 = \overline{P_{22} P_2} = -\frac{f d}{f_1} \qquad (3.15)$$

The cardinal planes can occur in any order, for example, it is common that the order of the principal planes P_1 and P_2 becomes reversed with lenses located closely together. Table 3.2 gives an overview of the order of the cardinal planes of a system of two lenses of positive focal length.

3.3.7 Matrix optics

Tracing rays through an optical system allows for in-depth analysis of the optics, taking into account all surfaces and materials. An ele-

Table 3.2: *Overview of the most important parameters of the combined lens and the order of the cardinal planes in case of $d, f_1, f_2 > 0$; L_i indicates the position of lens i*

Focal length	$d < f_1 + f_2$	$d > f_1 + f_2$
	$f > 0$	$f < 0$
p_1	$p_1 > 0$	$p_1 < 0$
p_2	$p_2 < 0$	$p_2 > 0$
	$\|v_1\| + \|v_2\| > d$	$\|v_1\| + \|v_2\| < d$
Relative position	P_1 is behind P_2	P_1 is in front of P_2
Order	$f_1 \leq d, f_2 \leq d \rightarrow P_2 L_1 L_2 P_1$	
of	$f_1 \leq d, f_2 \geq d \rightarrow P_2 L_1 P_1 L_2$	$P_1 \ L_1 \ L_2 \ P_2$
cardinal	$f_1 \geq d, f_2 \leq d \rightarrow L_1 P_2 L_2 P_1$	
planes	$f_1 \geq d, f_2 \geq d \rightarrow L_1 P_2 P_1 L_2$	

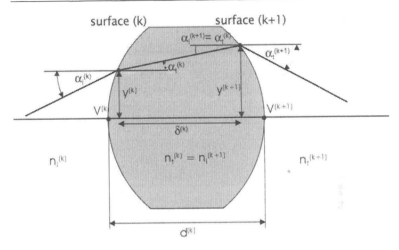

Figure 3.8: *Notation used for the matrix optic calculations.*

gant method to describe ray propagation between the surfaces of the system has been introduced by T. Smith [2]. Within the paraxial domain, it is possible to describe both refraction and ray propagation by simple matrix operations. The ray tracing can be achieved by matrix multiplication of the matrices describing the optical elements and their distances. In order to describe this method, all surfaces are numbered consecutively from left to right and are denoted by superscripts. Rays incoming to a surface are denoted by i; outgoing rays are denoted by t. The notation is illustrated in Fig. 3.8.

Vector notation for rays. A ray of angle α and distance y with respect to the optical axis is denoted by the vector

$$r = \begin{pmatrix} n\alpha \\ y \end{pmatrix} \tag{3.16}$$

Refraction at a single surface. Refraction of a ray of incident angle n_i and distance y_i to the optical axis can be written using the power $\mathcal{D}$ of a single surface

$$n_t^{(k)} \alpha_t^{(k)} = n_i^{(k)} \alpha_i^{(k)} - \mathcal{D}^{(k)} y_i^{(k)} \tag{3.17}$$

$$y_t^{(k)} = y_i^{(k)} \tag{3.18}$$

$$\mathcal{D}^{(k)} = \frac{n_t^{(k)} - n_i^{(k)}}{R^{(k)}} \tag{3.19}$$

Equation (3.20) can be rewritten as a matrix equation

$$r_t^{(k)} = \begin{pmatrix} n_t^{(k)} \alpha_t^{(k)} \\ y_t^{(k)} \end{pmatrix} = \begin{pmatrix} 1 & -\mathcal{D}^{(k)} \\ 0 & 1 \end{pmatrix} \begin{pmatrix} n_i^{(k)} \alpha_i^{(k)} \\ y_i^{(k)} \end{pmatrix} =: \mathcal{R}^{(k)} r_i^{(k)} \tag{3.20}$$

whereas the matrix $\mathcal{R}^{(k)}$ denotes the *refraction matrix* of the surface (k).

Ray propagation. The propagation of a ray between two consecutive surfaces (k) and $(k + 1)$ is linear due to the fact that no change in the refractive index can occur. Therefore replacing the true distance $\delta^{(k)}$ by its paraxial approximation $d^{(k)}$ yields $y_i^{(k+1)} = d^{(k)} \alpha_t^{(k)} + y_t^{(k)}$, and thus ray propagation towards the next surface can be expressed by the *transfer matrix* $\mathcal{T}^{()}$

$$r_i^{(k+1)} = \begin{pmatrix} n_i^{(k+1)} \alpha_i^{(k+1)} \\ y_i^{(k+1)} \end{pmatrix} = \begin{pmatrix} 1 & 0 \\ \frac{d^{(k)}}{n_t^{(k)}} & 1 \end{pmatrix} \begin{pmatrix} n_t^{(k)} \alpha_t^{(k)} \\ y_t^{(k)} \end{pmatrix} =: \mathcal{T}^{(k)} r_t^{(k)} \tag{3.21}$$

System matrix. Now refraction at single surfaces (Eq. (3.20)) is combined with ray propagation between two surfaces (Eq. (3.21)) to grasp the behavior of a lens consisting of two surfaces. A ray emerging from the second lens surface can be calculated from the incident ray by applying the refraction matrix of the first surface, the transfer matrix between the surfaces, and finally the refraction matrix of the second surface. This is done by simple matrix multiplication:

$$r_t^{(k+1)} = \mathcal{R}^{(k+1)} \mathcal{T}^{(k)} \mathcal{R}^{(k)} r_i^{(k)} =: S^{(k+1,k)} = \mathcal{R}^{(k+1)} \mathcal{T}^{(k)} \mathcal{R}^{(k)} \tag{3.22}$$

with system matrix $S^{(k+1,k)}$ of the optical element. It transforms an incident ray at the first surface (k) to an emerging ray at the next surface

Table 3.3: *System matrices for various optical elements*

Optics	System matrix	Optics	System matrix
Straight section	$\begin{pmatrix} 1 & 0 \\ \frac{d}{n} & 1 \end{pmatrix}$	Dielectric interface	$\begin{pmatrix} 1 & 0 \\ 0 & 1 \end{pmatrix}$
Plate in air	$\begin{pmatrix} 1 & 0 \\ \frac{d}{n} & 1 \end{pmatrix}$	Spherical interface	$\begin{pmatrix} 1 & -\mathcal{D} \\ 0 & 1 \end{pmatrix}$
Thin lens in air	$\begin{pmatrix} 1 & -1/f \\ 0 & 1 \end{pmatrix}$	Thick lens in air	$\begin{pmatrix} 1 - \frac{p_1}{f} & -\frac{1}{f} \\ \frac{p_1 p_2}{f} + p_1 - p_2 & 1 + \frac{p_2}{f} \end{pmatrix}$
Spherical mirror	$\begin{pmatrix} 1 & -\frac{2}{R} \\ 0 & 1 \end{pmatrix}$	Two thin lenses in air	$\begin{pmatrix} 1 - d/f_2 & 1/f \\ d & 1 - d/f_1 \end{pmatrix}$
Spherical lens	$\begin{pmatrix} 1 - \frac{d}{n}\mathcal{D}^{(2)} & \frac{d}{n}\mathcal{D}^{(1)}\mathcal{D}^{(2)} - (\mathcal{D}^{(1)} + \mathcal{D}^{(2)}) \\ \frac{d}{n} & 1 - \frac{d}{n}\mathcal{D}^{(2)} \end{pmatrix}$		

$(k+1)$. In general, any optical element with an arbitrary number of surfaces is described by a single system matrix. Assuming N surfaces, the system matrix is denoted $S^{(N,1)}$ in order to indicate the number of surfaces. It is given by

$$S^{(N,1)} = \mathcal{R}^{(N)} \mathcal{T}^{(N-1)} \mathcal{R}^{(N-1)} ... \mathcal{T}^{(1)} \mathcal{R}^{(1)} = \mathcal{R}^{(N)} \prod_{k=1}^{N-1} \mathcal{T}^{(k)} \mathcal{R}^{(k)} \qquad (3.23)$$

Equation (3.23) can be split at any surface (k) between the first and the last and rewritten as

$$S^{(N,1)} = S^{(N,k)} \mathcal{T}^{(k-1)} S^{(k-1,1)} \qquad \text{with} \quad 1 < k < N \qquad (3.24)$$

Equation (3.24) makes it easy to combine optical elements into more and more complex optical systems by reusing the known system matrices of the simpler elements.

Table of system matrices. The system matrix is the fundamental description of optical elements, and therefore is the basis of matrix optics calculation. Table 3.3 provides an overview of the most important system matrices of simple optical elements consisting of two surfaces. Elements of higher complexity can be calculated according to Eq. (3.24). To simplify notation, the index of refraction of the lens material is denoted by n, and the thickness of the lens is denoted by d.

Table 3.4: *Most important Fraunhofer spectral lines*

Symbol	Wavelength [nm]	Color	Element
i	365.0	UV	Hg
h	404.7	violet	Hg
g	435.8	blue	Hg
F'	480.0	blue	Cd
F	486.1	blue/green	H
e	546.1	yellow/green	Hg
d or D_3	587.6	orange	He
D_2	589.0	orange	Na
D	589.3	orange	Na
D_1	589.6	orange	Na
C'	643.8	orange	Cd
C	656.3	red	H
r	706.5	red	He
A'	768.2	red	K

3.4 Optical properties of glasses

3.4.1 Dispersion

Glasses and other material are characterized mainly by two properties: refractive index and dispersion. Dispersion means that the refractive index depends on the wavelength of the light. Therefore, in order to describe the refractive properties of any material, the dispersion curve $n(\lambda)$ has to be given. In practice, the refractive index is given only for a number of standardized wavelengths. These wavelengths correspond to spectral lines of specific chemical elements in which wavelengths are known with great precision. A table of the widely used wavelengths, together with their international symbol and the chemical element from which they arise, are given in Table 3.4.

For any other wavelengths in the visible, near UV and in the near IR range, the refractive index can be calculated by several common interpolation formulas. The most widely used are summarized in Table 3.5. The coefficients needed for the formulas are available in the glass catalogs of all major glass manufacturers, such as Schott [3]. It is often recommended to check the exact definitions of the formulas used before inserting coefficients from glass catalogs. This is because the formulas are often slightly modified by the manufacturers.

Table 3.5: *Dispersion formulas for glasses*

Name	Formula
Schott[1]	$n(\lambda) = a_0 + a_1\lambda^2 + a_2\lambda^{-2} + a_3\lambda^{-4} + a_4\lambda^{-6} + a_5\lambda^{-8}$
Sellmeier 1	$n^2(\lambda) = 1 + \dfrac{K_1\lambda^2}{\lambda^2 - L_1} + \dfrac{K_2\lambda^2}{\lambda^2 - L_2} + \dfrac{K_3\lambda^3}{\lambda^3 - L_3}$
Sellmeier 2	$n^2(\lambda) = 1 + A + \dfrac{B_1\lambda^2}{\lambda^2 - \lambda_1^2} + \dfrac{B_2\lambda^2}{\lambda^2 - \lambda_2^2}$
Herzberger[2]	$n(\lambda) = A + BL(\lambda) + CL^2(\lambda) + D\lambda^2 + E\lambda^4 + F\lambda^4$ with $L(\lambda) = \dfrac{1}{\lambda^2 - 0.028)}$
Conrady[3]	$n(\lambda) = n_0 + \dfrac{A}{\lambda} + \dfrac{B}{\lambda^{3.5}}$

[1]Schott no longer uses this formula, but it is still widely used.
[2]Mainly used in the infrared.
[3]Mainly used for fitting of sparse data.

3.4.2 Technical characterization of dispersion

In many cases, it is not necessary to know the complete dispersion relation $n(\lambda)$. Instead, a usable and short characterization of the glass is more useful. Usually, the *main refractive index* is employed as a characterization of the glass. It is defined as the refractive index at the wavelength λ_d or λ_e according to Table 3.5. As a code for the dispersion, *Abbe number* is widely used. Two definitions according to the use of either n_e or n_d as the main refractive index are common:

$$V_d = \frac{n_d - 1}{n_F - n_C} \qquad V_e = \frac{n_e - 1}{n_{F'} - n_{C'}} \tag{3.25}$$

Main refractive index and the Abbe number are combined in order to form a 6-digit number, the so-called *MIL number*. The first three digits of the MIL number are the d-light refractive index minus one, without the decimal place. The last three digits are the Abbe number V_d times 10; for example, the MIL-number of BK7 glas is 517642.

3.5 Aberrations

So far, lenses have been described by the paraxial approximation. Within their limits perfect image quality is achieved. In practice, an optics never reaches this ideal behavior, but shows degradations of image quality caused by *aberrations*. These are divided into two main classes

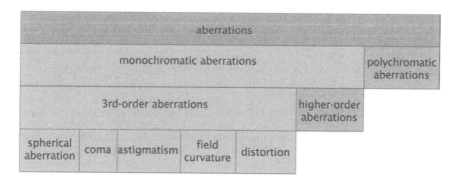

Figure 3.9: *Classification of aberrations.*

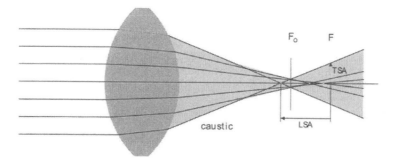

Figure 3.10: *Spherical aberration of a convex lens. To obtain the best image quality, the image plane has to be moved from the paraxial focal plane F to the optimal position F_o. The caustic is the envelope of the outgoing ray bundle.*

according to their cause. The change of refractive index with wavelength causes *polychromatic aberrations* that even exist in paraxial optics. Nonparaxial rays, which appear in any real optics, are the cause of *monochromatic aberrations*. The latter can be described by taking into account the higher-order terms in the series expansion equation (Eq. (3.6)). The third-order aberrations are divided into the five *primary aberrations* (see Fig. 3.9), also known as *Seidel aberrations*. Three of them, namely, spherical aberration, coma and astigmatism, cause image degradations by blurring, while field curvature and distortion deform the image. Understanding aberrations helps to achieve the best possible image quality, and leads to the suppression of aberrations by corrected optics.

3.5.1 Spherical aberrations

Outside the paraxial domain, a spherical surface no longer focuses parallel ray bundles onto a single point. On the contrary, rays hitting the

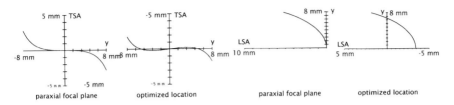

Figure 3.11: *Longitudinal and transversal spherical aberration for the lens from Fig. 3.10. Only TSA can be reduced by relocating the image plane.*

surface at a greater distance to the axis are focused on a point closer to the surface than rays nearer to the axis. The focal length then depends on the radial distance y of the ray to the optical axis.

To describe the strength of a spherical aberration, the axial distance from the true focal point to the paraxial focal point is used; this is called the *longitudinal spherical aberration* (LSA). The sign of the LSA equals the sign of the focal length of the lens. Thus a convex lens with positive focal length bends nonparaxial rays too much, so they intersect the axis in front of the paraxial focus. Diverging lenses with negative focal length focus tend to focus behind the paraxial focus.

To represent the influence of spherical aberrations on image quality, the *transversal spherical aberration* (TSA) can be used. It is defined as the radial distance of the intersection of the outgoing ray with the rear paraxial focal plane, as illustrated in Fig. 3.10. Due to the aberration, exact focusing become impossible.

For practical purposes, it is necessary to minimize the influence of the aberration. This can be done by several methods:

- **Low aperture.** Choosing a larger f-number reduces SA, but causes an unavoidable loss of brightness. Nevertheless, because LSA $\sim y^2$ and TSA $\sim y^3$, this is a very effective way to suppress SA.

- **Image plane shift.** To minimize blur while maintaining the aperture setting, it is optimal to move the image plane to the position I_o where the diameter of the caustic is minimal. The minimal but unavoidable blur circle is called the circle of least confusion. The suppression of spherical aberration is illustrated in Fig. 3.10. It is important to note that the location of the image plane I_o depends on the imaging conditions, in particular on object distance and f-number.

- **Optimal lens arranging.** Reducing spherical aberration can also be achieved by arranging the surfaces of the system in such a manner that the angles of the rays to the surfaces are as small as possible. This is because SA is caused by the violation of the small angle approximation. The refraction should be evenly distributed among the various surfaces.

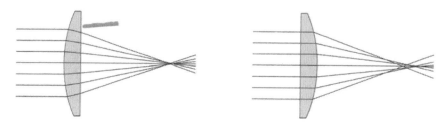

Figure 3.12: *The SA of a planoconvex lens (left: correct lens orientation; right: incorrect lens orientation). Turning the lens to the correct orientation strongly reduces SA.*

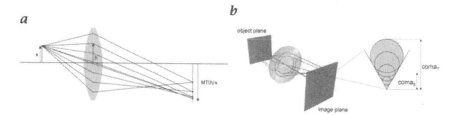

Figure 3.13: *a Illustration of negative coma. The transversal magnification decreases with ray height h. b Positive coma of a single point source.*

As a general rule, a single lens should always be used with its flat side pointing towards the rays with the higher angles of incidence. When imaging distant objects, a planoconvex lens with an almost flat rear side will produce the best results. For close range imaging a more symmetric lens is more preferable. The reduction of SA by simply turning the lens is illustrated in Fig. 3.12.

3.5.2 Coma

Coma is an aberration associated with off-axis object points. Even a small distance from the axis can cause visible coma in the image. Because of its asymmetric shape, coma is often considered the worst of all aberrations. It is caused by the dependence of the transversal magnification M_T on the ray height. Even in the absence of spherical aberration, this inhibits a focusing of the object point onto a single image point (Fig. 3.13a). Coma is considered positive if the magnification increases with increasing ray height h. The image of a point source formed by a lens flawed with coma only shows a comet tail-like shape. The pattern can be seen as a series of nonconcentric circles, whereby each circle is formed from the rays passing the lens at the same radial distance h (Fig. 3.13b). The centers of the circles are shifted according to the change of M_T with h. Notice that as the rays go around the aperture

a 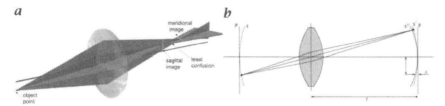 *b*

***Figure 3.14: a** Astigmatism. The focal length differs for the sagittal and the meridional plane. **b** Effect of field curvature. Instead of the planes P and P' being conjugated, the spheres S and S' are conjugated. Thus, the parabolic Petzval surface S'' is conjugated to the object plane P.*

circle on the lens once, they go around the circle in the coma patch twice. This is why both the tangential as well as the sagittal ray fan form a radial line in the patch. Consequently, the length of both lines is used in order to describe the amount of coma, denoted as sagittal and tangential coma (see Fig. 3.13b).

3.5.3 Astigmatism

Astimatism is associated with nonskew ray bundles emerging from nonaxial source points. It is convenient to look at two planar ray bundles in the meridional and in the sagittal planes. The meridional plane is defined as the plane containing the optical axis and the chief ray, while the sagittal plane contains the chief ray and is perpendicular to the meridional plane. Both planes change with the source point of the rays. In addition, the sagittal plane changes with each surface, while the meridional plane remains the same within the optical system. Assuming an optical element of axial symmetry, for an on-axis point there is no difference between the sagittal and the meridional plane. An off-axis point will show the lens under different angles, causing the effective focal lengths in the two planes to be different. The difference of the focal length increases with the paraxial focal length of the lens and the skew angle of the rays. The shape of the caustic of the outgoing ray bundle changes from circular shape near the lens to a line in the meridional plane at the meridional image distance. The shape changes further to a perpendicular line at the sagittal image (see Fig. 3.14a and Fig. 3.15). Of course, astigmatism is present for on-axis object points in systems without axial symmetry such as optics containing cylindrical lenses.

3.5.4 Field curvature

With an optical system otherwise free of aberrations, the fact that the cardinal planes are not truly plane causes a primary aberration called the *Petzval field curvature*. Because of the absence of other aberrations

sagittal   meridional
focus   focus

Figure 3.15: *Spot diagrams showing the change of the cross section of the caustic with increasing distance from the lens. The circle of least confusion is located between the two foci.*

the image of a point source is again a point. Within the paraxial domain, all points on the object plane would be imaged exactly to points on the image plane. Because the cardinal planes are spheres outside the paraxial domain, the conjugate planes turn into conjugate spheres (Fig. 3.14b). Consequently, forcing the source points on a plane surface deforms the image surface to a parabolic surface, the *Petzval surface*. A lens with positive focal length bends the Petzval surface towards the lens while a negative lens bends the Petzval surface away from it. Combining lenses with positive and negative focal length can therefore eliminate field curvature by flattening the Petzval surface to a plane. A system of two thin lenses of focal lengths f_1 and f_2 fulfilling the Petzval condition

$$n_1 f_1 + n_2 f_2 = 0 \qquad\qquad (3.26)$$

is therefore free of any field curvature. Field curvature can also be corrected by moving the stop. Such methods are often combined by using an additional meniscus lens according to Eq. (3.26) and a stop near that lens.

3.5.5 Distortions

Displacement of image points with respect to their paraxial locations causes distortions of the image geometry without degrading sharpness. Usually, the displacement increases with the object height as the rays become more inclined. For an optical system of rotational symmetry, the shift of the image points is purely radial and distortion can also be seen as a dependence of the transversal magnification of the distance of the object to the axis. Figure 3.16 illustrates this by imaging a rectangular grid with a complex wide angle lens. As always typical for a wide angle lens, it is flawed with heavy radial distortion. It is important to note that reversing the lens elements causes the distortion change from barrel to pincushion or vice versa. This can be used to eliminate distortion in slides by using the same lens for imaging and for projection.

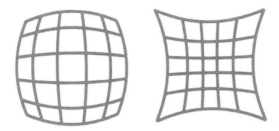

Figure 3.16: *Distortion illustrated by imaging a rectangular grid. Positive distortion causes a pincushion-like shape (right), negative distortion a barrel-shaped image (left).*

Table 3.6: *Distortion caused by stop position*

Focal length	Stop in front of lens	Stop behind lens
Positive	Negative distortion (barrel)	Positive distortion (pincushion)
Negative	Positive distortion (pincushion)	Negative distortion (barrel)

Distortion is influenced by the thickness of the lens and the position of the aperture stop. However, stopping down the aperture does not reduce distortion but it reduces the other aberrations. Therefore, positioning the stop at an appropriate position is often done to correct for distortion.

A complex lens system consisting of several lenses or lens groups tends to show distortions because the front lens group acts as an aperture stop in front of the rear lens group. Telephoto lenses typically consist of a positive front group and a negative rear group that can be moved against each other in order to focus or change focal length. Distortion can therefore change with the focal length, even from positive to negative distortion.

3.5.6 Chromatic aberrations

So far, we have only considered monochromatic aberrations caused by the nonlinearity of the law of refraction. The dependence of the refractive index of almost all materials on the wavelength of the light introduces a new type of aberration, because rays of different colors travel on different paths through the optics. Therefore, the images of

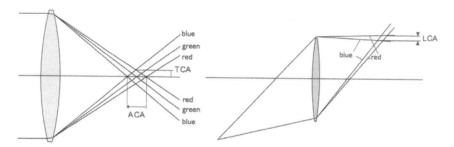

Figure 3.17: *Axial, transverse and longitudinal chromatic aberrations. Different rays correspond to different wavelengths.*

a point source are different for light of different wavelengths. In particular, the focal length of a lens varies with wavelength.

The effects of chromatic aberration are similar to those of spherical aberration (SA) and in analogy to SA described as axial (ACA) and transverse (TCA) chromatic aberration. As shown in Fig. 3.17, ACA is defined as the axial distance of the focal points corresponding to two different wavelengths. ACA is called positive if the focal length increases with wavelength, otherwise it is denoted as negative. A positive lens generally shows positive ACA because of the positive Abbe number of all glasses. As then expected, negative lenses cause negative ACA. The radius of the blur circle caused by the different focal lengths is called the transverse chromatic aberration TCA. In addition, CA causes the transversal magnification to become wavelength dependent. This is described by the lateral chromatic aberration (LCA), defined as the axial distance of the different image points.

3.5.7 Reducing aberrations

In the previous sections the primary aberrations have been explained in detail. It is obvious that the image degradation caused by the aberrations has to be suppressed as much as possible in order to achieve a good image quality. This in normally done during the design process of an optics, where ray tracing techniques are used in order to calculate the aberrations and to optimize the system for its desired purpose. Besides these inner parameters of the optics, the strength of aberration is influenced by outer parameters such as f-number or field angle. Image quality can therefore be improved by paying attention to some basic design rules. First of all, aberrations can be influenced by the aperture size h, which is the radial height of the ray hitting the aperture stop, and the radial distance of the object source point from the axis, the field height y. Table 3.7 summarizes the dependence of the Seidel and chromatic aberration from these two parameters. Thus it can be seen

Table 3.7: *Summary of the strength of primary aberrations by field height h and aperture y, according to [4]*

Aberration	Radial (blur)	Axial (focal shift)
Spherical aberration	y^3	y^2
Coma	y^2h	
Astigmatism	yh^2	h^2
Field curvature	yh^2	h^2
Distortion	h^3	
Axial chromatic aberration		y
Lateral chromatic aberration	h	

that distortion is the only primary aberration that cannot be suppressed by stopping down the aperture. Spherical aberration does not depend on the field height and is therefore the only monochromatic aberration that occurs for on-axis points. In order to estimate the strength of image blur, the radial column of Table 3.7 can be used. For example, if the f-number is increased one step, the aperture size is decreased by a factor of $\sqrt{2}$, meaning that blur circle according to SA is decreased by nearly a factor of three.

3.6 Optical image formation

3.6.1 Geometry of image formation

This section summarizes the most important lens equations used in order to calculate image position and size for imaging optics using the paraxial approximation. The terms used in the following formulas are illustrated in Fig. 3.18a. The distance d of the object point P from the front principal plane and its conjugate distance d' of the image point P' from the back principal plane both have positive sign in the particular direction away from the lens. The radial distance of image and source point are denoted by y' and y, respectively. As the refractive index of the medium can change from n to n' at the lens, its vacuum focal length f changes to $f' = n'f$ or $\tilde{f} = nf$. Because rays can be thought of as being axis-parallel between the two principal planes, these have been collapsed into a single one for simplicity in the drawing.

The lens equations are commonly expressed either in terms of distances related to the principal planes (d, d') or related to the focal points (z, z'), defined as $z = d - \tilde{f}$ and $z' = d' - f'$. The basic lens equation relates the object and source distances with the focal length:

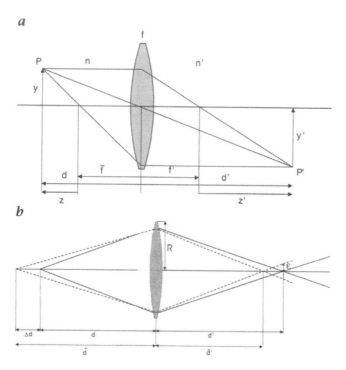

Figure 3.18: a *Terms used for the lens equations.* **b** *Geometry of image formation for depth-of-field calculations.*

Distances related to principal planes	Distances related to focal planes
$\dfrac{f'}{d'} + \dfrac{\tilde{f}}{d} = 1$ or $\dfrac{1}{f} = \dfrac{n}{d} + \dfrac{n'}{d'}$	$zz' = \tilde{f}f'$

Besides the distances, the image and source heights are related by the *transversal magnification* M_T, defined as the ratio of image to source height; M_T is therefore given by

Distances related to principal planes	Distances related to focal planes
$M_T = \dfrac{y'}{y} = -\dfrac{d'n}{dn'}$	$M_T = -\sqrt{\dfrac{z'n}{zn'}}$

It is sometimes convenient to express image space quantities only in object space terms and vice versa.

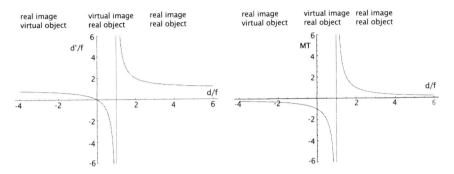

Figure 3.19: *Dependence of the image distance and the transversal magnification with object location. Note that all axes are drawn in units of the focal length of the lens. Their signs will be reversed if a negative lens is considered.*

Distances related to principal planes		Distances related to focal planes	
Image space	Object space	Image space	Object space
$d' = \dfrac{n'fd}{d - nf}$	$d = \dfrac{nfd'}{d' - n'f}$		
$d' = f'(1 - M_T)$	$d = \tilde{f}\left(1 - \dfrac{1}{M_T}\right)$	$z' = -f'M_T$	$z = -\dfrac{\tilde{f}}{M_T}$
$M_T = \dfrac{n'f}{d - nf}$	$M_T = -\dfrac{d' - n'f}{nf}$		

Imaging an object extended in all three dimensions results in a 3-D image filling the image space. In addition to the transversal magnification therefore, the axial extent of the image has to be related to the axial extent of the object. This is done by the *longitudinal magnification*

$$M_L := \frac{\partial d'}{\partial d} = M_T^2 \qquad (3.27)$$

which is the square of the transversal magnification.

Figure 3.19 gives an overview of the image distance and the magnification with respect to the object distance. It can be seen that depending on the object distance, the image distance can have positive or negative values. A positive image distance corresponds to a *real image* at which position the rays are focused to form an image.

A *virtual image*, associated with negative image distances, means that the rays in the image space behave as if they would emerge from a point in the object space. There is no point where the rays physically intersect each other, meaning that a virtual image cannot be recorded directly. This is summarized in Table 3.8.

Table 3.8:

Object location	Image location	Image type	Image orientation	M_T
Convex lens ($f > 0$)				
$\infty > d > 2f$	$f < d' < 2f$	real	inverted	$-1 < M_T < 0$
$d = 2f$	$d' = 2f$	real	inverted	$M_T = -1$
$f < d < 2f$	$\infty > d' > 2f$	real	inverted	$M_T < -1$
$d = f$	$d' = \infty$			
$d < f$	$d' > d$	virtual	erected	$M_T > 1$
Concave lens ($f < 0$)				
$0 < d \leq \infty$	$|d'| < \min(|f|, d)$	virtual	erected	$0 < M_T < 1$

3.6.2 Depth-of-field and focus

A paraxial lens of focal length f focuses all rays emerging from a point P onto its corresponding point P' in image space according to the basic lens equation

$$\frac{1}{f} = \frac{1}{d} + \frac{1}{d'} \tag{3.28}$$

Therefore only objects located at a given distance d are well focused onto the image plane at the fixed position d', whereas objects at other distances $\tilde{d}$ appear blurred (see Fig. 3.18b). The distance range in which the blur does not exceed a certain value is called the depth-of-field. A good value to characterize the depth-of-field is f-number $f/2R$, which gives the ratio of the focal length to the diameter of the lens. At a zero order approximation, blurring is described by the radius ϵ of the blur circle for an object point at $\tilde{d} = d + \Delta d$, which is controlled by the ratio of the image distances

$$\frac{\epsilon}{R} = \frac{d'}{\tilde{d}'} - 1 = d' \frac{\Delta d}{d\tilde{d}} \tag{3.29}$$

The depth-of-field is now determined by the choice of a maximal radius of the blur circle, the so-called circle of confusion. If ϵ_c denotes the circle of confusion, the depth-of-field can be expressed in terms of the magnification $M = b/g$, the f-number $O = f/2R$, and the object distances:

$$\Delta d = \frac{2O}{M_T f} \tilde{d}\epsilon_c = \frac{d}{\frac{M_T f}{2O\epsilon_c} - 1} \quad \Leftrightarrow \quad |\Delta d| = \frac{2O}{M_T f} \tilde{d}|\epsilon_c| = \frac{d}{1 \mp \frac{M_T f}{2O\epsilon_c}} \tag{3.30}$$

In Eq. (3.29) we combined the two distinct cases of Δd being positive or negative by understanding ϵ having the same sign as Δd. Distinguishing between positive and negative signs now shows the inherent asymmetry for the depth-of-field, caused by the nonlinearity of Eq. (3.28). Therefore it is a common practice to assume $M_T R \gg \epsilon_c$, leading to the approximation of $\tilde{d} \approx d$ in Eq. (3.30) and removing the asymmetry.

Moving the image plane instead of moving the object plane also causes a defocused image. Equivalent to the depth-of-field in object space the term depth of focus in image space denotes the maximal dislocation of the image plane with respect to a given circle of confusion. Again, with the approximation of the circle of confusion being small compared to the lens radius, the depth of focus is given by

$$\Delta d' = \frac{2O}{f} d' \epsilon_c \qquad (3.31)$$

The relation between depth of focus and depth-of-field is given by the longitudinal magnification M_T^2.

$$\Delta d = M_T^2 \Delta d' = M_L \Delta d' \qquad (3.32)$$

For far-field imaging, M_T is small and therefore a small depth-of-field causes a small depth of focus. In contrast, both close-up and microscopic imaging with large magnifications show a large depth of focus and a small depth-of-field at the same time. Finding the position of best focus may be difficult in this particular situation.

3.6.3 Telecentric optics

With this setup, the aperture stop is located at the rear focal point of the respective optics. The effect is that all principal rays in object space are parallel to the optical axis (Fig. 3.20). Only narrow and axis-parallel ray bundles contribute to image formation. This is often used in precision measuring, where an object is viewed by a screen or camera at a fixed position. If the object is moved slightly away from the optimal position, its image becomes blurred, but also the transversal magnification changes so that a different object size is obtained. A telecentric setup corrects this by making the principal ray independent of the object position, therefore preserving magnification. Obviously only an object smaller than the lens diameter can be viewed. Therefore the use of telecentric optics is normally restricted to close-range imaging. To achieve the best results, the illumination system should be telecentric as well, and the aperture of both the illumination and the imaging system should be the same.

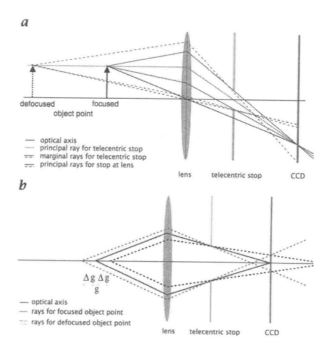

Figure 3.20: *a As the principal ray is independent of the object position blur does not cause size changes; b independence of the radius of the blur circle from the location.*

3.7 Wave and Fourier optics

Pure geometric optics, as we have considered so far, is limited to the calculation of the paths of bundles of light rays through an optical system and the parameters that can be extracted from these. Intensity of these bundles is especially important for imaging optics but is not readily quantified with geometric optics. The depth-of-field calculations explained in Section 3.6 clearly demonstrate this drawback, and while it is possible to obtain the size of the blur circle, the intensity distribution of the image of a blurred spot cannot be calculated exactly. Fourier optics provide a better means of understanding the behavior of an optical system without the need to delve deeply into the details of wave optics.

3.7.1 Linear optical systems

Point spread function. The point spread function is one of the central concepts used in Fourier optics because it allows the description of a complex optical system as a linear superposition of images of single spot sources. This concept allows the handling of different imaging

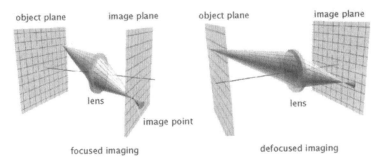

object plane image plane object plane image plane

lens lens

image point

focused imaging defocused imaging

Figure 3.21: *Focused and defocused imaging of an object point onto the image plane.*

problems such as quantitative description of image blurring, depth-from-focus reconstruction, and 3-D imaging of nonopaque volume objects as they occur with light or confocal microscopy, using the same mathematical description. The image of an object is the superposition of the images of all object points. Figure 3.21 illustrates the situation for both a well-focused and an ill-focused setup. An ideal aberration-free optics would image every object point onto its conjugate point in the image plane. In the case of defocus the rays emerging from the object point no longer intersect at the image plane but at the plane conjugate to the actual object plane. The image of the object point is therefore an intensity distribution at the image plane, which is is called the *point spread function* (PSF) of the lens.

Assuming that the PSF does not change for various object points, the effect of blurring can be described as a convolution of the well-focused image, as it would be achieved by a pinhole camera, with the PSF:

$$g(\boldsymbol{x}') = \int f(\boldsymbol{x}(\vec{\xi}'))PSF(\vec{\xi}' - \boldsymbol{x})d^2\xi' = f(\boldsymbol{x}(\boldsymbol{x}')) * PSF(\boldsymbol{x}') \quad (3.33)$$

It is important to note that the description by a convolution is only valid in case of a linear, shift-invariant system.

Shape of the PSF. In many cases the shape of the PSF remains unchanged for every object point, independent of its distance from the plane of best focus. Then, the PSF can be described by a shape function S and a scaling factor σ that varies with the distance g':

$$PSF_Z(\boldsymbol{x}) = \frac{S(\boldsymbol{x}/\sigma(Z))}{\int S(\boldsymbol{x}/\sigma(Z)) \, d^2x} \quad (3.34)$$

The denominator normalizes the PSF to $\int PSF_Z(\boldsymbol{x})d^2x = 1$, forcing gray-value preservation. In many cases it is sufficient to replace σ by the radius of the blur circle ϵ. The shape function can be completely different for different optical setups. Nevertheless, only a few

Table 3.9: *Standard functions for point spread functions of optical systems*

Function	PSF	Used for
Box $\dfrac{1}{\pi\sigma^2}\Pi\left(\dfrac{|\boldsymbol{x}|}{2\sigma}\right)$		Optical systems with circular aperture stop that are not dominated by wave optics.
Noncircular Box $\dfrac{1}{\pi\sigma^2}\Pi\left(\dfrac{|\boldsymbol{x}|}{2\sigma}\right)$		Optics with the same properties as above, but with a noncircular aperture stop, as with adjustable iris diaphragms. The shape function reflects the shape of the aperture stop.
Gaussian $\dfrac{1}{2\pi\sigma}\exp\left(-\dfrac{\boldsymbol{x}^2}{2\sigma^2}\right)$		Widley used in order to describe the PSF. It can be shown that the Gaussian results from the superposition of Airy functions for a wavelength range in the case of polychromatic illumination.
Airy $\dfrac{2J_1(|\boldsymbol{x}|/\sigma)}{x/\sigma}$		Optical systems that are dominated by wave optics, with coherent and monochromatic illumination, mainly microscopic systems; σ depends on the wavelength.

shape functions are sufficient in order to describe the main properties of standard optics as summarized in Table 3.9.

Optical transfer function. In Fourier space, convolution turns into a multiplication of the Fourier transform of the object function with the Fourier transform of the PSF (Section 8.6.3). The latter is called the *optical transfer function* (OTF). Its values give the transfer coefficient for spatial structures of different wavelength through the optical system. A value of zero indicates that this particular wavelength cannot be seen by the optics

$$
\begin{array}{rcccc}
\text{spatial domain} & G(\boldsymbol{x}) & = & PSF(\boldsymbol{x}) & \otimes & O(\boldsymbol{x}) \\[2mm]
& \updownarrow & & \updownarrow & & \updownarrow \\[2mm]
\text{Fourier domain} & \hat{G}(\boldsymbol{k}) & = & \widehat{PSF}(\boldsymbol{k}) & \cdot & \hat{O}(\boldsymbol{k})
\end{array}
\tag{3.35}
$$

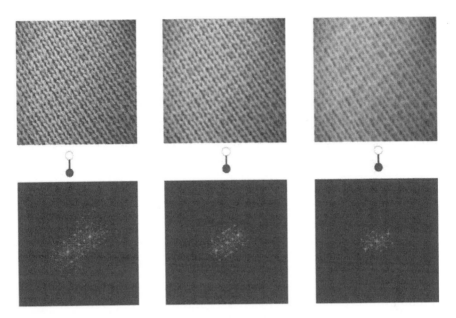

Figure 3.22: *Effect of defocus on images and their Fourier transforms. The cutoff of the higher wavelength is clearly observed with increasing defocus.*

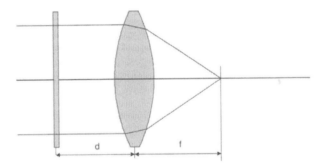

Figure 3.23: *Setup for optical Fourier transformation.*

A typical OTF will act as a low-pass filter, eliminating higher spatial frequencies, that is, high resolution details. This is illustrated in Fig. 3.22 showing a series of images of fabric, taken with different focus settings, together with the corresponding Fourier transforms. A telecentric optics has been used in order to avoid scaling of the Fourier space due to change in image magnification. Clearly, the suppression of the higher spatial frequencies with defocus can be seen.

3.7.2 Optical Fourier transform

One of the most useful properties of a convex lens is its ability to perform a 2-D Fourier transformation [5]. The input image to be transformed has to modulate the amplitude of the incoming light. The simplest possible input would therefore be a monochromatic slide placed in front of the lens (Fig. 3.23). Of course, it is also possible to work with modulation by reflection instead of transmission.

For an infinite lens the intensity distribution in the rear focal plane is given by

$$I(\xi,\eta) = \frac{I_o}{\lambda^2 f^2} \left| \int_{-\infty}^{\infty} \int_{-\infty}^{\infty} T(x,y) e^{-2\pi i(x\xi+y\eta)/(\lambda f)} \, dx \, dy \right|^2 \tag{3.36}$$

which is proportional to the power spectrum of the transmission function $T(x,y)$, that is, the input image. Changing the distance d between the input image and the lens only causes a phase shift and therefore has no influence on the intensity distribution.

To take into account the finite dimensions of the lens, a *pupil function P* is used that is 1 inside the lens and 0 outside the aperture. Thus arbitrarily shaped aperture stops can be described.

The amplitude and phase distribution in the rear focal plane correspond to the Fourier spectrum of the input image, and the intensity distribution to the power spectrum.

3.8 References

[1] Schröder, G., (1990). *Technische Optik*, 7th edition. Würzburg: Vogel Buchverlag.

[2] Hecht, E. and Zajac, A., (1977). *Optics*, 2nd edition. Addison Wesley World Student Series. Reading, MA: Addison Wesley.

[3] Schott. *Schott'96—Schott Optical Glass Catalog*. Schott Glass Technologies Inc., 400 York Avenue Duryea, PA 18642 USA, (1996). http://www.schottglasstech.com/SGTDnLoad.html.

[4] Smith, W. J., (1990). *Modern Optical Design—The Design of Optical Systems*. Optical and Electro-Optical Engineering Series. New York: McGraw Hill.

[5] Goodman, J. W., (1996). *Introduction to Fourier Optics*, 2nd edition. New York: McGraw-Hill Publishing Company.

4 Radiometry of Imaging

Horst Haußecker

Xerox Palo Alto Research Center (PARC)

4.1 Introduction

Radiometry is the measurement of some radiometric quantity, such as radiance L, irradiance E, or intensity I. In terms of computer vision, it relates quantitatively the image brightness to radiometric properties of the observed objects. Thus, a radiometric analysis of images can be used to obtain important information about the underlying physical processes and object properties. In Chapter 2 we defined the relevant radiometric and photometric quantities and detailed the basics of radiation. We also showed how the radiation emitted from objects interacts with all materials that are encountered before it finally reaches the imaging system. In Chapter 3 the fundamentals of optical imaging were introduced. This chapter concludes the radiometric considerations by combining the fundamental radiometric properties with the process

85

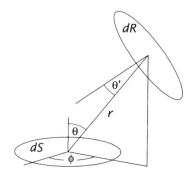

Figure 4.1: *Source-receiver geometry.*

of image formation and shows how quantitative radiometric measurements can be carried out with the imaging detector systems used in computer vision. Starting at the object surface, we follow the radiation on its way through the camera system and analyze how it is changed by the optical imaging, converted into irradiance at the detector plane, and finally detected, thereby contributing to a digital image.

4.2 Observing surfaces

Most applications of computer vision have to deal with images of opaque objects, which corresponds to images of object surfaces moving within the 3-D scenes. The "brightness" of these surfaces is usually taken for granted with the inherent assumption that they are Lambertian. This assumption is frequently confused with constant brightness, although even Lambertian surfaces are subject to brightness changes under general conditions in terms of 3-D motion and illumination setups. But what do surfaces look like, and which radiometric quantity can be remotely measured by an optical detector? In this section, we will address the following fundamental question: Which radiometric property of a surface is measured when it is observed by an optical detector system? We will conclude that an imaging detector acts as a *radiance meter*, with an output proportional to the *radiance* of the imaged surface.

4.2.1 Source-detector flux calculations

In order to measure radiation quantitatively, we need to know which portion of the radiation leaving the surface of an object finally reaches the detector. To derive the basic relations, we consider the geometric setup where the radiative flux of a source is directly transferred (radiated) onto the detector without any imaging device (Fig. 4.1).

Let dS and dR be infinitesimal surface elements of the source and the receiver (detector), respectively, separated by a distance r. The *radiance L* leaving the source element dS in the direction of the receiving surface dR can be computed from its initial definition Eq. (2.12) as

$$L = \frac{d^2\Phi}{d\Omega\, dS \cos\theta} \qquad (4.1)$$

where θ is the angle between the surface normal on dS, and the direction of the line connecting dS and dR. With $d\Omega$ we denote the element of solid angle subtended by the area dR as observed from the source dS. If dR is further inclined under an angle θ' with respect to the direction connecting the two surface elements, $d\Omega$ is given by

$$d\Omega = \frac{dR \cos\theta'}{r^2} \qquad (4.2)$$

Combining Eqs. (4.1) and (4.2), we get the infinitesimal element of radiative flux transferred between dS and dR:

$$d^2\Phi = L\frac{dS\, dR \cos\theta \cos\theta'}{r^2} \qquad (4.3)$$

From this equation we can immediately infer the following basic properties of radiative transfer: The transfer of radiative flux is:

1. directly proportional to the *radiance L* of the emitting surface dS;
2. directly proportional to the areas of the emitting and receiving surfaces dS, and dR, respectively;
3. inversely proportional to the square of the distance r between emitting and receiving surface (inverse square law); and
4. finally, it depends upon the orientation of the surface normals of dS and dR with respect to the direction connecting the two surfaces.

The most important fact is that the received flux is directly proportional to the radiance of the emitting surface. We will further show that this proportionality remains for an imaging detector. Thus, the basic property to be measured by radiometry is the *radiance* of the objects!

For finite size sources and detectors, we need to integrate Eq. (4.3) over the surface areas S and R of source and detector, respectively,

$$\Phi = \int_S \int_R L\frac{\cos\theta \cos\theta'}{r^2}\, dS\, dR \qquad (4.4)$$

The average *irradiance E* of the receiving detector element is given by:

$$E = \frac{d\Phi}{dR} = \int_S L\frac{\cos\theta \cos\theta'}{r^2}\, dS \qquad (4.5)$$

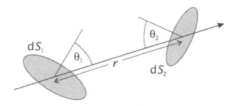

Figure 4.2: *Illustration of the radiance invariance.*

The integrals Eqs. (4.4) and (4.5) are the fundamental equations describing the transfer of radiation from a source surface to a detector surface [1]. These integrals, however, can only be solved analytically for simple geometrical setups.

If we just place a detector into a scene, all surface areas within the 3-D enclosure contribute to detector irradiance. Thus, we have to integrate Eq. (4.5) over the entire surface of all surrounding—arbitrarily shaped—objects. Apart from the mathematical difficulties, this integration yields the average irradiance of the detector surface element, rather than an "image" of the individual object surfaces. In order to resolve spatial variations of emitting surfaces, we need to restrict the allowed angles of incidence. Section 4.4 outlines the basic radiometric properties of imaging systems.

4.3 Propagating radiance

In Section 4.2 we learned that a radiometer serves as a *radiance meter*, which produces an output proportional to the radiance of the observed surfaces. Before we turn towards the question of how the radiance *distribution* of an object surface is converted into *irradiance* of the sensor plane by the optical image formation process, we need to consider exactly what happens to radiance when propagating through space and passing the camera lens system. We will derive a fundamental law of radiometry—referred to as *radiance invariance*—which constitutes the basis for all radiometric measurements. The derivation of this law follows McCluney [1] and Nicodemus [2].

4.3.1 Radiance invariance

The concept of *radiance* is sometimes hard to grasp, as we intuitively think about radiation as either absolutely parallel—in that case, we do not have a geometrical spreading and, hence, no radiance—or diverging in space. As radiance is defined as flux emitted into a unit solid angle, we always tend to think that it is diverging and, hence, becoming smaller, the farther it travels. An important question in the context of imaging systems is whether the measured brightness is decreasing with increasing object distance or, in general, how the radiance is distributed over the lens system at all.

In order to derive the law of radiance invariance, we consider two "virtual" infinitesimal surface elements dS_1 and dS_2 placed along the propagation direction of the measured radiation (Fig. 4.2) at distance r. The surface normals of the two elements with respect to the direction of the connecting line are inclined under the angles θ_1 and θ_2, respectively. The incident flux on either of the two elements is considered to leave the element in exactly the same direction at the opposite side, without attenuation.

The flux *leaving* surface element dS_1 is given by Eq. (4.3)

$$d^2\Phi_1 = L_1 \frac{dS_1 \cos\theta_1 \, dS_2 \cos\theta_2}{r^2} \tag{4.6}$$

where L_1 denotes the incident radiance on the surface element dS_1. Similarly, the *incident* flux on surface element dS_2 is given by

$$d^2\Phi_2 = L_2 \frac{dS_2 \cos\theta_2 \, dS_1 \cos\theta_1}{r^2} \tag{4.7}$$

Conservation of energy requires that both fluxes must be the same if no losses occur within the medium between dS_1 and dS_2, that is, $\Phi_1 = \Phi_2$. Using Eqs. (4.6) and (4.7) we get

$$L_1 = L_2 \tag{4.8}$$

As we have made no restrictions on the locations, orientations, or sizes of the surface elements, nor on the origin of the radiance, Eq. (4.8) constitutes a fundamental law, called *radiance invariance.*

Although this solution seems to be trivial, it is of major importance, as it proves that the quantity of radiance is not changed along the ray of propagation in space. Thus, it makes absolutely no difference where we measure the emitted radiance of objects.

4.3.2 Radiance invariance at interfaces

In this section, we consider the question as to how radiance is changed at the interface between objects with different refractive indices. This extension of the radiance invariance constitutes the basis for radiometric measurements with optical systems.

At the interface between two media with different indices of refraction, not only the direction of propagation changes but also the radiance because the geometric spreading of the beam is altered. Figure 4.3 illustrates the geometric quantities at the transition from n_1 to n_2, for

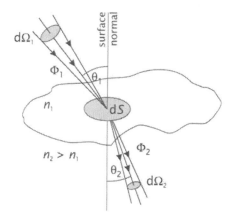

Figure 4.3: *Geometry for definition of radiance invariance at interfaces.*

$n_2 > n_1$. As refraction is not linear in angle, the two bounding rays are refracted under different angles due to the slightly different angles of incidence.

The element of incident flux $d\Phi_1$ is given by

$$d\Phi_1 = L_1 \, dS \cos \theta_1 \, d\Omega_1 = L_1 \, dS \cos \theta_1 \sin \theta_1 \, d\theta_1 \, d\phi \qquad (4.9)$$

where dS denotes an infinitesimal surface area, and the element of solid angle $d\Omega_1$ is replaced by spherical coordinates. Correspondingly, the element of refracted flux $d\Phi_2$ is given by

$$d\Phi_2 = L_2 \, dS \cos \theta_2 \, d\Omega_2 = L_2 \, dS \cos \theta_2 \sin \theta_2 \, d\theta_2 \, d\phi \qquad (4.10)$$

Conservation of energy requires

$$d\Phi_2 = (1 - \tilde{\rho}) \, d\Phi_1 \qquad (4.11)$$

accounting for reflection at the interface. Thus

$$1 = \frac{(1 - \tilde{\rho}) \, d\Phi_1}{d\Phi_2} = \frac{(1 - \tilde{\rho}) \, L_1 \cos \theta_1 \sin \theta_1 \, d\theta_1}{L_2 \cos \theta_2 \sin \theta_2 \, d\theta_2} \qquad (4.12)$$

The relation between the angles of incidence and refraction is given by Snell's law (Eq. (2.42), see Chapter 2.5)

$$n_1 \sin \theta_1 = n_2 \sin \theta_2 \qquad (4.13)$$

Differentiating both sides of this expression with respect to the angle yields

$$\frac{n_1}{n_2} = \frac{\cos \theta_1 \, d\theta_1}{\cos \theta_2 \, d\theta_2} = \frac{\sin \theta_1}{\sin \theta_2} \qquad (4.14)$$

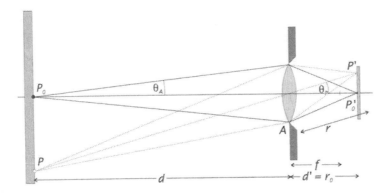

Figure 4.4: *Illustration of image formation by a perfect lens.*

Combining Eq. (4.14) with Eq. (4.12) yields

$$\frac{(1 - \tilde{\rho}) L_1}{n_1^2} = \frac{L_2}{n_2^2} \tag{4.15}$$

Ignoring reflection losses, the radiance is changed at the transition between two interfaces, but the quantity L/n^2 stays constant in any medium[1].

This leads to the conclusion that the radiance is not altered by optical components such as lenses and windows. Although the radiance within a lens is changed, the initial radiance is restored after exiting the lens at the second face. However, if the lens system is not loss-less due to reflections at all faces and internal absorption, only the fraction $\tilde{\tau}$ of the incident radiance is transmitted:

$$L_2 = \tilde{\tau} L_1 \tag{4.16}$$

4.4   Radiance of imaging

Now that we know that the radiance is conserved by passing through the optical system of a camera (with the exception of absorption and reflection losses), we need to know how the optical system changes the direction of propagation and the geometric spreading and how it turns the radiance distribution into an image.

4.4.1   Radiance and irradiance of images

Consider the imaging system to consist of a single circular lens, as illustrated in Fig. 4.4. We assume the lens to be perfect in terms of

---

[1]This fundamental law of radiometry can be compared to the invariance of the optical path nd in geometrical optics (see Chapter 3).

accurately focusing all radiation emerging from a point P at the object surface and collected by the lens aperture A, onto a single point P' on the sensor plane.

Let P'_o be the center point on the optical axis of the lens, that is, in the center of the image, and P_o the corresponding point at the object surface. The solid angles subtended by the lens aperture A, as observed from the point P_o, and from its image P'_o, are denoted by Ω and Ω', respectively.

The irradiance E' of the image point P'_o is simply given by integrating the radiance impinging onto this point from all angles within the solid angle Ω':

$$E'(P'_o) = \int_{\Omega'} L'(\theta', \phi') \cos \theta' \, d\Omega' \qquad (4.17)$$

where the primed letters refer to the quantities at the sensor side of the lens, that is, after passing the lens (Fig. 4.4).

Using the radiance invariance Eq. (4.16), we can replace L' by $L' = \tilde{\tau} L$, if we assume the lens to have a transmittance $\tilde{\tau}$, and L denotes the object radiance before reaching the lens. As the lens focuses all radiation, which is emitted by the point P_o into the solid angle Ω, we can replace the integration over the primed quantities in the image domain by an integration over the solid angle Ω in the object domain:

$$E'(P'_o) = \tilde{\tau} \int_{\Omega} L(\theta, \phi) \cos \theta \, d\Omega \qquad (4.18)$$

where $L(\theta, \phi)$ denotes the excitant radiance at the object point P_o.

For Lambertian surfaces, L is independent of the direction and can be removed from the integral. Thus,

$$E'(P'_o) = \tilde{\tau} L \int_{\Omega} \cos \theta \, d\Omega = \pi \tilde{\tau} L \sin^2 \theta_A \qquad (4.19)$$

with θ_A denoting the half angle of the lens aperture, as viewed from point P_o (Fig. 4.4). The larger the lens aperture, the more radiance is collected by the lens and the more irradiance is produced at the sensor. Hence, an optical imaging system allows the amount of collected radiative flux to be increased without reducing the spatial resolution. The maximum possible irradiance is collected for $\sin \theta_A = 1$, that is, for an infinite sized lens:

$$\max_{\theta_A} E'(P'_o) = \pi \tilde{\tau} L \qquad (4.20)$$

which equals the *radiant excitance* of the surface at the point P_o (see Chapter 2, Eq. (2.14)), reduced by the transmittance of the lens.

Using the *f-number* n_f of the lens (Chapter 3), Eq. (4.19) can be rewritten as

$$E'(P_o') = \pi \tilde{\tau} L \left(\frac{1}{1 + n_f^2} \right) \qquad (4.21)$$

4.4.2 Field darkening

So far, we have considered only the central point P_o in the image, located on the optical axis of the lens. This section shows how the sensitivity of an extended detector decreases towards the edges of the sensor.

Off-axis irradiance. Let P' be an arbitrary image point located off-axis in the sensor plane. The corresponding point in object domain is denoted by P. Further, let P have the same radiance as the center point P_o, that is, we assume the object to have a constant radiance over the imaged area.

Now, the distance r from the center of the lens to the point P' will depend on the angle θ_P,

$$r = \frac{r_o}{\cos \theta_P} \qquad (4.22)$$

where θ_P denotes the angle between the line connecting P and P' (passing through the center of the lens) and the optical axis, and r_o is the distance between the center of the lens and P_o' (Fig. 4.4).

According to the inverse square law Eq. (4.2), the irradiance is proportional to $1/r^2$, which reduces the off-axis irradiance $E'(P')$ by the factor $\cos^2 \theta_P$, compared to $E'(P_o')$.

Another factor further reducing the irradiance $E'(P')$ is given by the fact that the solid angle Ω, subtended by the lens, decreases proportional to $\cos \theta_P$ (Eq. (2.5), see Chapter 2). Thus, the effective lens aperture is reduced by the projection onto the viewing direction.

Finally, the irradiance $E'(P')$ at the detector plane is proportional to the angle of incidence, which is also given by $\cos \theta_P$.

Combining all influences decreasing the irradiance E', we get the following result for off-axis points:

$$E'(P') = E'(P_o') \cos^4 \theta_P \qquad (4.23)$$

This $\cos^4$-dependence is known as *field darkening*, reducing the irradiance towards the edge of the sensor plane.

Typical values of the relative decrease of irradiance at the edge of the image compared to the center point are in the order of 10% and 0.5% for $f = 25\,\text{mm}$ and $100\,\text{mm}$, respectively. With increasing focal length, the field darkening is expressed less. For wide-angle lenses, however, this effect can not be neglected.

Vignetting. In addition to the $\cos^4$-dependence of the irradiance across the sensor plane, other optical effects contribute to the resulting field darkening of an image. The term *vignetting* is used for effects blocking off-axis rays by internal aperture stops of the lens system or other beam-delimiting components [1]. Such effects produce an additional decline of the image irradiance towards the edge of the image.

4.5 Detecting radiance

The final step in the chain of radiometric imaging is the detection of radiation at the imaging sensor. Here, the irradiance of the sensor plane is converted into an electronic signal. Without going into details of solid state physics, this section outlines the basic properties of imaging detectors relevant for a quantitative radiometric interpretation of images. More detailed overviews of detectors for electromagnetic radiation can be found in the following excellent textbooks [1, 3, 4], as well as in standard handbooks on radiometry, such as [5].

4.5.1 Detector performance: figures of merit

Before we turn towards a classification of optical detectors in terms of their operational principle, we will summarize commonly used figures of merit, which allow us to compare the relative performance between detectors. These quantities also constitute the link between the radiometric quantities of radiation impinging on the detector material and the final electrical detector output.

Quantum efficiency. *Quantum efficiency* $\eta(\lambda)$ relates the number of photons incident on the detector to the number of independent electrons generated. It counts only primary charge carriers directly related to the initial absorption process and does not count electrical amplification. Quantum efficiency takes into account all processes related to photon losses, such as absorptance of the detector material, scattering, reflectance and electron recombination.

In a more general sense, the CIE vocabulary defines quantum efficiency as the ratio of elementary events contributing to the detector output to the number of incident photons. This also accounts for detectors in which no charge carriers are directly released by photon absorption. The quantum efficiency can be expressed as

$$\eta(\lambda) = \frac{n_o}{n_p} \tag{4.24}$$

where n_p is the number of incident photons; n_o defines the number of output events, such as photoelectrons in photodiodes, and electron-hole pairs in semiconductors (Section 4.5.2).

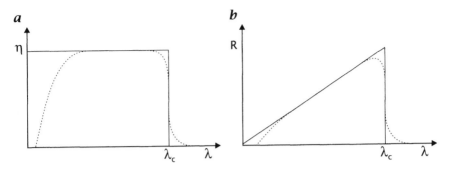

Figure 4.5: *Response of an ideal photodetector. **a** Quantum efficiency; and **b** responsivity. Solid lines correspond to ideal detectors and dashed lines to typical departures from ideal curves (After [3]).*

The quantum efficiency is always smaller than one and is commonly expressed in per cent. Figure 4.5a shows the spectral quantum efficiency for an ideal photodetector. The ideal quantum efficiency is a binary function of wavelength. Above a certain *cutoff wavelength* λ_c, photons have insufficient energy to produce photogenerated charge carriers (Section 4.5.2). All photons with higher energy (smaller wavelengths) should produce the same output. Real photodetectors show a slightly different behavior. Near λ_c the thermal excitation of the detector material can affect the production of charge carriers by photon absorption. Thus, the sharp transition is rounded, as illustrated by the dashed line. Another typical behavior of photodetectors is the decreasing quantum efficiency at short wavelengths.

Responsivity. An important quantity relating the final detector output to the irradiance is the *responsivity R* of the detector. It is defined as the electrical output signal divided by the input radiative flux ϕ:

$$R(\lambda, f) = \frac{V(\lambda, f)}{\phi_\lambda(f)} \qquad (4.25)$$

where V denotes the output voltage and f is the temporal frequency at which the input signal is chopped. The frequency dependency accounts for the finite response time of detectors and shows the detector's response to fast changing signals. If the detector output is current, rather than voltage, V has to be replaced by current I. Depending on the type of detector output, the units are given as $V\,W^{-1}$ (volts per watt) or $A\,W^{-1}$ (amperes per watt).

For a photon detector (Section 4.5.2), the responsivity can be expressed by the quantum efficiency η and the photon energy $e_p = hc/\lambda$

as

$$R(\lambda) = \frac{\eta \lambda q G}{hc} \qquad (4.26)$$

where q denotes the electron charge, $q = 1.602 \times 10^{-19}$ C. The *photoconductive gain* G depends on the geometrical setup of the detector element and material properties. The frequency dependent responsivity is given by

$$R(\lambda, f) = \frac{\eta \lambda q G}{hc\sqrt{2\pi f \tau}} \qquad (4.27)$$

where τ denotes the time constant of the detector.

The ideal spectral responsivity of a photodetector is illustrated in Fig. 4.5b. As R is proportional to the product of the quantum efficiency η and the wavelength λ, an ideal photodetector shows a linear increase in the responsivity with wavelength up to the cutoff wavelength λ_c, where it drops to zero. Real detectors show typical deviations from the ideal relationship as illustrated by the dashed line (compare to Fig. 4.5a).

Noise equivalent power. Another important figure of merit quantifies the detector noise output in the absence of incident flux. The signal output produced by the detector must be above the noise level of the detector output to be detected. Solving Eq. (4.25) for the incident radiative flux yields

$$\phi_\lambda = \frac{V}{R} \qquad (4.28)$$

where R is the responsivity of the detector. The *noise equivalent power* NEP is defined as the signal power, that is, radiative flux, which corresponds to an output voltage V given by the root-mean-square (rms) noise output, σ_n:

$$NEP = \frac{\sigma_n}{R} \qquad (4.29)$$

In other words, NEP defines the incident radiant power that yields a signal-to-noise ratio (SNR) of unity. It indicates the lower limit on the flux level that can be measured. It depends on the wavelength of the radiation, the modulation frequency, the optically active detector area, the noise-equivalent electrical bandwidth Δf, and the detector operating temperature. Thus, it depends on a large number of situation-dependent quantities.

Detectivity. The *detectivity* D of a detector is the reciprocal of the *NEP*:

$$D = \frac{1}{NEP} \tag{4.30}$$

A more useful property can be obtained by incorporating the detector area and the noise-equivalent bandwidth Δf. The corresponding quantity, called *normalized detectivity* D^* or D-star is defined as:

$$D^* = \frac{\sqrt{A_d \Delta f}}{NEP} \tag{4.31}$$

where A_d denotes the optically active detector area. It normalizes the detectivity to a 1-Hz bandwidth and a unit detector area. The units of D^* are $\mathrm{cm\,Hz}^{1/2}\,\mathrm{W}^{-1}$, which is defined as the unit "Jones." The normalized detectivity can be interpreted as the SNR of a detector when 1 W of radiative power is incident on a detector with an area of $1\,\mathrm{cm}^2$.

Again, the normalized detectivity depends on the remaining quantities, the wavelength of the radiation, the modulation frequency, and the detector operating temperature.

4.5.2 Classification of optical detectors

Over the last decades a variety of detectors for electromagnetic radiation have been developed. Recent developments in semiconductor technology have led to an increasing integration of large sensor arrays to produce high-quality focal-plane arrays suitable for computer vision applications. Other types of detectors are used as single-point measuring sensors, which scan the image area to produce higher-dimensional image data sets. Independent from the geometrical setup, they all rely on inherent changes of a physical property of the detector material by absorption of radiation, which can be quantitatively measured.

According to the underlying physical process of converting radiative energy into an electrical signal, all detectors can be classified into three major types:

1. **Photon detectors.** These types of detectors respond directly to individual photons. Any absorbed photon releases charge carriers in the detector that produce an electric signal. Photon detectors are among the most important sensor types for computer vision applications. They cover the entire range of electromagnetic radiation from x-rays, to ultraviolet and visible light, up to the infrared region. The most prominent examples are photographic films and CCD arrays. Other important applications include light-amplifying cameras, such as microchannel plate detectors and modern infrared focal plane array cameras.

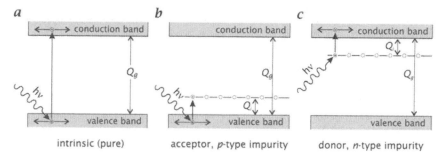

Figure 4.6: *Energy-band diagrams for **a** intrinsic photoconductors; **b** extrinsic p-type photoconductors; and **c** extrinsic n-type photoconductors.*

2. **Thermal detectors.** Optical radiation incident on a thermal detector causes the detector temperature to increase due to the absorbed energy. The increased temperature changes some electrical property of the detector material. The output signal of thermal detectors is proportional to the total energy stored in the detector as opposed to the number of absorbed photons in photon detectors. The wavelength of the radiation is irrelevant, as the same output signal can be produced by photons at different wavelengths if the photon number compensates for the different photon energies. Thus, the responsivity of thermal detectors exhibits a broad wavelength dependency, dominated by the spectral absorptance of the photon-absorbing material.

3. **Coherent detectors.** The third class of detectors directly respond to the electric field strength of the electromagnetic radiation by interference of the electric field of the incident photon with the electric field of a reference oscillator. Coherent detectors can be used only for "low-frequency" radiation, primarily for detection of radio and submillimeter radiation down to the infrared region. Prominent examples of detector systems are radar satellites operating at microwave frequencies and radio telescopes used in astronomy.

In the remainder of this section we will give an overview of the most common detector types, relevant for computer vision, with regard to the principal physical mechanisms and radiometric properties.

4.5.3 Photon detectors

The class of photon detectors contains the most important detector types for computer vision. Apart from a few exceptions, such as photographic films, most photon detectors are solid state detectors, which make use of the fact that electrical properties of semiconductors are dramatically altered by the absorption of ultraviolet, visible and infrared photons.

Intrinsic photoconductors. *Photoconductors* respond to light by either changing resistance or conductance of the detector material. *Intrinsic photoconductors* are the most straightforward way to design a solid state electronic detector. They make use of the inherent electrical property of pure semiconductor materials without additional manipulations. At normal temperatures, relatively few electrons will be in the conduction band of a semiconductor, which results in a low electric conductivity of the material. Figure 4.6a illustrates the energy-band diagram for an intrinsic photoconductor.

In order to move from the valence band into the conduction band, an electron must have sufficient energy. By absorbing a photon whose energy is greater than that of the bandgap energy Q_g, an electronic bond can be broken and the electron can be lifted into the conduction band, creating an electron/hole pair (Fig. 4.6a). Both the electron and the corresponding hole can migrate through the detector material and contribute to the conductivity. If an electric field is maintained across the detector, any absorbed photon results in a small electric current, which can be measured by a high-impedance amplifier.

As thermal excitation contributes to the conductivity in the same way as absorbed radiation, thermal noise will corrupt the signal, especially at high temperatures and low illumination levels. The number of thermally excited electrons follows the *Boltzmann distribution*:

$$n_t \propto \exp\left(-\frac{Q_g}{k_B T}\right) \qquad (4.32)$$

where Q_g, k_B, and T are the bandgap energy, the Boltzmann constant, and the absolute temperature, respectively. As Q_g becomes smaller, the number of thermally excited charge carriers increases. One way to overcome this problem is to cool the detector down to cryogenic temperatures below 77 K (liquid nitrogen temperature), where thermal excitation is negligible.

The minimum photon energy that can be detected is given be the bandgap energy Q_g of the detector material. With the photon energy (Eq. (2.2))

$$e_p = h\nu = \frac{hc}{\lambda} \qquad (4.33)$$

the maximum detectable wavelength λ_c, commonly referred to as *cutoff wavelength*, is given by

$$\lambda_c = \frac{hc}{Q_g} \qquad (4.34)$$

Substituting for the constants, and correcting for units such that wavelengths are in microns and energy gap in electron volts yields the following rule of thumb:

$$\lambda_c[\mu m] = \frac{1.238}{Q_g[eV]} \qquad (4.35)$$

Intrinsic photoconductor detectors can be made in large arrays and they have good uniformity and high quantum efficiency, typically in the order of 60%. They are the basic components of CCD-arrays (charge coupled devices), which are the most widely used 2-D detectors in the visible, the near infrared, and—to some extent—in the x-ray and ultraviolet region using special semiconductor compounds. In the infrared region, semiconductors with a small bandgap have to be used. For highly energetic radiation, such as x-rays, the energy exceeds the bandgap of any semiconductor. However, the absorption coefficient of most materials is extremely low at these wavelengths, which makes most sensors almost transparent to shortwave radiation. In order to deposit the energy in the detector, the semiconductor material must contain heavy atoms, which have a higher absorptivity in the x-ray region.

Extrinsic photoconductors. For longer wavelengths toward the infrared region, it is hard to find suitable intrinsic semiconductor materials with sufficiently small bandgaps. For wavelengths beyond 15 μm, materials tend to become unstable and difficulties occur in achieving high uniformity and making good electrical contacts. A solution to this problem is to use *extrinsic photoconductors*, that is, semiconductors doped with either p-type or n-type impurities.

The addition of impurities places available electron states in the previously forbidden gap and allows conductivity to be induced by freeing impurity-based charge carriers. Thus, smaller energy increments are required. As illustrated in Fig. 4.6b and c, only the gap between the valence band and the impurity level (p-type semiconductors) or the gap between the impurity level and the conduction band (n-type semiconductors) has to be overcome by absorption of a photon. In the former case, the conductivity is carried by holes and in the latter case free electrons in the conduction band contribute to the conductivity. The basic operation of extrinsic photoconductors is similar to that of intrinsic photoconductors, except that the bandgap energy Q_g has to be replaced by the excitation energy Q_i (Fig. 4.6b and c).

Although extrinsic photoconductors are an elegant way to get long wavelength response, they have some less desirable characteristics:

- Due to the smaller bandgap, extrinsic semiconductors are much more sensitive to thermal noise, which can be inferred from Eq. (4.32), and, therefore, require a much lower operating temperature than do intrinsic photoconductors.

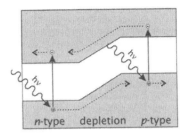

Figure 4.7: *Band diagram of the p-n junction in a photovoltaic detector (photodiode). In the p-type material, photogenerated electrons diffuse into the depletion region and are swept into the n-type region by the electric field. The same process occurs in the n-type material, except the roles of the holes and electrons are reversed.*

- Extrinsic photoconductors have a quantum efficiency that is substantially smaller than that of intrinsic materials (30% compared to 60% in average). This results from the fact that the impurities are necessarily more sparse than the host material, which leads to a smaller optical absorption cross section.

- The electrical conductivity of extrinsic materials differs fundamentally from that of intrinsic materials. In intrinsic photoconductors, electron/hole pairs are generated by the excitation process, both contributing to the charge transport (Fig. 4.6a). In extrinsic photoconductors, individual charge carriers are generated whose complementary charge resides in an ionized atom, which remains immobile in the crystal structure and cannot carry current (Fig. 4.6a and b).

As the number of semiconductor atoms always outnumbers the impurity atoms, the intrinsic effect dominates in both types of extrinsic material at high temperatures (where all impurity charge carriers are thermally excited) and for wavelengths smaller than the cutoff wavelength of the intrinsic material. To reduce the response from intrinsic conduction, all wavelengths below the anticipated long-wave radiation have to be blocked by spectral filters.

Photodiodes (photovoltaic detectors). A *photovoltaic detector* actively generates a voltage or current from incident electromagnetic radiation. The most common realization is based on a junction between two oppositely doped zones (*p-n* junction) in a semiconductor material. As this setup acts as a diode, this type of detector is also called *photodiode.*

Photodiodes allow large resistance and simultaneously high photoconductive gain within a small volume to be obtained. The *n*-type material has a surplus (and the *p*-type material has a deficiency) of electrons compared to the crystal bond of the semiconductor material. In the adjacent region of both oppositely doped zones, electrons migrate from the n- to the p-region acceptor atoms and holes migrate from the p- to the n-region donors, if thermal excitation frees them. Within the contact region all bonds are complete and the material is depleted of potential charge carriers. This results in a high resistance of this region, as opposed to the relatively high conductivity of the p- and n-type material. As the charge carriers diffuse, a voltage is established across the depletion region, called the *contact potential*, which opposes the diffusion of additional electrons. The net result is a permanent equilibrium voltage across the p-n junction. The resulting bandstructure across the contact zone is shown in Fig. 4.7.

When photons of energies greater than the forbidden gap energy are absorbed in, or close to a p-n junction of a photodiode, the resulting electron/hole pairs are pulled by the electric field of the contact potential across the p-n junction. Electrons are swept from the p-region into the n-region, and holes in the opposite direction (Fig. 4.7). As the charge carriers are spatially separated across the detector, a resulting voltage can be measured. If the n- and the p-type region are connected, a small current will flow between both regions. This phenomenon is called the *photovoltaic effect*.

Because photodiodes operate through intrinsic rather than extrinsic absorption, they can achieve a high quantum efficiency in small volumes. Photodiodes can be constructed in large arrays of many thousands of pixels. They are the most commonly used detectors in 1-6-μm region [3] (e. g., InSb infrared focal plane arrays) and are also used in the visible and near ultraviolet.

Photoemissive detectors. *Photoemissive detectors* operate with external photoelectric emission. The excited electron physically leaves the detector material and moves to the detecting anode. Figure 4.8a illustrates the principal setup. A conduction electron is produced in the photocathode by absorption of a photon with an energy greater than the intrinsic bandgap of the detector material. This electron diffuses through the detector material until it reaches the surface. At the surface of the photocathode it might escape into the vacuum. Using an electric field between the photocathode and the anode helps to accelerate the electron into the vacuum, where it is driven towards the anode and counted as current. Suitable photocathode materials must have the following properties:

- high-absorption coefficient for photons
- long mean-free path for the electron in the cathode material (low transport losses of electrons migrating to the surface of the cathode)
- low electron affinity, that is, low barrier inhibiting the electron emission

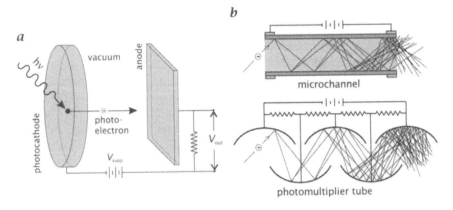

Figure 4.8: *Photoemissive detectors.* **a** *Detection process for a vacuum photodiode;* **b** *light amplification by a microchannel (top) and a photomultiplier tube (bottom).*

The simple vacuum photodiode (Fig. 4.8a) can be improved by electron multipliers, increasing the number of electrons contributing to the output current for each detected photon. A commonly used photoemissive detector is the *photomultiplier*, illustrated in Fig. 4.8b. It consists of a vacuum tube including several intermediate anodes. Each anode, called a *dynode*, is given a voltage higher than the previous one. The geometrical arrangement is such that emitted electrons are accelerated towards the next adjacent dynode. If the voltage difference is high enough, each photoelectron leaving a dynode gets fast enough to eject multiple electrons from the next dynode upon impact. This process is repeated until the avalanche of electrons finally reaches the anode. The voltages required for operation are provided by a single supply, divided by a chain of resistors. The photocathode is held at a large negative voltage in the order of several thousand volts relative to the anode.

Photomultipliers are large devices, restricted mainly to single detectors. A different form of electron multipliers, which is of practical relevance for computer vision, are made from thin tubes of lead-oxide glass. These *microchannels* have diameters of 8-45 μm and a length-to-diameter ratio of about 40 [3], and are suitable for integration into small-scale detector arrays. *Microchannel plates* are arrays of approximately one million channel electron multipliers, fused into solid wafers [6]. Figure 4.8b illustrates the principal mechanism of a single microchannel. The microchannel wall consists of three layers: an emitting layer; a conducting layer; and bulk glass. The conductive layer has a high resistance and allows a large voltage to be maintained across the ends of the tube. Electrons that enter the tube are accelerated along the tube until they collide with the wall. The inner surface layer, called the emitting layer, is made from PbO, which acts as an electron multiplier. Upon impact, the accelerated electrons create multiple secondary electrons that are accelerated by the voltage along the tube until they strike the walls again and produce more free electrons. This operation is comparable to a continuous dynode chain and the gains are nearly as large as those of photomultipliers.

Microchannel plates are used in modern light intensifying cameras, suitable for low-illumination applications, such as fluorescence imaging and night vision devices.

4.5.4 Thermal detectors

The first detectors discovered were thermal detectors, which showed a response to the heating effect of radiation. Unlike photon detectors, they do not respond to charge carriers, directly excited by absorbed photons. Instead, the thermal energy of absorbed photons is detected by temperature-dependent physical processes. A thermal detector can be thought of as two essential parts: the absorber and the temperature sensor.

It is important to note that the net energy stored by absorption is given by the photon energy times the number of absorbed photons. Thus, low-energy photons can create the same detector output as high-energy photons, if the photon flux is higher and compensates for the lower energy. For this reason, the spectral response of thermal detectors is flat and determined by the spectral dependence of the surface absorptance.

Thermal detectors are either bulk devices or metal junction devices. The junction devices, such as the thermocouple and thermopile, rely upon the *Seebeck effect* or *thermoelectric effect*. Two separate junctions of two dissimilar metals generate a voltage proportional to the difference in temperature between them [1]. If one junction is kept at reference temperature, the series output will be proportional to the temperature of the other junction. In practical realizations of thermocouples, one junction is embedded into an absorbing material, while the other junction is thermally connected to the radiometer housing with a high thermal mass. *Thermopiles* are series of individual thermocouples, which substantially increase the sensitivity.

While thermopiles are mostly used as single detectors, another type of thermal detector, called a *bolometer*, is a bulk-type detector and can be easily integrated into large detector arrays. Bolometers take advantage of the high-temperature coefficient of resistance in semiconductors, which is similar to the principle of photoconductors. A detailed treatment of recent developments in the fabrication of microbolometer arrays is given in [7].

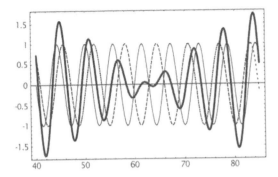

Figure 4.9: *Mixing of two periodic signals* S_i, *and* S_m *with slightly different wavelengths,* $\lambda_i = 1.1\,\lambda_m$. *The bold line shows the resulting signal* $S = S_i + S_m$. *The amplitude of the mixed signal is modulated by the difference, or* beat *frequency.*

Recent developments in high-temperature (about 77 K) superconductivity made another type of thermal detector available, which relies on the sharp resistance change with temperature in the superconducting transition region. These superconducting bolometers can also be operated in two other modes that involve the breaking of *Cooper pairs* by the incident photons, thus destroying superconductivity [4].

Coherent detectors. Coherent receivers directly measure the electromagnetic field of the incident radiation. They mix the electromagnetic field of the incoming photons with an internal reference field of similar frequency, produced by a high-frequency oscillator. The resulting signal shows a strong modulation of the amplitude, which is given by the difference frequency of both signals—a physical effect commonly referred to as *beating*.

Let S_i and S_m be the incident, and the mixing signal (electric field), respectively, given in complex notation by

$$S_m = A_m \exp[i\omega t], \quad \text{and} \quad S_i = A_i \exp[i(\omega + \epsilon)t] \qquad (4.36)$$

where ϵ is a small frequency shift compared to the main frequency ω. Linear superposition yields the following mixed signal:

$$\begin{aligned}
S &= S_m + S_i = A_m \exp[i\omega t] + A_i \exp[i(\omega + \epsilon)t] \\
&= \exp[i\omega t]\,(A_m + A_i \exp[i\epsilon t])
\end{aligned} \qquad (4.37)$$

which can be interpreted as an oscillation at the frequency ω, with an amplitude modulation at the difference (beat) frequency ϵ. This effect is illustrated in Fig. 4.9.

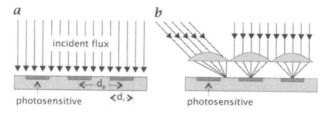

Figure 4.10: *Schematic illustration of the fill factor and microlens arrays on detector arrays. **a** Detector without a microlens array; **b** Detector with a microlens array.*

From the mixed field, the exact frequency can be extracted, as well as the amplitude and phase of the incident signal. In order to measure the electric field, the mixed field has to be passed through a nonlinear electrical element, called *mixer*, that converts power from the original frequency to the beat frequency.

Unlike all other types of (incoherent) receivers, these *coherent* receivers obtain additional information about the wave number and phase of the signal. As the phase information is given, they can correlate measurements of different receivers to reconstruct the incoming wavefront by interferometry. Intercontinental baseline radio telescopes use this ability to combine several telescopes spread over the entire globe to enhance the resolution up to milliarc-seconds for astronomical applications.

A more detailed treatment of the theory of coherent receivers can be found in References [8] and [3].

4.5.5 Characteristics of detector arrays

Fill factor. Most detector arrays used in computer vision are not photosensitive over the entire detector area. As all electrical contacts and microelectronic components have to be integrated into the chip surface, only a small portion is retained for the actual photosensitive detector area. Exceptions are 1-D detector arrays, where all electronic components and bonds can be arranged alongside the detector, or back-illuminated detector arrays.

The basic quantities defining the *fill factor* of the sensor are the pixel pitch d_p, which describes the center distance of two neighboring pixels, and the pixel size d_s, which is the extension of the photosensitive area. For nonsquare pixels, the dimensions on both directions have to be known.

Given a local irradiance $E_i(\boldsymbol{x})$ on the sensor, only the portion

$$E(\boldsymbol{x}) = E_i(\boldsymbol{x}) \frac{d_s^2}{d_p^2} \tag{4.38}$$

actually contributes to the signal at the point x (Fig. 4.10a). For non-square pixels/arrays, the squared quantities have to be replaced by the products of the corresponding quantities in the x- and y-direction, respectively.

Microlens arrays. A common technique to overcome the problem of reduced fill factor is to place microlens arrays over the detector area. An optimal microlens array covers the entire sensor surface, such that incident radiation is focused onto the individual photosensitive areas, as illustrated in Fig. 4.10b. In that way, the maximum possible radiative flux can be collected with low fill factors.

There are, however, two basic problems that have to be acknowledged, even for perfectly transparent lens-arrays:

• The incident radiation is focused onto a spot smaller than the photosensitive area, with the exact position depending on the angle of incidence (Fig. 4.10b). If the photosensitive area exhibits local inhomogeneities in the sensitivity, the detector output shows an angular dependence, given by the sensitivity distribution of the photosensitive area.

• For large angles of incidence, it might happen that the incident radiation is focused onto a point in between two photosensitive areas (Fig. 4.10b). Thus, the angular response suddenly drops to zero for a certain cutoff angle. This effect can be avoided if the geometric setup is such that no radiation beyond the critical angle can enter the optical system. The larger the focal lens of the optical system is, the smaller the maximum inclination angle.

Static noise pattern. It is impossible to manufacture large detector arrays in such a way that all individual sensor elements will be absolutely identical. Each pixel usually exhibits slightly different sensitivities, offsets, and gains. Thus, even absolutely uniform surfaces are imaged according to the intrinsic structure of the sensor array inhomogeneities. These patterns overlay all images and constitute some kind of "noise." Unlike other types of noise, this *fixed pattern noise* is static and remains stable over a certain time span.

In principle, the fixed pattern noise can be corrected for by radiometric calibration of the sensor. This procedure is commonly referred to as *flat fielding*, as a surface with uniform radiance is used to compute the local inhomogeneities.

If the fixed pattern noise remains stable over the expected lifetime of the camera, it can be calibrated once by the manufacturer, and all pixel readouts can be automatically corrected for local offsets and gains. If the static noise pattern changes over longer periods, it might be necessary to repeat the calibration procedure more frequently.

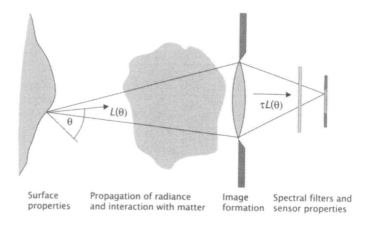

Surface   Propagation of radiance   Image   Spectral filters and
properties   and interaction with matter formation   sensor properties

Figure 4.11: *The chain of radiometric imaging.*

4.6 Concluding summary

This chapter concludes with a summary of the basic results of the previous considerations about quantitative radiometry of imaging. Figure 4.11 summarizes the chain of events leading from emission of radiation to the final image formation. The basic steps and results can
be summarized as follows:

1. The detected flux is proportional to the radiance of the emitting
   surface with a proportionality constant given by the geometry of
   the optical setup.

2. The radiance stays invariant as it propagates through space. Thus,
   the radiometric measurement can be carried out at any position
   along the direction of propagation. This result, however, assumes
   that no losses occur along the propagation path. For effects such
   as scattering, absorption, refraction, etc., the radiance is decreased
   according to the interaction of radiation with matter (this was presented in Chapter 2).

3. The radiance is changed at the transition of interfaces separating
   two media with different refractive indices. In case the radiation
   penetrates a second interface (into a medium with the same refractive index as the initial one), this process is reversed. Thus, the initial radiance is restored after passing a lens system, but attenuated
   by the transmittance of the optical system.

4. By optical imaging, the radiance entering a camera lens is converted
   into irradiance of the detector. The irradiance distribution on the
   detector plane shows a natural field darkening with decreasing irradiance towards the edges of the detector. This field darkening can

be further amplified by having vignetting and other optical effects block parts of the radiation.

5. The final output of the imaging detector depends on a variety of detector properties. If the conversion from incident flux to an electrical signal is linear, the output remains proportional to the object irradiance.

4.7 References

[1] McCluney, W. R., (1994). *Introduction to Radiometry and Photometry.* Boston: Artech House.

[2] Nicodemus, F. E., (1963). Radiance. *Am. J. Phys.,* **31**:368–377.

[3] Rieke, G. H., (1994). *Detection of Light: From the Ultraviolet to the Submillimeter.* Cambridge: Cambridge University Press.

[4] Dereniak, E. L. and Boreman, G. D., (1996). *Infrared Detectors and Systems.* New York: John Wiley & Sons, Inc.

[5] Wolfe, W. L. and Zissis, G. J. (eds.), (1989). *The Infrared Handbook,* 3rd edition. Michigan: The Infrared Information Analysis (IRIA) Center, Environmental Research Institute of Michigan.

[6] Laurin Publishing, (1998). *The Photonics Design and Applications Handbook,* 44th edition. Pittsfield, MA: Laurin Publishing CO.

[7] Sedky, S. and Fiorini, P., (1999). Poly SiGe Bolometers. In *Handbook of Computer Vision and Applications,* B. Jähne, H. Haußecker, and P. Geißler, eds., Vol. 1: Sensors and Imaging, pp. 271–308. San Diego, London, Boston, New York, Sydney, Tokyo, Toronto: Academic Press.

[8] Torrey, H. C. and Whitmer, C. A., (1948). *Crystal Rectifiers,* Vol. 15. New York: Massachusetts Institute of Technology Radiation Laboratory Series, McGraw-Hill.

5 Solid-State Image Sensing

Peter Seitz

Centre Suisse d'Électronique et de Microtechnique, Zürich, Switzerland

Computer Vision and Applications

5.1 Introduction

As the name indicates, the field of *computer vision* has long been viewed as an essentially computational science, concerned only with the mathematical treatment of images whose origins are effectively ignored. This conventional view of computer vision (or machine vision), as perceived, for example, in the textbook by Gonzalez and Wintz [1], has slowly given way to a different, holistic comprehension of machine vision as the science of systems that extract information from wave fields (see also Chapters 2–4). This systems approach, sometimes also called *electronic imaging* [2], has two immediate consequences: first, in a well-designed system, different components can compensate for the deficiencies in other components; practical examples of this capability include the digital correction of imaging lens distortions in photogrammetric applications (Chapter 6 or [3]), the significant increase of a system's dynamic range by nonlinear compression of the photosignal in the image sensor [4], and the digital compensation of offset and gain nonuniformities in the image sensor [5]. Second, the image acquisition process can become dynamic and adaptive, reacting to changes in the outside world by adapting the properties of the image capture and processing components in an optimal fashion. This powerful concept of *active vision* has already been proposed previously [6] but only now, with the recent development of custom solid-state image sensors, is it possible for active vision to reach its full potential. At the same time, new research opportunities are occurring in machine vision because new types of image processing algorithms are required that not only influence the image acquisition process but are also capable of exploiting novel imaging modalities [7].

This contribution should represent a comprehensive introduction to solid-state image sensing for machine vision and for optical microsystems, with an emphasis on custom image sensors that can be tailored to the requirements of individual imaging applications in research and industrial use.

The material presented here is organized in the form of a systematic exploration of the photosensing chain in Sections 5.2–5.5: Incident photons are followed on their paths into the interior of a semiconductor where most of the photons interact by producing electron-hole pairs. These photocharge pairs need to be separated in an electric field before they recombine again, leading to the flow of a photocurrent, which is proportional to the incident light intensity over many orders of magnitude (Section 5.2). The photocurrent can be manipulated and processed in many different ways before it is converted into a storable quantity at each pixel site. It is actually this large variety of processing capabilities that represents the true value of custom solid-state image sensing: By selecting and combining the required functionality for an imaging problem at hand, drawing from an extended "toolbox" of functional modules, the properties and the performance of an image sensor can be optimized for the given problem (Section 5.3). Finally, the preprocessed image information is stored at each pixel, often in the form of a voltage signal. During readout the individual pixels are interrogated either sequentially or several of them in parallel (Section 5.4). The stored pixel information is transmitted off-chip to the outside world, or additional processing steps (for example analog-to-digital conversion or even digital image processing) can be performed on the image sensor chip itself. An important part of the presented fundamentals of solid-state photosensing is the analysis of noise sources, noise reduction schemes, and the achievable signal-to-noise ratios (SNR) (Section 5.5). This leads us naturally to the basic reason for the development of modern *charge-coupled device* (CCD) technology and to the discussion of in which applications CCD image sensors might be replaced by CMOS-compatible image sensors in the near future.

Section 5.6 is devoted to an introduction of image sensor architectures. It covers the various types of CCDs employed today, the traditional photodiode array image sensor, and the active pixel sensor (APS) architecture. After an introduction to the basics of color vision Section 5.7 outlines the technical realization of color chips and color cameras.

Often ignored in the design of machine vision systems, the practical limitations of today's solid-state image sensors require special considerations for optimum system solutions. As described in Section 5.8, most of the shortcomings of the image sensors can be compensated by suitable calibration or correction procedures in an accompanying digital processor.

The concluding Section 5.9 reviews the most important aspects of custom image sensors, leading to the prediction that the large degree of freedom offered by the wide choice of image sensing functionality will result in many more applications where smart machine vision systems will be inexpensive, reliable, and yet provide high-performance solutions to optical measurement and visual inspection problems.

For the interested reader, more detailed information on camera and video standards, semiconductor technology for image sensing, and the future of sensor technology can be found in the full edition of this handbook [CVA1, Chapter 7].

5.2 Fundamentals of solid-state photosensing

A generic machine vision or optical measurement system consists of the elements illustrated in Fig. 5.1. A suitable source of radiation, for example a light bulb, creates a wave field that can interact with the

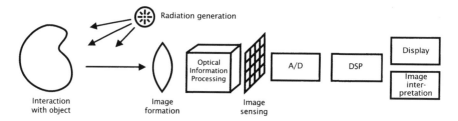

Figure 5.1: *Illustration of the photosensing ("electronic imaging") chain. It consists of a source of radiation, an interaction mechanism of the object under study with this radiation, shaping of the radiation field, conversion of radiation into electronic charge, the processing of this information, and the display for a human observer or the automatic extraction of pictorial information content.*

object under study. The part of the radiation that interacted with the object now carries information about it, which can be contained, for example, in the spatial, temporal, spectral, or polarization modulation of the radiation. The returning information-carrying radiation is partially collected, often by making use of an imaging (lens) subsystem. A sensor converts the collected radiation into an electronic charge, which can be preprocessed using analog or digital electronics. The preprocessed information is converted into digital form for treatment in a specialized or general-purpose computer. The purpose of this image processing step is either to enhance certain aspects of the image information and display the modified image for inspection by a human observer, or to extract automatically certain types of pictorial content. This information can then be used to react to the perceived information content: for example, by interacting with the environment employing suitable actuators.

This chapter concentrates on the sensor and electronic preprocessing part of the whole electronic imaging chain using solid-state image sensors. The radiation that can be captured with these types of image sensors is restricted to electromagnetic waves extending from the x-ray region to the near infrared. This large spectral range covers most wavelength regions of practical importance, notably the visible spectrum.

Although any type of high-quality semiconductor can be employed for the conversion of electromagnetic radiation into photocharge and its electronic processing, the presentation in this work will be concerned mainly with *silicon*, due to its almost exclusive use in the semiconductor industry. As we will see, in most aspects this is not a real restriction, and the use of silicon for photoconversion and electronic processing is really an excellent choice.

In the following, a systematic exploration of the photosensing chain is presented ("from photons to bits"), as illustrated in Fig. 5.2. Incident

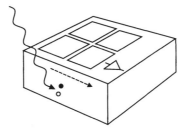

Figure 5.2: *Simplified sequence of events in semiconductor photodetection. Incoming radiation is converted into charge pairs in the bulk of the semiconductor, the charge pairs are separated in an electric field, and they are either stored in the pixel or the photocurrent is processed locally. The photosignal is subsequently transported to an electronic amplification circuit for detection.*

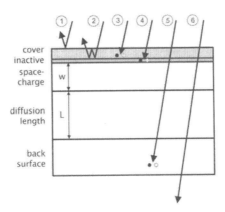

Figure 5.3: *Schematic representation of the optical losses encountered in semiconductor photosensors: (1) surface reflection; (2) thin-film interference; (3) absorption in the cover; (4) photocharge loss in inactive regions; (5) interaction deep in the semiconductor bulk; and (6) transmission through the semiconductor.*

photons are converted into charge pairs, leading finally to preprocessed image information at the output of the semiconductor chip.

5.2.1 Propagation of photons in the image sensor

Two types of interactions of photons with solid-state materials have to be considered for an understanding of an image sensor's properties: absorption and reflection (see also Sections 2.5.2 and 2.5.3). Before an incident photon can interact measurably in the bulk of a piece of semiconductor, it has to arrive there safely, crossing the interface between air and semiconductor surface. What can happen to an incident photon is illustrated schematically in Fig. 5.3, depicting the cross section

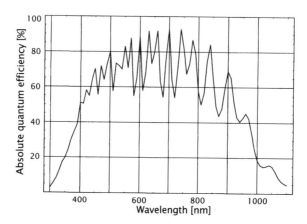

Figure 5.4: *Absolute quantum efficiency measurement of a silicon p-n junction realized with a standard CMOS process. This example illustrates the decay towards the blue (surface absorption) and red spectral region (interaction too deep in the semiconductor), as well as the oscillations due to thin-film interference.*

through an image sensor. On top of the image sensor, we find scratch-resistant transparent covering and protective materials, often in the form of dielectric layers such as silicon dioxide or silicon nitride, with a typical thickness of a few μm. At the interface between cover and actual semiconductor, there is a thin, essentially inactive zone. In the bulk of the semiconductor one encounters first a region that has been swept clean of mobile electronic charges. In this so-called space-charge region, usually a few microns deep, an electric field is present. Below this, the field-free bulk of the semiconductor follows, which can be as thin as a few μm or as thick as many 100 μm. The following identifies six different effects that prevent photons from being detected by the image sensor:

1. Due to the mismatch between the refractive index of top surface and ambient (often air), the incident photon is reflected and does not enter the image sensor. A typical value for this *reflection loss* is obtained in the following way: using an index of refraction of $n=1.5$ for silicon dioxide, 4 % of the photons are reflected at normal incidence from air [8].

2. Multiple reflections in the covering thin layer lead to a strong spectral oscillation of the transmittance, as is apparent in the measurement shown in Fig. 5.4.
   Depending on the wavelength of the incident photon it is either transmitted well or it is preferentially reflected back. In good image sensors, this disturbing effect is virtually eliminated by the deposi-

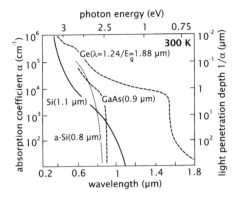

Figure 5.5: *Optical absorption coefficient and light penetration depth as a function of wavelength for various semiconductor materials. Data taken from Sze [10].*

tion of additional dielectric antireflection layers on top of the image sensor [8].

3. The covering layers are not perfectly transparent, leading to *absorption* of part of the incident photons already at this stage. The reduced blue response of CCD image sensors is a good example of this effect, caused by the low transmission of the covering polysilicon electrodes on the pixels.

4. Inactive regions near the surface of the semiconductor consist of semiconductor material with a very short lifetime of charge pairs. This is either caused by defects right at the interface (less than 1 nm), or by very high doping concentration near contacts [9]. Photogenerated charge pairs recombine so fast that their collection and electronic detection is improbable.

5. Photons that are absorbed very deeply in the bulk of the semiconductor result in photocharge that does not have a chance to reach the surface of the image sensor for collection in a pixel. As will be described in what follows, the critical distance is the so-called diffusion length L, which can be many times $10\,\mu m$ deep for low-doped semiconductors [9].

6. Finally, photons might travel through the image sensor without interaction, leaving it again at the back end.

5.2.2 Generation of photocharge pairs

Because of the sequential process of *photocharge generation*, virtually all photons that are absorbed in the semiconductor material are converted into an electronic charge [8]. There is a strong spectral depen-

dence, however, of the mean absorption depth at which this photoconversion takes place, as illustrated in Fig. 5.5. Short-wavelength light
is predominantly absorbed at the surface, while red light penetrates
deeply into the bulk of the semiconductor. A major consequence of this
effect is that the achievable spatial resolution degrades significantly
with wavelength [11]: images taken in the red or infrared spectral region show much less contrast compared to images taken in green or
blue light. For this reason, image sensors are often covered with an
optical filter, cutting off the infrared portion of the incident light.

In the absorption process, a photon loses its energy by creating one
or more charge pairs. In a photodetection event, no net charge is created and neutrality is always maintained. For this reason, charge pairs
are created, consisting of an electron and a (positively charged) quasi-
particle called hole [8]. The overall charge conversion efficiency of this
process is usually measured with the *quantum efficiency* η, describing
how many charge pairs are created and electronically detected per incident photon. Alternatively, this conversion efficiency can be described
with the *responsivity* R in units A/W, measuring how much current is
flowing out of a photosensor per incident light power. The relationship
between R and η is given by

$$R = \eta \frac{\lambda q}{hc} \tag{5.1}$$

using Planck's constant h, the speed of light c, the unit charge q, and
the photons' wavelength λ. As an example, consider a photodetector
with an η of 0.9, illuminated with red light (λ =633 nm) from a HeNe
laser. The corresponding responsivity is R =0.46 A/W.

In the visible and infrared portion of the spectrum, η is less than
unity. This is illustrated in Fig. 5.4 with the actual measurement of an
$n^-\,p^-$ photodiode, manufactured with a standard CMOS process using
silicon. The η decreases towards both the blue (incident light is already absorbed in the covering layers) and the infrared portion of the
spectrum (light penetrates and interacts so deeply in the semiconductor that the created charge pairs recombine and disappear before they
reach the surface where they could have been collected and measured).
In the visible part of the spectrum, a rather high η of close to 100% is
observed. As no special antireflection coating is used in this photodiode, spectral oscillations can be seen in the η curve, caused by multiple
reflections of the incident light within the covering layers [8], so-called
thin-film interference. For improved performance, antireflection coatings are employed, reducing this effect significantly.

If a photon has a sufficiently high energy such as in x-rays, one photon can create many charge pairs. In silicon a mean energy of 3.8 eV is
required for the creation of one electron-hole pair [12]. As an example,

consider a soft x-ray photon with an energy of 1000 eV, corresponding to a wavelength of 1.24 nm. The absorption of this x-ray photon
results in the creation of 263 charge pairs. Because silicon starts to become transparent for x-ray photons with an energy of more than a few
1000 eV, silicon is not an efficient solid state detector for such energies.
Other semiconductors, consisting of high-density materials with atoms
of high atomic numbers, are more appropriate for x-ray detection [13].

5.2.3 Separation of photogenerated charge pairs: photocurrents

Once a charge (electron-hole) pair has been created, it must be separated within a certain time before it recombines again and loses all
information about the previous presence of the photon that generated
the charge pair. This recombination lifetime τ depends critically on
the quality and purity of the semiconductor [9]. In high-quality low-
doped silicon used in CMOS processes, for example, the lifetime can be
as large as several tens of microseconds. This is the time available for
separating the photocharge and moving the different charge types to
suitable storage areas.

Two physical effects dominate the motion of electronic charge in
semiconductors: drift in an electric field and diffusion caused by the
random thermal motion of the charge carriers. The presence of an
electric field E causes charge carriers to move with the velocity v

$$v = \mu E \tag{5.2}$$

with the *mobility* μ. As an example, the mobility of electrons in low-
doped silicon at room temperature is about 1350 cm^2/Vs. Above a
certain field strength, the velocity saturates, taking on a constant value
v_{sat}. For silicon, this saturation velocity is about 10^5 m/s [10].

Even in the absence of an electric field, charge can move: the thermal
random motion causes diffusion, a tendency of charge carriers to equi-
librate their distribution. The thermally induced velocity v_{diff} of the
charge carriers can be very high: an electron at room temperature has
an average velocity of $v_{\text{diff}} = 10^5$ m/s. This random motion causes an
average [root-mean-square] (rms)] displacement L of a single electron,
depending on the time t given for the diffusion process

$$L = \sqrt{Dt} \tag{5.3}$$

with the diffusion constant D. Silicon exhibits a typical electron diffusion constant of about 45 cm^2/s at room temperature. For the recombination lifetime τ already mentioned, the corresponding average
displacement L is called *diffusion length*. This is the average distance

over which a charge carrier can move without the influence of an electric field and without recombining. As an example, consider $\tau = 10\,\mu s$ and $D = 45\,cm^2/s$, resulting in $L = 212\,\mu m$. This implies that the diffusion process can be extremely important for the collection of charge carriers over significant distances. This also means that charge carriers photogenerated deeply in the semiconductor have a high chance of reaching the surface, where they can be collected and where they contribute to a severe reduction of the contrast, especially for small pixel periods. As mentioned in the preceding, this can be counteracted only by filtering out the long-wavelength photons that would penetrate deeply into the semiconductor.

Photogenerated charge carriers moving under the influence of an electric field represent a current, the so-called *photocurrent*. This photocurrent is proportional to the incident light intensity over 10 orders of magnitude and more [14]. It is this strict linearity of photocurrent with incident light over a wide dynamic range that makes semiconductor photosensors so attractive for many applications in image sensors and optical measurement systems.

5.3   Photocurrent processing

All the information a photosensor can extract from the light distribution in a scene is contained in the spatial and temporal modulation of the photocurrent in the individual pixels. For this reason, it is of much interest to process the pixels' photocurrents accordingly, in order to obtain the relevant modulation parameters in the most efficient manner [7]. Traditionally, only the integrated photocurrent could be extracted; today a large variety of photocurrent preprocessing is available, making it possible to optimize the photosensor acquisition parameters to a given problem. In the following, a few examples of such photocurrent preprocessing are presented.

5.3.1   Photocharge integration in photodiodes CCDs

The simplest type of photocurrent processing is the integration of the photocurrent during a certain time, the exposure time. In this way an integrated charge is obtained that is proportional to the number of photons incident on the pixel's sensitive area during the exposure time. This functionality is very easy to implement by employing the capacitance of the device used for generating the electric field for photocharge separation. Figure 5.6 illustrates this principle for the two most important photosensitive structures, the *photodiode* (PD) and the *metal-oxide-semiconductor* (MOS) capacitor as used in the *charge-coupled device*

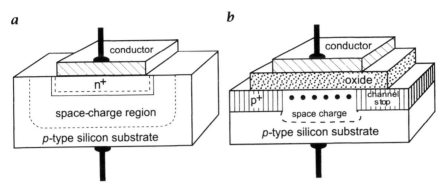

Figure 5.6: *Cross sections through the two major types of electrical field generating and charge storing devices in semiconductors: **a** photodiode, consisting of a reverse-biased p-n junction; **b** MOS capacitance, consisting of a (transparent) electrode on the semiconductor material, separated by a dielectric insulation.*

(CCD) image sensors. Both devices are easily fabricated with standard semiconductor processes.

A photodiode consists of a combination of two different conductivity types of semiconductor, as illustrated in Fig. 5.6a. In the junction between the two types of semiconductor, an electric field in the so-called space-charge region exists, as required for the separation of photogenerated charge carriers. At the same time, this space-charge region has a certain capacitance, varying with the inverse of the space-charge region width. Photodiodes are typically operated by biasing ("resetting") them to a certain potential and exposing them to light. Photocharge pairs entering the space-charge region are separated in the PD's electric field, a photocurrent is produced, and the photocharge is accumulated on the PD's capacitance, lowering the voltage across it. After the exposure time, the residual voltage is measured, and the voltage difference compared with the reset voltage level is a measure of the amount of light incident on the pixel during the exposure time.

The MOS-capacitance illustrated in Fig. 5.6b consists of a thin layer of oxide on top of a piece of semiconductor. The oxide is covered with a conductive material, often a metal or highly doped polycrystalline silicon (polysilicon). As in the case of the PD, the MOS structure is biased to a suitable voltage, leading to a space-charge region of a certain extent in the semiconductor. Again, photocharge is separated in the electric field and it is integrated on the MOS capacitance, collected at the interface between semiconductor and oxide.

A typical value for the PD and MOS area capacitance is 0.1 fF/μm^2. Assuming a maximum voltage swing of a few volts, this implies a storage capacity of a few thousand photoelectrons per μm^2. Once this storage capacity is exceeded, additional photocharge in the corresponding

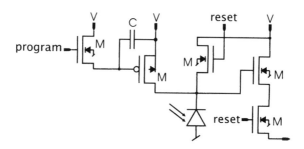

Figure 5.7: *Schematic diagram of the offset pixel with current source transistor* M_{cur}, *reset transistor* M_r, *row-select transistor* M_{sel}, *and sense transistor* M_s. *The value of the offset current is stored on the switched offset memory capacitor* C_M *with the programming switch* M_p *[16].*

pixel starts to spill over to neighboring pixels. This effect is called *blooming*, and well-designed image sensors provide special collecting ("*antiblooming*") structures for a reduction of this effect [15].

5.3.2 Programmable offset subtraction

Several machine vision and optical metrology problems suffer from small spatial contrast [7]. In such cases in which the spatial signal modulation is small compared to the background light level, one would profit from an *offset subtraction* mechanism in each pixel. This can be realized, even programmable in each pixel, with the offset subtraction mechanism proposed by Vietze and Seitz [16]. Each pixel contains a photodiode in series with a programmable current source, as illustrated in Fig. 5.7. This current source is easily realized with a MOSFET, whose gate voltage can be preset to a certain voltage level with a second MOS-FET, and by using a capacitance for the storage of this gate voltage. The MOSFET is operated in the so-called weak-inversion regime, where the drain current depends exponentially on the gate voltage; the current typically doubles with each increase of gate voltage by about 30 mV. In this way, the offset current can be varied easily between 1 fA up to several tens of μA [17]. The same integration mechanism as presented in Section 5.3.2 is employed for the collection of signal photocharge, representing the difference between total photocharge minus offset photocharge. Using this method, a dynamic range exceeding 150 dB can be reached, and several interesting applications can be realized very easily. An example of this is a simple *change detector*, implemented as a two-stage process. In a first stage, the offset current in each pixel is programmed such that the net result is zero; the offset currents effectively cancel the local photocurrents. In a second stage, the image is simply observed for nonzero pixels, indicating that there was a change in the

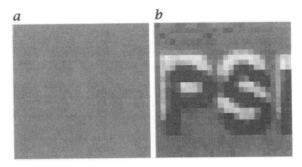

Figure 5.8: *Application example of the offset pixel—motion detector realized with a 26 × 28 pixel CMOS image sensor [17]: **a** sensor image of a simple scene (black letters "PSI" on white paper) after adjusting the pixels' individual offset current to a medium gray level; **b** sensor image after moving the scene slightly downwards and to the right. Pixels with changed values appear either black or white.*

present scene compared to the original "reference" scene: a change in the scene has occurred!

The realization of such a change detector is illustrated with an experimental offset pixel image sensor with 28 × 26 pixels, fabricated with standard CMOS technology [17]. In Fig. 5.8a the result of offset cancellation for a stationary scene containing the letters PSI is shown: a uniform gray picture. Once the object is moved (the letters are shifted downwards), the resulting pixels appear as bright where the dark object was, or as dark where the bright background was, see Fig. 5.8b.

5.3.3 Programmable gain pixels

Another local operation desirable in an image sensor is the individual multiplication of the photocurrent with a programmable factor. This can be achieved with a modification of a simple electronic circuit called *current-mirror*, consisting of two transistors. In the standard configuration, the gate terminals of the two transistors are connected. In the modification proposed in Vietze [17], a voltage difference between the two gates is applied, as illustrated in Fig. 5.9. This voltage difference is either fixed (e.g., by semiconductor process parameters), or it can be implemented as individually programmable potential differences across a storage capacitor. The photocurrent produced by a photodiode in the first branch of the modified current mirror results in current in the second branch that is given by the photocurrent times a factor. By using a similar physical mechanism as in the offset pixel, the gain pixel shows a current doubling (or halving) for each increase (decrease) of the voltage difference by about 30 mV. In this way, current multiplication (division) by several orders of magnitude can easily be obtained. As before, the

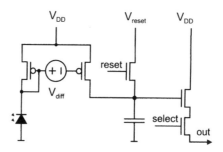

Figure 5.9: Schematic diagram of the gain pixel, consisting of a modified current mirror [17], with which a photocurrent multiplication with a factor ranging between 10^{-4} up to more than 10^4 can be realized.

multiplied photocurrent is integrated on a storage capacitor and read out using conventional circuitry.

An application of this is a high-sensitivity image sensor as described in Reference [17], in which each pixel has a fixed gain of about 8500. In this way, a sensitivity (see Section 5.5.1 for the definition) of 43 mV per photoelectron has been obtained, and an input-referred rms charge noise of better than 0.1 electrons at room temperature. As will be discussed in Section 5.5, this impressive performance must come at a price. In this case it is the reduced bandwidth of the pixel, reflected in the low-pass filter characteristics at low photocurrents with response times of several milliseconds.

5.3.4 Avalanche photocurrent multiplication

The multiplication mechanism described in the foregoing is based strictly on the use of electronic circuitry to achieve gain. In semiconductors there is a physical mechanism that can be exploited to multiply charge carriers before they are detected. This effect is called avalanche multiplication, and it is used in so-called *avalanche photodiodes* (APDs) [18]. If the electric field is increased to a few times 10^5 V/cm, charge carriers are multiplied with a strongly field-dependent factor. Depending on the specific doping conditions in the semiconductor, the necessary electric fields correspond to breakdown voltages of between a few volts and a few hundred volts. The strong dependency of the multiplication factor on voltage is illustrated with a model calculation for a breakdown voltage of 40 V, shown in Fig. 5.10 [19].

The APDs are commercially available and, because of high achievable gains, they are even suitable for single-photon light detection [20]. Due to the unusual voltages, the complex voltage stabilization/homogenization circuits, and the nontrivial readout electronics in each pixel, most APDs are only of the single-pixel type. The development of APD

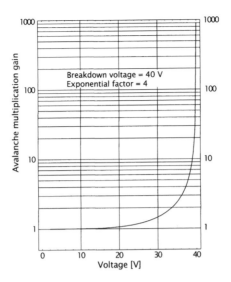

Figure 5.10: *Empirical relationship between applied voltage and obtained current gain in an avalanche photodiode, for which a breakdown voltage of $V_B = 40$ V and an exponent of $n = 4$ have been assumed.*

line and image sensor arrays has only just started. Nevertheless, the fabrication of reliable APD image sensors with CMOS processes is an active topic of research, and promising results have already been obtained (see, for example, Mathewson [21].

5.3.5   Nonlinear photocurrent to signal voltage conversion

Image processing algorithms are often motivated by solutions found in biological vision systems. The same is true for different types of photodetection strategies, especially for the realization of image sensors offering a similarly large dynamic range already inherent in animal vision. The fact that the human eye shows a nonlinear, close to *logarithmic sensitivity* has been exploited, for example, in the artificial retina described in Mahowald [22].

The realization of CMOS pixels offering a logarithmic sensitivity is particularly easy to achieve: One can use the logarithmic relationship between gate voltage and drain current in a MOSFET operated in weak inversion, already described in Section 5.3.2. The resulting pixel architecture, shown in Fig. 5.11 and exploited in CVA1 [Chapter 8], is particularly easy to implement in a CMOS process because a pixel consists of just a photodiode and three MOS transistors [23]. A typical photoresponse of about 40 mV per decade of optical input power is obtained with such logarithmic pixels, and their useful dynamic range exceeds 120 dB. Practical examples of scenes requiring such a high dy-

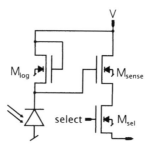

Figure 5.11: *Schematic diagram of a pixel with logarithmic response, consisting of just one photodiode and three MOSFETs. Implemented with a standard CMOS process, such a pixel shows an output voltage increase of about 40 mV per decade of incident light power.*

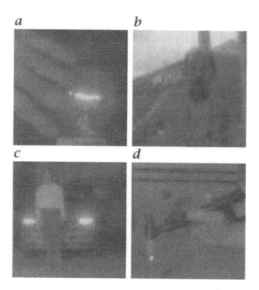

Figure 5.12: *Pictures taken with a small-area logarithmic image sensor with 64×64 pixels: **a** Electric light bulb where the glowing filament and the background are visible simultaneously; **b** Back-illuminated scene of a portrait in front of a window; **c** Parking garage application with its notoriously high dynamic range (headlights compared to dark corners) and low average light levels; **d** Welding application in which the object and the welding arc can be observed at the same time without blooming.*

namic range are illustrated in Fig. 5.12, with the actual measurements taken with a logarithmic image sensor exhibiting 64×64 pixels. In the image of a light bulb, the glowing filament as well as the background are clearly visible at the same time. Back-illuminated scenes, such as a portrait in front of a window, are dreaded by photographers, but they are easily handled by logarithmic pixels. In a parking garage, it is difficult to image dark corners and the interior of cars without being blinded by car headlights. Welding applications profit from the simultaneous imaging of the welding arc and its environment.

In contrast to other pixel types in which photocharge is integrated as discussed in Section 5.3.1, the logarithmic pixel measures the *voltage* at the drain of the MOSFET in series with the photodiode. For this reason, the dynamic behavior of such a logarithmic pixel depends on the photocurrent: the darker a scene (the lower a diode's photocurrent), the longer it takes until this MOSFET is in equilibrium again. Therefore, logarithmic pixels react much more slowly at low than at high illumination levels.

Besides their high dynamic range, logarithmic pixels have a property that should make them extremely interesting for image processing applications: An object with a given local contrast, which is imaged with a logarithmic sensor, results in an image with local pixel differences that are independent of the scene illumination level. This property is easily explained with the observation that a (local) light intensity ratio I_1/I_2 results in a signal given by $\log(I_1) - \log(I_2)$, and a proportional intensity change of $c \times I$ results in a signal given by $\log(c) + \log(I)$. The same object under brighter illumination looks the same in the logarithmic image, except for an additive shift of the background level.

5.4   Transportation of photosignals

The different types of image sensors described in the preceding produce an electrical quantity as a measure for a certain property of the incident light. The electrical quantity can be an amount of charge (e. g., the integrated photocharge), a current (e. g., the photocurrent) or a voltage level (e. g., the voltage difference of a discharged photodiode). This signal has to be transported as efficiently as possible to an output amplifier, responsible for making this signal available to the off-chip electronics.

5.4.1   Charge-coupled-device photocharge transportation

In the case of CCDs, the photocharge is stored under a precharged MOS capacitance. The basic *CCD* idea is to combine a linear array of such MOS capacitances, so that a stored photocharge can be moved laterally under the influence of appropriate MOS electrode voltage patterns. This principle is illustrated in Fig. 5.13, showing a *surface-channel CCD* (S-CCD). In the semiconductor, photocharge pairs are created under the influence of light. Moving by diffusion and by drift, the photoelectrons can find their way to positively biased MOS electrodes, also called gates, where they are stored at the interface between semiconductor and thin

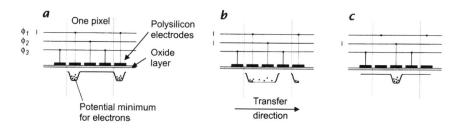

Figure 5.13: *Illustration of the charge transport principle in CCDs. Different stages of the electrode clocking and charge shifting sequence are shown in **a**, **b**, and **c**.*

oxide. The photogenerated holes are repelled by the positive gate voltage, and they move around by diffusion until they finally combine in the silicon substrate.

It is important to note that a CCD pixel is not represented only by the positively biased gate because this electrode can receive diffusing and drifting photoelectrons from its environment. A pixel's geometry is therefore rather defined in terms of "effective photocharge collection area," extending about halfway to the next positively biased electrode. This also shows that a pixel does not have sharply defined edges; the extent of the charge collection area representing a pixel depends on the wavelength, the electric field distribution, and the diffusion properties of the semiconductor. Generally, longer wavelength light results in a lower contrast and offers reduced resolution, as discussed in Section 5.2.2.

In Fig. 5.13, the potential distribution under the electrodes right at the surface is indicated. Photocharge accumulates in the shown "potential wells." By changing the gate voltage patterns, the potential wells can be widened, leading to a broadened distribution of photoelectrons. Using a suitable gate voltage pattern, one can also reduce the extent of the potential wells, and photoelectrons move again to regions with the lowest potential. As illustrated in Fig. 5.13, it is physically possible to transport photocharge. This transport mechanism works rather well up to frequencies of a few MHz. In good S-CCDs, only about 0.01 % of the photocharge is lost on average in transporting a photoelectron packet from one gate to another, neighboring gate. Instead of this charge transport loss, one often uses the *charge transfer efficiency* (CTE) concept, defined as the complement to 100 %. The CTE amounts to 99.99 % in the case of a good S-CCD.

In long CCD lines, a CTE of 99.99 % is still not good enough. Charge is trapped at the surface, making it hard to improve the CTE. For this reason, another type of CCD has been invented, the *buried-channel CCD* (B-CCD), in which the transport takes place in the bulk of the semiconductor, a few 100 nm away from the surface. In this way CTEs of up to 99.99995 % can be obtained in B-CCDs, and all commercially available CCD line- and image sensors are of this type.

Above a limiting clock frequency a CCD's CTE starts to degrade rapidly. Nevertheless, CCDs have been operated successfully at very high clock frequencies. For silicon, 1 GHz has been achieved [24], while GaAs CCDs have reached 18 GHz clocking frequency [25]. Such high clock rates require special precautions in the CCD fabrication process, usually not available for standard video sensors. Today's technology limits the analog bandwidth of CCDs to about 40 MHz. This is sufficient for standard video imagers according to the European CCIR or the American RS-170 black-and-white video standard. For HDTV sensors, however, the required pixel rate is around 75 MHz, making it necessary to operate two outputs in parallel in HDTV CCD imagers.

5.4.2 Photodiode photocharge signal transmission

The CCD technology provides a clean separation of the acquisition of photocharge and its electronic detection. This is achieved by transporting the photocharge with the almost perfect CCD transportation principle. Traditional photodiode arrays operate differently, by supplying each PD with its individual switch (see also Fig. 5.17 and Section 5.6.4), and by connecting many switches to a common signal ("video") line. This video line is most often realized using a well-conducting metal strip, leading to a common output amplifier structure. In a PD array, the image acquisition process proceeds in the following way: Assume that all PDs are initially precharged to a certain reverse bias, typically a few volts and that all switches are closed. Incident light generates photocharge pairs in each pixel, leading to the flow of a photocurrent due to the separation of photocharge pairs in the electrical field region of the PDs. As a PD also represents a capacitance, this capacitance is discharged by the photocurrent. After a certain time (the exposure time), a pixel can be interrogated by connecting the PD via the appropriate switch to the video line. The output amplifier resets the photodiode to its initial voltage value through the conducting line, while measuring how much charge is necessary to do so. This charge is (apart from noise effects) the same as the accumulated photocharge in this pixel. This means that—in contrast to CCDs where the actual photocharge is transmitted and detected—a PD array works by charge equilibration in a usually long conducting line. As we will see in Section 5.5.2, this charge equilibration process introduces noise in the signal detection process, which is proportional to the video line's total capacitance: the larger the number of pixels, the larger the video line capacitance and the larger the image noise. It is this physical effect that made PD image sensors so unattractive compared to CCDs in the early 1980s and which led to their almost complete replacement by CCD image sensors.

5.4.3 Voltage signal transmission

Not all pixel types depend on the transmission of charge signals, as indicated by several examples of pixel functionality discussed in Section 5.3. Voltage signals are sometimes generated in the individual pixels and these voltage signals must be transmitted to an output amplifier structure. A similar architecture as described in the preceding is used for this, consisting of individual switches in each pixel that connect the local voltages to a common amplifier structure. In such an architecture the voltage signal transmission task is much easier to accomplish than the charge signal transmission just discussed here: Johnson noise in the conducting video line, filtered with the video line's RC low-pass filter characteristics results in voltage noise that is proportional to one over the square root of the video line's capacitance [26]. The larger this capacitance, the lower the voltage noise. For this reason, voltage signals can be transmitted with much less noise and higher measurement precision than (small) charge signals. This implies that image sensor types offering voltage transmission architectures, such as that provided by the logarithmic pixel described in Section 5.3.5, have an inherent noise advantage over conventional PD architectures. This will be discussed in more detail in Section 5.5.3.

5.5 Electronic signal detection

The basic task of electronic signal detection is the precise measurement of voltage signals offering low noise levels and a wide dynamic range. These input voltage signals have either been produced by the conversion of photocharge into a voltage, for example by employing a capacitance, or they are the result of more elaborate photocharge preprocessing as was already described here. The output of signal detection electronics is usually a voltage that should be proportional to the input voltage over a large dynamic range. An important property of the signal detection electronics is that its output should have very low impedance, that is, the output voltage should be stable and must not depend on the amount of current drawn. As we will see in what follows, the electronic signal detection noise is today's limiting factor in increasing an image sensor's sensitivity and its dynamic range.

5.5.1 Signal-to-noise (SNR) and dynamic range

For a numerical description of the voltage or charge-noise performance of an electronic circuit, two values are often used, the *signal-to-noise ratio* SNR and the *dynamic range* DR. The SNR is defined by comparing

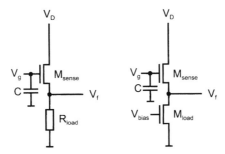

Figure 5.14: *Schematic diagram of the source follower circuit realized with a resistor (left) or with a so-called active load MOSFET (right). This is the most often used electronic circuit for photocharge detection in semiconductor image sensors. Photocharge deposited on the gate capacitance leads to a gate voltage V_g, which in turn produces a linear change in output voltage V_f.*

an actual signal level V with its rms noise ΔV, according to:

$$\mathrm{SNR} = 20^{10}\log\frac{V}{\Delta V} \tag{5.4}$$

The DR compares the maximum signal level V_{max} with the minimum rms noise level (ΔV_{min}), in an image sensor typically obtained in the dark

$$\mathrm{DR} = 20^{10}\log\frac{V_{max}}{\Delta V_{min}} \tag{5.5}$$

As an example, consider a CCD image sensor whose maximum charge ("*full well charge*") is 50,000 electrons, and for which a dark noise of 50 electrons rms is observed. This image sensor has a dynamic range of 60 dB.

It should be mentioned that the preceding definitions of SNR and DR in image sensors are not consistent with usage elsewhere in optical physics: As the measured voltage at the image sensor's output is usually proportional to the incident optical power, a factor of 10 in front of the logarithm should be used instead of the employed factor 20. However, because electrical engineers are used to associating power only with the square of voltage levels, the definitions given here are the ones employed almost exclusively for all image sensor specifications.

5.5.2 The basic MOSFET source follower

Although elaborate circuits exist for the desired conversion of voltage signals into other voltage signals, most image sensors employ the simplest type of voltage measurement circuits, the *MOSFET source follower*. As shown in Fig. 5.14, this circuit consists of just one transistor and one resistor, which is often implemented as another transistor called active load [27]. The output voltage of this source follower circuit is essentially given by

$$V_{out} = fV_{in} - V_0 \tag{5.6}$$

with a transistor-dependent multiplication factor f of 0.6-0.8 and an offset voltage V_0 of several hundred millivolts. In practice, one or a few such source follower stages are employed in series, to obtain low enough output impedance while maintaining the required read-out speed. At first sight it is surprising that such a simple circuit with a gain of less than unity is used in high-sensitivity image sensors. The reason for this is that the photocharge conversion gain is provided by the effective input capacitance, which is kept as small as possible. To-day's best image sensors have an effective input capacitance of around 15 fF, corresponding to a voltage increase of around $10 \mu V$ per electron. Taking the circuits' overall gain of less than unity into account, one arrives at the so-called sensitivity of the image sensor, expressed in μV per electrons. Typical sensitivities of state-of-the-art CCD and CMOS image sensors are between 5 and $10 \mu V$ per electron.

5.5.3   Noise sources in MOSFETs

Based on a source follower circuit, a typical output stage of an image sensor consists of the components shown in Fig. 5.15. The photocharge is transported to a diffusion (either the output diffusion of a CCD or the photodiode itself) that is connected to the gate of the source-follower MOSFET. Before measurement of each individual photocharge packet, the diffusion and the connected gate are biased to a reference voltage using a so-called reset MOSFET. Three main noise sources can be identified in such a circuit [26], whose influences are referenced back to the input of the source-follower MOSFET, contributing to an effective rms charge measurement uncertainty ΔQ.

Reset or kTC noise.   The channel of the reset transistor exhibits Johnson noise similar to an ordinary resistor. This causes statistical fluctuations in the observed reset voltage levels, which result in effective charge noise ΔQ_{reset} given by

$$\Delta Q_{reset} = \sqrt{kTC} \tag{5.7}$$

for the effective input capacitance C, at temperature T, and using Boltzmann's constant k.

Flicker or 1/f noise.   Statistical fluctuations in the mobility and charge carrier concentration of the source follower transistor's channel cause

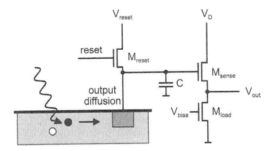

Figure 5.15: *Complete single-stage output circuit of a typical image sensor, consisting of a floating diffusion, a reset transistor, and a single-stage source follower as shown in Fig. 5.14.*

an effective charge noise $\Delta Q_{\text{flicker}}$ described by

$$\Delta Q_{\text{flicker}} \propto C \sqrt{\frac{I^A B}{g_m^2 f C_{ox} W L}} \qquad (5.8)$$

at frequency f, for current I, bandwidth B, transistor length L, and width W, oxide capacitance C_{ox}, process-dependent flicker noise constant A, which is typically between 0.5 and 2, and the transistor's transconductance g_m.

Thermal noise. Johnson noise in the source follower transistor's channel can also be referred back to the input, resulting in thermally generated charge noise $\Delta Q_{\text{thermal}}$ given by

$$\Delta Q_{\text{thermal}} = C \sqrt{\frac{4kTB\alpha}{g_m}} \qquad (5.9)$$

using the same parameters as in the preceding.

In practice, the first two noise sources can be essentially eliminated by a signal-processing technique called *correlated double sampling* (CDS) [28]: Reset noise is canceled by a two-stage process, in which the diffusion is preset to a reference voltage and a first measurement is made of this voltage level. In a second step, the photocharge is transferred to the diffusion, and a second measurement is made. The difference between these two measurements is free of reset noise and contains only information about the photocharge of interest. Because CDS is a temporal high-pass filter, flicker noise with its low-frequency dominance is effectively canceled at the same time.

The thermal noise contribution cannot be reduced using signal processing techniques, and it is obvious from Eq. (5.9) what can be done to minimize thermal noise. Reduction of temperature (in astronomical applications down to -120 °C) not only lowers charge noise levels [29] but the *dark current* contribution can be reduced to values as low as one electron per day per pixel. As a rule of thumb, dark current in silicon doubles for each increase in temperature of around 8–9 °C.

Often the reduction in temperature is combined with a reduction of the readout bandwidth to 50–100 kHz, leading to a charge noise level of around one electron [30]. Another technique of bandwidth reduction is the repetitive, nondestructive measurement of photocharge with output signal averaging, as carried out in the Skipper CCD [31]. Charge noise levels of 0.3 electrons rms have been obtained in this way. As can be seen in Eq. (5.9) the dominant factor in noise performance is the effective input capacitance. This has been lowered to values of less than 1 fF using the so-called double-gate MOSFET [32], corresponding to a sensitivity of more than 200 μV per electron and an effective charge noise level of less than one electron at room temperature and at video frequencies. The maximum photocharge such an output stage can handle is about 10,000 electrons, the DR is limited to about 80 dB.

5.6 Architectures of image sensors

For the acquisition of 1-D and 2-D distributions of incident light, arrays of pixel are required. Such arrays can be realized as an arrangement of CCD columns or as suitably placed and interconnected individual photodiodes as described in Section 5.3.1. Depending on the choice of arrangement and interconnection, different types of image sensors result.

5.6.1 Frame-transfer charge-coupled-devices

The simplest type of CCD image sensor is the *frame-transfer* (FT) CCD. As illustrated in Fig. 5.16, it consists of three CCD sections. One CCD area (A register) is used for the conversion of photons into photocharge during the exposure time and for the storage of this photocharge in the pixels. This 2-D photocharge distribution is subsequently shifted down into another CCD area (B register), which is covered with an opaque metal shield. From the B register, an image row at a time is shifted down into a CCD line (C register), with which the photocharges are transported laterally to the output amplifier, so that the content of this image row can be accessed sequentially.

The disadvantage of the FT-CCD principle is the afterexposure of bright areas that can occur when the photocharge pattern is transported from the A register into the light-shielded B register. This occurs because the A register remains light-sensitive during the vertical photocharge transportation time. The afterexposure effect in FT-CCDs can create saturated ("bright") columns without any contrast informa-

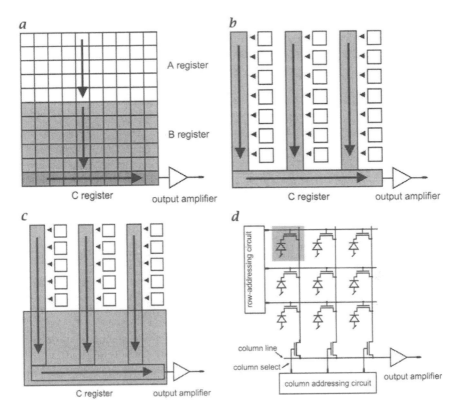

Figure 5.16: *The four most important architectures of solid-state image sensors: a frame-transfer (FT) CCD with its three registers; b interline-transfer (IT) CCD with column light shields for vertical charge transfer; c field-interline-transfer (FIT) CCD, combining FT-CCD and IT-CCD principles for studio and broadcast applications; d traditional photodiode array image sensor with one photodiode and one selection transistor per pixel.*

tion. For this reason, high-quality FT-CCD cameras employ a mechanical shutter, shielding the A register from incident light during the vertical photocharge transportation time.

The big advantage of the FT-CCD is that the whole A register area is photosensitive; one speaks of an *optical fill factor* of 100 %. Because the A register is covered with polysilicon CCD electrodes that tend to absorb in the blue and UV, an FT-CCD is not very sensitive in the blue spectral region. For special applications this can be remedied by thinning down an FT-CCD to about 10 µm thickness and by illuminating it from the back. Such back-side illuminated FT-CCDs offer 100 % fill factor, an excellent response over the whole visible spectrum, and they are the image sensors of choice for scientific and astronomical applications.

5.6.2   Interline-transfer charge-coupled-devices

In consumer applications, a mechanical shutter is impractical to use, and for this reason FT-CCDs are rarely used in video and surveillance cameras. Rather, the *interline-transfer* (IT) CCD principle is employed, as illustrated in Fig. 5.16b. Photocharge is collected in the individual pixels, and after the exposure time the photocharge is transferred via the pixels' transfer register into a corresponding vertical CCD column. These CCD columns are shielded from light with an opaque metal layer. A 2-D photocharge distribution can therefore be shifted downwards, one row at a time, into the horizontal output register, from where the photocharge packets are read out sequentially. As the vertical CCD columns are shielded, the afterexposure problem is much less severe than in FT-CCDs. One pays for this with a reduced fill factor, because the column light shields reduce the available photosensitive area on the image sensor's surface. The typical fill factor of an IT-CCD is about 30%, reducing the total sensitivity to about a third of that observed in FT-CCDs.

With the IT-CCD principle a very useful functionality becomes available: Because there is essentially no time-constraint in exposing the pixels and transferring their accumulated photocharge under the shielded columns, one can implement an *electronic shutter*. The exposure time can be as short as a few $10\,\mu s$, extending up to several seconds in cameras not conforming to a video standard. The exposure time is essentially bounded by the dark current, which depends strongly on temperature, as described in Section 5.5.2. The desirable properties of the IT-CCD make it the image sensor of choice for most of today's video and surveillance cameras, especially for consumer applications. In order to increase the optical fill factor of IT-CCDs, some manufacturers supply each pixel with its own *microlens*, so that more light can be directed to the IT-CCD's photosensitive surface. An even more efficient, albeit more expensive improvement is the coverage of an IT-CCD with amorphous silicon, with which the optical fill factor can be increased further, close to 100%.

5.6.3   Field-interline-transfer charged-coupled-devices

Although the column light shield in the IT-CCD is an efficient light blocker, there is always some residual photocharge seeping into the columns from the sides. For this reason, an IT-CCD can still show some afterexposure effects. For professional applications such as video broadcasting, this is considered not acceptable, and a combination FT- and IT-CCD principle has been invented to overcome this problem, the *field-interline-transfer* (FIT) CCD, illustrated in Fig. 5.16c. The upper part of a FIT-CCD really consists of an IT-CCD. The lower part, however, is realized like the B and C registers of an FT-CCD. The FIT-CCD is operated by acquiring an image conventionally, making use of the IT-CCD's variable exposure time functionality. The resulting 2-D photocharge distribution is then shifted quickly under the shielded vertical columns, from where it is transported very fast under the completely shielded intermediate storage register. The sequential row-by-row readout is then effectuated from the B and C registers, exactly as in FT-CCDs.

5.6.4 Conventional photodiode (MOS) arrays

A photodiode or MOS array image sensor consists of a 1-D or 2-D arrangement of PDs, each provided with its own selection transistor, as illustrated in Fig. 5.16d. For a description of the PD image sensor's operation, assume that all PDs are precharged to a certain reverse bias voltage, typically 5 V. Under the influence of the incident light, each pixel is discharged to a certain level. A pixel is read out by addressing the corresponding row and column transistors, providing a conducting line from the pixel to the output amplifier. Using this line the pixel is charged up again to the same reverse bias voltage as before. The amplifier measures how much charge is required to do so, and this charge is identical to the photocharge (plus dark current charge) accumulated at the pixel site. In this way, each pixel can be read out individually, at random, and the exposure time is completely under the control of the external addressing electronics.

The random addressing freedom, however, comes at the price of a large capacitance of the conducting line between pixel and output amplifier of several pF. As is obvious from the inspection of Eq. (5.9), this leads to noise levels one or two orders of magnitude larger than in corresponding CCDs image sensors. For this reason, the usage of such traditional PD image sensors has been restricted to applications where the random pixel access is an absolute must. In video applications, CCD technology is used almost exclusively.

5.6.5 Active pixel sensor technology

As just discussed, the noise performance of PD array image sensors is much worse than that of a CCD because of the large effective capacitance the first MOSFET in the output amplifier sees. The logical conclusion is that it should be possible to realize CMOS-compatible PD array image sensors with a noise performance comparable to CCD imagers when this first MOSFET is placed in each pixel. It took surprisingly long until this seemingly trivial observation was made. As a consequence, it led directly to what is called today *"active pixel sensor"* (APS) imaging technology [33]. It is apparently not sufficient just to move the first MOSFET into the pixel, because its input requires a reset mechanism.

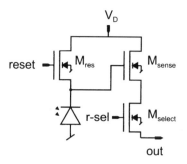

Figure 5.17: *Schematic diagram of an APS pixel, consisting of a photodiode, a reset transistor, a sense transistor, and a row-select transistor. The active load transistor that completes the source-follower circuit is shared by all pixels in a column, and it is therefore needed only once per column.*

For this reason, the simplest APS image sensor pixel consists of one photodiode and three MOSFETs as illustrated in Fig. 5.17.

With the reset MOSFET the photodiode and the gate of the source follower MOSFET are precharged to a voltage of typically 3-5 V. The photocurrent produced by the photodiode (plus the dark current) discharges the capacitance of the reverse-biased PD. The resulting voltage can then be sensed efficiently with the source-follower MOSFET with a sensitivity that is comparable to that of CCD image sensors. As in the PD array, the third MOSFET is employed as a selection switch with which a row is selected. The active load MOSFET of this APS pixel can be shared by all the pixels in a column, and it does not need to be included in the pixel itself.

The APS technology is very attractive for several reasons: (1) APS image sensors can be produced in standard CMOS technology, opening the way to image sensors with integrated electronic functionality and even complete digital processors; (2) The pixels offer random access similar to PD arrays; (3) The pixel readout is nondestructive, and it can be carried out repeatedly for different exposure times; (4) The exposure times can be programmed electronically; (5) APS image sensors dissipate one or two magnitudes less electrical power than CCDs; (6) APS imagers show less blooming (spilling of electronic charge to adjacent pixels); And (7) APS pixels are more robust under x-ray radiation.

Disadvantages of APS image sensors include the reduced optical fill factor (comparable to that of IT-CCDs), the increased offset noise due to MOSFET threshold variations (see Section 5.8), and the impossibility of performing correlated double sampling for noise reduction as discussed in Section 5.5.3. Fortunately, a combination of APS and CCD technology has been proposed, and the resulting photogate APS pixels offer this functionality [34].

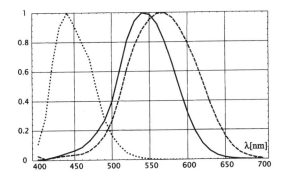

Figure 5.18: *Estimates of the relative cone sensitivities of the human eye after DeMarco et al. [35].*

Active pixel image sensors with up to $4k \times 4k$ pixels have been realized, with speeds of several thousand frames per second, with an input-referred charge noise of about 10 electrons at room temperature and video speed, and with a DR of up to 84 dB. Many experts do not doubt, therefore, that CMOS imagers using APS techniques can replace CCD image sensors in many practical applications, and several consumer products in the electronic still and video camera market already contain CMOS imagers.

5.7 Color vision and color imaging

5.7.1 Human color vision

Human color vision can be regarded as a parameter-based sampling. It does not measure the spectral radiant flux directly but rather properties of the spectral distribution such as the total radiant flux (*intensity*), the mean wavelength (*color*), and the width of the spectral distribution (*saturation* of the color). If the width of the spectral distribution is narrow we have a pure color with high saturation. If the spectral distribution is wide, the color has low saturation. If the spectral distribution is flat, we sense no color. With respect to this discussion, it appears that a 3-sensor system appears to be an ideal intensity-color-saturation sensor. It is ideal in the sense that it has a linear response and the wavelength (color) and width (saturation) resolution are independent of the wavelength. Thus it is interesting to compare this 3-sensor system with the color-sensing system of the human eye.

For color sensing, the human eye also has three types of photopigments in the photoreceptors known as cones with different spectral sensitivities (Fig. 5.18). The sensitivities cover different bands with maximal sensitivities at 445 nm, 535 nm, and 575 nm, respectively (band sampling), but overlap each other significantly (parameter-based sampling). The three sensor channels are unequally spaced and cannot simply be linearly related. Indeed, the color sensitivity of the human eye is uneven and all the nonlinearities involved make the science of color vision rather difficult. Here, only some basic facts are given—in as much as they are useful to handle color imagery.

Three-dimensional color space. With three color sensors, it is obvious that color signals cover a 3-D space. Each point in this space represents one color. From spectral sampling, it is clear that many spectral distributions called *metameric color stimuli* or short *metameres* map onto one point in this space. Generally, we can write the signal s_i received by a sensor with a spectral responsivity $R_i(\lambda)$ as

$$s_i = \int R_i(\lambda)\Phi(\lambda)\,d\lambda \tag{5.10}$$

With three primary color sensors, a triple of values is received, often called *tristimulus* and represented by the 3-D vector $\boldsymbol{s} = [s_1, s_2, s_3]^T$.

Primary colors. One of the most important questions in *colorimetry* is how to represent colors as linear combinations of some basic or *primary colors*. A set of three linearly independent spectral distributions $\Phi_j(\lambda)$ represents a set of primary colors and results in an array of responses that can be described by the matrix P with

$$P_{ij} = \int R_i(\lambda)\Phi_j(\lambda)\,d\lambda \tag{5.11}$$

Each vector $\boldsymbol{p}_j = \left[p_{1j}, p_{2j}, p_{3j}\right]^T$ represents the tristimulus of the primary colors in the 3-D color space. Then, it is obvious that any color can be represented by the primary colors that are a linear combination of the base vectors $\boldsymbol{p}_j$ in the following form:

$$\boldsymbol{s} = R\boldsymbol{p}_1 + G\boldsymbol{p}_2 + B\boldsymbol{p}_3 \quad \text{with} \quad 0 \le R, G, B \le 1 \tag{5.12}$$

where the coefficients are denoted by R, G, and B, indicating the three primary colors red, green, and blue. Note that these coefficients must be positive and smaller than one. Because of this condition, all colors can be presented as a linear combination of a set of primary colors only if the three base vectors are orthogonal to each other. This cannot be the case as soon as more than one of the color sensors responds to one primary color. Given the significant overlap in the spectral response of the three types of cones (Fig. 5.18), it is obvious that none of the color systems based on any type of real primary colors will be orthogonal. The colors that can be represented lie within the parallelepiped formed by the three base vectors of the primary colors. The more the primary

Table 5.1: *Most often used primary color systems. The second column gives also the conversion matrix of the corresponding color system to the XYZ color system (values taken from Wendland [36, Section 5.7.4] and Pratt [37, Table 3.5-1]).*

Name	Description
Monochromatic Primaries R_c, G_c, B_c	Adapted by C.I.E. in 1931 $\lambda_R = 700$ nm, $\lambda_G = 546.1$ nm, $\lambda_B = 435.8$ nm $\begin{bmatrix} 0.490 & 0.310 & 0.200 \\ 0.177 & 0.812 & 0.011 \\ 0.000 & 0.010 & 0.990 \end{bmatrix}$
NTSC Primary Receiver Standard R_N, G_N, B_N	FCC Standard, 1954, to match phosphors of RGB color monitors $\begin{bmatrix} 0.6070 & 0.1734 & 0.2006 \\ 0.2990 & 0.5864 & 0.1146 \\ 0.0000 & 0.0661 & 1.1175 \end{bmatrix}$
S.M.P.T.E. Primary Receiver Standard R_S, G_S, B_S	Better adapted to modern screen phosphors $\begin{bmatrix} 0.393 & 0.365 & 0.192 \\ 0.212 & 0.701 & 0.087 \\ 0.019 & 0.112 & 0.985 \end{bmatrix}$
EBU Primary Receiver Standard R_e, G_e, B_e	Adopted by EBU 1974 $\begin{bmatrix} 0.4303 & 0.3416 & 0.1780 \\ 0.2219 & 0.7068 & 0.0713 \\ 0.0202 & 0.1296 & 0.9387 \end{bmatrix}$

colors are correlated with each other (i. e., the smaller the angle between two of them is), the smaller is the color space that can be represented by them. Mathematically, colors that cannot be represented by a set of primary colors have at least one negative coefficient in Eq. (5.12). The most often used primary color systems are summarized in Table 5.1.

Chromaticity. One component in the 3-D color space is intensity. If a color vector is multiplied by a scalar, only its intensity is changed but not its color. Thus, all colors could be normalized by the intensity. This operation reduces the 3-D color space to a 2-D color plane or *chromaticity diagram*:

$$r = \frac{R}{R + G + B}, \quad g = \frac{G}{R + G + B}, \quad b = \frac{B}{R + G + B} \qquad (5.13)$$

with

$$r + g + b = 1 \qquad (5.14)$$

It is sufficient to use only the two components r and g. The third component is then given by $b = 1 - r - g$, according to Eq. (5.14).

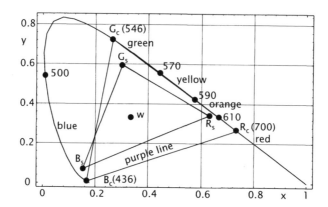

Figure 5.19: *Chromaticity diagram shown in the xy color space. The u-shaped curve of monochromatic colors with wavelengths in nm as indicated and the purple line includes all possible colors. Shown are also range of colors (triangles) that can be represented with monochromatic primaries R_c, G_c, B_c and the SMPTE primary receiver standard R_S, G_S, B_S.*

Thus, all colors that can be represented by the three primary colors R, G, and B are confined within a triangle. As already mentioned, some colors cannot be represented by the primary colors. The boundary of all possible colors is given by all visible monochromatic colors from deep red to blue. The line of monochromatic colors form a u-shaped curve (Fig. 5.19). Thus, most monochromatic colors cannot be represented by the monochromatic primaries. As all colors that lie on a straight line between two colors can be generated as a mixture of these colors, the space of all possible colors covers the area filled by the u-shaped spectral curve and the straight mixing line between its two end points for blue and red color (*purple line*).

In order to avoid negative color coordinate values, often a new co-ordinate system is chosen with virtual primary colors, that is, primary colors that cannot be realized by any physical colors. This color system is known as the *XYZ color system* and constructed in such a way that it includes just the curve of monochromatic colors with only positive coefficients (Fig. 5.19).

Hue and saturation. The color systems discussed so far do not directly relate to the human color sensing. From the rg or xy values, we cannot directly infer colors such as green, blue, etc. In addition to *luminance (intensity)*, a description of colors would also include the type of color such as green or blue (*hue*) and the purity of the color (*saturation*). From a pure color, we can obtain any degree of saturation by mixing it with white.

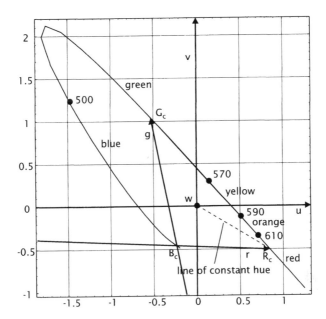

Figure 5.20: *Chromaticity diagram shown in the uv color difference system centered at the white point w. The color saturation is proportional to the distance from the center and the color hue is given by the angle to the x axis. Shown are also the axes of the rg color system marked with r and b.*

Hue and saturation can be extracted from chromaticity diagrams by simple coordinate transformations. The essential point is the *white point* in the middle of the chromaticity diagram (Fig. 5.20). If we draw a line from this point to a pure (monochromatic) color, it constitutes a mixing line for a pure color with white and is thus a line of constant hue. From the white point to the pure color, the saturation increases linearly. The *white point* is given in the rg chromaticity diagram by $w = (1/3, 1/3)$. A color system that has its center at the white point is called a *color difference system*. From a color difference system, we can infer a hue-saturation color system by simply using polar coordinate systems. Then, the radius coordinate is proportional to the saturation and the hue to the angle coordinate (Fig. 5.20).

Color science is, in the abstract, relatively simple. However, real difficulties arise from what is required to adapt the color system in an optimum way to display and print devices, for transmission by television signals, or to correct for the uneven color resolution of the human visual system that is apparent in the chromaticity diagrams of simple color spaces (Figs. 5.19 and 5.20). The result to date is a confusing manifold of different color systems. For a detailed treatment of color vision, the reader is referred to the monograph written by the Committee on Colorimetry of the Optical Society of America [38]. An excellent treatment of color with respect to digital image processing is given by Pratt [37] and with respect to video engineering by Inglis [39].

Intensity-hue-saturation color coordinate system. Here, we discuss only one further color coordinate system that is optimally suited to present vectorial image information as colors on monitors. With a gray scale image, only one parameter can be represented. In color, it is, however, possible to represent three parameters simultaneously, for instance as intensity, hue, and saturation (IHS). This representation is known as the IHS *color coordinate system.* The transformation is given by

$$
\begin{bmatrix} I \\ U \\ V \end{bmatrix} = \begin{bmatrix} 1/3 & 1/3 & 1/3 \\ 2/3 & -1/3 & -1/3 \\ -1/3 & 2/3 & -1/3 \end{bmatrix} \begin{bmatrix} R \\ G \\ B \end{bmatrix}
$$

$$
H = \arctan\left(\frac{V}{U}\right)
$$

$$
S = (U^2 + V^2)^{1/2}
$$

(5.15)

This transformation essentially means that the zero point in the chromaticity diagram has been shifted to the white point. The pairs $[U, V]^T$ and $[S, H]^T$ are the Cartesian and polar coordinates in this new coordinate system, respectively.

5.7.2 Color chips and color cameras

The task of most camera systems is accurately to capture the perceptible contents of a scene for subsequent faithful reproduction, viewed by a human observer. The black-and-white image sensors and cameras discussed so far can do this only for the brightness sensation; the very rich perception of *color* requires additional information, as described in Section 5.7.1: According to Grassman's Laws [40], a 3-D spectral representation of a scene is sufficient for the complete reproduction of a color scene as it can be perceived by a human observer. It is sufficient, therefore, to acquire a color scene through three different types of spectral filters, behind each of which a black-and-white camera system is placed. As described in Section 5.7.1 these filters correspond to the primary colors or a linear combination of them [41].

For the best performance, a color camera is built by providing special beam-splitting optics and by arranging three black-and-white image sensors so that they see an identical portion of a scene. Each image sensor is covered with its own color filter, as just described, and together the three image sensors acquire the complete colorimetric information

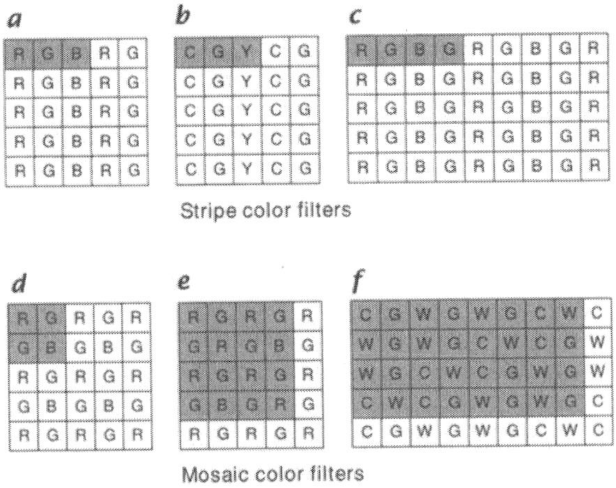

*Figure 5.21: Illustration of different color filter types for single-chip color sensors. The unit cell (basic arrangement of color filter patches that is periodically repeated on the image sensor) is shown as shaded rectangle: **a** primary color (RGB) stripe filter with 3×1 unit cell; **b** complementary color (CGY) stripe filter with 3×1 unit cell; **c** primary color (RGB) stripe filter with 4×1 unit cell; **d** Bayer color mosaic filter with 2×2 unit cell; **e** Bayer color mosaic filter with 4×4 unit cell; **f** shift-8 color mosaic filter using complementary colors in an 8×4 unit cell.*

about a scene. Such three-chip color cameras are employed in professional and studio cameras. They are quite expensive, unfortunately, because they have to employ costly beam-splitting objects, the three image sensors have to be aligned according to close tolerances (registration to sub-pixel accuracy), and three high-quality image sensors must be used, each requiring its proper driving electronics.

For these reasons, it is highly desirable to realize a color camera with just one single black-and-white image sensor and a suitable pattern of pixel-individual color filters on top. Several techniques have been used for the implementation of such a single-chip color camera. They are either based on 1-D color stripe filters (Fig. 5.21a-c) or on 2-D color mosaics (Fig. 5.21d-f).

The simplest arrangement is the RGB color stripe pattern shown in Fig. 5.21a. Its obvious drawback is its sensitivity to periodic objects, producing so-called moiré and color-aliasing effects [15]. Instead of the primary RGB filters, one can also use the complementary colors cyan (C=G+B), yellow (Y=R+G), and magenta (M=R+B), or even transparent white (W=R+G+B). An example of such a complementary stripe filter pattern is shown in Fig. 5.21b. Compared to the primary color stripe filter in Fig. 5.21a, this filter can be simpler to fabricate, and because it accepts more light, it might offer an improved SNR performance. Another example of a stripe filter is shown in Fig. 5.21c, illustrating the use of more green than red or blue information and the larger filter period of four pixels. This reflects the property of the human eye that spatial resolution is largest in the green, less pronounced in the red, and least developed in the blue spectral band. Much better performance is achieved with 2-D mosaic color filters. A popular color filter is the Bayer pattern with its 2×2 pixel unit cell shown in Fig. 5.21d [42]. An improved form makes even better use of the different spatial resolution for the three filter curves, resulting in the 4×4 pixel unit cell shown in Fig. 5.21e [42]. In this filter pattern, half of the color filters are green, 3/8 are red and only 1/8 are blue. The larger the unit cell period, the better a color filter's ability to prevent aliasing and moiré effect. A very effective color pattern making use of complementary colors is shown in Fig. 5.21f [43]. It uses a 4×8 pixel unit cell in such a way that the required signal processing is relatively simple to realize using conventional electronics [44]. The least amount of aliasing is produced by a color mosaic with an aperiodic color pattern. Although this is well known in theory, no commercial product has been offered yet with such a random color pattern, which would also require precise knowledge of the image sensor's complete color pattern for the accurate extraction of color information.

5.8   Practical limitations of semiconductor photosensors

Due to the analog nature of the pixels in a semiconductor photosensor, it is not possible to fabricate all pixels with identical properties, and often some pixels on an imager will be defective. It is therefore important for a machine vision system architect to have an idea about typical limitations and shortcomings of practical image sensors.

5.8.1   Pixel nonuniformity and dead pixels

Because of slightly varying geometries of CCD and APS pixels, their effective area and therefore their gain are not identical. These gain variations are of the order of 1-5 %, and for precision measurements, a multiplicative correction of this effect is required.

In APS pixels, where the individual source-follower transistors in the pixels show offset voltage fluctuations, an offset uncertainty of the order of 10 mV is observed. This results in APS pixel offset variations of around 1-2 %. These offset variations have to be corrected additively for precision measurements. Because the CCD principle is based on the virtually complete transfer of photogenerated charge packets from pixel site to pixel site, CCD pixels do not show this type of offset variation.

In applications where dark currents become significant, offset variations are obtained in APS as well as in CCD image sensors because dark current densities can vary from pixel to pixel in any type of semiconductor image sensor. It might even be possible that the dark current is so high in a few so-called "hot pixels" that these pixels are completely filled with thermally generated charge during the exposure time. This effect can only be reduced by lowering the temperature or by shortening the exposure time.

Digital memories do not suffer from most localized defects on the semiconductor surface because there are redundant memory cells on the integrated circuit that can replace defective storage cells. In an image sensor, this is of course not possible. For this reason, it is rather difficult to produce a perfect image sensor without any defects. It is not uncommon, therefore, that a few defective ("*dead*") pixels can be encountered on an image sensor. Usually, the position of these dead pixels is stored, and the image content at this place is computed as a function of neighboring values. Such pixel defect densities occur quite infrequently with a percentage of typically less than 0.001-0.01 %.

In CCDs, another type of defect is more consequential, when complete dead columns are encountered; the required correction computation is much more expensive than with single dead pixels. Fortunately, dead columns usually are only encountered in megapixel CCDs of lower grade, while smaller area CCDs for video applications are free of this type of defect.

5.8.2 Sensor nonlinearity

The conversion of light into photocharge is a highly linear process. In silicon, this has been verified for a large dynamic range of at least 10 orders of magnitude [14]. Unfortunately, much of this linearity is lost in the photocharge detection principle that is mainly used in image sensors. Photocharge is stored as the state of discharge of a precharged capacitance, either an MOS capacitance or a photodiode. As the width of the space-charge region depends on the discharge level, the spectral sensitivity and the photometric linearity are a function of the amount of photocharge already stored.

The same problem is encountered in the electronic charge detection circuits that are implemented as source followers after a floating diffusion (see Fig. 5.15). The capacitance of the floating diffusion depends on the voltage on it and therefore on the charge state. This causes nonlinearities in charge sensing.

The degree of the nonlinearity depends very much on the charge detection (or voltage) range that is used. For differential measurements of over a few hundred mV in the middle region of the analog sensor output, nonlinearities can be below 0.1 % [45]. Over the full sensing

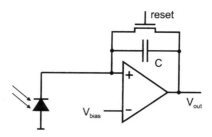

Figure 5.22: *Schematic diagram of a charge detection circuit, providing a high photodetection linearity by keeping the photodiode voltage constant. If the feedback capacitance is replaced by a resistor, a so-called transimpedance amplifier results, converting photocurrent in a proportional voltage with very high linearity.*

range, nonlinearities may be as large as a few percent. If the measurement should be highly linear, a proper electronic charge detector circuit must be used in which the voltage at the input is kept constant. Such a charge detector circuit, illustrated in Fig. 5.22, requires a certain amount of silicon floorspace. With state-of-the-art semiconductor technology, pixels become so large that only 1-D arrays have been realized with this technique [46]; in image sensors it is not yet realistic to implement such charge detectors in each pixel. For this reason, image sensing applications for optical metrology in which sub-percent linearity is demanded have to resort to accurate calibration and off-chip digital correction techniques [5].

5.9 Conclusions

It was only about a decade ago that a few researchers started to exploit one of the most exciting capabilities offered by modern silicon-based semiconductor technology, the monolithic integration of photosensitive, analog and digital circuits. Some of the results of these efforts are described in this work, representing just a small fraction of the many applications already demonstrated. They all support the main assertion of this chapter, that today's image sensors are no longer restricted to the acquisition of optical scenes. Image sensors can be supplied with custom integrated functionality, making them key components, application-specific for many types of optical measurement problems. It was argued that it is not always optimal to add the desired custom functionality in the form of highly-complex smart pixels, because an increase in functionality is often coupled with a larger fraction of a pixel's area being used for electronic circuit, at the cost of reduced light sensitivity. For this reason, each new optical measurement problem has to be inspected carefully, taking into account technical and economical issues. For optimum system solutions, not only smart pixels have to be considered. Functionality could also be provided by separate on-chip or off-chip circuits, perhaps by using commercially available electronic components.

Machine vision system architects can no longer ignore the freedom and functionality offered by smart image sensors, while being well aware of the shortcomings of semiconductor photosensing. It may be true that the seeing chips continue to be elusive for quite some time. The smart photosensor toolbox for custom imagers is a reality today, and a multitude of applications in optical metrology, machine vision, and electronic photography can profit from the exciting developments in this area. "Active vision," "integrated machine vision," "electronic eyes," and "artificial retinae" are quickly becoming more than concepts: the technology for their realization is finally here now!

5.10 References

[1] Gonzalez, R. and Wintz, P., (1987). *Digital Image Processing, 2nd edition.* Reading, MA: Addison-Wesley.

[2] Beck, R. (ed.), (1995). *Proc. AAAS Seminar on Fundamental Issues of Imaging Science, Atlanta (GA), February 16-17, 1995.*

[3] Beyer, H., (1992). *Geometric and radiometric analysis for a CCD-camera based photogrammetric close-range system.* PhD thesis No. ETH-9701, Federal Institute of Technology, Zurich, Switzerland.

[4] Chamberlain, S. and Lee, J., (1984). A novel wide dynamic range silicon photodetector and linear imaging array. *IEEE Jour. Solid State Circ.*, **SC-19**: 175-182.

[5] Lenz, R., (1996). *Ein Verfahren zur Schätzung der Parameter geometrischer Bildtransformationen.* Dissertation, Technical University of Munich, Munich, Germany.

[6] Schenker, P. (ed.), (1990). *Conference on Active Vision,* Vol. 1198 of *Proc. SPIE.*

[7] Seitz, P., (1995). Smart image sensors: An emerging key technology for advanced optical measurement and microsystems. In *Proc. SPIE*, Vol. 2783, pp. 244-255.

[8] Saleh, B. and Teich, M., (1991). *Fundamentals of Photonics.* New York: John Wiley and Sons, Inc.

[9] Wong, H., (1996). Technology and device scaling considerations for CMOS imagers. Vol. 43, pp. 2131-2142. ISPRS.

[10] Sze, S., (1985). *Semiconductor Devices.* New York: John Wiley and Sons.

[11] Spirig, T., (1997). *Smart CCD/CMOS based image sensors with programmable, real-time temporal and spatial convolution capabilities for applications in machine vision and optical metrology.* PhD thesis No. ETH-11993, Federal Institute of Technology, Zurich, Switzerland.

[12] Heath, R., (1972). Application of high-resolution solid-state detectors for X-ray spectrometry—a review. *Advan. X-Ray Anal.*, **15**:1-35.

[13] Bertin, E., (1975). *Principles and Practice of X-Ray Spectrometric Analysis.* New York: Plenum Press.

[14] Budde, W., (1979). Multidecade linearity measurements on Si photodiodes. *Applied Optics*, **18**:1555-1558.

[15] Theuwissen, A., (1995). *Solid-State Imaging with Charge-Coupled Devices.* Dordrecht, The Netherlands: Kluwer Academic Publishers.

[16] Vietze, O. and Seitz, P., (1996). Image sensing with programmable offset pixels for increased dynamic range of more than 150 dB. In *Conference on Solid State Sensor Arrays and CCD Cameras, Jan. 28–Feb. 2, 1996, San Jose, CA*, Vol. 2654A, pp. 93-98.

[17] Vietze, O., (1997). *Active pixel image sensors with application specific performance based on standard silicon CMOS processes.* PhD thesis No. ETH-12038, Federal Institute of Technology, Zurich, Switzerland.

[18] Webb, P., McIntyre, R., and Conradi, J., (1974). Properties of Avalanche Photodiodes. *RCA Review*, **35**:234-277.

[19] Seitz, P., (1997). Image sensing with maximum sensitivity using industrial CMOS technology. In *Conference on Micro-Optical Technologies for Measurement Sensors and Microsystems II, June 16–June 20, 1997, Munich, Germany*, Vol. 3099, pp. 22-33.

[20] Zappa, F., Lacatia, A., Cova, S., and Lovati, P., (1996). Solid-state single-photon detectors. *Optical Engineering*, **35**:938-945.

[21] Mathewson, A., (1995). *Integrated avalanche photo diode arrays.* Ph.D. thesis, National Microelectronics Research Centre, University College, Cork, Ireland.

[22] Mahowald, M., (1991). Silicon retina with adaptive photodetectors. In *Conference on Visual Information Processing: From Neurons to Chips Jan. 4, 1991, Orlando, FL*, Vol. 1473, pp. 52-58.

[23] Graf, H., Höfflinger, B., Seger, Z., and Siggelkow, A., (1995). Elektronisch Sehen. *Elektronik*, **3**:3-7.

[24] Sankaranarayanan, L., Hoekstra, W., Heldens, L., and Kokshoorn, A., (1991). 1 GHz CCD transient detector. In *International Electron Devices Meeting 1991*, Vol. 37, pp. 179-182.

[25] Colbeth, R. and LaRue, R., (1993). A CCD frequency prescaler for broadband applications. *IEEE J. Solid-State Circ.*, **28**:922-930.

[26] Carnes, J. and Kosonocky, W., (1972). Noise sources in charge-coupled devices. *RCA Review*, **33**:327-343.

[27] Allen, P. and Holberg, D., (1987). *CMOS Analog Circuit Design.* Fort Worth: Saunders College Publishing.

[28] Hopkinson, G. and Lumb, H., (1982). Noise reduction techniques for CCD image sensors. *J. Phys. E: Sci. Instrum*, **15**:1214-1222.

[29] Knop, K. and Seitz, P., (1996). Image Sensors. In *Sensors Update*, W. G. Baltes, H. and J. Hesse, eds., pp. 85-103. Weinheim, Germany: VCH-Verlagsgesellschaft.

[30] Chandler, C., Bredthauer, R., Janesick, J., Westphal, J., and Gunn, J., (1990). Sub-electron noise charge coupled devices. In *Conference on Charge-Coupled Devices and Solid State Optical Sensors, Feb. 12–Feb. 14, 1990, Santa Clara, CA*, Vol. 1242, pp. 238–251.

[31] Janesick, J., Elliott, T., Dingizian, A., Bredthauer, R., Chandler, C., Westphal, J., and Gunn, J., (1990). New advancements in charge-coupled device technology. Sub-electron noise and 4096 X 4096 pixel CCDs. In *Conference on Charge-Coupled Devices and Solid State Optical Sensors, Feb. 12–Feb. 14, 1990, Santa Clara, CA*, Vol. 1242, pp. 223–237.

[32] Matsunaga, Y., Yamashita, H., and Ohsawa, S., (1991). A highly sensitive on-chip charge detector for CCD area image sensor. *IEEE J. Solid State Circ.*, **26**:652–656.

[33] Fossum, E., (1993). Active pixel sensors (APS)—are CCDs dinosaurs? In *Conference on Charge-Coupled Devices and Solid-State Optical Sensors III, Jan. 31–Feb. 2, 1993, San Jose, CA*, Vol. 1900, pp. 2–14.

[34] Mendis, S., Kemeny, S., Gee, R., Pain, B., Staller, C., Kim, Q., and Fossum, E., (1997). CMOS active pixel image sensors for highly integrated imaging systems. *IEEE J. Solid-State Circ.*, **32**:187–197.

[35] DeMarco, P., Pokorny, J., and Smith, V. C., (1992). Full-spectrum cone sensitivity functions for X-chromosome-linked anomalous trichromats. *J. Optical Society*, **A9**:1465–1476.

[36] Wendland, B., (1988). *Fernsehtechnik I: Grundlagen*. Heidelberg: Hüthig.

[37] Pratt, W., (1991). *Digital image processing*. New York: Wiley.

[38] Committee on Colorimetry, Optical Society of America, (1953). *The Science of Color*. Washington, D. C.: Optical Society of America.

[39] Inglis, A. F., (1993). *Video engineering*. New York: McGraw-Hill.

[40] Pritchard, D. H., (1984). U.S. color television fundamentals — a review. *RCA Engineer*, **29**:15–26.

[41] Hunt, R. W. G., (1991). *Measuring Colour*, 2nd edition. Ellis Horwood.

[42] Bayer, B. E., (1976). Color imaging array, U.S. patent No. 3,971,065.

[43] Knop, K., (1985). Two-dimensional color encoding patterns for use in single chip cameras. *Proc. SPIE*, **594**:283–286.

[44] Aschwanden, F., Gale, M. T., Kieffer, P., and Knop, K., (1985). Single-chip color camera using a frame-transfer CCD. *IEEE Trans. Electron. Devices*, **ED-32**:1396–1401.

[45] Flores, J., (1992). An analytical depletion-mode MOSFET model for analysis of CCD output characteristics. In *Conference on High-Resolution Sensors and Hybrid Systems, Feb. 9–Feb. 14, 1992, San Jose, CA*, Vol. 1656, pp. 466–475.

[46] Raynor, J. and Seitz, P., (1997). A linear array of photodetectors with wide dynamic range and near photon quantum noise limit. *Sensors and Actuators A*, **61**:327–330.

6 Geometric Calibration of Digital Imaging Systems

Robert Godding

AICON GmbH, Braunschweig, Germany

6.1 Introduction

The use of digital imaging systems for metrology purposes implies the necessity to calibrate or check these systems. While simultaneous calibration of cameras during the measurement is possible for many types of photogrammetric work, separate calibration is particularly useful in the following cases:

Computer Vision and Applications

- when information is desired about the attainable accuracy of the measurement system and thus about the measurement accuracy at the object;
- when simultaneous calibration of the measurement system is impossible during the measurement for systemic reasons so that some or all other system parameters have to be predetermined;
- when complete imaging systems or components are to be tested by the manufacturer for quality-control purposes; and
- when digital images free from the effects of the imaging system are to be generated in preparation of further processing steps (such as rectification).

In addition, when setting up measurement systems it will be necessary to determine the positions of cameras or other sensors in relation to a higher-order world coordinate system to allow 3-D determination of objects within these systems.

The following chapters describe methods of calibration and orientation of imaging systems, focusing primarily on photogrammetric techniques as these permit homologous and highly accurate determination of the parameters required.

6.2 Calibration terminology

6.2.1 Camera calibration

Camera calibration in photogrammetric terminology refers to the determination of the parameters of interior orientation of individual cameras. When dealing with digital images, it is advisable to analyze the complete imaging system, including camera, transfer units and possibly frame grabbers. The parameters to be found by calibration depend on the type of camera used. Once the imaging system has been calibrated, measurements can be made after the cameras have been carefully oriented.

6.2.2 Camera orientation

Camera orientation usually includes determination of the parameters of exterior orientation to define the camera station and camera axis in the higher-order object-coordinate system, frequently called the *world coordinate system*. This requires the determination of three rotational and three translational parameters, that is, a total of six parameters for each camera.

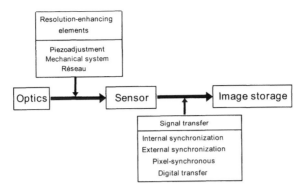

Figure 6.1: *Components of digital imaging systems.*

6.2.3 System calibration

In many applications, fixed setups of various sensors are used for measurement. Examples are online measurement systems in which, for example, several cameras, laser pointers, pattern projectors, rotary stages, etc., may be used. If the entire system is used as an integrated measuring tool, then the simultaneous calibration and orientation of all components involved maybe defined as *system calibration*.

6.3 Parameters influencing geometrical performance

6.3.1 Interior effects

All components of a digital imaging system leave their marks on the image of an object and thus on the measurement results obtained from processing this image. The following is a brief description of the relevant components (Fig. 6.1).

Optical system. Practically all lenses exhibit typical *radial-symmetrical distortion* that may vary greatly in magnitude. On the one hand, the lenses used in optical measurement systems are nearly distortion-free [1]. On the other hand, wide-angle lenses, above all, frequently exhibit distortion of several 100 μm at the edges of the field. Fisheye lenses are in a class of their own; they frequently have extreme distortion at the edges. Because radial-symmetrical distortion is a function of design, it cannot be considered an aberration. By contrast, centering errors often unavoidable in lens making cause aberrations reflected in radial-asymmetrical and tangential distortion components [2].

Additional optical elements in the light path, such as the IR barrier filter and protective filter of the sensor, also leave their mark on the image and have to be considered in the calibration of a system.

A more detailed treatment of optical systems and the corresponding distortions can be found in Chapter 3.

Resolution-enhancing elements. The image size and the possible resolution of CCD sensors are limited. Currently on the market are digital cameras with up to 4000×4000 sensor elements. Regarding the stability of the camera-body and the quality of the lenses, some of them are designed especially for measuring purposes, for example, the Rollei Q16 MetricCamera [3]. Other, less frequent approaches use techniques designed to attain higher resolution by shifting commercial sensors in parallel to the image plane. Essentially, there are two different techniques. In the case of "microscanning," the interline transfer CCD sensors are shifted by minute amounts by means of piezoadjustment so that the light-sensitive sensor elements fall within the gaps between elements typical of this type of system, where they acquire additional image information [4, 5]. Alternatively, in "macroscanning," the sensors may be shifted by a multiple of their own size, resulting in a larger image format. Individual images are then oriented with respect to the overall image either by a highly precise mechanical system [6, 7] or opto-numerically as in the RolleiMetric Réseau Scanning Camera by measuring a glass-based reference grid in the image plane ("*réseau scanning*") [8].

All resolution-enhancing elements affect the overall accuracy of the imaging system. In scanner systems with purely mechanical correlation of individual images, the accuracy of the stepping mechanism has a direct effect on the geometry of the high-resolution imagery. In the case of réseau scanning, the accuracy of the réseau is decisive for the attainable image-measuring accuracy [9].

Sensor and signal transfer. Due to their design, *charge-coupled device* (CCD) sensors usually offer high geometrical accuracy [10]. When judging an imaging system, its sensor should be assessed in conjunction with the frame grabber used. Geometrical errors of different magnitude may occur during A/D conversion of the video signal, depending on the type of *synchronization*, above all if *pixel-synchronous* signal transfer from camera to image storage is not guaranteed [9, 11]. However, in the case of pixel-synchronous readout of data, the additional transfer of the pixel clock pulse ensures that each sensor element will precisely match a picture element in the image storage. Very high accuracy has been proved for these types of cameras [1]. However, even with this type of transfer the square shape of individual pixels cannot be taken for granted. As with any kind of synchronization, most sensor-storage combinations make it necessary to account for an affinity factor; in other words, the pixels may have different extension in the direction of lines and columns.

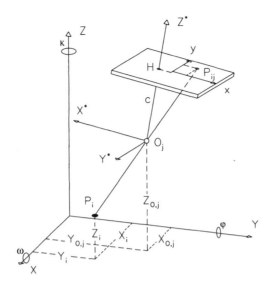

Figure 6.2: *Principle of central perspective [12].*

6.3.2 Exterior effects

If several cameras are used in an online metrology system, both the parameters of interior orientation and those of exterior orientation may vary, the former, for example, caused by refocusing and changes of temperature, the latter caused by mechanical effects or fluctuations of temperature. The resulting effects range from scale errors during object measurement all the way up to complex model deformation. This is why all systems of this kind should make it possible to check or redetermine all relevant parameters.

6.4 Optical systems model of image formation

Image formation by an optical system can, in principle, be described by the mathematical rules of *central perspective*. According to these rules, an object is imaged in a plane so that the object points P_i and the corresponding image points P_i' are located on straight lines through the perspective center O_j (Fig. 6.2). The following holds under idealized conditions for the formation of a point image in the image plane:

$$\begin{bmatrix} x_{ij} \\ y_{ij} \end{bmatrix} = \frac{-c}{Z_{ij}^*} \begin{bmatrix} X_{ij}^* \\ Y_{ij}^* \end{bmatrix} \tag{6.1}$$

with

$$
\begin{bmatrix} X_{ij}^* \\ Y_{ij}^* \\ Z_{ij}^* \end{bmatrix} = D(\omega, \varphi, \kappa)_j \begin{bmatrix} X_i - X_{oj} \\ Y_i - Y_{oj} \\ Z_i - Z_{oj} \end{bmatrix} \tag{6.2}
$$

where X_i, Y_i, Z_i are the coordinates of an object point P_i in the object-coordinate system K; X_{oj}, Y_{oj}, Z_{oj} are the coordinates of the perspective center O_j in the object-coordinate system K; X_{ij}^*, Y_{ij}^*, Z_{ij}^* are the coordinates of the object point P_i in the coordinate system K_j^*; x_{ij}, y_{ij} are the coordinates of the image point in the image-coordinate system K_B; and $D(\omega, \varphi, \kappa)_j$ is the rotation matrix between K and K_j^*; and c is the distance between perspective center and image plane, the system K_j^* being parallel to the system K_B with the origin in the perspective center O_j [13].

The representation of the central perspective as described in Eq. (6.1) and Eq. (6.2) splits up the process of computation from image-space to object space in two steps:

- Within Eq. (6.1) mainly the parameters of image-space like camera parameters (interior orientation) and measured image coordinates are used.

- In Eq. (6.2) the transformation to the world coordinate system is done by using three parameters of translation and three parameters of rotation (exterior orientation).

This ideal concept is not attained in reality where many influences are encountered due to the different components of the imaging system. These can be modeled as departures from rigorous central perspective. The following section describes various approaches to mathematical camera models.

6.5 Camera models

When optical systems are used for measurement, modeling the entire process of image formation is decisive in obtaining accuracy. Basically, the same ideas apply, for example, to projection systems for which models can be set up similarly to imaging systems.

Before we continue, we have to define an *image-coordinate system* K_B in the image plane of the camera. In most electro-optical cameras, this image plane is defined by the sensor plane; only in special designs (e. g., in réseau scanning cameras [8]), is this plane defined differently. While in the majority of analog cameras used for metrology purposes the image-coordinate system is defined by projected fiducial marks or réseau crosses, this definition is not required for digital cameras. Here

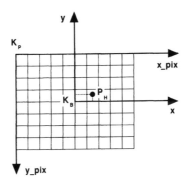

Figure 6.3: *Definition of image-coordinate system.*

it is entirely sufficient to place the origin of image-coordinate system in the center of the digital images in the storage (Fig. 6.3). Because the pixel interval in column direction in the storage is equal to the interval of the corresponding sensor elements, the unit "pixel in column direction" may serve as a unit of measure in the image space. All parameters of interior orientation can be directly computed in this unit, without conversion to metric values.

6.5.1 Calibrated focal length and principal-point location

The reference axis for the camera model is not the optical axis in its physical sense, but a principal ray, which on the object side is perpendicular to the image plane defined in the foregoing and intersects the latter at the *principal point* $P_H(x_H, y_H)$. The perspective center O_j is located at distance c_K (also known as *calibrated focal length*) perpendicularly in front of the principal point [14].

The original formulation of Eq. (6.1) is thus expanded as follows:

$$\begin{bmatrix} x_{ij} \\ y_{ij} \end{bmatrix} = \frac{-c_k}{Z_{ij}^*} \begin{bmatrix} X_{ij}^* \\ Y_{ij}^* \end{bmatrix} + \begin{bmatrix} x_H \\ y_H \end{bmatrix} \tag{6.3}$$

6.5.2 Distortion and affinity

The following additional correction function can be applied to Eq. (6.3) for radial symmetrical, radial asymmetrical and tangential distortion:

$$\begin{bmatrix} x_{ij} \\ y_{ij} \end{bmatrix} = \frac{-c_k}{Z_{ij}^*} \begin{bmatrix} X_{ij}^* \\ Y_{ij}^* \end{bmatrix} + \begin{bmatrix} x_H \\ y_H \end{bmatrix} + \begin{bmatrix} dx(V,A) \\ dy(V,A) \end{bmatrix} \tag{6.4}$$

Here, dx and dy may now be defined differently, depending on the type of camera used, and are made up of the following different components:

$$
\begin{aligned}
\mathrm{d}x &= \mathrm{d}x_{\text{sym}} + \mathrm{d}x_{\text{asy}} + \mathrm{d}x_{\text{aff}} \\
\mathrm{d}y &= \mathrm{d}y_{\text{sym}} + \mathrm{d}y_{\text{asy}} + \mathrm{d}y_{\text{aff}}
\end{aligned} \tag{6.5}
$$

Radial-symmetrical distortion. The *radial-symmetrical distortion* typical of a lens can generally be expressed with sufficient accuracy by a polynomial of odd powers of the image radius (x_{ij} and y_{ij} are henceforth called x and y for the sake of simplicity):

$$
\mathrm{d}r_{\text{sym}} = A_1(r^3 - r_0^2 r) + A_2(r^5 - r_0^4 r) + A_3(r^7 - r_0^6 r) \tag{6.6}
$$

where $\mathrm{d}r_{\text{sym}}$ is the radial-symmetrical distortion correction; r is the image radius from $r^2 = x^2 + y^2$; A_1, A_2, A_3 are the polynomial coefficients; and r_0 is the second zero crossing of the distortion curve, so that we obtain

$$
\mathrm{d}x_{\text{sym}} = \frac{\mathrm{d}r_{\text{sym}}}{r} x \quad \text{and} \quad \mathrm{d}y_{\text{sym}} = \frac{\mathrm{d}r_{\text{sym}}}{r} y \tag{6.7}
$$

A polynomial with two coefficients is generally sufficient to describe radial symmetrical distortion. Expanding this distortion model, it is possible to describe even lenses with pronounced departure from perspective projection (e. g., fisheye lenses) with sufficient accuracy. In the case of very pronounced distortion it is advisable to introduce an additional point of symmetry $P_S(x_S, y_S)$. Figure 6.4 shows a typical distortion curve.

For numerical stabilization and far-reaching avoidance of correlations between the coefficients of the distortion function and the calibrated focal lengths, a linear component of the distortion curve is split off by specifying a second zero crossing [15].

Lenz [16] proposes a different formulation for determining radial-symmetrical distortion, which includes only one coefficient. We thus obtain the following equation:

$$
\mathrm{d}r_{\text{sym}} = r \frac{1 - \sqrt{1 - 4Kr^2}}{1 + \sqrt{1 - 4Kr^2}} \tag{6.8}
$$

where K is the distortion coefficient to be determined.

Radial-asymmetrical and tangential distortion. To handle *radial-asymmetrical* and *tangential distortion*, various different formulations are possible. Based on Conrady [17], these distortion components may be formulated as follows [2]:

$$
\begin{aligned}
\mathrm{d}x_{\text{asy}} &= B_1(r^2 + 2x^2) + 2B_2 xy \\
\mathrm{d}y_{\text{asy}} &= B_2(r^2 + 2y^2) + 2B_1 xy
\end{aligned} \tag{6.9}
$$

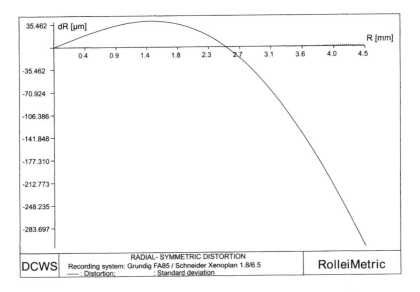

Figure 6.4: *Typical distortion curve of a lens.*

In other words, these effects are always described with the two additional parameters B_1 and B_2.

This formulation is expanded by Brown [18], who adds parameters to describe overall image deformation or the lack of image-plane flatness:

$$
\begin{aligned}
dx_{asy} &= (D_1(x^2 - y^2) + D_2x^2y^2 + D3(x^4 - y^4))x/c_K \\
&+ E_1xy + E_2y^2 + E_3x^2y + E_4xy^2 + E_5x^2y^2 \\
dy_{asy} &= (D_1(x^2 - y^2) + D_2x^2y^2 + D3(x^4 - y^4))y/c_K \\
&+ E_6xy + E_7x^2 + E_8x^2y + E_9xy^2 + E_10x^2y^2
\end{aligned}
\tag{6.10}
$$

In view of the large number of coefficients, however, this formulation implies a certain risk of too many parameters. Moreover, because this model was primarily developed for large-format analog imaging systems, some of the parameters cannot be directly interpreted for applications using digital imaging systems. Equation (6.7) is generally sufficient to describe asymmetrical effects. Figure 6.5 shows typical effects for radial-symmetrical and tangential distortion.

Affinity and nonorthogonality. The differences in length and width of the pixels in the image storage caused by synchronization can be taken into account by an *affinity factor*. In addition, an affinity direction may be determined, which primarily describes the orthogonality of the axes of the image-coordinate system K_B. An example may be a line scanner that does not move perpendicularly to the line direction. Allowance for

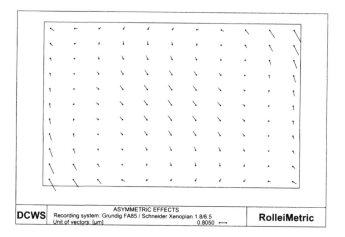

Figure 6.5: Radial symmetrical and tangential distortion.

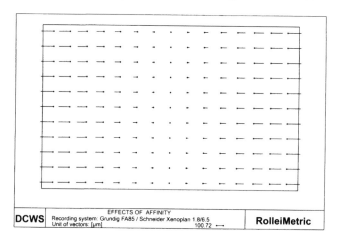

Figure 6.6: Effects of affinity.

these two effects can be made as follows:

$$dx_{\text{aff}} = C_1 x + C_2 x \quad \text{and} \quad dy_{\text{aff}} = 0 \tag{6.11}$$

Figure 6.6 gives an example of the effect of affinity.

Additional parameters. The introduction of additional parameters may be of interest for special applications. Fryer [19] and Fraser and Shortis [20] describe formulations that also make allowance for distance-related components of distortion. However, these are primarily effective with medium- and large-image formats and the corresponding lenses and are of only minor importance for the wide field of digital uses.

Gerdes et al. [21] use a different camera model in which an additional two parameters have to be determined for the oblique position of the sensor.

6.6 Calibration and orientation techniques

6.6.1 In the laboratory

Distortion parameters can be determined in the laboratory under clearly defined conditions.

In the goniometer method, a highly precise grid plate is positioned in the image plane of a camera. Then, the goniometer is used to sight the grid intersections from the object side and to determine the corresponding angles. Distortion values can then be obtained by a comparison between nominal and actual values.

In the collimator technique, test patterns are projected onto the image plane by several collimators set up at defined angles to each other. Here also, the parameters of interior orientation can be obtained by a comparison between nominal and actual values, though only for cameras focused at infinity [14].

Apart from this restriction, there are more reasons weighing against the use of the aforementioned laboratory techniques for calibrating digital imaging systems, including the following:

- The equipment layout is high;
- The interior orientation of the cameras used normally is not stable, requiring regular recalibration by the user; and
- Interior orientation including distortion varies at different focus and aperture settings so that calibration under practical conditions appears more appropriate.

6.6.2 Bundle adjustment

All the parameters required for calibration and orientation may be obtained by means of photogrammetric bundle adjustment. In *bundle adjustment*, two so-called observation equations are set up for each point measured in an image, based on Eqs. (6.2) and (6.4). The total of all equations for the image points of all corresponding object points results in a system that makes it possible to determine the unknown parameters [22]. Because this is a nonlinear system of equations, no linearization is initially necessary. The computation is made iteratively by the method of least squares, the unknowns being determined in such a way that the squares of deviations are minimized at the image

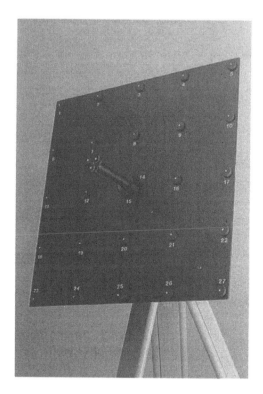

Figure 6.7: *Test array for camera calibration.*

coordinates observed. Newer approaches are working with modern algorithms such as balanced parameter estimation [23]. Bundle adjustment thus allows simultaneous determination of the unknown object coordinates, exterior orientation and interior orientation with all relevant system parameters of the imaging system. In addition, standard deviations are computed for all parameters, which give a measure of the quality of the imaging system.

Calibration based exclusively on image information. This method is particularly well suited for calibrating individual imaging systems. It requires a survey of a field of points in a geometrically stable photogrammetric assembly. The points need not include any points with known object coordinates (control points); the coordinates of all points need only be known approximately [22]. It is, however, necessary that the point field be stable for the duration of image acquisition. The scale of the point field likewise has no effect on the determination of the desired image-space parameters. Figure 6.7 shows a point field suitable for calibration.

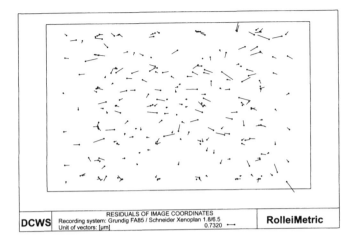

DCWS	RESIDUALS OF IMAGE COORDINATES Recording system: Grundig FA85 / Schneider Xenoplan 1.8/6.5 Unit of vectors: [μm] 0.7320	RolleiMetric

Figure 6.8: Residual mismatches after bundle adjustment.

The accuracy of the system studied can be judged from the residual mismatches of the image coordinates as well as the standard deviation of the unit of weight after adjustment (Fig. 6.8). The effect of synchronization errors, for example, becomes immediately apparent, for instance, by larger residual mismatches of different magnitude in line and column direction.

Figure 6.9 gives a diagrammatic view of the minimum setup for surveying a point array with which the aforementioned system parameters can be determined. The array may be a 3-D test field with a sufficient number of properly distributed, circular, retroreflecting targets. This test field is first recorded in three frontal images, with camera and field at an angle of 90° for determining affinity and 180° for determining the location of the principal point. In addition, four convergent images of the test field are used to give the assembly the necessary geometric stability for determination of the object coordinates and to minimize correlation with exterior orientation.

Optimum use of the image format is a precondition for the determination of distortion parameters. However, this requirement need not be satisfied for all individual images. It is sufficient if the image points of all images cover the format uniformly and completely.

If this setup is followed, seven images will be obtained roughly as shown in Fig. 6.10; their outer frame stands for the image format, the inner frame for the image of the square test field, and the arrowhead for the position of the test field. It is generally preferable to rotate the test field with the aid of a suitable suspension in front of the camera instead of moving the camera for image acquisition. The use of retroreflecting targets and a ring light guarantee proper, high-contrast reproduction

Figure 6.9: *Imaging setup for calibration [1].*

Figure 6.10: *Test field.*

of the object points, which is indispensable for precise and reliable measurement. A complete, commercially available software package offering far-reaching automation of the process is described in Godding [1].

Additional object information for calibration and orientation. Once the imaging system has been calibrated, its orientation can be found by resection in space. The latter may be seen as a special bundle adjustment in which the parameters of interior orientation and the object coordinates are known. This requires a minimum of three control points in space whose object coordinates in the world coordinate system are known and whose image points have been measured with the imaging system to be oriented.

In addition to orientation, calibration of an imaging system is also possible with a single image. However, as a single image does not allow the object coordinates to be determined, suitable information within the object has to be available in the form of a 3-D control-point array [24]. But constructing, maintaining and regularly checking such an array is rather costly, all the more so as it should be mobile so that it may be used for different applications. The control pattern should completely fill the measurement range of the cameras to be calibrated and oriented to ensure good agreement between calibration and measurement volumes.

a   *b*

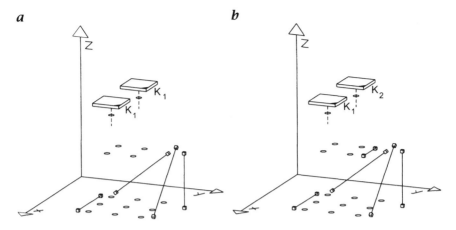

Figure 6.11: *Scale setup for calibrating **a** one camera and **b** two cameras.*

The expense is considerably less if several images are available. For a two-image assembly and one camera, a spatial array of points that need to be known only approximately plus, as additional information, several known distances (scales) distributed in the object space will be sufficient; this is similar to the previous paragraph. In an ideal case, one scale on the camera axis, another one perpendicular to it, and two oblique scales in two perpendicular planes parallel to the camera axis are required (Fig. 6.11a). This will considerably reduce the object-side expense, because the creation and checking of scales is much simpler than that of an extensive 3-D array of control points.

A similar setup is possible if the double-image assembly is recorded with several cameras instead of just one. This is, in principle, the case with online measurement systems. An additional scale is then required in the foreground of the object space, bringing the total number of scales to five (Fig. 6.11b).

If at least one of the two cameras can be rolled, the oblique scales can be dispensed with, provided that the rolled image is used for calibration [24].

The setups described in Fig. 6.11 are, of course, applicable to more than two cameras as well. In other words, all the cameras of a measurement system can be calibrated if the aforementioned conditions are created for each of the cameras. At least two cameras have to be calibrated in common, with the scales set up as described. Simultaneous calibration of all cameras is also possible, but then the scale information must also be simultaneously available to all the cameras. If all cameras also are to be calibrated in common, this will have to be done via common points.

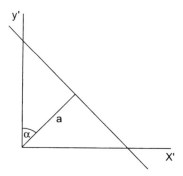

Figure 6.12: Principle of the plumbline method.

System calibration. As we have seen from the previous two paragraphs, joint calibration and orientation of all cameras involved and thus calibration of the entire system are possible if certain conditions are met. With the aid of bundle adjustment, the two problems can, in principle, be solved jointly with a suitable array of control points or a spatial point array of unknown coordinates plus additional scales. The cameras then already are in measurement position during calibration. Possible correlations between the exterior and interior orientations required are thus neutralized because the calibration setup is identical to the measurement setup.

Apart from the imaging systems, other components can be calibrated and oriented within the framework of system calibration. Godding and Luhmann [25] describe a technique in which a suitable procedure in an *online measurement system* allows both the interior and exterior orientation of the cameras involved as well as the orientation of a rotary stage to be determined with the aid of a spatial point array and additional scales. The calibration of a line projector within a measurement system using photogrammetric techniques was, for example, presented by Strutz [26].

6.6.3 Other techniques

Based on the fact that straight lines in the object space have to be reproduced as straight lines in the image, the so-called *plumbline method* serves to determine distortion. The technique is predicated on the fact that the calibrated focal length and principal-point location are known [27].

According to Fig. 6.12, each of the straight-line points imaged are governed by the relationship

$$x' \sin \alpha + y' \cos \alpha = a \qquad (6.12)$$

where x' and y' can be expressed as follows:

$$\begin{aligned} x' &= x_{ij} + dx_{sym} + dx_{asy} \\ y' &= y_{ij} + dy_{sym} + dy_{asy} \end{aligned} \qquad (6.13)$$

where dx_{sym}, dy_{sym}, dx_{asy}, and dy_{asy} correspond to the formulations in Eq. (6.7), (6.9), and (6.10). It is an advantage of this method that, assuming suitable selection of the straight lines in the object, a large number of observations is available for determining distortion, and measurement of the straight lines in the image lends itself to automation. A disadvantage of the technique is the fact that simultaneous determination of all relevant parameters of interior orientation is impossible.

Lenz [16] presented a technique in which an imaging system was similarly calibrated and oriented in several steps. The technique requires a plane test field with known coordinates, which generally should not be oriented parallel to the image plane. Modeling radial symmetrical distortion with only one coefficient (see also Section 6.5.2) and neglecting asymmetrical effects allows the calibration to be based entirely on linear models. Because these do not need to be resolved interactively, the technique is very fast. It is a disadvantage, however, that here also it is impossible to determine all the parameters simultaneously and that, for example, the location of the principal point and pixel affinity have to be determined externally.

Gerdes et al. [21] describe a method in which cameras are permitted to be calibrated and oriented with the aid of parallel straight lines projected onto the image. A cube of known dimensions is required for the purpose as a calibrating medium. Vanishing points and vanishing lines can be computed from the cube edges projected onto the image and used to determine the unknown parameters.

A frequently used formulation for the determination of the parameters of exterior and interior orientation is the method of direct linear transformation (DLT) first proposed by Abdel-Aziz and Karara [28]. This establishes a linear relationship between image and object points. The original imaging equation is converted to a transformation with 11 parameters that initially have no physical importance. By introducing additional relations between these coefficients it is then possible to derive the parameters of interior and exterior orientation, including the introduction of distortion models [29]. Because the linear formulation of DLT can be solved directly, without approximations for the unknowns, the technique is frequently used to determine approximations for bundle adjustment. The method requires a spatial test field with a minimum of six known control points, a sufficient number of additional points necessary to determine distortion. However, if more images are to be used to determine interior orientation or object coordinates, nonlinear models will have to be used here also.

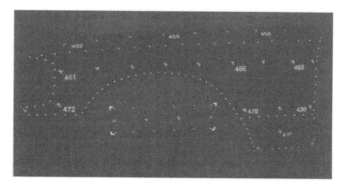

Figure 6.13: *Measurement of a fender.*

Figure 6.14: *Rollei Q16 MetricCamera.*

6.7 Photogrammetric applications

6.7.1 Applications with simultaneous calibration

The imaging setup for many photogrammetric applications allows *simultaneous calibration* of cameras. It is an advantage of this solution that no additional effort is required for external calibration of the cameras and that current camera data for the instant of exposure can be determined by bundle adjustment. This procedure, however, is possible only if the evaluation software offers the option of simultaneous calibration. As an example, let us look at measurement of an automobile part (Fig. 6.13).

A total of nine photos were taken with a Rollei Q16 MetricCamera (Fig. 6.14) with a resolution of 4096×4096 sensor elements. RolleiMetric Close-Range Digital Workstation software was used for evaluation. This allows fully automatic determination of 3-D coordinates, starting with measurement of image points right up to computation of all un-

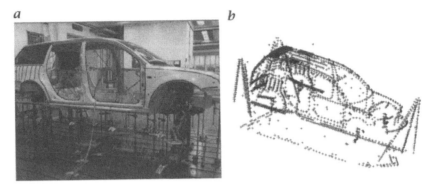

Figure 6.15: **a** *Measurement of a car;* **b** *3-D view of measured points.*

known parameters. In addition to target sizes and the 3-D coordinates of all measured points in the world coordinate system, these include the camera parameters and all camera stations. For this example the coordinates have an accuracy of approximately 1/100 mm in each of the three coordinate axes. Figure 6.15a, b illustrates another example from the automotive industry. Here, torsion tests were made in the course of deformation measurements. The data were obtained by photogrammetric means. A total of 3000 points all around the vehicle were recorded in a total of 170 images with the aid of a digital camera with a resolution of 3000 × 2000 sensor elements. Here also, the camera was simultaneously calibrated during image acquisition. The points measured were accurate to within about 5/100 mm. Most photogrammetric applications for high-precision 3-D industrial metrology work are based on simultaneous calibration. Numerous other uses can be found in the aviation industry (measuring aircraft components and fixtures), in the aeronautical industry (measuring satellites and antennas), and in civil engineering (measuring finished components). Some of these applications are discussed in Sections A2 and A7.

6.7.2 Applications with precalibrated camera

Robot calibration. At KUKA Robotertechnik of Augsburg industrial robots have been reliably measured, adjusted and calibrated on the assembly line at two specially installed workplaces during the past two years [30]. To measure the required positions and orientations, a photogrammetric metrology system consisting of one or two RolleiMetric Réseau Scanning Cameras (RSCs) are mounted on a rugged tripod (Fig. 6.16). Using a shiftable standard CCD sensor, these cameras reach a resolution of 4200 × 4200 picture elements at an image format of 50 × 50 mm² with an accuracy of better than 1 μm in image space. The orientation of the single images in relation to the entire image is done

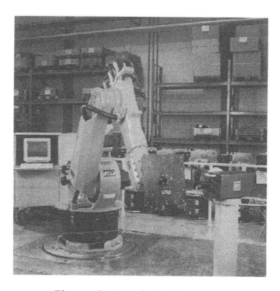

Figure 6.16: *Robot adjustment.*

in an optical-numerical way by a réseau measurement. Besides, this principle, which is described in Riechmann [8], allows the focusing of the camera without changing the interior orientation.

The cameras are controlled by a commercial PC with a standard frame grabber, running under Windows NT. The PC serves for operator prompting, for processing and outputting results and for connection to the robot control. The measurement system is basically independent of the robot control.

The interior orientation of the cameras is determined once in a special calibration measurement. With this known interior orientation, it is possible to determine the orientation of the cameras. Various target plates 450 mm × 450 mm in size are used, with reflective targets as control points, which are also identified as tools for the robot. A second target plate of 600 mm × 600 mm with an adapter serves for prior determination of the robot base and external orientation of the camera. To transfer the different coordinate systems, highly precise bores in the target plates are used with special adapters. A mechanical precision measuring machine serves as a higher-order metrology system for measuring the bores.

After orientation the online measurement of the robots is possible. The quality of the system orientation is verified by special measurements. A recalibration of the system normally is necessary only in time periods of some months.

Other applications. Other photogrammetric applications for the 3-D capture of objects can be found, for example, in accident photography and in architecture. In these fields, it is primarily scale drawings or rectified scale photos (orthophotos) that are obtained from the photograms. The cameras employed are generally calibrated for different focus settings using the methods described in the foregoing. An example is the RolleiMetric ChipPack with a resolution of 2000×2000 sensor elements. Special metric lenses, which guarantee reproducible focus setting by mechanical click stops of the focusing ring, keep interior orientation constant for prolonged periods. The data of interior orientation are entered in the software and thus used for plotting and all computations. This guarantees high-precision 3-D plotting with minimum expense in the phase of image acquisition.

6.8 Summary

The use of digital cameras for measurement purposes requires the knowledge about different parameters, describing the interior camera model and the exterior camera positions and orientations. The determination of the interior and exterior camera parameters is defined as calibration and orientation of the measuring system. It has been shown, that—depending on the application—different strategies for the calibration and orientation exist. Different mathematical models for the description of optical measuring systems are usable. A focal point has been the description of an integrated model, which defines the transformation from image-space to object-space by six parameters of the exterior orientation and different parameters for the camera geometry. Effects from electronical, mechanical or optical influences (e.g., lens distortion) are corrected by the model. The described models have been used for many applications and are sufficient for a wide range of cameras. Current developments of digital cameras for measuring purposes are using large image-sensors with higher resolution. On the other hand, accuracy requirements are increasing for many applications. For this reason future improvements and extensions of the mathematical camera model can be necessary and helpful, taking into account special problems of large sensors, such as sensor flatness or patching of smaller sensor parts to complete sensors.

6.9 References

[1] Godding, R., (1993). Ein photogrammetrisches Verfahren zur Überprüfung und Kalibrierung digitaler Bildaufnahmesysteme. *Zeitschrift für Photogrammetrie und Fernerkundung*, 2:82–90.

[2] Brown, D. C., (1966). Decentering distortion of lenses. *Photogrammetric Engineering*, **32**:444–462.

[3] Schafmeister, R., (1997). Erste Erfahrungen mit der neuen Rollei Q16 MetricCamera. In *Publikationen der Deutschen Gesellschaft für Photogrammetrie und Fernerkundung (DGPF)*, Vol. 1, pp. 367–378. Berlin: DGPF.

[4] Lenz, R. and Lenz, U., (1990). Calibration of a color CCD camera with 3000 × 2300 picture elements. ISPRS Symposium, Com. V. Close-Range Photogrammetry meets Machine Vision, Zürich. *Proc. SPIE*, **1395**:104–111.

[5] Richter, U., (1993). Hardware-Komponenten für die Bildaufnahme mit höchster örtlicher Auflösung. In *Publikationen der Deutschen Gesellschaft für Photogrammetrie und Fernerkundung.*, Vol. 1, pp. 367–378. Berlin: DGPF.

[6] Poitz, H., (1993). Die UMK SCAN von Carl Zeiss Jena, ein neues System für die digitale Industrie-Photogrammetrie. In *Tagungsband zur DGPF-Jahrestagung 1992 in Jena, DGPF; Berlin*.

[7] Holdorf, M., (1993). Höchstauflösende digitale Aufnahmesysteme mit Réseau Scanning und Line-Scan-Kameras. In *Symposium Bildverarbeitung '93,*, pp. 45–51. Esslingen: Technische Akademie Esslingen.

[8] Riechmann, W., (1993). *Hochgenaue photogrammetrische Online-Objekterfassung*. PhD thesis, Technical University of Brunswick.

[9] Bösemann, W., Godding, R., and Riechmann, W., (1990). Photogrammetric investigation of CCD cameras. ISPRS symposium, close-range photogrammetry meets machine vision, Zürich. *Com. V. Close-Proc. SPIE*, **1395**:119–126.

[10] Lenz, R., (1988). Zur Genauigkeit der Videometrie mit CCD-Sensoren. In *Proc. 10. DAGM-Symp. Mustererkennung 1988, Informatik Fachberichte 180*, H. Bunke, O. Kübler, and P. Stucki, eds., pp. 179–189, DAGM. Berlin: Springer.

[11] Beyer, H., (1992). Advances in characterization and calibration of digital imaging systems. International archives of photogrammetry and remote sensing. 17th ISPRS Congress, Washington. *Com. V*, **29**:545–555.

[12] Dold, J., (1994). Photogrammetrie. Vermessungsverfahren im Maschinen- und Anlagenbau. In *Schriftenreihe des Deutschen Vereins für Vermessungswesen DVW*, W. Schwarz, ed., Vol. 13. Stuttgart: Verlag Konrad Wittwer.

[13] Wester-Ebbinghaus, W., (1989). Mehrbild-Photogrammetrie — räumliche Triangulation mit Richtungsbündeln. In *Symposium Bildverarbeitung '89*, pp. 25.1–25.13. Technische Akademie Esslingen.

[14] Rüger, Pietschner, and Regensburger, (1978). *Photogrammetrie— Verfahren und Geräte*. Berlin: VEB Verlag für Bauwesen.

[15] Wester-Ebbinghaus, W., (1980). Photographisch-numerische Bestimmung der geometrischen Abbildungseigenschaften eines optischen Systems. *Optik*, **3**:253–259.

[16] Lenz, R., (1987). Linsenfehlerkorrigierte Eichung von Halbleiterkameras mit Standardobjektiven für hochgenaue 3D-Messungen in Echtzeit. In *Proc. 9. DAGM-Symp. Mustererkennung 1987, Informatik Fachberichte*

149, E. Paulus, ed., pp. 212–216, DAGM. Berlin: Springer.

[17] Conrady, A., (1919). Decentered lens systems. *Royal Astronomical Society, Monthly Notices*, **79**:384–390.

[18] Brown, D., (1976). The bundle adjustment—progress and perspectives. Helsinki 1976. In *International Archives of Photogrammetry*, Vol. 21(3), p. 303041.

[19] Fryer, J., (1989). Camera calibration in non-topographic photogrammetry. In *Handbook of Non-Topographic Photogrammetry*, 2nd edition, pp. 51–69. American Society of Photogrammetry and Remote Sensing.

[20] Fraser, C. and Shortis, M., (1992). Variation of distortion within the photographic field. *Photogrammetric Engineering and Remote Sensing*, **58(6)**: 851–855.

[21] Gerdes, R., Otterbach, R., and Kammüller, R., (1993). Kalibrierung eines digitalen Bildverarbeitungssystems mit CCD-Kamera. *Technisches Messen*, **60(6)**:256–261.

[22] Wester-Ebbinghaus, W., (1985). Bündeltriangulation mit gemeinsamer Ausgleichung photogrammetrischer und geodätischer Beobachtungen. *Zeitschrift für Vermessungswesen*, **3**:101–111.

[23] Fellbaum, M., (1996). PROMP —A new bundle adjustment program using combined parameter estimation. *International Archives of Photogrammetry and Remote Sensing*, **31(B3)**:192–196.

[24] Wester-Ebbinghaus, W., (1985). Verfahren zur Feldkalibrierung von photogrammetrischen Aufnahmekammern im Nahbereich. *DGK-Reihe B*, **275**: 106–114.

[25] Godding, R. and Luhmann, T., (1992). Calibration and accuracy assessment of a multi-sensor online-photogrammetric system. In *International Archives of Photogrammetry and Remote Sensing, Com. V, 17. ISPRS Congress, Washington*, Vol. XXIX, pp. 24–29. Bethesda, MD: American Society for Photogrammetry and Remote Sensing.

[26] Strutz, T., (1993). *Ein genaues aktives optisches Triangulationsverfahren zur Oberflächenvermessung.* PhD thesis, Magdeburg Technical University.

[27] Fryer, J. and Brown, D. C., (1986). Lens distortion for close-range photogrammetry. *Photogrammetric Engineering and Remote Sensing*, **52**:51–58.

[28] Abdel-Aziz, Y. J. and Karara, H. M., (1971). Direct linear transformation from comparator coordinates into object space coordinates in close-range photogrammetry. In *Symposium of the American Society of Photogrammetry on Close-Range Photogrammetry*. Virginia: Falls Church.

[29] Bopp, H. and Kraus, H., (1978). Ein Orientierungs- und Kalibrierungsverfahren für nichttopographische Anwendungen der Photogrammetrie. *Allgemeine Vermessungs-Nachrichten (AVN)*, **5**:182–188.

[30] Godding, R., Lehmann, M., and Rawiel, G., (1997). Robot adjustment and 3-D calibration—photogrammetric quality control in daily use. *Optical 3-D Measurement Techniques*, **4**:158–168.

7 Three-Dimensional Imaging Techniques

Rudolf Schwarte[1], Gerd Häusler[2], and Reinhard W. Malz[3]

[1]Zentrum für Sensorsysteme (ZESS), Siegen, Germany
[2]Lehrstuhl für Optik,Universität Erlangen-Nürnberg, Germany
[3]Fachhochschule Esslingen, Germany

Computer Vision and Applications

7.1   Introduction

Electronic imaging using charge coupled devices (CCD) cameras and digital image processing found widespread application in research, industrial production, communications, and consumer goods. Nowadays, 3-D image acquisition and processing appears to be on the verge of a comparably stormy and far-reaching development. Fast and non-contact optical shape measurements are of significant importance in industrial inspection, robot vision in automatic assembly, and *reverse engineering*. They are equally important for the surveillance of secured areas, 3-D object recognition and navigation. Another application requiring data about the geometrical shape of objects in 3-D space is *virtual reality*.

Three-dimensional optical shape measurements deliver the *absolute* 3-D geometry of objects that should be independent from the object's surface reflectivity, its distance from the sensor, and from illumination conditions. Thus, 3-D optical sensors deliver the shape and physical dimensions of an object, which are rotation-, translation-, and illumination-invariant.

From the knowledge of the underlying physical principles that define the limitations of measuring uncertainty, one can design optimal sensors that work just at those limits, as well as judge available sensors. We will show that the vast number of known 3-D sensors are based on only three different principles: *triangulation, time-of-flight measurement* (TOF) including broad-band interferometry, and classical *interferometry*.

The three principles are different in terms of how the measuring uncertainty scales with the object distance [1]. The measuring uncertainty ranges from about one nanometer to a few millimeters, depending on the principle and the measuring range.

It is the goal of this chapter to provide an overview of the techniques for optical shape measurements by means of CCD cameras in a well-organized and comparable hierarchical scheme. An insight is given into the basic problems, and new developments are pointed out. The reader will further learn that with only two or three different sensors a great majority of problems from automatic inspection or virtual reality can be solved. This chapter focuses on the applicability to real problems and addresses the interests of potential users of 3-D surface measurement sensors. It discusses the potentials and limitations of the major sensor principles and gives examples of sensor realizations. Other overviews of 3-D imaging techniques have previously been given [2, 3, 4, 5], and in extended versions of parts of this chapter in CVA1 [Chapter 18–20]. A scientific review was given in [6].

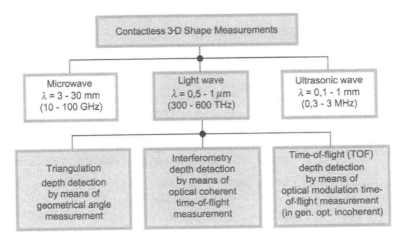

Figure 7.1: *Principles of noncontact 3-D shape measurements.*

7.2 Characteristics of 3-D sensors

7.2.1 Basic principles of depth sensing

As shown in Fig. 7.1, optical shape measurements are based on three different principles: (I) triangulation, (II) time-of-flight measurements and interferometry on rough surfaces, and (III) classical interferometry at smooth surfaces. The classification is based on the fact that the physically achievable measuring uncertainty δz of the three principles scales differently with the distance z:

$$\text{type I: } \delta z \propto z^2, \quad \text{type II: } \delta z \propto z^0, \quad \text{type III: } \delta z \propto z^{-1}$$

In Fig. 7.1, interferometry of type II and type III are put together into one box because in practice we get a measuring uncertainty of less than $1\,\mu\text{m}$, while time-of-flight measurements are less accuarte by more than one or two orders of magnitude.

Triangulation normally determines an unknown visual point within a triangle by means of a known optical basis and the related side angles pointing to the unknown point.

Continuous wave (CW) and pulse time-of-flight techniques measure the time of flight of the envelope of a modulated optical signal (group velocity). Figure 7.17 shows the hierarchical partitioning of this technique.

Interferometry measures depth also by means of the time-of-flight. Now, however, *coherent* mixing and correlation of the wavefront reflected from the 3-D object with a reference wavefront is required.

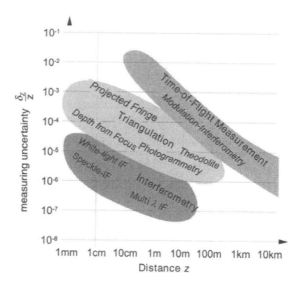

Figure 7.2: *Relative resolution of methods for optical shape measurements.*

7.2.2 Depth map

The depth information measured by a 3-D sensor constitutes a spatial point cloud. It can be given on a regular grid either in Cartesian coordinates $z(x, y)$, or in polar coordinates $R(\theta, \phi)$. This type of information is called a *depth map* or *depth image.* For many applications, this information is sufficient. Together with the depth map, most 3-D sensors also deliver a signal amplitude. Thus, we obtain a standard intensity or gray-scale 3-D surface image $G(x, y, z)$.

Given the tremendous advances in computer graphics, it is no longer a problem to compute realistic visualizations from 3-D object surfaces even in real time. The true problem remains the fast and precise acquisition of the depth map within a large volume and in a natural environment. Today, we are still far away from such a complete and video-rate depth image acquisition.

7.2.3 Measuring range and uncertainty

The most critical parameters of such systems are the depth-measuring range Δz and the depth resolution δ_z. Figure 7.2 illustrates the measuring and resolution ranges that are covered by the existing industrial measuring systems. The figure shows the relative uncertainty δ_z/z as a function of the object distance z. Due to electronic time drifts or mechanical instabilities, the systematic measuring error (accuracy) can be much larger than the measuring uncertainty (precision) δ_z. The increasing use of imaging systems for all three techniques reduces the measuring times significantly.

The lowest absolute measuring uncertainty δ_z is achieved by interferometry, which achieves values better than $\lambda/100$. Multiwavelength techniques increase the depth range Δz from micrometers to meters.

Triangulation techniques can be used with high accuracy from the millimeter range (depth of focus techniques, Chapter 11.3) to the 100 km range (classical photogrammetry), or even up to distances of light years with the earth orbit diameter as the optical baseline (astronomy).

So-called *active triangulation systems* with a projected fringe patterns work almost like a 3-D camera (see Section 7.3.2). Online photogrammetry with digital cameras enables fast 3-D measurements of special targets attached to the 3-D object (see Section 7.3.3). A complete surface 3-D reconstruction outside the targets, however, still requires several minutes if at all possible by naturally existing points appropriate for correspondence.

With only 6.7 ps time-of-flight per millimeter, time-of flight depth estimation is an extreme challenge for time measurements. The measuring uncertainty δ_z due to electronic time drifts are practically independent of the distance and are in the millimeter range. Significant improvements are possible if the time-consuming and error prone correlation process is transferred as much as possible from electronic components to optical components and done in parallel. This is realized in a new inherently mixing and correlating photodetector, the *photonic mixer device* (PMD), which makes possible a high-integral 3-D imaging sensor [7].

7.2.4 Types of radiation used in depth sensing

Microwaves are particularly suitable for large-scale 3-D measurements either by triangulation (e. g., *global positioning system* (GPS), determination of an unknown point of a triangle by three sides) or directly by time-of-flight measurements (e. g., conventional radar and synthetic aperture interferometry) (see [8, 9, 10]). For industrial production automation, these techniques, in general, do not reach the required angular resolution due to diffraction. A circular antenna with a diameter d generates a radiation cone (*Airy pattern*, see Chapter 3) with an angle 2α, where

$$\sin \alpha = 1.22\frac{\lambda}{d} = \frac{w}{2f} \tag{7.1}$$

If we use, for example, an antenna with $d = 122\,mm$ diameter and an extremely short microwave ($\lambda = 3\,mm$, $\nu = 100\,GHz$), the opening angle 2α of the radiation cone is 60 mrad and the minimum spot size or waist w is already 60 mm at 1 m distance, respectively, at the focal length f.

For *ultrasound* we get the same relations for the same wavelength of, for example, $\lambda = 3\,mm$ ($v = 110\,kHz$ in normal atmosphere). Additional difficulties with ultrasound are the significant sensitivity of the propagation speed of sound from pressure and temperature (with a relative change of about 2.2×10^{-3} per °C and only -0.93×10^{-6} per °C for light) and, moreover, the increasing attenuation at higher frequencies and a high reflectivity that is similar to a mirror of technical surfaces.

In contrast to microwave and ultrasound, optical 3-D sensors possess a 10^3 to 10^4 times higher lateral and angular resolution due to the shorter wavelength in the range of 300 nm (ultraviolet) to 3 μm (infrared) (Section 2.2.1).

7.2.5 Scanning versus staring image acquisition

Point-measuring sensor principles (laser triangulation, time-of-flight, laser heterodyne interferometers as shown in Figs. 7.4 and 7.16) can be used in scanning mode for surface measurements. As a major advantage compared to area-based sensors, parameter optimization is possible for every measured point. Dynamic control of lens focus, aperture, and signal amplification can, in principle, be used to overcome the physical limitations of fixed focus sensors, which need small apertures for a large depth of focus (Section 7.3.6, [11]).

7.3 Triangulation

Triangulation is the most widely used technique for optical shape measurements. Figure 7.3 shows the hierarchy of the most important variants, which, despite the same basic principle, partly appear extremely different. At the highest level, we distinguish the following: (1) focus techniques; (2) active triangulation with structured illumination; (3) passive triangulation techniques on the basis of digital photogrammetry and stereoscopy; (4) theodolite-measuring systems; and (5) shape-from-shading techniques. The rapid progress of optical triangulation, specifically active with structured light and passive with digital photogrammetry and with combinations of both, is already a big step towards the goal of a 3-D triangulation camera and real-time stereovision. In the following subsections, a survey of the five basic variants of triangulation techniques is given.

7.3.1 Focus techniques

The critical parameters of *focus techniques* are the diameter of the diffraction-limited spot or waist w in the focal plane

$$w = 2.44\frac{\lambda f}{d} = 2f \sin \alpha \qquad (7.2)$$

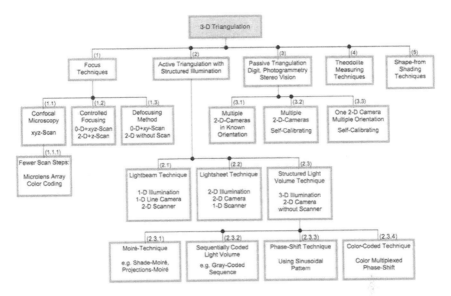

Figure 7.3: *Hierarchy of the most important principles of triangulation techniques.*

and the Rayleigh depth of focus

$$\Delta z_R = \frac{\lambda}{\sin^2 \alpha} \tag{7.3}$$

where $\sin \alpha$, f, and d are the numerical aperture, the focal length, and the free diameter of the optical system, respectively.

The technique of *confocal microscopy* (1.1 in Fig. 7.3) utilizes the double spatial filtering at the focal plane by both illumination and detection of the object using a pinhole. The detector "sees" only illuminated points at the focal plane. Because only one single point is measured at a time, the acquisition of a true 3-D image requires scanning in all three spatial directions x, y, and z. Confocal microscopy with a microlens array and a CCD matrix sensor acquires one image at a time and thus needs only a depth scan. Area-extended measurements are also achieved by the systems reported by Engelhardt and Häusler [12] and Engelhardt [13]. A detailed account on 3-D confocal microscopy is given in CVA1 [Chapter 21].

Controlled focusing (1.2 in Fig. 7.3) delivers a height profile of a surface $z(x, y)$ by scanning the xy plane with a fast Z control using, for example, a differential photodiode for high angular resolution [14, 15]. With the defocusing method (1.3 in Fig. 7.3), the distance can either be determined by the diameter or the intensity of the spot. A depth scan can be avoided by spectral analysis provided that the focal length f depends approximately linearly on the wavelength [16].

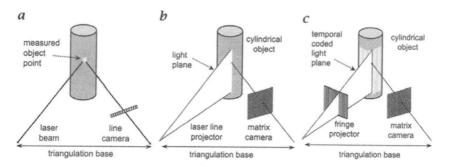

Figure 7.4: *Triangulation-based point and line sensors for surface measurement:* ***a*** *point triangulation sensor;* ***b*** *light sectioning with a single light plane;* ***c*** *active-optical sensors with a calibrated camera-projector pair perform highest sampling rate and lateral resolution. Every camera pixel can, in principle, produce a separate coordinate.*

7.3.2 Active triangulation

Active triangulation needs structured illumination (Fig. 7.4). Either a small light spot is projected onto the object (we call this a "point sensor" because it measures the distance of just one single point). Or we project a narrow line ("line sensor"; this method is known as *light sectioning* [17]). Or we project a grating (phase-measuring triangulation [18, 19]).

With light point or 1-D *laser triangulation* (2.1 in Fig. 7.3), the light source emitting a collimated beam (pencil beam), the detector, and the illuminated object point form the so-called triangulation triangle. On the side of the sender, the angle to the triangulation basis is fixed while on the side of the detector it is determined either by a CCD line sensor or a position-sensitive photodetector (PSD). From this angle, the depth can be determined. The principally achievable minimum distance uncertainty δ_z for laser illumination is given by

$$\delta_z = \frac{\lambda}{2\pi \sin\theta \sin\alpha_d} \tag{7.4}$$

and the measuring range Δz (two times the depth of focus [20]) by

$$\Delta z = \frac{2\lambda}{\sin^2 \alpha_d} \tag{7.5}$$

where $\sin\alpha_d$ and θ are the aperture of the detector optics and the triangulation angle, respectively. The acquisition of a depth image with this technique requires an xy scan [14, p. 6], [21, p. 1].

With the lightsheet technique (2.2 in Fig. 7.3) or 2-D laser triangulation, generally a laser beam is expanded via cylindrical lenses or by a scanning device to a light sheet. The cross section of the lightsheet

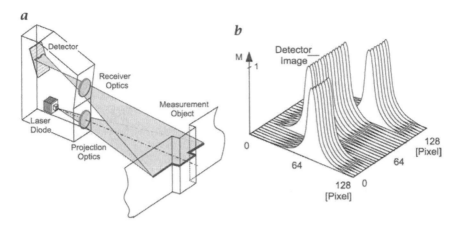

Figure 7.5: *Lightsheet triangulation: a instrument; b detector image.*

and of a 3-D object form a light line (the height profile) that is imaged onto a 2-D detector. Thus, only a 1-D scan perpendicular to the light plane is required for 3-D imaging [14, 22, p. 8], Section A5.

Figure 7.5 shows schematically such a *lightsheet triangulation* instrument. The height profile generates the charge image on the CCD detector shown in Fig. 7.5b. In order to obtain maximum depth resolution, the detector plane, the plane of the image-forming optics (perpendicular to the optical axis), and the plane of the object to be measured, have a common axis and, thus, meet the *Scheimpflug condition*.

The *light-volume triangulation* (2.3 in Fig. 7.3) illuminates the whole 3-D object to be measured with structured light. Thus, no scanning is required. For materials that scatter light from the surface (and not from subsurface regions), light projection can be used to produce textures on the surface. For example, the projection of pseudo-noise is often used in digital photogrammetry with two or more views. Other projection patterns include line grids, crossed lines and sine grids. Active triangulation by projected textures works quite well on smooth and nonspecular surfaces. The lateral continuity of the surface is important, because the image processing needs neighboring pixel values to find the center of the spot, the center line(s) or the absolute phase of the sine grid [23].

With the Moiré technique (see 2.3.1 in Fig. 7.3), the projected texture is observed through an adapted reference structure. The superposition of these two patterns produces spatial beat frequencies, respectively, and a beat pattern with much lower wave numbers that can be observed by a detector with a correspondingly lower spatial resolution. In this way, the depth resolution can be increased by one order of magnitude over conventional stripe projector systems [22, 24, p. 16].

All single pattern-based measuring principles use the intensity distribution in small image areas. This lateral image processing assumes lateral continuity of light remission and of the topology. Also, the lateral resolution of 3-D information will be reduced. This is not acceptable in industrial applications with nondiffuse and nonsmooth object surfaces. Only sensors that are based on local encoding/decoding principles instead of image correlation, can get results under such critical circumstances. The sequentially coded light-volume technique (2.3.2 in Fig. 7.3) illuminates the 3-D object with a sequence of binary patterns with increasing wavenumber in such a way that each pixel can be associated with a code, for example, a 10-digit Gray code, from which the *absolute* distance can be inferred [14, 25, p. 10].

Another variant of the fringe projection technique, which has also found widespread application, is the phase-shift or projected fringe technique (2.3.3 in Fig. 7.3). A programmable LCD projector illuminates the scene with sinusoidal patterns with different phase positions. In order to evaluate the phase information, at least 3 or 4 (120° or 90° phase shift) independent measurements are required [14, p. 12]. This technique also results in a significant depth resolution. In conjunction with an additional sequential binary coding (so-called *Gray-code phase-shift technique*), absolute depth can be measured with high resolution.

The color-coded light-volume technique (2.3.4 in Fig. 7.3) requires only one single image as three color channels are acquired simultaneously. The phase and thus the depth can, for example, be computed from red, blue, and green stripe patterns that are phase shifted from each other by 120° [26, 27].

In the following sections, we show how appropriate sequentially coded light can be realized in order to encode the depth of individual pixels by sequential illumination.

MZX-code. The first example uses all six permutations of the three patterns—black, white, and wedge (Fig. 7.6a). By using all combinations of three projector levels it fulfills the constraint that at least one value must be white and one must be black. A second property is that the spatial gradient of decoder output is constant and maximal. This code was named MZX for Maximum level, Zero level, Crossover [28]).

Phase shifting with a single-frequency sine pattern. A great variety of interferometrical *phase-shifting* techniques has been developed since the 1970s. Phase-calculating and phase-unwrapping algorithms can also be used in triangulation-based sensors where periodic patterns are projected [29, 30, 31, 32, 33].

The advantage of a set of phase-shifted patterns compared to a single pattern is the same as described for MZX code: from three gray values that are measured at the same pixel position, a local phase can

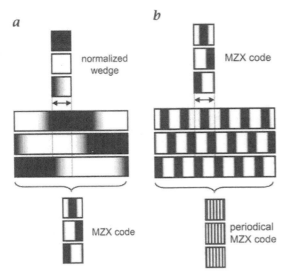

Figure 7.6: *a The permutation of a normalized wedge produces the MZX code with a six-times higher spatial resolution compared to a wedge. b The periodical repetition shows a pattern that is close to the phase-shift principle with sine functions (0°, 120°, and 240°)*

be evaluated that is independent from the lateral distribution of gray values.

This local phase value, which is always in the range $(0, 2\pi)$, can be seen as an absolute phase φ modulo 2π, where φ corresponds to the projector coordinate ζ_p. If the object surface is continuous, the absolute phase can be calculated by an incremental phase-unwrapping algorithm, which allows no phase increments between neighboring pixels larger than $\pi/2$.

Phase shifting with two or more frequencies. To produce absolute and local phase information $\varphi(x, y)$ at noncontinuous surfaces, multifrequency (heterodyne) principles have been used in interferometry [32]. Independent phase-shift measurements at slightly different light frequencies or wavelengths (Fig. 7.7) lead to an absolute distance measurement.

Gray codes. Binary *Gray codes* (Fig. 7.8) [34, 35] as well as multifrequency phase-shift techniques with periodical and continuous patterns [29] have been widely used to acquire dense (that is, in principle, for each camera pixel) and unique 3-D point data from objects in short range. To binarize the digitized images, it is necessary to know the local threshold (which may be different for each pixel). There are several ways of using additional images to calculate this threshold:

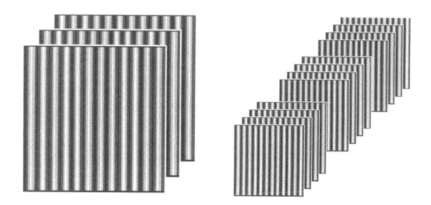

Figure 7.7: *Projected patterns with 0°, 120°, 240°phase shift) and 3 groups of slightly different frequencies, each with phase steps of 0°, 90°, 180°, and 270°.*

Figure 7.8: *Binary gray code (additional images for threshold generation are not shown).*

1. project unstructured gray with 50 % intensity and use the acquired image as threshold; or
2. project unstructured white and black and use the averaged images as threshold; or
3. project both normal and inverse patterns, and use the sign (1,0) of the difference as bit.

Hybrid codes. As developed by Malz [28], *hybrid codes* combine the advantages of digital and analogue principles and yield results close to

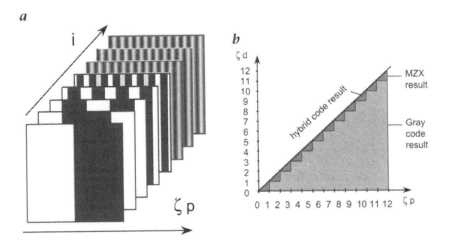

Figure 7.9: *a Hybrid code (binary Gray code, MZX code); b decoder function.*

the theoretical limits, which can be achieved with temporally encoded light structures.

The trapezoid light distribution of the MZX subcode is continuous in space and intensity. Hybrid codes can be used with variable numbers of images ($w \geq 3$) and also with variable digital code bases (binary, ternary, quarternary gray codes). It has the highest resolution compared to all other temporal principles (under equal conditions, namely, the number of images used, and the lowest acceptable number of separable gray levels. See also Fig. 7.9).

Light fringe projectors. An important factor in the signal chain is the programmable light projector. The decoder result can only be linear and noiseless, if the spatial projector modulation is exact. Hybrid codes need analog projecting devices for best results. At least, the decoder function has to be strictly monotone with no steps.

Some technical light projectors, however, are not able to produce continuous sine or MZX-modulation. For example, a rectangular projection pattern used for a phase-shifting with 90° produces a step-by-step decoder function. This causes systematic errors of the detector signal in the range of $\pm \pi/4$ (Fig. 7.10). A projection device for accurate sinusoidal fringes was realized by Häusler et al. [36].

7.3.3 Passive triangulation

Passive triangulation techniques (3 in Fig. 7.3) basically include the different forms of *digital photogrammetry* and (as a special subclass *stereovision*). Passive in this context means that the geometrical arrange-

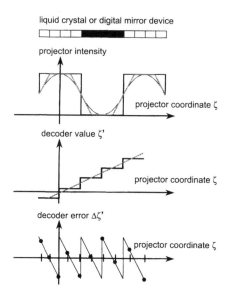

Figure 7.10: *Binary light modulators produce systematic errors in the detector signal.*

ment of the illumination is not considered (Fig. 7.11). In the area of industrial inspection, the classical photogrammetric techniques for evaluation of aerial photographs have been optimized for close distances. These techniques have formed the new field of *close-range photogrammetry* (Chapter 6). For photogrammetric techniques, at least three different views of a point are required to determine its 3-D position. For dynamic processes, often multiple cameras with known relative positions (3.1 in Fig. 7.3) or self-calibrating methods (3.2 in Fig. 7.3) are used. For static scenes, a single camera that takes images from three or more different unknown views is sufficient (3.3 in Fig. 7.3) [37]. The numerical problem is solved by *bundle adjustment*, which calculates all unknown parameters for camera(s) position(s), and object points simultaneously.

If a 3-D object is imaged from different perspectives with a high-resolution digital camera, relative standard deviations in the positions σ_X/X, σ_Y/Y, and σ_Z/Z of better than 10^{-5} come close to time-consuming classical photographic techniques of photogrammetry. High computing power and optimized algorithms make online inspection with about 50 targets and a period of 4 s possible. Photogrammetric camera calibration and orientation estimation is dealt with in Chapter 6.

Feature-based target points. A fundamental concept in photogrammetry is the intersection of rays in object space. The quality of inter-

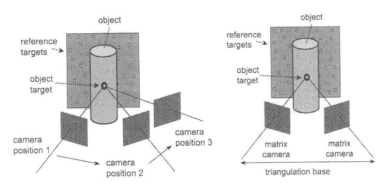

Figure 7.11: *a To measure static scenes and objects a single (still video) camera can be used for sequential image acquisition.* ***b*** *Static and dynamic scenes can be measured in snapshots with two or more synchronized cameras.*

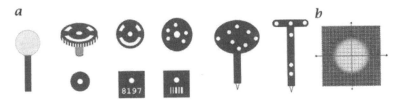

Figure 7.12: *a Different target types for point coordinate measurement with subpixel precision.* ***b*** *Subpixeling with circular targets needs extended image regions of interest (e. g., 16 × 16 pixels for the central blob).*

section "points" determines the quality of measurement. In fact, these points can be represented by any spatial physical features or optical phenomena, provided that there are models that fit precisely independent from viewing angle. Temporal invariance is also required, if sequential imaging is used. Good physical representations of points can be characteristic coordinates of geometrical primitives (like spheres, circles, etc.) or radiometric primitives (as edges between areas of different diffuse scattering materials). It is important that the borders between regions in the image are borders between different diffuse materials only.

Artificial targets. Well-designed artificial targets are used to establish stable intersection points in the scene or on the object. With *retroreflecting targets* or diffuse white flat or spherical targets of good optical quality (homogeneous and symmetrical intensity distribution) and sufficient size (5–10 pixels diameter) standard deviations of 1/20–1/50 pixels in the image plane can be achieved [38] (Fig. 7.12).

The advantages of close-range photogrammetry with targets are

- high accuracy of target measurement, and
- short measuring time.

However, some disadvantages have to be accepted:

- the object has to be prepared and cleaned,
- the measured coordinate points are target coordinates, but not co-ordinates of the object itself,
- interesting object features like edges, corners or holes are discontinuities and cannot be prepared with standard targets,
- high densities of coordinates cannot be achieved with targets, because there is always a need for extended image regions of interest for each point.

Simple errors on targets, illumination, optics, sensor chips, sensor electronics reduce the accuracy substantially. For example, mechanical and optical errors on targets can be:

- variable thickness of attached retroreflective targets,
- enclosed particles and bubbles,
- dirty target surface and frayed target edges,
- virtual dislocations from inhomogeneous illumination.

Texture-based matching. Obviously, target-based measurement is good for a limited number of selected points. But how can we measure surfaces and produce point clouds with thousands of points? Higher spatial sampling rates can be achieved using textures on the object surface. To define and find homologue points from different views, these textures should be dense, high frequency and aperiodic to get unique and narrow correlation peaks for different scales. Texture analysis needs correlation windows of sufficient sizes (typically 10–25 pixels diameter) to get stable and unique results with high precision. This reduces the lateral resolution and the available number of independent coordinate points.

Remote sensing applications need and use natural textures on the surface. Parts in industrial production processes, however, are often made from one material with low texture contrast. Such surfaces cannot be measured directly with passive photogrammetric techniques. Painted or printed diffuse textures would be optimal, but this kind of object manipulation would not be acceptable in most applications.

7.3.4 Theodolites

So far, *theodolites* are still the most accurate triangulation systems available with a relative distance error of about 5×10^{-6}. However, they require long measuring times. A target is focused with at least two theodolites. The horizontal and vertical angles are measured electronically, and the 3-D coordinates of the target are computed from the measured angle and the known positions of the theodolites [14, p. 14]. Theodolites are used for accurate measurements of large-scale objects. In modern systems, sometimes a 1-D laser radar distance is integrated.

7.3.5 Shape from shading

The *shape-from-shading* techniques delivers 3-D information as surface normals of the surface elements from the image irradiance and the known position of the camera and the light sources. From this information, the 3-D shape can be computed [39, p. 39]. The various types of shape-from-shading techniques including extensions using multiple images with different illuminations or image sequences with moving light sources (*photometric stereo*) are discussed in detail in CVA2 [Chapter 19].

7.3.6 Limits and drawbacks of triangulation

Random localization errors. The object surface can be either optically smooth like a mirror, or it can be optically rough like a ground glass. It is important to note that the attribute smooth or rough depends on the lateral resolution of the observation optics: If we resolve the lateral structure of a ground glass, for example, by a high-aperture microscope, the surface is smooth for our purpose. "Smooth" means for us that the elementary waves that are collected from the object to form a diffraction-limited image spot contribute only with minor phase variations of less than $\pm\lambda/4$. If there are larger phase variations within the elementary waves, then we have diffuse reflection, or scattering (Chapter 2).

The weakness of point triangulation is obvious: it is not robust against shape variation of the spot image. And just such a variation is introduced by speckle, as shown in Fig. 7.13. As the shape of the spot image depends on the unknown *microtopology* of the surface, there will be a principal random localization error, theoretically and experimentally determined in Dorsch et al. [40]. Its standard deviation δz_m will be given by

$$\delta z_m = \frac{C\lambda}{2\pi \sin u_{obs} \sin \Theta} \tag{7.6}$$

where θ is the angle of triangulation, $\sin u_{obs}$ is the aperture of observation, λ is the wavelength of light, and C is the *speckle* contrast. The speckle contrast is unity for laser illumination. We have to emphasize that it is not the monochromaticity that causes speckle. It is the spatial coherence. And strong spatial coherence is always present,

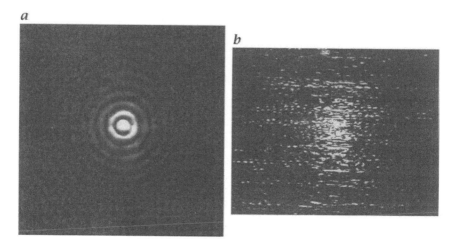

Figure 7.13: a Spot image after reflection at a smooth surface; b spot image after reflection at a rough surface. The localization of the spot image is possible only with some uncertainty, introduced by the surface microtopology to which we have no access.

if the aperture of the illumination u_{ill} is smaller than the aperture of observation. With a small light source we can achieve high contrast speckles, even if the source emits white light! Hence, Eq. (7.6) is valid for phase-measuring triangulation as well; we just have to use the correct speckle contrast, which is smaller than unity for properly designed PMT systems [41].

Equation (7.6) introduces a physical lower limit of the measuring uncertainty of triangulation sensors (type I). For a macroscopically planar ground glass with a surface roughness of 1 μm, using a sensor with an aperture of observation of 1/100, an angle of triangulation of 20°, and a wavelength of 0.8 μ, from laser illumination, we will find a standard deviation of the measured distance of about 37 μ, which is much larger than the surface roughness. Such a large statistical error is not acceptable for many applications.

In order to overcome this problem, we have to destroy spatial coherence! For a point sensor this can be done only at the object surface. Figure 7.14 displays the result of an experiment that proves the importance of spatial coherence for distance uncertainty by using a fluorescent coating producing perfectly incoherent reflection. A different method of destroying spatial coherence is to heat up the surface and make it thermally radiant. This happens in laser material processing. We make use of the thermal radiation from the laser-induced plasma, to measure the material wear on line, with very low aperture, through the laser beam, with an uncertainty of less than 5 μm [41].

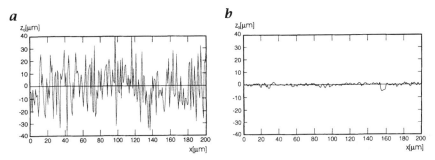

Figure 7.14: a *Observed image spot from a rough surface, measured with spatially coherent triangulation (laser illumination).* **b** *The same object measured in fluorescent light: the surfaces were covered with a very thin fluorescent film. Because fluorescence is perfectly incoherent, the noise is dramatically reduced. This experiment proves the large role of spatial coherence as a limiting factor in triangulation.*

As the two preceding possibilities are not generally applicable, the question arises as to whether we can reduce spatial coherence by illumination with a large source. This can be done principally for phase-measuring triangulation. However, for practical reasons, the size of the illumination aperture can not be much larger than that of the observation aperture. Hence, there will always be a residual speckle contrast of $c = 0.1$ or more. Introducing this into Eq. (7.6), we will get a reduced measuring uncertainty [41].

Shape alterations of the spot image. Triangulation usually does not even reach the physical limit on real technical surfaces, because the microtopology of the milling or turning process causes errors much larger than that of good ground surfaces. The reason is again the sensitivity of triangulation against shape alterations of the spot image. For real triangulation sensors that can measure macroscopic objects, it turns out that, in practice, we cannot get a better uncertainty than about $5\,\mu m$.

Inhomogeneous spatial resolution and shading. A further drawback is that in triangulation, illumination and observation are not coaxial. Hence, we cannot avoid shading: some parts of the object are either not illuminated or cannot be seen by the observation system. From Fig. 7.15, we see that in close-range applications, object-camera and object-projector distances can vary greatly, and this affects the lateral image and the longitudinal range resolution in a more geometrical sense. Throughout the measurement space there is a variety of voxel sizes and shapes. Voxels are more square near N, more rhomboid near F, and more rectangular near L and R. Diffraction and defocusing, as well as the variation of surface orientation relative to camera and pro-

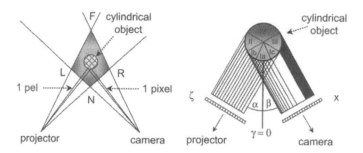

Figure 7.15: a *Variable spatial discretization.* **b** *Variable spatial frequency transfer function.*

jector axes lead to additional problems. The apertures of camera and projector lenses are rather poor compromises: they should be open for higher contrast and signal-to-noise ratios at limited projector intensities. On the other hand, they should be reduced for a wide depth of focus reaching from N to F.

Another critical effect is the variable frequency transfer from projector to camera. Figure 7.15b shows the variation in the projector-to-camera frequency transfer function for a cylindrical object. Only the regions Ia and b fulfill the Nyquist criteria (e. g., the sampling frequency must be at least twice the upper limit of the object spectrum). The increasing spatial frequency seen by the camera in region I_c leads to a strong undersampling and crosstalk between neighboring pixels and finally results in decoding errors. Regions II, III and IV are not measurable with this sensor position and have to be measured from different views.

In addition to optical resolution effects, the variation of surface orientation relative to camera and projector causes extreme intensity variations on nondiffuse surfaces. Even on a perfect lambertian surface, the camera sees lower intensities in region I_a. Finally, there remains a small measurable region I_b on the cylinder. In the center of the sensor workspace, we find the best conditions for the measurement.

7.4 Time-of-flight (TOF) of modulated light

The distance of an object or the depth z can easily be determined by the echo *time-of-flight* (TOF) τ of a light signal sent by the sensor and reflected back from the object to the sensor via

$$z = c\tau/2 \qquad (7.7)$$

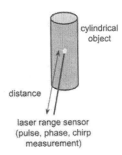

Figure 7.16: *Principle of a time-of-flight sensor.*

This basic relation is valid for both time-of-flight and interferometric distance measurements of type II (Fig. 7.16). In the first case, the time-of-flight of a modulated optical signal, that is, the *group velocity*, is measured. Generally, this is done by *correlation* with a suitable reference signal. Therefore, the partitioning in Fig. 7.17 distinguishes between the different types of signals: (1) pulse modulation; (2) continuous wave (CW) modulation; (3) and pseudo-random modulation. The basic problem of all TOF techniques is the extremely high speed of light of $300\,\text{m}/\mu\text{s}$ or $300\,\mu\text{m/ps}$, which requires correspondingly high temporal resolutions for the measuring techniques.

7.4.1 Pulse modulation

With *pulse modulation*, the time of flight is measured directly by correlating a start-and-stop signal with a parallel running counter. Pulse-modulating techniques can distinguish multiple targets. A disadvantage is the temperature-sensitive time delay and the nonlinearity of the transients of pulsed laser diodes in addition to the high demands in bandwidth and dynamics for the amplifiers.

7.4.2 Continuous wave (CW) modulation

This principle of TOF measurement can be understood as a sort of radio wave (RF) interferometry based on an optical carrier modulation and in that way as "Optical RF Interferometry" (ORFI). All imaginable variations are similar to that of structured illumination interferometry in triangulation as well as to that in rear optical interferometry. The echo-TOF τ of sine wave modulation can be determined either by *heterodyne mixing* (different frequencies are mixed, resulting in the beat frequency and phase difference $\varphi = 2\pi\nu\tau$) or by *homodyne mixing* (same frequencies are mixed, resulting in a baseband signal proportional to $\cos\varphi$). The frequency-modulated chirp modulation is used

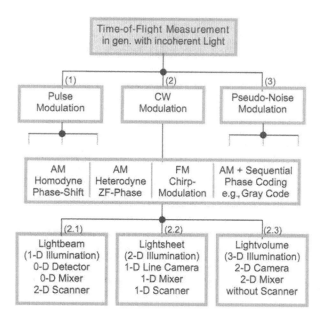

Figure 7.17: *Hierarchy of the most important principles of modulation-based optical depth measurements [42, 43]; [14, p. 26].*

for higher resolution or to determine the TOF-dependent frequency shift or to expect pulse compression for multitarget detection. The low range of a unique depth determination of only $\Delta z = \lambda_m/2$ can be extended by rectangular 0° to 180° switching of the phase of the rectangular frequency. A definite distance measurement is then possible using several measurements with different switching frequencies according to a Gray code in the same way as with the sequentially coded structured light-projection technique (Section 7.3.2). Because of the variety of modulation techniques, Fig. 7.17 further partitions only the sinusoidal modulation techniques.

Three-dimensional optical shape measurements with TOF techniques is (in contrast to 1-D geodetic distance measurements) not frequently used in industrial applications. This is due to the principal technical problems discussed at the beginning of this section. The block (2.1) in Fig. 7.17, labeled "Lightbeam," describes 1-D TOF instruments that require a 2-D scanning system for the acquisition of depth images. If a modulated lightsheet or plane is used (2.2 in Fig. 7.17), we get 2-D information as a light stripe in space. In this case, a 1-D scanner is sufficient. With a modulated light volume, no scanning is required at all. In this case, the receiver requires a 2-D mixer for CW demodulation. It produces a radio-frequency modulation interferogram in which the

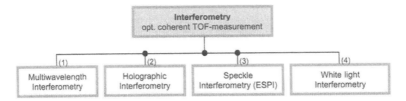

Figure 7.18: *Hierarchy of the most important measuring principles for depth measurements on the basis of optical interferometry.*

depth information is encoded and can be detected by a CCD camera [44]. This field of ORFI is of growing importance [45].

7.5 Optical Interferometry (OF)

Classical *interferometry* is a technique to measure smooth (polished) surfaces. A coherent wavefront is split into a measuring (or object) and a reference wavefront. These are superimposed (correlated) again in a detector as illustrated in Fig. 7.23. If a 2-D detector is used, an interferogram or correlogram is generated, indicating the phase shift over the detector area. With at least three measurements with different phase positions of the reference, the phase shift between the reference and the signal wavefronts can be determined according to the phase-shift principle. Unfortunately, this technique cannot determine absolute depth. Because of the ambiguity of the signal in multiples of $\lambda/2$, a unique depth determination is only possible in this narrow depth range. With homodyne and heterodyne interferometry, a resolution better than $\lambda/100$ and $\lambda/1000$, respectively, can be reached. The high depth accuracy of interferometric measurements requires a mechanically very stable instrument.

A large number of different interferometric depth-measuring systems with different measuring properties is currently available [46, p. 23], [47, p. 66]. For practical applications in 3-D shape measurements, several types of instruments are predominantly used and continuously improved (Fig. 7.18).

7.5.1 Multiwavelength interferometry

Multiwavelength interferometry (1 in Fig. 7.18) offers exceptional features for industrial applications. It is possible to perform *absolute* distance measurements over up to several ten meters with resolutions in the nanometer range under ideal conditions. A basic characteristic of multiwavelength interferometry is the generation of beat frequencies in the gigahertz and megahertz range by the superposition of two closely

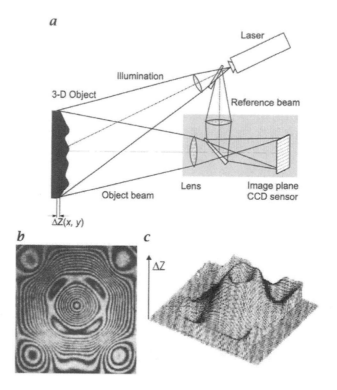

Figure 7.19: *Speckle interferometry:* **a** *Schematic illustration of the instrument setup;* **b** *Difference interferogram showing a form change;* **c** *3-D reconstruction.*

spaced wavelengths. The "synthetic" wavelengths of these beat frequencies determine (instead of the wavelength of the light itself) the range in which distances can be measured without ambiguity [47, 48].

7.5.2 Holographic interferometry

Holographic interferometry (2 in Fig. 7.18) enables deformation of 3-D objects caused, for example, by thermal or mechanical stress to be measured in the nanometer range. A hologram of the original object is coherently superimposed by the one under deformation. The resulting interferogram describes the deformation and can be captured or observed online, for example, by a video camera [14, p. 32].

7.5.3 Speckle interferometry

Speckle interferometry (3 in Fig. 7.18) utilizes an otherwise disturbing effect in optical metrology for exact deformation measurements. Speckles are generated when coherent light is reflected from a rough surface. The reflected wavefronts interfere with each other on the detector surface and generate a speckle pattern that is characteristic for the surface roughness elements. If an additional reference beam generates a second speckle pattern, this is coherently superimposed on the first one and produces a speckle interferogram.

Figure 7.19a shows the typical setup of a so-called electronic speckle interferometer (ESPI). After the object is deformed, a second speckle interferogram is captured. If this interferogram is subtracted from the previous interferogram of the original object, a difference interferogram is obtained as shown in Fig. 7.19b. The distance between the stripes corresponds to a height difference of $\lambda/2$. At least three exposures are required to obtain a difference height image $\Delta Z(x, y)$ as shown in Fig. 7.19c [2 S.34][31].

7.5.4 White-light interferometry

White-light interferometry or the has a unique properties, as time-of-flight measurements: the achievable measuring uncertainty does not depend on the distance z nor the aperature of illumination. Hence this method, called *coherency radar* (4 in Fig. 7.18) can measure with high accuracy the depth of narrow boreholes. The setup equals a Michelson interferometer. In one arm of the interferometer the object to be measured is located, and in the other arm a CCD camera is located.

Until recently, rough surface interferometry was not possible because the speckles in the image plane of the interferometer display an arbitrary phase, with the phase within each speckle independent from the phase in other speckles [49]. Therefore, we cannot see fringes if we replace one mirror in a Michelson interferometer by the rough object. And it is useless to evaluate the phase of the interference contrast within each speckle. There is no useful information within that phase.

However, there is a way to measure rough surfaces with an uncertainty in the 1 μm regime [50]:

1. The phase is *constant* within one speckle, allowing us to generate *interference contrast* in each speckle separately if *only* speckles are generated. This can be accomplished by using a sufficiently small *aperture of illumination* (as explained in preceding material)—even in the case of a white, extended light source.

2. *Broadband illumination* is used to exploit the limited *coherence length* of the light. It turns out that interference contrast can be observed only within those speckles that satisfy the equal path length condition: The path length in the object arm of the interferometer has to be approximately the same as that in the reference arm. For a certain object position on the z-axis, we will see interference contrast at one certain contour line of equal distance (or "height"). To

a

b

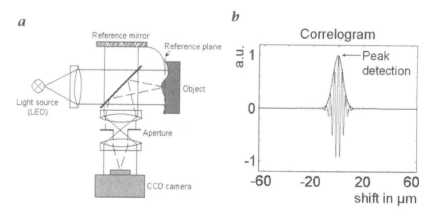

Figure 7.20: *a Principle of the "coherence radar." b The correlogram shows the (temporal) interference pattern in one single speckle while scanning the object along the z-axis.*

acquire the shape of the object, we have to scan the distance (along the z-axis; see Fig. 7.20).

While scanning through the z-axis, each pixel of our observation system displays a modulated periodic time signal, which is called "correlogram." It is displayed in Fig. 7.20b. The length of this correlogram signal is about coherence length, and the time of occurrence, or the position $z_m(x,y)$ of the scanning device at that time, is individual for each pixel: The correlogram has its maximum modulation, if the equal path-length condition is satisfied. We store z_m for each pixel separately and find the shape of the surface.

White light interferometry on rough surfaces, as it is realized in the coherence radar, is extremely powerful. There are unique features that will be summarized and illustrated by measuring examples:

- The coherence radar is a coaxial method: illumination and observation can be on the same axis. No shading occurs.

- The coherence radar is inherently telecentric, independently from the size of the object. All depths are imaged with the same scale.

- The distance measuring uncertainty on rough surfaces is not given by the apparatus or limited by the observation aperture. It is given only by the *roughness of the surface* itself.

Because the measuring uncertainty is independent of the aperture, it is independent of distance from objects (standoff), as well. Hence, we can measure distant objects with the same longitudinal accuracy as close objects. In particular, we can measure within deep boreholes without loss of accuracy (see Fig. 7.22).

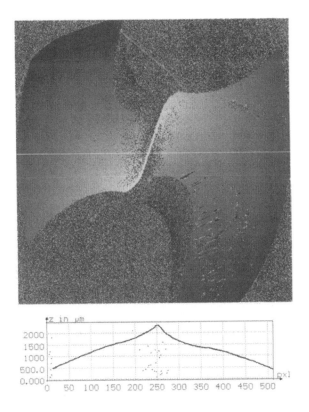

Figure 7.21: *Depth map of a drill, seen from the top, and cross section.*

One more feature that cannot be achieved by triangulation is the ability of the coherence radar to measure translucent objects such as ceramics, paint or even skin. The reason is that we measure essentially the time of flight (with the reference wave as a clock). Thus, we can distinguish light scattered from the surface from light scattered from the bulk of the object. Further examples and modifications of white-light interferometry are shown in CVA1 [Chapter 19] and Ammon et al. [51].

7.5.5 Comparison of TOF and interferometry

Because the modulation-based and interferometric depth measurements are based on the same TOF principles, the question arises of why modulation-based techniques already encounter significant measuring problems at resolutions in the centimeter range, while interferometric techniques can easily reach resolutions in the nanometer range.

The answer to this question is illustrated in Fig. 7.23. A conventional TOF measurement according to Fig. 7.23a includes (besides the optical

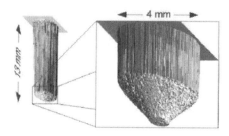

Figure 7.22: *As the measuring uncertainty of the coherence radar does not depend on the observation aperture, we can measure within deep boreholes, with about 1 μm accuracy.*

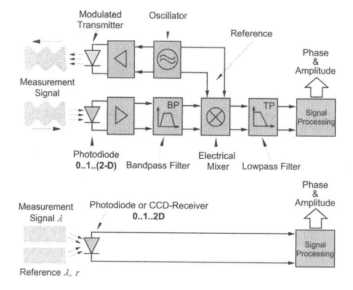

Figure 7.23: *Principle of optical depth measurements by:* **a** *incoherent (modulation); and* **b** *coherent (interferometry) time-of-flight measurements.*

path) a considerable time delay in the high-frequency electronics *before* the signal is mixed and correlated. Especially the entrance amplifier and the electronic mixer give rise to such high errors in the temporal delay that either a continuous time-consuming mechanical calibration or a compensation by a costly second reference channel (not shown in the figure) is required [52]. In practice, the latter reference channel eliminates the unsatisfying time drifts mentioned in the foregoing.

With an interferometric TOF measurement, the mixing and correlation of the signal and reference channel take place directly within the photodetector by coherent field superposition, practically without any errors or temporal delay. As a direct consequence, this means that good TOF measurements require the high-frequency mixing process to take place not in the RF electronics but either in an optical component or in the detector itself. In this way, not only can the significant errors due to the time delays in the wideband amplifier, the electronic mixer, and cross-talk be avoided, but also the high costs associated with these components.

7.6 Conclusion

The measuring technologies for 3-D optical shape measurements have been in a phase of rapid development for a number of years. It is expected that this development will continue for some time to come. Better and new components, higher computing power, and faster and more accurate algorithms are on the horizon as well as the fusion of various depth-measuring principles.

Designing good optical sensors requires an understanding of physical limits. Properly designed, optical 3-D sensors supply accurate data about the geometrical shape of objects that are as accurate as physics allows. The *dynamic range* allows researchers to distinguish 1000-10,000 different depths. Two main sensor principles, active triangulation and White-light interferometry at rough surfaces ("coherence radar") can measure a majority of objects with different surface structures. Once acquired, the geometrical shape complements intelligent algorithms very well in solving inspection problems, because the algorithms do not have to be concerned with the variable appearance of objects, as is the case in 2-D image processing.

7.7 References

[1] Häusler, G., (1997). About the scaling behavior of optical range sensors. In *Proc. 3rd Int. Workshop on Automatic Processing of Fringe Patterns.* Bremen, September 15–17, 1997.

[2] Jiang, X. and Bunke, H., (1997). *Dreidimensionales Computersehen.* Berlin, Heidelberg, New York: Springer-Verlag.

[3] Küchel, M., (1995). Dreidimensionale Meßverfahren. In *Tagungsband Bildverarbeitung '95*, pp. 315–348. Technische Akademie Esslingen.

[4] Häusler, G., (1997). Möglichkeiten und Grenzen optischer 3D-Sensoren in der industriellen Praxis. In *Optische Meßtechnik an diffus reflektierenden Medien*, Koch, Rupprecht, Toedter, and Häusler, eds. Renningen-Malmsheim, Germany: Expert-Verlag.

[5] Deutsche Gesellschaft für zerstörungsfreie Materialprüfung e. V. (ed.), (1995). *Handbuch OF1: Verfahren für die optische Formerfassung.* Deutsche Gesellschaft für zerstörungsfreie Materialprüfung e. V.

[6] Besl, P. J., (1988). Active, optical range imaging sensors. *Machine Vision and Application*, **1**:127–152.

[7] Schwarte, R., Xu, Z., Heinol, H. G., Olk, J., Klein, R., Buxbaum, B., Fischer, H., and Schulte, J., (1997). A new electrooptical Mixing and Correlating Sensor: Facilities and Applications of this Photonic Mixer Device (PMD). In *SPIE-EOS: Sensors, Sensor Systems, and Sensor Data Processing, München*, Vol. 3100.

[8] Hein, A., (1998). *Verarbeitung von SAR-Daten unter besonderer Berücksichtigung interferometrischer Anwendungen.* Phd thesis, INV, Universiät-GH, Siegen.

[9] Fitch, J. P., (1995). *Synthetic Aperture Radar.* Springer.

[10] Leick, A., (1995). *GPS Satellite Surveying.* New York: John Wiley and Sons.

[11] Häusler, G., (1990). About fundamental limits of three-dimensional sensing. *SPIE Optics in Complex Systems*, **1319**:352–353.

[12] Engelhardt, K. and Häusler, G., (1988). Acquisition of 3-D data by focus sensing. *Appl. Opt.*, **27(22)**:4684.

[13] Engelhardt, K., (1991). Acquisition of 3-D data by focus sensing utilizing the moire effect of CCD cameras. *Appl. Opt.*, **30(11)**:1401.

[14] Breitmeier, U., Daum, W., Häusler, G., Heinrich, G., Küchel, M., Mollath, G., Nadeborn, W., Schlemmer, H., Schulze-Willbrenning, B., Schwarte, R., Seib, M., Sowa, P., and Steinbichler, R., (1995). Verfahren für die optische Formerfassung. In *Handbuch OF 1*, Vol. 38. Deutsche Gesellschaft für zerstörungsfreie Prüfung e.V. DGZfP, 1.HE11/95.

[15] Breitmeier, U., (1993). Laserprofilometrie-Meßanlage für biomedizinische Fragestellungen. *Biomedizinische Technik*, pp. 35–45.

[16] Jurca, (1997). Firmenunterlagen der Fa. Jurca Optoelektronik, Rodgau.

[17] Häusler, G. and Heckel, W., (1988). Light sectioning with large depth and high resolution. *Applied Optics*, **27**:5165–5169.

[18] Halioua, M., Liu, H., and Srinivasan, V., (1984). Automated phase-measuring profilometry of 3-D diffuse objects. *Applied Optics*, **23**(18): 3105–3108.

[19] Malz, R. W., (1992). *Codierte Lichtstrukturen für 3-D-Meßtechnik und Inspektion*, Vol. 14 of *Berichte aus dem Institut für Technische Optik*. University of Stuttgart.

[20] Dorsch, R. G., Häusler, G., and Herrmann, J. M., (1994). Laser triangulation: fundamental uncertainty in distance measurement. *Applied Optics*, **33(7)**.

[21] Pfeiffer, T. and Sowa, P., (1994). Optoelektronische Meßverfahren sichern die Produktqualität. In *Tagungsband Optisches Messen von Länge und Gestalt, GMA-Bericht 23*. Düsseldorf: VDI.

[22] Klicker, J., (1992). *Ein zweidimensionales Triangulationsmeßsystem mit Online-Meßwertverarbeitung bei hoher Bildrate.* Phd thesis, ZESS, Universität-GH Siegen.

[23] Takeda, M. and et al., (1982). Fourier-transform method of fringe pattern analysis for computer-based topography and interferometry. *Jour. Opt. Soc. of America*, **72**.

[24] Seib, M. and Höfler, H., (1990). Überblick über die verschiedenen Moiré-Techniken. *Vision & Voice-Magazine*, **4(2)**.

[25] Wolf, H., (1996). Aufrüstung von 2D-Bildverarbeitungssystemen zu 3D-Systemen mit aktiver strukturierter Beleuchtung. In *Tagungsunterlagen Aktuelle Entwicklungen und industrieller Einsatz der Bildverarbeitung*, p. 1. Aachen: MIT Management.

[26] Schubert, E., (1996). *Mehrfachfarbcodierte Triangulationsverfahren zur topometrischen Erfassung und Vermessung von 3D-Objekten*. PhD thesis, ZESS, Universität-GH Siegen.

[27] Häusler, G. and Ritter, D., (1993). Parallel 3D-sensing by color coded triangulation. *Applied Optics*, **32**:7164–7169.

[28] Malz, R., (1989). Adaptive light encoding for 3-D sensing with maximum measurement efficiency. In *Proc. 11th DAGM-Symposium, Hamburg, Informatik-Fachberichte*, Vol. 219. Springer.

[29] Zumbrunn, R., (1987). Automatic fast shape determination of diffuse reflecting objects at close range, by means of structured light and digital phase measurement. In *Proc. ISPRS Intercommission Conference on Fast Proc. of Photogrammetric Data, Interlaken, Switzerland*.

[30] Bruning, J. et al., (1974). Digital wavefront measuring for testing optical surfaces and lenses. *Applied Optics*, **13**.

[31] Creath, K., (1988). Phase-measurement interferometry techniques. In *Progress in Optics*, E. Wolf, ed. Amsterdam: North-Holland.

[32] Takeda, M., (1997). The philosophy of fringes—analogies and dualities in fringe generation and analysis. In *Proc. 3rd Intl. Workshop on Automatic Processing of Fringe Patterns*, W. Jüptner and W. Osten, eds., pp. 18–26. Berlin: Akademie Verlag.

[33] Küchel, M. F., (1997). Some progress in phase measurement techniques. In *Proc. 3rd Intl. Workshop on Automatic Processing of Fringe Patterns*, W. Jüptner and W. Osten, eds., pp. 27–44. Berlin: Akademie Verlag.

[34] Yamamoto, H., Sato, K., and Inokuchi, S., (1986). Range imaging systems based on binary image accumulation. *IEEE*, pp. 233–235.

[35] Wahl, F. M., (1986). A coded light approach for depth map acquisition. In *Proc. DAGM-Symposium Mustererkennung 1986. Informatik-Fachberichte*, Vol. 125. Springer.

[36] Häusler, G., Hernanz, M. B., Lampalzer, R., and Schönfeld, H., (1997). 3D real real time camera. In *Proc. 3rd Int. Workshop on Automatic Processing of Fringe Patterns*. Bremen, September 15–17, 1997.

[37] Grün, A., (1995). High Accuracy Object Reconstruction With Least Squares Matching. In *Tagungsband Bildverarbeitung 95 an der Technischen Akademie Esslingen*, pp. 277–296.

[38] Luhmann, T., (1995). Punktmessung in digitalen Bildern mit Subpixel-Genauigkeit. In *Proc. Bildverarbeitung '95 - Forschen, Entwickeln, Anwenden*, R. Ahlers, ed. Esslingen: Technische Akademie.

[39] Hauske, G., (1994). *Systhemtheorie der visuellen Wahrnehmung*. Stuttgart: Teubner Verlag.

[40] Dorsch, R., Herrmann, J., and Häusler, G., (1994). Laser triangulation: fundamental uncertainty of distance measurement. *Applied Optics*, **33** (7):1306–1314.

[41] Häusler, G., Kreipl, S., Lampalzer, R., Schielzeth, A., and Spellenberg, B., (1997). New range sensors at the physical limit of measuring uncertainty. In *Proc. of the EOS, Topical Meeting on Optoelectronic Distance Measurements and Applications, Nantes, July 8–10*. Orsay, France: European Optical Society.

[42] Schwarte, R., Hartmann, K., Klein, R., and Olk, J., (1994). *Neue Konzepte für die industrielle 3D-Objektvermessung nach dem Laufzeitverfahren*. PhD thesis, Düsseldorf.

[43] Schwarte, R., Heinol, H. G., Xu, Z., Olk, J., and Tai, W., (1997). Schnelle und einfache 3D-Formerfassung mit einem neuartigen Korrelations-Photodetektor-Array. In *Tagungsband Optische Formerfassung, DGZfP und VDI-GMA, Langen, 1997*.

[44] Heinol, H. G., Schwarte, R., Xu, Z., Neuhaus, H., and Lange, R., (1996). First Experimental Results of a New 3D-Vision System Based on RF-Modulation Interferometry. In *Kongreßband OPTO96-Optische Sensorik Meßtechnik Elektronik*. Leipzig, Germany: AMA Fachverband für Sensorik.

[45] Yu, Z., (1998). *Investigation of a 3D-Imaging System based on ORF-Modulation*. PhD thesis, INV, Universität-GH, Siegen.

[46] Gruen, A. and Kahmen, H., (1993). *Optical 3D-Measurement Techniques II*. Karlsruhe: Wichmann-Verlag.

[47] Breuckmann, B., (1993). *Bildverarbeitung und optische Meßtechnik in der industriellen Praxis*. München: Franzis-Verlag.

[48] Dändliker, R., Hug, K., Politch, J., and Zimmermann, E., (1995). High accuracy distance measurements with multiple-wavelength interferometry. *Optical Engineering*, **34(8)**:2407.

[49] Goodman, J. W., (1984). Statistical properties of laser speckle patterns. In *Laser Speckle and Related Phenomena*, J. C. Dainty, ed., p. 46 ff. Berlin: Springer-Verlag.

[50] Dresel, T., Häusler, G., and Venzke, H., (1992). 3D sensing of rough surfaces by coherence radar. *Applied Optics*, **33**:919–925.

[51] Ammon, G., Andretzky, P., Blossey, S., Bohn, G., Ettl, P., Habermeier, H. P., Harand, B., Häusler, G., Laszlo, I., and Schmidt, B., (1997). New modifications of the coherence radar. In *Proc. 3rd Int. Workshop on Automatic Processing of Fringe Patterns*. Bremen, September 15–17, 1997.

[52] Olk, J., (1997). *Untersuchung von Laufzeitentfernungsmeßsystemen unter besonderer Berücksichtigung des Referenzproblems*. PhD thesis, INV, Universität-GH Siegen.

Part II

Signal Processing and Pattern Recognition

8 Representation of Multidimensional Signals

Bernd Jähne

Interdisziplinäres Zentrum für Wissenschaftliches Rechnen (IWR)
Universität Heidelberg, Germany

Computer Vision and Applications

8.1   Introduction

Images are signals with two spatial dimensions. This chapter deals with signals of arbitrary dimensions. This generalization is very useful because computer vision is not restricted solely to 2-D signals. On the one hand, higher-dimensional signals are encountered. Dynamic scenes require the analysis of image sequences; the exploration of 3-D space requires the acquisition of volumetric images. Scientific exploration of complex phenomena is significantly enhanced if images not only of a single parameter but of many parameters are acquired. On the other hand, signals of lower dimensionality are also of importance when a computer vision system is integrated into a larger system and image data are fused with time series from point-measuring sensors.

8.2   Continuous signals

8.2.1   Types of signals

An important characteristic of a signal is its *dimension.* A zero-dimensional signal results from the measurement of a single quantity at a single point in space and time. Such a single value can also be averaged over a certain time period and area. There are several ways to extend a zero-dimensional signal into a 1-D signal (Table 8.1). A *time series* records the temporal course of a signal in time, while a *profile* does the same in a spatial direction or along a certain path.

A 1-D signal is also obtained if certain experimental parameters of the measurement are continuously changed and the measured parameter is recorded as a function of some control parameters. With respect to optics, the most obvious parameter is the wavelength of the electromagnetic radiation received by a radiation detector. When radiation is recorded as a function of the *wavelength,* a *spectrum* is obtained. The

Table 8.1: *Some types of signals g depending on D parameters*

D	Type of signal	Function
0	Measurement at a single point in space and time	g
1	Time series	$g(t)$
1	Profile	$g(x)$
1	Spectrum	$g(\lambda)$
2	Image	$g(x, y)$
2	Time series of profiles	$g(x, t)$
2	Time series of spectra	$g(\lambda, t)$
3	Volumetric image	$g(x, y, z)$
3	Image sequence	$g(x, y, t)$
3	Hyperspectral image	$g(x, y, \lambda)$
4	Volumetric image sequence	$g(x, y, z, t)$
4	Hyperspectral image sequence	$g(x, y, \lambda, t)$
5	Hyperspectral volumetric image sequence	$g(x, y, z, \lambda, t)$

wavelength is only one of the many parameters that could be considered. Others could be temperature, pressure, humidity, concentration of a chemical species, and any other properties that may influence the measured quantity.

With this general approach to multidimensional signal processing, it is obvious that an image is only one of the many possibilities of a 2-D signal. Other 2-D signals are, for example, time series of profiles or spectra. With increasing dimension, more types of signals are possible as summarized in Table 8.1. A 5-D signal is constituted by a *hyperspectral* volumetric image sequence.

8.2.2 Unified description

Mathematically, all these different types of multidimensional signals can be described in a unified way as continuous scalar functions of multiple parameters or generalized coordinates q_d as

$$g(\boldsymbol{q}) = g(q_1, q_2, \dots, q_D) \quad \text{with} \quad \boldsymbol{q} = [q_1, q_2, \dots, q_D]^T \quad (8.1)$$

that can be summarized in a D-dimensional *parameter vector* or generalized coordinate vector $\boldsymbol{q}$. An element of the vector can be a spatial direction, the time, or any other parameter.

As the signal g represents physical quantities, we can generally assume some properties that make the mathematical handling of the signals much easier.

Continuity. Real signals do not show any abrupt changes or discontinuities. Mathematically, this means that signals can generally be regarded as arbitrarily often differentiable.

Finite range. The physical nature of both the signal and the imaging sensor ensures that a signal is limited to a finite range. Some signals are restricted to positive values.

Finite energy. Normally a signal corresponds to the amplitude or the energy of a physical process. As the energy of any physical system is limited, any signal must be square integrable:

$$\int_{-\infty}^{\infty} |g(\boldsymbol{q})|^2 \, \mathrm{d}^D q < \infty \tag{8.2}$$

With these general properties of physical signals, it is obvious that the continuous representation provides a powerful mathematical approach. The properties imply, for example, that the Fourier transform (Section 8.6) of the signals always exist.

Depending on the underlying physical process the observed signal can be regarded as a stochastic signal. More often, however, a signal is a mixture of a deterministic and a stochastic signal. In the simplest case, the measured signal of a deterministic process g_d is corrupted by additive *zero-mean homogeneous noise*. This leads to the simple signal model

$$g(\boldsymbol{q}) = g_d(\boldsymbol{q}) + n \tag{8.3}$$

where n has the *variance* $\sigma_n^2 = \langle n^2 \rangle$. In most practical situations, the noise is not homogeneous but rather depends on the level of the signal. Thus in a more general way

$$g(\boldsymbol{q}) = g_d(\boldsymbol{q}) + n(g) \quad \text{with} \quad \langle n(g) \rangle = 0, \quad \langle n^2(g) \rangle = \sigma_n^2(g) \tag{8.4}$$

A detailed treatment of noise in various types of imaging sensors can be found in Section 5.5; see also CVA1 [Chapter 9 and 10].

8.2.3 Multichannel signals

So far, only scalar signals have been considered. If more than one signal is taken simultaneously, a *multichannel signal* is obtained. In some cases, for example, taking time series at different spatial positions, the multichannel signal can be considered as just a sampled version of a higher-dimensional signal. In other cases, the individual signals cannot be regarded as samples. This is the case when they are parameters with different units and/or meaning.

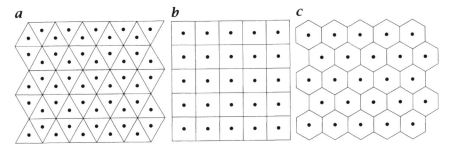

Figure 8.1: *Representation of 2-D digital images by meshes of regular polygons:* **a** *triangles;* **b** *squares;* **c** *hexagons.*

Table 8.2: *Properties of tessellations of the 2-D space with regular triangular, square, and hexagonal meshes;* N_e: *number of neighbors with common edge;* N_c: *number of neighbors with common edge and/or corner;* l: *basis length* l *of regular polygon;* d: *distance* d *to nearest neighbor; and* A: *area of cell*

	Triangular	Square	Hexagonal
N_e	3	4	6
N_c	12	8	6
l	$l = \sqrt{3}d = \sqrt{\sqrt{16/3A}}$	$l = d = \sqrt{A}$	$l = \frac{1}{3}\sqrt{3}d = \sqrt{\sqrt{4/27A}}$
d	$d = \frac{1}{3}\sqrt{3}l = \sqrt{\sqrt{16/27A}}$	$d = l = \sqrt{A}$	$d = \sqrt{3}l = \sqrt{\sqrt{4/3A}}$
A	$A = \frac{3}{4}\sqrt{3}d^2 = \frac{1}{4}\sqrt{3}l^2$	$A = d^2 = l^2$	$A = \frac{1}{2}\sqrt{3}d^2 = \frac{3}{2}\sqrt{3}l^2$

A multichannel signal provides a vector at each point and is therefore sometimes denoted as a *vectorial signal* and written as

$$g(q) = [q_1(q), q_2(q), \ldots, q_D(q)]^T \qquad (8.5)$$

A multichannel signal is not necessarily a vectorial signal. Depending on the mathematical relation between its components, it could also be a higher-order signal, for example, a *tensorial signal*. Such types of multichannel images are encountered when complex features are extracted from images. One example is the tensorial description of local structure discussed in Section 9.8.

8.3 Discrete signals

8.3.1 Regular two-dimensional lattices

Computers cannot handle continuous signals but only arrays of digital numbers. Thus it is required to represent signals as D-dimensional arrays of points. We first consider images as 2-D arrays of points. A

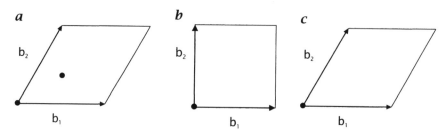

Figure 8.2: *Elementary cells of regular grids for 2-D digital images: **a** triangle grid; **b** square grid; **c** hexagonal grid.*

point on the 2-D grid is called a *pixel* or *pel*. Both words are abbreviations of *picture element*. A pixel represents the irradiance at the corresponding grid position. There are two ways to derive 2-D lattices from continuous signals.

First, the continuous 2-D space can be partitioned into space-filling cells. For symmetry reasons, only *regular polygons* are considered. Then there are only three possible *tesselations* with regular polygons: triangles, squares, and hexagons as illustrated in Fig. 8.1 (see also Table 8.2). All other regular polygons do not lead to a space-filling geometrical arrangement. There are either overlaps or gaps. From the mesh of regular polygons a 2-D array of points is then formed by the symmetry centers of the polygons. In case of the square mesh, these points lay again on a square grid. For the hexagonal mesh, the symmetry centers of the hexagons form a triangular grid. In contrast, the symmetry centers of the triangular grid form a more complex pattern, where two triangular meshes are interleaved. The second mesh is offset by a third of the base length l of the triangular mesh.

A second approach to regular lattices starts with a *primitive cell*. A primitive cell in 2-D is spanned by two not necessarily orthogonal base vectors $\boldsymbol{b}_1$ and $\boldsymbol{b}_2$. Thus, the primitive cell is always a parallelogram except for square and rectangular lattices (Fig. 8.2). Only in the latter case are the base vectors $\boldsymbol{b}_1$ and $\boldsymbol{b}_2$ orthogonal. Translating the primitive cell by multiples of the base vectors of the primitive cell then forms the lattice. Such a *translation vector* or *lattice vector* $\boldsymbol{r}$ is therefore given by

$$\boldsymbol{r} = n_1\boldsymbol{b}_1 + n_2\boldsymbol{b}_2 \quad n_1, n_2 \in \mathbb{Z} \tag{8.6}$$

The primitive cells of the square and hexagonal lattices (Fig. 8.2b and c) contains only one grid located at the origin of the primitive cell. This is not possible for a triangular grid, as the lattice points are not arranged in *regular* distances along two directions (Fig. 8.1a). Thus, the construction of the triangular lattice requires a primitive cell with

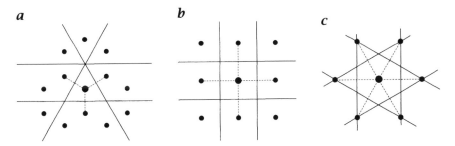

Figure 8.3: *Construction of the cells of a regular lattice from the lattice points: a triangle lattice; b square lattice; and c hexagonal lattice.*

two grid points. One grid point is located at the origin of the cell, the other is offset by a third of the length of each base vector (Fig. 8.2a)

The construction scheme to generate the elementary cells of regular shape from the lattice points is illustrated in Fig. 8.3. From one lattice point straight lines are drawn to all other lattice points starting with the nearest neighbors (dashed lines). Then the smallest cell formed by the lines perpendicular to these lines and dividing them into two halves results in the primitive cell. For all three lattices, only the nearest neighbors must be considered for this construction scheme.

The mathematics behind the formation of regular lattices in two dimensions is the 2-D analog to 3-D lattices used to describe crystals in solid state physics and mineralogy. The primitive cell constructed from the lattice points is, for example, known in solid state physics as the *Wigner-Seitz cell.*

Although there is a choice of three lattices with regular polygons—and many more if irregular polygons are considered—almost exclusively square or rectangular lattices are used for 2-D digital images.

The position of the pixel is given in the common notation for matrices. The first index m denotes the position of the row, the second, n, the position of the column (Fig. 8.4a); M gives the number of rows, and N the number of columns. In accordance with the matrix notation, the vertical axis (y axis) runs from top to bottom and not vice versa as is common in graphs. The horizontal axis (x axis) runs as usual from left to right.

8.3.2 Regular higher-dimensional lattices

The considerations in the previous section can be extended to higher dimensions. In 3-D space, lattices are identical to those used in solidstate physics to describe crystalline solids. In higher dimensions, we have serious difficulty in grasping the structure of discrete lattices because we can visualize only projections onto 2-D space. Given the fact that

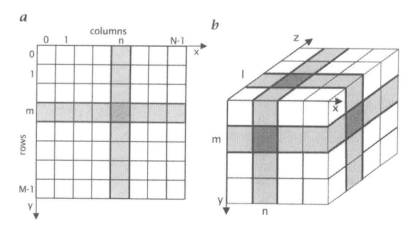

Figure 8.4: *Representation of digital images by orthogonal lattices: **a** square lattice for a 2-D image; and **b** cubic lattice for a volumetric or 3-D image.*

already 2-D discrete images are almost exclusively represented by rectangular lattices (Section 8.3.1), we may ask what we lose if we consider only hypercubic lattices in higher dimensions. Surprisingly, it turns out that this lattice has significant advantages. Thus it is hardly necessary to consider any other lattice.

Orthogonal lattice. The base vectors of the hypercubic primitive cell are orthogonal to each other. As discussed in CVA1 [Chapter 6], this is a significant advantage for the design of filters. If separable filters are used, they can easily be extended to arbitrary dimensions.

Valid for all dimensions. The hypercubic lattice is the most general solution for digital data as it is the only geometry that exists in arbitrary dimensions. In practice this means that it is generally quite easy to extend image processing algorithms to higher dimensions. We will see this, for example, with the discrete Fourier transform in Section 8.7, with multigrid data structures in Section 8.10, with averaging in Section 9.5, and with the analysis of local structure in Section 9.8.

Only lattice with regular polyhedron. While in 2-D three lattices with regular polyhedrons exist (Section 8.3.1), the cubic lattice is the only lattice with a regular polyhedron (the hexahedron) in 3-D. None of the other four regular polyhedra (tetrahedron, octahedron, dodecahedron, and icosahedron) is space filling.

These significant advantages of the hypercubic lattice are not outweighed by the single disadvantage that the neighborhood relations, discussed in Section 8.3.4, are more complex on these lattices than, for example, the 2-D hexagonal lattice.

In 3-D or *volumetric images* the elementary cell is known as a *voxel*, an abbreviation of *volume element*. On a rectangular grid, each voxel represents the mean gray value of a cuboid. The position of a voxel is given by three indices. The first, l, denotes the depth, m the row, and n the column (Fig. 8.4b). In higher dimensions, the elementary cell is denoted as a *hyperpixel*.

8.3.3   Metric in digital images

Based on the discussion in the previous two sections, we will focus in the following on hypercubic or orthogonal lattices and discuss in this section the metric of discrete images. This constitutes the base for all length, size, volume, and distance measurements in digital images. It is useful to generalize the *lattice vector* introduced in Eq. (8.6) that represents all points of a D-dimensional digital image and can be written as

$$\boldsymbol{r_n} = [n_1\Delta x_1, n_2\Delta x_2, \ldots, n_D\Delta x_D]^T \qquad (8.7)$$

In the preceding equation, the lattice constants Δx_d need not be equal in all directions. For the special cases of 2-D images, 3-D volumetric images, and 4-D spatiotemporal images the lattice vectors are

$$\boldsymbol{r}_{m,n} = \begin{bmatrix} n\Delta x \\ m\Delta y \end{bmatrix}, \boldsymbol{r}_{l,m,n} = \begin{bmatrix} n\Delta x \\ m\Delta y \\ l\Delta z \end{bmatrix}, \boldsymbol{r}_{k,l,m,n} = \begin{bmatrix} n\Delta x \\ m\Delta y \\ l\Delta z \\ k\Delta t \end{bmatrix} \qquad (8.8)$$

To measure distances, the *Euclidean distance* can be computed on an orthogonal lattice by

$$d_e(\boldsymbol{x}, \boldsymbol{x'}) = \|\boldsymbol{x} - \boldsymbol{x'}\| = \left[\sum_{d=1}^{D} (n_d - n_d')^2 \Delta x_d^2\right]^{1/2} \qquad (8.9)$$

On a square lattice, that is, a lattice with the same grid constant in all directions, the Euclidean distance can be computed more efficiently by

$$d_e(\boldsymbol{x}, \boldsymbol{x'}) = \|\boldsymbol{x} - \boldsymbol{x'}\| = \left[\sum_{d=1}^{D} (n_d - n_d')^2\right]^{1/2} \Delta x \qquad (8.10)$$

The Euclidean distance on discrete lattices is somewhat awkward. Although it is a discrete quantity, its values are not integers. Moreover, it cannot be computed very efficiently.

Therefore, two other metrics are sometimes considered in image processing. The *city-block distance*

$$d_b(\pmb{x}, \pmb{x}') = \sum_{d=1}^{D} |n_d - n'_d| \qquad (8.11)$$

simply adds up the magnitude of the component differences of two lattice vectors and not the squares as with the Euclidean distance in Eq. (8.10). Geometrically, the city block distance gives the length of a path between the two lattice vectors if we can only walk in directions parallel to axes. The *chessboard distance* is defined as the maximum of the absolute difference between two components of the corresponding lattice vectors:

$$d_c(\pmb{x}, \pmb{x}') = \max_{d=1,\dots,D} |n_d - n'_d| \qquad (8.12)$$

These two metrics have gained some importance for morphological operations (Section 14.2.4). Despite their simplicity they are not of much use as soon as lengths and distances are to be measured. The Euclidean distance is the only metric on digital images that preserves the *isotropy* of the continuous space. With the city block and chessboard distance, distances in the direction of the diagonals are longer and shorter than the Euclidean distance, respectively.

8.3.4 Neighborhood relations

The term *neighborhood* has no meaning for a continuous signal. How far two points are from each other is simply measured by an adequate metric such as the Euclidean distance function and this distance can take any value. With the cells of a discrete signal, however, a ranking of the distance between cells is possible. The set of cells with the smallest distance to a given cell are called the nearest neighbors. The triangular, square, and hexagonal lattices have three, four, and six nearest neighbors, respectively (Fig. 8.5). The figure indicates also the ranking in distance from the central cell.

Directly related to the question of neighbors is the term *adjacency*. A *digital object* is defined as a *connected region*. This means that we can reach any cell in the region from any other by walking from one neighboring cell to the next. Such a walk is called a *path*.

On a square lattice there are two possible ways to define neighboring cells (Fig. 8.5b). We can regard pixels as neighbors either when they have a joint edge or when they have at least one joint corner. Thus a pixel has four or eight neighbors and we speak of a *4-neighborhood* or an *8-neighborhood*. The definition of the 8-neighborhood is somewhat awkward, as there are neighboring cells with different distances.

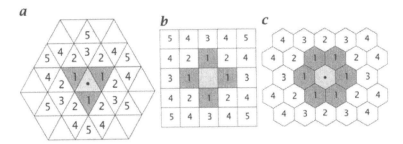

Figure 8.5: *Classification of the cells according to the distance from a given cell for the **a** triangular, **b** square, and **c** hexagonal lattices. The central cell is shaded in light gray, the nearest neighbors in darker gray. The numbers give the ranking in distance from the central cell.*

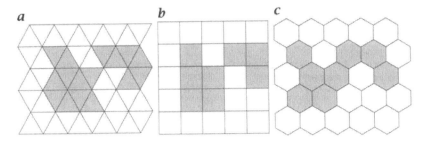

Figure 8.6: *Digital objects on a **triangular, b** square, and **c** hexagonal lattice; **a** and **b** show either two objects or one object (connected regions) depending on the neighborhood definition.*

The triangular lattice shows an equivalent ambivalence with the 3- and 12-neighborhoods with cells that have either only a joint edge or at least a joint corner with the central cell (Fig. 8.5a). In the 12-neighborhood there are three different types of neighboring cells, each with a different distance (Fig. 8.5a).

Only the hexagonal lattice gives a unique definition of neighbors. Each cell has six neighboring cells at the same distance joining one edge and two corners with the central cell.

A closer look shows that unfortunately both types of neighborhood definitions are required on triangular and square grids for a proper definition of connected regions. A region or an object is called connected when we can reach any pixel in the region by walking from one neighboring pixel to the next. The black object shown in Fig. 8.6b is one object in the 8-neighborhood, but constitutes two objects in the 4-neighborhood. The white background, however, shows the same property. Thus we have either two connected regions in the 8-neighborhood crossing each other or four separated regions in the 4-neighborhood.

This inconsistency between objects and background can be overcome if we declare the objects as 4-neighboring and the background as 8-neighboring, or vice versa.

These complications occur also on a triangular lattice (Fig. 8.6b) but not on a hexagonal lattice (Fig. 8.6c). The photosensors on the retina in the human eye, however, have a more hexagonal shape, see Wandell [1, Fig. 3.4, p. 49].

8.3.5 Errors in object position and geometry

The tessellation of space in discrete images limits the accuracy of the estimation of the position of an object and thus all other geometrical quantities such as distance, area, circumference, and orientation of lines. It is obvious that the accuracy of the position of a single point is only in the order of the lattice constant. The interesting question is, however, how this error propagates into position errors for larger objects and other relations. This question is of significant importance because of the relatively low spatial resolution of images as compared to other measuring instruments. Without much effort many physical quantities such as frequency, voltage, and distance can be measured with an accuracy better than 1 ppm, that is, 1 in 1,000,000, while images have a spatial resolution in the order of 1 in 1000 due to the limited number of pixels. Thus only highly accurate position estimates in the order of 1/100 of the pixel size result in an accuracy of about 1 in 100,000.

The discussion of position errors in this section will be limited to orthogonal lattices. These lattices have the significant advantage that the errors in the different directions can be discussed independently. Thus the following discussion is not only valid for 2-D images but any type of multidimensional signals and we must consider only one component.

In order to estimate the accuracy of the position estimate of a single point it is assumed that all positions are equally probable. This means a constant probability density function in the interval Δx. Then the variance σ_x^2 introduced by the position discretization is given by Papoulis [2, p. 106]

$$\sigma_x^2 = \frac{1}{\Delta x} \int_{x_n - \Delta x/2}^{x_n + \Delta x/2} (x - x_n)^2 \, dx = \frac{(\Delta x)^2}{12} \qquad (8.13)$$

Thus the standard deviation σ_x is about $1/\sqrt{12} \approx 0.3$ times the lattice constant Δx. The maximum error is, of course, $0.5\Delta x$.

All other errors for geometrical measurements of segmented objects can be related to this basic position error by statistical error propagation. We will illustrate this with a simple example computing the area and center of gravity of an object. For the sake of simplicity, we start with the unrealistic assumption that any cell that contains even the smallest fraction of the object is regarded as a cell of the object. We further assume that this segmentation is exact, that is, the signal itself does not contain noise and separates without errors from the background. In this way we separate all other errors from the errors introduced by the discrete lattice.

The area of the object is simply given as the product of the number N of cells and the area A_c of a cell. This simple estimate is, however, biased towards a larger area because the cells at the border of the object are only partly covered by the object. In the mean, half of the border cells are covered. Hence an unbiased estimate of the area is given by

$$A = A_c(N - 0.5N_b) \tag{8.14}$$

where N_b is the number of border cells. With this equation, the variance of the estimate can be determined. Only the statistical error in the area of the border cells must be considered. According to the laws of error propagation with independent random variables, the variance of the area estimate σ_A^2 is given by

$$\sigma_A^2 = 0.25A_c^2 N_b \sigma_x^2 \tag{8.15}$$

If we assume a compact object, for example, a square, with a length of D pixels, it has D^2 pixels and $4D$ border pixels. Using $\sigma_x \approx 0.3$ (Eq. (8.13)), the absolute and relative standard deviation of the area estimate are given by

$$\sigma_A \approx 0.3A_c\sqrt{D} \quad \text{and} \quad \frac{\sigma_A}{A} \approx \frac{0.3}{D^{3/2}} \quad \text{if } D \gg 1 \tag{8.16}$$

Thus the standard deviation of the area error for an object with a length of 10 pixels is just about the area of the pixel and the relative error is about 1 %. Equations (8.14) and (8.15) are also valid for volumetric images if the area of the elementary cell is replaced by the volume of the cell. Only the number of border cells is now different. If we again assume a compact object, for example, a cube, with a length of D, we now have D^3 cells in the object and $6D^2$ border cells. Then the absolute and relative standard deviations are approximately given by

$$\sigma_V \approx 0.45V_cD \quad \text{and} \quad \frac{\sigma_V}{V} \approx \frac{0.45}{D^2} \quad \text{if } D \gg 1 \tag{8.17}$$

Now the standard deviation of the volume for an object with a diameter of 10 pixels is about 5 times the volume of the cells but the relative error is about 0.5 %. Note that the absolute/relative error for volume measurements in/decreases faster with the size of the object than for area measurements.

The computations for the error of the center of gravity are quite similar. With the same assumptions about the segmentation process, an unbiased estimate of the center of gravity is given by

$$\boldsymbol{x}_g = \frac{1}{N} \left(\sum_{n=1}^{N-N_b} \boldsymbol{x}_n + \frac{1}{2} \sum_{n'=1}^{N_b} \boldsymbol{x}_{n'} \right) \tag{8.18}$$

Again the border pixels are counted only half. As the first part of the estimate with the nonborder pixels is exact, errors are caused only by the variation in the area of the border pixels. Therefore the variance of the estimate for each component of the center of gravity is given by

$$\sigma_g^2 = \frac{N_b}{4N^2} \sigma^2 \tag{8.19}$$

where σ is again the variance in the position of the fractional cells at the border of the object. Thus the standard deviation of the center of gravity for a compact object with the diameter of D pixels is

$$\sigma_g \approx \frac{0.3}{D^{3/2}} \quad \text{if } D \gg 1 \tag{8.20}$$

Thus the standard deviation for the center of gravity of an object with 10 pixel diameter is only about 0.01 pixel. For a volumetric object with a diameter of D pixel, the standard deviation becomes

$$\sigma_{gv} \approx \frac{0.45}{D^2} \quad \text{if } D \gg 1 \tag{8.21}$$

This result clearly shows that the position of objects and all related geometrical quantities such as the distances can be performed even with binary images (segmented objects) well into the range of 1/100 pixel. It is interesting that the relative errors for the area and volume estimates of Eqs. (8.16) and (8.17) are equal to the standard deviation of the center of gravity Equations (8.20) and (8.21). Note that only the *statistical error* has been discussed. A bias in the segmentation might easily result in much higher systematic errors.

8.4 Relation between continuous and discrete signals

A continuous function $g(\boldsymbol{q})$ is a useful mathematical description of a signal as discussed in Section 8.2. Real-world signals, however, can only be represented and processed as discrete or digital signals. Therefore a detailed knowledge of the relation between these two types of signals is required. It is not only necessary to understand the whole chain of the image-formation process from a continuous spatial radiance distribution to a digital image but also to perform subpixel-accurate image

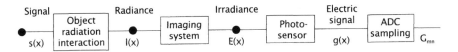

Figure 8.7: Steps from a continuous to a discrete signal.

interpolation (Section 9.6) and warping of images [CVA2, Chapter 9] as it is, for example, required for multiscale image operations [CVA2, Chapter 14].

The chain of processes that lead from the "true" signal to the digital signal include all the steps of the image-formation process as illustrated in Fig. 8.7. First, the signal of interest $s(\boldsymbol{x})$, such as reflectivity, temperature, etc., of an object, is somehow related to the radiance $L(x)$ emitted by the object in a generally nonlinear function (Section 2.5). In some cases this relation is linear (e. g., reflectivity), in others it is highly nonlinear (e. g., temperature). Often other parameters that are not controlled or not even known influence the signal as well. As an example, the radiance of an object is the product of its reflectivity and the irradiance. Moreover, the radiance of the beam from the object to the camera may be attenuated by absorption or scattering of radiation (Section 2.5.3). Thus the radiance of the object may vary with many other unknown parameters until it finally reaches the radiation-collecting system (optics).

The optical system generates an irradiance $E(\boldsymbol{x})$ at the image plane that is proportional to the object radiance (Chapter 4). There is, however, not a point-to-point correspondence. Because of the limited resolution of the optical systems due to physical limitation (e. g., diffraction) or imperfections of the optical systems (various aberrations; Section 3.5). This blurring of the signal is known as the *point spread function (PSF)* of the optical system and described in the Fourier domain by the *optical transfer function*. The nonzero area of the individual sensor elements of the sensor array (or the scanning mechanism) results in a further spatial and temporal blurring of the irradiance at the image plane.

The conversion to electrical signal U adds noise and possibly further nonlinearities to the signal $g(\boldsymbol{x},t)$ that is finally measured. In a last step, the analog electrical signal is converted by an *analog-to-digital converter (ADC)* into digital numbers. The basic relation between continuous and digital signals is established by the sampling theorem. It describes the effects of spatial and temporal sampling on continuous signals and thus also tells us how to reconstruct a continuous signal from its samples.

The image-formation process itself thus includes two essential steps. First, the whole image-formation process blurs the signal. Second, the continuous signal at the image plane is sampled. Although both processes often occur together, they can be separated for an easier mathematical treatment.

8.4.1 Image formation

If we denote the undistorted original signal projected onto the image plane by $g'(x,t)$, then the signal $g(x,t)$ modified by the image-formation process is given by

$$g(x,t) = \int_{-\infty}^{\infty} g'(x',t')h(x,x',t,t') \, d^2x' \, dt' \qquad (8.22)$$

The function h is the PSF. The signal $g'(x,t)$ can be considered as the image that would be obtained by a perfect system, that is, an optical system whose PSF is a δ-distribution. Equation (8.22) indicates that the signal at the point $[x,t]^T$ in space and time is composed of the radiance of a whole range of points $[x',t']^T$ nearby, which linearly add up weighted with the signal h at $[x',t']^T$. The integral can significantly be simplified if the point-spread function is the same at all points (*homogeneous system* or *shift-invariant system*). Then the point-spread function h depends only on the distance of $[x',t']^T$ to $[x,t]^T$ and the integral in Eq. (8.22) reduces to the *convolution* integral

$$g(x,t) = \int_{-\infty}^{\infty} g'(x',t')h(x - x', t - t') \, d^2x' \, dt' = (g' * h)(x,t) \quad (8.23)$$

For most optical systems the PSF is not strictly shift-invariant because the degree of blurring is increasing with the distance from the optical axis (Chapter 3). However, as long as the variation is continuous and does not change significantly over the width of the PSF, the convolution integral in Eq. (8.23) still describes the image formation correctly. The PSF and the system transfer function just become weakly dependent on x.

8.4.2 Sampling theorem

Sampling means that all information is lost except at the grid points. Mathematically, this constitutes a multiplication of the continuous function with a function that is zero everywhere except for the grid points. This operation can be performed by multiplying the image function $g(x)$ with the sum of δ distributions located at all lattice vectors $r_{m,n}$ as in Eq. (8.7). This function is called the two-dimensional δ comb, or "nail-board function." Then sampling can be expressed as

$$g_s(\boldsymbol{x}) = g(\boldsymbol{x}) \sum_{m=-\infty}^{m=\infty} \sum_{n=-\infty}^{n=\infty} \delta(\boldsymbol{x} - \boldsymbol{r}_{m,n}) \tag{8.24}$$

This equation is only valid as long as the elementary cell of the lattice contains only one point. This is the case for the square and hexagonal grids (Fig. 8.2b and c). The elementary cell of the triangular grid, however, includes two points (Fig. 8.2a). Thus for general regular lattices, p points per elementary cell must be considered. In this case, a sum of P δ combs must be considered, each shifted by the offsets $\boldsymbol{s}_p$ of the points of the elementary cells:

$$g_s(\boldsymbol{x}) = g(\boldsymbol{x}) \sum_{p=1}^{P} \sum_{m=-\infty}^{\infty} \sum_{n=-\infty}^{\infty} \delta(\boldsymbol{x} - \boldsymbol{r}_{m,n} - \boldsymbol{s}_p) \tag{8.25}$$

It is easy to extend this equation for sampling into higher-dimensional spaces and into the time domain:

$$g_s(\boldsymbol{x}) = g(\boldsymbol{x}) \sum_p \sum_n \delta(\boldsymbol{x} - \boldsymbol{r}_n - \boldsymbol{s}_p) \tag{8.26}$$

In this equation, the summation ranges have been omitted. One of the coordinates of the D-dimensional space and thus the vector $\boldsymbol{x}$ and the lattice vector $\boldsymbol{r}_n$

$$\boldsymbol{r}_n = [n_1 \boldsymbol{b}_1, n_2 \boldsymbol{b}_2, \dots, n_D \boldsymbol{b}_D]^T \quad \text{with} \quad n_d \in \mathbb{Z} \tag{8.27}$$

is the time coordinate. The set of fundamental translation vectors $\{\boldsymbol{b}_1, \boldsymbol{b}_2, \dots, \boldsymbol{b}_D\}$ form a not necessarily orthogonal base spanning the D-dimensional space.

The sampling theorem directly results from the Fourier transform of Eq. (8.26). In this equation the continuous signal $g(\boldsymbol{x})$ is multiplied by the sum of delta distributions. According to the convolution theorem of the Fourier transform (Section 8.6), this results in a convolution of the Fourier transforms of the signal and the sum of delta combs in Fourier space. The Fourier transform of a delta comb is again a delta comb (see Table 8.5). As the convolution of a signal with a delta distribution simply replicates the function value at the zero point of the delta functions, the Fourier transform of the sampled signal is simply a sum of shifted copies of the Fourier transform of the signal:

$$\hat{g}_s(\boldsymbol{k}, v) = \sum_p \sum_v \hat{g}(\boldsymbol{k} - \hat{\boldsymbol{r}}_v) \exp\left(-2\pi i \boldsymbol{k}^T \boldsymbol{s}_p\right) \tag{8.28}$$

The phase factor $\exp(-2\pi i \boldsymbol{k}^T \boldsymbol{s}_p)$ results from the shift of the points in the elementary cell by $\boldsymbol{s}_p$ according to the shift theorem of the Fourier transform (see Table 8.4). The vectors $\hat{\boldsymbol{r}}_v$

$$\hat{\boldsymbol{r}}_v = v_1\hat{\boldsymbol{b}}_1 + v_2\hat{\boldsymbol{b}}_2 + \ldots + v_D\hat{\boldsymbol{b}}_D \quad \text{with} \quad v_d \in \mathbb{Z} \qquad (8.29)$$

are the points of the so-called *reciprocal lattice*. The fundamental translation vectors in the space and Fourier domain are related to each other
by

$$\boldsymbol{b}_d^T\hat{\boldsymbol{b}}_{d'} = \delta_{d-d'} \qquad (8.30)$$

This basically means that the fundamental translation vector in the
Fourier domain is perpendicular to all translation vectors in the spatial
domain except for the corresponding one. Furthermore, the distances
are reciprocally related to each other. In 3-D space, the fundamental
translations of the reciprocial lattice can therefore be computed by

$$\hat{\boldsymbol{b}}_d = \frac{\boldsymbol{b}_{d+1} \times \boldsymbol{b}_{d+2}}{\boldsymbol{b}_1^T(\boldsymbol{b}_2 \times \boldsymbol{b}_3)} \qquad (8.31)$$

The indices in the preceding equation are computed modulo 3, $\boldsymbol{b}_1^T(\boldsymbol{b}_2 \times \boldsymbol{b}_3)$ is the volume of the primitive elementary cell in the spatial domain.
All these equations are familiar to solid state physicists or cristallogra-
phers [3]. Mathematicians know the lattice in the Fourier domain as the
dual base or *reciprocal base* of a vector space spanned by a nonorthogonal base. For an orthogonal base, all vectors of the dual base show into
the same direction as the corresponding vectors and the magnitude is
given by $\left|\hat{\boldsymbol{b}}_d\right| = 1/|\boldsymbol{b}_d|$. Then often the length of the base vectors is de-
noted by Δx_d, and the length of the reciprocal vectors by $\Delta k_d = 1/\Delta x_d$.
Thus an orthonormal base is dual to itself.

For further illustration, Fig. 8.8 shows the lattices in both domains
for a triangular, square, and hexagonal grid. The figure also includes
the primitive cell known as the *Wigner-Seitz cell* (Section 8.3.1 and
Fig. 8.3) and first *Brillouin zone* in the spatial and Fourier domain, respectively.

Now we can formulate the condition where we get no distortion of
the signal by sampling, known as the *sampling theorem*. If the image
spectrum $\hat{g}(\boldsymbol{k})$ contains such high wave numbers that parts of it overlap
with the periodically repeated copies, we cannot distinguish whether
the spectral amplitudes come from the original spectrum at the center
or from one of the copies. In other words, a low wave number can be
an alias of a high wave number and assume an incorrect amplitude of
the corresponding wave number. In order to obtain no distortions, we
must avoid overlapping. A safe condition to avoid overlapping is as
follows: the spectrum must be zero outside of the primitive cell of the
reciprocal lattice, that is, the first Brillouin zone.

On a rectangular grid, this results in the simple condition that the
maximum wave number (or frequency) at which the image spectrum

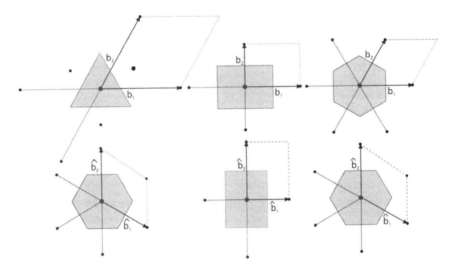

Figure 8.8: *Lattices with the fundamental translation vectors and primitive cell in the spatial and Fourier domain for a triangular (left), square (middle), and hexagonal (right) 2-D lattice.*

is not equal to zero must be restricted to less than half of the grid constants of the reciprocal grid. Therefore the sampling theorem is as follows:

Theorem 8.1 (Sampling Theorem) *If the spectrum $\hat{g}(\mathbf{k})$ of a continuous function $g(\mathbf{x})$ is band-limited, that is,*

$$\hat{g}(\mathbf{k}) = 0 \ \forall \ |k_d| \geq \Delta k_d/2 \tag{8.32}$$

then it can be reconstructed exactly from samples with a distance

$$\Delta x_d = 1/\Delta k_d \tag{8.33}$$

In other words, we will obtain a periodic structure correctly only if we take at least two samples per wavelength (or period). The maximum wave number that can be sampled without errors is called the *Nyquist* or *limiting* wave number (or frequency). In the following, we will often use dimensionless wave numbers (frequencies), which are scaled to the limiting wave number (frequency). We denote this scaling with a tilde:

$$\tilde{k}_d = \frac{k_d}{\Delta k_d/2} = 2k_d\Delta x_d \quad \text{and} \quad \tilde{\nu} = \frac{\nu}{\Delta\nu/2} = 2\nu\Delta T \tag{8.34}$$

In this scaling all the components of the wave number $\tilde{k}_d$ fall into the interval $]-1, 1[$.

8.4.3 Aliasing

If the conditions of the sampling theorem are not met, it is not only impossible to reconstruct the original signal exactly but also distortions are introduced into the signal. This effect is known in signal theory as *aliasing* or in imaging as the *Moiré effect*.

The basic problem with aliasing is that the band limitation introduced by the blurring of the image formation and the nonzero area of the sensor is generally not sufficient to avoid aliasing. This is illustrated in the following example with an "ideal" sensor.

Example 8.1: Standard sampling

An "ideal" imaging sensor will have a nonblurring optics (the PSF is the delta distribution) and a sensor array that has a 100% fill factor, that is, the sensor elements show a constant sensitivity over the whole area without gaps inbetween. The PSF of such an imaging sensor is a box function with the width Δx of the sensor elements and the transfer function (TF) is a sinc function:

$$
\begin{array}{ll}
\text{PSF} & \dfrac{1}{\Delta x_1}\Pi(x_1/\Delta x_1)\dfrac{1}{\Delta x_2}\Pi(x_2/\Delta x_2) \\[2ex]
\text{TF} & \dfrac{\sin(\pi k_1 \Delta x_1)}{\pi k_1 \Delta x_1}\dfrac{\sin(\pi k_2 \Delta x_2)}{\pi k_2 \Delta x_2}
\end{array}
\tag{8.35}
$$

The sinc function has its first zero crossings when the argument is $\pm\pi$. This is when $k_d = \pm\Delta x_d$ or at twice the Nyquist wave number, see Eq. (8.34). At the Nyquist wave number the value of the transfer function is still $1/\sqrt{2}$. Thus standard sampling is not sufficient to avoid aliasing. The only safe way to avoid aliasing is to ensure that the imaged objects do not contain wave numbers and frequencies beyond the Nyquist limit.

8.4.4 Reconstruction from samples

The sampling theorem ensures the conditions under which we can reconstruct a continuous function from sampled points, but we still do not know how to perform the reconstruction of the continuous image from its samples, that is, the inverse operation to sampling.

Reconstruction is performed by a suitable *interpolation* of the sampled points. Again we use the most general case: a nonorthogonal primitive cell with P points. Generally, the interpolated points $g_r(\boldsymbol{x})$ are calculated from the values sampled at $\boldsymbol{r_n}+\boldsymbol{s_p}$ weighted with suitable factors that depend on the distance from the interpolated point:

$$
g_r(\boldsymbol{x}) = \sum_p \sum_n g_s(\boldsymbol{r_n} + \boldsymbol{s_p})h(\boldsymbol{x} - \boldsymbol{r_n} - \boldsymbol{s_p})
\tag{8.36}
$$

Using the integral property of the δ distributions, we can substitute the sampled points on the right-hand side by the continuous values and then interchange summation and integration:

$$g_r(\boldsymbol{x}) = \sum_p \sum_n \int_{-\infty}^{\infty} g(\boldsymbol{x}')h(\boldsymbol{x} - \boldsymbol{x}')\delta(\boldsymbol{r}_n + \boldsymbol{s}_p - \boldsymbol{x}')\,\mathrm{d}^D x'$$

$$= \int_{-\infty}^{\infty} h(\boldsymbol{x} - \boldsymbol{x}')\sum_p \sum_n \delta(\boldsymbol{r}_n + \boldsymbol{s}_p - \boldsymbol{x}')g(\boldsymbol{x}')\,\mathrm{d}^D x'$$

The latter integral is a convolution of the weighting function h with a function that is the sum of the product of the image function g with shifted δ combs. In Fourier space, convolution is replaced by complex multiplication and vice versa. If we further consider the shift theorem and that the Fourier transform of a δ comb is again a δ comb, we finally obtain

$$\hat{g}_r(\boldsymbol{k}) = \hat{h}(\boldsymbol{k})\sum_p \sum_v \hat{g}(\boldsymbol{k} - \hat{\boldsymbol{r}}_v)\exp\left(-2\pi\mathrm{i}\boldsymbol{k}^T \boldsymbol{s}_p\right) \qquad (8.37)$$

The interpolated function can only be equal to the original image if the periodically repeated image spectra are not overlapping. This is nothing new; it is exactly what the sampling theorem states. The interpolated image function is only equal to the original image function if the weighting function is one within the first Brillouin zone and zero outside, eliminating all replicated spectra and leaving the original band-limited spectrum unchanged. On a D-dimensional orthogonal lattice Eq. (8.37) becomes

$$\hat{g}_r(\boldsymbol{k}) = \hat{g}(\boldsymbol{k})\prod_{d=1}^{D}\Pi(k_d\Delta x_d) \qquad (8.38)$$

and the ideal interpolation function h is the sinc function

$$h(\boldsymbol{x}) = \prod_{d=1}^{D}\frac{\sin(\pi x_d/\Delta x_d)}{\pi x_d/\Delta x_d} \qquad (8.39)$$

Unfortunately, this function decreases only with $1/x$ towards zero. Therefore, a correct interpolation requires a large image area; mathematically, it must be infinitely large. This condition can be weakened if we "overfill" the sampling theorem, that is, ensure that $\hat{g}(\boldsymbol{k})$ is already zero before we reach the Nyquist limit. According to Eq. (8.37), we can then choose $\hat{h}(\boldsymbol{k})$ arbitrarily in the region where $\hat{g}$ vanishes. We can use this freedom to construct an interpolation function that decreases more quickly in the spatial domain, that is, has a minimum-length interpolation mask. We can also start from a given interpolation formula. Then the deviation of its Fourier transform from a box function tells us to what extent structures will be distorted as a function of the wave number. Suitable interpolation functions will be discussed in detail in Section 9.6.

8.5   Vector spaces and unitary transforms

8.5.1   Introduction

An $N \times M$ digital image has NM individual pixels that can take arbitrary values. Thus it has NM degrees of freedom. Without mentioning it explicitly, we thought of an image as being composed of individual pixels. Thus, we can compose each image of *basis images* ${}^{m,n}P$ where just one pixel has a value of one while all other pixels are zero:

$$
{}^{m,n}P_{m',n'} = \delta_{m-m'}\delta_{n-n'} = \begin{cases} 1 & \text{if } m = m' \wedge n = n' \\ 0 & \text{otherwise} \end{cases} \tag{8.40}
$$

Any arbitrary image can then be composed of all basis images in Eq. (8.40) by

$$
G = \sum_{m=0}^{M-1} \sum_{n=0}^{N-1} G_{m,n} \, {}^{m,n}P \tag{8.41}
$$

where $G_{m,n}$ denotes the gray value at the position $[m, n]$. The *inner product* (also known as *scalar product*) of two "vectors" in this space can be defined similarly to the scalar product for vectors and is given by

$$
(G, H) = \sum_{m=0}^{M-1} \sum_{n=0}^{N-1} G_{m,n} H_{m,n} \tag{8.42}
$$

where the parenthesis notation $(\cdot, \cdot)$ is used for the inner product in order to distinguish it from matrix multiplication. The basis images ${}^{m,n}P$ form an *orthonormal base* for an $N \times M$-dimensional vector space. From Eq. (8.42), we can immediately derive the *orthonormality relation* for the basis images ${}^{m,n}P$:

$$
\sum_{m=0}^{M-1} \sum_{n=0}^{N-1} {}^{m',n'}P_{m,n} \, {}^{m'',n''}P_{m,n} = \delta_{m'-m''}\delta_{n'-n''} \tag{8.43}
$$

This states that the inner product between two base images is zero if two different basis images are taken. The scalar product of a basis image with itself is one. The MN basis images thus span an $M \times N$-dimensional vector space $\mathbb{R}^{N \times M}$ over the set of real numbers.

An $M \times N$ image represents a point in the $M \times N$ vector space. If we change the coordinate system, the image remains the same but its coordinates change. This means that we just observe the same piece of information from a different point of view. All these representations are equivalent to each other and each gives a complete representation of the image. A coordinate transformation leads us from one representation to the other and back again. An important property of such a transform is that the *length* or (*magnitude*) of a vector

$$\|G\|_2 = (G, G)^{1/2} \tag{8.44}$$

is not changed and that orthogonal vectors remain orthogonal. Both requirements are met if the coordinate transform preserves the inner product. A transform with this property is known as a *unitary transform*.

Physicists will be reminded of the theoretical foundations of *quantum mechanics*, which are formulated in an inner product vector space of infinite dimension, the *Hilbert space*.

8.5.2 Basic properties of unitary transforms

The two most important properties of a unitary transform are [4]:

Theorem 8.2 (Unitary transform) *Let V be a finite-dimensional inner product vector space. Let U be a one-one linear transformation of V onto itself. Then*

1. *U preserves the inner product, that is, $(G, H) = (UG, UH)$, $\forall G, H \in V$.*
2. *The inverse of U, U^{-1}, is the adjoin U^{*^T} of $U : UU^{*^T} = I$.*

Rotation in $\mathbb{R}^2$ or $\mathbb{R}^3$ is an example of a transform where the preservation of the length of vectors is obvious.

The product of two unitary transforms $U_1 U_2$ is unitary. Because the identity operator I is unitary, as is the inverse of a unitary operator, the set of all unitary transforms on an inner product space is a *group* under the operation of composition. In practice, this means that we can compose/decompose complex unitary transforms of/into simpler or elementary transforms.

8.5.3 Significance of the Fourier transform (FT)

A number of unitary transforms have gained importance for digital signal processing including the cosine, sine, Hartley, slant, Haar, and Walsh transforms [5, 6, 7]. But none of these transforms matches the *Fourier transform* in importance.

The uniqueness of the Fourier transform is related to a property expressed by the *shift theorem*. If a signal is shifted in space, its Fourier transform does not change in amplitude but only in phase, that is, it is multiplied with a complex phase factor. Mathematically, this means that all base functions of the Fourier transform are *eigenvectors* of the *shift operator* $S(s)$:

$$S(s) \exp(-2\pi ikx) = \exp(-2\pi iks) \exp(-2\pi ikx) \qquad (8.45)$$

The phase factor $\exp(-2\pi iks)$ is the *eigenvalue* and the complex exponentials $\exp(-2\pi ikx)$ are the base functions of the Fourier transform spanning the infinite-dimensional vector space of the square integrable complex-valued functions over $\mathbb{R}$. For all other transforms, various base functions are mixed with each other if one base function is shifted. Therefore, the base functions of all these transforms are not an eigenvector of the shift operator.

The base functions of the Fourier space are the eigenfunctions of *all linear shift-invariant operators* or *convolution* operators. If an operator is shift-invariant, the result is the same at whichever point in space it is applied. Therefore, a periodic function such as the complex exponential is not changed in period and does not become an aperiodic function. If a convolution operator is applied to a periodic signal, only its phase and amplitude change, which can be expressed by a complex factor. This complex factor is the (wave-number dependent) eigenvalue or transfer function of the convolution operator.

At this point, it is also obvious why the Fourier transform is complex valued. For a real periodic function, that is, a pure sine or cosine function, it is not possible to formulate a shift theorem, as both functions are required to express a shift. The complex exponential $\exp(ikx) = \cos kx + i \sin kx$ contains both functions and a shift by a distance s can simply be expressed by the complex phase factor $\exp(iks)$.

Each base function and thus each point in the Fourier domain contains two pieces of information: the *amplitude* and the *phase*, that is, relative position, of a periodic structure. Given this composition, we ask whether the phase or the amplitude contains the more significant information on the structure in the image, or whether both are of equal importance.

In order to answer this question, we perform a simple experiment. Figure 8.9 shows two images of a street close to Heidelberg University taken at different times. Both images are Fourier transformed and then the phase and amplitude are interchanged as illustrated in Fig. 8.9c, d. The result of this interchange is surprising. It is the phase that determines the content of an image. Both images look somewhat patchy but the significant information is preserved.

From this experiment, we can conclude that the phase of the Fourier transform carries essential information about the image structure. The amplitude alone implies only *that* such a periodic structure is contained in the image but not *where*.

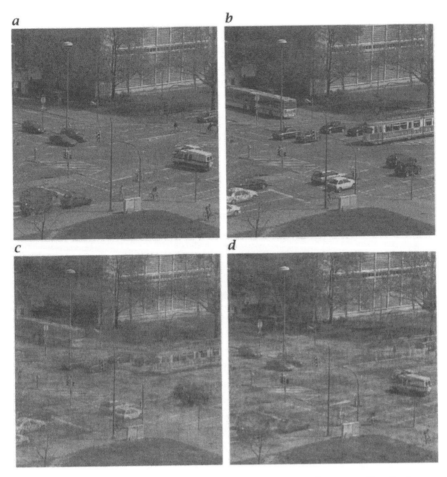

Figure 8.9: *Importance of phase and amplitude in Fourier space for the image content: **a, b** two images of a traffic scene taken at different times; **c** composite image using the phase from image **b** and the amplitude from image **a**; **d** composite image using the phase from image **a** and the amplitude from image **b**.*

8.5.4 Dynamical range and resolution of the FT

While in most cases it is sufficient to represent an image with rather few quantization levels, for example, 256 values or one byte per pixel, the Fourier transform of an image needs a much larger dynamical range. Typically, we observe a strong decrease of the Fourier components with the magnitude of the wave number, so that a dynamical range of at least 3–4 decades is required. Consequently, at least 16-bit integers or 32-bit floating-point numbers are necessary to represent an image in the Fourier domain without significant rounding errors.

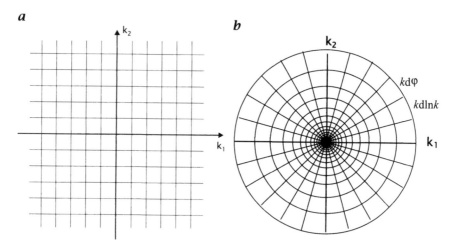

Figure 8.10: *Tessellation of the 2-D Fourier domain into:* **a** *Cartesian; and* **b** *logarithmic-polar lattices.*

The reason for this behavior is not the insignificance of high wave numbers in images. If we simply omitted them, we would blur the image. The decrease is caused by the fact that the *relative* resolution is increasing with the wave number. With the discrete Fourier transform (see Section 8.7), the Fourier transform contains only wave numbers that fit exactly integer times into the image:

$$k_{vp} = \frac{v}{d_p} \tag{8.46}$$

where $d = [d_1, \ldots, d_D]^T$ is the size of the D-dimensional signal. Therefore, the absolute wave number resolution $\Delta k = 1/\Delta x$ is constant, equivalent to a Cartesian tessellation of the Fourier space (Fig. 8.10a). Thus the smallest wave number ($v = 1$) has a wavelength of the size of the image, and the next coarse wave number has a wavelength of half the size of the image. This is a very low resolution for large wavelengths. The smaller the wavelength, the better the resolution.

This ever increasing *relative resolution* is not natural. We can, for example, easily see the difference of 10 cm in 1 m, but not in 1 km. It is more natural to think of relative resolutions, because we are better able to distinguish relative distance differences than absolute ones. If we apply this concept to the Fourier domain, it seems to be more natural to tessellate the Fourier domain in intervals increasing with the wave number, a *log-polar coordinate system*, as illustrated in Fig. 8.10b. Such a lattice partitions the space into angular and ln$k$ intervals. Thus, the cell area is proportional to k^2. In order to preserve the norm, or—physically speaking—the energy, of the signal in this representation, the increase in the area of the cells proportional to k^2 must be considered:

$$\int_{-\infty}^{\infty} |\hat{g}(\boldsymbol{k})|^2 \, dk_1 \, dk_2 = \int_{-\infty}^{\infty} k^2 |\hat{g}(\boldsymbol{k})|^2 \, d\ln k \, d\varphi \qquad (8.47)$$

Thus, the *power spectrum* $|\hat{g}(\boldsymbol{k})|^2$ in the log-polar representation is multiplied by k^2 and falls off much less steep than in the Cartesian representation. The representation in a log-polar coordinate system allows a much better evaluation of the directions of the spatial structures and of the smaller scales. Moreover, a change in scale or orientation just causes a shift of the signal in the log-polar representation. Therefore, it has gained importance in representation object for shape analysis ([CVA3, Chapter 8]).

8.6 Continuous Fourier transform (FT)

In this section, we give a brief survey of the continuous Fourier transform and we point out the properties that are most important for signal processing. Extensive and excellent reviews of the Fourier transform are given by Bracewell [8], Poularikas [7, Chapter 2], or Madisetti and Williams [9, Chapter 1]

8.6.1 One-dimensional FT

Definition 8.1 (1-D FT) *If $g(x) : \mathbb{R} \mapsto \mathbb{C}$ is a square integrable function, that is,*

$$\int_{-\infty}^{\infty} |g(x)| \, dx < \infty \qquad (8.48)$$

then the Fourier transform *of $g(x)$, $\hat{g}(k)$ is given by*

$$\hat{g}(k) = \int_{-\infty}^{\infty} g(x) \exp(-2\pi ikx) \, dx \qquad (8.49)$$

The Fourier transform maps the vector space of absolutely integrable functions onto itself. The inverse Fourier transform of $\hat{g}(k)$ results in the original function $g(x)$:

$$g(x) = \int_{-\infty}^{\infty} \hat{g}(k) \exp(2\pi ikx) \, dk \qquad (8.50)$$

It is convenient to use an operator notation for the Fourier transform. With this notation, the Fourier transform and its inverse are simply written as

$$\hat{g}(k) = \mathcal{F}g(x) \quad \text{and} \quad g(x) = \mathcal{F}^{-1}\hat{g}(k) \tag{8.51}$$

A function and its transform, a *Fourier transform pair* is simply denoted by $g(x) \Longleftrightarrow \hat{g}(k)$.

In Eqs. (8.49) and (8.50) a definition of the wave number *without* the factor 2π is used, that is $k = 1/\lambda$, in contrast to the notation often used in physics with $k' = 2\pi/\lambda$. For signal processing, the first notion is more useful, because k directly gives the number of periods per unit length.

With the notation that includes the factor 2π in the wave number, two forms of the Fourier transform are common: the asymmetric form

$$\hat{g}(k') = \int_{-\infty}^{\infty} g(x) \exp(-ik'x) \, dx$$

$$g(x) = \frac{1}{2\pi} \int_{-\infty}^{\infty} \hat{g}(k) \exp(ik'x) \, dk \tag{8.52}$$

and the symmetric form

$$\hat{g}(k') = \frac{1}{\sqrt{2\pi}} \int_{-\infty}^{\infty} g(x) \exp(-ik'x) \, dx$$

$$g(x) = \frac{1}{\sqrt{2\pi}} \int_{-\infty}^{\infty} \hat{g}(k') \exp(ik'x) \, dk' \tag{8.53}$$

As the definition of the Fourier transform takes the simplest form in Eqs. (8.49) and (8.50), most other relations and equations also become simpler than with the definitions in Eqs. (8.52) and (8.53). In addition, the relation of the continuous Fourier transform with the discrete Fourier transform (Section 8.7) and the Fourier series (Table 8.3) becomes more straightforward.

Because all three versions of the Fourier transform are in common use, it is likely that wrong factors in Fourier transform pairs will be obtained. The rules for conversion of Fourier transform pairs between the three versions can directly be inferred from the definitions and are summarized here:

$$
\begin{array}{lll}
k \text{ without } 2\pi, \text{ Eq. (8.49)} & g(x) \Longleftrightarrow \hat{g}(k) & \\
k' \text{ with } 2\pi, \text{ Eq. (8.52)} & g(x) \Longleftrightarrow \hat{g}(k'/2\pi) & (8.54) \\
k' \text{ with } 2\pi, \text{ Eq. (8.53)} & g(x/\sqrt{(2\pi)}) \Longleftrightarrow \hat{g}(k'/\sqrt{(2\pi)}) &
\end{array}
$$

Table 8.3: *Comparison of the continuous Fourier transform (FT), the Fourier series (FS), the infinite discrete Fourier transform (IDFT), and the discrete Fourier transform (DFT) in one dimension*

Type	Forward transform	Backward transform
FT: $\mathbb{R} \Longleftrightarrow \mathbb{R}$	$\displaystyle\int_{-\infty}^{\infty} g(x)\exp(-2\pi ikx)\,dx$	$\displaystyle\int_{-\infty}^{\infty} \hat{g}(k)\exp(2\pi ikx)\,dk$
FS: $[0,\Delta x] \Longleftrightarrow \mathbb{Z}$	$\displaystyle\frac{1}{\Delta x}\int_{0}^{\Delta x} g(x)\exp\left(-2\pi i\frac{vx}{\Delta x}\right)\,dx$	$\displaystyle\sum_{v=-\infty}^{\infty} \hat{g}_v\exp\left(2\pi i\frac{vx}{\Delta x}\right)$
IDFT: $\mathbb{Z} \Longleftrightarrow [0,1/\Delta x]$	$\displaystyle\sum_{n=-\infty}^{\infty} g_n\exp(-2\pi in\Delta xk)$	$\displaystyle\Delta x\int_{0}^{1/\Delta x} \hat{g}(k)\exp(2\pi in\Delta xk)\,dk$
DFT: $\mathbb{N}_N \Longleftrightarrow \mathbb{N}_N$	$\displaystyle\frac{1}{N}\sum_{n=0}^{N-1} g_n\exp\left(-2\pi i\frac{vn}{N}\right)$	$\displaystyle\sum_{v=0}^{N-1} \hat{g}_v\exp\left(2\pi i\frac{vn}{N}\right)$

8.6.2 Multidimensional FT

The Fourier transform can easily be extended to multidimensional signals.

Definition 8.2 (Multidimensional FT) *If $g(\boldsymbol{x}) : \mathbb{R}^D \mapsto \mathbb{C}$ is a square integrable function, that is,*

$$\int_{-\infty}^{\infty} |g(\boldsymbol{x})|\,d^D x < \infty \tag{8.55}$$

then the Fourier transform *of $g(\boldsymbol{x})$, $\hat{g}(\boldsymbol{k})$ is given by*

$$\hat{g}(\boldsymbol{k}) = \int_{-\infty}^{\infty} g(\boldsymbol{x})\exp\left(-2\pi i\boldsymbol{k}^T\boldsymbol{x}\right)\,d^D x \tag{8.56}$$

and the inverse Fourier transform *by*

$$g(\boldsymbol{x}) = \int_{-\infty}^{\infty} \hat{g}(\boldsymbol{k})\exp\left(2\pi i\boldsymbol{k}^T\boldsymbol{x}\right)\,d^D k \tag{8.57}$$

The scalar product in the exponent of the kernel $\boldsymbol{x}^T\boldsymbol{k}$ makes the kernel of the Fourier transform separable, that is, it can be written as

$$\exp\left(-2\pi i\boldsymbol{k}^T\boldsymbol{x}\right) = \prod_{d=1}^{D} \exp(-ik_d x_d) \tag{8.58}$$

Table 8.4: *Summary of the properties of the continuous D-dimensional Fourier transform; $g(\boldsymbol{x})$ and $h(\boldsymbol{x})$ are complex-valued functions, the Fourier transforms of which, $\hat{g}(\boldsymbol{k})$ and $\hat{h}(\boldsymbol{k})$, do exist; s is a real and a and b are complex constants; A and U are $D \times D$ matrices, U is unitary ($\boldsymbol{U}^{-1} = \boldsymbol{U}^T$, see Section 8.5.2)*

Property	Spatial domain	Fourier domain
Linearity	$ag(\boldsymbol{x}) + bh(\boldsymbol{x})$	$a\hat{g}(\boldsymbol{k}) + b\hat{h}(\boldsymbol{k})$
Similarity	$g(s\boldsymbol{x})$	$\hat{g}(\boldsymbol{k}/s)/\lvert s\rvert$
Similarity	$g(\boldsymbol{Ax})$	$\hat{g}\left((\boldsymbol{A}^{-1})^T\boldsymbol{k}\right)/\lvert\boldsymbol{A}\rvert$
Rotation	$g(\boldsymbol{Ux})$	$\hat{g}(\boldsymbol{Uk})$
Separability	$\displaystyle\prod_{d=1}^{D} g(x_d)$	$\displaystyle\prod_{d=1}^{D} \hat{g}(k_d)$
Shift in x space	$g(\boldsymbol{x} - \boldsymbol{x}_0)$	$\exp(-2\pi\mathrm{i}\boldsymbol{kx}_0)\hat{g}(\boldsymbol{k})$
Shift in k space	$\exp(2\pi\mathrm{i}\boldsymbol{k}_0\boldsymbol{x})g(\boldsymbol{x})$	$\hat{g}(\boldsymbol{k} - \boldsymbol{k}_0)$
Differentiation in x space	$\dfrac{\partial g(\boldsymbol{x})}{\partial x_p}$	$2\pi\mathrm{i}k_p\hat{g}(\boldsymbol{k})$
Differentiation in k space	$-2\pi\mathrm{i}x_p g(\boldsymbol{x})$	$\dfrac{\partial \hat{g}(\boldsymbol{k})}{\partial k_p}$
Definite integral	$\displaystyle\int_{-\infty}^{\infty} g(\boldsymbol{x}')\,\mathrm{d}^D x'$	$\hat{g}(0)$
Moments	$\displaystyle\int_{-\infty}^{\infty} x_p^m x_q^n g(\boldsymbol{x})\,\mathrm{d}^D x$	$\left(\dfrac{1}{-2\pi\mathrm{i}}\right)^{m+n}\left(\dfrac{\partial^m \hat{g}(\boldsymbol{k})}{\partial k_p^m}\dfrac{\partial^n \hat{g}(\boldsymbol{k})}{\partial k_q^n}\right)\bigg\vert_0$
Convolution	$\displaystyle\int_{-\infty}^{\infty} h(\boldsymbol{x}')g(\boldsymbol{x} - \boldsymbol{x}')\,\mathrm{d}^D x'$	$\hat{h}(\boldsymbol{k})\hat{g}(\boldsymbol{k})$
Multiplication	$h(\boldsymbol{x})g(\boldsymbol{x})$	$\displaystyle\int_{-\infty}^{\infty} \hat{h}(\boldsymbol{k}')\hat{g}(\boldsymbol{k} - \boldsymbol{k}')\,\mathrm{d}^D k'$
Finite difference	$g(\boldsymbol{x} + \boldsymbol{Vx}_0) - g(\boldsymbol{x} - \boldsymbol{Vx}_0)$	$2\mathrm{i}\sin(2\pi\boldsymbol{x}_0\boldsymbol{k})$
Modulation	$\cos(2\pi\boldsymbol{k}_0\boldsymbol{x})g(\boldsymbol{x})$	$(\hat{g}(\boldsymbol{k} - \boldsymbol{k}_0) + \hat{g}(\boldsymbol{k} + \boldsymbol{k}_0))/2$
Spatial correlation	$\displaystyle\int_{-\infty}^{\infty} g(\boldsymbol{x}')h(\boldsymbol{x}' + \boldsymbol{x})\,\mathrm{d}^D x'$	$\hat{g}(\boldsymbol{k})\hat{h}^*(\boldsymbol{k})$
Inner product	$\displaystyle\int_{-\infty}^{\infty} g(\boldsymbol{x})h^*(\boldsymbol{x})\,\mathrm{d}^D x$	$\displaystyle\int_{-\infty}^{\infty} \hat{g}(\boldsymbol{k})\hat{h}^*(\boldsymbol{k})\,\mathrm{d}^D k$

8.6.3 Basic properties

For reference, the basic properties of the Fourier transform are summarized in Table 8.4. An excellent review of the Fourier transform and its applications are given by [8]. Here we will point out some of the properties of the FT that are most significant for multidimensional signal processing.

Symmetries. Four types of symmetries are important for the Fourier transform:

$$
\begin{array}{lll}
\text{even} & g(-\boldsymbol{x}) = g(\boldsymbol{x}), \\
\text{odd} & g(-\boldsymbol{x}) = -g(\boldsymbol{x}), \\
\text{Hermitian} & g(-\boldsymbol{x}) = g^*(\boldsymbol{x}), \\
\text{anti-Hermitian} & g(-\boldsymbol{x}) = -g^*(\boldsymbol{x})
\end{array}
\tag{8.59}
$$

Any function $g(\boldsymbol{x})$ can be split into its even and odd parts by

$$
{}^e g(\boldsymbol{x}) = \frac{g(\boldsymbol{x}) + g(-\boldsymbol{x})}{2} \quad \text{and} \quad {}^o g(\boldsymbol{x}) = \frac{g(\boldsymbol{x}) - g(-\boldsymbol{x})}{2}
\tag{8.60}
$$

With this partition, the Fourier transform can be parted into a cosine and a sine transform:

$$
\hat{g}(\boldsymbol{k}) = 2 \int_0^\infty {}^e g(\boldsymbol{x}) \cos(2\pi \boldsymbol{k}^T \boldsymbol{x}) \, \mathrm{d}^D x + 2\mathrm{i} \int_0^\infty {}^o g(\boldsymbol{x}) \sin(2\pi \boldsymbol{k}^T \boldsymbol{x}) \, \mathrm{d}^D x \tag{8.61}
$$

It follows that if a function is even or odd, its transform is also even or odd. The full symmetry results are:

$$
\begin{array}{lll}
\text{real} & \Longleftrightarrow & \text{Hermitian} \\
\text{real and even} & \Longleftrightarrow & \text{real and even} \\
\text{real and odd} & \Longleftrightarrow & \text{imaginary and odd} \\
\text{imaginary} & \Longleftrightarrow & \text{anti-Hermitian} \\
\text{imaginary and even} & \Longleftrightarrow & \text{imaginary and even} \\
\text{imaginary and odd} & \Longleftrightarrow & \text{real and odd} \\
\text{Hermitian} & \Longleftrightarrow & \text{real} \\
\text{anti-Hermitian} & \Longleftrightarrow & \text{imaginary} \\
\text{even} & \Longleftrightarrow & \text{even} \\
\text{odd} & \Longleftrightarrow & \text{odd}
\end{array}
\tag{8.62}
$$

Separability. As the kernel of the Fourier transform (Eq. (8.58)) is separable, the transform of a separable function is also separable:

$$
\prod_{d=1}^D g(x_d) \Longleftrightarrow \prod_{d=1}^D \hat{g}(k_d) \tag{8.63}
$$

This property is essential to compute transforms of multidimensional functions efficiently from 1-D transforms because many of them are separable.

Convolution. Convolution is one of the most important operations for signal processing. It is defined by

$$(h * g)(\boldsymbol{x}) = \int\limits_{-\infty}^{\infty} g(\boldsymbol{x}')h(\boldsymbol{x} - \boldsymbol{x}')\, \mathrm{d}^D x' \tag{8.64}$$

In signal processing, the function $h(\boldsymbol{x})$ is normally zero except for a small area around zero and is often denoted as the *convolution mask*. Thus, the convolution with $h(\boldsymbol{x})$ results in a new function $g'(\boldsymbol{x})$ whose values are a kind of weighted average of $g(\boldsymbol{x})$ in a small neighborhood around $\boldsymbol{x}$. It changes the signal in a defined way, that is, makes it smoother, etc. Therefore it is also called a *filter operation*. The *convolution theorem* states:

Theorem 8.3 (Convolution) *If $g(\boldsymbol{x})$ has the Fourier transform $\hat{g}(\boldsymbol{k})$ and $h(\boldsymbol{x})$ has the Fourier transform $\hat{h}(\boldsymbol{k})$ and if the convolution integral (Eq. (8.64)) exists, then it has the Fourier transform $\hat{h}(\boldsymbol{k})\hat{g}(\boldsymbol{k})$.*

Thus, convolution of two functions means multiplication of their transforms. Likewise, convolution of two functions in the Fourier domain means multiplication in the space domain. The simplicity of convolution in the Fourier space stems from the fact that the base functions of the Fourier domain, the complex exponentials $\exp\left(2\pi i \boldsymbol{k}^T \boldsymbol{x}\right)$, are joint eigenfunctions of all convolution operators. This means that these functions are not changed by a convolution operator except for the multiplication by a factor.

From the convolution theorem, the following properties are immediately evident. Convolution is

commutative	$h * g = g * h$,	
associative	$h_1 * (h_2 * g) = (h_1 * h_2) * g$,	(8.65)
distributive over addition	$(h_1 + h_2) * g = h_1 * g + h_2 * g$	

In order to grasp the importance of these properties of convolution, we note that two operations that do not look so at first glance, are also convolution operations: the shift operation and all derivative operators. This can immediately be seen from the shift and derivative theorems (Table 8.4; [8, Chapters 5 and 6]).

In both cases the Fourier transform is just multiplied by a complex factor. The convolution mask for a shift operation S is a shifted δ distribution:

$$S(\boldsymbol{s})g(\boldsymbol{x}) = \delta(\boldsymbol{x} - \boldsymbol{s}) * g(\boldsymbol{x}) \tag{8.66}$$

The transform of the first derivative operator in x_1 direction is $2\pi i k_1$. The corresponding inverse Fourier transform of $2\pi i k_1$, that is, the convolution mask, is no longer an ordinary function ($2\pi i k_1$ is not absolutely integrable) but the derivative of the δ distribution:

$$2\pi i k_1 \quad \Longleftrightarrow \quad \delta'(x) = \frac{d\delta(x)}{dx} = \lim_{a \to 0} \frac{d}{dx}\left(\frac{\exp(-\pi x^2/a^2)}{a}\right) \qquad (8.67)$$

Of course, the derivation of the δ distribution exists—as all properties of distributions—only in the sense as a limit of a sequence of functions as shown in the preceding equation.

With the knowledge of derivative and shift operators being convolution operators, we can use the properties summarized in Eq. (8.65) to draw some important conclusions. As any convolution operator commutes with the shift operator, convolution is a shift-invariant operation. Furthermore, we can first differentiate a signal and then perform a convolution operation or vice versa and obtain the same result.

The properties in Eq. (8.65) are essential for an effective computation of convolution operations [CVA2, Section 5.6]. As we already discussed qualitatively in Section 8.5.3, the convolution operation is a linear shift-invariant operator. As the base functions of the Fourier domain are the common eigenvectors of all linear and shift-invariant operators, the convolution simplifies to a complex multiplication of the transforms.

Central-limit theorem. The central-limit theorem is mostly known for its importance in the theory of probability [2]. It also plays, however, an important role for signal processing as it is a rigorous statement of the tendency that cascaded convolution tends to approach Gaussian form ($\propto \exp(-ax^2)$). Because the Fourier transform of the Gaussian is also a Gaussian (Table 8.5), this means that *both* the Fourier transform (the transfer function) and the mask of a convolution approach Gaussian shape. Thus the central-limit theorem is central to the unique role of the Gaussian function for signal processing. The sufficient conditions under which the central-limit theorem is valid can be formulated in different ways. We use here the conditions from [2] and express the theorem with respect to convolution.

Theorem 8.4 (Central-limit theorem) *Given N functions $h_n(x)$ with zero mean $\int_{-\infty}^{\infty} h_n(x)\,dx$ and the variance $\sigma_n^2 = \int_{-\infty}^{\infty} x^2 h_n(x)\,dx$ with $z = x/\sigma$, $\sigma^2 = \sum_{n=1}^{N} \sigma_n^2$ then*

$$h = \lim_{N \to \infty} h_1 * h_2 * \ldots * h_N \propto \exp(-z^2/2) \qquad (8.68)$$

provided that

$$\lim_{N \to \infty} \sum_{n=1}^{N} \sigma_n^2 \to \infty \tag{8.69}$$

and there exists a number $\alpha > 2$ and a finite constant c such that

$$\int_{-\infty}^{\infty} x^\alpha h_n(x) \, dx < c < \infty \quad \forall n \tag{8.70}$$

The theorem is of much practical importance because—especially if h is smooth—the Gaussian shape is approximated sufficiently accurate already for values of n as low as 5.

Smoothness and compactness. The smoother a function is, the more compact is its Fourier transform. This general rule can be formulated more quantitatively if we express the smoothness by the number of derivatives that are continuous and the compactness by the asymptotic behavior for large values of k. Then we can state: If a function $g(x)$ and its first $n - 1$ derivatives are continuous, its Fourier transform decreases at least as rapidly as $|k|^{-(n+1)}$ for large k, that is, $\lim_{|k| \to \infty} |k|^n g(k) = 0$.

As simple examples we can take the box and triangle functions (see next section). The box function is discontinuous ($n = 0$), its Fourier transform, the sinc function, decays with $|k|^{-1}$. In contrast, the triangle function is continuous, but its first derivative is discontinuous. Therefore, its Fourier transform, the sinc^2 function, decays steeper with $|k|^{-2}$. In order to include also impulsive functions (δ distributions) in this relation, we note that the derivative of a discontinous function becomes impulsive. Therefore, we can state: If the nth derivative of a function becomes impulsive, the function's Fourier transform decays with $|k|^{-n}$.

The relation between smoothness and compactness is an extension of reciprocity between the spatial and Fourier domain. What is strongly localized in one domain is widely extended in the other and vice versa.

Uncertainty relation. This general law of reciprocity finds another quantitative expression in the classical *uncertainty relation* or the *bandwidth-duration product*. This theorem relates the mean square width of a function and its Fourier transform. The mean square width $(\Delta x)^2$ is defined as

$$(\Delta x)^2 = \frac{\int_{-\infty}^{\infty} x^2 |g(x)|^2}{\int_{-\infty}^{\infty} |g(x)|^2} - \left(\frac{\int_{-\infty}^{\infty} x |g(x)|^2}{\int_{-\infty}^{\infty} |g(x)|^2} \right)^2 \tag{8.71}$$

Table 8.5: *Functions and distributions that are invariant under the Fourier transform; the table contains 1-D and multidimensional functions with the dimension D*

Space domain	Fourier domain
Gauss, $\exp\left(-\pi x^T x\right)$	Gauss, $\exp\left(-\pi k^T k\right)$
$\operatorname{sech}(\pi x) = \dfrac{1}{\exp(\pi x) + \exp(-\pi x)}$	$\operatorname{sech}(\pi k) = \dfrac{1}{\exp(\pi k) + \exp(-\pi k)}$
Pole, $\lvert x \rvert^{-D/2}$	Pole, $\lvert k \rvert^{-D/2}$
δ comb, $\mathrm{III}(x/\Delta x) = \displaystyle\sum_{n=-\infty}^{\infty} \delta(x - n\Delta x)$	δ comb, $\mathrm{III}(k\Delta x) = \displaystyle\sum_{v=-\infty}^{\infty} \delta(k - v/\Delta x)$

It is essentially the variance of $\lvert g(x) \rvert^2$, a measure of the width of the distribution of the "energy" of the signal. The uncertainty relation states:

Theorem 8.5 (Uncertainty relation) *The product of the variance of* $\lvert g(x) \rvert^2$, $(\Delta x)^2$, *and of the variance of* $\lvert \hat{g}(k) \rvert^2$, $(\Delta k)^2$, *cannot be smaller than* $1/4\pi$:

$$\Delta x \Delta k \geq \frac{1}{4\pi} \tag{8.72}$$

The relations between compactness and smoothness and the uncertainty relation give some basic guidance for the design of linear filter (convolution) operators [CVA2, Chapter 6].

Invariant functions. It is well known that the Fourier transform of a Gaussian function is again a Gaussian function with reciprocal variance:

$$\exp\left(\frac{-\pi x^2}{a^2}\right) \quad \Longleftrightarrow \quad \exp\left(\frac{-\pi k^2}{a^{-2}}\right) \tag{8.73}$$

But it is less well known that there are other functions that are invariant under the Fourier transform (Table 8.5). Each of these functions has a special meaning for the Fourier transform. The δ-comb function III is the basis for the sampling theorem and establishes the relation between the lattice in the spatial domain and the *reciprocal* lattice in the Fourier domain. The functions with a pole at the origin, $\lvert x \rvert^{D/2}$ in a D-dimensional space, are the limiting signal form for which the integral over the square of the function diverges (physically speaking, the total energy of a signal just becomes infinite). Tables with Fourier transform pairs can be found in Bracewell [8].

8.7 The discrete Fourier transform (DFT)

8.7.1 One-dimensional DFT

Definition 8.3 (1-D DFT) *If* g *is an N-dimensional complex-valued vector,*

$$g = [g_0, g_1, \ldots, g_{N-1}]^T \tag{8.74}$$

then the discrete Fourier transform of g, $\hat{g}$ *is defined as*

$$\hat{g}_v = \frac{1}{\sqrt{N}} \sum_{n=0}^{N-1} g_n \exp\left(-\frac{2\pi i n v}{N}\right), \quad 0 \le v < N \tag{8.75}$$

The DFT maps the vector space of N-dimensional complex-valued vectors onto itself. The index v denotes how often the wavelength of the corresponding discrete exponential $\exp(-2\pi i n v / N)$ with the amplitude $\hat{g}_v$ fits into the interval $[0, N]$.

The back transformation is given by

$$g_n = \frac{1}{\sqrt{N}} \sum_{v=0}^{N-1} \hat{g}_v \exp\left(\frac{2\pi i n v}{N}\right), \quad 0 \le n < N \tag{8.76}$$

We can consider the DFT as the inner product of the vector g with a set of M orthonormal basis vectors, the *kernel* of the DFT:

$$b_v = \frac{1}{\sqrt{N}} \left[1, W_N^v, W_N^{2v}, \ldots, W_N^{(N-1)v}\right]^T \text{ with } W_N = \exp\left(\frac{2\pi i}{N}\right) \tag{8.77}$$

Using the base vectors b_v, the DFT reduces to

$$\hat{g}_v = b^{*T} g \quad \text{or} \quad \hat{g} = Fg \quad \text{with} \quad F = \begin{bmatrix} b_0^{*T} \\ b_1^{*T} \\ \cdots \\ b_{N-1}^{*T} \end{bmatrix} \tag{8.78}$$

This means that the coefficient $\hat{g}_v$ in the Fourier space is obtained by projecting the vector g onto the basis vector b_v. The N basis vectors b_v form an *orthonormal base* of the vector space:

$$b_v^{*T} b_v' = \delta_{v-v'} = \begin{cases} 1 & \text{if} \quad v = v' \\ 0 & \text{otherwise} \end{cases} \tag{8.79}$$

The real and imaginary parts of the basis vectors are sampled sine and cosine functions of different wavelengths with a characteristic periodicity:

$$\exp\left(\frac{2\pi i n + pN}{N}\right) = \exp\left(\frac{2\pi i n}{N}\right), \quad \forall p \in \mathbb{Z} \tag{8.80}$$

The basis vector $\boldsymbol{b}_0$ is a constant real vector.

With this relation and Eqs. (8.75) and (8.76) the DFT and the inverse DFT extend the vectors $\hat{\boldsymbol{g}}$ and $\boldsymbol{g}$, respectively, periodically over the whole space:

$$
\begin{array}{lll}
\text{Fourier domain} & \hat{g}_{v+pN} = \hat{g}_v, & \forall p \in \mathbb{Z} \\
\text{space domain} & g_{n+pN} = g_n & \forall p \in \mathbb{Z}
\end{array}
\tag{8.81}
$$

This periodicity of the DFT gives rise to an interesting geometric interpretation. According to Eq. (8.81) the border points g_{M-1} and $g_M = g_0$ are neighboring points. Thus it is natural to draw the points of the vector not on a finite line but on a unit circle, or *Fourier ring*.

With the double periodicity of the DFT, it does not matter which range of N indices we chose. The most natural choice of wave numbers is $v \in [-N/2, N/2 - 1]$, N even. With this index range the 1-D DFT and its inverse are defined as

$$
\hat{g}_v = \frac{1}{\sqrt{N}} \sum_{n=0}^{N-1} g_n W_N^{-nv} \iff g_n = \frac{1}{\sqrt{N}} \sum_{v=-N/2}^{N/2-1} \hat{g}_v W_N^{nv}
\tag{8.82}
$$

Then the wave numbers are restricted to values that meet the sampling theorem (Section 8.4.2), that is, are sampled at least two times per period. Note that the exponentials $\boldsymbol{b}_{N-v} = \boldsymbol{b}_{-v} = \boldsymbol{b}_v^*$ according to Eqs. (8.77) and (8.80).

As in the continuous case further variants for the definition of the DFT exist that differ by the factors applied to the forward and backward transform. Here again a symmetric definition was chosen that has the benefit that the base vectors become unit vectors. Other variants use the factor $1/N$ either with the forward or backward transform and not, as we did $1/\sqrt{N}$ with both transforms. The definition with the factor $1/N$ has the advantage that the zero coefficient of the DFT, $\hat{g}_0 = (1/N) \sum_{n=0}^{N-1} g_n$, directly gives the mean value of the sequence. The various definitions in use are problematic because they cause considerable confusion with factors in DFT pairs and DFT theorems.

8.7.2 Multidimensional DFT

As with the continuous FT (Section 8.6.2), it is easy to extend the DFT to higher dimensions. In order to simplify the equations, we use the abbreviation for the complex exponentials already used in Eq. (8.77)

$$
W_N = \exp\left(\frac{2\pi i}{N}\right) \quad \text{with} \quad W_N^{n+pN} = W_N^n, \; W_N^{-n} = W_N^{*n}
\tag{8.83}
$$

In two dimensions the DFT operates on $M \times N$ matrices.

Definition 8.4 (2-D DFT) *The 2-D DFT:* $\mathbb{C}^{M \times N} \mapsto \mathbb{C}^{M \times N}$ *is defined as*

$$\hat{G}_{u,v} = \frac{1}{\sqrt{MN}} \sum_{m=0}^{M-1} \left(\sum_{n=0}^{N-1} G_{m,n} W_N^{-nv} \right) W_M^{-mu} \qquad (8.84)$$

and the inverse DFT as

$$G_{mn} = \frac{1}{\sqrt{MN}} \sum_{u=0}^{M-1} \sum_{v=0}^{N-1} \hat{G}_{u,v} W_M^{mu} W_N^{nv} \qquad (8.85)$$

As in the 1-D case, the DFT expands a matrix into a set of NM orthonormal basis matrices $\boldsymbol{B}_{u,v}$, which span the $N \times M$-dimensional vector space over the field of complex numbers:

$$\boldsymbol{B}_{u,v} = \frac{1}{\sqrt{MN}} W_N^{-nv} W_M^{-mu} = \frac{1}{\sqrt{MN}} \boldsymbol{b}_u \boldsymbol{b}_v^T \qquad (8.86)$$

In this equation, the basis matrices are expressed as an *outer product* of the column and the row vector that form the basis vectors of the 1-D DFT. Thus as in the continuous case, the kernel of the multidimensional DFTs are *separable*.

As in the 1-D case (Section 8.7.1), the definition of the 2-D DFT implies a periodic extension in both domains beyond the original matrices into the whole 2-D space.

8.7.3 Basic properties

The theorems of the 2-D DFT are summarized in Table 8.6. They are very similar to the corresponding theorems of the continuous Fourier transform, which are listed in Table 8.4 for a D-dimensional FT. As in Section 8.6.3, we discuss some properties that are of importance for signal processing in more detail.

Symmetry. The DFT shows the same symmetries as the FT (Eq. (8.59)). In the definition for even and odd functions $g(-\boldsymbol{x}) = \pm g(\boldsymbol{x})$ only the continuous functions must be replaced by the corresponding vectors $g_{-n} = \pm g_n$ or matrices $G_{-m,-n} = \pm G_{m,n}$. Note that because of the periodicity of the DFT, these symmetry relations can also be written as

$$G_{-m,-n} = \pm G_{m,n} \equiv G_{M-m,N-n} = \pm G_{m,n} \qquad (8.87)$$

for even (+ sign) and odd (− sign) functions. This is equivalent to shifting the symmetry center from the origin to the point $[M/2, N/2]^T$.

The study of symmetries is important for practical purposes. Careful consideration of symmetry allows storage space to be saved and algorithms to speed up. Such a case is real-valued images. Real-valued

Table 8.6: *Summary of the properties of the 2-D DFT;* G *and* H *are complex-valued* $M \times N$ *matrices,* $\hat{G}$ *and* $\hat{H}$ *their Fourier transforms, and* a *and* b *complex-valued constants; for proofs see Poularikas [7], Cooley and Tukey [10]*

Property	Space domain	Wave-number domain
Mean	$\dfrac{1}{MN}\displaystyle\sum_{m=0}^{M-1}\sum_{n=0}^{N-1} G_{mn}$	$\hat{G}_{0,0}/\sqrt{MN}$
Linearity	$aG + bH$	$a\hat{G} + b\hat{H}$
Shifting	$G_{m-m',n-n'}$	$W_M^{-m'u} W_N^{-n'v}\hat{G}_{uv}$
Modulation	$W_M^{u'm} W_N^{v'n} G_{m,n}$	$\hat{G}_{u-u',v-v'}$
Finite differences	$(G_{m+1,n} - G_{m-1,n})/2$ $(G_{m,n+1} - G_{m,n-1})/2$	$i\sin(2\pi u/M)\hat{G}_{uv}$ $i\sin(2\pi v/N)\hat{G}_{uv}$
Spatial stretching	$G_{Pm,Qn}$	$\hat{G}_{uv}/(\sqrt{PQ})$
Frequency stretching	$G_{m,n}/(\sqrt{PQ})$	$\hat{G}_{Pu,Qv}$
Spatial sampling	$G_{m/P,n/Q}$	$\dfrac{1}{\sqrt{PQ}}\displaystyle\sum_{p=0}^{P-1}\sum_{q=0}^{Q-1}\hat{G}_{u+pM/P,v+qN/Q}$
Frequency sampling	$\dfrac{1}{\sqrt{PQ}}\displaystyle\sum_{p=0}^{P-1}\sum_{q=0}^{Q-1} G_{m+pM/P,n+qN/Q}$	$\hat{G}_{pu,qv}$
Convolution	$\displaystyle\sum_{m'=0}^{M-1}\sum_{n'=0}^{N-1} H_{m'n'} G_{m-m',n-n'}$	$\sqrt{MN}\,\hat{H}_{uv}\hat{G}_{uv}$
Multiplication	$\sqrt{MN}\,G_{mn}H_{mn}$	$\displaystyle\sum_{u'=0}^{M-1}\sum_{v'=0}^{N-1} H_{u'v'} G_{u-u',v-v'}$
Spatial correlation	$\displaystyle\sum_{m'=0}^{M-1}\sum_{n'=0}^{N-1} H_{m'n'} G_{m+m',n+n'}$	$\sqrt{N}\,\hat{H}_{uv}\hat{G}_{uv}^{*}$
Inner product	$\displaystyle\sum_{m=0}^{M-1}\sum_{n=0}^{N-1} G_{mn}H_{mn}^{*}$	$\displaystyle\sum_{u=0}^{M-1}\sum_{v=0}^{N-1} \hat{G}_{uv}\hat{H}_{uv}^{*}$
Norm	$\displaystyle\sum_{m=0}^{M-1}\sum_{n=0}^{N-1} |G_{mn}|^2$	$\displaystyle\sum_{u=0}^{M-1}\sum_{v=0}^{N-1} |\hat{G}_{uv}|^2$

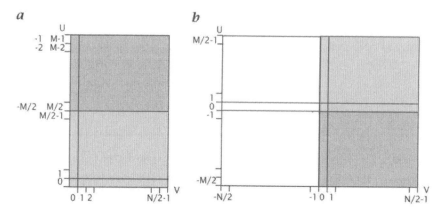

Figure 8.11: *a Half-space as computed by an in-place Fourier transform algorithm; the wave number zero is in the upper left corner; b FT with the missing half appended and remapped so that the wave number zero is in the center.*

images can be stored in half of the space as complex-valued images. From the symmetry relations Eq. (8.62) we can conclude that real-valued functions exhibit a Hermitian DFT:

$$G_{mn} = G_{mn}^* \quad \Longleftrightarrow \quad \hat{G}_{M-u,N-v} = \hat{G}_{uv}^* \qquad (8.88)$$

The complex-valued DFT of real-valued matrices is, therefore, completely determined by the values in one half-space. The other half-space is obtained by mirroring at the symmetry center $(M/2, N/2)$. Consequently, we need the same amount of storage space for the DFT of a real image as for the image itself, as only half of the complex spectrum needs to be stored.

In two and higher dimensions, matters are slightly more complex. The spectrum of a real-valued image is determined completely by the values in one half-space, but there are many ways to select the half-space. This means that all except for one component of the wave number can be negative, but that we cannot distinguish between k and $-k$, that is, between wave numbers that differ only in sign. Therefore, we can again represent the Fourier transform of real-valued images in a half-space where only one component of the wave number includes negative values. For proper representation of the spectra with zero values of this component in the middle of the image, it is necessary to interchange the upper (positive) and lower (negative) parts of the image as illustrated in Fig. 8.11.

For real-valued image sequences, again we need only a half-space to represent the spectrum. Physically, it makes the most sense to choose the half-space that contains positive frequencies. In contrast to a single image, we obtain the full wave-number space. Now we can identify the spatially identical wave numbers k and $-k$ as structures propagating in opposite directions.

Convolution. One- and two-dimensional discrete convolution are defined by

$$g'_n = \sum_{n'=0}^{N-1} h_{n'} g_{n-n'}, \quad G'_{m,n} = \sum_{m'=0}^{M-1} \sum_{n'=0}^{N-1} H_{m'n'} G_{m-m',n-n'} \quad (8.89)$$

The *convolution theorem* states:

Theorem 8.6 (Discrete convolution) *If g (G) has the Fourier transform $\hat{g}$ ($\hat{G}$) and h (H) has the Fourier transform $\hat{h}$ ($\hat{H}$), then $h * g$ ($H * G$) has the Fourier transform $\sqrt{N}\hat{h}\hat{g}$ ($\sqrt{MN}\hat{H}\hat{G}$).*

Thus, also in the discrete case convolution of two functions means multiplication of their transforms. This is true because the *shift theorem* is still valid, which ensures that the eigenfunctions of all convolution operators are the basis functions b_v of the Fourier transform.

Convolution for arbitrary dimensional signals is also

commutative	$h * g = g * h,$
associative	$h_1 * (h_2 * g) = (h_1 * h_2) * g,$
distributive over addition	$(h_1 + h_2) * g = h_1 * g + h_2 * g$

(8.90)

These equations show only the 1-D case.

8.7.4 Fast Fourier transform algorithms (FFT)

Without an effective algorithm to calculate the discrete Fourier transform, it would not be possible to apply the FT to images and other higher-dimensional signals. Computed directly after Eq. (8.84), the FT is prohibitively expensive. Not counting the calculations of the cosine and sine functions in the kernel, which can be precalculated and stored in a lookup table, the FT of an $N \times N$ image needs in total N^4 complex multiplications and $N^2(N^2 - 1)$ complex additions. Thus it is an operation of $O(N^4)$ and the urgent need arises to minimize the number of computations by finding a suitable fast algorithm. Indeed, the fast Fourier transform (FFT) algorithm first published by Cooley and Tukey [10] is the classical example of a fast algorithm. A detailed discussion on FFT-algorithms can be found in Bracewell [8], Blahut [11], and Besslich and Lu [6].

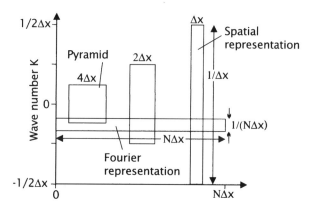

Figure 8.12: *Illustration of the interdependence of resolution in the spatial and wave-number domain in one dimension. Representations in the space domain, the wave-number domain, and the space/wave-number domain (2 planes of pyramid with half and quarter resolution) are shown.*

8.8   Scale of signals

8.8.1   Basics

In Sections 8.5 and 8.7 the representation of images in the spatial and wave-number domain were discussed. If an image is represented in the *spatial domain*, we do not have any information at all about the wave numbers contained at a point in the image. We know the position with an accuracy of the lattice constant Δx, but the local wave number at this position may be anywhere in the range of the possible wave numbers from $-1/(2\Delta x)$ to $1/(2\Delta x)$ (Fig. 8.12).

In the *wave-number domain* we have the reverse case. Each pixel in this domain represents one wave number with the highest wave-number resolution possible for the given image size, which is $-1/(N\Delta x)$ for an image with N pixels in each coordinate. But any positional information is lost, as one point in the wave-number space represents a periodic structure that is spread over the whole image (Fig. 8.12). Thus, the position uncertainty is the linear dimension of the image $N\Delta x$. In this section we will revisit both representations under the perspective of how to generate a multiscale representation of an image.

The foregoing discussion shows that the representations of an image in either the spatial or wave-number domain constitute two opposite extremes. Although the understanding of both domains is essential for any type of signal processing, the representation in either of these domains is inadequate to analyze objects in images.

In the wave-number representation the spatial structures from various independent objects are mixed up because the extracted periodic structures cover the whole image. In the spatial representation we have no information about the spatial structures contained in an object, we just know the local pixel gray values.

What we thus really need is a type of joint representation that allows for a separation into different wave-number ranges (scales) but still preserves as much spatial resolution as possible. Such a representation is called a multiscale or *multiresolution representation.*

The limits of the joint spatial/wave-number resolution are given by the *uncertainty relation* discussed in Section 8.6.3. It states that the product of the resolutions in the spatial and wave-number domain cannot be beyond a certain threshold. This is exactly what we observed already in the spatial and wave-number domains. However, besides these two domains any other combination of resolutions that meets the uncertainty relation can be chosen. Thus the resolution in wave numbers, that is, the distinction of various scales in an image, can be set to any value with a corresponding spatial resolution (Fig. 8.12). As the uncertainty relation gives only the lower limit of the joint resolution, it is important to devise efficient data structures that approach this limit.

In the last two decades a number of various concepts have been developed for multiresolution signal processing. Some trace back to the early roots of signal processing. This includes various techniques to filter signals for certain scale ranges such as the windowed Fourier transform, Gabor filters, polar separable quadrature filters, and filters steerable in scale (Section 8.8).

Some of these techniques are directly suitable to compute a *local wave number* that reflects the dominant scale in a local neighborhood. Multigrid image structures in the form of pyramids are another early and efficient multiresolution [12]. More recent developments are the *scale space* (Section 8.8) and *wavelets* [13, 14].

Although all of these techniques seem to be quite different at first glance, this it not the case. They have much in common; they merely look at the question of multiresolutional signal representation from a different point of view. Thus an important issue in this chapter is to work out the relations between the various approaches.

An early account on multiresolution imaging was given by Rosenfeld [15]. The standard work on linear scale space theory is by Lindeberg [16] (see also CVA2 [Chapter 11]), and nonlinear scale space theory is treated by Weickert [17] (see also Chapter 12).

8.8.2 Windowed Fourier transform

One way to a multiresolutional signal representation starts with the Fourier transform. If the Fourier transform is applied only to a section of the image and this section is moved around through the whole image, then a joint spatial/wave-number resolution is achieved. The spatial resolution is given by the size of the window and due to the uncertainty relation (Section 8.6.3), the wave-number resolution is reduced by the ratio of the image size to the window size. The window function $w(x)$ must not be a box function. Generally, a useful window function has a maximum at the origin, is even and isotropic, and decreases monotonically with increasing distance from the origin. This approach to a joint space/wave-number representation is the *windowed Fourier transform*. It is defined by

$$\hat{g}(x, k_0) = \int_{-\infty}^{\infty} g(x') w(x' - x) \exp(-2\pi i k_0 x') \, dx'^2 \qquad (8.91)$$

The integral in Eq. (8.91) looks almost like a convolution integral (Section 8.6.3). To convert it into a convolution integral we make use of the fact that the window function is even ($w(-k) = w(k)$) and rearrange the second part of Eq. (8.91):

$$w(x' - x) \exp(-2\pi i k_0 x') =$$
$$w(x - x') \exp(2\pi i k_0 (x - x')) \exp(-2\pi i k_0 x)$$

Then we can write Eq. (8.91) as a convolution:

$$\hat{g}(x, k_0) = [g(x) * w(x) \exp(2\pi i k_0 x)] \exp(-2\pi i k_0 x) \qquad (8.92)$$

This means that the local Fourier transform corresponds to a convolution with the complex convolution kernel $w(x) \exp(2\pi i k_0 x)$ except for a phase factor $\exp(-2\pi i k_0 x)$. Using the *shift theorem* (Table 8.4), the transfer function of the convolution kernel can be computed to be

$$w(x) \exp(2\pi i k_0 x) \iff \hat{w}(k - k_0) \qquad (8.93)$$

This means that the convolution kernel is a *bandpass filter* with a peak wave number of k_0. The width of the bandpass is inversely proportional to the width of the window function. In this way, the spatial and wave-number resolutions are interrelated to each other. As an example, we take a Gaussian window function

$$w(x) = \frac{1}{\sigma^D} \exp\left(-\pi \frac{|x|^2}{\sigma^2}\right) \iff \hat{w}(k) = \exp\left(-\pi \frac{|k|^2}{\sigma^{-2}}\right) \qquad (8.94)$$

The Gaussian window function reaches the theoretical limit set by the uncertainty relation and is thus an optimal choice; a better wave-number resolution cannot be achieved with a given spatial resolution.

The windowed Fourier transform Equation (8.91) delivers a complex filter response. This has the advantage that both the phase and the amplitude of a bandpass-filtered signal are retrieved.

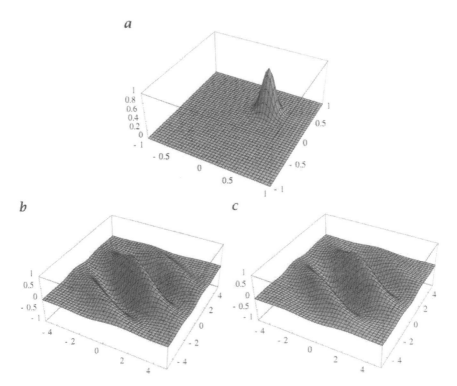

Figure 8.13: *a Transfer function (Eq. (8.95)); **b** even; and **c** odd part of the filter mask (Eq. (8.97)) of a Gabor filter.*

8.8.3 Gabor filter

Definition. A *Gabor filter* is a bandpass filter that selects a certain wavelength range around the center wavelength k_0 using the Gaussian function. The Gabor filter is very similar to the windowed Fourier transform if the latter is used with a Gaussian window function. The transfer function of the Gabor filter is real but asymmetric and defined as

$$\hat{G}(k) = \exp\left(-\pi|k - k_0)|^2 \sigma_x^2\right) \tag{8.95}$$

From this equation it is obvious that a Gabor filter is only a useful bandpass filter if it does not include the origin, that is, it is $\hat{G}(0) = 0$. This condition is met in good approximation if $|k_0|\sigma_x > 3$.

The filter mask (point spread function) of these filters can be computed easily with the shift theorem (Table 8.4):

$$G(x) = \frac{1}{\sigma^D} \exp(2\pi i k_0 x) \exp\left(-\frac{\pi|x|^2}{\sigma_x^2}\right) \tag{8.96}$$

The complex filter mask can be split into an even real and an odd imaginary part:

$$G_+(\boldsymbol{x}) \;=\; \frac{1}{\sigma^D} \cos(\boldsymbol{k}_0 \boldsymbol{x}) \exp\left(-\frac{\pi |\boldsymbol{x}|^2}{\sigma_x^2}\right)$$

$$G_-(\boldsymbol{x}) \;=\; \frac{1}{\sigma^D} \sin(\boldsymbol{k}_0 \boldsymbol{x}) \exp\left(-\frac{\pi |\boldsymbol{x}|^2}{\sigma_x^2}\right) \tag{8.97}$$

Quadrature filters and analytic signals. Gabor filters are examples of quadrature filters. This general class of filters generates a special type of signal known as the *analytic signal* from a real-valued signal.

It is the easiest way to introduce the quadrature filter with the complex form of its transfer function. Essentially, the transfer function of a D-dimensional quadrature filter is zero for one half-space of the Fourier domain parted by the hyperplane $\boldsymbol{k}^T\bar{\boldsymbol{n}} = 0$:

$$\hat{q}(\boldsymbol{k}) = \begin{cases} 2h(\boldsymbol{k}) & \boldsymbol{k}^T\bar{\boldsymbol{n}} > 0 \\ 0 & \text{otherwise} \end{cases} \tag{8.98}$$

where $h(\boldsymbol{k})$ is a real-valued function. Equation (8.98) can be separated into an even and odd function:

$$\hat{q}_+(\boldsymbol{k}) \;=\; (\hat{q}(\boldsymbol{k}) + \hat{q}(-\boldsymbol{k}))/2$$

$$\hat{q}_-(\boldsymbol{k}) \;=\; (\hat{q}(\boldsymbol{k}) - \hat{q}(-\boldsymbol{k}))/2 \tag{8.99}$$

The relation between the even and odd part of the signal response can be described by the *Hilbert transform*:

$$\hat{q}_-(\boldsymbol{k}) = \mathrm{i}\,\mathrm{sgn}(\boldsymbol{k}^T\bar{\boldsymbol{n}})\hat{q}_+(\boldsymbol{k}) \iff q_-(\boldsymbol{x}) = \frac{\mathrm{i}}{\pi} \int\limits_{-\infty}^{\infty} \frac{q_+(\boldsymbol{x}')}{(\boldsymbol{x}' - \boldsymbol{x})^T\bar{\boldsymbol{n}}}\, \mathrm{d}^D\boldsymbol{x}' \tag{8.100}$$

The even and odd part of a quadrature filter can be combined into a complex-valued signal by

$$q_A = q_+ - \mathrm{i}q_- \tag{8.101}$$

From Eq. (8.100) we can then see that this combination is consistent with the definition of the transfer function of the quadrature filter in Eq. (8.98).

The basic characteristic of the analytic filter is that its even and odd part have the *same* magnitude of the transfer function but that one is even and real and the other is odd and imaginary. Thus the filter responses of the even and odd part are shifted in phase by 90°. Thus the even part is cosine-like and the odd part is sine-like—as can be seen

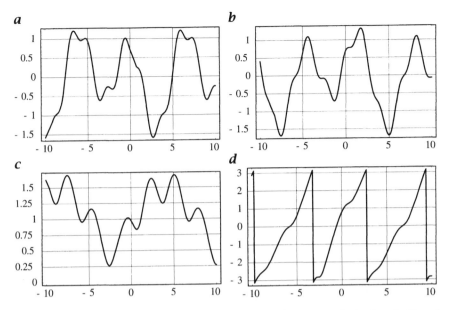

Figure 8.14: *Representation of a filtered 1-D signal as an analytic signal: Signal filtered with **a** the even and **b** the odd part of a quadrature filter; **c** amplitude; and **d** phase signal.*

from the Gabor filter (Fig. 8.13b and c)—and they are shifted in phase by 90° (Fig. 8.14).

Although the transfer function of the analytic filter is real, it results in a complex signal because it is asymmetric. For a real signal no information is lost by suppressing the negative wave numbers. They can be reconstructed as the Fourier transform of a real signal is Hermitian (Section 8.6.3).

The analytic signal can be regarded as just another representation of a real signal with two important properties. The magnitude of the analytic signal gives the *local amplitude* (Fig. 8.14c)

$$|q_A|^2 = q_+^2 + q_-^2 \qquad (8.102)$$

and the argument the *local phase* (Fig. 8.14d)

$$\arg(\mathcal{A}) = \arctan\left(\frac{-\mathcal{H}}{\mathcal{I}}\right) \qquad (8.103)$$

While the concept of the analytic signal works with any type of 1-D signal, it must be used with much more care in higher-dimensional signals. These problems are related to the fact that an analytical signal cannot be defined for all wave numbers that lie on the hyperplane defined by $k^T \bar{n} = 0$ partitioning the Fourier domain in two half-spaces.

For these wave numbers the odd part of the quadrature filter is zero. Thus it is not possible to compute the local amplitude nor the local phase of the signal. This problem can only be avoided if the transfer function of the quadrature filter is zero at the hyperplane. For a phase definition in two dimensions that does not show these restrictions, see CVA3 [Chapter 10].

8.8.4 Local wave number

The key to determining the local wave number is the *phase* of the signal. As an introduction we discuss a simple example and consider the 1-D periodic signal $g(x) = g_0 \cos(kx)$. The argument of the cosine function is known as the phase $\phi(x) = kx$ of the periodic signal. This is a linear function of the position and the wave number. Thus, we obtain the wave number of the periodic signal by computing the first-order spatial derivative of the phase signal

$$\frac{\partial \phi(x)}{\partial x} = k \qquad (8.104)$$

These simple considerations emphasize the significant role of the phase in signal processing.

Local wave number from phase gradients.   In order to determine the local wave number, we need to compute just the first spatial derivative of the phase signal. This derivative has to be applied in the same direction as the Hilbert or quadrature filter. The phase is given by

$$\phi(\boldsymbol{x}) = \arctan\left(\frac{-g_+(\boldsymbol{x})}{g_-(\boldsymbol{x})}\right) \qquad (8.105)$$

Direct computation of the partial derivatives from Eq. (8.105) is not advisable, however, because of the inherent discontinuities in the phase signal. A phase computed with the inverse tangent restricts the phase to the main interval $[-\pi, \pi[$ and thus inevitably leads to a wrapping of the phase signal from π to $-\pi$ with the corresponding discontinuities. As pointed out by Fleet [18], this problem can be avoided by computing the phase gradient directly from the gradients of $q_+(\boldsymbol{x})$ and $q_-(\boldsymbol{x})$:

$$\begin{aligned}
k_p &= \frac{\partial \phi(\boldsymbol{x})}{\partial x_p} \\[2mm]
&= \frac{\partial}{\partial x_p} \arctan(-q_+(\boldsymbol{x})/q_-(\boldsymbol{x})) \qquad (8.106) \\[2mm]
&= \frac{1}{q_+^2(\boldsymbol{x}) + q_-^2(\boldsymbol{x})} \left(\frac{\partial q_+(\boldsymbol{x})}{\partial x_p} q_-(\boldsymbol{x}) - \frac{\partial q_-(\boldsymbol{x})}{\partial x_p} q_+(\boldsymbol{x})\right)
\end{aligned}$$

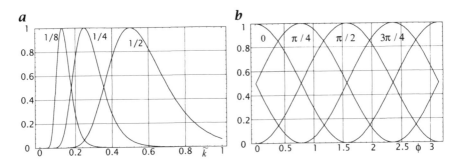

Figure 8.15: *a Radial and b angular part of quadrature filter according to Eq. (8.107) with l = 2 and B = 2 in different directions and with different peak wave numbers.*

This formulation of the phase gradient also eliminates the need for using trigonometric functions to compute the phase signal and is, therefore, significantly faster.

Local wave number from filter ratios. With *polar separable* quadrature filters $(\hat{r}(k)\hat{d}(\phi))$ as introduced by Knutsson [19] another scheme for computation of the local scale is possible. These classes of filters are defined by

$$\hat{r}(k) = \exp\left[-\frac{(\ln k - \ln k_0)^2}{(B/2)^2 \ln 2}\right]$$

$$\hat{d}(\phi) = \begin{cases} \cos^{2l}(\phi - \phi_k) & |\phi - \phi_k| < \pi/2 \\ 0 & \text{otherwise} \end{cases} \tag{8.107}$$

In this equation, the complex notation for quadrature filters is used as introduced at the beginning of this section. The filter is directed into the angle ϕ_k.

The filter is continuous, as the cosine function is zero in the partition plane for the two half-spaces ($|\phi - \phi_k| = \pi/2$). The constant k_0 denotes the peak wave number. The constant B determines the half-width of the wave number in number of octaves and l the angular resolution of the filter. In a logarithmic wave-number scale, the filter has the shape of a Gaussian function. Therefore, the radial part has a *lognormal* shape. Figure 8.15 shows the radial and angular part of the transfer function.

The *lognormal* form of the radial part of the quadrature filter sets is the key for a direct estimate of the *local wave number* of a narrowband signal. According to Eq. (8.107), we can write the radial part of the transfer function as

$$\hat{r}_l(k) = \exp\left[-\frac{(\ln k - \ln k_l)^2}{2\sigma^2 \ln 2}\right] \tag{8.108}$$

We examine the ratio of the output of two different radial center frequencies k_1 and k_2 and obtain:

$$
\begin{aligned}
\frac{\hat{r}_2}{\hat{r}_1} &= \exp\left[-\frac{(\ln k - \ln k_2)^2 - (\ln k - \ln k_1)^2}{2\sigma^2 \ln 2} \right] \\
&= \exp\left[\frac{2(\ln k_2 - \ln k_1)\ln k + \ln^2 k_2 - \ln^2 k_1}{2\sigma^2 \ln 2} \right] \\
&= \exp\left[\frac{(\ln k_2 - \ln k_1)[\ln k - 1/2(\ln k_2 + \ln k_1)]}{\sigma^2 \ln 2} \right] \\
&= \exp\left[\frac{\ln(k/\sqrt{k_2 k_1})\,\ln(k_2/k_1)}{\sigma^2 \ln 2} \right] \\
&= \left(\frac{k}{\sqrt{k_1 k_2}} \right)^{\ln(k_2/k_1)/(\sigma^2 \ln 2)}
\end{aligned}
$$

Generally, the ratio of two different radial filters is directly related to the local wave number. The relation becomes particularly simple if the exponent in the last expression is one. This is the case, for example, if the wave-number ratio of the two filters is two ($k_2/k_1 = 2$ and $\sigma = 1$). Then

$$
\frac{\hat{r}_2}{\hat{r}_1} = \frac{k}{\sqrt{k_1 k_2}} \tag{8.109}
$$

8.9 Scale space and diffusion

As we have seen with the example of the windowed Fourier transform in the previous section, the introduction of a characteristic *scale* adds a new coordinate to the representation of image data. Besides the spatial resolution, we have a new parameter that characterizes the current resolution level of the image data. The scale parameter is denoted by ξ. A data structure that consists of a sequence of images with different resolutions is known as a *scale space*; we write $g(x, \xi)$ to indicate the scale space of the image $g(x)$. Such a sequence of images can be generated by repeated convolution with an appropriate smoothing filter kernel.

This section is considered a brief introduction into scale spaces. For an authoritative monograph on scale spaces, see Lindeberg [16].

8.9.1 General properties of a scale space

In this section, we discuss some general conditions that must be met by a filter kernel generating a scale space. We will discuss two basic requirements. First, new details must not be added with increasing scale parameter. From the perspective of information theory, we may say that the information content in the signal should continuously decrease with the scale parameter.

The second property is related to the general principle of *scale invariance*. This basically means that we can start smoothing the signal at any scale parameter in the scale space and still obtain the same scale space.

Minimum-maximum principle. The information-decreasing property of the scale space with ξ can be formulated mathematically in different ways. We express it here with the *minimum-maximum principle*, which states that local extrema must not be enhanced. This means that the gray value at a local maximum or minimum must not increase or decrease, respectively. For the physical process of diffusion this is an intuitive property. For example, in a heat transfer problem, a hot spot must not become hotter or a cool spot cooler.

Semigroup property. The second important property of the scale space is related to the *scale invariance* principle. We want to start the generating process at any scale parameter and still obtain the same scale space. More quantitatively, we can formulate this property as

$$\mathcal{B}(\xi_2)\mathcal{B}(\xi_1) = \mathcal{B}(\xi_1 + \xi_2) \qquad (8.110)$$

This means that the smoothing of the scale space at the scale ξ_1 by an operator with the scale ξ_2 is equivalent to the application of the scale space operator with the scale $\xi_1 + \xi_2$ to the original image. Alternatively, we can state that the representation at the coarser level ξ_2 can be computed from the representation at the finer level ξ_1 by applying

$$\mathcal{B}(\xi_2) = \mathcal{B}(\xi_2 - \xi_1)\mathcal{B}(\xi_1) \quad \text{with} \quad \xi_2 > \xi_1 \qquad (8.111)$$

In mathematics the properties Eqs. (8.110) and (8.111) are referred to as the *semigroup property*.

Conversely, we can ask what scale space generating kernels exist that meet both the minimum-maximum principle and the semigroup property. The answer to this question may be surprising. As shown by Lindeberg [16, Chapter 2], the Gaussian kernel is the *only* convolution kernel that meets both criteria and is in addition isotropic and homogeneous. From yet another perspective this feature puts the Gaussian convolution kernel into a unique position for signal processing. With respect to the Fourier transform we have already discussed that the Gaussian function is one of the few functions with a shape that is invariant under the Fourier transform (Table 8.5) and optimal in the sense of the uncertainty relation (Section 8.6.3). In Section 9.5.4 we will see in addition that the Gaussian function is the only function that is separable and isotropic.

8.9.2 Linear scale spaces

Generation by a diffusion process. The generation of a scale space requires a process that can blur images to a controllable degree. Diffusion is a transport process that tends to level out concentration differences. In physics, diffusion processes govern the transport of heat, matter, and momentum [20] leading to an ever increasing equalization of spatial concentration differences. If we identify the time with the scale parameter ξ, the diffusion process thus establishes a scale space.

To apply a diffusion process to an image, we regard the gray value g as the concentration of a scalar property. The elementary law of diffusion states that the flux density j is directed against the concentration gradient ∇g and is proportional to it:

$$j = -D\nabla g \qquad (8.112)$$

where the constant D is known as the *diffusion coefficient*. Using the continuity equation

$$\frac{\partial g}{\partial t} + \nabla j = 0 \qquad (8.113)$$

the diffusion equation is

$$\frac{\partial g}{\partial t} = \nabla(D\nabla g) \qquad (8.114)$$

For the case of a homogeneous diffusion process (D does not depend on the position), the equation reduces to

$$\frac{\partial g}{\partial t} = D\Delta g \quad \text{where} \quad \Delta = \sum_{d=1}^{D} \frac{\partial^2}{\partial x_d^2} \qquad (8.115)$$

It is easy to show that the general solution to this equation is equivalent to a convolution with a smoothing mask. To this end, we perform a spatial Fourier transform that results in

$$\frac{\partial \hat{g}(k)}{\partial t} = -4\pi^2 D|k|^2 \hat{g}(k) \qquad (8.116)$$

reducing the equation to a linear first-order differential equation with the general solution

$$\hat{g}(k, t) = \exp(-4\pi^2 Dt|k|^2)\hat{g}(k, 0) \qquad (8.117)$$

where $\hat{g}(k, 0)$ is the Fourier-transformed image at time zero.

Multiplication of the image in Fourier space with the Gaussian function in Eq. (8.117) is equivalent to a convolution with the same function but of reciprocal width. Using

$$\exp\left(-\pi a|k|^2\right) \iff \frac{1}{a^{d/2}} \exp\left(-\frac{|x|^2}{a/\pi}\right) \qquad (8.118)$$

we obtain with $a = 4\pi Dt$ for a d-dimensional space

$$g(\boldsymbol{x}, t) = \frac{1}{(2\pi)^{d/2}\sigma^d(t)} \exp\left(-\frac{|\boldsymbol{x}|^2}{2\sigma^2(t)}\right) * g(\boldsymbol{x}, 0) \qquad (8.119)$$

with

$$\sigma(t) = \sqrt{2Dt} \qquad (8.120)$$

Now we can replace the physical time coordinate by the scale parameter ξ with

$$\xi = 2Dt = \sigma^2 \qquad (8.121)$$

and finally obtain

$$g(\boldsymbol{x}, \xi) = \frac{1}{(2\pi\xi)^{d/2}} \exp\left(-\frac{|\boldsymbol{x}|^2}{2\xi}\right) * g(\boldsymbol{x}, 0) \qquad (8.122)$$

We have written all equations in such a way that they can be used for signals of any dimension. Thus, Eqs. (8.117) and (8.119) can also be applied to scale spaces of image sequences. The scale parameter is *not* identical to the time although we used a physical diffusion process that proceeds with time to derive it. If we compute a scale-space representation of an image sequence, it is useful to scale the time coordinate with a characteristic velocity u_0 so that it has the same dimension as the spatial coordinates: $t' = u_0 t$. For digital signals (Section 8.3), of course, no such scaling is required. It is automatically fixed by the spatial and temporal sampling intervals: $u_0 = \Delta x / \Delta t$.

As an illustration, Fig. 8.16 shows some individual images of the scale space of a 2-D image at values of ξ as indicated. This example nicely demonstrates a general property of scale spaces. With increasing scale parameter ξ, the signals become increasingly blurred, more and more details are lost. This feature can be most easily seen by the transfer function of the scale-space representation in Eq. (8.117). The transfer function is always positive and monotonically decreasing with the increasing scale parameter ξ for all wave numbers. This means that no structure is amplified. All structures are attenuated with increasing ξ, and smaller structures always faster than coarser structures. In the limit of $\xi \to \infty$ the scale space converges to a constant image with the mean gray value. A certain feature exists only over a certain scale range. We can observe that edges and lines disappear and two objects merge into one.

Accelerated scale spaces. Despite the mathematical beauty of scale-space generation with a Gaussian convolution kernel, this approach has

Figure 8.16: *Scale space of a 2-D image:* **a** *original image;* **b**, **c**, *and* **d** *at scale parameters σ 1, 2, and 4, respectively.*

one significant disadvantage. The standard deviation of the smoothing increases only with the square root of the scale parameter ξ (see Eq. (8.121)). While smoothing goes fast for fine scales, it becomes increasingly slower for larger scales.

There is a simple cure for this problem. We need a diffusion process where the diffusion constant increases with time. We first discuss a diffusion coefficient that increases linearly with time. This approach results in the differential equation

$$\frac{\partial g}{\partial t} = D_0 t \Delta g \qquad (8.123)$$

A spatial Fourier transform results in

$$\frac{\partial \hat{g}(\boldsymbol{k})}{\partial t} = -4\pi^2 D_0 t |\boldsymbol{k}|^2 \hat{g}(\boldsymbol{k}) \qquad (8.124)$$

This equation has the general solution

$$\hat{g}(\boldsymbol{k}, t) = \exp(-2\pi^2 D_0 t^2 |\boldsymbol{k}|^2) \hat{g}(\boldsymbol{k}, 0) \qquad (8.125)$$

which is equivalent to a convolution in the spatial domain as in Eq. (8.121) with $\xi = \sigma^2 = D_0 t^2$. Now the standard deviation for the smoothing is proportional to time for a diffusion process with a diffusion coefficient that increases linearly in time. As the scale parameter ξ is proportional to the time squared, we denote this scale space as the *quadratic scale space*. This modified scale space still meets the minimum-maximum principle and the semigroup property.

For even more accelerated smoothing, we can construct a *logarithmic scale space*, that is, a scale space where the scale parameter increases logarithmically with time. We use a diffusion coefficient that increases exponentially in time:

$$\frac{\partial g}{\partial t} = D_0 \exp(t/\tau)\Delta g \tag{8.126}$$

A spatial Fourier transform results in

$$\frac{\partial \hat{g}(k)}{\partial t} = -4\pi^2 D_0 \exp(t/\tau)|k|^2 \hat{g}(k) \tag{8.127}$$

The general solution of this equation in the Fourier domain is

$$\hat{g}(k, t) = \exp(-4\pi^2 D_0 (\exp(t/\tau)/\tau)|k|^2)\hat{g}(k, 0) \tag{8.128}$$

Again, the transfer function and thus the convolution kernel have the same form as in Eqs. (8.117) and (8.125), now with the scale parameter

$$\xi_l = \sigma^2 = \frac{2D_0}{\tau} \exp(t/\tau) \tag{8.129}$$

This means that the logarithm of the scale parameter ξ is now proportional to the limiting scales still contained in the scale space. Essentially, we can think of the quadratic and logarithmic scale spaces as a coordinate transform of the scale parameter that efficiently compresses the scale space coordinate:

$$\xi_q \propto \sqrt{\xi}, \qquad \xi_l \propto \ln(\xi) \tag{8.130}$$

8.9.3 Differential scale spaces

The interest in a *differential scale space* stems from the fact that we want to select optimum scales for processing of features in images. In a differential scale space, the change of the image with scale is emphasized. We use the transfer function of the scale-space kernel Equation (8.117), which is also valid for quadratic and logarithmic scale spaces. The general solution for the scale space can be written in the Fourier space as

$$\hat{g}(k, \xi) = \exp(-2\pi^2 |k|^2 \xi)\hat{g}(k, 0) \tag{8.131}$$

Differentiating this signal with respect to the scale parameter ξ yields

$$
\begin{aligned}
\frac{\partial \hat{g}(\boldsymbol{k}, \xi)}{\partial \xi} &= -2\pi^2 |\boldsymbol{k}|^2 \exp(-2\pi^2 |\boldsymbol{k}|^2 \xi) \hat{g}(\boldsymbol{k}, 0) \\
&= -2\pi^2 |\boldsymbol{k}|^2 \hat{g}(\boldsymbol{k}, \xi)
\end{aligned}
\tag{8.132}
$$

The multiplication with $-4\pi^2 |\boldsymbol{k}|^2$ is equivalent to a second-order spatial derivative (Table 8.4), the *Laplacian operator*. Thus we can write in the spatial domain

$$
\frac{\partial g(\boldsymbol{x}, \xi)}{\partial \xi} = \frac{1}{2} \Delta g(\boldsymbol{x}, \xi)
\tag{8.133}
$$

Equations (8.132) and (8.133) constitute a basic property of the differential scale space. The differential scale space is equivalent to a second-order spatial derivation with the Laplacian operator and thus leads to an isotropic *bandpass decomposition* of the image. This is, of course, not surprising as the diffusion equation in Eq. (8.115) relates just the first-order temporal derivative with the second-order spatial derivative. The transfer function at the scale ξ is

$$
-2\pi^2 |\boldsymbol{k}|^2 \exp(-2\pi^2 \xi |\boldsymbol{k}|^2)
\tag{8.134}
$$

For small wave numbers, the transfer function is proportional to $-|\boldsymbol{k}|^2$. It reaches a maximum at

$$
k_{\max} = \frac{1}{\sqrt{2\pi^2 \xi}}
\tag{8.135}
$$

and then decays exponentially.

8.9.4 Discrete scale spaces

The construction of a *discrete scale space* requires a discretization of the diffusion equation and *not* of the convolution kernel [16]. We start with a discretization of the 1-D diffusion equation

$$
\frac{\partial g(x, \xi)}{\partial \xi} = \frac{\partial^2 g(x, \xi)}{\partial x^2}
\tag{8.136}
$$

The derivatives are replaced by discrete differences in the following way:

$$
\begin{aligned}
\frac{\partial g(x, \xi)}{\partial \xi} &\approx \frac{g(x, \xi + \Delta\xi) - g(x, \xi)}{\Delta\xi} \\
\frac{\partial^2 g(x, \xi)}{\partial x^2} &\approx \frac{g(x + \Delta x, \xi) - 2g(x, \xi) + g(x - \Delta x, \xi)}{\Delta x^2}
\end{aligned}
\tag{8.137}
$$

This leads to the following iteration scheme for computing a discrete scale space:

$$g(x, \xi + \Delta\xi) = \Delta\xi g(x + \Delta x, \xi) + (1 - 2\Delta\xi)g(x, \xi) + \Delta\xi g(x - \Delta x, \xi)$$
$$(8.138)$$

or written with discrete coordinates

$$g_{n,\xi+1} = \Delta\xi g_{n+1,\xi} + (1 - 2\Delta\xi)g_{n,\xi} + \Delta\xi g_{n-1,\xi} \qquad (8.139)$$

Lindeberg [16] shows that this iteration results in a discrete scale space that meets the minimum-maximum principle and the semi-group property if and only if

$$\Delta\xi \le \frac{1}{4} \qquad (8.140)$$

The limit case of $\Delta\xi = 1/4$ leads to the especially simple iteration

$$g_{n,\xi+1} = 1/4 g_{n+1,\xi} + 1/2 g_{n,\xi} + 1/4 g_{n-1,\xi} \qquad (8.141)$$

Each step of the scale-space computation is given by a smoothing of the signal with the binomial mask $\boldsymbol{B}^2 = [1/4 \ 1/2 \ 1/4]$ (Section 9.5.4). We can also formulate the general scale-space generating operator in Eq. (8.139) using the convolution operator $\mathcal{B}$. Written in the operator notation introduced in Section 9.1.3, the operator for one iteration step to generate the discrete scale space is

$$(1 - \epsilon)\mathcal{I} + \epsilon\mathcal{B}^2 \quad \text{with} \quad \epsilon \le 1 \qquad (8.142)$$

where $\mathcal{I}$ denotes the identy operator.

This expression is significant, as it can be extended directly to higher dimensions by replacing $\mathcal{B}^2$ with a correspondingly higher-dimensional smoothing operator. The convolution mask $\boldsymbol{B}^2$ is the simplest mask in the class of smoothing binomial filters. These filters will be discussed in Section 9.5.4. A detailed discussion of discrete linear scale spaces is given by Lindeberg [16, Chapters 3 and 4].

8.10 Multigrid representations

8.10.1 Basics

The scale space discussed in Section 8.9 has one significant disadvantage. The use of the additional scale parameter adds a new dimension to the images and thus leads to an explosion of the data storage requirements and, in turn, the computational overhead for generating the scale space and for analyzing it. Thus, it is not surprising that before the evolution of the scale space more efficient multiscale storage schemes, especially pyramids, found widespread application in image processing. With data structures of this type, the resolution of the images decreases to such an extent as the scale increases. In this way an optimum balance between spatial and wave-number resolution is achieved in the sense of the *uncertainty relation* (Section 8.6.3). Data structures of this type are known as *multiresolution representations* [15].

The basic idea is quite simple. While the representation of fine scales requires the full resolution, coarser scales can be represented at lower resolution. This leads to a scale space with smaller and smaller images as the scale parameter increases. In the following two sections we will discuss the *Gaussian pyramid* (Section 8.10.2) and the *Laplacian pyramid* (Section 8.10.3) as efficient discrete implementations of discrete scale spaces. In addition, while the Gaussian pyramid constitutes a standard scale space, the Laplacian pyramid is a discrete version of a differential scale space (Section 8.9.3). The Gaussian and Laplacian pyramids are examples of multigrid data structures, which were introduced into digital image processing in the early 1980s and since then have led to a tremendous increase in speed of image-processing algorithms. A new research area, *multiresolutional image processing*, was established [15].

8.10.2 Gaussian pyramid

When *subsampling* an image, for example, by taking every second pixel in every second line it is important to consider the *sampling theorem* (Section 8.4.2). Before subsampling, the image must be smoothed to an extent that no aliasing occurs in the subsampled image. Consequently, for subsampling by a factor two, we must ensure that all structures, which are sampled less than four times per wavelength, are suppressed by an appropriate smoothing filter. This means that size reduction must go hand-in-hand with appropriate smoothing.

Generally, the requirement for the smoothing filter can be formulated as

$$\hat{B}(\tilde{\boldsymbol{k}}) = 0 \quad \forall \tilde{k}_d \geq \frac{1}{r_d} \tag{8.143}$$

where r_d is the subsampling rate in the direction of the dth coordinate.

The combined smoothing and size reduction can be expressed in a single operator by using the following notation to compute the $q + 1$th level of the Gaussian pyramid from the qth level:

$$\boldsymbol{G}^{(q+1)} = \mathcal{B}_{\downarrow 2}\boldsymbol{G}^{(q)} \tag{8.144}$$

The number behind the $\downarrow$ in the index denotes the subsampling rate. Level 0 of the pyramid is the original image: $\boldsymbol{G}^{(0)} = \boldsymbol{G}$.

If we repeat the smoothing and subsampling operations iteratively, we obtain a series of images, which is called the *Gaussian pyramid*. From level to level, the resolution decreases by a factor of two; the size of the images decreases correspondingly. Consequently, we can think of the series of images as being arranged in the form of a pyramid.

The pyramid does not require much storage space. Generally, if we consider the formation of a pyramid from a D-dimensional image with a subsampling factor of two and N pixels in each coordinate direction, the total number of pixels is given by

$$N^D \left(1 + \frac{1}{2^D} + \frac{1}{2^{2D}} + \cdots\right) < N^D \frac{2^D}{2^D - 1} \qquad (8.145)$$

For a 2-D image, the whole pyramid needs just $1/3$ more space than the original image, for a 3-D image only $1/7$ more. Likewise, the computation of the pyramid is equally effective. The *same* smoothing filter is applied to each level of the pyramid. Thus the computation of the *whole* pyramid needs only $4/3$ and $8/7$ times more operations than for the first level of a 2-D and 3-D image, respectively.

The pyramid brings large scales into the range of local neighborhood operations with small kernels. Moreover, these operations are performed efficiently. Once the pyramid has been computed, we can perform neighborhood operations on large scales in the upper levels of the pyramid—because of the smaller image sizes—much more efficiently than for finer scales.

The Gaussian pyramid constitutes a series of low-pass filtered images in which the cutoff wave numbers decrease by a factor of two (an octave) from level to level. Thus the Gaussian pyramid resembles a logarithmic scale space. Only a few levels of the pyramid are necessary to span a wide range of wave numbers. If we stop the pyramid at an 8×8 image, we can usefully compute only a seven-level pyramid from a 512×512 image.

8.10.3 Laplacian pyramid

From the Gaussian pyramid, another pyramid type can be derived, that is, the *Laplacian pyramid*. This type of pyramid is the discrete counterpart to the *differential scale space* discussed in Section 8.9.3 and leads to a sequence of bandpass-filtered images. In contrast to the Fourier transform, the Laplacian pyramid leads only to a coarse wave-number decomposition without a directional decomposition. All wave numbers, independently of their direction, within the range of about an octave (factor of two) are contained in one level of the pyramid.

Because of the coarse wave number resolution, we can preserve a good spatial resolution. Each level of the pyramid contains only matching scales, which are sampled a few times (two to six) per wavelength.

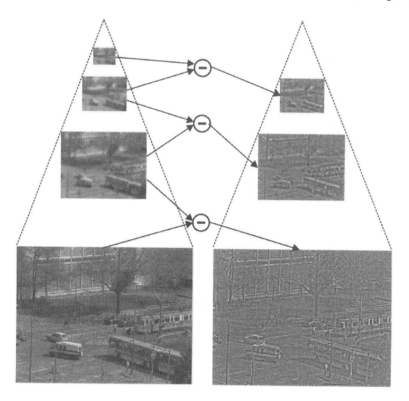

Figure 8.17: *Construction of the Laplacian pyramid (right column) from the Gaussian pyramid (left column) by subtracting two consecutive planes of the Gaussian pyramid.*

In this way, the Laplacian pyramid is an efficient data structure well adapted to the limits of the product of wave number and spatial resolution set by the *uncertainty relation* (Section 8.6.3).

The differentiation in scale direction in the continuous scale space is approximated by subtracting two levels of the Gaussian pyramid in the discrete scale space. In order to do so, first the image at the coarser level must be expanded. This operation is performed by an *expansion operator* $\mathcal{E}_{\uparrow 2}$. As with the reducing smoothing operator, the degree of expansion is denoted by the figure after the $\uparrow$ in the index.

The expansion is significantly more difficult than the size reduction because the missing information must be interpolated. For a size increase of two in all directions, first, every second pixel in each row must be interpolated and then every second row. Interpolation is discussed in detail in Section 9.6. With the introduced notation, the generation of the pth level of the Laplacian pyramid can be written as:

$$\mathcal{L}^{(p)} = G^{(p)} - \mathcal{E}_{\uparrow 2} G^{(p+1)} \tag{8.146}$$

The Laplacian pyramid is an effective scheme for a *bandpass decomposition* of an image. The center wave number is halved from level to level. The last image of the Laplacian pyramid is a low-pass-filtered image containing only the coarsest structures.

The Laplacian pyramid has the significant advantage that the original image can be reconstructed quickly from the sequence of images in the Laplacian pyramid by recursively expanding the images and summing them up. In a Laplacian pyramid with $p + 1$ levels, the level p (counting starts with zero!) is the coarsest level of the Gaussian pyramid. Then the level $p - 1$ of the Gaussian pyramid can be reconstructed by

$$G^{(p-1)} = \mathcal{L}^{(p-1)} + \mathcal{E}_{\uparrow 2} G^p \tag{8.147}$$

Note that this is just the inversion of the construction scheme for the Laplacian pyramid. This means that even if the interpolation algorithms required to expand the image contain errors, they affect only the Laplacian pyramid and not the reconstruction of the Gaussian pyramid from the Laplacian pyramid, because the same algorithm is used. The recursion in Eq. (8.147) is repeated with lower levels until level 0, that is, the original image, is reached again. As illustrated in Fig. 8.17, finer and finer details become visible during the reconstruction process.

8.11 References

[1] Wandell, B. A., (1995). *Foundations of Vision.* Sunderland, MA: Sinauer Associates.

[2] Papoulis, A., (1991). *Probability, Random Variables, and Stochastic Processes.* New York: McGraw-Hill.

[3] Kittel, C., (1971). *Introduction to Solid State Physics.* New York: Wiley.

[4] Hoffman, K. and Kunze, R., (1971). *Linear Algebra,* 2nd edition. Englewood Cliffs, NJ: Prentice-Hall.

[5] Jaroslavskij, J. P., (1985). *Einführung in die digitale Bildverarbeitung.* Berlin: VEB Deutscher Verlag der Wissenschaften.

[6] Besslich, P. W. and Lu, T., (1990). *Diskrete Orthogonaltransformation. Algorithmen und Flußgraphen für die Signalverarbeitung.* Berlin: Springer.

[7] Poularikas, A. D. (ed.), (1995). *The Transforms and Applications Handbook.* Boca Raton, FL: CRC Press.

[8] Bracewell, R., (1986). *The Fourier Transform and Its Applications,* 2nd edition, revised. New York: McGraw-Hill.

[9] Madisetti, V. K. and Williams, D. B. (eds.), (1997). *The Digital Signal Processing Handbook.* Boca Raton, FL: CRC Press.

[10] Cooley, J. W. and Tukey, J. W., (1965). An algorithm for the machine calculation of complex Fourier series. *Math. Comp.*, **19**:297–301.

[11] Blahut, R., (1985). *Fast Algorithms for Digital Signal Processing.* Reading, MA: Addison-Wesley.

[12] Burt, P. J., (1984). The pyramid as a structure for efficient computation. In *Multiresolution Image Processing and Analysis*, A. Rosenfeld, ed., Vol. 12 of *Springer Series in Information Sciences*, pp. 6–35. New York: Springer.

[13] Meyer, Y., (1993). *Wavelets: Algorithms & Applications.* Philadelphia: SIAM.

[14] Kaiser, G., (1994). *A Friendly Guide to Wavelets.* Boston, MA: Birkhäuser.

[15] Rosenfeld, A. (ed.), (1984). *Multiresolution Image Processing and Analysis.* New York: Springer.

[16] Lindeberg, T., (1994). *Scale-space Theory in Computer Vision.* Boston: Kluwer Academic Publishers.

[17] Weickert, J., (1998). *Anisotropic Diffusion in Image Processing.* Stuttgart: Teubner-Verlag.

[18] Fleet, D. J., (1990). *Measurement of Image Velocity.* PhD Dissertation, University of Toronto.

[19] Knutsson, H., (1982). *Filtering and Reconstruction in Image Processing.* PhD Dissertation, Linköping Univ.

[20] Crank, J., (1975). *The Mathematics of Diffusion.* 2nd edition. Oxford: Oxford University Press.

9 Neighborhood Operators

Bernd Jähne

Interdisziplinäres Zentrum für Wissenschaftliches Rechnen (IWR)
Universität Heidelberg, Germany

Computer Vision and Applications

9.1   Basics

The extraction of features from multidimensional signals requires the analysis of at least a local neighborhood. By analysis of the local neighborhood a rich set of features can already be extracted. We can distinguish areas of constant gray values from those that contain an edge, a texture, or just noise. Thus this chapter gives an important theoretical basis for low-level signal processing.

9.1.1   Definition of neighborhood operators

A neighborhood operator takes the gray values of the neighborhood around a point, performs some operations with them, and writes the result back on the pixel. This operation is repeated for all points of the signal. Therefore, we can write a neighborhood operation with a multidimensional continuous signal $g(\boldsymbol{x})$ as

$$g'(\boldsymbol{x}) = N(\{g(\boldsymbol{x}')\}, \forall (\boldsymbol{x} - \boldsymbol{x}') \in M) \qquad (9.1)$$

where M is an area, called *mask, region of support*, or *structure element*. The size and shape of M determines the neighborhood operation by specifying the input values of g in the area M shifted with its origin to the point $\boldsymbol{x}$. The neighborhood operation N itself is not specified here. It can be of any type; its result determines the value of the output g' at $\boldsymbol{x}$. For symmetry reasons the mask is often symmetric and has its center of gravity in the origin.

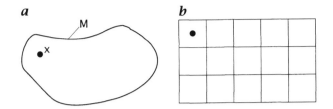

Figure 9.1: *Mask or structure element with **a** continuous; and **b** digital 2-D signals on a square lattice. The point that receives the result is marked.*

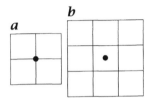

Figure 9.2: *Various types of symmetric masks on 2-D lattices: **a** 2×2 mask; and **b** 3×3 mask on a square lattice.*

For digital signals a general neighborhood operation can be expressed as

$$G'_{m,n} = N(G_{m'-m,n'-n}, \forall [m,n]^T \in M) \tag{9.2}$$

or by equivalent expressions for dimensions other than two.

Although these equations do not specify in any way the type of neighborhood operation that is performed, they still reveal the common structure of all neighborhood operations. Thus very general strategies can be developed to compute them efficiently [CVA2, Section 5.6].

9.1.2 Shape and symmetry of neighborhoods

As we have seen, any type of neighborhood operator is first determined by the size of the mask. With continuous signals, the mask may take any shape. With digital data on orthogonal lattices, the mask is normally of rectangular shape. In any case, we must also specify the point relative to the mask that receives the result of the operation (Fig. 9.1).

With regard to symmetry, the most natural choice is to place the result of the operation at the pixel in the center of the mask. While this is straightforward for continuous masks, it requires more thought for digital signals. Natural choices for masks on an orthogonal lattice are rectangles. Basically, there are two types of symmetric masks: masks with an even or odd size of pixels in each direction. For odd-sized masks, the symmetry center coincides with the central pixel and, thus, seems to be a good choice (Fig. 9.2b). The smallest size of odd-sized masks includes only the directly neighboring pixels. In one, two, and three dimensions, the mask includes 3, 9, and 27 pixels, respectively.

In contrast, even-sized masks seem not to be suitable for neighborhood operations because there is no pixel that lies in the center of the mask. With adroitness, we can apply them nevertheless, and they turn out to be useful for certain types of neighborhood operations. The result of the neighborhood operation is simply written back to pixels that lay between the original pixels (Fig. 9.2a). Thus, the resulting image is shifted by half the pixel distance into every direction and the receiving central pixel lays directly in the center of the neighborhoods. In effect, the resulting image has one pixel less in every direction. It is very important to be aware of this shift by half the pixel distance. Therefore, image features computed by even-sized masks should never be combined with original gray values because this would lead to considerable errors. Also, a mask must either be even-sided or odd-sized in *all* directions for multidimensional digital signals. Otherwise, the output lattices do not coincide.

The number of pixels contained in the masks increases considerably with their size. If R is the linear size of a mask in D dimensions, the mask has R^D elements. The higher the dimension, the faster the number of elements with the size of the mask increases. Even small neighborhoods include hundreds or thousands of elements. Therefore, it will be a challenging task for higher-dimensional signal processing to develop efficient schemes to compute a neighborhood operation with as few computations as possible. Otherwise, it would not be possible to use them at all.

The challenge for efficient computation schemes is to decrease the number of computations from $O(R^D)$ to a lower order. This means that the number of computations is no longer proportional to R^D but rather to a lower order of the size R of the mask. The ultimate goal is to achieve computation schemes that increase only linearly with the size of the mask ($O(R^1)$) or, even better, do not depend at all on the size of the mask ($O(R^0)$).

9.1.3 Operator notation

In this section, we introduce an *operator notation* for signal-processing operations. It helps us to make complex composite neighbor operations easily comprehensible. All operators will be written in calligraphic letters, such as $\mathcal{B}, \mathcal{D}, \mathcal{H}, \mathcal{S}$. We write

$$G' = \mathcal{H}\,G \qquad\qquad (9.3)$$

for an operator $\mathcal{H}$, which transforms the image G into the image G'. Note that this notation can be used for any type of signal. It can be used for continuous as well as digital signals and for signals of any dimension.

Consecutive application is denoted by writing the operators one after the other. The rightmost operator is applied first. Consecutive application of the same operator is expressed by an exponent

$$\underbrace{\mathcal{H}\,\mathcal{H}\ldots\mathcal{H}}_{p\text{ times}} = \mathcal{H}^p \tag{9.4}$$

If the operator acts on a single image, the operand, which is to the right in the equations, will be omitted. In this way we can write operator equations without targets. Furthermore, we will use braces in the usual way to control the order of execution.

The operator notation leads to a *representation-independent notation* of signal-processing operations. A linear shift-invariant operator (see Section 8.6.3) performs a convolution operation in the spatial domain and a complex multiplication in the Fourier domain. With the operator notation, we can write the basic properties of the linear shift-invariant operator (Eq. (8.65)) in an easily comprehensible way and without specifying a target as

commutativity	$\mathcal{H}_1\mathcal{H}_2 = \mathcal{H}_2\mathcal{H}_1$	
associativity	$\mathcal{H}_1(\mathcal{H}_2\mathcal{H}_3) = (\mathcal{H}_1\mathcal{H}_2)\mathcal{H}_3$	(9.5)
distributivity over addition	$(\mathcal{H}_1 + \mathcal{H}_2)\mathcal{H}_3 = \mathcal{H}_1\mathcal{H}_2 + \mathcal{H}_2\mathcal{H}_3$	

As can be seen from these equations, other operations such as addition can also be used in the operator notation. Care must be taken with any *nonlinear* operator. As soon as nonlinear operators are involved, the order in which the operators are executed must strictly be given. We retain the notation that operators are executed from the left to the right, provided that braces are not used to change the order of execution.

The point operation of pixelwise multiplication in the spatial domain is a simple example for a nonlinear operator. As this operator occurs frequently, it is denoted by a special symbol, a centered dot ($\cdot$). A special symbol is required in order to distinguish it from successive application of operators. The operator expression $\mathcal{B}(\mathcal{D} \cdot \mathcal{D})$, for instance, means: apply the operator $\mathcal{D}$ to the signal, square the result pixelwise, and then apply the operator $\mathcal{B}$. Without parentheses the expression $\mathcal{B}\mathcal{D} \cdot \mathcal{D}$ would mean: apply the operator $\mathcal{D}$ to the image and apply the operator $\mathcal{B}\mathcal{D}$ to the image and then multiply the results point by point. This notation thus gives precedence to the pointwise multiplication over consecutive operator execution. As a placeholder for an object onto which an operator is acting, we will use the symbol ":." In this notation, the forementioned operator combination is written as $\mathcal{B}(\mathcal{D} : \cdot \mathcal{D} :)$.

9.2   Linear shift-invariant filters

9.2.1   Linearity

Linear operators are defined by the *principle of superposition*. If a and b are two complex-valued scalars, and $\mathcal{H}$ is an operator that maps an image onto another image of the same dimension, then the operator is linear if and only if

$$\mathcal{H}(a:+b:) = a\mathcal{H}:+b\mathcal{H}: \tag{9.6}$$

We can generalize Eq. (9.6) to the superposition of many inputs

$$\mathcal{H}\left(\sum_k a_k:\right) = \sum_k a_k\mathcal{H}: \tag{9.7}$$

The superposition property makes linear operators very useful. We can decompose a complex image into simpler components for which we can easily derive the response of the operator and then compose the resulting response from that of the components.

It is especially useful to decompose an image into its individual pixels as discussed in Section 8.5.1.

9.2.2   Shift invariance and convolution

Another important property of an operator is shift invariance or homogeneity. It means that the response of the operator does not explicitly depend on the position. If we shift a signal, the output image is the same but for the shift applied. We can formulate this property more elegantly with a *shift operator* S. For 2-D images, for example, the shift operator is defined as

$$^{mn}SG_{m'n'} = G_{m'-m,n'-n} \tag{9.8}$$

An operator is then *shift-invariant* if and only if it commutes with the shift operator, that is,

$$\mathcal{H}S = S\mathcal{H} \tag{9.9}$$

Note that the shift operator S itself is a shift-invariant operator. An operator that is both linear and shift-invariant is known as a *linear shift-invariant operator* or short *LSI* operator. This important class of operators is also known as *linear time-invariant* or *LTI* operators for time series.

It can be proven [1] that a linear shift-invariant operator must *necessarily* be a convolution operation in the space domain. There is *no* other operator type that is both linear and shift-invariant. Thus, linear shift-invariant neighborhood operators share all the useful features of convolution that were discussed in Section 8.6.3. They are commutative, associative, and distribute over addition (see also Eq. (9.5)). These properties are very useful for an efficient design of filter operations [CVA2, Chapter 6].

9.2.3 Point spread function

As just discussed in the previous section, an LSI filter can be represented in the space domain as a convolution operation. In two dimensions the image G is convolved with another image H that represents the LSI operator:

$$G'_{mn} = \sum_{m'=0}^{M-1} \sum_{n'=0}^{N-1} H_{m',n'} G_{m-m',n-n'} \tag{9.10}$$

Because for a neighborhood operation H is zero except for a small neighborhood, this operation can also be written as

$$G'_{mn} = \sum_{m'=-R}^{R} \sum_{n'=-R}^{R} H_{-m',-n'} G_{m+m',n+n'} \tag{9.11}$$

In this equation it is assumed that coefficients of H are nonzero only in a $(2R+1) \times (2R+1)$ window. Both representations are equivalent if we consider the periodicity in the space domain (Section 8.7.1). The latter representation is much more practical and gives a better comprehension of the operator. For example, the following $M \times N$ matrix and 3×3 filter mask are equivalent:

$$\begin{bmatrix} 0. & -1 & 0 & \ldots & 0 & 1 \\ 1 & 0 & 0 & \ldots & 0 & 2 \\ 0 & 0 & 0 & \ldots & 0 & 0 \\ \vdots & \vdots & \vdots & \vdots & \vdots & \vdots \\ 0 & 0 & 0 & \ldots & 0 & 0 \\ -1 & -2 & 0 & \ldots & 0 & 0 \end{bmatrix} \equiv \begin{bmatrix} 0 & -1 & -2 \\ 1 & 0. & -1 \\ 2 & 1 & 0 \end{bmatrix} \tag{9.12}$$

For a D-dimensional signal, the convolution sum can be written with a simplified vector indexing as also used in Section 8.4.4:

$$G'_{\boldsymbol{n}} = \sum_{n'=-R}^{R} H_{-\boldsymbol{n}'} G_{\boldsymbol{n}+\boldsymbol{n}'} \tag{9.13}$$

with $\boldsymbol{n} = [n_1, n_2, \ldots, n_D]$, $\boldsymbol{R} = [R_1, R_2, \ldots, R_D]$, where $G_{\boldsymbol{n}}$ is an element of a D-dimensional signal $G_{n_1, n_2, \ldots, n_D}$. The notation for the sums in this equation is an abbreviation for

$$\sum_{n'=-R}^{R} = \sum_{n'_1=-R_1}^{R_1} \sum_{n'_2=-R_2}^{R_2} \cdots \sum_{n'_D=-R_D}^{R_D} \tag{9.14}$$

The vectorial indexing introduced here allows writing most of the relations for arbitary dimensional signals in a simple way. Moreover, it can also be used for skewed coordinate systems if n are regarded as the indices of the corresponding *lattice vectors* (see Eq. (8.27), Section 8.4.2).

The filter mask is identical to another quantity known as the *point spread function*, which gives the response of the filter to a point image:

$$P'_n = \sum_{n'=-R}^{R} H_{n'} P_{n-n'} = H_n \tag{9.15}$$

where

$$P_n = \begin{cases} 1 & n = 0 \\ 0 & \text{otherwise} \end{cases} \tag{9.16}$$

The central importance of the point spread function is based on the fact that the convolution operation is linear. If we know the response to a point image, we can compute the response to any image, as any image can be composed of point images as discussed in Section 8.5.1. With respect to the analysis of time series, the point spread function is known as the *impulse response*, with respect to the solution of partial differential equations as the *Green's function* [2].

9.2.4 Transfer function

The Fourier transform of the convolution mask is known as the *transfer function* of a linear filter. The transfer function has an important practical meaning. For each wave number, it gives the factor by which a periodic structure is multiplied using the filter operation. This factor is generally a complex number. Thus, a periodic structure experiences not only a change in the amplitude but also a phase shift:

$$\hat{G}'_v = \hat{H}_v \hat{G}_v = r_H \exp(i\varphi_H) \, r_G \exp(i\varphi_G)$$
$$= r_H r_G \exp[i(\varphi_H + \varphi_G)] \tag{9.17}$$

where the complex numbers are represented by their magnitude and phase as complex exponentials.

Using the wave number normalized to the Nyquist limit (Eq. (8.34) in Section 8.4.2), the transfer function is given by

$$\hat{h}(\tilde{k}) = \sum_{n'=-R}^{R} h_{n'} \exp(-\pi i n' \tilde{k}) \tag{9.18}$$

for a 1-D signal and by

$$\hat{h}(\tilde{\boldsymbol{k}}) = \sum_{n'=-R}^{R} H_{n'} \exp(-\pi i n'^{T} \tilde{\boldsymbol{k}}) \qquad (9.19)$$

for a multidimensional signal. For a nonorthogonal, that is, skewed lattice, the vectorial index $\boldsymbol{n}'$ has to be replaced by the reciprocal lattice vector (Eq. (8.29)), and Eq. (9.19) becomes

$$\hat{h}(\boldsymbol{k}) = \sum_{v=-R}^{R} H_{r} \exp(-2\pi i \hat{\boldsymbol{r}}_{v}^{T} \boldsymbol{k}) \qquad (9.20)$$

9.2.5 Symmetries

Symmetries play a central rule for linear shift-invariant filters in the processing of higher-dimensional signal processing. This is because of the simplified transfer function of symmetric masks. According to Section 8.6.3, filters of even and odd symmetry have a real and purely imaginary transfer function, respectively. The symmetry of a filter is most generally expressed by:

$$H_{R-r} = \pm H_{r} \qquad (9.21)$$

This is a necessary and sufficient condition for a real or imaginary transfer function. Filters normally meet a stronger symmetry condition for each direction d:

$$H_{r_1,\dots,R_d-r_d,\dots,r_D} = \pm H_{r_1,\dots,r_d,\dots,r_D} \qquad (9.22)$$

For separable symmetric filters, the symmetry conditions can be expressed for each 1-D component separately:

$$h_{R_d-r_d} = \pm h_{r_d} \qquad (9.23)$$

As the transfer functions of the 1-D components of separable filters are combined multiplicatively, an even and odd number of odd components results in an even and odd filter according to Eq. (9.21) and thus into a real and imaginary transfer function, respectively.

Because of the significance of separable filters for effective computing of convolution operations [CVA2, Section 5.6], we focus on the symmetry of 1-D filters. Besides odd and even symmetry, it is necessary to distinguish filters with an even and odd number of coefficients.

The situation is straightforward for filters with an odd number of coefficients. Then the central coefficient is the center of symmetry and the result of a filter operation is written for the position of this central coefficient. This symmetry is implicitly considered in Eqs. (9.13) and

(9.18) where the central coefficient has the index 0. With this indexing of the filter coefficients, the convolution sum and transfer function of even 1-D filters with $2R + 1$ coefficients—also known as *type I FIR filter* [3]—can be expressed as

$$g'_n = h_0 g_n + \sum_{n'=1}^{R} h'_n (g_{n+n'} + g_{n-n'}), \quad \hat{h}(\tilde{k}) = h_0 + \sum_{n'=1}^{R} 2h_{n'} \cos(n' \pi \tilde{k}) \tag{9.24}$$

and for odd filters with $2R + 1$ coefficients or *type III FIR filters* as

$$g'_n = \sum_{n'=1}^{R} h'_n (g_{n-n'} - g_{n+n'}), \quad \hat{h}(\tilde{k}) = i \sum_{n'=1}^{R} 2h_{n'} \sin(n' \pi \tilde{k}) \tag{9.25}$$

For filters with an even number of coefficients, there is no central pixel. The symmetry center rather is inbetween two pixels. This means that the results of a filter operation with such a filter are to be placed on a grid that is shifted by half a pixel distance. Because of this shift between the output pixel and the input pixels, the transfer function of an even filter with $2R$ coefficients *type II FIR filter* is

$$\hat{h}(\tilde{k}) = h_0 + \sum_{n'=1}^{R} 2h_{n'} \cos((n' - 1/2)\pi \tilde{k}) \tag{9.26}$$

The transfer function of an odd filter with $2R$ coefficients or *type IV FIR filter* is

$$\hat{h}(\tilde{k}) = i \sum_{n'=1}^{R} 2h_{n'} \sin((n' - 1/2)\pi \tilde{k}) \tag{9.27}$$

The equations for symmetric filters for two and more dimensions are significantly more complex and are discussed in Jähne [4].

9.2.6 LSI operators as least squares estimators

The LSI operators compute a new value at each point in a signal from a linear combination of neighboring points. Likewise, a least squares estimator computes the estimate of a quantity from a linear combination of the input values. Thus it appears that a close relationship should exist between LSI operators and least squares estimators.

We assume that we want to fit a certain function with linear parameters a_p

$$f(\boldsymbol{x}) = \sum_{p=0}^{P-1} a_p f_p(\boldsymbol{x}) \tag{9.28}$$

to the local spatial gray-value variation $g(x)$. For 2-D digital signals, the continuous functions $f_p(x)$ have to be replaced by matrices F_p. All of the following equations are also valid for digital signals but it is more convenient to stay with the continuous case. In the least squares sense, the following error measure $e^2(x)$ should be minimized:

$$e^2(x) = \int_{-\infty}^{\infty} w(x') \left(\sum_{p=0}^{P-1} a_p(x) f_p(x') - g(x + x') \right)^2 d^D x' \qquad (9.29)$$

In this integral the window function $w(x')$ has been introduced to limit the fit to a local neighborhood around the point x. Therefore, the fit coefficients $a_p(x)$ depend on the position. Normally, the window function is an isotropic even function with a maximum at the origin monotonically decreasing with increasing distance from the origin. We further assume that the window function is normalized, that is,

$$\int_{-\infty}^{\infty} w(x') d^D x' = 1 \qquad (9.30)$$

For the sake of simpler equations, the following abbreviations will be used in this section:

$$\langle f_p g_x \rangle = \int_{-\infty}^{\infty} w(x') f_p(x') g(x + x') d^D x'$$

$$\langle f_p f_q \rangle = \int_{-\infty}^{\infty} w(x') f_p(x') f_q(x') d^D x' \qquad (9.31)$$

Setting all derivatives of Eq. (9.29) with respect to the parameters $a_p(x)$ zero, the following linear equation system is obtained as the standard least squares solution of the minimization problem:

$$a(x) = M^{-1} d(x) \qquad (9.32)$$

with

$$M_{p,q} = \langle f_p f_q \rangle, \quad a = [a_0(x), a_1(x), \ldots, a_{P-1}(x)]^T \quad d_p = \langle f_p g_x \rangle$$

The solution of Eq. (9.32) becomes most simplistic if the functions $f_p(x)$ are orthogonal to each other, that is, $\langle f_p f_q \rangle = \langle f_p^2 \rangle \delta_{p-q}$. Then the matrix M is diagonal and

$$a_p(x) = \langle f_p g_x \rangle / \langle f_p^2 \rangle \qquad (9.33)$$

This expression can also be written as a convolution integral by using Eq. (9.31) and substituting x' by $-x'$:

$$a_p(x) = \int_{-\infty}^{\infty} w(x')f_p(-x')g(x-x')\,d^Dx' \qquad (9.34)$$

This means that the fit coefficient for each point is computed by convolving the windowed and mirrored orthonormal function with the signal.

Example 9.1: Plane fit

As a simple example we discuss the local plane fit, that is, the local approximation of the gray-scale variation by a plane. The fit function is

$$f(x) = a_0 + a_1x_1 + a_2x_2, \quad f_0 = 1, f_1 = x_1, f_2 = x_2 \qquad (9.35)$$

It is easy to verify that these three functions are orthogonal to each other. Therefore,

$$a_0 = \int_{-\infty}^{\infty} w(x')g(x-x')\,d^Dx'$$

$$a_1 = -\int_{-\infty}^{\infty} w(x')x_1'g(x-x')\,d^Dx' \Big/ \int_{-\infty}^{\infty} w(x')x_1'^2\,d^Dx' \qquad (9.36)$$

$$a_2 = -\int_{-\infty}^{\infty} w(x')x_2'g(x-x')\,d^Dx' \Big/ \int_{-\infty}^{\infty} w(x')x_2'^2\,d^Dx'$$

As a special case for 2-D digital signals we take a binomial 3×3 window and obtain

$$W = \frac{1}{16}\begin{bmatrix} 1 & 2 & 1 \\ 2 & 4 & 2 \\ 1 & 2 & 1 \end{bmatrix}, \qquad F_0 = \begin{bmatrix} 1 & 1 & 1 \\ 1 & 1 & 1 \\ 1 & 1 & 1 \end{bmatrix}$$

$$F_1 = 2\begin{bmatrix} -1 & -1 & -1 \\ 0 & 0 & 0 \\ 1 & 1 & 1 \end{bmatrix}, \qquad F_2 = 2\begin{bmatrix} -1 & 0 & 1 \\ -1 & 0 & 1 \\ -1 & 0 & 1 \end{bmatrix} \qquad (9.37)$$

The three matrices F_0, F_1, and F_2 are already normalized, that is,

$$\sum_{m=0}^{M-1}\sum_{n=0}^{N-1} W_{m,n}((F_p)_{m,n})^2 = 1 \qquad (9.38)$$

so that the division in Eq. (9.36) is not required. Then the convolution masks to obtain the fit coefficients a_0, a_1, and a_2 are

$$\frac{1}{16}\begin{bmatrix} 1 & 2 & 1 \\ 2 & 4 & 2 \\ 1 & 2 & 1 \end{bmatrix}, \frac{1}{8}\begin{bmatrix} 1 & 2 & 1 \\ 0 & 0 & 0 \\ -1 & -2 & -1 \end{bmatrix}, \frac{1}{8}\begin{bmatrix} 1 & 0 & -1 \\ 2 & 0 & -2 \\ 1 & 0 & -1 \end{bmatrix} \qquad (9.39)$$

and we end up with the well-known binomial smoothing mask and the Sobel operator for the estimate of the mean and slopes of a local plane fit, respectively.

Thus, the close relationship between LSI operators and least squares fits is helpful in determining what kind of properties an LSI operator is filtering out from a signal.

The case with nonorthogonal fit functions is slightly more complex. As the matrix M (Eq. (9.32)) depends only on the fit functions and the chosen window and not on the signal $g(x)$, the matrix M can be inverted once for a given fit. Then the fit coefficients are given as a linear combination of the results from the convolutions with all P fit functions:

$$a_p(x) = \sum_{p'=0}^{P-1} M_{p,p'}^{-1} \int_{-\infty}^{\infty} w(x') f_{p'}(-x') g(x - x') \, d^D x' \qquad (9.40)$$

9.3 Recursive filters

9.3.1 Definition

Recursive filters are a special form of the linear convolution filters. This type of filter includes results from previous convolutions at neighboring pixels into the convolution sum. In this way, the filter becomes directional. Recursive filters can most easily be understood if we apply them first to a 1-D discrete signal, a *time series*. Then we can write

$$g'_n = -\sum_{n''=1}^{S} a_{n''} g'_{n-n''} + \sum_{n'=-R}^{R} h_{n'} g_{n-n'} \qquad (9.41)$$

While the neighborhood of the nonrecursive part (coefficients h) is symmetric around the central point, the recursive part is asymmetric, using only previously computed values. A filter that contains only such a recursive part is called a *causal filter*. If we put the recursive part on the left hand side of the equation, we observe that the recursive filter is equivalent to the following difference equation, also known as an ARMA(S,R) process (*autoregressive-moving average process*):

$$\sum_{n''=0}^{S} a_{n''} g'_{n-n''} = \sum_{n'=-R}^{R} h_{n'} g_{n-n'} \quad \text{with} \quad a_0 = 1 \qquad (9.42)$$

9.3.2 Transfer function and z-transform

The transfer function of such a filter with a recursive and a nonrecursive part can be computed by applying the *discrete-space Fourier transform*

(Section 8.5.1, Table 8.3) to Eq. (9.42). In the Fourier space the convolution of g' with a and of g with h is replaced by a multiplication of the corresponding Fourier transforms:

$$\hat{g}'(k) \sum_{n''=0}^{S} a_{n''} \exp(-2\pi in''k) = \hat{g}(k) \sum_{n'=-R}^{R} h_{n'} \exp(-2\pi in'k) \quad (9.43)$$

Thus the transfer function is

$$\hat{h}(k) = \frac{\hat{g}'(k)}{\hat{g}(k)} = \frac{\displaystyle\sum_{n'=-R}^{R} h_{n'} \exp(-2\pi in'k)}{\displaystyle\sum_{n''=0}^{S} a_{n''} \exp(-2\pi in''k)} \quad (9.44)$$

The nature of the transfer function of a recursive filter becomes more evident if we consider that both the numerator and the denominator can have zeros. Thus the nonrecursive part of the transfer function may cause zeros and the recursive part poles.

A deeper analysis of the zeros and thus the structure of the transfer function is not possible in the form as Eq. (9.44) is written. It requires an extension similar to the extension from real numbers to complex numbers that was necessary to introduce the Fourier transform (Section 8.5.3). We observe that the expressions for both the numerator and the denominator are polynomials in the *complex exponential* $\exp(2\pi ik)$. The complex exponential has a magnitude of one and thus covers the unit circle in the complex plane. It covers the whole complex plane if we add a radius r to the expression: $z = r \exp(2\pi ik)$.

With this extension, the expressions become polynomials in z. As such we can apply the fundamental law of algebra that any *complex polynomial* of degree n can be factorized in n factors containing the roots or zeros of the polynomial. Thus we can write a new expression in z, which becomes the transfer function for $z = \exp(2\pi ik)$:

$$\hat{h}(z) = \frac{\displaystyle\prod_{n'=-R}^{R} (1 - c_{n'} z^{-1})}{\displaystyle\prod_{n''=0}^{S} (1 - d_{n''} z^{-1})} \quad (9.45)$$

Each of the factors $c_{n'}$ and $d_{n''}$ is a zero of the corresponding polynomial ($z = c_{n'}$ or $z = d_{n''}$).

The inclusion of the factor r in the extended transfer function results in an extension of the Fourier transform, the *z-transform* that is defined as

$$\hat{g}(z) = \sum_{n=-\infty}^{\infty} g_n z^{-n} \quad (9.46)$$

The z-transform of the series g_n can be regarded as the Fourier transform of the series $g_n r^{-n}$ [5]. The z-transform is the key mathematical tool to understand recursive filters. Detailed accounts of the z-transform are given by Oppenheim and Schafer [3] and Poularikas [6]; the 2-D z-transform is discussed by Lim [5].

The factorization of the z-transform of the filter in Eq. (9.45)—and in turn of the transfer function—is an essential property. Multiplication of the individual factors of the transfer function means that we can decompose any filter into elementary filters containing only one factor because multiplication of transfer functions is equivalent to cascaded convolution in the spatial domain (Section 8.6.3). The basic filters that are equivalent to a single factor in Eq. (9.45) will be discussed further in Section 9.3.6.

Recursive filters can also be defined in higher dimensions with the same type of equations as in Eq. (9.42); also the transfer function and z-transform of higher-dimensional recursive filters can be written in the very same way as in Eq. (9.44). However, it is generally *not* possible to factorize the z-transform as in Eq. (9.45) [5]. From Eq. (9.45) we can immediately conclude that it will be possible to factorize a *separable* recursive filter because then the higher-dimensional polynomials can be factorized into 1-D polynomials. Given these inherent difficulties of higher-dimensional recursive filters we will restrict the further discussion on 1-D recursive filters that can be extended by cascaded convolution into higher-dimensional filters.

9.3.3 Infinite and unstable response

The *impulse response* or *point spread function* of a recursive filter is no longer identical to the filter coefficients as for nonrecursive filters (Section 9.2.3). It must rather be computed as the inverse Fourier transform of the transfer function. The impulse response of nonrecursive filters has only a finite number of nonzero samples. A filter with this property is called a *finite-duration impulse response* or FIR filter. In contrast, recursive filters have an *infinite-duration impulse response* (IIR).

The *stability* of the filter response is not an issue for nonrecursive filters but of central importance for recursive filters. A filter is said to be *stable* if and only if *each* bound input sequence generates a bound output sequence. In terms of the impulse response this means that a filter is stable if and only if the impulse response is absolutely summable [3]. For 1-D filters the analysis of the stability is straightforward because the conditions are well established by the same basic algebraic theorems. A filter is stable and causal if and only if all poles and zeros of the z-transform $\hat{h}(z)$ (Eq. (9.45)) are inside the unit circle [3].

9.3.4 Relation between recursive and nonrecursive filters

Any stable recursive filter can be replaced by a nonrecursive filter, in general, with an infinite-sized mask. Its mask is given by the point spread function of the recursive filter. In practice, the masks cannot be infinite and also need not be infinite. This is due to the fact that the envelope of the impulse response of any recursive filter decays exponentially (Section 9.3.6).

Another observation is of importance. From Eq. (9.44) we see that the transfer function of a recursive filter is the ratio of its nonrecursive and recursive part. This means that a purely recursive and a nonrecursive filter with the same coefficients are inverse filters to each other. This general relation is a good base to construct inverse filters from nonrecursive filters.

9.3.5 Zero-phase recursive filtering

The causal 1-D recursive filters are of not much use for processing of higher-dimensional spatial data. While a filter that uses only previous data is natural and useful for real-time processing of time series, it makes not much sense for spatial data. There is no "before" and "after" in spatial data. Even worse, the spatial shift (delay) associated with recursive filters is not acceptable because it causes phase shifts and thus objects to be shifted depending on the filters applied.

With a single recursive filter it is impossible to construct a zero-phase filter. Thus it is required to combine multiple recursive filters. The combination should either result in a zero-phase filter suitable for smoothing operations or a derivative filter that shifts the phase by 90°. Thus the transfer function should either be purely real or purely imaginary (Section 8.6.3).

We start with a 1-D causal recursive filter that has the transfer function

$$^{+}\hat{h}(\tilde{k}) = a(\tilde{k}) + ib(\tilde{k}) \tag{9.47}$$

The superscript "+" denotes that the filter runs in positive coordinate direction. The transfer function of the same filter but running in the opposite direction has a similar transfer function. We replace $\tilde{k}$ by $-\tilde{k}$ and note that $a(-\tilde{k}) = a(+\tilde{k})$ and $b(-\tilde{k}) = -b(\tilde{k})$) because the transfer function of a real PSF is Hermitian (Section 8.6.3) and thus obtain

$$^{-}\hat{h}(\tilde{k}) = a(\tilde{k}) - ib(\tilde{k}) \tag{9.48}$$

Thus, only the sign of the imaginary part of the transfer function changes when the filter direction is reversed.

We now have three possibilities to combine the two transfer functions (Eqs. (9.47) and (9.48)) either into a purely real or imaginary transfer function:

Addition $\quad {}^e\hat{h}(\tilde{k}) = \frac{1}{2}\left({}^+\hat{h}(\tilde{k}) + {}^-\hat{h}(\tilde{k})\right) = a(\tilde{k})$

Subtraction $\quad {}^o\hat{h}(\tilde{k}) = \frac{1}{2}\left({}^+\hat{h}(\tilde{k}) - {}^-\hat{h}(\tilde{k})\right) = ib(\tilde{k})$ $\qquad$ (9.49)

Multiplication $\quad \hat{h}(\tilde{k}) = {}^+\hat{h}(\tilde{k})\,{}^-\hat{h}(\tilde{k}) = a^2(\tilde{k}) + b^2(\tilde{k})$

Addition and multiplication (consecutive application) of the left and right running filter yields filters of even symmetry, while subtraction results in a filter of odd symmetry. This way to cascade recursive filters gives them the same properties as zero- or $\pi/2$-phase shift nonrecursive filters with the additional advantage that they can easily be tuned, and extended point spread functions can be realized with only a few filter coefficients.

9.3.6 Basic recursive filters

In Section 9.3.2 we found that the factorization of the generalized recursive filter is a key to analyze its transfer function and stability properties (Eq. (9.45)). The individual factors contain the poles and zeros. From each factor, we can compute the impulse response so that the resulting impulse response of the whole filter is given by a cascaded convolution of all components.

As the factors are all of the form

$$f_n(\tilde{k}) = 1 - c_n \exp(-2\pi i \tilde{k}) \qquad (9.50)$$

the analysis becomes quite easy. Still we can distinguish two basic types of partial factors. They result from the fact that the impulse response of the filter must be real. Therefore, the transfer function must be Hermitian, that is, $f^*(-k) = f(k)$. This can only be the case when either the zero c_n is real or a pair of factors exists with complex-conjugate zeros. This condition gives rise to two basic types of recursive filters, the relaxation filter and the resonance filter that are discussed in detail in what follows. As these filters are only useful for image processing if they are applied both in forward and backward direction, we discuss also the resulting symmetric transfer function and point spread function.

Relaxation filter. The transfer function of the relaxation filter running in forward or backward direction is

$$\pm\hat{r}(\tilde{k}) = \frac{1 - \alpha}{1 - \alpha\exp(\mp\pi i\tilde{k})} \quad \text{with} \quad \alpha \in \mathbb{R} \qquad (9.51)$$

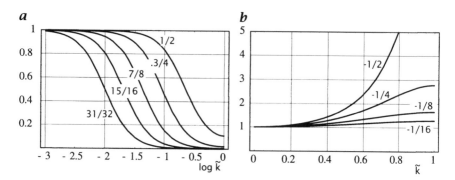

Figure 9.3: *Transfer function of the relaxation filter $g'_n = \alpha g'_{n\mp 1} + (1 - \alpha) g_n$ applied first in forward and then in backward direction for **a** positive; and **b** negative values of α as indicated.*

In this equation, the wave number has been replaced by the wave number normalized with the Nyquist limit (see Section 8.4.2, Eq. (8.34)). It also has been normalized so that $\hat{r}(0) = 1$. Comparing Eqs. (9.42) and (9.43) it is evident that the transfer function Eq. (9.51) belongs to the simple recursive filter

$$g'_n = \alpha g'_{n\mp 1} + (1 - \alpha) g_n = g_n + \alpha(g'_{n\mp 1} - g_n) \qquad (9.52)$$

with the point spread function

$$^{\pm}r_{\pm n} = \begin{cases} (1 - \alpha)\alpha^n & n \geq 0 \\ 0 & \text{else} \end{cases} \qquad (9.53)$$

This filter takes the fraction α from the previously calculated value and the fraction $1 - \alpha$ from the current pixel.

The transfer function Eq. (9.51) is complex and can be divided into its real and imaginary parts as

$$^{\pm}\hat{r}(\tilde{k}) = \frac{1 - \alpha}{1 - 2\alpha \cos \pi \tilde{k} + \alpha^2} \left[(1 - \alpha \cos \pi \tilde{k}) \mp i\alpha \sin \pi \tilde{k} \right] \qquad (9.54)$$

From this transfer function, we can compute the multiplicative ($\hat{r}$) application of the filters by running it successively in positive and negative direction; see Eq. (9.49):

$$\hat{r}(\tilde{k}) = \frac{(1 - \alpha)^2}{1 - 2\alpha \cos \pi \tilde{k} + \alpha^2} = \frac{1}{1 + \beta - \beta \cos \pi \tilde{k}} \qquad (9.55)$$

with

$$\beta = \frac{2\alpha}{(1 - \alpha)^2} \quad \text{and} \quad \alpha = \frac{1 + \beta - \sqrt{1 + 2\beta}}{\beta}$$

From Eq. (9.53) we can conclude that the relaxation filter is stable if $|\alpha| < 1$, which corresponds to $\beta \in] - 1/2, \infty[$. As already noted, the transfer function is one for small wave numbers. A Taylor series in $\tilde{k}$ results in

$$\hat{r}(\tilde{k}) \approx= 1 - \frac{\alpha}{(1-\alpha)^2}(\pi\tilde{k})^2 + \frac{\alpha((1+10\alpha+\alpha^2)}{12(1-\alpha^2)^2}(\pi\tilde{k})^4 \qquad (9.56)$$

If α is positive, the filter is a low-pass filter (Fig. 9.3a). It can be tuned by adjusting α. If α is approaching 1, the averaging distance becomes infinite. For negative α, the filter enhances high wave numbers (Fig. 9.3b).

This filter is the discrete analog to the first-order differential equation $\dot{y} + \tau y = 0$ describing a relaxation process with the relaxation time $\tau = -\Delta t / \ln \alpha$ [4].

Resonance filter. The transfer function of a filter with a pair of complex-conjugate zeros running in forward or backward direction is

$$^{\pm}\hat{s}(\tilde{k}) = \frac{1}{1-r\exp(i\pi\tilde{k}_0)\exp(\mp i\pi\tilde{k})} \cdot \frac{1}{1-r\exp(-i\pi\tilde{k}_0)\exp(\mp i\pi\tilde{k})}$$

$$= \frac{1}{1-2r\cos(\pi\tilde{k}_0)\exp(\mp i\pi\tilde{k})+r^2\exp(\mp 2i\pi\tilde{k})} \qquad (9.57)$$

The second row of the equation shows that this is the transfer function of the recursive filter

$$g'_n = g_n + 2r\cos(\pi\tilde{k}_0)g'_{n\mp 1} - r^2 g'_{n\mp 2} \qquad (9.58)$$

The impulse response of this filter is [3]

$$h_{\pm n} = \begin{cases} \dfrac{r^n}{\sin\pi\tilde{k}_0}\sin[(n+1)\pi\tilde{k}_0] & n \geq 0 \\ 0 & n < 0 \end{cases} \qquad (9.59)$$

If we run the filter back and forth, the resulting transfer function is

$$\hat{s}(\tilde{k}) = \frac{1}{\left(1-2r\cos[\pi(\tilde{k}-\tilde{k}_0)]+r^2\right)\left(1-2r\cos[\pi(\tilde{k}+\tilde{k}_0)]+r^2\right)} \qquad (9.60)$$

From this equation, it is evident that this filter is a bandpass filter with a center wave number of $\tilde{k}_0$. The parameter r is related to the width of the bandpass. If $r = 1$, the transfer function has two *poles* at $\tilde{k} = \pm\tilde{k}_0$. If $r > 1$, the filter is unstable; even the slightest excitement will cause infinite amplitudes of the oscillation. The filter is only stable for $r \leq 1$.

The response of this filter can be normalized to obtain a bandpass filter with a unit response at the center wave number. The transfer function of this normalized filter is

$$\hat{s}(\tilde{k}) = \frac{(1-r^2)^2\sin^2(\pi\tilde{k}_0)}{(1+r^2)^2+2r^2\cos(2\pi\tilde{k}_0)-4r(1+r^2)\cos(\pi\tilde{k}_0)\cos(\pi\tilde{k})+2r^2\cos(2\pi\tilde{k})} \qquad (9.61)$$

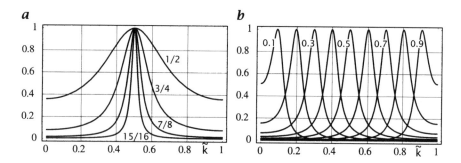

Figure 9.4: *Transfer function of the zero-phase recursive resonance filter for* **a** $\tilde{k}_0 = 1/2$ *and values of* r *as indicated; and* **b** $r = 7/8$ *and values of* $\tilde{k}_0$ *as indicated.*

The denominator in Eq. (9.61) is still the same as in Eq. (9.60); it has only been expanded in terms with $\cos(n\pi\tilde{k}_0)$. The corresponding recursive filter coefficients are:

$$g'_n = (1 - r^2)\sin(\pi\tilde{k}_0)g_n + 2r\cos(\pi\tilde{k}_0)g'_{n\mp1} - r^2 g'_{n\mp2} \qquad (9.62)$$

Figure 9.4 shows the transfer function of this filter for values of $\tilde{k}_0$ and r as indicated.

For symmetry reasons, the factors become most simple for a resonance wave number of $\tilde{k}_0 = 1/2$. Then the recursive filter is

$$g'_n = (1 - r^2)g_n - r^2 g'_{n\mp2} = g_n - r^2(g_n + g'_{n\mp2}) \qquad (9.63)$$

with the transfer function

$$\hat{s}(\tilde{k}) = \frac{(1 - r^2)^2}{1 + r^4 + 2r^2 \cos(2\pi\tilde{k})} \qquad (9.64)$$

The maximum response of this filter at $\tilde{k} = 1/2$ is one and the minimum response at $\tilde{k} = 0$ and $\tilde{k} = 1$ is $((1 - r^2)/(1 + r^2))^2$.

This resonance filter is the discrete analog to a linear system governed by the second-order differential equation $\ddot{y} + 2\tau\dot{y} + \omega_0^2 y = 0$, the damped harmonic oscillator. The circular eigenfrequency ω_0 and the time constant τ of a real-world oscillator are related to the parameters of the discrete oscillator, r and $\tilde{k}_0$ by [4]

$$r = \exp(-\Delta t/\tau) \quad \text{and} \quad \tilde{k}_0 = \omega_0 \Delta t/\pi \qquad (9.65)$$

9.4 Classes of nonlinear filters

9.4.1 Limitations of linear filters

In the previous sections, the theory of linear shift-invariant filters was discussed in detail. Although the theory of these filters is well established and they can be applied, they still have some severe limitations. Basically, linear filters cannot distinguish between a useful feature and noise. This property can be best demonstrated with a simple example. We assume a simple signal model with additive noise:

$$g'(\boldsymbol{x}) = g(\boldsymbol{x}) + n(\boldsymbol{x}) \Longleftrightarrow \hat{g}'(\boldsymbol{k}) = \hat{g}(\boldsymbol{k}) + \hat{n}(\boldsymbol{k}) \qquad (9.66)$$

The signal to noise ratio (SNR) is defined by $|\hat{g}(\boldsymbol{k})| / |\hat{n}(\boldsymbol{k})|$. If we now apply a linear filter with the transfer function $\hat{h}(\boldsymbol{k})$ to this signal, the filtered signal is

$$\hat{h}(\boldsymbol{k})\hat{g}'(\boldsymbol{k}) = \hat{h}(\boldsymbol{k})(\hat{g}(\boldsymbol{k}) + \hat{n}(\boldsymbol{k})) = \hat{h}(\boldsymbol{k})\hat{g}(\boldsymbol{k}) + \hat{h}(\boldsymbol{k})\hat{n}(\boldsymbol{k}) \qquad (9.67)$$

It is immediately evident that the noise and the signal are damped by the same factor. Consequently, the SNR does not increase at all by linear filtering, it just stays the same.

From the preceding considerations, it is obvious that more complex approaches are required than linear filtering. Common to all these approaches is that in one or another way the filters are made dependent on the context or are tailored for specific types of signals. Often a control strategy is an important part of such filters that controls which filter or in which way a filter has to be applied at a certain point in the image. Here, we will outline only the general classes for nonlinear filters. Pitas and Venetsanopoulos [7] give a detailed survey on this topic.

9.4.2 Rank-value filters

Rank-value filters are based on a quite different concept than linear-shift invariant operators. These operators consider all pixels in the neighborhood. It is implicitly assumed that each pixel, distorted or noisy, carries still useful and correct information. Thus, convolution operators are not equipped to handle situations where the value at a pixel carries incorrect information. This situation arises, for instance, when an individual sensor element in a CCD array is defective or a transmission error occurred.

To handle such cases, operations are required that apply selection mechanisms and do not use all pixels in the neighborhood to compute the output of the operator. The simplest class of operators of this type are rank-value filters. While the convolution operators may be characterized by "weighting and accumulating," rank-value filters may be characterized by "comparing and selecting."

For this we take all the gray values of the pixels that are within the filter mask and sort them by ascending gray value. This sorting is common to all rank-value filters. They only differ by the position in the list from which the gray value is picked out and written back to the center pixel. The filter operation that selects the medium value is called the *median filter*. The median filter is an excellent example for a filter that is adapted to a certain type of signal. It is ideally suited for removing a single pixel that has a completely incorrect gray value because of a transmission or data error. It is less well suited, for example, to reduce white noise.

Other known rank-value filters are the *minimum filter* and the *maximum filter*. As the names indicate, these filters select out of a local neighborhood, either the minimum or the maximum gray value forming the base for gray-scale *morphological filters* (Chapter 14).

As rank-value filters do not perform arithmetic operations but select pixels, we will never run into rounding problems. These filters map a discrete set of gray values onto itself. The theory of rank-value filters has still not been developed to the same extent as convolution filters. As they are nonlinear filters, it is much more difficult to understand their general properties. Rank-value filters are discussed in detail by Pitas and Venetsanopoulos [7].

9.4.3   Pixels with certainty measures

Linear filters as discussed in Section 9.2 treat each pixel equally. Implicitly, it is assumed that the information they are carrying is of equal significance. While this seems to be a reasonable first approximation, it is certain that it cannot be generally true. During image acquisition, the sensor area may contain bad sensor elements that lead to erroneous gray values at certain positions in the image. Furthermore, the sensitivity and noise level may vary from sensor element to sensor element. In addition, transmission errors may occur so that individual pixels may carry wrong information. Thus we may attach in one way or another a certainty measurement to each picture element.

Once a certainty measurement has been attached to a pixel, it is obvious that the normal convolution operators are no longer a good choice. Instead, the certainty has to be considered when performing any kind of operation with it. A pixel with suspicious information should only get a low weighting factor in the convolution sum. This kind of approach leads us to what is known as *normalized convolution* [8, 9].

This approach seems to be very natural for a scientist or engineer who is used to qualifying any measurement with an error. A measurement without a careful error estimate is of no value. The standard deviation of a measured value is required for the further analysis of any quantity that is related to the measurement. In normalized convolution this common principle is applied to image processing.

The power of this approach is related to the fact that we have quite different possibilities to define the certainty measurement. It need not only be related to a direct measurement error of a single pixel. If we are, for example, interested in computing an estimate of the mean gray value in an object, we can take the following approach. We devise a kind of certainty measurement that analyzes neighborhoods and attaches low weighting factors where we may suspect an edge so that these pixels do not contribute much to the mean gray value or feature of the object.

In a similar way, we can, for instance, also check how likely the gray value of a certain pixel is if we suspect some distortion by transmission errors or defective pixels. If the certainty measurement of a certain pixel is below a critical threshold, we replace it by a value interpolated from the surrounding pixels.

9.4.4   Adaptive and steerable filters

Adaptive filters can be regarded as a linear filter operation that is made dependent on the neighborhood. Adaptive filtering can best be explained by a classical application, that is, the suppression of noise without significant blurring of image features.

The basic idea of adaptive filtering is that in certain neighborhoods we could very well apply a smoothing operation. If, for instance, the neighborhood is flat, we can assume that we are within an object with constant features and thus apply an isotropic smoothing operation to this pixel to reduce the noise level. If an edge has been detected in the neighborhood, we could still apply some smoothing, namely, along the edge. In this way, some noise is still removed but the edge is not blurred. With this approach, we need a set of filters for various unidirectional and directional smoothing operations and choose the most appropriate smoothing filter for each pixel according to the local structure around it. Because of the many filters involved, adaptive filtering may be a very computational-intensive approach. This is the case if either the coefficients of the filter to be applied have to be computed for every single pixel or if a large set of filters is used in parallel and after all filters are computed it is decided at every pixel which filtered image is chosen for the output image.

With the discovery of steerable filters [10], however, adaptive filtering techniques have become attractive and computationally much more efficient.

9.4.5   Nonlinear combinations of filters

Normalized convolution and adaptive filtering have one strategy in common. Both use combinations of linear filters and nonlinear point operations such as pointwise multiplication and division of images. The combination of linear filter operations with nonlinear point operations makes the whole operation nonlinear.

The combination of these two kinds of elementary operations is a very powerful instrument for image processing. Operators containing combinations of linear filter operators and point operators are very attractive as they can be composed of very simple and elementary operations that are very well understood and for which analytic expressions are available. Thus, these operations in contrast to many others can be the subject of a detailed mathematical analysis. Many advanced signal and image-processing techniques are of that type. This includes operators to compute local structure in images and various operations for texture analysis.

9.5 Local averaging

Averaging is an elementary neighborhood operation for multidimensional signal processing. Averaging results in better feature estimates by including more data points. It is also an essential tool to regularize otherwise ill-defined quantities such as derivatives (Chapters 10 and 12). Convolution provides the framework for all elementary averaging filters. In this chapter averaging filters are considered for continuous signals and for discrete signals on square, rectangular and hexagonal lattices. The discussion is not restricted to 2-D signals. Whenever it is possible, the equations and filters are given for signals with arbitrary dimension.

The common properties and characteristics of all averaging filters are discussed in Section 9.5.1. On lattices two types of averaging filters are possible [3, Section 5.7.3]. Type I filters generate an output on the same lattice. On a rectangular grid such filters are of odd length in all directions. Type II filters generate an output on a grid with lattice points between the original lattice points (intermediate lattice). On a rectangular grid such filters are of even length in all directions. In this chapter two elementary averaging filters for digital multidimensional signals are discussed—box filters (Section 9.5.3) and binomial filters (Section 9.5.4). Then we will deal with techniques to cascade these elementary filters to large-scale averaging filters in Section 9.5.5, and filters with weighted signals (normalized convolution) in Section 9.5.6.

9.5.1 General properties

Transfer function. Any averaging filter operator must preserve the mean value. This condition means that the transfer function for zero wave number is 1 or, equivalently, that the sum of all coefficients of the mask is 1:

$$\hat{h}(\mathbf{0}) = 1 \iff \int_{-\infty}^{\infty} h(\mathbf{x})\, \mathrm{d}^D x = 1 \quad \text{or} \quad \sum_{\mathbf{n} \in \text{mask}} H_{\mathbf{n}} = 1 \qquad (9.68)$$

Intuitively, we expect that any smoothing operator attenuates smaller scales more strongly than coarser scales. More specifically, a smoothing operator should not completely annul a certain scale while smaller scales still remain in the image. Mathematically speaking, this means that the transfer function decreases monotonically with the wave number. Then for any direction, represented by a unit vector $\bar{r}$

$$\hat{h}(k_2\bar{r}) \le \hat{h}(k_1\bar{r}) \quad \text{if} \quad k_2 > k_1 \tag{9.69}$$

We may impose the more stringent condition that the transfer function approaches zero in all directions,

$$\lim_{k\to\infty} \hat{h}(k\bar{r}) = 0 \tag{9.70}$$

On a discrete lattice the wave numbers are limited by the *Nyquist* condition, that is, the wave number must lay within the first Brillouin zone (Section 8.4.2). Then it makes sense to demand that the transfer function of an averaging filter is zero at the border of the Brillouin zone. On a rectangular lattice this means

$$\hat{h}(k) = 0 \quad \text{if} \quad k\hat{b}_d = |\hat{b}_d|/2 \tag{9.71}$$

where $\hat{b}_d$ is any of the D-basis vectors of the reciprocal lattice (Section 8.4.2). Together with the monotonicity condition and the preservation of the mean value, this means that the transfer function decreases monotonically from one to zero for each averaging operator.

For a 1-D filter we can easily use Eq. (9.24) to relate the condition in Eq. (9.71) to a condition for the coefficients of type I filters:

$$\hat{h}(1) = 0 \iff h_0 + 2 \sum_{r \text{ even}} h_r = 2 \sum_{r \text{ odd}} h_r \tag{9.72}$$

One-dimensional type II filters are, according to Eq. (9.24), always zero for $\tilde{k} = 1$.

Even filters in continuous space. With respect to object detection, the most important feature of an averaging operator is that it must not shift the object position. Any shift introduced by a preprocessing operator would cause errors in the estimates of the position and possibly other geometric features of an object. In order not to cause a spatial shift, a filter must not induce any phase shift in the Fourier space. A filter with this property is known as a *zero-phase filter*. This implies that the transfer function is real and this is equivalent with an *even symmetry* of the filter mask (Section 8.6.3):

$$h(-x) = h(x) \iff \hat{h}(k) \quad \text{real} \tag{9.73}$$

Averaging filters normally meet a stronger symmetry condition in the sense that each axis is a symmetry axis. Then Eq. (9.73) is valid for each component of $\boldsymbol{x}$:

$$h([x_1,\ldots,-x_d,\ldots,x_D]^T) = h([x_1,\ldots,x_d,\ldots,x_D]^T) \qquad (9.74)$$

Even filters on 1-D lattices. For digital signals we distinguish filters with odd and even numbers of coefficients in *all* directions (Section 9.2.5). For both cases, we can write the symmetry condition for a filter with $R_d + 1$ coefficients in the direction d as

$$H_{r_0,r_1,\ldots,R_d-r_d,\ldots,r_D} = H_{r_0,r_1,\ldots,r_d,\ldots,r_D} \qquad \forall d \in [1,D] \qquad (9.75)$$

when we count the coefficients in each direction from left to right from 0 to R_d. This is not the usual counting but it is convenient as only one equation is required to express the evenness for filters with even and odd numbers of coefficients. For a 1-D filter the symmetry conditions reduce to

$$H_{R-r} = H_r \qquad (9.76)$$

The symmetry relations significantly ease the computation of the transfer functions because for real transfer functions only the cosine term of the complex exponential from the Fourier transform remains in the equations (Sections 8.6 and 9.2.5). The transfer function for 1-D even masks with either $2R + 1$ (type I filter) or $2R$ coefficients (type II filter) is

$$
\begin{aligned}
{}^I\hat{h}(\tilde{k}) &= h_0 + 2\sum_{r=1}^{R} h_r \cos(r\pi\tilde{k}) \\
{}^{II}\hat{h}(\tilde{k}) &= 2\sum_{r=1}^{R} h_r \cos((r - 1/2)\pi\tilde{k})
\end{aligned}
\qquad (9.77)
$$

Note that in these equations only pairs of coefficients are counted from 1 to R. The central coefficient of a filter with an odd number of coefficients has the index zero. As discussed in Section 9.2.5, filters with an odd number of coefficients output the filter results to the same lattice while filters with an even number of coefficients output the filter result to the intermediate lattice. A further discussion of the properties of symmetric filters up to three dimensions can be found in Jähne [4].

Isotropic filters. In most applications, the averaging should be the same in all directions in order not to prefer any direction. Thus, both the filter mask and the transfer function should be isotropic. Consequently, the filter mask depends only on the magnitude of the distance from the center pixel and the transfer function on the magnitude of the wave number:

$$H(\mathbf{x}) = H(|\mathbf{x}|) \iff \hat{H}(\tilde{\mathbf{k}}) = \hat{H}(|\tilde{\mathbf{k}}|) \tag{9.78}$$

This condition can also be met easily in discrete space. It means that the coefficients at lattice points with an equal distance from the center point are the same. However, the major difference now is that a filter whose coefficients meet this condition does not necessarily have an isotropic transfer function. The deviations from the isotropy are stronger the smaller is the filter mask. We will discuss the deviations from isotropy in detail for specific filters.

9.5.2 Separable averaging filters

The importance of separable filters for higher-dimensional signals is related to the fact that they can be computed much faster than non-separable filters [CVA2, Section 5.6]. The symmetry conditions for separable averaging filters are also quite simple because only the symmetry condition Equation (9.76) must be considered. Likewise, the equations for the transfer functions of separable filters are quite simple. If we apply the same 1-D filter in all directions, the resulting transfer function of a D-dimensional filter is given after Eq. (9.77) by

$$
\begin{aligned}
{}^{I}\hat{h}(\tilde{\mathbf{k}}) &= \prod_{d=1}^{D} \left(h_0 + 2\sum_{r=1}^{R} h_r \cos(r\pi\tilde{k}_d) \right) \\
{}^{II}\hat{h}(\tilde{\mathbf{k}}) &= \prod_{d=1}^{D} \left(2\sum_{r=1}^{R} h_r \cos((r-1/2)\pi\tilde{k}_d) \right)
\end{aligned}
\tag{9.79}
$$

With respect to isotropy, there exists only a single separable filter that is also isotropic, that is, the Gaussian function

$$
\begin{aligned}
\frac{1}{a^D} \exp(-\pi \mathbf{x}^T\mathbf{x}/a^2) &= \frac{1}{a^D} \prod_{d=1}^{D} \exp(-\pi x_d^2/a^2) \iff \\
\exp(-\pi a^2 \tilde{\mathbf{k}}^T\tilde{\mathbf{k}}/4) &= \prod_{d=1}^{D} \exp(-\pi a^2 \tilde{k}_d^2/4)
\end{aligned}
\tag{9.80}
$$

This feature shows the central importance of the Gaussian function for signal processing from yet another perspective.

To a good approximation, the Gaussian function can be replaced on orthogonal discrete lattices by the binomial distribution. The coefficients of a 1-D binomal filter with $R + 1$ coefficients and its transfer

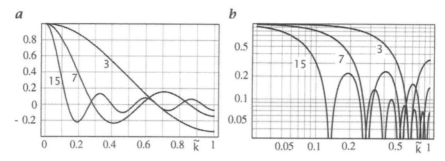

Figure 9.5: *Transfer functions of type I box filters with 3, 7, and 15 coefficients in **a** a linear plot; and **b** a log-log plot of the absolute value.*

function are given by

$$B^R = \frac{1}{2^R}\left[b_0 = 1,\dots,b_r = \binom{R}{r},\dots,b_{R+1} = 1\right] \iff \hat{B}^R(\tilde{k}) = \cos^R(\pi\tilde{k}/2) \tag{9.81}$$

With the comments on the isotropy of discrete filters in mind (Section 9.5.1), it is necessary to study the deviation of the transfer function of binomial filters from an isotropic filter.

9.5.3 Box filters

The simplest method is to average pixels within the filter mask and to divide the sum by the number of pixels. Such a simple filter is called a *box filter*. It is also known under the name *running mean*. In this section, only type I box filters are discussed. For type II box filters and box filters on hexagonal lattices see CVA2 [Section 7.3].

The simplest type I 1-D box filter is

$$^3R = \frac{1}{3}[1,1,1] \iff {}^3\hat{R}(\tilde{k}) = \frac{1}{3} + \frac{2}{3}\cos(\pi\tilde{k}) \tag{9.82}$$

The factor 1/3 scales the result of the convolution sum in order to preserve the mean value (see Eq. (9.68) in Section 9.5.1). Generally, a type I 1-D box filter with $2R + 1$ coefficients has the transfer function

$$
\begin{aligned}
{}^I\hat{R}(\tilde{k}) &= \frac{1}{2R+1} + \frac{2}{2R+1}\sum_{r=1}^{R}\cos(\pi r\tilde{k}) \\[2mm]
&= \frac{1}{2R+1}\frac{\cos(\pi R\tilde{k}) - \cos(\pi(R+1)\tilde{k})}{1 - \cos(\pi\tilde{k})}
\end{aligned}
\tag{9.83}
$$

For small wave numbers the transfer function can be approximated by

$$^I\hat{R}(\tilde{k}) \approx 1 - \frac{R(R+1)}{6}(\pi\tilde{k})^2 + \frac{R(R+1)(3R^2+3R-1)}{360}(\pi\tilde{k})^4 \tag{9.84}$$

Figure 9.5 shows that the box filter is a poor averaging filter. The transfer function is not monotonical and the envelope of the transfer function is only decreasing with k^{-1} (compare Section 8.6.3). The highest wave number is not completely suppressed even with large filter masks. The box filter also shows significant oscillations in the transfer function. The filter ${}^{2R+1}\mathcal{R}$ completely eliminates the wave numbers $\tilde{k} = 2r/(2R + 1)$ for $1 \leq r \leq R$. In certain wave-number ranges, the transfer function becomes negative. This corresponds to a 180° phase shift and thus a contrast inversion.

Despite all their disadvantages, box filters have one significant advantage. They can be computed very fast with only one addition, subtraction, and multiplication independent of the size of the filter, that is, $O(R^0)$. Equation (9.83) indicates that the box filter can also be understood as a filter operation with a recursive part according to the following relation:

$$g'_n = g'_{n-1} + \frac{1}{2R + 1}(g_{n+R} - g_{n-R-1}) \tag{9.85}$$

This recursion can easily be understood by comparing the computations for the convolution at neighboring pixels. When the box mask is moved one position to the right, it contains the same weighting factor for all pixels except for the last and the first pixel. Thus, we can simply take the result of the previous convolution (g'_{n-1}), subtract the first pixel that just moved out of the mask (g_{n-R-1}), and add the gray value at the pixel that just came into the mask (g_{n+R}). In this way, the computation of a box filter does not depend on its size.

Higher-dimensional box filters can simply be computed by cascading 1-D box filters running in all directions, as the box filter is separable. Thus the resulting transfer function for a D-dimensional filter is

$$^{2R+1}\hat{R}(\tilde{k}) = \frac{1}{(2R + 1)^D} \prod_{d=1}^{D} \frac{\cos(\pi R \tilde{k}_d) - \cos(\pi (R + 1)\tilde{k}_d)}{1 - \cos(\pi \tilde{k}_d)} \tag{9.86}$$

For a 2-D filter, we can approximate the transfer function for small wave numbers and express the result in cylinder coordinates by using $k_1 = k \cos \phi$ and $k_2 = k \sin \phi$ and obtain

$$
\begin{aligned}
^1\hat{R}(\tilde{k}) \quad \approx \quad & 1 - \frac{R(R + 1)}{6}(\pi \tilde{k})^2 + \frac{R(R + 1)(14R^2 + 14R - 1)}{1440}(\pi \tilde{k})^4 \\
& - \frac{R(R + 1)(2R^2 + 2R + 1)}{1440} \cos(4\phi)(\pi \tilde{k})^4
\end{aligned}
$$

$$\tag{9.87}$$

This equation indicates that—although the term with $\tilde{k}^2$ is isotropic— the term with $\tilde{k}^4$ is significantly anisotropic. The anisotropy does not

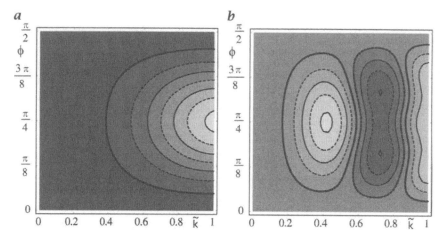

Figure 9.6: *Absolute deviation of the 2-D transfer functions of type I 2-D box filters from the transfer function along the x axis (1-D transfer function shown in Fig. 9.5) for a **a** 3×3 and **b** 7×7 filter. The distance of the contour lines is 0.05. The area between the thick contour lines marks the range around zero.*

improve for larger filter masks because the isotropic and anisotropic terms in $\tilde{k}^4$ grow with the same power in R.

A useful measure for the anisotropy is the deviation of the 2-D filter response from the response in the direction of the x_1 axis:

$$\Delta \hat{R}(\tilde{\boldsymbol{k}}) = \hat{R}(\tilde{\boldsymbol{k}}) - \hat{R}(\tilde{k}_1) \qquad (9.88)$$

For an isotropic filter, this deviation is zero. Again in an approximation for small wave numbers we obtain by Taylor expansion

$$\Delta^I \hat{R}(\tilde{\boldsymbol{k}}) \quad \approx \quad \frac{2R^4 + 4R^3 + 3R^2 + R}{720} \sin^2(2\phi)(\pi \tilde{k})^4 \qquad (9.89)$$

The anisotropy for various box filters is shown in Fig. 9.6. Clearly, the anisotropy does not become weaker for larger box filters. The deviations are significant and easily reach 0.25. This figure means that the attenuation for a certain wave number varies up to 0.25 with the direction of the wave number.

9.5.4 Binomial filters

In Section 9.5.2 we concluded that only the Gaussian function meets the most desirable features of an averaging filter: separability and isotropy. In this section we will investigate to which extent the binomial filter, which is a discrete approximation to the Gaussian filter, still meets these criteria. The coefficients of the one-dimensional binomial filter

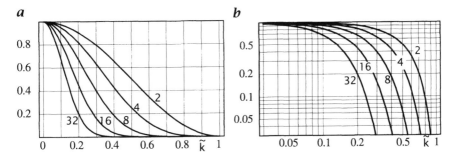

Figure 9.7: *Transfer functions of binomial filters $\mathcal{B}^R$ in **a** a linear plot and **b** a log-log plot of the absolute value with values of R as indicated.*

can be generated by repeatedly convolving the simple $1/2\,[1\ 1]$ mask:

$$B^R = \underbrace{1/2\,[1\ 1] * \ldots * 1/2\,[1\ 1]}_{R\ \text{times}} \tag{9.90}$$

This cascaded convolution is equivalent to the scheme in *Pascal's triangle*. The transfer function of the elementary $B = 1/2\,[1\ 1]$ filter is

$$\hat{B} = \cos(\pi\tilde{k}/2) \tag{9.91}$$

There is no need to distinguish type I and type II binomial filters in the equations because they can be generated by cascaded convolution as in Eq. (9.90). Therefore, the transfer function of the B^R binomial filter is

$$\hat{B}^R = \cos^R(\pi\tilde{k}/2) \tag{9.92}$$

The most important features of binomial averaging filters are:

Monotonic transfer function. The transfer function decreases monotonically from 1 to 0 (Fig. 9.7).

Spatial variance. The coefficients of the binomial filter quickly approach with increasing mask size a sampled normal distribution. The spatial variance is

$$\sigma_x^2 = R/4 \tag{9.93}$$

A binomial filter effectively averages over a width of $2\sigma_x$. In contrast to the box filters, the effective averaging width increases only with the square root of the filter length.

Variance. Also the transfer function of the binomial filter quickly approaches the Gaussian function with increasing mask size (Fig. 9.7a). It is instructive to compare the Taylor expansion of the Gaussian

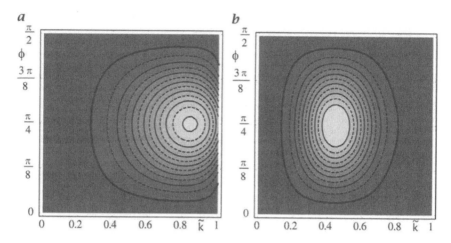

Figure 9.8: *Absolute deviation of the 2-D transfer functions of binomial filters from the transfer function along the x axis (1-D transfer function shown in Fig. 9.7) for a **a** 3×3 ($\mathcal{B}^2$) and **b** 9×9 ($\mathcal{B}^8$) filter. The distance of the contour lines is 0.005 in **a** and 0.001 in **b**. The area between the thick contour lines marks the range around zero.*

function for small wave numbers with those of the transfer functions of binomial filters:

$$
\begin{aligned}
\exp(-\tilde{k}^2/(2\sigma_k^2)) &\approx 1 \;-\; \frac{1}{2\sigma_k^2}\tilde{k}^2 \;+\; \frac{1}{8\sigma_k^4}\tilde{k}^4 \\
\hat{B}^R(\tilde{k}) &\approx 1 \;-\; \frac{R\pi^2}{8}\tilde{k}^2 \;+\; \left(\frac{R^2\pi^4}{128} - \frac{R\pi^4}{192}\right)\tilde{k}^4
\end{aligned}
\tag{9.94}
$$

For large R both expansions are the same with

$$
\sigma_k = \frac{2}{\sqrt{R\pi}}
\tag{9.95}
$$

Higher-dimensional binomial filters can be composed from 1-D binomial filters in all directions:

$$
\mathcal{B}^R = \prod_{d=1}^{D} \mathcal{B}_d^R
\tag{9.96}
$$

Thus the transfer function of the multidimensional binomial filter $\mathcal{B}^R$ with $(R+1)^D$ coefficients is given by

$$
\hat{B}^R = \prod_{d=1}^{D} \cos^R(\pi\tilde{k}_d/2)
\tag{9.97}
$$

The isotropy of binomial filters can be studied by expanding Eq. (9.97) in a Taylor series using cylindrical coordinates $\tilde{\boldsymbol{k}} = [\tilde{k}, \phi]^T$:

$$\hat{B}^R \approx 1 - \frac{R}{8}(\pi\tilde{k})^2 + \frac{2R^2 - R}{256}(\pi\tilde{k})^4 - \frac{R\cos 4\phi}{768}(\pi\tilde{k})^4 \qquad (9.98)$$

Only the second-order term is isotropic. In contrast, the fourth-order term contains an anisotropic part, which increases the transfer function in the direction of the diagonals. A larger filter (larger R) is less anisotropic as the isotropic term with $\tilde{k}^4$ increases quadratically with R while the anisotropic term with $\tilde{k}^4 \cos 4\theta$ increases only linearly with R. The anisotropy deviation according to Eq. (9.88) is given by

$$\Delta\hat{B}^R \approx \frac{R}{384}\sin^2(2\phi)(\pi\tilde{k})^4 + \frac{5R^2 - 4R}{15360}\sin^2(2\phi)(\pi\tilde{k})^6 \qquad (9.99)$$

and shown in Fig. 9.8.

Three-dimensional binomial filters and binomial filters on hexagonal grids are discussed in CVA2 [Section 7.4.3].

9.5.5 Cascaded averaging

The approaches discussed so far for local averaging are no solution if the averaging should cover large neighborhoods for the following reasons: First, binomial filters are not suitable for large-scale averaging—despite their efficient implementation by cascaded convolution with $\mathcal{B}$—because the averaging distance increases only with the square root of the mask size (see Eq. (9.93) in Section 9.5.4). Second, box filters and recursive filters are, in principle, suitable for large-scale averaging because the number of operations does not increase with the size of the point spread function (operation of the order $O(R^0)$). However, both types of filters have a nonideal transfer function. The transfer function of the box filter is not monotonically decreasing with the wave number (Section 9.5.3) and both filters show overly large deviations from an isotropic response. In this section, several techniques are discussed for large-scale averaging that overcome these deficits and limitations.

Multistep averaging. The problem of slow large-scale averaging originates from the small distance between the pixels averaged by small masks. In order to overcome this problem, we may use the same elementary averaging process but with more distant pixels. As the box, binomial and recursive averaging filters are separable and thus are applied as cascaded filter operations running one after the other in all coordinate directions through a multidimensional signal, it is sufficient to discuss increasing the step width for 1-D filter operations. A 1-D convolution with a mask that operates only with every S-th pixel can

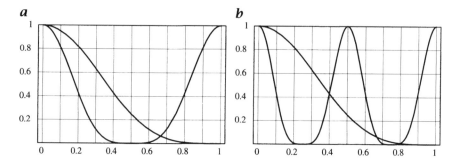

Figure 9.9: *Transfer functions of the binomial filter $\mathcal{B}^4$ ($\boldsymbol{B} = 1/16[1\,4\,6\,4\,1]$) and the same filter stretched by a a factor of two, $\mathcal{B}_2^4$ ($\boldsymbol{B}_2 = 1/16[1\,0\,4\,0\,6\,0\,4\,0\,1]$), and b a factor of four, $\mathcal{B}_4^4$.*

be written as a stretched mask

$$(h_S)_n = \begin{cases} h_{n'} & n = Sn' \\ 0 & \text{else} \end{cases} \quad \Longleftrightarrow \quad \hat{h}_S(\tilde{k}) = \hat{h}(\tilde{k}/S) \tag{9.100}$$

Because of the reciprocity between the spatial and Fourier domains the stretching of the filter mask by a factor S results in a corresponding shrinking of the transfer function. This shrinking goes—because of the periodicity of the transfer function of discrete samples—along with an S-fold replication of the transfer function as illustrated in Fig. 9.9.

An averaging filter that is used with a larger step width is no longer a good averaging filter for the whole wave-number range but only for wave numbers up to $\tilde{k} = 1/S$. Used individually, these filters are thus not of much help. But we can use them in cascade in such a way that previous smoothing has already removed all wave numbers beyond $\tilde{k} = 1/S$. This is the basic principle for the design of cascaded filters.

For practical design there are two degrees of freedom. First, we can select the basic filter that is used repeatedly with different step widths. Here, box, binomial and relaxation filters are investigated. Second, we can choose the way in which the step width is increased. We will consider both a linear and an exponential increase in the step width. Generally, a cascaded filter operation consists of the following chain of P operations with the filter operation $\mathcal{B}$:

$$\underbrace{\mathcal{B}_{a_P} \ldots \mathcal{B}_{a_p} \ldots \mathcal{B}_{a_2} \mathcal{B}_{a_1}}_{P \text{ times}} \tag{9.101}$$

where a_p consists of a sequence of step widths. Whereas in each step the same operator $\mathcal{B}$ with the spatial variance σ^2 is used and only the

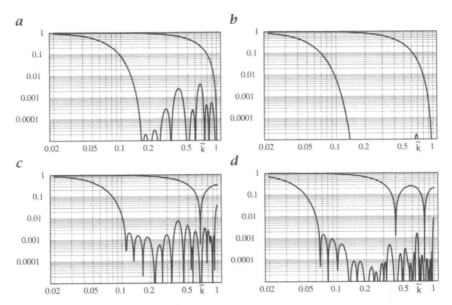

Figure 9.10: *Transfer functions of cascaded filtering with linear increase in step width with a $\mathcal{B}^2$, b $\mathcal{B}^4$, c $^3\mathcal{R}$, and d $^5\mathcal{R}$. Shown are the transfer functions of the original filters and of the cascaded filtering up to the six-fold step size with a resulting averaging width $\sqrt{91} \approx 9.54$ times larger than the original filter.*

step width is changed, the resulting step width can be computed by

$$\sigma_c^2 = \sigma^2 \sum_{p=1}^{P} a_p^2 \qquad (9.102)$$

From this equation it is also obvious that efficient filter cascading requires an increasing step width. If we keep the step width constant, the averaging width given by σ_c increases only with $\sqrt{P}$ and not linearly with P.

Linearly increasing step width. In the simplest case, the step width is increased linearly, that is, $a_p = p$. This results in the following sequence of P step widths: $1, 2, 3, 4, \ldots, P$. According to Eq. (9.102), the resulting series of variances is

$$\sigma_c^2 = \sigma^2 \sum_{p=1}^{P} p^2 = \frac{P(P+1)(2P+1)}{6} \sigma^2 \qquad (9.103)$$

For large P, $\sigma_c = P^{3/2}\sigma/\sqrt{3}$. Thus the averaging width increases even stronger than linear with the number of steps. With only six steps, the resulting averaging width is $\sqrt{91} \approx 9.54$ times larger than that of the

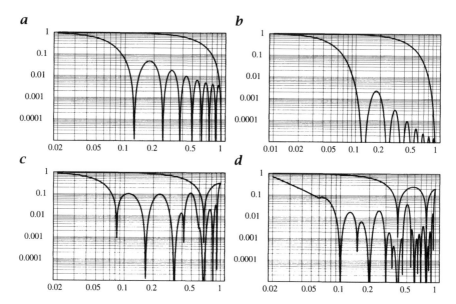

Figure 9.11: *Transfer functions of cascaded filtering with exponential increase in step width with* **a** $\mathcal{B}^2$, **b** $\mathcal{B}^4$, **c** $^3\mathcal{R}$, *and* **d** $^5\mathcal{R}$. *Shown are the transfer functions of the original filters and of four cascaded filters (up to step size 8) with a resulting averaging width* $\sqrt{85} \approx 9.22$ *times larger than the original filter.*

original filter (Fig. 9.10). To achieve this averaging width, the same filter would have to be applied 91 times.

The quality of the cascaded filtering, that is, the degree of deviation from a monotonic transfer function, is determined by the basic filter. Figure 9.10 shows the transfer functions for a number of different filters in a double-logarithmic plot. Only the binomial filter $\mathcal{B}^4$ shows negligible secondary peaks well beyond 10^{-4}. The other filters in Fig. 9.10 have significantly more pronounced secondary peaks in the 10^{-4} to 10^{-2} range.

Exponentially increasing step width. A linear increase in the step width is still too slow to achieve averaging over very large scales. It is also disadvantageous in that the increase in the averaging width is of the odd order $P^{3/2}$. This means that filtering does not increase the width of the averaging linearly. The increase is slightly stronger. Both difficulties are overcome with an exponential increase in the step width. The easiest way is to increase the step width by a factor of two from filtering to filtering. The resulting mask has the standard deviation

$$\sigma_c^2 = \sigma^2 \sum_{p=1}^{P} 2^{2p-2} = \frac{2^{2P}-1}{3}\sigma^2 \tag{9.104}$$

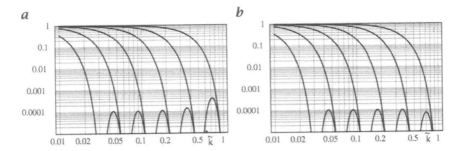

Figure 9.12: *a Sequence of transfer functions of cascaded filtering with exponential increase in step width using the $\mathcal{B}^6$ binomial filter. b Shows the same sequence except that the first filter with step width 1 is $\mathcal{B}^8$.*

Thus the standard deviation grows exponentially to $\approx (2^P/\sqrt{3})\sigma$ with only P filtering steps. In other words, the number of computations increases only logarithmically with the averaging width.

As for the linear increase of the step width, the basic filter determines the quality of the resulting transfer function of the cascaded filtering. Figure 9.11 shows that only the binomial filter $\mathcal{B}^4$ results in an acceptable transfer function of the cascaded filtering. All other filters show too high secondary peaks.

Figure 9.12a shows a sequence of transfer functions for the cascading of the binomial filter $\mathcal{B}^6$. It can be observed that the filters are not of exactly the same shape but that the secondary peak is higher for the first steps and only gradually levels off to a constant value. This effect is caused by the constant term in Eq. (9.104). It can be compensated if the first filter ($p = 1$) does not have variance σ^2 but has variance $4/3\sigma^2$. Indeed, if a $\mathcal{B}^8$ filter is used instead of the $\mathcal{B}^6$ filter in the first step, the filters in the different steps of the filter cascade are much more similar (Fig. 9.12b).

For higher-dimensional signals the isotropy of the averaging is of significance. As we already know that all filters except for the binomial filters are significantly anisotropic, only binomial filters are discussed. While the $\mathcal{B}^2$ filter still shows a pronounced anisotropy of several percent (Fig. 9.13a), the anisotropy is already just slightly more than 0.01 for a $\mathcal{B}^4$ filter (Fig. 9.13b).

Multigrid averaging. Multistep cascaded averaging can be further enhanced by converting it into a multiresolution technique. The idea of multigrid smoothing is very simple. If a larger step mask is involved, this operation can be applied on a correspondingly coarser grid. This means that the last operation before using the larger step mask needs to compute the convolution only at the grid points used by the following coarser grid operator. This sampling procedure is denoted by a special syntax in the operator index; $\mathcal{O}_{\downarrow 2}$ means: Apply the operator in

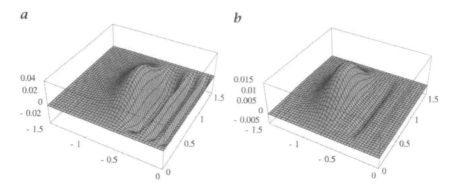

Figure 9.13: *Anisotropy of cascaded filtering with exponential increase of the step width in a log-polar plot. Shown is the deviation from the transfer function in the direction of the x axis for* **a** $\mathcal{B}_4^2 \mathcal{B}_2^2 \mathcal{B}_1^2$ *and* **b** $\mathcal{B}_4^4 \mathcal{B}_2^4 \mathcal{B}_1^4$.

all directions and advance the mask two pixels in all directions. Thus, the output of the filter operator has only half as many pixels in every direction as the input.

Multigrid smoothing makes the number of computations essentially independent of the standard deviation of the smoothing mask. We again consider a sequence of 1-D averaging filters:

$$\underbrace{\mathcal{B}_{12} \cdots \mathcal{B}_{12} \mathcal{B}_{12}}_{P \text{ times}}$$

The standard deviation of the filter cascade is the same as for the multistep approach with exponential increase of the step width (Eq. (9.104)). Also, as long as the sampling condition is met, that is, $\hat{B}^p(\tilde{k}) = 0$ $\forall \tilde{k} \geq 1/2$, the transfer functions of the filters are the same as for the multistep filters.

If $\mathcal{B}_{12}$ takes q operations, the operator sequence takes

$$q \sum_{p=1}^{P} \frac{1}{2^{p-1}} = 2q \left(1 - \frac{1}{2^{P-1}}\right) < 2q \qquad (9.105)$$

Thus, smoothing to any degree takes no more than twice as many operations as smoothing at the first step.

9.5.6 Weighted averaging

Image data, just like any other experimental data, may be characterized by individual errors that have to be considered in any further processing. As an introduction, we first discuss the averaging of a set of N data g_n with standard deviations σ_n. From elementary statistics, it is known that appropriate averaging requires the weighting of each data point g_n with the inverse of the variance $w_n = 1/\sigma_n^2$. Then, an estimate of the mean value is given by

$$\langle g \rangle = \sum_{n=1}^{N} g_n/\sigma_n^2 \left/ \sum_{n=1}^{N} 1/\sigma_n^2 \right. \tag{9.106}$$

while the standard deviation of the mean is

$$\sigma_{\langle g \rangle}^2 = 1 \left/ \sum_{n=1}^{N} 1/\sigma_n^2 \right. \tag{9.107}$$

The application of *weighted averaging* to image processing is known as *normalized convolution* [9]. The averaging is now extended to a local neighborhood. Each pixel enters the convolution sum with a weighting factor associated with it. Thus, normalized convolution requires two signals. One is the image G to be processed, the other an image W with the weighting factors.

By analogy to Eqs. (9.106) and (9.107), normalized convolution with the mask H is defined as

$$G' = \frac{H * (W \cdot G)}{H * W} \tag{9.108}$$

A normalized convolution with the mask H essentially transforms the image G and the weighting image W into a new image G' and a new weighting image $W' = H * W$, which can undergo further processing.

Normalized convolution is just adequate consideration of pixels with spatially variable statistical errors. "Standard" convolution can be regarded as a special case of normalized convolution. Then all pixels are assigned the same weighting factor and it is not required to use a weighting image, because the factor remains a constant.

The flexibility of normalized convolution is given by the choice of the weighting image. The weighting image is not necessarily associated with an error. It can be used to select and/or amplify pixels with certain features. In this way, normalized convolution becomes a versatile nonlinear operator. The application of normalized convolution is discussed in a number of contributions in the application gallery: Sections A18, A20, A16, and A23.

9.6 Interpolation

Interpolation of digital signals is required for a wide range of signal-processing tasks whenever any operation shifts the digital points of the output signal so that they no longer coincide with the grid points of the input signal. This occurs, among others, with the following operations:

Geometric operations. For many applications, the geometrical distortions introduced by optical systems [CVA1, Chapter 4]) are not acceptable and must be corrected. For satellite images, it is often required to recompute the image data to a different projective mapping.

Signal registration. If data are taken with different sensors, these sensors will almost never be in perfect spatial alignment. Thus it is required to map them onto common spatial coordinates for further joint processing.

Multiresolution signal processing. For multigrid data structures, such as pyramids (Section 8.10), signals are represented at different resolution levels. On such data structures it is necessary to interpolate missing points from coarser levels to be able to process them at a finer level.

Coarse-to-fine strategies. Coarse-to-fine strategies are an often used concept on multigrid data structures if the processing involves images that are shifted to each other either because of a different sensor (image registration), a different perspective (stereo images) or motion of objects (Chapter 10). In all these cases it is required to warp the images with the determined displacement vector field before processing at the next finer resolution [CVA2, Chapter 14].

Test image generation. In order to evaluate algorithms, it is important to apply them to known signals. For image-sequence processing, for example, it is useful to simulate displacement vector fields by warping images correspondingly.

For a long time there was little effort put into interpolation algorithms for computer vision. Thus most of the available procedures have been invented for computer graphics in the framework of *photorealistic rendering*. An excellent survey in this respect is provided by Wolberg [11]. Only with increasing demand for subpixel-accurate computer vision algorithms have the researchers become aware of the importance of accurate interpolation algorithms. The demands are quite high. As a rule of thumb, interpolation should neither change the amplitude of a signal by more than 1 % nor shift any signal by more than 0.01.

The analysis of the structure in small neighborhoods is a key element in higher-dimensional signal processing. Changes in the gray values reveal either the edge of an object or the type of texture.

9.6.1 Interpolation as convolution

The basis of interpolation is the sampling theorem (Section 8.4.2). This theorem states that the digital signal *completely* represents the continuous signal provided the sampling conditions are met. This basic fact suggests the following general framework for interpolation:

Reconstruction of continuous signal. From the sampled signal a continuous or a higher-resolution representation is reconstructed.

Filtering. Before a resampling can be performed, it is necessary to check whether a prefiltering of the data is required. Whenever the data are to be resampled with a coarser resolution, aliasing could occur because the sampling condition is no longer met (Section 8.4.3).

Resampling. This step finally forms the new digital signal.

Of course, a certain procedure for interpolation can perform two or even all of these steps in a single operation. However, it is still helpful for a better understanding of the procedure to separate it into these steps.

Although these procedures sound simple and straightforward, they are not. The problem is related to the fact that the reconstruction of the continuous signal from the sampled signal in practice is quite involved and can be performed only approximately. Thus, we need to balance the computational effort with the residual error for a given interpolation task.

Generally, a continuous multidimensional signal is interpolated from values at all points of a lattice by (Section 8.4.4)

$$g_r(x) = \sum_{p=1}^{P} \sum_n g_s(r_n + s_p) h(x - (r_n + s_p)) \tag{9.109}$$

In this equation r_n are the translation vectors of the lattice and s_p the offsets of the P points in the *primitive cell* of the lattice. If a continuous signal is required but only the value at a shifted point p (Eq. (9.109)) reduces to

$$g_r(p) = \sum_{p=1}^{P} \sum_n g_s(r_n + s_p) h(p - (r_n + s_p)) \tag{9.110}$$

This equation reveals that interpolation is nothing else but a generalized convolution operation of the points on a discrete lattice with sampled values from the interpolation kernel. The only difference is that the result of the operation is not written back to the same lattice but to a shifted lattice. Thus an interpolation operation can be described by a transfer function. According to the discussion of the *sampling theorem* in Sections 8.4.2 and 8.4.4, the ideal interpolation function has a transfer function that is constantly one within the first Brillouin zone and zero outside.

For the rest of this section, we will restrict all considerations to orthogonal lattices because interpolation of multidimensional signals is much easier to handle on these grids. On an orthogonal lattice with only one point per primitive cell ($P = 1$), the interpolation in Eq. (9.109) reduces to

$$g_r(\tilde{\pmb{x}}) = \sum_n g_s(\pmb{n})h(\tilde{\pmb{x}} - \pmb{n}) \tag{9.111}$$

In this equation all vectors in the spatial domain are expressed in units of the lattice constants: $\tilde{x}_d = x_d/\Delta x_d$. Thus, the components of the translation vector $\pmb{r}$ are integers and are replaced by $\pmb{n} = [n_1, \ldots, n_D]^T$, the vectorial index that counts the translations vectors on a D-dimensional lattice.

The ideal transfer function for interpolation of a D-dimensional signal is then a D-dimensional box function

$$\hat{g}_r(\tilde{\pmb{k}}) = \hat{g}(\tilde{\pmb{k}}) \prod_{d=1}^{D} \Pi(2\tilde{\pmb{k}}) \tag{9.112}$$

where $\tilde{\pmb{k}}$ is the wave number normalized to the Nyquist limit according to Eq. (8.34). It follows that the ideal interpolation function h is the Fourier transform of the box function, the sinc function

$$h(\tilde{\pmb{x}}) = \prod_{d=1}^{D} \frac{\sin(\pi\tilde{x}_d)}{\pi\tilde{x}_d} = \prod_{d=1}^{D} \mathrm{sinc}(\tilde{x}_d) \tag{9.113}$$

This ideal interpolation mask cannot be used in practice as it is infinite. Thus an optimal approximation must be found that minimizes the deviations from the ideal transfer function.

9.6.2 General properties of interpolation kernels

In this section some general properties of interpolation are summarized that are useful for the design of optimal interpolation masks.

Symmetries. An interpolation mask can have an even or odd number of coefficients. Because of symmetry reasons, the interpolation interval of these two types of interpolation masks is different. For a mask with an even number of coefficients (Fig. 9.14a), the symmetry center is between the two central points of the interpolation mask. Because any interpolation mask can have an interpolation interval of one distance between two points of the mask, the interpolation interval is limited to the interval between the two central points of the mask. For points outside of this range, the mask is shifted a corresponding number of points on the lattice, so that the point to be interpolated again is within this central interval.

For a mask with an odd number of coefficients (Fig. 9.14b), the symmetry center coincides with the central point. Thus the interpolation interval is now half the distance between points on the lattice on both

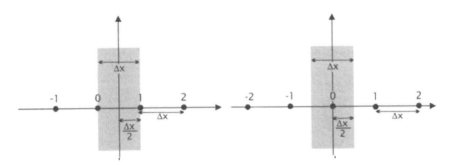

Figure 9.14: *Interpolation interval for interpolation masks with **a** an even and **b** an odd number of coefficients.*

sides of the central point. The symmetry conditions for these two types of interpolation filters are analogous to type I and type II averaging filters discussed in Sections 9.2.5 and 9.5.3.

Interpolation condition.   There are some general constraints that must be met by any interpolation filter. They result from the simple fact that the interpolated values in Eq. (9.111) at the lattice points n should reproduce the lattice points and not depend on any other lattice points. From this condition, we can infer the *interpolation condition*:

$$h(n) = \begin{cases} 1 & n = 0 \\ 0 & \text{otherwise} \end{cases} \tag{9.114}$$

Therefore any interpolation mask must have zero crossings at all grid points except the zero point where it is one. The ideal interpolation mask in Eq. (9.113) meets this interpolation condition.

More generally, we can state that any discrete interpolation mask sampled from the continuous interpolation kernel should meet the following condition:

$$^{\check{x}}H_n = \sum_n h(n + \tilde{x}) = 1 \quad \Longleftrightarrow \quad {}^{\check{x}}\hat{H}_0 = 1 \tag{9.115}$$

This generalized condition indicates only that a constant signal ($\tilde{k} = 0$) is not changed by an interpolation operation.

Separability.   The ideal interpolation function in Eq. (9.113) is separable. Therefore, interpolation can as easily be formulated for higher-dimensional images. We can expect that all solutions to the interpolation problem will also be separable. Consequently, we need only dis-

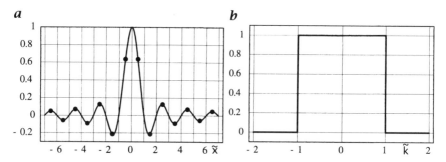

Figure 9.15: *a Ideal 1-D interpolation mask and b its transfer function. The values for the coefficients of the discrete mask to interpolate intermediate lattice points ($\tilde{x} = 1/2$) are marked by dots.*

cuss the 1-D interpolation problem

$$g_r(\tilde{x}) = \sum_{n=-R}^{R} g_n h(\tilde{x} - n) \tag{9.116}$$

where n and R take half-integer values for interpolation masks with an even number of coefficients and integer values for interpolation masks with an odd number of coefficients; x is given here in units of the lattice constant $\tilde{x} = x/\Delta x$. The 1-D ideal interpolation mask sinc($\tilde{x}$) and its transfer function $\Pi(2\tilde{k})$ are illustrated in Fig. 9.15.

Once a good interpolation mask is found for 1-D interpolation, we also have a solution for the D-dimensional interpolation problem.

An important special case is the interpolation to intermediate lattice points half-way between the existing lattice points. This scheme doubles the resolution and image size in all directions in which it is applied. The coefficients of the corresponding interpolation mask are the values of the sinc($\tilde{x}$) function sampled at all half-integer values:

$$h = \left[\frac{(-1)^{r-1} 2}{(2r - 1)\pi} \quad \cdots \quad -\frac{2}{3\pi} \frac{2}{\pi} \frac{2}{\pi} -\frac{2}{3\pi} \quad \cdots \quad \frac{(-1)^{r-1} 2}{(2r - 1)\pi} \right] \tag{9.117}$$

The coefficients are of alternating sign.

Interpolation error analysis. The fact that interpolation is a convolution operation and thus can be described by a transfer function in Fourier space Equation (9.113) gives us a tool to rate the errors associated with an interpolation technique. The box-type transfer function for the ideal interpolation function simply means that all wave numbers within the range of possible wave numbers $|k_d| \leq \Delta x_d/\pi$ experience neither a phase shift nor amplitude damping. Also, no wave number beyond the allowed interval is present in the interpolated signal, because the transfer function is zero there.

9.6.3   Interpolation in Fourier space

Interpolation reduces to a simple operation in the Fourier domain. The transfer function of an ideal interpolation kernel is a box function that is zero outside the wave numbers that can be represented (see Eq. (9.113)). This basic fact suggests the following interpolation procedure in Fourier space:

1. *Enlargement of the Fourier transform of the signal.* If the discrete Fourier transform of an M^D multidimensional signal is increased to an M'^D array, the array in the spatial domain is also increased to the same size. Because of the reciprocity of the Fourier transform, the image *size* remains unchanged. Only the spacing between pixels in the spatial domain is decreased, resulting in a higher spatial resolution:

$$M\Delta k_d \to M'\Delta k_d \quad \Longleftrightarrow \quad \Delta x = \frac{2\pi}{M\Delta k} \to \Delta x' = \frac{2\pi}{M'\Delta k} \qquad (9.118)$$

The padded area in the Fourier space is filled with zeroes.

2. *Inverse Fourier transform.* All that needs to be done is the computation of an inverse Fourier transform to obtain a higher resolution signal.

The Fourier transform can also be used to shift a signal by any distance without changing the signal resolution. Then the following three-step procedure must be applied.

1. *Forward Fourier transform.*

2. *Multiplication with a phase factor.* According to the *shift theorem* (Table 8.6), a shift in the spatial domain by a distance x_s corresponds to the multiplication of the Fourier transform by the following phase factor:

$$g(x) \to g(x - s) \quad \Longleftrightarrow \quad \hat{G}_u \to \exp(-2\pi i u s)\hat{G}_u \qquad (9.119)$$

where the vectorial shift s is given in units of the lattice constants Δx_d.

3. *Inverse Fourier transform.*

Theoretically, these simple procedures result in perfectly interpolated signals. A closer look, however, reveals that these techniques have some serious drawbacks.

First, the Fourier transform of a finite image implies a cyclic repetition of the image both in the spatial and Fourier domain. Thus, the convolution performed by the Fourier transform is also cyclic. This means that at the right or left edge of the image, convolution continues with the image at the opposite side. Because the real world is not

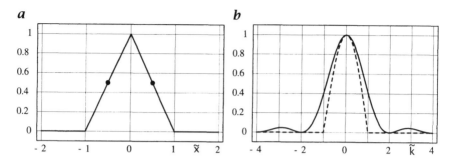

Figure 9.16: *a One-dimensional linear interpolation:* ***a*** *continuous interpolation mask and* ***b*** *its transfer function. The values for the coefficients of the discrete mask to interpolate intermediate lattice points ($\tilde{x} = 1/2$) are marked by dots.*

periodic and interpolation masks are large, this may lead to significant distortions of the interpolation even at quite large distances from the edges of the image.

Second, the Fourier transform can be computed efficiently only for a specified number of values for M' [CVA2, Section 3.4]. Therefore, the Fourier-transform based interpolation is limited to scaling factors of powers of two.

Third, the Fourier transform is a global transform. Thus it can be applied only to a global scaling of the signal by an integer factor.

9.6.4 Polynomial interpolation

Linear interpolation. *Linear interpolation* is the classic approach to interpolation. The interpolated points are on pieces of straight lines connecting neighboring grid points. In order to simplify the expressions in the following, we use normalized spatial coordinates $\tilde{x} = x/\Delta x$. We locate the two grid points at $-1/2$ and $1/2$. This yields the interpolation equation

$$g(\tilde{x}) = \frac{g_{1/2} + g_{-1/2}}{2} + \left(g_{1/2} - g_{-1/2}\right)\tilde{x} \quad \text{for} \quad |\tilde{x}| \le 1/2 \qquad (9.120)$$

By comparison of Eq. (9.120) with Eq. (9.116), we can conclude that the continuous interpolation mask for linear interpolation is the triangle function

$$h_1(\tilde{x}) = \Lambda(\tilde{x}) = \begin{cases} 1 - |\tilde{x}| & |\tilde{x}| \le 1 \\ 0 & \text{otherwise} \end{cases} \qquad (9.121)$$

The transfer function of the interpolation mask for linear interpolation, the triangle function $h_1(x)$ Eq. (9.121), is the squared sinc function

$$\hat{h}_1(\tilde{k}) = \frac{\sin^2(\pi\tilde{k}/2)}{(\pi\tilde{k}/2)^2} = \text{sinc}^2(\tilde{k}/2) \qquad (9.122)$$

A comparison with the ideal transfer function for interpolation Equation (9.112) (see also Fig. 9.15b and Fig. 9.16b), shows that two distortions are introduced by linear interpolation:

1. While low wave numbers (and especially the mean value $\tilde{k} = 0$) are interpolated correctly, high wave numbers are reduced in amplitude, resulting in some degree of smoothing. At $\tilde{k} = 1$, the transfer function is reduced to about 40%: $\hat{h}_1(1) = (2/\pi)^2 \approx 0.4$.

2. As $\hat{h}_1(\tilde{k})$ is not zero at wave numbers $\tilde{k} > 1$, some spurious high wave numbers are introduced. If the continuously interpolated image is resampled, this yields moderate aliasing. The first sidelobe has an amplitude of $(2/3\pi)^2 \approx 0.045$.

If we interpolate only the intermediate grid points at $\tilde{x} = 0$, the continuous interpolation function Eq. (9.121) reduces to a discrete convolution mask with values at $\tilde{x} = [\ldots -3/2 \; -1/2 \; 1/2 \; 3/2 \ldots]$. As Eq. (9.121) is zero for $|\tilde{x}| \geq 1$, we obtain the simple interpolation mask $H = 1/2[1\ 1]$ with the transfer function

$$\hat{H}_1(\tilde{k}) = \cos \pi \tilde{k}/2 \tag{9.123}$$

The transfer function is real, so no phase shifts occur. The significant amplitude damping at higher wave numbers, however, shows that structures with high wave numbers are not correctly interpolated.

Higher-order polynomial interpolation. Given the significant limitations of linear interpolation, we ask whether higher-order interpolation schemes perform better. The basic principle of linear interpolation was that a straight line was drawn to pass through two neighboring points. In the same way, we can use a polynomial of degree P with $P + 1$ unknown coefficients a_p to pass through $P + 1$ points:

$$g_r(\tilde{x}) = \sum_{p=0}^{P} a_p \tilde{x}^p \tag{9.124}$$

For symmetry reasons, the lattice points are placed at the positions

$$\tilde{k}_p = \frac{2p - P}{2} \tag{9.125}$$

For an even number of points (P is odd), the lattice points are located at half-integer values.

From the interpolation condition at the grid points $g_r(\tilde{k}_p) = g_p$, we obtain a linear equation system with $P+1$ equations and $P+1$ unknowns

a_P of the following form when P is odd:

$$
\begin{bmatrix}
g_0 \\
\vdots \\
g_{(P-1)/2} \\
g_{(P+1)/2} \\
\vdots \\
g_P
\end{bmatrix}
=
\begin{bmatrix}
1 & -P/2 & P^2/4 & -P^3/8 & \cdots \\
& \vdots & & & \\
1 & -1/2 & 1/4 & -1/8 & \cdots \\
1 & 1/2 & 1/4 & 1/8 & \cdots \\
& \vdots & & & \\
1 & P/2 & P^2/4 & P^3/8 & \cdots
\end{bmatrix}
\begin{bmatrix}
a_0 \\
\vdots \\
a_{(P-1)/2} \\
a_{(P+1)/2} \\
\vdots \\
a_P
\end{bmatrix}
\tag{9.126}
$$

or written as a matrix equation:

$$
\boldsymbol{g} = \boldsymbol{M}\boldsymbol{a} \quad \text{with} \quad M_{pq} = \left(\frac{2q-P}{2}\right)^p, \quad p,q \in [0,P]
\tag{9.127}
$$

For a cubic polynomial ($P = 3$), the solution of the equations system is

$$
\begin{bmatrix}
a_0 \\
a_1 \\
a_2 \\
a_3
\end{bmatrix}
=
\frac{1}{48}
\begin{bmatrix}
-3 & 27 & 27 & -3 \\
2 & -54 & 54 & -2 \\
12 & -12 & -12 & 12 \\
-8 & 24 & -24 & 8
\end{bmatrix}
\begin{bmatrix}
g_0 \\
g_1 \\
g_2 \\
g_3
\end{bmatrix}
\tag{9.128}
$$

Using Eqs. (9.124) and (9.128) we can express the interpolated values for the position ϵ in the interval $[-1/2, 1/2]$ as

$$
\begin{aligned}
g(\epsilon) &= \frac{9 - 4\epsilon^2}{16}(g_1 + g_2) \quad\quad - \frac{1 - 4\epsilon^2}{16}(g_0 + g_3) \\[2mm]
&+ \frac{\epsilon(9 - 4\epsilon^2)}{8}(g_2 - g_1) \quad - \frac{\epsilon(1 - 4\epsilon^2)}{24}(g_3 - g_0)
\end{aligned}
\tag{9.129}
$$

Thus the interpolation mask is

$$
\left[\frac{-\alpha}{16} + \frac{\epsilon\alpha}{24}, \quad \frac{8+\alpha}{16} + \frac{\epsilon(8+\alpha)}{8}, \quad \frac{8+\alpha}{16} - \frac{\epsilon(8+\alpha)}{8}, \quad \frac{-\alpha}{16} - \frac{\epsilon\alpha}{24} \right]
\tag{9.130}
$$

with $\alpha = 1 - 4\epsilon^2$. For $\epsilon = 0$ ($\alpha = 1$), the mask reduces to

$$
\frac{1}{16}[-1 \; 9 \; 9 \; -1]
\tag{9.131}
$$

It is not very helpful to go to higher-order polynomial interpolation. With increasing degree P of the interpolating polynomial, the transfer function approaches the ideal transfer function better but convergence is too slow (Fig. 9.17). Less than 1% amplitude error is given only for a polynomial of degree 7 for $\tilde{k} < 0.45$. Thus the extra effort of higher-order polynomial interpolation does not pay off.

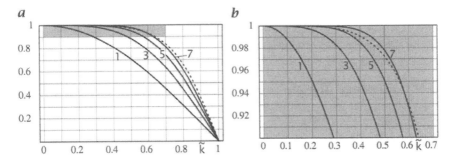

Figure 9.17: *Transfer function of polynomial interpolation filters to interpolate the value between two grid points (ε = 0). The degree of the polynomial (1 = linear, 3 = cubic, etc.) is marked in the graph. The dashed line marks the transfer function for cubic B-spline interpolation (Section 9.6.5): a Full range; b sector as marked in a.*

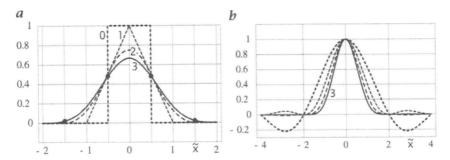

Figure 9.18: *a B-spline interpolation kernels of order 0 (nearest neighbor), 1 (linear interpolation), 2 (quadratic B-spline), and 3 (cubic B-spline); b corresponding transfer functions.*

9.6.5 Spline-based interpolation

Besides the still limited accuracy, polynomial interpolation has another significant disadvantage. The interpolated curve is not continuous at the grid points already in its first derivative. This is due to the fact that for each interval between grid points another polynomial is taken. Thus, only the interpolated function is continuous at the grid points but not the derivatives.

Splines avoid this disadvantage by additional constraints for the continuity of derivatives at the grid points. From the many classes of splines, we will here discuss only one class, *B-splines*, and introduce *cubic B-spline interpolation*. From the background of signal processing, the easiest access to B-splines is their convolution property. The kernel of a *P*-order B-spline curve is generated by convolving the box function

P times with itself (Fig. 9.18a):

$$\beta_P(\tilde{x}) = \underbrace{\Pi(\tilde{x}) * \ldots * \Pi(\tilde{x})}_{(P+1) \text{ times}} \tag{9.132}$$

The transfer function of the box function is the sinc function (see Fig. 9.15). Therefore, the transfer function of the P-order B-spline is

$$\hat{\beta}_P(\hat{k}) = \left(\frac{\sin \pi \tilde{k}/2}{(\pi \tilde{k}/2)} \right)^{P+1} \tag{9.133}$$

Figure 9.18b shows that the B-spline function does not make a suitable interpolation function. The transfer function decreases too early, indicating that B-spline interpolation performs too much averaging. Moreover, the B-spline kernel does not meet the interpolation condition Eq. (9.114) for $P > 1$. Thus, B-splines can be used only for interpolation if the discrete grid points are first transformed in such a way that a following convolution with the B-spline kernel restores the original values at the grid points.

This transformation, known as the B-spline transformation, is constructed from the following condition:

$$g_P(x) = \sum_n c_n \beta_P(x - x_n) \quad \text{with} \quad g_P(x_n) = g(x_n) \tag{9.134}$$

If centered around a grid point, the cubic B-spline interpolation kernel is unequal to zero for only three grid points. The coefficients $\beta_3(-1) = \beta_{-1}, \beta_3(0) = \beta_0$, and $\beta_3(1) = \beta_1$ are 1/6, 2/3, and 1/6. The convolution of this kernel with the unknown B-spline transform values c_n should result in the original values g_n at the grid points. Therefore,

$$g = c * \beta_3 \quad \text{or} \quad g_n = \sum_{n'=-1}^{1} c_{n+n'} \beta_{n'} \tag{9.135}$$

Equation (9.134) constitutes the sparse linear equation system

$$\begin{bmatrix} g_0 \\ g_1 \\ \vdots \\ g_{N-1} \end{bmatrix} = \frac{1}{6} \begin{bmatrix} 4 & 1 & 0 & \cdots & 0 & 1 \\ 1 & 4 & 1 & 0 & \cdots & 0 \\ 0 & 1 & 4 & 1 & 0 & \cdots \\ \vdots & & & & \ddots & \ddots \\ \cdots & \cdots & 1 & 4 & 1 & 0 \\ 0 & \cdots & 0 & 1 & 4 & 1 \\ 1 & 0 & \cdots & 0 & 1 & 4 \end{bmatrix} \begin{bmatrix} c_0 \\ c_1 \\ \vdots \\ c_{N-1} \end{bmatrix} \tag{9.136}$$

using cyclic boundary conditions. The determination of the B-spline transformation thus requires the solution of a linear equation system with N unknowns. The special form of the equation system as a convolution operation, however, allows for a more efficient solution. In Fourier space, Eq. (9.135) reduces to

$$\hat{g} = \hat{\beta}_3 \hat{c} \tag{9.137}$$

The transfer function of β_3 is $\hat{\beta}_3(\tilde{k}) = 2/3 + 1/3\cos(\pi\tilde{k})$. As this function has no zeroes, we can compute c by inverse filtering, that is, convoluting g with a mask that has the transfer function

$$\hat{\beta}_3^{-1}(\tilde{k}) = \hat{\beta}_T(\tilde{k}) = \frac{1}{2/3 + 1/3\cos(\pi\tilde{k})} \tag{9.138}$$

This is the transfer function of a recursive relaxation filter (Section 9.3.6) that is applied first in the forward and then in the backward direction with the following recursion [12]:

$$\begin{aligned} g'_n &= g_n - (2 - \sqrt{3})(g'_{n-1} - g_n) \\ c'_n &= g'_n - (2 - \sqrt{3})(c_{n+1} - g'_n) \end{aligned} \tag{9.139}$$

The entire operation takes only two multiplications and four additions.

The B-spline interpolation is applied after the B-spline transformation. In the continuous cubic case this yields the effective transfer function using Eqs. (9.133) and (9.138),

$$\hat{\beta}_I(\tilde{k}) = \frac{\sin^4(\pi\tilde{k}/2)/(\pi\tilde{k}/2)^4}{(2/3 + 1/3\cos(\pi\tilde{k}))} \tag{9.140}$$

Essentially, the B-spline transformation performs an amplification of high wave numbers (at $\tilde{k} = 1$ by a factor 3), which compensates the smoothing of the B-spline interpolation to a large extent.

We investigate this compensation at both the grid points and the intermediate points. From the equation of the cubic B-spline interpolating kernel (Eq. (9.132); see also Fig. 9.18a) the interpolation coefficients for the grid points and intermediate grid points are

$$1/6\,[1\ 4\ 1] \quad \text{and} \quad 1/48\,[1\ 23\ 23\ 1] \tag{9.141}$$

respectively. Therefore, the transfer functions are

$$2/3 + 1/3\cos(\pi\tilde{k}) \quad \text{and} \quad 23/24\cos(\pi\tilde{k}/2) + 1/24\cos(3\pi\tilde{k}/2) \tag{9.142}$$

respectively. At the grid points, the transfer functions compensate exactly—as expected—the application of the B-spline transformation

Equation (9.138). Thus, the interpolation curve goes through the values at the grid points. At the intermediate points the effective transfer function for the cubic B-spline interpolation is then

$$\hat{\beta}_I(1/2, \tilde{k}) = \frac{23/24 \cos(\pi\tilde{k}/2) + 1/24 \cos(3\pi\tilde{k}/2)}{2/3 + 1/3 \cos \pi\tilde{k}} \tag{9.143}$$

The interpolation errors are better than even for an interpolation with a polynomial of order 7 (Fig. 9.17), but still too high for algorithms that ought to be accurate in the 1/100 pixel range. If no better interpolation technique can be applied, the maximum wave number should be lower than 0.5. Then, the maximum phase shift is lower than 0.01 and the amplitude damping is less than 3 %.

9.6.6 Optimized interpolation

Filter design for interpolation—like any filter design problem—can be treated in a mathematically more rigorous way as an optimization problem [CVA2, Chapter 6]. The general idea is to vary the filter coefficients in such a way that the derivation from a *target function* reaches a minimum.

The target function for an interpolation filter is the box function Equation (9.112) as depicted in Fig. 9.15b. The ansatz functions for an interpolation filter include the following constraints. First, the transfer function is real. Thus only cos terms must be considered. Second, the mean value should be preserved by the interpolation function. This implies the condition $\hat{h}(0) = 1$. With these two conditions, the ansatz function for a nonrecursive filter technique is

$$\hat{h}(\tilde{k}) = \cos\left(\frac{1}{2}\pi\tilde{k}\right) + \sum_{r=2}^{R} h_r \left[\cos\left(\frac{2r-3}{2}\pi\tilde{k}\right) - \cos\left(\frac{1}{2}\pi\tilde{k}\right)\right] \tag{9.144}$$

The filters (Fig. 9.19a, c) are significantly better than those obtained by polynomial and cubic B-spline interpolation (Fig. 9.17). Even better interpolation masks can be obtained by using a combination of nonrecursive and recursive filters, as with the cubic B-spline interpolation:

$$\hat{h}(\tilde{k}) = \frac{\cos\left(1/2\,\pi\tilde{k}\right) + \sum_{r=2}^{R} h_r \left[\cos\left((2r-3)/2\,\pi\tilde{k}\right) - \cos\left(1/2\,\pi\tilde{k}\right)\right]}{1 - \alpha + \alpha\cos\left(\pi\tilde{k}\right)} \tag{9.145}$$

Figure 9.19b, d shows the transfer functions for $R = 1$ to 4. A more detailed discussion of interpolation filters including tables with optimized filters can be found in Jähne [4].

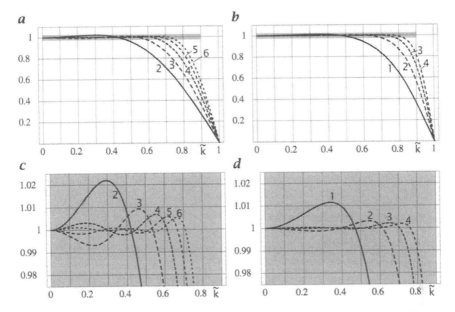

Figure 9.19: *Transfer function of interpolation kernels optimized with the weighted least squares technique of **a** Eq. (9.144) with R = 2 to 6 and **b** Eq. (9.145) with R = 1 to 4 (solid line). **c** and **d** show a narrow sector of the plots in **a** and **b** for a better estimation of small deviations from ideal values.*

9.7 Edge detection

Detection of edges is one of the most important tasks of low-level multi-dimensional signal processing. An edge marks the border of an object that is characterized by a different feature (gray value, color, or any other property) than the background. In the context of simple neighborhoods, an edge is a special type of simple neighborhood with a sharp transition. Low-level edge detection thus means to detect the strength of such a transition and the direction of the edge.

9.7.1 Edge detection by first-order derivatives

First-order derivative filters are one way for low-level edge detection. A first-order derivative operator corresponds to a multiplication by $2\pi i k_d$ in the wave-number space (Section 8.6.3). Thus, a first-order derivative operator in the direction d is represented by the following operations in the space and wave-number domain:

$$\frac{\partial}{\partial x_d} \iff 2\pi i k_d \qquad (9.146)$$

where $\tilde{k}$ is the dimensionless wave number normalized to the Nyquist limit Equation (8.34). One-dimensional first-order derivative operators are not sufficient for edge detection in higher-dimensional signals because they predominantly detect edges that are perpendicular to the direction of the operator. As shown with Eq. (9.186) in Section 9.8.1, the *gradient vector*

$$\nabla g = \left[\frac{\partial g}{\partial x_1}, \frac{\partial g}{\partial x_2}, ..., \frac{\partial g}{\partial x_D} \right]^T \tag{9.147}$$

is parallel to the direction in which the gray values change. Thus it is a good low-level measure for edges. In the operator notation introduced in Section 9.1.3, the gradient can be written as a vector operator. In 2-D and 3-D space this is

$$\mathcal{D} = \left[\begin{array}{c} \mathcal{D}_x \\ \mathcal{D}_y \end{array} \right] \quad \text{or} \quad \mathcal{D} = \left[\begin{array}{c} \mathcal{D}_x \\ \mathcal{D}_y \\ \mathcal{D}_z \end{array} \right] \tag{9.148}$$

The magnitude of the gradient vector

$$|\nabla g| = \left(\sum_{d=1}^{D} \left(\frac{\partial g}{\partial x_d} \right)^2 \right)^{1/2} \tag{9.149}$$

is rotation-invariant and a measure for the edge strength. Because of the rotation invariance, this measure is isotropic. The computation of the magnitude of the gradient can be expressed in operator notation as

$$|\mathcal{D}| = \left[\sum_{d=1}^{D} \mathcal{D}_d \cdot \mathcal{D}_d \right]^{1/2} \tag{9.150}$$

The principal problem with all types of edge detectors is that a derivative operator can only be approximated on a discrete grid. This is one of the reasons why there is such a wide variety of solutions for edge detectors available.

General properties. With respect to object detection, the most important feature of a derivative convolution operator is that it must not shift the object position. For a first-order derivative filter, a real transfer function makes no sense, because extreme values should be mapped onto zero crossings and the steepest slopes to extreme values. This mapping implies a 90° phase shift, a purely imaginary transfer function and an antisymmetric or odd filter mask. According to the classification of *linear shift-invariant* (LSI) filters established in Section 9.2.5, first-order derivative filters are either type III or type IV filters. Thus the simplified equations, Eqs. (9.25) and (9.27), can be used to compute the transfer function.

A derivative filter of any order must not show response to constant values or an offset in a signal. This condition implies that the sum of the coefficients must be zero and that the transfer function is zero for a zero wave number:

$$\sum_n H_n = 0 \Longleftrightarrow \hat{H}(\mathbf{0}) = 0 \qquad (9.151)$$

Intuitively, we expect that any derivative operator amplifies smaller scales more strongly than coarser scales, as the transfer function of a first-order derivative operator goes with k. However, this condition is too restrictive. Imagine that we first apply a smoothing operator to an image before we apply a derivative operator. Then the resulting transfer function would not increase monotonically with the wave number but decrease for higher wave numbers. We would, however, still recognize the joint operation as a derivation because the mean gray value is suppressed and the operator is only sensitive to spatial gray-value changes.

Thus a more general condition is required. Here we suggest

$$\hat{H}(\tilde{\mathbf{k}}) = i\pi \tilde{k}_d \hat{B}(|\tilde{\mathbf{k}}|) \quad \text{with} \quad \hat{B}(0) = 1 \text{ and } \nabla\hat{B} = \mathbf{0} \qquad (9.152)$$

This condition ensures that the transfer function is still zero for the wave number zero and increases in proportion to $\tilde{k}_d$ for small wave numbers. One can regard Eq. (9.152) as a first-order derivative filter regularized by an isotropic smoothing filter.

For good edge detection, it is important that the response of the operator does not depend on the direction of the edge. If this is the case, we speak of an isotropic edge detector. The isotropy of an edge detector can best be analyzed by its transfer function. Equation (9.152), which we derived from the condition of nonselective derivation, gives a general form for an isotropic first-order derivative operator.

First-order difference operators. This is the simplest of all approaches to compute a gradient vector. For the first partial derivative in the x direction, one of the following approximations may be used:

$$\frac{\partial g(\mathbf{x})}{\partial x_d} \approx \frac{g(\mathbf{x}) - g(\mathbf{x} - \Delta x_d \bar{\mathbf{e}}_d)}{\Delta x_d} \qquad \text{backward}$$

$$\approx \frac{g(\mathbf{x} + \Delta x_d \bar{\mathbf{e}}_d) - g(\mathbf{x})}{\Delta x_d} \qquad \text{forward} \qquad (9.153)$$

$$\approx \frac{g(\mathbf{x} + \Delta x_d \bar{\mathbf{e}}_d) - g(\mathbf{x} - \Delta x_d \bar{\mathbf{e}}_d)}{2\Delta x_d} \qquad \text{symmetric}$$

where $\bar{e}_d$ is a unit vector in the direction d. These approximations correspond to the filter masks

$$^-\!\boldsymbol{D}_d = [1. \; -1], \, ^+\!\boldsymbol{D}_d = [1 \; -1.], \boldsymbol{D}_{2d} = 1/2 \; [1 \; 0 \; -1] \qquad (9.154)$$

The subscript "•" denotes the pixel of the asymmetric masks to which the result is written. The symmetric difference operator results in a type III operator (odd number of coefficients, odd symmetry, see Section 9.2.5). The forward and backward difference operators are asymmetric and thus not of much use in signal processing. They can be transformed in a type IV LSI operator if the result is not stored at the position of the right or left pixel but at a position half-way between the two pixels. This corresponds to a shift of the grid by half a pixel distance. The transfer function for the backward difference is then

$$^-\!\hat{D}_d = \exp(i\pi\tilde{k}_d/2)\left[1 - \exp(-i\pi\tilde{k}_d)\right] = i\sin(\pi\tilde{k}_d/2) \qquad (9.155)$$

where the first term results from the shift by half a lattice point.

According to Eq. (9.25), the transfer function of the symmetric difference operator is given by

$$\hat{D}_{2d} = i\sin(\pi\tilde{k}_d) \qquad (9.156)$$

This operator can also be computed from

$$\boldsymbol{D}_{2d} = \,^-\!\boldsymbol{D}_d\boldsymbol{B}_d = [1. \; -1] * 1/2 \; [1 \; 1.] = 1/2\,[1 \; 0 \; -1]$$

Unfortunately, these simple difference filters are only poor approximations for an edge detector. From Eq. (9.156), we infer that the magnitude and direction of the gradient ϕ' are given by

$$|\nabla g| = \left[\sin^2(\pi\tilde{k}\cos\phi) + \sin^2(\pi\tilde{k}\sin\phi)\right]^{1/2} \qquad (9.157)$$

and

$$\phi' = \arctan\frac{\sin(\pi\tilde{k}\sin\phi)}{\sin(\pi\tilde{k}\cos\phi)} \qquad (9.158)$$

when the wave number is written in polar coordinates (k, ϕ). The magnitude of the gradient decreases quickly from the correct value. A Taylor expansion of Eq. (9.157) in $\tilde{k}$ yields for the anisotropy in the magnitude

$$\Delta|\nabla g| = |\nabla g(\phi)| - |\nabla g(0)| \approx \frac{(\pi\tilde{k})^3}{12}\sin^2(2\phi) \qquad (9.159)$$

The resulting errors are shown in Fig. 9.20 as a function of the magnitude of the wave number and the angle to the x axis. The decrease

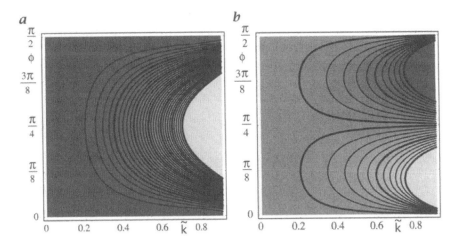

Figure 9.20: *Anisotropy of the **a** magnitude and **b** error in the direction of the gradient based on the symmetrical gradient operator* $[\mathcal{D}_{2x}, \mathcal{D}_{2y}]^T$. *The parameters are the magnitude of the wave number (0 to 0.9) and the angle to the x axis (0 to $\pi/2$). Distance of contour lines: **a** 0.02 (thick lines 0.1); **b** 2°.*

is also anisotropic; it is slower in the diagonal direction. The errors in the direction of the gradient are also large (Fig. 9.20b). While in the direction of the axes and diagonals the error is zero, in the directions inbetween it reaches values of about $\pm 10°$ already at $\tilde{k} = 0.5$. A Taylor expansion of Eq. (9.158) in $\tilde{k}$ gives in the approximation of small $\tilde{k}$ the angle error

$$\Delta\phi \approx \frac{(\pi\tilde{k})^2}{24} \sin 4\phi \qquad (9.160)$$

From this equation, we see that the angle error is zero for $\phi = n\pi/4$ with $n \in \mathbb{Z}$, that is, for $\phi = 0°, 45° \ 90°, \ldots$.

Regularized difference operators. It is a common practice to regularize derivative operators by presmoothing the signal (see, e. g., Chapter 12). We will investigate here to what extent the direction and isotropy of the gradient is improved.

One type of regularized derivative filter is the derivate of a Gaussian. On a discrete lattice this operator is best approximated by the derivative of a binomial mask (Section 9.5.4) as

$$^{(B,R)}\mathcal{D}_d = \mathcal{D}_{2d}\mathcal{B}^R \qquad (9.161)$$

with the transfer function

$$^{(B,R)}\hat{D}_d(\tilde{k}) = i \sin(\pi\tilde{k}_d) \prod_{d=1}^{D} \cos^R(\pi\tilde{k}_d/2) \qquad (9.162)$$

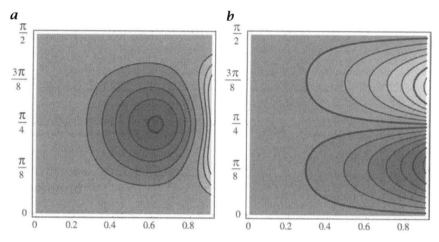

Figure 9.21: *Anisotropy of the **a** magnitude and **b** error in the direction of the gradient based on the Sobel operator Equation (9.166). Distance of contour lines as in Fig. 9.20.*

for even R. This approach leads to nonsquare masks and results in some improvement of the isotropy of the gradient magnitude. However, the error in the direction of the gradient is the same as for the symmetric difference operator because the smoothing terms in Eq. (9.162) cancel out in Eq. (9.158).

Slightly better are Sobel-type difference operators

$$^R S_d = \mathcal{D}_{2d} \mathcal{B}_d^{R-1} \prod_{d' \neq d} \mathcal{B}_{d'}^R \tag{9.163}$$

with the transfer function

$$^R \hat{S}_d(\tilde{k}) = i \tan(\pi \tilde{k}_d/2) \prod_{d=1}^{D} \cos^R(\pi \tilde{k}_d/2) \tag{9.164}$$

that lead to square masks by reducing the smoothing in the direction of the derivation. The smallest operator of this type ($R = 1$) has in two dimensions the masks

$$^1 S_x = \frac{1}{2} \begin{bmatrix} 1 & -1 \\ 1 & -1 \end{bmatrix}, \quad ^1 S_y = \frac{1}{2} \begin{bmatrix} 1 & 1 \\ -1 & -1 \end{bmatrix} \tag{9.165}$$

The best known example of this class of filters is the *Sobel operator*

$$^2 S_x = D_x B_x B_y^2 = \frac{1}{8} \begin{bmatrix} 1 & 0 & -1 \\ 2 & 0 & -2 \\ 1 & 0 & -1 \end{bmatrix}, \quad ^2 S_y = \frac{1}{8} \begin{bmatrix} 1 & 2 & 1 \\ 0 & 0 & 0 \\ -1 & -2 & -1 \end{bmatrix} \tag{9.166}$$

The errors in the magnitude and direction of the gradient based on Eq. (9.164) are given by

$$\Delta |\nabla g| \approx -\frac{(\pi \tilde{k})^3}{24} \sin^2(2\phi) \tag{9.167}$$

and

$$\Delta \phi = \arctan \frac{\tan(\pi(\tilde{k}_d/2) \sin \phi)}{\tan(\pi(\tilde{k}_d/2) \cos \phi)} - \phi \approx -\frac{(\pi \tilde{k}_d)^2}{48} \sin 4\phi \tag{9.168}$$

and shown in Fig. 9.21. The results are remarkable in two respects. First, the error in the direction does not depend at all on the degree of smoothing as for the derivatives of Gaussians and is only about two times lower than that for the simple symmetric difference operator. Second, Fig. 9.21b shows that the anisotropy of the magnitude of the gradient is surprisingly low as compared to the symmetric difference filter in Fig. 9.20b. This could not be expected from the Taylor expansion because the term with $\tilde{k}^2$ is only a factor of two lower than that for the symmetric difference operator in Eq. (9.160). Thus the extrapolation of the transfer functions from small wave numbers to high wave numbers is not valid. The example of the Sobel operator shows that oscillating higher-order terms may cancel each other and lead to much better results as could be expected from a Taylor expansion.

The disadvantage of all approaches discussed so far is that they give no clear indication whether the achieved solution is good or whether any better exists. The filter design problem can be treated in a rigorously mathematical way as an optimization problem [CVA2, Chapter 6]. These techniques not only allow the design of optimal filters but they make it easier to decide precisely which criterion creates an optimal solution.

9.7.2 Edge detection by zero crossings

General properties. First-order derivative operators detect edges by maxima in the magnitude of the gradient. Alternatively, edges can be detected as zero crossings of second-order derivative operators. This technique is attractive because only *linear* operators are required to perform an isotropic detection of edges by zero crossings. In contrast, the magnitude of the gradient is only obtained after squaring and adding first-order derivative operators in all directions.

For an isotropic zero-crossing detector, only all second-order partial derivatives must be added up. The resulting operator is called the *Laplace operator* and denoted by Δ

$$\Delta = \sum_{d=1}^{D} \frac{\partial^2}{\partial x_w^2} \quad \Longleftrightarrow \quad -\sum_{d=1}^{D} 4\pi^2 k_d^2 = -4\pi^2 |\boldsymbol{k}|^2 \tag{9.169}$$

From this equation it is immediately evident that the Laplace operator is an isotropic operator.

A second-order derivative filter detects curvature. Extremes in function values should thus coincide with extremes in curvature. Consequently, a second-order derivative filter should be of even symmetry similar to a smoothing filter and all the properties for filters of even symmetry discussed in Sections 9.2.5 and 9.5.1 should also apply to second-order derivative filters. In addition, the sum of the coefficients must be zero as for first-order derivative filters:

$$\sum_n H_n = 0 \quad \Longleftrightarrow \quad \hat{H}(\mathbf{0}) = 0 \tag{9.170}$$

Also, a second-order derivative filter should not respond to a constant slope. This condition implies no further constraints as it is equivalent to the conditions that the sum of the coefficients is zero and that the filter is of even symmetry.

Laplace of Gaussian. The standard implementations for the Laplace operator are well known and described in many textbooks (see, e. g., [1]). Thus, we will discuss here only the question of an optimal implementation of the Laplacian operator. Because of a transfer function proportional to $\tilde{k}^2$ (Eq. (9.169)), Laplace filters tend to enhance the noise level in images considerably. Thus, a better edge detector may be found by first smoothing the image and then applying the Laplacian filter. This leads to a kind of regularized edge detection and to two classes of filters known as *Laplace of Gaussian* or LoG filters and *difference of Gaussian* or DoG filters. While these filters reduce the noise level it is not clear to what extent they improve or even optimize the isotropy of the Laplace operator.

In the discrete case, a LoG filter is approximated by first smoothing the image with a binomial mask and then applying the discrete Laplace filter. Thus we have the operator combination $\mathcal{L}\mathcal{B}^R$ with the transfer function

$$\hat{\text{LoG}} = \hat{\mathcal{L}}\hat{\mathcal{B}}^R = -4 \sum_{d=1}^{D} \sin^2(\pi \tilde{k}_d/2) \prod_{d=1}^{D} \cos^R(\pi \tilde{k}_d/2) \tag{9.171}$$

For $R = 0$ this is the transfer function of the Laplace operator. In this equation, we used the standard implementation of the Laplace operator, which has in two dimensions the mask

$$\mathbf{L} = \begin{bmatrix} 0 & 1 & 0 \\ 1 & -4 & 1 \\ 0 & 1 & 0 \end{bmatrix} \tag{9.172}$$

and the transfer function

$$\hat{L} = \sin^2(\pi\tilde{k}_1/2) + \sin^2(\pi\tilde{k}_2/2) \tag{9.173}$$

For small wave numbers, the 2-D transfer function in Eq. (9.171) can be approximated in polar coordinates by

$$\hat{LoG}(\tilde{k}, \phi) \approx -(\pi\tilde{k})^2 + \left[\frac{1}{16} + \frac{R}{8} + \frac{1}{48}\cos(4\phi) \right](\pi\tilde{k})^4 \tag{9.174}$$

Difference of Gaussian filters. The multidimensional *difference of Gaussian* type of Laplace filter, or *DoG* filter, is defined as

$$\text{DoG} = 4(\mathcal{B}^2 - 1)\mathcal{B}^R = 4(\mathcal{B}^{R+2} - \mathcal{B}^R) \tag{9.175}$$

and has the transfer function

$$\hat{DoG}(\tilde{k}) = 4\prod_{d=1}^{D}\cos^{R+2}(\pi\tilde{k}_d/2) - 4\prod_{d=1}^{D}\cos^R(\pi\tilde{k}_d/2) \tag{9.176}$$

For small wave numbers it can be approximated by

$$\hat{DoG}(\tilde{k}, \phi) \approx -(\pi\tilde{k})^2 + \left[\frac{3}{32} + \frac{R}{8} - \frac{1}{96}\cos(4\phi) \right](\pi\tilde{k})^4 \tag{9.177}$$

The transfer function of the LoG and DoG filters are quite similar. Both have a significant anisotropic term. Increased smoothing (larger R) does not help to decrease the anisotropy. It is obvious that the DoG filter is significantly more isotropic but neither of them is really optimal with respect to a minimal anisotropy. That second-order derivative operators with better isotropy are possible is immediately evident by comparing Eqs. (9.174) and (9.177). The anisotropic $\cos 4\phi$ terms have different signs. Thus they can easily be compensated by a mix of LoG and DoG operators of the form $2/3\text{DoG} + 1/3\text{LoG}$, which corresponds to the operator $(8/3\mathcal{B}^2 - 8/3\mathcal{I} - 1/3\mathcal{L})\mathcal{B}^P$.

This *ad hoc* solution is certainly not the best. Examples of optimized second-order differential operators are discussed in CVA2 [Chapter 6].

9.7.3 Edges in multichannel images

In multichannel images, it is significantly more difficult to analyze edges than to perform averaging, which simply can be performed channel by channel. The problem is that the different channels may contain conflicting information about edges. In channel A, the gradient can point to a different direction than in channel B. Thus a simple addition of the gradients in all channels

$$\sum_{p=1}^{P} \nabla g_p(\boldsymbol{x}) \tag{9.178}$$

is of no use. It may happen that the sum of the gradients over all channels is zero although the gradients themselves are not zero. Then we would be unable to distinguish this case from constant areas in all channels.

A more suitable measure of the total edge strength is the sum of the squared magnitudes of gradients in all channels

$$\sum_{p=1}^{P} |\nabla g_p|^2 = \sum_{p=1}^{P} \sum_{d=1}^{D} \left(\frac{\partial g_p}{\partial x_d} \right)^2 \tag{9.179}$$

While this expression gives a useful estimate of the overall edge strength, it still does not solve the problem of conflicting edge directions. An analysis of how edges are distributed in a D-dimensional multichannel image with P channels is possible with the following symmetric $D \times D$ matrix S (where D is the dimension of the image):

$$S = J^T J \tag{9.180}$$

where J is known as the *Jacobian matrix*. This $P \times D$ matrix is defined as

$$J = \begin{bmatrix} \dfrac{\partial g_1}{\partial x_1} & \dfrac{\partial g_1}{\partial x_2} & \cdots & \dfrac{\partial g_1}{\partial x_D} \\[2mm] \dfrac{\partial g_2}{\partial x_1} & \dfrac{\partial g_2}{\partial x_2} & \cdots & \dfrac{\partial g_2}{\partial x_D} \\[2mm] \vdots & & \ddots & \vdots \\[2mm] \dfrac{\partial g_P}{\partial x_1} & \dfrac{\partial g_P}{\partial x_2} & \cdots & \dfrac{\partial g_P}{\partial x_D} \end{bmatrix} \tag{9.181}$$

Thus the elements of the matrix S are

$$S_{kl} = \sum_{p=1}^{P} \frac{\partial g_p}{\partial x_k} \frac{\partial g_p}{\partial x_l} \tag{9.182}$$

Because S is a symmetric matrix, we can diagonalize it by a suitable coordinate transform. Then, the diagonals contain terms of the form

$$\sum_{p=1}^{P} \left(\frac{\partial g_p}{\partial x_d'} \right)^2 \tag{9.183}$$

In the case of an ideal edge, only one of the diagonal terms of the matrix will be nonzero. This is the direction perpendicular to the discontinuity. In all other directions it will be zero. Thus, S is a matrix of rank one in this case.

By contrast, if the edges in the different channels point randomly in all directions, all diagonal terms will be nonzero and equal. In this way, it is possible to distinguish random changes by noise from coherent edges. The trace of the matrix S

$$\text{trace}(S) = \sum_{d=1}^{D} S_{dd} = \sum_{d=1}^{D} \sum_{p=1}^{P} \left(\frac{\partial g_p}{\partial x_d}\right)^2 \tag{9.184}$$

gives a measure of the edge strength that we have already defined in Eq. (9.179). It is independent of the orientation of the edge because the trace of a symmetric matrix is invariant to a rotation of the coordinate system.

In conclusion, the matrix S is the key for edge detection in multi-channel signals. Note that an arbitrary number of channels can be processed and that the number of computations increases only linearly with the number of channels. The analysis is, however, of order $O(D^2)$ in the dimension of the signal.

9.8 Tensor representation of simple neighborhoods

9.8.1 Simple neighborhoods

The mathematical description of a local neighborhood by continuous functions has two significant advantages. First, it is much easier to formulate the concepts and to study their properties analytically. As long as the corresponding discrete image satisfies the sampling theorem, all the results derived from continuous functions remain valid because the sampled image is an exact representation of the continuous gray-value function. Second, we can now distinguish between errors inherent to the chosen approach and those that are only introduced by the discretization.

A simple local neighborhood is characterized by the fact that the gray value only changes in one direction. In all other directions it is constant. Because the gray values are constant along lines and form oriented structures this property of a neighborhood is denoted as *local orientation* [13] or *linear symmetry* [14]. Only more recently, the term *simple neighborhood* has been coined by Granlund and Knutsson [9].

If we orient the coordinate system along the principal directions, the gray values become a 1-D function of only one coordinate. Generally, we will denote the direction of local orientation with a unit vector $\bar{r}$ perpendicular to the lines of constant gray values. Then, a simple neighborhood is mathematically represented by

$$g(\boldsymbol{x}) = g(\boldsymbol{x}^T \bar{\boldsymbol{r}}) \tag{9.185}$$

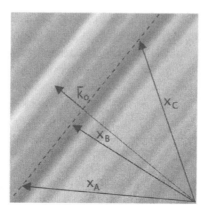

Figure 9.22: *Illustration of a linear symmetric or simple neighborhood. The gray values depend only on a coordinate given by a unit vector $\bar{r}$.*

Equation Eq. (9.185) is also valid for image data with more than two dimensions. The projection of the vector $\boldsymbol{x}$ onto the unit vector $\bar{r}$ makes the gray values depend only on a scalar quantity, the coordinate in the direction of $\bar{r}$ (Fig. 9.22). The essential relation now is that the gradient is parallel to the direction $\bar{r}$ into which the gray values change:

$$
\nabla g(\boldsymbol{x}^T \bar{r}) = \begin{bmatrix} \dfrac{\partial g(\boldsymbol{x}^T \bar{r})}{\partial x_1} \\ \cdots \\ \dfrac{\partial g(\boldsymbol{x}^T \bar{r})}{\partial x_W} \end{bmatrix} = \begin{bmatrix} \bar{r}_1 g'(\boldsymbol{x}^T \bar{r}) \\ \cdots \\ \bar{r}_D g'(\boldsymbol{x}^T \bar{r}) \end{bmatrix} = \bar{r} g'(\boldsymbol{x}^T \bar{r}) \qquad (9.186)
$$

The term g' denotes the derivative of g with respect to the scalar variable $\boldsymbol{x}^T \bar{r}$. In the hyperplane perpendicular to the gradient, the values remain locally constant.

A simple neighborhood has a special form in Fourier space. Let us first assume that the whole image is described by Eq. (9.185), that is, $\bar{r}$ does not depend on the position. Then, from the very fact that a simple neighborhood is constant in all directions except $\bar{r}$, we infer that the Fourier transform must be confined to a line. The direction of the line is given by $\bar{r}$:

$$
g(\boldsymbol{x}^T \bar{r}) \qquad \Longleftrightarrow \qquad \hat{g}(k)\delta(\boldsymbol{k} - \bar{r}(\boldsymbol{k}^T \bar{r})) \qquad (9.187)
$$

where k denotes the coordinate in the Fourier domain in the direction of $\bar{r}$. The argument in the δ function is only zero when $\boldsymbol{k}$ is parallel to $\bar{r}$.

In a second step, a window function $w(\boldsymbol{x} - \boldsymbol{x}_0)$ is used to restrict the area to a local neighborhood around a point $\boldsymbol{x}_0$. Thus $g(\boldsymbol{x}^T \bar{r})$ in

Eq. (9.187) is multiplied by the window function $w(\boldsymbol{x} - \boldsymbol{x}_0)$ in the spatial domain. The size and shape of the neighborhood is determined by the window function. Multiplication in the space domain corresponds to a convolution in the Fourier domain (Section 8.6.3). Thus,

$$ w(\boldsymbol{x} - \boldsymbol{x}_0)g(\boldsymbol{x}^T\bar{\boldsymbol{r}}) \quad \Longleftrightarrow \quad \hat{w}(\boldsymbol{k}) * \hat{g}(k)\delta(\boldsymbol{k} - \bar{\boldsymbol{r}}(\boldsymbol{k}^T\bar{\boldsymbol{r}})) \quad (9.188) $$

where $\hat{w}(\boldsymbol{k})$ is the Fourier transform of the window function.

The limitation to a local neighborhood thus blurs the line in Fourier space to a "sausage-like" shape. Because of the reciprocity of scales between the two domains, its thickness is inversely proportional to the size of the window. From this elementary relation, we can already conclude qualitatively that the accuracy of the orientation estimate is directly related to the ratio of the window size to the wavelength of the smallest structures in the window.

9.8.2 Direction versus orientation

For an appropriate representation of simple neighborhoods, it is first important to distinguish *orientation* from *direction*. The direction is defined over the full angle range of 2π (360°). Two vectors that point in opposite directions, that is, differ by 180°, are different. The gradient vector, for example, always points into the direction into which the gray values are increasing. With respect to a bright object on a dark background, this means that the gradient at the edge is pointing towards the object. In contrast, to describe the direction of a local neighborhood, an angle range of 360° makes no sense. We cannot distinguish between patterns that are rotated by 180°. If a pattern is rotated by 180°, it still has the same direction. Thus, the direction of a simple neighborhood is different from the direction of a gradient. While for the edge of an object gradients pointing in opposite directions are conflicting and inconsistent, for the direction of a simple neighborhood this is consistent information.

In order to distinguish the two types of "directions," we will speak of *orientation* in all cases where an angle range of only 180° is required. Orientation is still, of course, a *cyclic* quantity. Increasing the orientation beyond 180° flips it back to 0°. Therefore, an appropriate representation of orientation requires an angle doubling.

In his pioneering paper on a general picture processing operator Granlund [13] introduced a vectorial representation of the local orientation. The magnitude of the *orientation vector* is set to the certainty with which the orientation could be determined and its direction to the doubled orientation angle. This vector representation of orientation has two significant advantages.

First, it is more suitable for further processing than a separate representation of the orientation by two scalar quantities. Take, for example, averaging. Vectors are summed up by chaining them together, and the resulting sum vector is the vector from the starting point of the first vector to the end point of the last vector. The weight of an individual vector in the vector sum is given by its length. In this way, the certainty of the orientation measurement is adequately taken into account.

9.8.3 First-order tensor representation; structure tensor

The vectorial representation discussed in Section 9.8.2 is incomplete. Although it is suitable for representing the orientation of simple neighborhoods, it cannot distinguish between neighborhoods with constant values and isotropic orientation distribution (e. g., uncorrelated noise). Both cases result in an orientation vector with zero magnitude.

Therefore, it is obvious that an adequate representation of gray-value changes in a local neighborhood must be more complex. Such a representation should be able to determine a unique orientation and to distinguish constant neighborhoods from neighborhoods without local orientation.

A suitable representation can be introduced by a optimization strategy to determine the orientation of a *simple neighborhood* in a slightly more general way as performed by Kass and Witkin [15]. The optimum orientation is defined as the orientation that shows the least deviations from the directions of the gradient. A suitable measure for the deviation must treat gradients pointing in opposite directions equally. The squared scalar product between the gradient vector and the unit vector representing the local orientation $\bar{r}$ meets this criterion

$$(\nabla g^T \bar{r})^2 = |\nabla g|^2 \cos^2 (\angle(\nabla g, \bar{r})) \tag{9.189}$$

This quantity is proportional to the cosine squared of the angle between the gradient vector and the orientation vector and is thus maximal when ∇g and $\bar{r}$ are parallel or antiparallel, and zero if they are perpendicular to each other. Therefore, the following integral is maximized in a D-dimensional local neighborhood:

$$\int w(\boldsymbol{x} - \boldsymbol{x}') \left(\nabla g(\boldsymbol{x}')^T \bar{r} \right)^2 d^D x' \tag{9.190}$$

where the window function w determines the size and shape of the neighborhood around a point $\boldsymbol{x}$ in which the orientation is averaged. The maximization problem must be solved for each point $\boldsymbol{x}$. Equation Eq. (9.190) can be rewritten in the following way:

$$\bar{r}^T J \bar{r} \to \max \tag{9.191}$$

with

$$J = \int_{-\infty}^{\infty} w(\boldsymbol{x} - \boldsymbol{x}') \left(\nabla g(\boldsymbol{x}') \nabla g(\boldsymbol{x}')^T \right) d^D x'$$

The components of this symmetric $D \times D$ tensor are

$$J_{pq}(\boldsymbol{x}) = \int_{-\infty}^{\infty} w(\boldsymbol{x} - \boldsymbol{x}') \left(\frac{\partial g(\boldsymbol{x}')}{\partial x'_p} \frac{\partial g(\boldsymbol{x}')}{\partial x'_q} \right) \mathrm{d}^D x' \qquad (9.192)$$

At this point it is easy to extend the tensor for multichannel signals. It is only needed to sum the tensor components for all channels. The weighting function might be different for each channel in order to consider the significance and spatial resolution of a certain channel. With all this, Eq. (9.192) extends to

$$J_{r,s}(\boldsymbol{x}) = \sum_{p=1}^{P} \int_{-\infty}^{\infty} w_p(\boldsymbol{x} - \boldsymbol{x}') \left(\frac{\partial g_p(\boldsymbol{x}')}{\partial x'_r} \frac{\partial g_p(\boldsymbol{x}')}{\partial x'_s} \right) \mathrm{d}^D x' \qquad (9.193)$$

These equations indicate that a tensor is an adequate first-order representation of a local neighborhood. The term first-order has a double meaning. First, only first-order derivatives are involved. Second, only simple neighborhoods can be described in the sense that we can analyze in which direction(s) the gray values change. More complex structures such as structures with multiple orientations cannot be distinguished.

The complexity of Eqs. (9.191) and (9.192) somewhat obscures their simple meaning. The tensor is symmetric. By a rotation of the coordinate system, it can be brought into a diagonal form. Then, Eq. (9.191) reduces to

$$J = [\bar{r}'_1, \bar{r}'_2, \ldots, \bar{r}'_D] \begin{bmatrix} J_{1'1'} & 0 & \cdots & 0 \\ 0 & J_{2'2'} & \cdots & 0 \\ \vdots & \vdots & \ddots & \vdots \\ 0 & \cdots & \cdots & J_{D'D'} \end{bmatrix} \begin{bmatrix} \bar{r}'_1 \\ \bar{r}'_2 \\ \cdots \\ \bar{r}'_D \end{bmatrix} \rightarrow \text{max}$$

or

$$J = \sum_{d'=1}^{D} J_{d'd'} (\bar{r}'_{d'})^2$$

Without loss of generality, we assume that $J_{1'1'} \geq J_{d'd'} \ \forall d' \neq 1$. Then, it is obvious that the unit vector $\bar{r}' = [1 \ 0 \ \ldots \ 0]^T$ maximizes the foregoing expression. The maximum value is $J_{1'1'}$. In conclusion, this approach not only yields a tensor representation for the local neighborhood but also shows the way to determine the orientation. Essentially, we have to solve an *eigenvalue problem*. The eigenvalues λ_d and eigenvectors $\boldsymbol{k}_d$ of a $D \times D$ matrix are defined by

$$\boldsymbol{J}\boldsymbol{k}_d = \lambda_d \boldsymbol{k}_d \qquad (9.194)$$

An eigenvector k_d of J is thus a vector that is not turned in direction by multiplication with the matrix J, but is only multiplied by a scalar factor, the eigenvalue λ_w. This implies that the structure tensor becomes diagonal in a coordinate system that is spanned by the eigenvectors. For our further discussion it is important to keep in mind that the eigenvalues are all real and nonnegative and form an orthogonal basis [16, 17, 18].

9.8.4 Classification of local neighborhoods

The power of the tensor representation becomes apparent if we classify the eigenvalues of the structure tensor. The classifying criterion is the number of eigenvalues that are zero. If an eigenvalue is zero, this means that the gray values in the direction of the corresponding eigenvector do not change. The number of zero eigenvalues is also closely related to the rank of a matrix. The *rank* of a matrix is defined as the dimension of the subspace for which $Jk \neq 0$. The space for which $Jk = 0$ is denoted as the *null space*. The dimension of the null space is the dimension of the matrix minus the rank of the matrix and equal to the number of zero eigenvalues. We will perform an analysis of the eigenvalues for two and three dimensions. In two dimensions, we can distinguish the following cases:

$\lambda_1 = \lambda_2 = 0$, *rank 0 tensor*. Both eigenvalues are zero. The mean square magnitude of the gradient $(\lambda_1 + \lambda_2)$ is zero. The local neighborhood has constant values. It belongs to an object with a homogeneous feature;

$\lambda_1 > 0, \lambda_2 = 0$, *rank 1 tensor*. One eigenvalue is zero. The values do not change in the direction of the corresponding eigenvector. The local neighborhood is a simple neighborhood with ideal orientation. This could either be the *edge* of an object or an *oriented texture*;

$\lambda_1 > 0, \lambda_2 > 0$, *rank 2 tensor*. Both eigenvalues are unequal to zero. The gray values change in all directions as at the *corner* of an object or a texture with a distributed orientation. In the special case of $\lambda_1 = \lambda_2$, we speak of an isotropic gray-value structure as it changes equally in all directions.

The classification of the eigenvalues in three dimensions is similar to the 2-D case:

$\lambda_1 = \lambda_2 = \lambda_3 = 0$, *rank 0 tensor*. The gray values do not change in any direction; constant neighborhood.

$\lambda_1 > 0, \lambda_2 = \lambda_3 = 0$, *rank 1 tensor*. The gray values change only in one direction. This direction is given by the eigenvector to the nonzero eigenvalue. The neighborhood includes a boundary between two objects (*surface*) or a *layered texture*. In a space-time image, this means a constant motion of a spatially oriented pattern ("planar wave");

$\lambda_1 > 0, \lambda_2 > 0, \lambda_3 = 0$, *rank 2 tensor.* The gray values change in two directions and are constant in a third. The eigenvector to the zero eigenvalue gives the direction of the constant gray values. This happens at the edge of a three-dimensional object in a volumetric image, or if a pattern with distributed spatial orientation moves with constant speed; and

$\lambda_1 > 0, \lambda_2 > 0, \lambda_3 > 0$, *rank 3 tensor.* The gray values change in all three directions as at the corner of an object or a region with isotropic noise.

In practice, it will not be checked whether the eigenvalues are zero but below a critical threshold that is determined by the noise level in the image.

9.8.5 Computation of the structure tensor

The structure tensor (Section 9.8.3) can be computed straightforwardly as a combination of *linear convolution* and *nonlinear point operations.* The partial derivatives in Eq. (9.192) are approximated by discrete derivative operators. The integration weighted with the window function is replaced by a convolution with a smoothing filter that has the shape of the window function. If we denote the discrete partial derivative operator with respect to the coordinate p by the operator $\mathcal{D}_p$ and the (isotropic) smoothing operator by $\mathcal{B}$, the local structure of a gray-value image can be computed with the structure tensor operator

$$\mathcal{J}_{pq} = \mathcal{B}(\mathcal{D}_p \cdot \mathcal{D}_q) \qquad (9.195)$$

The equation is written in the operator notation introduced in Section 9.1.3. Pixelwise multiplication is denoted by a centered dot "·" to distinguish it from successive application of convolution operators. Equation (9.195) expresses in words that the $\mathcal{J}_{pq}$ component of the tensor is computed by convolving the image independently with $\mathcal{D}_p$ and $\mathcal{D}_q$, multiplying the two images pixelwise, and smoothing the resulting image with $\mathcal{B}$. For the inertia tensor method, a similar tensor operator can be formulated

$$\mathcal{J}'_{pp} = \sum_{q \neq p} \mathcal{B}(\mathcal{D}_q \cdot \mathcal{D}_q), \quad \mathcal{J}'_{pq} = -\mathcal{B}(\mathcal{D}_p \cdot \mathcal{D}_q) \qquad (9.196)$$

These operators are valid in images of any dimension $D \geq 2$. In a D-dimensional image, the structure tensor has $D(D+1)/2$ independent components, hence 3 in 2-D and 6 in 3-D images. These components are best stored in a multichannel image with $D(D+1)/2$ channels.

The smoothing operations consume the largest number of operations. Therefore, a fast implementation must, in the first place, apply a fast smoothing algorithm. A fast algorithm can be established based on the general observation that higher-order features always show a lower resolution than the features from which they are computed. This means that the structure tensor can be stored on a coarser grid and thus in a smaller image. It is convenient and appropriate to reduce the scale by a factor of two by storing only every second pixel in every second row.

These procedures lead us in a natural way to multigrid data structures that are discussed in detail in Chapter 8.10. Multistep averaging is discussed in detail in Section 9.5.5.

Storing higher-order features on coarser scales has another significant advantage. Any subsequent processing is sped up simply by the fact that many fewer pixels have to be processed. A linear scale reduction by a factor of two results in a reduction in the number of pixels and the number of computations by a factor of 4 in two and 8 in three dimensions.

The accuracy of the orientation angle strongly depends on the implementation of the derivative filters. It is critical to use a derivative filter that has been optimized for a minimum error in the direction of the gradient. Such filters are discussed in Section 9.7.1.

9.8.6 Orientation vector

With the simple convolution and point operations discussed in the previous section, we computed the components of the structure tensor. In this section, we solve the eigenvalue problem to determine the orientation vector. In two dimensions, we can readily solve the eigenvalue problem. The orientation angle can be determined by rotating the inertia tensor into the principal axes coordinate system. As shown, for example, by Jähne [1], the orientation angle is given by

$$\tan 2\phi = \frac{2J_{12}}{J_{22} - J_{11}} \qquad (9.197)$$

Without defining any prerequisites, we have obtained the anticipated angle doubling for orientation as discussed in Section 9.8.2 at the beginning of this chapter. Because $\tan 2\phi$ is gained from a quotient, we can regard the dividend as the y and the divisor as the x component of a vector and can form the *orientation vector* o, as introduced by Granlund [13]

$$o = \begin{bmatrix} J_{22} - J_{11} \\ 2J_{12} \end{bmatrix} \qquad (9.198)$$

The argument of this vector gives the orientation angle and the magnitude a certainty measure for local orientation.

The result of Eq. (9.198) is remarkable in that the computation of the components of the orientation vector from the components of the orientation tensor requires just one subtraction and one multiplication by two. As these components of the orientation vector are all we need for further processing steps, we do not need the orientation angle or the magnitude of the vector. Thus, the solution of the eigenvalue problem in two dimensions is trivial.

9.8.7 Coherency

The orientation vector reduces local structure to local orientation. From three independent components of the symmetric tensor still only two are used. When we fail to observe an orientated structure in a neighborhood, we do not know whether any gray-value variations or distributed orientations are encountered. This information is included in the not yet used component of the tensor $J_{11} + J_{22}$, which gives the mean square magnitude of the gradient. Consequently, a well-equipped structure operator needs to include also the third component. A suitable linear combination is

$$S = \begin{bmatrix} J_{11} + J_{22} \\ J_{11} - J_{22} \\ 2J_{12} \end{bmatrix} \tag{9.199}$$

This structure operator contains the two components of the orientation vector and, as an additional component, the mean square magnitude of the gradient, which is a rotation-invariant parameter. Comparing the latter with the magnitude of the orientation vector, a constant gray-value area and an isotropic gray-value structure without preferred orientation can be distinguished. In the first case, both squared quantities are zero; in the second, only the magnitude of the orientation vector. In the case of a perfectly oriented pattern, both quantities are equal. Thus their ratio seems to be a good *coherency measure* c_c for local orientation

$$c_c = \frac{(J_{22} - J_{11})^2 + 4J_{12}^2}{(J_{11} + J_{22})^2} = \left(\frac{\lambda_1 - \lambda_2}{\lambda_1 + \lambda_2} \right)^2 \tag{9.200}$$

The coherency c_c ranges from 0 to 1. For ideal local orientation ($\lambda_2 = 0, \lambda_1 > 0$) it is one, for an isotropic gray-value structure ($\lambda_1 = \lambda_2 > 0$) it is zero.

9.8.8 Color coding of the two-dimensional structure tensor

A symmetric 2-D tensor has three independent pieces of information (Eq. (9.199)), which fit well to the three degrees of freedom available to represent color, for example, luminance, hue, and saturation. First, the squared magnitude of the gradient is mapped onto the intensity. Second, the coherency measure Equation (9.200) is used as the saturation. The angle of the orientation vector is represented as the hue.

In practice, a slight modification of this color representation is useful. The squared magnitude of the gradient shows variations too large to be displayed in the narrow dynamic range of a display screen with only 256 luminance levels. Therefore, a suitable normalization is required. The basic idea of this normalization is to compare the squared magnitude of the gradient with the noise level. Once the gradient is well above the noise level it is regarded as a significant piece of information. This train of thoughts suggests the following normalization for the intensity I:

$$I = \frac{J_{11} + J_{22}}{(J_{11} + J_{22}) + y\sigma_n^2} \tag{9.201}$$

where σ_n is an estimate of the standard deviation of the noise level. This normalization provides a rapid transition of the luminance from one, when the magnitude of the gradient is larger than σ_n, to zero when the gradient is smaller than σ_n. The factor y is used to optimize the display.

A demonstration of the structure tensor technique is given by the heurisko image processing workspace `orient.ws` in `/software/09`.

9.9 References

[1] Jähne, B., (1997). *Digital Image Processing—Concepts, Algorithms, and Scientific Applications,* 4th edition. New York: Springer.

[2] Zachmanoglou, E. C. and Thoe, D. W., (1986). *Introduction to Partial Differential Equations with Applications.* New York: Dover Publications.

[3] Oppenheim, A. V. and Schafer, R. W., (1989). *Discrete-Time Signal Processing. Prentice-Hall Signal Processing Series.* Englewood Cliffs, NJ: Prentice-Hall.

[4] Jähne, B., (1997). *Handbook of Digital Image Processing for Scientific Applications.* Boca Raton, FL: CRC Press.

[5] Lim, J. S., (1990). *Two-dimensional Signal and Image Processing.* Englewood Cliffs, NJ: Prentice-Hall.

[6] Poularikas, A. D. (ed.), (1996). *The Transforms and Applications Handbook.* Boca Raton, FL: CRC Press.

[7] Pitas, I. and Venetsanopoulos, A. N., (1990). *Nonlinear Digital Filters. Principles and Applications.* Norwell, MA: Kluwer Academic Publishers.

[8] Knutsson, H. and Westin, C.-F., (1993). Normalized and differential convolution. In *Proceedings CVPR'93, New York City, NY,* pp. 515-523, IEEE. Washington, DC: IEEE Computer Society Press.

[9] Granlund, G. H. and Knutsson, H., (1995). *Signal Processing for Computer Vision.* Norwell, MA: Kluwer Academic Publishers.

[10] Freeman, W. T. and Adelson, E. H., (1991). The design and use of steerable filters. *IEEE Trans. Patt. Anal. Mach. Intell.,* **13**:891-906.

[11] Wolberg, G., (1990). *Digital Image Warping.* Los Alamitos, CA: IEEE Computer Society Press.

[12] Unser, M., Aldroubi, A., and Eden, M., (1991). Fast B-spline transforms for continuous image representation and interpolation. *IEEE Trans. PAMI,* **13**: 277-285.

[13] Granlund, G. H., (1978). In search of a general picture processing operator. *Comp. Graph. Imag. Process.,* **8**:155-173.

[14] Bigün, J. and Granlund, G. H., (1987). Optimal orientation detection of linear symmetry. In *Proceedings ICCV'87, London 1987,* pp. 433-438, IEEE. Washington, DC: IEEE Computer Society Press.

[15] Kass, M. and Witkin, A., (1987). Analysing oriented patterns. *Comp. Vis. Graph. Im. Process.,* **37**:362-385.

[16] Hoffman, K. and Kunze, R., (1971). *Linear Algebra,* 2nd edition. Englewood Cliffs, NJ: Prentice-Hall.

[17] Golub, G. H. and van Loan, C. F., (1989). *Matrix Computations. Johns Hopkins Series in the Mathematical Sciences, No. 3.* Baltimore: The Johns Hopkins University Press.

[18] Press, W. H., Flannery, B. P., Teukolsky, S. A., and Vetterling, W. T., (1992). *Numerical Recipes in C: The Art of Scientific Computing.* New York: Cambridge University Press.

10 Motion

Horst Haußecker[1] and Hagen Spies[2]

[1]Xerox Palo Alto Research Center (PARC)
[2]Interdisziplinäres Zentrum für Wissenschaftliches Rechnen (IWR)
Universität Heidelberg, Germany

10.1 Introduction

Motion is a powerful feature of image sequences, revealing the dynamics of scenes by relating spatial image features to temporal changes. The task of motion analysis remains a challenging and fundamental problem of computer vision. From sequences of 2-D images, the only accessible motion parameter is the *optical flow* f, an approximation of the 2-D *motion field* u, on the image sensor [1]. The motion field is given as the projection of the 3-D motion of points in the scene onto the

Computer Vision and Applications

image sensor. The estimated optical flow field can be used as input for a variety of subsequent processing steps including motion detection, motion compensation, motion-based data compression, 3-D scene reconstruction, autonomous navigation, and the analysis of dynamical processes in scientific applications.

The difficulties in motion estimation are manifold and originate in the inherent differences between the optical flow and the real motion field. As only the apparent motion in the sequence can be extracted, further *a priori* assumptions on brightness changes, object properties, and the relation between relative 3-D scene motion and the projection onto the 2-D image sensor are necessary for quantitative scene analysis. Horn [2] gives an optimistic view of the possibility of 3-D reconstruction from motion fields. He shows that the motion field can almost always be unambiguously related to translational and rotational velocities of rigid surfaces. However, the motion field itself is often inaccessible. This can be nicely demonstrated by a simple example illustrated in Fig. 10.1. Consider a rigid sphere with homogeneous surface reflectance, spinning around an axis through the center of the sphere. If the surface is not textured and the illumination stays constant, the apparent optical flow field would equal zero over the entire sphere. If a directional light source moves around the same sphere the apparent illumination changes would be falsely attributed to motion of the sphere surface. This rather academic problem shows that even very simple experimental setups under perfect conditions can render motion estimation impossible. This and other examples are given by Horn [3]. Problems frequently encountered in real-world sequences include transparent overlay of multiple motions, occlusions, illumination changes, nonrigid motion, stop-and-shoot motion, low signal-to-noise (SNR) levels, aperture problem, and correspondence problem—to mention only some of them. For this reason, Verri and Poggio [4] conclude that the true motion field is hardly ever accessible and suggest that only qualitative properties of the motion field should be computed [5].

These problems, however, are not always present and are usually not spread over the entire image area. Thus, there exist many applications where motion analysis becomes feasible. At the same time, they pose a constraint on optical flow computation that is often disregarded: Errors have to be detected and quantified! This is especially important for quantitative scientific measurement tasks. In contrast to the more qualitative requirements of standard computer vision applications, such as motion detection or collision avoidance, quantitative measurements of dynamic processes require precise and dense optical flow fields in order to reduce the propagation of errors into subsequent processing steps. In addition to the optical flow field, measures of confidence have to be provided to discard erroneous data points and quantify measurement precision.

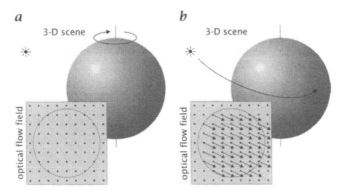

Figure 10.1: *Physical vs visual correspondence: **a** a spinning sphere with fixed illumination leads to zero optical flow; **b** a moving illumination source causes an apparent optical flow field without motion of the sphere.*

This chapter will focus on the algorithmic aspects of low-level motion estimation. We first discuss the principal differences between optical flow-based techniques and correlation approaches (Section 10.2). In Section 10.3 optical flow-based techniques will be detailed including differential and tensor-based techniques. Sections 10.4 and 10.5 deal with quadrature filter-based and correlation-based techniques, respectively. In Section 10.6 we try to introduce different attempts to improve accuracy and overcome intrinsic problems of motion estimation by an appropriate model of the underlying motion field.

10.2 Basics: flow and correspondence

10.2.1 Optical flow

Moving patterns cause temporal variations of the image brightness. The relationship between brightness changes and the optical flow field f constitutes the basis for a variety of approaches, such as differential, spatiotemporal energy-based, tensor-based, and phase-based techniques. Analyzing the relationship between the temporal variations of image intensity or the spatiotemporal frequency distribution in the Fourier domain serves as an attempt to estimate the optical flow field. This section introduces the fundamental relation between motion and brightness variations and its representation in image sequences and Fourier domain. All optical flow-based, as well as quadrature filter-based techniques rely inherently on the coherence of motion. Therefore, a basic prerequisite relating the scale of patterns to the frame rate of image acquisition is given by the temporal sampling theorem, detailed at the end of this section.

Brightness change constraint. A common assumption on optical flow is that the image brightness $g(x, t)$ at a point $x = [x, y]^T$ at time t should only change because of motion. Thus, the total time derivative,

$$\frac{dg}{dt} = \frac{\partial g}{\partial x}\frac{dx}{dt} + \frac{\partial g}{\partial y}\frac{dy}{dt} + \frac{\partial g}{\partial t} \tag{10.1}$$

needs to equal zero. With the definitions $f_1 = dx/dt$ and $f_2 = dy/dt$, this directly yields the well-known *motion constraint equation* or *brightness change constraint equation*, BCCE [6]:

$$(\nabla g)^T f + g_t = 0 \tag{10.2}$$

where $f = [f_1, f_2]^T$ is the optical flow, ∇g defines the spatial gradient, and g_t denotes the partial time derivative $\partial g/\partial t$.

This relation poses a single local constraint on the optical flow at a certain point in the image. It is, however, ill-posed as Eq. (10.2) constitutes only one equation of two unknowns. This problem is commonly referred to as the *aperture problem* of motion estimation, illustrated in Fig. 10.2a. All vectors along the *constraint line* defined by Eq. (10.2) are likely to be the real optical flow f. Without further assumptions only the flow $f_\perp$,

$$f_\perp(x, t) = -\frac{g_t(x, t)}{\|\nabla g(x, t)\|}\, n, \quad n = \frac{\nabla g(x, t)}{\|\nabla g(x, t)\|} \tag{10.3}$$

perpendicular to the constraint line can be estimated. This vector is referred to as *normal flow* as it points normal to lines of constant image brightness, parallel to the spatial gradient.

Although Eq. (10.2) is formulated for a single point in the image, any discrete realization of the spatial and temporal derivatives requires some neighborhood of the image point to be considered. From this fact, the question arises, should the search for f be extended to a neighborhood of finite size instead of focusing on a single point? If the spatial gradient changes within this region, additional constraints can be used to find the 2-D optical flow f. This is the common representation of the aperture problem as illustrated in Fig. 10.2b and c. If the spatial structure within an aperture of finite size shows directional variations, the optical flow f can be estimated unambiguously (Fig. 10.2b). In this case the constraint lines of several points within the neighborhood have a joint intersection. If, on the other hand, all gradient vectors within the aperture are pointing into the same direction, all constraint lines fall together and the aperture problem persists (Fig. 10.2c). A variety of approaches have been proposed that directly use Eq. (10.2) by trying to minimize an objective function pooling constraints over a small finite area. They can be subdivided into differential techniques, using both local and global constraints (Section 10.3).

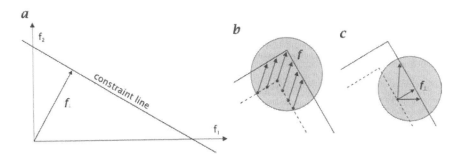

Figure 10.2: *Illustration of the aperture problem: a constraint line defined by Eq. (10.2). The normal optical flow vector $f_\perp$ is pointing perpendicular to the line and parallel to the local gradient $\nabla g(x, t)$; b no aperture problem for local neighborhoods with spatially distributed structures (moving corner); c within a local neighborhood all gradients are parallel (moving edge). The optical flow cannot be determined unambiguously.*

In order to overcome the aperture problem, the size of the region of interest has to be enlarged, as with the growing size of the local neighborhood the chances for distributed spatial structure increase. At the same time it becomes more likely that the region extends over motion boundaries. These two competing obstacles of optical flow computation are referred to as the generalized *aperture problem* [7]. Recent approaches to overcome this problem use robust statistics to avoid averaging independent optical flow fields [8] (Section 10.6.2).

Optical flow in spatiotemporal images. In the previous section we derived the brightness change constraint Equation (10.2), relating temporal and spatial derivatives of the image brightness to the optical flow. Another basic relation can be found if we do not restrict the analysis to two consecutive images but rather assume the brightness pattern $g(x, t)$ to be extended in both space and time, forming a 3-D *spatiotemporal image*. The displacement of brightness patterns within consecutive images of a sequence yields inclined structures with respect to the temporal axis of spatiotemporal images. Figure 10.3 shows examples of spatiotemporal images for synthetic test patterns moving with constant velocity.

Let $r = [r_1, r_2, r_3]^T = a\,[\delta_x, \delta_y, \delta_t]^T$ be the vector pointing into the direction of constant brightness within the 3-D xt-domain. With δ_x and δ_y we denote infinitesimal shifts of the brightness pattern within the infinitesimal time step δ_t. The (arbitrary) scaling factor a will be set to 1 in the remainder of this chapter, as only the fractions, r_1/r_3 and r_2/r_3 are relating r to the optical flow f. The relation between the orientation angles, the spatiotemporal vector r, and the optical flow

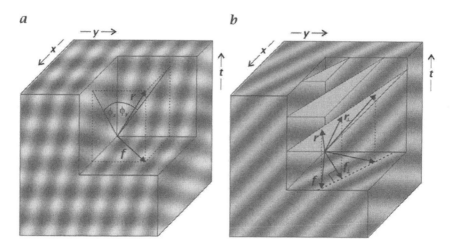

Figure 10.3: *Illustration of the spatiotemporal brightness distribution of moving patterns: **a** moving sinusoidal plaid pattern (no aperture problem); **b** moving planar wave pattern (aperture problem). The upper right portions of the 3-D xt-cubes have been cut off, revealing the internal structure of the spatiotemporal images.*

can be derived from Fig. 10.3a to be

$$f = \left[\frac{r_1}{r_3}, \frac{r_2}{r_3}\right]^T = -\left[\tan \phi_x, \tan \phi_y\right]^T \qquad (10.4)$$

where ϕ_x and ϕ_y denote the angles between the t-axis and the projection of the vector r onto the xt- and yt-plane, respectively. Thus, optical flow computation reduces to an *orientation analysis* in spatiotemporal images, that is, an estimate of the 3-D vector r.

The direction r of constant brightness at a certain point within a spatiotemporal image is pointing perpendicular to the spatiotemporal gradient vector $\nabla_{xt}g = [g_x, g_y, g_t]^T$. Using the relation Eq. (10.4), the brightness change constraint Eq. (10.2) can be formulated as:

$$[g_x, g_y, g_t]\begin{bmatrix} f_1 \\ f_2 \\ 1 \end{bmatrix} = r_3^{-1}(\nabla_{xt}g)^T r = 0 \qquad (10.5)$$

As soon as an aperture persists within a local spatial neighborhood the direction r of smallest brightness changes is no longer unambiguous and the local spatiotemporal neighborhood consists of layered structures instead of lines. This can be observed in Fig. 10.3b, which shows the spatiotemporal structure of a moving planar wave pattern. Without further constraints only the normal flow $f_\perp$ can be computed.

It is important to note that Eqs. (10.2) and (10.5) are mathematically equivalent and no constraint is added by extending the formulation of the brightness conservation into 3-D space.

Motion constraint in Fourier domain. The concept of image sequences as spatiotemporal images allows one to analyze motion in the corresponding *spatiotemporal frequency domain* (*Fourier domain*).

Let $g(\mathbf{x}, t)$ be an image sequence of any pattern moving with constant velocity, causing the optical flow $\mathbf{f}$ at any point in the image plane. The resulting spatiotemporal structure can be described by

$$g(\mathbf{x}, t) = g(\mathbf{x} - \mathbf{f}t) \tag{10.6}$$

The spatiotemporal Fourier transform $\hat{g}(\mathbf{k}, \omega)$ of Eq. (10.6) is given by [9]

$$\hat{g}(\mathbf{k}, \omega) = \hat{g}(\mathbf{k})\delta(\mathbf{k}^T \mathbf{f} - \omega) \tag{10.7}$$

where $\hat{g}(\mathbf{k})$ is the spatial Fourier transform of the pattern, and $\delta(\cdot)$ denotes Dirac's delta distribution. Equation (10.7) states that the 3-D Fourier spectrum of a pattern moving with constant velocity condenses to a plane in Fourier space. The 2-D Fourier spectrum of the pattern is being projected parallel to the temporal frequency ω onto the plane. Figure 10.4a shows the spatiotemporal image of a 1-D random pattern moving with 1 pixel/frame into positive x-direction. The corresponding Fourier (power) spectrum is shown in Fig. 10.4b.

The equation of the plane in Fourier domain is given by the argument of the delta distribution in Eq. (10.7):

$$\omega(\mathbf{k}, \mathbf{f}) = \mathbf{k}^T \mathbf{f} \tag{10.8}$$

The normal vector of the plane is pointing parallel to the 3-D vector $[f_1, f_2, 1]^T$. The plane constraint relation Equation (10.8) is an equivalent formulation of the brightness change constraint equation, BCCE Eq. (10.2). It is the basis for all spatiotemporal energy-based techniques (Section 10.4) that attempt to fit a plane to the Fourier spectrum of an image sequence. From the inclination of the plane the optical flow can be estimated. Taking the derivatives of $\omega(\mathbf{k}, \mathbf{f})$ Eq. (10.8) with respect to k_x and k_y yields both components of the optical flow:

$$\nabla_k \omega(\mathbf{k}, \mathbf{f}) = \mathbf{f} \tag{10.9}$$

The Fourier transform does not necessarily have to be applied to the whole image. For local estimates, multiplication with an appropriate window function prior to transformation restricts the spectrum to a local neighborhood (Fig. 10.4c). It is, however, not possible to perform a Fourier transformation for a single pixel. The smaller the window, the more blurred the spectrum becomes [10] (compare Fig. 10.4b

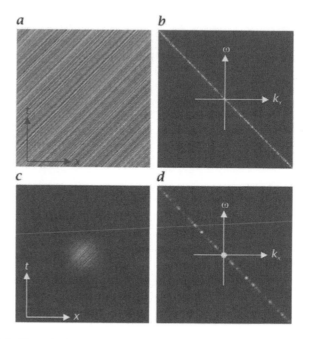

Figure 10.4: *Translating 1-D random pattern moving at 1 pixel/frame:* **a** *2-D xt-image (256 × 256);* **b** *power spectrum of the xt-image, with k_x and ω ranging from $-\pi$ to π. The star-shaped patterns are due to the finite size of the image;* **c** *windowed 2-D xt-image;* **d** *power spectrum of the windowed xt-image.*

with Fig. 10.4d). With the spatiotemporal window function $w(\mathbf{x}, t)$, the resulting Fourier spectrum is blurred by the Fourier transform of w, according to

$$\widehat{g \cdot w}(\mathbf{k}, \omega) = \hat{w}(\mathbf{k}, \omega) * [\hat{g}(\mathbf{k})\delta(\mathbf{k}f - \omega)] \qquad (10.10)$$

where $\hat{w}(\mathbf{k}, \omega)$ denotes the Fourier transform of the window function $w(\mathbf{x}, t)$, and $*$ defines the convolution

$$a(\mathbf{k}, \omega) * b(\mathbf{k}, \omega) = \int\limits_{-\infty}^{\infty} a(\mathbf{k} - \mathbf{k}', \omega - \omega')b(\mathbf{k}', \omega')d\mathbf{k}'d\omega' \qquad (10.11)$$

Without additional windowing, $w(\mathbf{x}, t)$ is given by the size of the image and the number of frames, that is, a box function with the size of the spatiotemporal image. Its Fourier transform corresponds to a 2-D sinc function, which can be observed in the star-shaped patterns of Fig. 10.4b.

Hence, the Fourier domain formulation Eq. (10.8) intrinsically extends the motion constraint to a local neighborhood of a pixel. In case

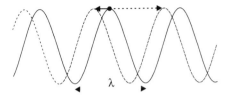

Figure 10.5: *Illustration of the temporal sampling theorem for a sinusoidal pattern of wavelength λ. Without restrictions on the magnitude of the displacement between two consecutive frames, both displacements indicated by arrows and all multiples of λ are equally likely to be the real displacement.*

of an *aperture problem*, the moving pattern shows spatial orientation within the local neighborhood. This causes the 3-D Fourier spectrum to reduce to a line instead of a plane. From the line, only one inclination angle can be extracted, corresponding to the normal optical flow.

Temporal sampling theorem.   In all cases in which spatial and temporal derivatives are directly related, it is inherently assumed that the shift between two consecutive frames is small compared to the scale of the pattern. In other words: the time derivative has to be unambiguously related to the moving brightness pattern within a small spatiotemporal neighborhood. This corresponds to the fact that derivatives are always realized by finite differences in image sequence processing although they are defined as infinitesimal quantities. For overly large displacements, no coherent structures can be detected in the spatiotemporal image. How fast are patterns of a certain size allowed to move? The answer is given by the *temporal sampling theorem*.

Consider a moving sinusoidal pattern of wavelength λ (Fig. 10.5). If no restrictions on the magnitude of shifts within consecutive frames apply, the real shift cannot be unambiguously determined. It is further undetermined up to multiples of the wavelength λ. The displacement stays unambiguous if it can be restricted to less than half the wavelength λ. In this case the correct optical flow can be estimated by the *minimal motion*, indicated by the solid arrow in Fig. 10.5.

From the spatial sampling theorem we know that any periodic signal has to be sampled at least twice per wavelength (Section 8.4.2). For temporal periodic signals, the wavelength corresponds to the cycle T with $T = 2\pi/\omega$. Using Eq. (10.8) the temporal sampling theorem is given by

$$\Delta t < \frac{T}{2} = \frac{\pi}{\omega} = \frac{\pi}{k^T f} \tag{10.12}$$

where Δt denotes the minimum frame rate necessary to estimate the optical flow f of a periodic signal with wave number k. The smaller the scale of a pattern, the more slowly it is allowed to move if the frame rate cannot be increased. As all patterns can be decomposed into periodic signals, Eq. (10.12) applies for any moving object. It is important to note that it is not the size of the object, but rather the smallest wave number contained in the Fourier spectrum of the object that is the limiting factor. A large disk-shaped object can suffer from temporal aliasing right at its edge, where high wave numbers are located.

If the temporal sampling theorem is violated by too large displacements, temporal aliasing appears. In spatiotemporal images it shows up as patterns with false inclinations or as distributed structures without any relation at all. A prominent example of temporal aliasing is one in which the wheels of horse-drawn carriages in movies seem to spin around in the wrong direction.

Performing a low-pass filtering to remove all small scale spatial frequencies beyond the critical limit is the basic idea of multiscale optical flow computation techniques [CVA2, Chapter 14]. Starting from coarse patterns, large displacements can be computed, which can be iteratively refined from smaller scales. Such an approach, however, assumes that patterns at all scales are moving with the same velocity. This is not true for physical processes showing dispersion, such as water surface waves.

10.2.2 Physical and visual correspondence

From the aperture problem we learned that only normal optical flow can be computed in the case of linear symmetry of the brightness distribution within a local neighborhood. Translations parallel to lines of constant gray values do not contribute to brightness variations and are thus not detectable. The temporal sampling theorem states that large displacements cannot be estimated from small-scale patterns. Both problems of motion estimation can be considered as special cases of a more general problem, commonly referred to as the *correspondence problem*. The motion of patterns does not always allow for relating corresponding features in consecutive frames in an unambiguous manner. The physical correspondence of features can remain undetectable due to an aperture problem, missing texture (recall the example of the spinning sphere in Fig. 10.1), or overly large displacements. Conversely, the apparent motion can lead to false correspondence. Variation in scene intensity may not be due to motion but instead may be caused by variations in illumination.

If local constraints are violated, *correspondence*-based techniques try to estimate a best match of features within consecutive frames (Chapter 10.5). Depending on the kind of features under consideration, these techniques can be classified into *correlation methods* and *token tracking* techniques [11]. Correlation techniques are computationally costly and therefore restricted to short-range displacements. Token tracking methods extract features, such as corners, straight line segments, or blobs [12] and track them over time. The search can be extended to the entire image area, which enables estimates of long-range displacements. All correspondence-based techniques consider only two single images. They do not use any information about the continuous temporal domain.

10.2.3 Flow versus correspondence

There has been much discussion of the pros and cons of optical flow-based techniques in contrast to correspondence-based techniques. We do not want to contribute to this dispute but rather recall which method seems to be best suited under certain circumstances.

In order to solve the aperture problem a variety of optical flow-based approaches have been proposed that try to minimize an objective function pooling constraints over a small finite area. An excellent overview of the current state of the art is given by Barron et al. [13]. They conclude that differential techniques, such as the local weighted least squares method proposed by Lucas and Kanade [14] (Section 10.3.1), perform best in terms of efficiency and accuracy. Phase-based methods [15] (Section 10.4.3) show slightly better accuracy but are less efficient in implementation and lack a single useful confidence measure. Bainbridge-Smith and Lane [16] come to the same conclusion in their comparison of the performance of differential methods. Performing analytical studies of various motion estimation techniques, Jähne [17] and [9] showed that the 3-D structure tensor technique (Section 10.3.2) yields the best results with respect to systematic errors and noise sensitivity. This could be verified by Jähne et al. [18], in their analysis of a calibrated image sequence with ground truth data provided by Otte and Nagel [19].

On the other hand, correspondence-based techniques (Section 10.5) are less sensitive to illumination changes. They are also capable of estimating long-range displacements of distinct features that violate the temporal sampling theorem. In this case any optical flow-based technique will fail. However, correlation-based approaches are extremely sensitive to periodic structures. With nearly periodic inputs (such as textures or bandpass filtered signals) they tend to find multiple local minima [13]. Comparative studies show that correlation-based techniques produce unpredictable output for straight edges (aperture problem), while optical flow-based techniques correctly estimate normal flow. Correlation techniques also perform less effectively in estimating subpixel displacements than do optical flow-based techniques [13, 20]. Especially at very small displacements in the order of less than $1/10$ pixel/frame, optical flow-based techniques yield better results.

Before we turn towards a detailed description of the various techniques, we want to draw the conclusion that neither correlation nor optical flow-based techniques are perfect choices in any case. If the temporal sampling theorem can be assured to be fulfilled, optical flow-based techniques are generally the better choice. In other cases, when large displacements of small structures are expected, correlation-based approaches usually perform better.

For both kind of techniques, it is important to get *confidence measures* in addition to the optical flow. No technique is without errors in any case. Only if errors can be detected and quantified can the result be reliably interpreted. It also shows that differences in precision, attributable to details of the initial formulation, are in fact, a result of different minimization procedures and a careful numerical discretization of the used filters.

10.3 Optical flow-based motion estimation

In this section we want to focus on common optical flow-based techniques. We can not detail all facets of the spectrum of existing techniques, but rather try to give a concise overview of the basic principles.

10.3.1 Differential techniques

Local weighted least squares. Assuming the optical flow f to be constant within a small neighborhood U Lucas and Kanade [14] propose a local weighted least squares estimate of the constraint Equation (10.2) on individual pixels within U. Similar approaches are reported in [21, 22, 23, 24]. The estimated optical flow is given by the solution of the following minimization problem:

$$f = \arg\min\|e\|_2^2, \quad \|e\|_2^2 = \int_{-\infty}^{\infty} w(x - x') \left[(\nabla g)^T f + g_t \right]^2 \, dx' \quad (10.13)$$

with a weighting function $w(x)$ selecting the size of the neighborhood. In practical implementations the weighting is realized by a Gaussian smoothing kernel. Additionally, w could weight each pixel according to some kind of confidence measure, for example, the magnitude of the gradient. In that way, *a priori* known errors are not propagated into the optical flow computation.

In the initial formulation of [14], Eq. (10.13) was given by a discrete sum of the squared *residuals* $(\nabla g)^T f + g_t$, which have to be minimized. The mathematically equivalent *continuous least squares* formulation Eq. (10.13) replaces the weighted sum by a convolution integral [9, 17]. This formulation enables us to use linear filter theory, which allows, for example, optimizing the convolution kernels independently from the minimization procedure. In this way practical implementations of different approaches can be quantitatively compared without confusing discretization errors with intrinsic errors of the algorithms.

The minimization of Eq. (10.13) is carried out by standard least squares estimation. Both partial derivatives of $\|e\|_2^2$ with respect to the two components f_1 and f_2 of the optical flow f have to equal zero at the minimum of $\|e\|_2^2$:

$$\frac{\partial\|e\|_2^2}{\partial f_1} = 2\int_{-\infty}^{\infty} w(x - x')g_x\left[(\nabla g)^T f + g_t\right] dx' \overset{!}{=} 0 \qquad (10.14)$$

$$\frac{\partial\|e\|_2^2}{\partial f_2} = 2\int_{-\infty}^{\infty} w(x - x')g_y\left[(\nabla g)^T f + g_t\right] dx' \overset{!}{=} 0 \qquad (10.15)$$

If the optical flow f is assumed to be constant within the area of influence of w, it can be drawn out of the integral. Combining Eqs. (10.14) and (10.15) yields the following linear equation system

$$\underbrace{\begin{bmatrix} \langle g_x\,g_x\rangle & \langle g_x\,g_y\rangle \\ \langle g_x\,g_y\rangle & \langle g_y\,g_y\rangle \end{bmatrix}}_{A} \underbrace{\begin{bmatrix} f_1 \\ f_2 \end{bmatrix}}_{f} = -\underbrace{\begin{bmatrix} \langle g_x\,g_t\rangle \\ \langle g_y\,g_t\rangle \end{bmatrix}}_{b} \qquad (10.16)$$

with the abbreviation

$$\langle a\rangle = \int_{-\infty}^{\infty} w(x - x')\,a\,dx' \qquad (10.17)$$

In operator notation, the components of Eq. (10.16) are given by

$$\langle g_p\,g_q\rangle = \mathcal{B}(\mathcal{D}_p \cdot \mathcal{D}_q), \quad \text{and} \quad \langle g_p\,g_t\rangle = \mathcal{B}(\mathcal{D}_p \cdot \mathcal{D}_t) \qquad (10.18)$$

where $\mathcal{B}$ is a smoothing operator and $\mathcal{D}_p$, $\mathcal{D}_q$, and $\mathcal{D}_t$ are discrete first-order derivative operators in the spatial directions p and q and in time direction t, respectively. The solution of Eq. (10.16) is given by

$$f = A^{-1}b \qquad (10.19)$$

provided the inverse of A exists. If all gradient vectors within U are pointing into the same direction, A gets singular. Then, the brightness distribution can be expressed locally as

$$g(x) = g(d^T x) \qquad (10.20)$$

where $d = [d_1, d_2]^T$ is a vector pointing perpendicular to lines of constant brightness. From Eq. (10.20) the first-order partial derivatives can be computed as $g_x = d_1 g'$ and $g_y = d_2 g'$, where the abbreviation $g' = \partial g / \partial (d^T x)$ is used. The determinant

$$\det(A) = \langle g_x\, g_x \rangle \langle g_y\, g_y \rangle - \langle g_x\, g_y \rangle^2 \tag{10.21}$$

equals zero and A cannot be inverted. Thus, averaging Eq. (10.2) over a small neighborhood does not yield more information than a single point if the aperture problem persists within the neighborhood. In this case, only the normal flow $f_\perp$ is computed according to Eq. (10.3).

Instead of zero determinant, singularity of A can be identified by analyzing the eigenvalues of the symmetric matrix A prior to inversion. While Simoncelli [24] suggests using the sum of eigenvalues, Barron et al. [13] conclude that the smallest eigenvalue constitutes a more reliable measure.

Jähne [9] shows that an extension of the integration in Eq. (10.13) into the temporal domain yields a better local regularization, provided that the optical flow is modeled constant within the spatiotemporal neighborhood U. However, this does not change the minimization procedure and results in the same linear equation system Equation (10.16). All that needs to be changed are the components $\langle a \rangle$

$$\langle a \rangle = \int_{-\infty}^{\infty} w(x - x', t - t')\, a\, dx'\, dt' \tag{10.22}$$

where both the integration as well as the window function w have been extended into the temporal domain.

While the presence of an aperture problem can be identified by the singularity of the matrix A, the initial assumption of constant optical flow within U remains to be proved. In any case, an averaged optical flow will be computed by the solution of Eq. (10.19). This leads to over-smoothing of the optical flow field at motion discontinuities and false estimation at the presence of transparent motion overlay. Such cases lead to nonzero values of the expression $[(\nabla g)^T f + g_t]$, which is called the measurement *innovation*, or the *residual*. The residual reflects the discrepancy between the predicted measurement $(\nabla g)^T f$ and the actual measurement g_t. A residual of zero means that both are in complete agreement. Thus, a nonconstant optical flow field can be detected by analyzing the variance of the data σ^2, given by the squared magnitude of the residuals [9]

$$\sigma^2 = \|e\|_2^2 = \left\langle \left[(\nabla g)^T f + g_t \right]^2 \right\rangle \tag{10.23}$$

where f is the *estimated* optical flow. In case of constant f within U, the residuals in Eq. (10.23) vanish and σ^2 reduces to the variance caused by noise in the image. Thus, a variance significantly larger than the noise variance is a clear indicator of a violation of the assumption of constant optical flow. In real applications, f will never be constant over the whole image. If it varies smoothly over the image area, it can be considered locally constant and the local least squares estimate can be applied. Other models of the spatial distribution of $f(x)$, such as linear (affine) motion, can be incorporated into the least squares approach as well. This will be the subject of Section 10.6.1.

From a probabilistic point of view, the minimization of Eq. (10.13) corresponds to a maximum likelihood estimation of the optical flow, given Gaussian-distributed errors at individual pixels [25]. Black and Anandan [8] show that the Gaussian assumption does not hold for motion discontinuities and transparent motions. By replacing the least squares estimation with robust statistics they come up with an iterative estimation of multiple motions (Section 10.6.2).

Second-order techniques. Instead of grouping constraints over a local neighborhood, it has been proposed to use second-order information to solve for both components of f [26, 27, 28]. This can be motivated by extending the brightness constancy assumption to an assumption on the conservation of the gradient ∇g under translation:

$$\frac{d(\nabla g)}{dt} = 0 \qquad (10.24)$$

Evaluating Eq. (10.24) yields the following linear equation system for a single point:

$$\underbrace{\begin{bmatrix} g_{xx} & g_{xy} \\ g_{xy} & g_{yy} \end{bmatrix}}_{H} \underbrace{\begin{bmatrix} f_1 \\ f_2 \end{bmatrix}}_{f} = - \underbrace{\begin{bmatrix} g_{tx} \\ g_{ty} \end{bmatrix}}_{b} \qquad (10.25)$$

The matrix H is the *Hessian* of the image brightness function, containing all second-order partial spatial derivatives $g_{pq} = \partial^2 g / \partial p \partial q$. The second-order spatiotemporal derivatives in b are abbreviated by $g_{tp} = \partial^2 g / \partial t \partial p$. The linear equation system Eq. (10.25) can be solved by

$$f = H^{-1} b \qquad (10.26)$$

if the Hessian matrix is not singular. This happens if the determinant vanishes,

$$\det(H) = g_{xx} g_{yy} - g_{xy}^2 = 0 \qquad (10.27)$$

The trivial solution of Eq. (10.27) is given for vanishing second-order derivatives, $g_{xx} = g_{yy} = g_{xy} = 0$, that is, local planar brightness distribution. Equation (10.27) also holds, if the image brightness shows *linear symmetry* within the local area supporting the second-order derivative operators. In this case, the brightness distribution can be expressed locally as

$$g(\boldsymbol{x}) = g(\boldsymbol{d}^T \boldsymbol{x}) \tag{10.28}$$

where $\boldsymbol{d} = [d_1, d_2]^T$ is a vector pointing perpendicular to lines of constant brightness. From Eq. (10.28) the second-order partial derivatives can be computed as

$$g_{xx} = d_1^2 g'', \quad g_{yy} = d_2^2 g'', \quad \text{and} \quad g_{xy} = d_1 d_2 g'' \tag{10.29}$$

where the abbreviation $g'' = \partial^2 g / \partial (\boldsymbol{d}^T \boldsymbol{x})^2$ is used. With Eq. (10.29) the condition Eq. (10.27) is satisfied and the Hessian $\boldsymbol{H}$ cannot be inverted.

Thus, second-order techniques, just as first-order techniques, do not allow for estimating the 2-D optical flow field $\boldsymbol{f}$ in case of an aperture problem within a local neighborhood. Although no local averaging has been performed to obtain the solution Equation (10.25), a local neighborhood is introduced by the region of support of the second-order derivative operators. In order to obtain second-order differential information, first-order properties of the image area need to be related over an increased area compared to first-order differentiation. From first-order information the full 2-D optical flow can only be extracted if the spatial orientation changes within the region of interest. Bainbridge-Smith and Lane [16] conclude that first-order differential techniques, such as proposed by Lucas and Kanade [14], are in fact generalized second-order techniques, because they implicitly require variation of the gradient within the region of support.

The initial assumption (Eq. (10.24)) requests that first-order (affine) motions, such as dilation, rotation or shear, are not allowed in the optical flow field. This constraint is much stronger than the brightness conservation assumption of Eq. (10.2) and is fulfilled only rarely for real motion fields. Hence, second-order techniques generally lead to sparser optical flow fields than those of first-order techniques [13]. If the assumption of conserved gradient is violated, the residual error

$$\|\boldsymbol{e}\|_2^2 = [\boldsymbol{H}\boldsymbol{f} - \boldsymbol{b}]^2 \tag{10.30}$$

will increase beyond the noise variance σ^2 (compare to Eq. (10.23)), which allows one to identify erroneous estimates of $\boldsymbol{f}$.

Global constraints. Local least squares techniques minimize the brightness change constraint Equation (10.2) over a localized aperture, defined by the size of the spatial window function w (Eq. (10.13)).

Global constraint methods extend the integration to the entire image area and combine the local gradient constraint Equation (10.2) with a spatial coherence assumption. The resulting objective function $\|e_t\|_2^2$ to be minimized consists of two terms. The first one, $\|e_d\|_2^2$, contains the local data (brightness) conservation constraint Equation (10.2) at each pixel and a second one, $\|e_s\|_2^2$, expresses the spatial relation between optical flow vectors:

$$\|e_t\|_2^2 = \|e_d\|_2^2 + \lambda^2 \|e_s\|_2^2 = \int_D \left[(\nabla g)^T f + g_t \right]^2 \, d\mathbf{x}' + \lambda^2 \|e_s\|_2^2 \quad (10.31)$$

The integration is carried out over the domain D, which can be extended to the entire image. The parameter λ controls the influence of the spatial coherence term. The optical flow f is estimated by minimizing $\|e_t\|_2^2$,

$$f = \arg \min \|e_t\|_2^2 \quad (10.32)$$

The introduction of a regularizing spatial coherence constraint $\|e_s\|_2^2$ restricts the class of admissible solutions and makes the problem well-posed [8]. A variety of approaches have been proposed in the literature, dealing with the choice of an appropriate spatial constraint. In general, it should interpolate optical flow estimates at regions suffering from the aperture problem or without sufficient brightness variations. At the same time spatial oversmoothing of motion boundaries should be prevented. Both are competing requirements.

The most common formulation of $\|e_s\|_2^2$ has been introduced by Horn and Schunk [6]. They propose a *global smoothness* constraint of the form

$$\|e_s\|_2^2 = \int_D \left[\left(\frac{\partial f_1}{\partial x}\right)^2 + \left(\frac{\partial f_1}{\partial y}\right)^2 + \left(\frac{\partial f_2}{\partial x}\right)^2 + \left(\frac{\partial f_2}{\partial y}\right)^2 \right] d\mathbf{x}' \quad (10.33)$$

Minimizing Eq. (10.32) by means of *Gauss-Seidel iteration* [29] yields an iterative solution for the optical flow $f^{(k+1)}$ at time step $k + 1$ given the flow $f^{(k)}$ at time k:

$$f^{(k+1)} = \left\langle f^{(k)} \right\rangle - \nabla g \frac{\nabla g \left\langle f^{(k)} \right\rangle + g_t}{\|\nabla g\|_2^2 + \lambda^2} \quad (10.34)$$

where $\left\langle f^{(k)} \right\rangle$ denotes a local average of $f^{(k)}$. The initial estimate $f^{(0)}$ is usually set to zero for the entire image. It is important to note that the gradient ∇g apparently controls the influence of both terms in Eq. (10.34). If the gradient vanishes, that is, at regions with low spatial structure, the optical flow is interpolated from adjacent estimates. In regions with high contrast the local brightness change constraint (numerator of the right term in Eq. (10.34)) becomes dominant.

The propagation of the flow field into regions with low contrast is an important feature of Horn and Schunck's smoothness constraint. However, as no directional selectivity is included in Eq. (10.33) the resulting flow field is blurred over motion discontinuities. It also has the drawback that a localized error can have a far-reaching effect if the surrounding gradients are small [16].

In order to reduce smoothing across edges, Nagel [26, 30, 31] suggests an *oriented smoothness* constraint:

$$\|e_s\|_2^2 = \int_D \frac{1}{\|\nabla g\|_2^2 + 2\delta} [E_1 + \delta E_2] \, \mathrm{d}x' \qquad (10.35)$$

$$
\begin{aligned}
E_1 &= \left[\frac{\partial f_1}{\partial x} g_y - \frac{\partial f_1}{\partial y} g_x\right]^2 + \left[\frac{\partial f_2}{\partial x} g_y - \frac{\partial f_2}{\partial y} g_x\right]^2 \\
E_2 &= \left(\frac{\partial f_1}{\partial x}\right)^2 + \left(\frac{\partial f_1}{\partial y}\right)^2 + \left(\frac{\partial f_2}{\partial x}\right)^2 + \left(\frac{\partial f_2}{\partial y}\right)^2
\end{aligned}
\qquad (10.36)
$$

The additional parameter δ controls the relative influence of the oriented smoothness term E_1 compared to E_2, which constitutes Horn and Schunck's global smoothness constraint. Again, the solution is given by an iterative Gauss-Seidel method. As an interesting feature, the rather complicated solution equations implicitly contain second-order derivatives [13].

In a more restrictive way, Hildreth [32, 33] reduces all computations to zero crossings of a Laplace-filtered image. Along these contour lines C, an objective function is defined according to

$$\|e_t\|_2^2 = \int_C \left[(\nabla g)^T f + g_t\right]^2 + \lambda^2 \left[\left(\frac{\partial f_1}{\partial s}\right)^2 + \left(\frac{\partial f_2}{\partial s}\right)^2\right] \mathrm{d}s' \qquad (10.37)$$

where the first term in the integral is given by the standard data conservation constraint Equation (10.31) and $\partial f_p / \partial s$ denotes the directional derivative of f_p into the direction s along the contour C. In contrast to other approaches, all integrations are carried out along contour lines instead of by 2-D averaging. Thus, no information is smoothed across brightness edges. However, the approach inherently assumes that all edges belong to the same object. If contours of independently moving objects merge, the resulting optical flow field is blurred along the contour line as well.

All approaches incorporating global constraints have in common that they result in systems of differential equations relating spatial variations of the optical flow within the entire domain D. Such a system can only be solved iteratively using numerical iteration methods, such as *Gauss-Seidel iteration* or *successive overrelaxation* [25, 34]. Although

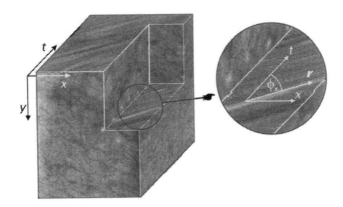

Figure 10.6: *Illustration of the spatiotemporal brightness distribution of moving patterns. The sequence shows infrared images of the ocean surface moving mainly in positive x-direction. The upper right portion of the 3-D **x**t-cube has been cut off, revealing the internal structure of the spatiotemporal image.*

efficient iterative solutions have been developed in numerical mathematics, they are still slower than closed solutions. Another problem of iterative solutions is the question of convergence, which may depend on image content. Further information on global constraints can be found in Chapter 13, where a general toolbox for variational approaches is proposed, together with an efficient numerical iteration scheme.

10.3.2 Tensor-based techniques

In Section 10.2.1 we have shown that optical flow computation can be formulated as orientation analysis in spatiotemporal images. A practical example of such a spatiotemporal image and the corresponding structures is shown in Fig. 10.6. This application example has been chosen for illustration because it demonstrates nicely how any moving gray-value structure causes inclined patterns, regardless of certain object properties.

In order to determine local orientation Bigün and Granlund [35] proposed a *tensor representation* of the local image brightness distribution. Starting with a different idea, Kass and Witkin [36] came to a solution that turned out to be equivalent to the tensor method. Searching for a general description of local orientation in multidimensional images, Knutsson [37, 38] concluded that local structure in an n-dimensional domain can be represented by a symmetric $n \times n$ tensor of second-order. In the analysis of data with a dimensionality higher than two it turns out that using scalars and vectors is no longer always convenient [39]. Tensors—a generalization of the vector concept—are perfectly suited to describe symmetries within local neighborhoods in multidimensional spatial and spatiotemporal signals.

This section outlines the practical application of tensor representations to optical flow computation and its relation to other optical flow-based techniques. We will show how a local least squares estimation of optical flow, such as the approach of Lucas and Kanade [14], can be improved by using total least squares estimation instead of standard least squares. This leads directly to the *structure tensor technique* for optical flow computation [40, 41, 42, 43], which constitutes the most direct approach to linear symmetry detection in spatiotemporal images. Another tensor representation, based on combinations of quadrature filters, will be outlined in Section 10.4.2.

The structure tensor approach. The optical flow f and the direction r of constant brightness within a spatiotemporal image are related by $f = r_3^{-1} [r_1, r_2]^T$ (Eq. (10.4)). Within a local neighborhood U, the vector r has to be as perpendicular as possible to the spatiotemporal gradient $\nabla_{xt}g = [g_x, g_y, g_t]^T$. Thus, the scalar product $(\nabla_{xt}g)^T r$ has to vanish at any point within U for the optimum estimate of r (Eq. (10.5)). In a least squares sense, r can be found by minimizing

$$r = \arg \min_{r^T r = 1} \|e\|_2^2, \quad \|e\|_2^2 = \int_{-\infty}^{\infty} w(x - x') \left[(\nabla_{xt}g)^T r \right]^2 dx' \quad (10.38)$$

which is equivalent to Eq. (10.13). In order to avoid the trivial solution $r = 0$, the constraint $r^T r = 1$ has to be imposed on r. The information within a local neighborhood U around the central point $x = [x, y, t]^T$ is weighted by a window-function $w(x - x')$. In practical applications the size of the local neighborhood U represents the area over which the optical flow is averaged. Again, the spatial integration can be extended into the time domain for local regularization without changing the results of the following minimization procedure [9].

Using the abbreviation Eq. (10.17), the objective function $\|e\|_2^2$ can be transformed into

$$\|e\|_2^2 = \left\langle \left[(\nabla_{xt}g)^T r \right]^2 \right\rangle = \left\langle r^T (\nabla_{xt}g)(\nabla_{xt}g)^T r \right\rangle \quad (10.39)$$

Under the assumption of constant r (that is, constant f) within U, Eq. (10.39) reduces to the following quadratic form:

$$\|e\|_2^2 = r^T \left\langle (\nabla_{xt}g)(\nabla_{xt}g)^T \right\rangle r = r^T J r \quad (10.40)$$

with the 3-D symmetric *structure tensor*

$$J = \begin{bmatrix} \langle g_x g_x \rangle & \langle g_x g_y \rangle & \langle g_x g_t \rangle \\ \langle g_x g_y \rangle & \langle g_y g_y \rangle & \langle g_y g_t \rangle \\ \langle g_x g_t \rangle & \langle g_y g_t \rangle & \langle g_t g_t \rangle \end{bmatrix} \quad (10.41)$$

The components of J are given by

$$J_{pq} = \langle g_p\,g_q \rangle = \int_{-\infty}^{\infty} w(x - x')\,g_p g_q\, \mathrm{d}x' \qquad (10.42)$$

where g_p, $p \in \{x, y, t\}$, denotes the partial derivative along the coordinate p. The implementation of the tensor components can be carried out very efficiently by standard image processing operators. Identifying the convolution in Eq. (10.42) with a smoothing of the product of partial derivatives, each component of the structure tensor can be computed as

$$J_{pq} = \mathcal{B}(\mathcal{D}_p \cdot \mathcal{D}_q) \qquad (10.43)$$

with the smoothing operator $\mathcal{B}$ and the differential operator $\mathcal{D}_p$ in the direction of the coordinate p.

The minimization of Eq. (10.40) subject to the constraint $r^T r = 1$ can be carried out by the method of *Lagrange multiplier*, minimizing the combined objective function $L(r, \lambda)$

$$f = \arg \min L(r, \lambda), \quad L(r, \lambda) = r^T J r + \lambda\left(1 - r^T r\right) \qquad (10.44)$$

The *Lagrange parameter* λ has to be chosen such that the partial derivatives of $L(r, \lambda)$ with respect to all three components of r equal zero:

$$\frac{\partial L(r, \lambda)}{\partial r_i} = 2\sum_k J_{ik} r_k - 2\lambda r_i \overset{!}{=} 0, \quad i \in \{1, 2, 3\} \qquad (10.45)$$

Combining the three equations in Eq. (10.45) yields the following linear equation system

$$Jr = \lambda r \qquad (10.46)$$

Thus, the minimization reduces to an *eigenvalue problem* of the symmetric matrix J. Once a minimizing r is found, Eq. (10.40) reduces to

$$\|e\|_2^2 = r^T J r = r^T \lambda r = \lambda \qquad (10.47)$$

which shows that the minimum of Eq. (10.40) is reached if the vector r is given by the *eigenvector* of the tensor J to the *minimum eigenvalue* λ.

Total least squares versus standard least squares. Although the local least squares technique (Eq. (10.13)) and the structure tensor technique (Eq. (10.38)) are based on the same initial formulation, the corresponding solutions Equations (10.19) and (10.46) are quite different. Practical implementations of both techniques also show that the structure tensor technique is more accurate [CVA2, Chapter 13]. Performing analytical studies Jähne [9] showed that the local least squares technique is biased towards lower values of f in the presence of noise, while the structure tensor technique yields an unbiased estimate for isotropic noise.

The reason for the differences between both techniques lies in the numerical minimization procedure. While the local least squares technique uses standard least squares (LS) the solution of the structure tensor technique mathematically corresponds to a total least squares solution (TLS). A detailed comparison of both techniques with respect to optical flow computation can be found in CVA2 [Chapter 13]. Without going into details we want to emphasize two important differences between LS and TLS in terms of optical flow computation:

- Instead of only the two parameters f_1 and f_2, the total least squares technique varies all three parameters of the vector $\boldsymbol{r}$. This leads to a robust estimate of the spatiotemporal orientation in contrast to a fixed temporal component using standard least squares.

- Both techniques yield matrices with components of the form $\langle g_p g_q \rangle$, where g_p denotes partial derivatives in x, y, and t. Comparing the structure tensor Equation (10.41) to the least squares solution Equation (10.16) shows that the purely temporal component $\langle g_t g_t \rangle$ of Eq. (10.41) is missing in Eq. (10.16). This component, however, allows to separate isotropic noise, occlusions, and fast accelerations from coherent motion [CVA2, Chapter 13]. Such regions violating the model assumption of constant f within U are detected by analyzing the residual errors in the standard least squares estimation.

Eigenvalue analysis.   In order to estimate optical flow from the structure tensor J we need to carry out an *eigenvalue analysis* of the symmetric 3×3 tensor in Eq. (10.46). The symmetry of J implies that all three eigenvalues are real and it further implies that there is an orthonormal basis of eigenvectors [34]. These vectors are pointing into the directions of minimal and maximal brightness changes, respectively, spanning the principal-axes coordinate system of the local 3-D spatiotemporal neighborhood U. In the principal-axes system, the transformed structure tensor J' is diagonal and contains the eigenvalues of J as diagonal elements. Four different classes of 3-D spatiotemporal structures can be distinguished and identified by analyzing the rank of the structure tensor (Table 10.1), which is given by the number of nonzero eigenvalues. The eigenvalues of J constitute the squared partial derivatives of the spatiotemporal brightness structure along the corresponding principal axis (averaged over U). Thus, rank (J) can be identified as the number of directions (principal axes) with nonzero brightness derivatives, which is directly related to the optical flow. A detailed analysis of the structure tensor technique and its practical application to optical flow computation can be found in CVA2 [Chapter 13].

Table 10.1: Classification of motion types by the rank of the structure tensor,
rank (J)

Motion type	rank (J)
Constant brightness, no apparent motion	0
Spatial orientation and constant motion (aperture problem)	1
Distributed spatial structure and constant motion	2
Distributed spatiotemporal structure (no coherent motion)	3

10.3.3 Multifeature-based techniques

The basic problem of optical flow estimation is to solve the under-constrained brightness change constrained Equation (10.2) for both components of f. Two basic approaches to this problem have been introduced in this chapter. Second-order differential techniques extend the continuity of optical flow to the spatial gradient Equation (10.24) to obtain two equations in two unknowns Eq. (10.25). Another approach was to model the optical flow and to group constraints over a local neighborhood (so far the model assumption was restricted to constant f, which will be extended in Section 10.6). Both kinds of approaches fail, however, if the local neighborhood is subject to spatial orientation. In this case the matrices in the resulting algebraic equations—which are obtained by any technique—become singular. Thus, the aperture problem corresponds to a linear dependence of the rows in the corresponding solution matrix, that is, to linearly dependent constraint equations.

Multifeature (or multiconstraint) techniques try to use two or more features to obtain overconstrained equation systems at the same location. These features have to be linearly independent in order to solve for both components of f. Otherwise the aperture problem remains, leading to singularities in the overconstrained system of equations. Multiple features can be obtained by using multiple light sources and/or multispectral cameras; visualizing independent physical properties of the same object; and using results of (nonlinear) functions of the image brightness.

Of course, all features have to move with the same velocity. Otherwise the estimated optical flow exhibits the motion of the combined feature vector rather than the real object motion. This prerequisite can be violated for features showing different physical properties that are subject to *dispersion*.

Within the scope of this book, we can give only a concise overview of the principal possibilities of multifeature-based techniques, illustrated by two examples, which relate to the previous results of Section 10.3.

Augmented second-order solution. The second-order approach of Tretiak and Pastor [27] and Uras et al. [28] can be interpreted as a two-feature method, applying the optical flow constraint to the horizontal and vertical spatial derivative Equation (10.24).

Equation (10.25) can be extended by incorporating the first-order BCCE Eq. (10.2) to form an overdetermined system of equations,

$$
\begin{bmatrix} g_x & g_y \\ g_{xx} & g_{xy} \\ g_{xy} & g_{yy} \end{bmatrix} \begin{bmatrix} f_1 \\ f_2 \end{bmatrix} = - \begin{bmatrix} g_t \\ g_{xt} \\ g_{yt} \end{bmatrix}
\tag{10.48}
$$

The relative influence of first- and second-order terms in Eq. (10.48) can be changed by attaching weights to the corresponding equations. In a least squares sense this entails multiplying each side of Eq. (10.48) with

$$
W = \begin{bmatrix} g_x & g_y \\ g_{xx} & g_{xy} \\ g_{xy} & g_{yy} \end{bmatrix}^T \begin{bmatrix} w_1 & 0 & 0 \\ 0 & w_2 & 0 \\ 0 & 0 & w_2 \end{bmatrix}
\tag{10.49}
$$

where the diagonal matrix contains the weights w_1 and w_2 of the first- and second-order terms, respectively [16]. Using the fractional weight $w = w_1/w_2$ and carrying out the matrix multiplication yields the following system of equations

$$
\begin{bmatrix} w g_x^2 + g_{xx}^2 + g_{xy}^2 & w g_x g_y + g_{xx} g_{xy} + g_{yy} g_{xy} \\ w g_x g_y + g_{xx} g_{xy} + g_{yy} g_{xy} & w g_y^2 + g_{yy}^2 + g_{xy}^2 \end{bmatrix} \begin{bmatrix} f_1 \\ f_2 \end{bmatrix}
$$

$$
= - \begin{bmatrix} w g_y g_t + g_{xx} g_{xt} + g_{xy} g_{yt} \\ w g_x g_t + g_{xy} g_{xt} + g_{yy} g_{yt} \end{bmatrix}
\tag{10.50}
$$

This approach is referred to as *augmented second-order technique* by Bainbridge-Smith and Lane [16]. They demonstrate that the first-order weighted least squares approach of Lucas and Kanade [14] (Eq. (10.13)) becomes equivalent to Eq. (10.50) if the aperture is restricted to a size where the brightness distribution can be adequately described by a second-order Taylor series. For larger apertures, the effect of higher-order derivatives leads to a more robust performance of the first-order local weighted least squares technique.

Multifeature structure tensor technique. The effect of linearly dependent constraint equations on the solubility of the corresponding algebraic equations can be demonstrated by a simple example using the structure tensor technique.

Let $\mathbf{G}(\mathbf{x}) = [g(\mathbf{x}), h(\mathbf{x})]^T$ be a vector-valued image (e.g., color image) that contains only two components with 1-D horizontal and vertical brightness changes

$$\mathbf{G}(\mathbf{x}) = \begin{bmatrix} g(\mathbf{x}) \\ h(\mathbf{x}) \end{bmatrix} = \begin{bmatrix} ax \\ by \end{bmatrix} \tag{10.51}$$

moving with the velocity $\mathbf{u} = [u_1, u_2]^T$.

The temporal derivatives of g and h are given by the brightness change constraint Equation (10.2), that is, $g_t = -(\nabla g)^T \mathbf{u} = -au_1$ and $h_t = -(\nabla h)^T \mathbf{u} = -bu_2$, with $\nabla g = [a, 0]^T$ and $\nabla h = [0, b]^T$. As all partial derivatives are constant over the entire image area, the structure tensor Equation (10.41) of g and h computes directly to

$$J_g = \begin{bmatrix} a^2 & 0 & -a^2 u_1 \\ 0 & 0 & 0 \\ -a^2 u_1 & 0 & a^2 u_1^2 \end{bmatrix}, \quad \text{and} \quad J_h = \begin{bmatrix} 0 & 0 & 0 \\ 0 & b^2 & -b^2 u_2 \\ 0 & -b^2 u_2 & b^2 u_2^2 \end{bmatrix} \tag{10.52}$$

respectively. As one row equals zero and the two remaining rows are linearly dependent, $\text{rank}(J_g) = \text{rank}(J_h) = 1$. Thus, both components are subject to the aperture problem over the entire image area due to the linear brightness variation (Table 10.1). Estimating the optical flow from g and h independently yields $\mathbf{f}_g = [u_1, 0]^T$ and $\mathbf{f}_h = [0, u_2]^T$. Without further assumptions, the connection between $\mathbf{f}_g$ and $\mathbf{f}_h$ remains unknown.

The vector-valued image, $\mathbf{G}$, however, allows one to extract the 2-D optical flow in an unambiguous fashion. How can the information from both components be adequately combined to accomplish this?

Simply adding up both component images results in a third image with linear spatial brightness distribution

$$g(\mathbf{x}) + h(\mathbf{x}) = ax + by \tag{10.53}$$

which suffers from the aperture problem as well. This can be verified by computing the structure tensor J_{g+h}

$$J_{g+h} = \begin{bmatrix} a^2 & ab & -a(au_1 + bu_2) \\ ab & b^2 & -b(au_1 + bu_2) \\ -a(au_1 + bu_2) & -b(au_1 + bu_2) & (au_1 + bu_2)^2 \end{bmatrix} \tag{10.54}$$

where any two rows are collinear. Hence, $\text{rank}(J_{g+h}) = 1$, that is, the sum of both components does not yield additional information.

By adding up the structure tensors of both components (Eq. (10.52)), we obtain

$$
J_g + J_h = \begin{bmatrix} a^2 & 0 & -a^2 u_1 \\ 0 & b^2 & -b^2 u_2 \\ -a^2 u_1 & -b^2 u_2 & -(a^2 u_1^2 + b^2 u_2^2) \end{bmatrix} \tag{10.55}
$$

In this matrix the third row can be expressed by a linear combination of the two first rows, which reduces the rank by one. As no other linear dependency exists, rank $(J_g + J_h) = 2$, which allows for unambiguously determining the 2-D optical flow $f = u$ (Table 10.1).

This example demonstrates the importance of the order in which linear and nonlinear operations are carried out. Adding features with linear brightness variations retains the linear relationship. Adding up the structure tensors of individual components (which consists of nonlinear operations), regularizes the combined structure tensor of linearly independent (uncorrelated) features. This technique can be easily extended to multiple features.

10.4 Quadrature filter techniques

This section deals with different approaches based on the motion constraint in Fourier domain, detailed in Section 10.2.1. As the Fourier spectrum of moving patterns falls onto a plane (Eq. (10.7)), quadrature filter techniques try to estimate the orientation of this plane by using velocity-tuned filters in the Fourier domain. A variety of approaches have been proposed that differ in both the design of frequency-selective filters and the combination of the filter outputs. All approaches have in common that the 3-D frequency distribution is interpolated from the response of a finite number of smoothly varying window functions, subsampling the 3-D spectrum.

A certain wave number/frequency band can be extracted by multiplying the Fourier spectrum with an appropriate window function $\hat{w}(k, \omega)$. The result of this operation, however, would be an oscillating signal with the selected wave numbers and frequencies, rather than quantification of the "presence" of the selected frequency band. In order to reduce these oscillations and omit zero crossings, we need to find a second signal with the same amplitude but a phase shift of $\pm\pi/2$ for every wave number and frequency. At zero crossings of the bandpass filtered signal, the phase-shifted signal shows extremes. A filter that performs such a phase shift is known as the *Hilbert filter*. It has an imaginary transfer function with odd symmetry, while the bandpass filter has a real-valued transfer function with even symmetry.

A frequency selective filter and its Hilbert transform is called a *quadrature filter* (Section 8.8.3). The output q of the quadrature filter G is a complex valued number,

$$q = G * g = q_+ - i q_- \qquad (10.56)$$

where g denotes the spatiotemporal image, q_+ the bandpass filtered signal and q_- its Hilbert transform, with the indices '+' and '-' referring to the even and odd symmetry of the corresponding filters. The magnitude

$$\|q\| = q_+^2 + q_-^2 \qquad (10.57)$$

minimizes the sensitivity to phase changes in the signal and provides an estimate of the *spectral density* or *energy* of the corresponding periodic image structure. For this reason, quadrature filter-based approaches are commonly referred to as *spatiotemporal energy-based approaches* in the literature. For the simple case of a sinusoidal signal $a \sin(k^T x + \omega t)$ (corresponding to a delta peak in the Fourier spectrum), the magnitude of q will be completely phase invariant:

$$q = \hat{w}(k, \omega) a \sin(k^T x + \omega t) - i \hat{w}(k, \omega) a \cos(k^T x + \omega t) \qquad (10.58)$$

$$\|q\| = \hat{w}^2(k, \omega) a^2 \left[\sin^2(k^T x + \omega t) + \cos^2(k^T x + \omega t) \right] = \hat{w}^2(k, \omega) a^2$$

The most common quadrature filter pair is the Gabor filter. It selects a certain spatiotemporal frequency region with a Gaussian window function centered at (k_0, ω_0) (Fig. 8.13, Section 8.8.3). The corresponding complex filter mask is given by

$$G(x, t) = \exp\left[i(k_0 x + \omega_0 t)\right] \exp\left[-\left(\frac{x^2}{2\sigma_x^2} + \frac{y^2}{2\sigma_y^2} + \frac{t^2}{2\sigma_t^2}\right)\right] \qquad (10.59)$$

More detailed information about the basic concept of quadrature filters can be found in [9, 39]. In the following sections we will outline how these filters can be used for optical flow estimation.

10.4.1 Spatiotemporal energy models

A quadrature filter technique for the computation of 2-D optical flow was developed by Heeger [44, 45]. At each of several spatial scales, he used 12 Gabor filters tuned to different spatial orientation at three different temporal frequencies. The filters are arranged in three layers with cylindrical symmetry about the temporal frequency axis (Fig. 10.7a).

The expected response of a Gabor filter (Eq. (10.59)) tuned to frequency (k_x, k_y, ω) for translating white noise, as a function of the velocity $f = [f_1, f_2]^T$, is given by:

$$R_{k,\omega}(f_1, f_2) = \exp\left[-\frac{4\pi^2 \sigma_x^2 \sigma_y^2 \sigma_t^2 (f_1 k_x + f_2 k_y + \omega)}{(f_1 \sigma_x \sigma_t)^2 + (f_2 \sigma_y \sigma_t)^2 + (\sigma_x \sigma_y)^2}\right] \qquad (10.60)$$

a   b

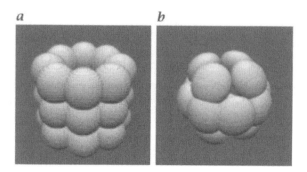

Figure 10.7: *Illustration of 3-D spatiotemporal filters in Fourier domain. Shown are level surfaces of the power spectra of the filters. Surfaces are rendered assuming a fixed point light source and a Lambertian surface: **a** arrangement of the twelve Gabor filters used in the approach of Heeger [44]. The ω axis is pointing along the cylindrical axis of symmetry; **b** spatiotemporal frequency spectra of the directional derivative filters used in the local least squares approach of Lucas and Kanade [14]. (Images courtesy of E. P. Simoncelli, New York University, [24].)*

In order to find the optical flow f that best fits the measured filter energy responses, Heeger [44] performed a least squares plane fit of the 12 different $R_{k,\omega}$, using a numerical optimization procedure.

The Gabor filters used in this approach are, however, not symmetrically arranged about the origin. This leads to systematic errors in velocity estimates if the wave number of the moving pattern does not match the center response of the filters [24]. The choice of Gabor filters has been motivated by the fact that they minimize a joint space-frequency localization criterion and have been suggested for use in biological vision modeling [24, 46, 47].

The 2-D first-order least squares solution can be interpreted as a spatiotemporal energy-based approach. Simoncelli [24] showed that the components of Eq. (10.16) can be reformulated as local averages of squares of directional filters and differences of two such squares. This corresponds to eight different spatiotemporally oriented bandpass filters. The local average of squared bandpass filters approximates the magnitude of quadrature filters. Level contours of the eight transfer functions are symmetrically arranged about the origin (Fig. 10.7b), in contrast to the Gabor filters of Heeger [44] (Fig. 10.7a). Thus, the velocity estimate computed with the first-order least squares solution will be invariant to scaling of the spatial frequency of the input signal.

10.4.2 Tensor from quadrature filter sets

In Section 10.3.2 we pointed out that *tensors* are perfectly suited to describe symmetries within local neighborhoods of spatiotemporal signals. In this section we discuss how to design optimal quadrature filters that detect both spatiotemporal orientation and wave number. We further show how these filters can be combined to compute the *structure tensor* introduced in Section 10.3.2. This section is based on the work of Knutsson [37, 38], summarized in an excellent monograph by Granlund and Knutsson [39] that details the theory of tensors for local structure analysis.

Spherically separable filters. In order to interpolate the spatiotemporal frequency distribution optimally from the frequency responses of directionally selective filters, they are required to have particular interpolation properties. Directional filters having the necessary properties were first suggested by Knutsson [37] for the 2-D case and further extended by Knutsson [38] for the 3-D case. He found that an optimal filter should be *polar separable*, that is, the transfer function should separate into a function of radius R and a function of direction D

$$\hat{Q}(\boldsymbol{k}) = R(k)D(\bar{\boldsymbol{k}}) \quad \text{with} \quad \boldsymbol{k} = [k_1, k_2, \omega]^T \qquad (10.61)$$

Here $\boldsymbol{k}$ denotes the 3-D spatiotemporal frequency vector. The arguments $k = \|\boldsymbol{k}\|$ and $\bar{\boldsymbol{k}} = \boldsymbol{k}/k$ are the magnitude of $\boldsymbol{k}$ and the unit directional vector, respectively.

The radial function $R(k)$ can be chosen arbitrarily without violating the basic requirements. Typically, $R(k)$ is a bandpass function with a certain center frequency and bandwidth. Knutsson et al. [48] suggested the following radial function:

$$R(k) = \exp\left[-\frac{(\ln k - \ln k_0)^2}{(B/2)^2 \ln 2} \right] \qquad (10.62)$$

which is a *lognormal function*, that is, a Gaussian function on a logarithmic scale. The constant B is the relative bandwidth of the filter and k_0 the peak frequency.

The following directional function $D(\bar{\boldsymbol{k}})$ incorporating the necessary interpolation properties was suggested by Knutsson [38]:

$$D(\bar{\boldsymbol{k}}) = \begin{cases} (\bar{\boldsymbol{k}}^T \bar{\boldsymbol{d}}_i)^{2l} & \text{if } \bar{\boldsymbol{k}}^T \bar{\boldsymbol{d}}_i > 0 \\ 0 & \text{otherwise} \end{cases} \qquad (10.63)$$

where $\bar{\boldsymbol{d}}_i$ is the unit vector pointing into the direction of the filter. The directional function has a maximum at the filter direction $\bar{\boldsymbol{d}}_i$ and varies as $\cos^{2l}(\phi)$, where ϕ is the difference in angle between an arbitrary direction $\boldsymbol{k}$ and $\bar{\boldsymbol{d}}_i$.

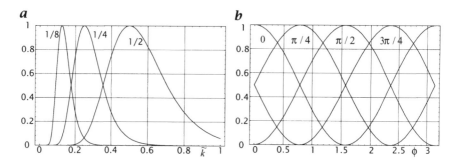

Figure 10.8: a *Radial and* **b** *angular part of the 2-D polar separable quadrature filter according to Eqs. (10.62) and (10.64) with l = 1 and B = 2 with different peak wave numbers k_0 and four directions (0°, 45°, 90°, and 125°)*

For the real even and the imaginary odd filter of the quadrature filter, the radial part R is the same and only the directional part D differs:

$$D_+(\bar{\boldsymbol{k}}) = (\bar{\boldsymbol{k}}^T \bar{\boldsymbol{d}}_i)^{2l}$$
$$D_-(\bar{\boldsymbol{k}}) = \mathrm{i}\,(\bar{\boldsymbol{k}}^T \bar{\boldsymbol{d}}_i)^{2l}\,\mathrm{sign}(\bar{\boldsymbol{k}}^T \bar{\boldsymbol{d}}_i) \tag{10.64}$$

Figure 10.8 illustrates the transfer function of this quadrature filter with different peak wave number k_0 and in four directions.

Number and direction of filters. The filters used to compute local spatiotemporal structure have to be symmetrically distributed in the 3-D Fourier domain. It is shown in [38] that the minimum number of filters has to be greater than 4. However, as there is no way of distributing 5 filters symmetrically in 3-D space, the next possible number is 6. The orientations of these filters are given by the following 6 normal vectors:

$$\bar{\boldsymbol{d}}_1 = c\,[a,0,b]^T \quad \bar{\boldsymbol{d}}_2 = c\,[-a,0,b]^T$$
$$\bar{\boldsymbol{d}}_3 = c\,[b,a,0]^T \quad \bar{\boldsymbol{d}}_4 = c\,[b,-a,0]^T \tag{10.65}$$
$$\bar{\boldsymbol{d}}_5 = c\,[0,b,a]^T \quad \bar{\boldsymbol{d}}_6 = c\,[0,b,-a]^T$$

where

$$a = 2,\ b = (1 + \sqrt{5}),\ \text{and}\ c = (10 + 2\sqrt{5})^{-1/2} \tag{10.66}$$

Tensor construction. From the responses of the 6 directional filters, the *structure tensor* $\boldsymbol{J}$ (Section 10.3.2) can be computed. According to Granlund and Knutsson [39], $\boldsymbol{J}$ can be obtained by linear summation of the quadrature filter output magnitudes:

$$\boldsymbol{J}(\boldsymbol{x}) = \sum_{i=0}^{5} q_i M_i, \quad M_i = \left(\alpha \bar{\boldsymbol{d}}_i \bar{\boldsymbol{d}}_i^T - \beta \boldsymbol{I}\right) \tag{10.67}$$

where q_i is the magnitude of the complex-valued output of the quadrature filter in the direction $\bar{d}_i$, M_i is a tensor associated with the quadrature filter i, and I is the identity tensor (matrix). The two constants are given by $\alpha = 5/4$ and $\beta = 1/4$. As the elements M_i are constant tensors, they can be precalculated. Thus, the structure tensor can be estimated by a weighted summation of the tensors M_i, where the weights are the quadrature filter outputs q_i.

Optical flow computation. Given the structure tensor J, the optical flow can be computed analogously to that shown in Section 10.3.2. After an eigenvalue analysis of the structure tensor, the corresponding eigenvectors are pointing into the directions of minimal and maximal brightness changes, respectively. They can be used to compute either the normal flow $f_\perp$ or the 2-D optical flow f depending on the distribution of the eigenvalues.

10.4.3 Phase techniques

Another class of techniques, based on the work of Fleet and Jepson [15], uses quadrature filters to estimate the local *phase* of the spatiotemporal image. The use of phase information is motivated by the fact that the phase component of a bandpass filtered signal is less sensitive to illumination changes than the amplitude component of the filter output [49]. This corresponds to the fact that the phase of the Fourier transform carries the essential information: An image can still be recognized when the amplitude information is lost, but not vice versa [50].

Consider a planar spatiotemporal wave with a wave number k and a temporal frequency ω, corresponding to a delta peak in the 3-D Fourier domain:

$$g(x,t) = g_0 \exp\left[-i\phi(x,t)\right] = g_0 \exp\left[-i(k^T x - \omega t)\right] \qquad (10.68)$$

This spatiotemporal signal corresponds to a planar 2-D wave, traveling with a phase speed u, with $\omega = k^T u$ (Eq. (10.8)). The *phase* of the signal

$$\phi(x,t) = k^T x - \omega t = k^T x - k^T u t \qquad (10.69)$$

varies linearly in space and time. The projection f_c of the 2-D velocity u onto the wave number unit vector $\bar{k}$,

$$f_c = \bar{k}^T u = \frac{1}{\|k\|} k^T u \qquad (10.70)$$

is called *component velocity*. It is the instantaneous motion normal to level phase contours of a periodic structure (the output of a bandpass filter), as opposed to *normal velocity*, which constitutes the velocity component normal to the local intensity structure.

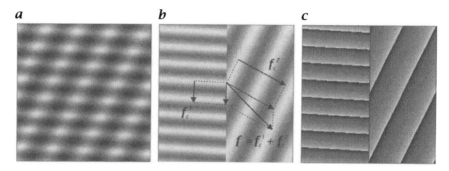

a   *b*   *c*

Figure 10.9: *Illustration of the phase technique:* **a** *sinusoidal plaid pattern composed of two sinusoids moving with the optical flow* f; **b** *the two individual components allow one to extract the corresponding component velocities* f_c^1 *and* f_c^2, *respectively. The 2-D optical flow* f *is reconstructed from the component velocities;* **c** *phase images of the two sinusoidal patterns.*

The component velocity f_c is pointing parallel to the phase gradient and can be computed by

$$f_c = -\frac{\phi_t(x,t)}{\|\nabla\phi(x,t)\|}\frac{\nabla\phi(x,t)}{\|\nabla\phi(x,t)\|} \qquad (10.71)$$

which can be directly verified using Eq. (10.69). Comparing Eq. (10.71) to Eq. (10.3) shows that, in fact, the phase-based technique is a differential technique applied to phase rather than intensity. The phase-based technique, however, allows one to estimate multiple component velocities at a single image location, compared to only one normal velocity in Eq. (10.3). If the wave-number vectors k of the different components are linear independent, the full 2-D optical flow can be recovered. Figure 10.9 illustrates the phase and component velocity for a simple pattern composed of two periodical signals.

The phase ϕ can be computed using a quadrature filter. As with any complex number, the argument $\arg(q)$ of the filter output represents the local phase of the signal:

$$\phi(x,t) = \arg(q) = \arctan\frac{q_-(x,t)}{q_+(x,t)} \qquad (10.72)$$

Unfortunately, a phase computed with the inverse tangent is restricted to the main interval $[-\pi, \pi[$ and jumps at the transition from $-\pi$ to π (Fig. 10.9c). Computing the derivative of such a discontinuous signal would inevitably lead to errors in the velocity estimate.

Fleet and Jepson [15] found a solution to avoid this problem by directly computing the phase derivatives from the quadrature filter pair, without prior computation of the phase. This can be performed using the identity

$$\nabla_{xt}\phi(\mathbf{x},t) = \frac{q_+(\mathbf{x},t)\nabla_{xt}q_-(\mathbf{x},t) - q_-(\mathbf{x},t)\nabla_{xt}q_+(\mathbf{x},t)}{q_+^2(\mathbf{x},t) + q_-^2(\mathbf{x},t)} \quad (10.73)$$

where ∇_{xt} denotes the spatiotemporal gradient $\nabla_{xt}\phi = [\phi_x, \phi_y, \phi_t]^T$. They also proposed decomposing the image into periodic structures by a set of Gabor filters. From the output of these filters, they use theoretical results on the stability of band-pass phase signals [49] to determine which outputs should provide reliable estimates of component velocity. When a band-pass filtered signal is reliable, the component velocity is computed by Eq. (10.71) using Eq. (10.73) for the partial derivatives. The 2-D optical flow is composed from these component velocities. It is estimated locally by solving a linear system of equations relating the component velocities to an affine model of optical flow (Section 10.6.1).

10.5 Correlation and matching

Differential and quadrature filter-based approaches are subject to errors, if the temporal sampling theorem is violated, that is, for large displacements of the moving pattern within two consecutive frames. In addition, optical flow estimates are biased if the illumination changes within the temporal region of support. Correspondence-based approaches are less sensitive to these error sources. They try to find the best match of a characteristic image feature and the corresponding feature in the consecutive frame. Correspondence techniques can be classified into *region-based matching* and *feature-based matching* techniques, respectively. Comprehensive overviews of feature-based matching techniques are given by Faugeras [51] and Murray [11]. These techniques are commonly extended into 3-D spaceto recover 3-D motion, and to track objects. In this section we focus on region-based matching techniques, such as *cross correlation* and *distance minimization*. Region-based matching techniques approximate the optical flow $\mathbf{f}$ by

$$\mathbf{f}(\mathbf{x}) = \frac{\mathbf{s}(\mathbf{x})}{t_2 - t_1} \quad (10.74)$$

where $\mathbf{s} = [s_1, s_2]^T$ is the displacement that yields the best match between two image regions in consecutive frames $g(\mathbf{x},t_1)$ and $g(\mathbf{x}-\mathbf{s},t_2)$. A best match is found by either *minimizing* a *distance measure*, or *maximizing* a *similarity measure*, with respect to the displacement $\mathbf{s}$.

10.5.1 Cross correlation

A suitable similarity measure of two image regions is given by the *cross-correlation function*

$$r(\mathbf{x}, \mathbf{s}) = \frac{\langle g(\mathbf{x}', t_1) g(\mathbf{x}' - \mathbf{s}, t_2) \rangle}{\left(\langle g^2(\mathbf{x}', t_1) \rangle \langle g^2(\mathbf{x}' - \mathbf{s}, t_2) \rangle \right)^{1/2}} \qquad (10.75)$$

which has to be maximized over $\mathbf{s}$. The abbreviation Eq. (10.17) has been used in Eq. (10.75) to simplify notation. The window function w in the terms $< \cdot >$ determines the size of the region to be matched. The cross-correlation function is independent of illumination changes. It is zero for totally dissimilar patterns and reaches a maximum of one for similar features.

The cross-correlation function is a 4-D function, depending on both the position $\mathbf{x}$ within the image as well as on the shift $\mathbf{s}$. In order to restrict the number of admissible matches and to minimize computational costs, the search range of $\mathbf{s}$ is restricted to a finite search window.

To speed up computations, a fast maximum search strategy has been proposed by Jähne [9]. Assuming the cross-correlation function $r(\mathbf{s})$ to be appropriately approximated by a second-order polynomial in $\mathbf{s}$, he shows that the $\mathbf{s}^m$ maximizing $r(\mathbf{s})$ can be estimated by the following linear system of equations:

$$\begin{bmatrix} r_{s_1 s_1} & r_{s_1 s_2} \\ r_{s_1 s_2} & r_{s_2 s_2} \end{bmatrix} \begin{bmatrix} s_1^m \\ s_2^m \end{bmatrix} = - \begin{bmatrix} r_{s_1} \\ r_{s_2} \end{bmatrix} \qquad (10.76)$$

with

$$r_{s_p} = \frac{\partial r}{\partial s_p} \quad \text{and} \quad r_{s_p s_q} = \frac{\partial^2 r}{\partial s_p \partial s_q} \qquad (10.77)$$

The first- and second-order partial derivatives of r with respect to the components s_1 and s_2 are taken at $\mathbf{s} = 0$. However, the fast maximum search according to Eq. (10.76) will fail, if r cannot be approximated by a second-order polynomial within the search region of $\mathbf{s}$. In order to overcome this problem, an iterative coarse-to-fine strategy can be applied. Beginning at the coarsest level of a Laplacian pyramid (Section 8.10.3), where displacements are assumed to be in the order of 1 pixel/frame or less, maxima of r can be located within a small search space of only 1-3 pixels. Within this region the second-order approximation of r is appropriate. Subpixel displacements are successively computed from finer levels of the Laplacian pyramid, by a quadratic approximation of r about $\mathbf{s}^m$ from coarser levels.

10.5.2 Distance minimization matching

An alternative approach to maximizing the cross-correlation function is to minimize a distance measure, quantifying the dissimilarity between two image regions. A common distance measure is given by the *sum-of-squared difference* (SSD):

$$d_{1,2}(\boldsymbol{x}, \boldsymbol{s}) = \left\langle [g(\boldsymbol{x}', t_1) - g(\boldsymbol{x}' - \boldsymbol{s}, t_2)]^2 \right\rangle \tag{10.78}$$

The indices 1 and 2 refer to times t_1 and t_2, respectively. Again the abbreviation Equation (10.17) has been used to simplify notation. Interestingly, Eq. (10.78) is closely related to the approach of Lucas and Kanade [14]. Approximating $g(\boldsymbol{x}' - \boldsymbol{s}, t_2)$ in Eq. (10.78) by a truncated Taylor expansion about $\boldsymbol{s} = 0$ and skipping all terms above first-order yields the gradient-based formulation Equation (10.13).

Approaches using SSD-based matching are reported by Anandan [52] and Singh [53, 54]. The matching technique of Anandan [52] uses a coarse-to-fine strategy based on a Laplacian pyramid. Similar to the maximum search for the cross-correlation function described in the preceding, the minimization of d is initially carried out on the coarsest level of the pyramid and then successively refined to subpixel accuracy.

An interesting extension of the two-frame matching techniques is proposed by Singh [53, 54]. He averages the SSD of two consecutive pairs of bandpass filtered images, that is, three frames, to average spurious SSD minima due to noise or periodic texture:

$$d_2(\boldsymbol{x}, \boldsymbol{s}) = d_{1,2}(\boldsymbol{x}, -\boldsymbol{s}) + d_{2,3}(\boldsymbol{x}, \boldsymbol{s}) \tag{10.79}$$

In a second stage, this error measure is converted into a probability response distribution using

$$R(\boldsymbol{x}, \boldsymbol{s}) = \exp\left[\frac{\ln(0.95)d_2(\boldsymbol{x}, \boldsymbol{s})}{\min(d_2(\boldsymbol{x}, \boldsymbol{s}))}\right] \tag{10.80}$$

The choice for an exponential function for converting error distribution into response distribution is motivated by the fact that the response obtained with an exponential function varies continuously between zero and unity over the entire range of error. Hence, finding a minimum of d_2 corresponds to maximizing the response function $R(\boldsymbol{x}, \boldsymbol{s})$ over $\boldsymbol{s}$. In order to avoid local maxima, Singh [54] suggests finding a best estimate $\boldsymbol{s}^m$ of the displacement $\boldsymbol{s}$ by computing the center of mass of R with respect to $\boldsymbol{s}$:

$$\boldsymbol{s}^m(\boldsymbol{x}) = \frac{\displaystyle\sum_{n=0}^{N-1} R(\boldsymbol{x}, \boldsymbol{s}_n)\boldsymbol{s}_n}{\displaystyle\sum_{n=0}^{N-1} R(\boldsymbol{x}, \boldsymbol{s}_n)} \tag{10.81}$$

where the summation is carried out over all N integer values $\boldsymbol{s}_n$ within the search window. The center of mass only approximates the maximum peak value if R is symmetrically centered about the peak. Thus, a coarse-to-fine strategy based on a Laplacian pyramid is used to ensure the surface of R is centered close to the true displacement [13].

10.6 Modeling of flow fields

In all optical flow techniques detailed in this chapter, tight restrictions have been imposed on the optical flow field $f(x)$. All techniques that group constraints over a local neighborhood U intrinsically assumed f to be constant within U. In order to fulfill this prerequisite, the local neighborhood tends to be chosen as small as possible to get a local estimate of f. The larger the neighborhood gets, the more likely it is that f varies within U, or that U contains multiple motions. At the same time, U has to be chosen sufficiently large as to contain enough information to constrain the solution, that is, to overcome the aperture problem. This competition of requirements is commonly referred to as the *generalized aperture problem* [55].

A variety of approaches use least-squares estimates (either LS or TLS) to group Eq. (10.2) or some other relation over a local neighborhood U. By using a quadratic objective function, they inherently assume Gaussian residual errors, locally independent with equal variance within U. The merit of this assumption is a fairly simple, closed solution. As soon as multiple motions (e. g., occlusion boundaries or transparent motion) are present within U, the residuals can not longer be considered Gaussian [8]. If these motions are independent, the error distribution might even become bimodal.

These considerations show that, in fact, we have already applied a model to optical flow computation, namely the most simple model of constant f and independent Gaussian errors within U. This section outlines two principal approaches to the forementioned problems. They try to model more appropriately the flow field and can be incorporated into techniques detailed so far. These approaches weaken the simple model assumptions by modeling both smooth spatial variations in the optical flow field as well as multiple motions.

10.6.1 Parameterization of flow fields

Parameterized flow field models assume the optical flow $f(x)$ to be modeled according to some parametric function in the image coordinates. An appropriate optical flow technique has to estimate the model parameters a, which include the mean optical flow, as well as spatial derivatives of f. If the model appropriately describes the spatial variation of f within a certain area, the local neighborhood can be increased up to this size without violating the model assumption. In fact, the local region of support has to be increased (compared to constant f within

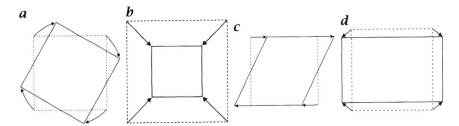

Figure 10.10: *Elementary geometric transformations of a planar surface element undergoing affine transformation:* **a** *rotation;* **b** *dilation;* **c** *shear;* **d** *stretching.*

U) in order to compute the model parameters reliably. The more parameters have to be estimated, the larger the local neighborhood has to be in order to regularize the solution. At the same time the computational complexity increases with the number of parameters.

Affine optical flow field. A more complicated model of the optical flow field assumes a linear variation of f, that is, an *affine transformation* of local image regions:

$$f(\boldsymbol{x}) = \begin{bmatrix} a_1 & a_2 \\ a_3 & a_4 \end{bmatrix} \begin{bmatrix} x \\ y \end{bmatrix} + \begin{bmatrix} a_5 \\ a_6 \end{bmatrix} = \boldsymbol{A}\boldsymbol{x} + \boldsymbol{t} \qquad (10.82)$$

with

$$a_1 = \frac{\partial f_1}{\partial x}, \quad a_2 = \frac{\partial f_1}{\partial y}, \quad a_3 = \frac{\partial f_2}{\partial x}, \quad \text{and} \quad a_4 = \frac{\partial f_2}{\partial y} \qquad (10.83)$$

This model appropriately describes the underlying optical flow field $f(\boldsymbol{x})$, if it can be locally expressed by a first-order Taylor expansion, which is always possible for smoothly varying $f(\boldsymbol{x})$. The size of the local neighborhood U must be chosen such that it is small enough for the first-order condition to hold, and simultaneously large enough to constrain the solution.

The vector $\boldsymbol{t} = [a_5, a_6]^T$ represents the translation of the center of the local neighborhood and corresponds to the constant optical flow vector f used so far. From the four components $a_1, \ldots, a_4$ the four elementary geometric transformations of the local neighborhood can be computed (see also Eq. (13.32) in Chapter 13):

- If the optical flow field has nonzero *vorticity*, the local neighborhood is subject to *rotation*, as illustrated in Fig. 10.10a and Fig. 10.11c. Rotation (vorticity) can be computed from the nondiagonal elements of $\boldsymbol{A}$ by

$$\text{rot}(\boldsymbol{f}) = \frac{\partial f_1}{\partial y} - \frac{\partial f_2}{\partial x} = a_3 - a_2 \qquad (10.84)$$

- If the optical flow field has nonzero *divergence*, the local neighborhood is subject to *dilation* (Fig. 10.10b and Fig. 10.11b). Dilation (divergence) can be computed by

$$\text{div}(\boldsymbol{f}) = \frac{\partial f_1}{\partial x} + \frac{\partial f_2}{\partial y} = a_1 + a_4 \qquad (10.85)$$

  which corresponds to the trace of the matrix $\boldsymbol{A}$.
- The *shear* of the local neighborhood (Fig. 10.10c and Fig. 10.11d) can be computed by

$$\text{sh}(\boldsymbol{f}) = \frac{\partial f_1}{\partial y} + \frac{\partial f_2}{\partial x} = a_2 + a_3 \qquad (10.86)$$

- The *stretching* of the local neighborhood (Fig. 10.10d and Fig. 10.11e) can be computed by

$$\text{str}(\boldsymbol{f}) = \frac{\partial f_1}{\partial x} - \frac{\partial f_2}{\partial y} = a_1 - a_4 \qquad (10.87)$$

In order to incorporate the affine model into optical flow estimation, we need to replace the constant flow vector $\boldsymbol{f}$ in the objective functions of any technique by the affine flow $\boldsymbol{f}(\boldsymbol{x}, \boldsymbol{a}) = \boldsymbol{A}\boldsymbol{x} + \boldsymbol{t}$.

Lie group transformations. Affine flow is only one possible model of local image transformations. A mathematical generalization of the theory of transformations can be found by using the formalism of *Lie algebra*. In fact, the *affine group* is a subgroup of the *Lie group* of continuous transformations. Without detailing all mathematical prerequisites of Lie group theory, we approach this concept in terms of coordinate transformations from Cartesian image coordinates into generalized coordinates, and outline the practical application to optical flow computation. A more detailed treatment of Lie algebra is found in [56, 57].

In the following, we assume the image brightness pattern to undergo a spatial transformation within a time interval δt, which can be expressed by

$$g(\boldsymbol{x}, t) = g(\boldsymbol{x}', t - \delta t) = g(\boldsymbol{S}^{-1}(\boldsymbol{x}, \boldsymbol{a}), t - \delta t) \qquad (10.88)$$

where $\boldsymbol{S} = [S_x, S_y]^T$ defines a 2-D invertible transformation acting on the image coordinates $\boldsymbol{x}$:

$$\boldsymbol{x} = \boldsymbol{S}(\boldsymbol{x}', \boldsymbol{a}), \quad \text{and} \quad \boldsymbol{x}' = \boldsymbol{S}^{-1}(\boldsymbol{x}, \boldsymbol{a}) \qquad (10.89)$$

With $\boldsymbol{a} = [a_1, \ldots, a_p]^T$ we denote the p-dimensional parameter vector of the transformation, which is assumed to be constant within the time

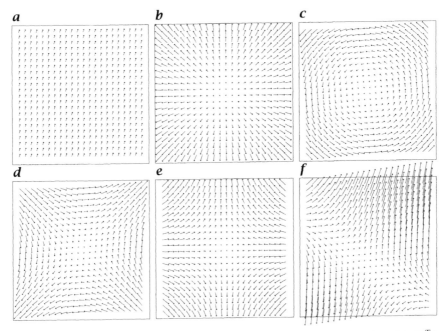

Figure 10.11: *Elementary affine flow fields:* **a** *pure translation (**t** = [1,2]^T);* **b** *pure divergence (div(**f**) = 1.0);* **c** *pure rotation (rot(**f**) = 1.0);* **d** *pure shear (sh(**f**) = 1.0);* **e** *pure stretching (str(**f**) = 1.0); and* **f** *example of a linear combination of all elementary transformations (**t** = [1,2]^T, div(**f**) = -1.0, rot(**f**) = 1.0, sh(**f**) = 0.3, str(**f**) = 0.8).*

interval δt. If S is chosen to form a *Lie group of transformations* it is infinitely differentiable in x and analytic in a. Applied to the image $g(x, t)$ at a certain time instant t, it gives a transformed image $g(x', t)$. Thus, successive application of the transformation $S(x, a(t))$ defines a trajectory through the sequence, along which the brightness of g remains constant (although being treated as constant within δt, we allow a to slowly vary over longer periods).

As S is analytic with respect to the parameters a_i, we can expand the coordinate transformation in a first-order Taylor series about $a = 0$, assuming the transformation to be infinitesimal within the time interval δt:

$$x = x' + \sum_{i=1}^{p} a_i \frac{\partial S(x', a)}{\partial a_i}, \quad \text{with} \quad x' = S(x', a = 0) \qquad (10.90)$$

where $a = 0$ is taken as the identity element of the transformation.

Using Eq. (10.90), we can determine how the spatiotemporal brightness distribution $g(x, t)$ depends on the individual parameters a_i by taking the partial derivative

$$\frac{\partial g(\boldsymbol{x},t)}{\partial a_i} = \frac{\partial g}{\partial x}\frac{\partial x}{\partial a_i} + \frac{\partial g}{\partial y}\frac{\partial y}{\partial a_i} = \frac{\partial g}{\partial x}\frac{\partial S_x}{\partial a_i} + \frac{\partial g}{\partial y}\frac{\partial S_y}{\partial a_i} \tag{10.91}$$

In operator notation, this expression can be reformulated for any $g(\boldsymbol{x},t)$ as

$$\frac{\partial g(\boldsymbol{x},t)}{\partial a_i} = \mathcal{L}_i g(\boldsymbol{x},t) \tag{10.92}$$

$$\text{with} \quad \mathcal{L}_i = \frac{\partial S_x}{\partial a_i}\frac{\partial}{\partial x} + \frac{\partial S_y}{\partial a_i}\frac{\partial}{\partial y} = \boldsymbol{\xi}_i^T \nabla, \quad \text{and} \quad \boldsymbol{\xi}_i = \left[\frac{\partial S_x}{\partial a_i}, \frac{\partial S_y}{\partial a_i}\right]^T \tag{10.93}$$

The operator $\mathcal{L}_i$, $i \in \{1,\dots,p\}$, is called an *infinitesimal generator* of the Lie group of transformations in a_i. As the explicit time dependency of g in Eq. (10.88) is formulated as 1-D "translation in time" with the fixed parameter $a_t = 1$, we can immediately infer the corresponding infinitesimal generator to be $\mathcal{L}_t = \partial/\partial t$.

An image sequence $g(\boldsymbol{x},t)$ is called an *invariant function* under the group of transformations in the parameter a_i, if and only if

$$\mathcal{L}_i g(\boldsymbol{x},t) = \frac{\partial g(\boldsymbol{x},t)}{\partial a_i} = 0 \tag{10.94}$$

Thus, an invariant function remains constant if it is subject to a transformation with respect to the parameter a_i. Examples of such patterns and the corresponding transformations are the translation of a pattern with linear symmetry parallel to lines of constant brightness, or a pattern containing concentric circles rotated about the center of circular symmetry. The set of parameters a_i, $i \in \{1,\dots,p\}$, can be regarded as *generalized coordinates* of the transformation, also referred to as *canonical coordinates*, spanning a p-dimensional space. Lie groups of transformations extend an arbitrary spatiotemporal transformation into a p-dimensional translation in the p canonical coordinates including the time t.

In a final step, we expand the spatiotemporal image at $g(\boldsymbol{x},t)$ with respect to the parameters a_i, that is, we compose the transformation by the set of infinitesimal transformations:

$$g(\boldsymbol{x},t) = g(\boldsymbol{x}',t-\delta t) + \sum_{i=1}^{p} a_i \frac{\partial g}{\partial a_i} = g(\boldsymbol{x}',t-\delta t) + \sum_{i=1}^{p} a_i \mathcal{L}_i g \tag{10.95}$$

With the initial assumption of brightness conservation (Eq. (10.88)), that is, $g(\boldsymbol{x},t) = g(\boldsymbol{x}',t-\delta t)$, we immediately get the relation between the infinitesimal transformations and g:

$$\sum_{i=1}^{p} a_i \mathcal{L}_i g = 0, \quad \forall \boldsymbol{x} \tag{10.96}$$

Equation (10.96) has to be solved for the parameter vector $\boldsymbol{a}$. In order to avoid the trivial solution $\boldsymbol{a} = 0$, we need to add the constraint $\boldsymbol{a}^T \boldsymbol{a} = 1$, which is possible, as a scaling of $\boldsymbol{a}$ does not change the group of transformations.

It is important to note that solution Equation (10.96) constitutes a *generalization* of the standard brightness change constraint Equation (10.2). Due to the presence of noise, Eq. (10.96) is usually not exactly satisfied. However, if we find an appropriate model for the optical flow field, which can be expressed by a Lie group of transformations, minimizing Eq. (10.96) with respect to the parameters $\boldsymbol{a}$ yields the underlying optical flow field. The minimization can be carried out by standard techniques of numerical linear algebra, such as LS and TLS estimation, as already pointed out earlier in this chapter.

An interesting relationship between Eq. (10.96) and previous approaches can be found, if we identify the sum in Eq. (10.96) by the scalar product

$$\boldsymbol{a}^T (\nabla_{\mathcal{L}} g), \quad \nabla_{\mathcal{L}} = [\mathcal{L}_1, \dots, \mathcal{L}_p]^T \tag{10.97}$$

where $\nabla_{\mathcal{L}}$ denotes the *generalized gradient*. This notation obviously constitutes a generalized extension of the spatiotemporal gradient constraint Equation (10.5), which has been directly used in the structure tensor technique (Eq. (10.38)) with $\boldsymbol{a} = \boldsymbol{r}$.

We will illustrate how the Lie group formalism translates into practical application with the help of two simple examples.

Example 10.1: Translation

A simple example of a flow field model is a constant translation within a neighborhood U. The corresponding coordinate transformation reads

$$S(\boldsymbol{x}, \boldsymbol{t}) = \boldsymbol{x} + \boldsymbol{t} \tag{10.98}$$

where $\boldsymbol{t} = [t_1, t_2]^T$ denotes the translation vector, which has to be estimated. Letting $\boldsymbol{a} = [\boldsymbol{t}, 1]^T$, the infinitesimal generators can be computed by Eq. (10.93) as

$$\mathcal{L}_1 = \mathcal{L}_x = \frac{\partial}{\partial x}, \quad \mathcal{L}_2 = \mathcal{L}_y = \frac{\partial}{\partial y}, \quad \text{and} \quad \mathcal{L}_3 = \mathcal{L}_t = \frac{\partial}{\partial t} \tag{10.99}$$

Thus, Eq. (10.96) yields nothing but the standard BCCE, Eq. (10.2):

$$t_1 \frac{\partial g}{\partial x} + t_2 \frac{\partial g}{\partial y} + \frac{\partial g}{\partial t} = 0 \tag{10.100}$$

Example 10.2: Affine flow

In this example we are going to revisit affine flow fields in the context of Lie group transformations. The affine coordinate transformation is given by Eq. (10.82)

$$S(x,a) = \begin{bmatrix} a_1 & a_2 \\ a_3 & a_4 \end{bmatrix} \begin{bmatrix} x \\ y \end{bmatrix} + \begin{bmatrix} a_5 \\ a_6 \end{bmatrix} = Ax + t \qquad (10.101)$$

With $a = [a_1, \ldots, a_6, 1]^T$, using Eq. (10.93), the infinitesimal generators can be derived as

$$\mathcal{L}_1 = x\frac{\partial}{\partial x}, \ \mathcal{L}_2 = y\frac{\partial}{\partial x}, \ \mathcal{L}_3 = x\frac{\partial}{\partial y}, \ \mathcal{L}_4 = y\frac{\partial}{\partial y}$$

$$\mathcal{L}_5 = \frac{\partial}{\partial x}, \ \mathcal{L}_6 = \frac{\partial}{\partial y}, \ \mathcal{L}_7 = \frac{\partial}{\partial t} \qquad (10.102)$$

The generators for the more intuitive transformations of divergence, rotation, shear, and stretching can be obtained as the following linear combinations of $\mathcal{L}_1, \ldots, \mathcal{L}_4$:

$$\mathcal{L}_d = \mathcal{L}_1 + \mathcal{L}_4 = x\frac{\partial}{\partial x} + y\frac{\partial}{\partial y}, \quad \mathcal{L}_r = \mathcal{L}_3 - \mathcal{L}_2 = x\frac{\partial}{\partial y} - y\frac{\partial}{\partial x}$$

$$\mathcal{L}_{st} = \mathcal{L}_1 - \mathcal{L}_4 = x\frac{\partial}{\partial x} - y\frac{\partial}{\partial y}, \quad \mathcal{L}_{sh} = \mathcal{L}_2 + \mathcal{L}_3 = y\frac{\partial}{\partial x} + x\frac{\partial}{\partial y}$$

$$(10.103)$$

where the indices d, r, sh, st denote the elementary transformations 'divergence', 'rotation', 'shear', and 'stretching', respectively. Thus, the Lie group formalism automatically decomposes the flow field into the elementary transformations, given the coordinate transformation Eq. (10.101).

The concept of Lie groups, outlined in this section, has been successfully used by Duc [56] for optical flow computation. Although more general than plain translation or affine flow, Lie groups of transformations do not account for brightness variations, as the image is only warped from the original image according to Eq. (10.88). They also do not model multiple motions and occlusions, a problem which can be addressed by using a robust estimation framework, which will be outlined in Section 10.6.2.

10.6.2 Robust techniques

Optical flow estimation is corrupted for all approaches pooling constraints over a finite-size spatial neighborhood in case it contains multiple motions, that is, at motion discontinuities and in the case of transparent motion overlay. Parameterized flow field models fail to handle these kinds of errors if they assume a smooth spatial transition of the optical flow field.

a   **b**

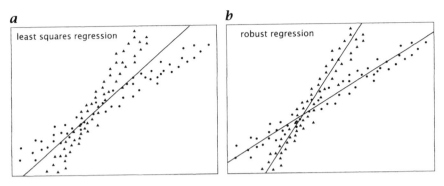

Figure 10.12: *Illustration of* **a** *least squares regression vs* **b** *robust regression of two independent data sets.*

The basic problem results from how the local constraints are combined. Least squares estimation tries to minimize the quadratic objective function

$$\|e\|_2^2 = \sum_{i=0}^{N-1} [e_i]^2 \tag{10.104}$$

where e_i denotes the residual error at point i. The summation is carried out over all N points within U. The influence of any residual error on the objective function can be computed as

$$\frac{\partial \|e\|_2^2}{\partial e_i} = 2e_i \tag{10.105}$$

which shows that the objective function $\|e\|_2^2$ depends linearly on the individual errors without bound. Hence, a single large error (outlier) is sufficient to corrupt the entire least squares solution.

In a statistical context, only a fraction of the pixels within U fits to the model assumptions, while another fraction can be viewed as *outliers*. Thus, we need to recover the model parameters that best fit the majority of data while outliers have to be detected and rejected. This is the main goal of *robust statistics* [58], which has been increasingly used for a variety of computer vision applications [59]. Figure 10.12 illustrates the difference between standard least squares (LS) and robust estimation for the example of linear regression. While LS regression fits a line to the entire cloud of data points, disregarding individual clusters, robust regression techniques separate the clusters. An excellent introduction into robust estimation that addresses its application to the problem of optical flow computation, is given by Black and Anandan [8]. They propose a unified framework to account for the different optical flow techniques outlined in this chapter.

The basic idea of *robust estimation* is to replace the quadratic weighting of the residuals by another analytical expression $\rho(e_i)$, which is referred to as an *M-estimator* in statistics. The ρ-function has to be designed to perform an unequal weighting depending on the magnitude of the residuals. Thus, we obtain the following minimization problem:

$$f = \arg\min \|e\|_\rho, \quad \|e\|_\rho = \sum_{i=0}^{N-1} \rho(e_i, \sigma_s) \qquad (10.106)$$

The optional scale parameter σ_s defines the range of residuals that are considered to belong to the set of 'inliers' (as opposed to 'outliers'). For a quadratic ρ, Eq. (10.106) corresponds to the standard least squares formulation.

In order to reduce the influence of outliers we search to minimize the influence of large residual errors on $\|e_\rho\|$. The influence of individual residuals is characterized by the *influence function* ψ, which is proportional to the derivative of the ρ-function [58]:

$$\psi(e_i, \sigma_s) = \frac{\partial \rho(e_i, \sigma_s)}{\partial e_i} \qquad (10.107)$$

corresponding to Eq. (10.105) for a quadratic function. In order to be robust against outliers, ψ needs to be *redescending*, that is, it has to approach zero for large residuals after an initial increase for small values. Thus, the corresponding ρ-functions show an asymptotic behavior. One of the most simple ρ-functions is a truncated quadratic (Fig. 10.13a). The corresponding influence function drops to zero beyond a certain threshold (Fig. 10.13b). The truncated quadratic has to be compared to the standard quadratic with an unbounded ψ-function (Fig. 10.13a and b). Another commonly used ρ-function, proposed by Geman and McClure [60], is given by (Fig. 10.13c and d)

$$\rho(e_i, \sigma) = \frac{e_i^2}{\sigma + e_i^2}, \quad \psi(e_i, \sigma) = \frac{2\sigma e_i}{(\sigma + e_i^2)^2} \qquad (10.108)$$

For practical application of the robust estimation framework to optical flow computation we simply need to replace the quadratic norm of the objective functions by a robust error norm ρ. As one example, the local least squares technique Eq. (10.13) can be reformulated as

$$f = \arg\min \|e\|_\rho, \quad \|e\|_\rho = \int_{-\infty}^{\infty} w(\boldsymbol{x} - \boldsymbol{x}') \rho \left((\nabla g)^T \boldsymbol{f} + g_t \right) d\boldsymbol{x}'$$

$$(10.109)$$

where ρ is a robust ρ-function. The discrete summation in Eq. (10.106) has been replaced by a weighted integration. Likewise, all other objective functions introduced in this chapter can be transformed into robust functions. Further details can be found in [8].

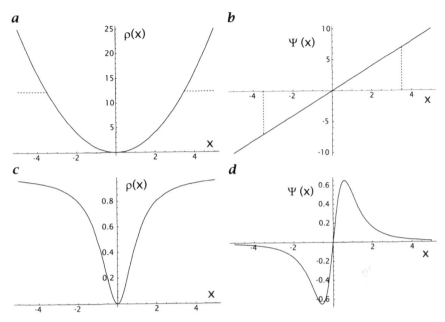

Figure 10.13: *Two examples of ρ and ψ functions:* **a** *quadratic (l₂ norm) and truncated quadratic (dashed);* **b** *derivative of the quadratic and truncated quadratic function;* **c** *Geman and McClure norm; and* **d** *derivative of the Geman and McClure norm [60].*

In general, robust formulations do not admit closed solutions and have to be solved iteratively. Black and Anandan [8] use over-relaxation techniques, such as the *Gauss-Seidel method*. This may be regarded as a disadvantage of robust estimation compared to LS estimation. It also has to be pointed out that robust techniques usually search for a dominant motion within U and attach a region of support to each motion. Although multiple motions can be iteratively found, the corresponding regions are disjoint. Thus, the image area is segmented into the individual motions, even in the case of transparency.

10.6.3 Summary

This chapter provided the general principles of motion estimation from image sequences and gave a concise overview of different approaches to optical flow computation. Due to space limitations we were not able to give a detailed discussion of results from the various techniques. A comprehensive overview of numerical results of selected optical flow techniques can be found in Barron et al. [13] and CVA2 [Chapter 13]. Without going into detail we will end this chapter with a brief summary of the performance of the most important techniques.

In summary we found that differential techniques give the best over-all performance with respect to both accuracy and density. If a distinction between normal and 2-D flow has to be made, the local and total least squares approaches [14, 41] are clearly favored. It seems that the theoretical advantages of the total vs local least squares algorithm only become apparent for low signal-to-noise ratios and small displacements.

The second-order differential method by Uras et al. [28] performs very well for pure translational motion over all velocities up to the temporal sampling limit and regardless of the movement direction. However, for other types of motion, such as divergence or rotation, this method should not be used.

The phase-based method by Fleet and Jepson [15] provides accurate but rather sparse velocity fields and the computational load for this method is far higher than for the other compared techniques.

Matching techniques are only useful for larger displacements, in particular for integer pixel displacements. However, in this case a differential multiscale approach as described by CVA2 [Chapter 14] might still be the better choice. Between the two compared matching techniques the method by Singh [53] was found to give more reliable results.

In general, good results on realistic data are not to be expected without a means to remove unreliable estimates. Depending on the image content, some way to distinguish normal from 2-D flow is essential for accurate motion estimation. Obviously, in cases without an aperture problem such a distinction is unnecessary. For software demonstrations see `lucas.ws`, `horn.ws`, and `tensor.ws` in /software/10.

10.7 References

[1] Gibson, J. J., (1950). *The Perception of the Visual World.* New York: Houghton Mifflin.

[2] Horn, B. K. P., (1987). Motion fields are hardly ever ambiguous. *Int. J. of Computer Vision*, 1:259-274.

[3] Horn, B. K., (1986). *Robot vision.* Cambridge, MA: MIT Press.

[4] Verri, A. and Poggio, T., (1987). Against quantitative optical flow. In *Proceedings ICCV'87, London*, pp. 171-180, IEEE. Washington, DC: Los Alamitos, CA: IEEE Computer Society Press.

[5] Verri, A. and Poggio, T., (1989). Motion field and optical flow: qualitative properties. *IEEE Trans. PAMI*, **11(5)**:490-498.

[6] Horn, B. K. P. and Schunk, B. G., (1981). Determining optical flow. *Artificial Intelligence*, 17:185-204.

[7] Jepson, A. and Black, M. J., (1993). Mixture models for optical flow computation. In *Proc. Computer Vision and Pattern Recognition, CVPR '93*, pp. 760-761. New York.

[8] Black, M. J. and Anandan, P., (1996). The robust estimation of multiple motions: parametric and piecewise-smooth flow fields. *Computer Vision and Image Understanding*, **63(1)**:75–104.

[9] Jähne, B., (1997). *Digital Image Processing-Concepts, Algorithms, and Scientific Applications, 4th edition*. New York: Springer.

[10] Bracewell, R., (1986). *The Fourier Transform and its Applications*, 2nd revised edition. New York: McGraw-Hill.

[11] Murray, B. F., D. W. Buxton, (1990). *Experiments in the Machine Interpretation of Visual Motion*. Cambridge, MA: MIT Press.

[12] Shi, J. and Tomasi, C., (1994). Good features to track. In *Proc. Conf. Comput. Vis. Patt. Recog.*, pp. 593–600. Seattle, Washington: IEEE Computer Society Press.

[13] Barron, J. L., Fleet, D. J., and Beauchemin, S. S., (1994). Performance of optical flow techniques. *Intern. J. Comput. Vis.*, **12(1)**:43–77.

[14] Lucas, B. and Kanade, T., (1981). An iterative image registration technique with an application to stereo vision. In *DARPA Image Understanding Workshop*, pp. 121–130.

[15] Fleet, D. J. and Jepson, A. D., (1990). Computation of component image velocity from local phase information. *Intern. J. Comput. Vis.*, 5:77–104.

[16] Bainbridge-Smith, A. and Lane, R. G., (1997). Determining optical flow using a differential method. *Image and Vision Computing*, 15:11–22.

[17] Jähne, B., (1993). *Spatio-temporal image processing*. Berlin: Springer.

[18] Jähne, B., Haussecker, H., Spies, H., Schmundt, D., and Schurr, U., (1998). Study of dynamical processes with tensor-based spatiotemporal image processing techniques. In *Computer Vision - ECCV '98*. Springer-Verlag, in press.

[19] Otte, M. and Nagel, H.-H., (1994). Optical flow estimation: advances and comparisons. In *Computer Vision—ECCV '94*, J.-O. Eklundh, ed., pp. 51–60. Springer.

[20] Hering, F., Haussecker, H., Dieter, J., Netzsch, T., and Jähne, B., (1997). A comprehensive study of algorithms for multi-dimensional flow field diagnostics. In *Proc. ISPRS Intercommision V/III Symposium*. Zurich, Switzerland.

[21] Adelson, E. H. and Bergen, J. R., (1986). The extraction of spatiotemporal energy in human and machine vision. In *Proc. IEEE Workshop on Visual Motion*, pp. 151–156. Charleston.

[22] Kearney, J. K., Thompson, W. B., and Boley, D. L., (1987). Optical flow estimation: an error analysis of gradient-based methods with local optimization. *IEEE Trans. PAMI*, **9(2)**:229–244.

[23] Simoncelli, E. P., Adelson, E. H., and Heeger, D. J., (1991). Probability distributions of optical flow. In *Proc. Conf. Comput. Vis. Patt. Recog.*, pp. 310–315. Maui.

[24] Simoncelli, E. P., (1993). *Distributed Representation and Analysis of Visual Motion*. Dissertation, MIT.

[25] Press, W. H., Teukolsky, S. A., Vetterling, W., and Flannery, B., (1992). *Numerical Recipes in C: The Art of Scientific Computing*. New York: Cam-

bridge University Press.

[26] Nagel, H., (1983). Displacement vectors derived from second-order intensity variations in image sequences. *Computer Vision, Graphics, and Image Processing (GVGIP)*, **21**:85–117.

[27] Tretiak, O. and Pastor, L., (1984). Velocity estimation from image sequences with second order differential operators. In *Proc. 7th Intern. Conf. Patt. Recogn., Montreal*, pp. 20–22.

[28] Uras, S., Girosi, F., Verri, A., and Torre, V., (1988). A computational approach to motion perception. *Biol. Cybern.*, **60**:79–97.

[29] Press, W. H., Vetterling, W. T., Teukolsky, S. A., and Flannery, B. P., (1994). *Numerical Recipes in C - The Art of Scientific Computing*, Second edition. Cambridge University Press.

[30] Nagel, H., (1986). Image sequences – ten (octal) years – from phenomenology towards a theoretical foundation. In *Proc. Int. Conf. Patt. Recogn., Paris 1986*, pp. 1174–1185. Washington: IEEE Computer Society Press.

[31] Nagel, H.-H., (1987). On the estimation of optical flow: relations between different approaches and some new results. *Artificial Intelligence*, **33**: 299–324.

[32] Hildreth, E. C., (1984). Computations underlying the measurement of visual motion. *Artificial Intelligence*, **23**:309–354.

[33] Hildreth, E. C., (1984). The computation of the velocity field. *Proc. Royal Soc. Lond.*, **B 221**:189–220.

[34] Golub, G. H. and Van Loan, C. F., (1989). *Matrix Computations*, second edition edition. Baltimore and London: The Johns Hopkins University Press.

[35] Bigün, J. and Granlund, G. H., (1987). Optimal orientation detection of linear symmetry. In *Proceedings ICCV'87, London 1987*, pp. 433–438, IEEE. Washington, DC: IEEE Computer Society Press.

[36] Kass, M. and Witkin, A., (1987). Analyzing oriented patterns. *Comp. Vision Graphics and Image Proc.*, **37**:362–385.

[37] Knutsson, H., (1982). *Filtering and Reconstruction in Image Processing*. Diss., Linköping Univ.

[38] Knutsson, H., (1998). Representing local structure using tensors. In *Proc. 6th Scandinavian Conf. on Image Analysis, Oulu, Finland*, pp. 244–251. Springer-Verlag.

[39] Granlund, G. H. and Knutsson, H., (1995). *Signal Processing for Computer Vision*. Kluwer.

[40] Bigün, J., Granlund, G. H., and Wiklund, J., (1991). Multidimensional orientation estimation with application to texture analysis and optical flow. *IEEE Trans. PAMI*, **13(8)**:775–790.

[41] Haussecker, H. and Jähne, B., (1997). A Tensor approach for precise computation of dense displacement vector fields. In *Mustererkennung 1997*, F. Wahl and E. Paulus, eds., pp. 199–208. Springer-Verlag.

[42] Haussecker, H., Spies, H., and Jähne, B., (1998). Tensor-based image sequence processing techniques for the study of dynamical processes. In *Proc. Intern. Symp. On Real-time Imaging and Dynamic Analysis*, Vol.

32(5), pp. 704–711. Hakodate, Japan: International Society of Photogrammetry and Remote Sensing, ISPRS, Commision V.

[43] Nagel, H.-H. and Gehrke, A., (1998). Spatiotemporal adaptive estimation and segmentation of OF-fields. In *Proc. Computer Vision - ECCV '98*, pp. 87–102. Lecture Notes in Computer Science, Springer-Verlag.

[44] Heeger, D. J., (1987). Model for the extraction of image flow. *J. Opt. Soc. Am. A*, 4:1455–1471.

[45] Heeger, D. J., (1988). Optical flow from spatiotemporal filters. *Int. J. Comp. Vis.*, 1:279–302.

[46] Gabor, D., (1941). Theory of communication. *J. IEE*, **93**:492–457.

[47] Daugman, J. G., (1985). Uncertainty relation for resolution in space, spatial frequency, and orientation optimized by two-dimensional visual cortex filters. *J. Opt. Soc. Am. A*, **2(7)**:1160–1169.

[48] Knutsson, H., von Post, B., and Granlund, G. H., (1980). Optimization of arithmetic neighborhood operations for image processing. In *Proc. First Scandinavian Conference on Image Analysis*. Linköping, Sweden.

[49] Fleet, D. J. and Jepson, A. D., (1993). Stability of phase information. *IEEE Trans. PAMI*, **15(12)**:1253–1268.

[50] Lim, J. S., (1990). *Two-Dimensional Signal and Image Processing*. Englewood Cliffs, NJ: Prentice-Hall.

[51] Faugeras, O., (1993). *Three-Dimensional Computer Vision: A Geometric Viewpoint*. Cambridge, MA: MIT Press.

[52] Anandan, P., (1989). A computational framework and an algorithm for the measurement of visual motion. *Int. J. Comp. Vis.*, 2:283–310.

[53] Singh, A., (1990). An estimation-theoretic framework for image-flow computation. In *Proceedings ICCV'90, Osaka, Japan*, pp. 168–177, IEEE. Washington, DC: IEEE Computer Society Press.

[54] Singh, A., (1992). *Optic Flow Computation: A Unified Perspective*. IEEE Computer Society Press.

[55] Black, M. J. and Anandan, P., (1993). A framework for the robust estimation of optical flow. In *Proceedings ICCV'93, Berlin*, pp. 231–236, IEEE. Washington, DC: IEEE Computer Society Press.

[56] Duc, B., (1997). *Feature Design: Applications to Motion Analysis and Identity Verification*. Dissertation, École Polytechnique Fédérale de Lausanne.

[57] Bluman, G. W. and Kumei, S., (1989). Symmetries and differential equations. *Applied Mathematical Sciences*, **81**.

[58] Hampel, F. R., Ronchetti, E. M., Rousseeuw, P. J., and Stahel, W. A., (1986). *Robust Statistics: The Approach Based on Influence Functions*. Wiley, New York.

[59] Meer, P., Mintz, D., and Rosenfeld, A., (1991). Robust regression methods for computer vision. *Int. J. Comp. Vision*, **6(1)**:59–70.

[60] Geman, S. and McClure, D. E., (1987). Statistical methods for tomographic image reconstruction. *Bull. Int. Statist. Inst.*, **LII-4**:721–741.

11 Three-Dimensional Imaging Algorithms

Peter Geißler[1,2], Tobias Dierig[1] and Hanspeter A. Mallot[3]

[1] Interdisziplinäres Zentrum für Wissenschaftliches Rechnen (IWR)
Universität Heidelberg, Germany
[2] Now with ARRI, München, Germany
[3] Max-Planck-Institut für biologische Kybernetik, Tübingen, Germany

11.1 Introduction

Image acquisition always contracts the 3-D information of the scene to 2-D information of the image due to the projection on the 2-D image plane. Therefore the reconstruction of the depth information from 2-D images is a fundamental problem in computer vision applications.

Many different approaches to the problem are known, including *stereo* (Dhond and Aggarwal [1], [CVA2, Chapter 17], [CVA2, Chapter 18]) or its generalization to multiview imaging, *shape-from-shading* and *photogrammetric stereo* [CVA2, Chapter 19], shape from motion, texture analysis and depth from focus.

Herein, we focus on two important approaches for the recovery of depth information: stereo reconstruction and depth-from-focus. Although not immediately apparent, these two methods are based on the same principle. Stereo uses the difference between images taken from

Computer Vision and Applications

different viewpoints, the so-called parallactic difference. The lateral shift of image points between the two images is directly correlated to the distance of the object point. Depth-from-focus uses the inherent blur in the images to correlate it with depth. Because blur cannot be directly separated from the image, further images that differ only in the grade of optical blur are required. So both methods gain the 3-D information from the difference of images taken from the same scene, but with different camera parameters in a general sense. In this sense both techniques have to be classified as a *triangulation* technique (Section 7.3). An overview of other triangulation methods is given in Fig. 7.3.

Concerning depth-from-focus, algorithms that need only a single image are possible, provided that additional information about the observed scene is present. These methods will be discussed at the end of this chapter. Whereas it focuses on 3D reconstruction from an algorithmic point of view, Chapter 7 gives an overview of methods suitable for 3-D image acquisition.

11.2 Stereopsis

Stereopsis is the perception of depth from the parallactic differences between the images seen by the left and the right eye. Wheatstone [2], using his mirror-stereoscope, was the first to demonstrate that image difference, or *disparity*, is indeed the crucial carrier of information.

Much work in stereovision has been devoted to one particular type of image differences, namely, the position differences of the images of individual points in the two cameras or eyes. In order to measure these point disparities, an image-matching procedure is required as reviewed, for example, by Dhond and Aggarwal [3], Jenkin et al. [4], Förstner [5]. Image matching and the associated correspondence problem [6, 7] will not be dealt with in this chapter. The traditional view that correspondence is the central problem in stereopsis has been challenged by recent psychophysical findings indicating that other types of disparity as well as global image comparisons play an important part at least in human vision [8, 9].

The different viewpoints used for recording the two half-images of a stereogram result in a number of different types of image differences, some of which are illustrated in Fig. 11.1. A comprehensive discussion is given in Arndt et al. [10] and Howard and Rogers [11].

1. *Horizontal disparity* is the horizontal offset of the images of an individual point projected into the two cameras. It can be measured as an angle or as a distance on the camera target (Fig. 11.1a).

2. *Vertical disparity* is the analogous offset in the vertical image direction. Because the stereo baseline between the two cameras is usually

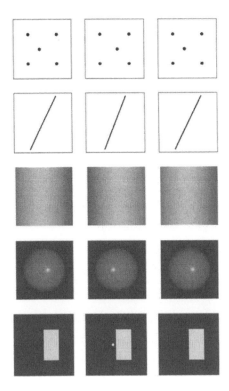

Figure 11.1: *Types of image differences or disparities:* **a** *point disparities;* **b** *orientation disparities;* **c** *intensity disparities;* **d** *disparate highlights (photometric disparities);* **e** *monocular occlusion ("amodal stereopsis"). For crossed fusion, use the left two columns, for uncrossed fusion the right ones. Readers not used to free stereoscopic fusion should cover up the left column and place a piece of cardboard vertically between the right two columns. By placing the head symmetrically over the cardboard, each eye is allowed to view one column only. In this situation, fusion is easily obtained.*

horizontal, vertical disparities are usually rather small. They vanish in nonverging camera systems, that is, systems with parallel view axes.

3. *Orientation disparities* occur if oblique lines are imaged. Generally, the resulting lines in the two images will have different slope (Fig. 11.1b). Related higher-order disparities include the projected movement of a point moving in space or the deformation (size, shear, rotation) of a planar figure.

4. *Disparate shading* as shown in Fig. 11.1c,d may result for purely geometrical reasons. Figure 11.1c shows a Lambertian shaded cylinder with horizontal disparities that cannot be pinpointed to feature points in the image. Still, depth perception is obtained. Figure 11.1d

shows a more complicated case where disparities are due to specular reflection, that is, to the fact that the same surface point looks different when observed from different directions. It is interesting to note that even though the highlight is the virtual image of the light source and its disparity therefore corresponds to a point behind the spherical surface, human observers are able to make correct use of disparate highlights. That is to say, they perceive a protruding surface when the highlight's disparity is uncrossed [12].

5. *Monocular occlusion*, also called amodal or *DaVinci stereopsis*, is another example of stereopsis without feature correspondence. In the case shown in Fig. 11.1e, the dot seems to float behind the rectangle as if it was occluded in the right image. When exchanging the two half-images, perceived depth is not inverted.

The image differences illustrated in Fig. 11.1a-c can be formalized by a so-called *disparity map*, that is, a continuous, one-to-one function $\delta(x', y')$ such that

$$I_r(x', y') = I_l(x' - \delta_1(x', y'), y' - \delta_2(x', y')) \tag{11.1}$$

where the components of δ are the horizontal and vertical disparities. Using first-order derivatives of δ leads to the orientation and deformation disparities. The global disparity map exists only if the imaged surface is completely visible from both eyes (no monocular occlusion) and if shading is Lambertian. It does not in general exist at the most interesting image regions, that is, at depth discontinuities.

11.2.1 Stereo geometry

In this section, we review the *geometry of binocular space*, as it has been developed in psychophysics and optometry [13]. We will argue that the formulation presented here is also advantageous for technical stereoheads. We will assume throughout this chapter that the view axes of the two cameras meet at some point in space, called the fixation point. The case of parallel camera axes is contained as a limiting case.

World coordinates will be given in a Cartesian system (x, y, z) whose origin is the midpoint of the camera nodal points. The horizontal x axis points to the right, the vertical y axis points upward, and the horizontal z axis marks the depth direction away from the observer. This coordinate system is not the head coordinate system in that it does not rotate with the head; it is, however, centered at the head. Image coordinates are denoted by (x'_l, y'_l) for the left and (x'_r, y'_r) for the right camera.

Hering coordinates. The basic variables describing a binocular head are illustrated in Fig. 11.2a. The heading direction is normal to the baseline connecting the camera nodal points and the pan-axis of the head.

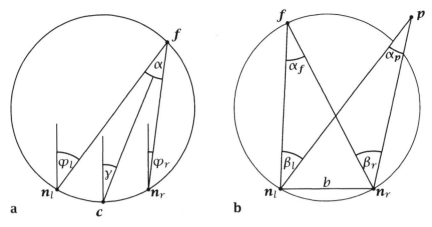

Figure 11.2: *Naming conventions for binocular geometry:* ***a*** *view axes and fixation;* ***b*** *image position of peripheral points.* ***f***: *Fixation point.* $\boldsymbol{n}_l, \boldsymbol{n}_r$: *nodal points;* ***c***: *"Cyclopean point" half-way between the nodal points;* ***b***: *baseline distance;* φ_r, φ_l: *azimuth angles of the cameras (viewing directions) in a head-centered system;* $\alpha = \alpha_f$: *Vergence;* y: *Version;* ***p***: *arbitrary point viewed while fixating at* ***f***; α_p: *target vergence of* ***p***; β_l, β_r: *azimuth angles of point* ***p*** *in camera-centered coordinate system.*

We assume for now that the nodal points are located at $\boldsymbol{n}_l = (-b/2, 0, 0)$ and $\boldsymbol{n}_r = (+b/2, 0, 0)$, respectively; the length of the baseline therefore is b. We consider first the geometry of the horizontal (epipolar, (x, z)) plane; for a more complete discussion, see Howard and Rogers [11]. The viewing directions of the camera φ_l and φ_r are defined with respect to the heading direction and positive turns are to the right. Rather than using these viewing directions themselves, we introduce the quantities

$$\alpha = \varphi_l - \varphi_r \tag{11.2}$$

$$y = \frac{1}{2}(\varphi_l + \varphi_r) \tag{11.3}$$

These quantities are known as the (Hering)-*vergence* (α) and (Hering)-*version* (y), respectively.

Vergence takes the value 0 if the camera axes are parallel. Negative values do not occur as long as the axes converge, that is, as long as there is an intersection point of the viewing axes. For each vergence $\alpha > 0$, a circle can be drawn through the nodal points and the intersection point of the two camera axes. This circle has the radius

$$R = \frac{b}{2 \sin \alpha} \tag{11.4}$$

and the center

$$\boldsymbol{v} = \left[0, 0, \frac{b}{2} \cot \alpha\right]^T \tag{11.5}$$

It is called the *Vieth-Müller circle* (VMC) of vergence α. As an application of the theorem of Thales, it is easy to show that whenever fixating a point on a fixed VMC, the same vergence angle α will result, that is, the VMCs are the iso-vergence lines.

Version as defined in Eq. (11.4) is the average, or "cyclopean," viewing direction of the two cameras. More formally, when fixating a point f with some vergence α, consider the corresponding Vieth-Müller-circle. The point on the circle half-way between the two nodal points may be called the "cyclopean point" c; the visual direction from this point to the fixation point is Hering's version y (see Fig. 11.2). To see this, consider the three triangles $\Delta n_l f n_r$ (apical angle α), $\Delta n_l f c$ (apical angle α_l), $\Delta c f n_r$ (apical angle α_r), all of which are inscribed into the same VMC. Therefore, from Eq. (11.4)

$$\frac{b}{2 \sin \alpha} = \frac{b_l}{2 \sin \alpha_l} = \frac{b_r}{2 \sin \alpha_r}$$

where b_l and b_r denote the length of the chords $\overline{n_l, c}$ and $\overline{c, n_r}$, respectively. If $b_l = b_r$, that is, if c is centered between n_l and n_r, it follows that $\alpha_l = \alpha_r$. Because, from simple trigonometry, $\alpha_l = \varphi_l - y$ and $\alpha_r = y - \varphi_r$, this implies $y = \frac{1}{2}(\varphi_l + \varphi_r)$.

Note that c depends on the current vergence angle. The lines of constant version are the so-called *hyperbolas of Hillebrand*. Simple trigonometric considerations yield the transformation rule from Hering vergence and version to Cartesian x, y, z coordinates:

$$H(\alpha, y) = \begin{bmatrix} x \\ y \\ z \end{bmatrix} = \frac{b}{2 \sin \alpha} \begin{bmatrix} \sin 2y \\ 0 \\ \cos \alpha + \cos 2y \end{bmatrix}$$

$$= R \begin{bmatrix} \cos \varphi_r \sin \varphi_l - \cos \varphi_l \sin \varphi_r \\ 0 \\ 2 \cos \varphi_r \cos \varphi_l \end{bmatrix} \quad (11.6)$$

The iso-curves of this transformation for constant vergence (circles) and constant version (hyperbolas) are plotted in Fig. 11.3a.

Horizontal disparity.   So far, we have considered only the camera axes and their intersection points. As camera movements are mostly rotations, the angular description seems rather natural. We now turn to points that are not currently fixated and to their images in the two cameras, and will show that the angular formulation applies here as well. Let the system fixate a point f and consider a second point p. The angles between the optical axis of each camera and the ray through point p will be called β_l and β_r, respectively (see Fig. 11.2b). They correspond to the image coordinates of the projection of p, which is

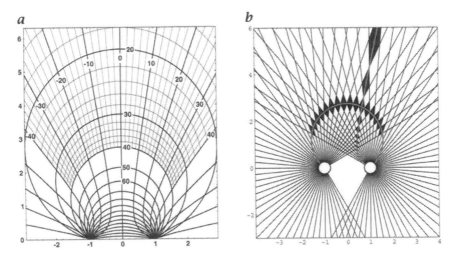

Figure 11.3: *a Curves of iso-vergence (Vieth-Müller circles) and iso-version (hyperbolas of Hillebrand). The nodal points are located at n = (±1,0). The bold lines are spaced at 10° both for version and vergence. The light line spacing is 2°. b Stereo geometry for collimated imaging devices (complex eyes). Each quadrangle corresponds to one pair of image points. Points in 3-D space can be distinguished if they fall into different quadrangles. A Vieth-Müller circle and an iso-version hyperbola are marked for comparison with Fig. 11.3a. (Redrawn based on figures from Burkhardt et al. [14])*

given by $x'_{l,r} = f \tan \beta_{l,r}$ where f is the focal length of the camera. The *disparity* of the point p is defined by angular difference:

$$\delta = \beta_l - \beta_r \tag{11.7}$$

Likewise, we define the average eccentricity

$$\eta = \frac{1}{2}(\beta_l + \beta_r) \tag{11.8}$$

It is quite clear that disparity δ depends on the current vergence angle of the system. If this is changed such as to fixate p, δ is obviously reduced to zero. To stress this dependence of disparity on vergence, δ is sometimes called *relative* disparity. Let us now denote by α_p the vergence angle obtained when fixating p, sometimes also called the *target vergence* of p. Let us further denote by $\delta_f(p)$ the disparity of point p when fixating f. It is then easy to show that

$$\delta_f(p) = \alpha_f - \alpha_p \tag{11.9}$$

Analogously, we have:

$$\eta_f(p) = \gamma_f - \gamma_p \tag{11.10}$$

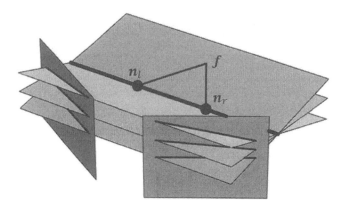

Figure 11.4: *Epipolar lines and vertical disparities in a verging stereo system.* n_l, n_r: *left and right nodal points;* f *fixation. The image planes are orthogonal to the "optical axes"* $\overline{n_l f}$ *and* $\overline{n_r f}$, *respectively. The epipolar lines diverge towards the midline of the system.*

With these relations, we can also use the coordinate system derived for eye movements for disparities. For example, when fixating a point with Hering coordinates (α_f, γ_f), the Cartesian coordinates of a point with disparity $\delta_f(\boldsymbol{p})$ and eccentricity $\eta_f(\boldsymbol{p})$ are $H(\alpha_f + \delta_f(\boldsymbol{p}), \gamma_f + \eta_f(\boldsymbol{p}))$, where H is the transformation defined in Eq. 11.6. In Fig. 11.3a disparities with respect to an arbitrary fixation point are immediately given by the distance from the fixation point in vergence direction. Hering coordinates thus provide a means for a unified evaluation of disparities at changing vergence conditions. As a consequence, we have shown that for each vergence state of the system, the corresponding VMC is the (theoretical) *horopter*, that is, the geometrical locus of all points having disparity zero with respect to the fixation point.

Figure 11.3b shows an alternative account of binocular geometry in the plane. While this approach applies most clearly to collimated imaging systems such as the complex eyes of insects [14], it is also useful for discussions of stereo resolution [15]. Resolution is inversely proportional to the size of the quadrilaterals in Fig. 11.3b.

Vertical disparity and epipolar lines. So far, we have considered only the horizontal plane together with camera movements about axes orthogonal to this plane. In this case, disparities are completely described by Eqs. (11.7) to (11.9). Points outside this plane are imaged to positions that may differ both in their horizontal and vertical coordinates. As an example, consider a point at height h above the horizontal plane. Its vertical coordinate in the two image planes will depend on the distance of the point from the camera nodal points. Therefore, disparity will have a vertical component.

Vertical disparities are closely related to the notion of epipolar lines (see Fig. 11.4). Consider a point p_l in the left image plane. The geometrical locus of all points p in 3-D space generating an image at point p_l is a ray from the left nodal point containing $\mathbf{p}_l$. When observed from the right camera, this ray is imaged at a certain line in the image. The plane spanned by all rays from the right nodal point to the ray of possible positions of p is identical to the plane passing through the two nodal points and p_l or any one of its generators p; it is called the epipolar plane of p. The intersections of the epipolar plane with the image planes form a pair of epipolar lines. Any point imaged on some epipolar line in one image must be imaged on the corresponding epipolar line in the other image. That is to say, horizontal and vertical disparity have a constant ratio, which corresponds to the slope of the epipolar lines. All epipolar lines of one image meet at a common intersection point, which is also the intersection of the image plane with the baseline connecting the two nodal points of the camera system. If the vergence angle is zero, that is, if the camera axes are parallel to each other and orthogonal to the baseline, the epipolar lines become parallel and horizontal and all vertical disparities vanish.

Epipolar lines are important in two respects. First, if the coordinates of the fixation point are known, epipolar lines can be predicted from camera geometry. In the stereo-matching process, this information can be used to simplify the matching process because corresponding image points must be localized along the respective epipolar lines. One way to do this is by means of the so-called *epipolar transformation* [16], a collineation applied to the images to make epipolar lines horizontal.

A second application of epipolar lines is the calibration of stereo camera systems. If vergence is symmetric, the vergence angle can be inferred from a single known stereo correspondence with nonzero vertical disparity. In symmetric vergence, the epipolar lines of the two half-images are mirror-symmetric with respect to the vertical midline of the images. The intersection points of all epipolar lines are located on the x' axis of the image coordinate system at $y'_{r,l} = \pm f \cot \alpha/2$ for the left and right image, respectively (see Fig. 11.5). As before, α denotes vergence and f is the focal length of the camera. If a pair of corresponding points is given by (x'_r, y'_r) in the right image and (x'_l, y'_l) in the left image, the slope of the epipolar line in the right image is

$$s_r = \frac{y'_r - y'_l}{x'_r + x'_l} \tag{11.11}$$

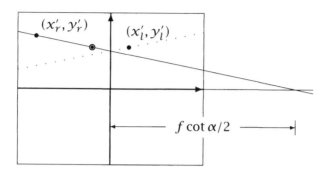

Figure 11.5: *Slope of an epipolar line in symmetrical vergence. The figure shows the two image planes superimposed. If a pair of corresponding points $((x'_l, y'_l), (x'_r, y'_r))$ is known, the slope of the right epipolar line can be determined by mirroring the point from the left image at the vertical image midline (y' axis), which results in a point $(-x'_l, y'_l)$, shown by an open dot. The line through (x'_r, y'_r) and $(-x'_l, y'_l)$ is the epipolar line. From its intersection with the horizontal axis, the vergence angle α (Eq. (11.2)) can be inferred.*

The epipolar line crosses the horizontal image axis at $x_r - y_r / s_r$. From this, we obtain:

$$\alpha = 2 \arctan \frac{y'_r - y'_l}{x'_l y'_r + x'_r y'_l} \tag{11.12}$$

Note that the numerator of the fraction in this equation is the vertical disparity in Cartesian coordinates. Equation (11.12) is undefined for points on the horizontal or vertical image axes. In conclusion, in symmetrically verging systems, one pair of corresponding image points suffices to determine the absolute position of the point in space, even if the vergence of the camera system is allowed to change.

Binocular camera movements. So far, we have considered cases where the camera rotation was confined to a pair of axes orthogonal to the horizontal plane. If we now turn to general fixation points, we first have to discuss the degrees of freedom of the required turns. The possible arrangements and naming conventions are summarized in Fig. 11.6. The human eye moves according to the Listing system shown in Fig. 11.6c.

We give rotation matrices for the three systems that rotate a space direction $[a, b, c]^T$ with $a^2 + b^2 + c^2 = 1$ and $c \neq 1$ into the straight-on direction of the camera, $[0, 0, 1]^T$. Additional roll movement about that axis of gaze is not included in these matrices.

In the *Fick system* (Fig. 11.6a), the first rotation is around a vertical axis, while the second uses a horizontal one. Technically, this is real-

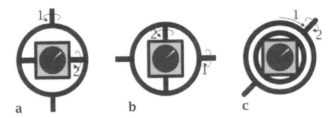

Figure 11.6: *Degrees of freedom of rotation for technical and biological camera systems. The central square with the pupil marks the camera: **a** Fick system. The first turn is about the vertical axis, the second about a horizontal one; **b** Helmholtz system. The first turn is about a vertical axis, the second turn about an axis orthogonal moving axis; **c** Listing system. The camera is placed in a bearing. In the first rotation the outside ring is moved, thereby selecting an axis for the second turn. All systems include a roll movement about the view axis as a third step. It is not shown here.*

ized by two independent pan-tilt camera systems. The equation reads:

$$F_{(a,b,c)} = \begin{bmatrix} c/\sqrt{a^2+c^2} & 0 & -a/\sqrt{a^2+c^2} \\ -ab/\sqrt{a^2+c^2} & \sqrt{a^2+c^2} & -bc/\sqrt{a^2+c^2} \\ a & b & c \end{bmatrix} \qquad (11.13)$$

The *Helmholtz system* starts with a turn about a fixed horizontal axis (Fig. 11.6b). *Stereo heads* using the Helmholtz geometry can thus be built with a common tilt axis. Additional turns are about an axis orthogonal to this tilt axis. The matrix is:

$$H_{(a,b,c)} = \begin{bmatrix} \sqrt{b^2+c^2} & -ab/\sqrt{b^2+c^2} & -ac/\sqrt{b^2+c^2} \\ 0 & c/\sqrt{b^2+c^2} & -b/\sqrt{b^2+c^2} \\ a & b & c \end{bmatrix} \qquad (11.14)$$

Finally, in the *Listing system*, movement starts by choosing an axis of rotation. The second step is a turn about that axis moving the gaze direction from the start to the goal position on a great circle. All possible axes lie in what is called Listing's plane, a plane orthogonal to the principal (straight-on) direction passing through the center of the eye:

$$L_{(a,b,c)} = \begin{bmatrix} (a^2c+b^2)/(1-c^2) & -ab/(1+c) & -a \\ -ab/(1+c) & (a^2+b^2c)/(1-c^2) & -b \\ a & b & c \end{bmatrix} \qquad (11.15)$$

In human vision, Listing's law states that the roll position at any one viewing direction is as if the eye had moved to this direction along a great circle from the straight-on position. Roll is independent of the actual way by which the current position is reached.

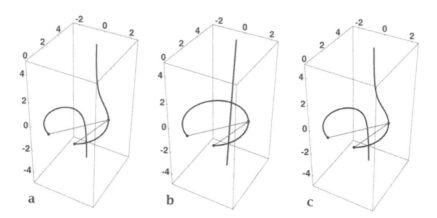

Figure 11.7: *Space horopter for a stereo camera system with nodal points* $(\pm 1, 0, 0)^{\top}$ *fixating at* $(2.0, 0.3, 3.0)^{\top}$*:* ***a*** *Fick system;* ***b*** *Helmholtz system;* ***c*** *Listing system.*

The space horopter. An important concept for understanding stereo geometry is the space *horopter*, that is, the set of points in the 3-D world whose vertical and horizontal disparity vanish simultaneously. It is clear that the space horopter passes through the point of fixation. Because the vanishing of both horizontal and vertical disparity poses a 2-D constraint on the horopter, one would expect it to be a curve, or some 1-D manifold. With the rotation matrices given in the foregoing, the problem can be formulated as follows.

Let $f = [f_1, f_2, f_3]^T$ denote a fixation point with $f_3 > 0$. Let M denote one of the forementioned rotation matrices. We write

$$M_l = M_{f - n_l}; \quad M_r = M_{f - n_r} \tag{11.16}$$

where the camera nodal points are denoted by n_l and n_r, respectively. $M_l(p - n_l)$ thus describes the coordinate transformation of a point p from world coordinates into the coordinate system centered around the left camera. A point on the horopter must then satisfy the equation

$$M_l(p - n_l) = \lambda M_r(p - n_r) \tag{11.17}$$

where λ is a positive real variable describing the ratio of the distances of point p to the two nodal points.

Figure 11.7 shows solutions of Eq. (11.17) for the three systems of camera axes. For the Helmholtz system, the space horopter is composed of a Vieth-Müller circle in a plane tilted away from the horizontal by the common elevation angle, and a medial line perpendicular to the circle. In the other cases, the space horopter is a space curve that degenerates to the circle plus line arrangement for fixation points in

Table 11.1: *Examples for stereo camera heads with various degrees of freedom. In the DoF column, the first number applies to the cameras, the second to the head, and the third to a further support system (body, vehicle, etc.)*

DoF	Type	Examples
HELMHOLTZ architectures (common tilt axis)		
$1 + 4 + 0$	symmetric vergence + head tilt, pan, x, y-translation	U Penn; Krotkov [18]
$1 + 2 + 0$	symmetric vergence + head tilt and pan (symmetric Helmholtz)	Harvard head; Clark and Ferrier [19]
$2 + 1 + 6$	camera pan + yoked tilt + Puma arm	Rochester head; Coombs and Brown [20]
FICK architectures (independent tilt and pan)		
$4 + 2 + 0$	camera pan and tilt about nodal points + eccentric pan and tilt of neck module	KTH head; Pahlavan and Eklundh [21]
$4 + 0 + 2$	camera pan and tilt + turn and z-translation of vehicle	Seelen et al. [22]
LISTING architecture (camera movement on great circles)		
$6 + 6 + 6$		human head

the horizontal or medial plane. For a derivation of the space horopter in the Listing case, see Solomons [17].

Stereo camera heads. The discussion of stereo geometry presented so far applies to stereo camera systems with a fair number of degrees of freedom to move. In human vision, these are the yoked variables, vergence and version, for the movements within the horizontal plane; for movements outside the horizontal plane, Listing's law applies. Mechanically, each eye has the full three degrees of freedom of rotation. Movements of head and body give additional flexibility to the system.

An overview of some technical camera heads is given in Table 11.1; for a more comprehensive discussion, see Murray et al. [23]. As an example of the design questions arising in the design of camera heads, we discuss one simple geometrical property of verging camera systems that seems to have been overlooked previously.

Consider a simple camera head with two degrees of freedom. These can be either the two viewing directions (pan) φ_l and φ_r of the individual cameras, or the symmetric vergence of the system α and the heading direction ξ. For simplicity, we assume that the head turns around a vertical axis through the midpoint between the two camera

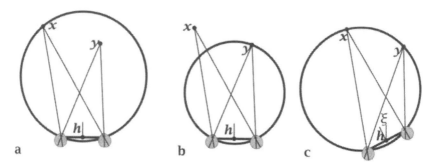

Figure 11.8: *Comparison of camera heads with two degrees of freedom. The center of rotation of the camera head is marked by* **h:** *a and b head with independently moving camera* ((φ_l, φ_r) *system); c head with symmetric version and yoked pan movements* ((α, ξ) *system). In the* (φ_l, φ_r) *system, the zero-disparity circle can be made passing through just one point* (**x** *or* **y**) *at any one time. In the* (α, ξ) *system, the disparity of both points can be compensated simultaneously. Note that the spatial relation of* **x**, **y** *and* **h** *is the same in all panels.*

nodal points and the cameras turn around parallel axes through their respective nodal points. Note that ξ is not identical to the version angle y previously introduced. Two criteria could be the following:

C1 Is it possible to fixate any point in the plane, thereby reducing its disparity to zero?

C2 Given two points in the plane, is it possible to simultaneously reduce both disparities to zero? In this case, a smooth surface passing through the two points would have low disparity values throughout.

With respect to criterion 1, the (φ_l, φ_r) system has a problem with points on the baseline. The (α, ξ) system can fixate any point in the plane without restriction. With respect to criterion 2, it is quite clear that for the (φ_l, φ_r) system, simultaneous disparity reduction of two points is possible only if the two points happen to be on a circle passing through the two nodal points. In the (α, ξ) system, however, simultaneous disparity reduction is always possible as long as the line through the two points **x** and **y** is neither the baseline nor the horizontal midline of the system. The corresponding settings for the camera head are:

$$\xi = \arctan \frac{(4x^2 - b^2)y_2 - (4y^2 - b^2)x_2}{(4y^2 - b^2)x_1 - (4x^2 - b^2)y_1} \qquad (11.18)$$

$$\alpha = \arctan \frac{b(x_1 \sin\xi + x_2 \cos\xi)}{x^2 - b^2/4}$$

$$= \arctan \frac{b(y_1 \sin\xi + y_2 \cos\xi)}{y^2 - b^2/4} \qquad (11.19)$$

An example of this relationship is shown in Fig. 11.8c.

11.2.2 Global stereopsis

Global disparity. In this section, we will briefly discuss global image difference as one interesting variable in stereovision. We will assume that the left and right images are related to each other by a 1-D disparity map $\delta(x', y')$ such that

$$I_r(x', y') = I_l(x' - \delta(x', y'), y') \tag{11.20}$$

Vertical disparities will be neglected in this analysis.

We will prove in this section that the global disparity or image shift minimizing the overall image difference equals the averaged true disparity, weighted by local image contrast. To see this, we introduce the global image *correlation*

$$\Phi(D) := \int \int [I_l(x', y') - I_r(x' + D, y')]^2 \, dx' \, dy' \tag{11.21}$$

Setting $I(x', y') := I_l(x', y')$ and substituting Eq. (11.20) into Eq. (11.21), we obtain:

$$\Phi(D) = \int \int [I(x', y') - I(x' - \delta(x', y') + D, y)]^2 \, dx' \, dy' \tag{11.22}$$

The minimization is now performed by calculating the derivative $\Phi'(D)$. Application of the chain rule yields:

$$\Phi'(D) = 2 \int \int I_{x'}(x' - \delta(x', y') + D, y') \tag{11.23}$$
$$[I(x', y') - I(x' - \delta(x', y') + D, y')] \, dx' \, dy'$$

Setting $\Phi'(D^*) = 0$ and linearly approximating the term in square brackets, we obtain:

$$0 \approx \int \int I_{x'}(x', y')[(D^* - \delta(x', y'))I_{x'}(x', y')] \, dx' \, dy' \tag{11.24}$$

This yields the final result:

$$D^* \approx \frac{\int \int \delta(x', y') I_{x'}^2(x', y') \, dx' \, dy'}{\int \int I_{x'}^2(x', y') \, dx' \, dy'} \tag{11.25}$$

As stated in the foregoing, Eq. (11.25) shows that the global disparity, that is, the image shift maximizing overall correlation between the left and the right image, is equivalent to the average of the local disparities, weighted by the squared partial derivative of the image intensity

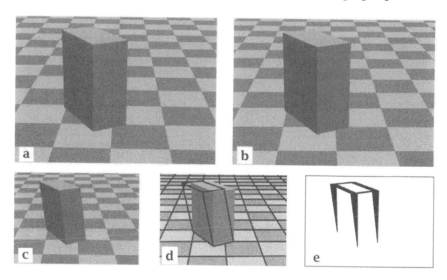

Figure 11.9: *Obstacle avoidance by inverse perspective mapping:* **a,b** *left and right images of a scene;* **c** *predicted right view based on inverse perspective mapping of the left view;* **d** *comparison of actual and predicted right image. The actual image is shown as gray values, whereas the prediction is shown by contours. The images coincide in the ground plane, but deviate increasingly for objects raising above the plane;* **e** *difference image of actual and predicted right image. The obstacle can easily be segmented from the ground plane.*

function $I_{x'}^2(x', y')$, which may be considered a measure of image contrast in the "disparity direction."

In verging camera systems, global disparities can be used to adjust the vergence angle and thus the working point of stereopsis to some point of interest in space. In biological vision, disparities are considered only in a narrow range around zero, called *Panum's fusional area*. The advantage of this is that high disparity resolution can be deployed to regions in space where it is actually needed. In terms of stereo-correspondence algorithms, the ability to verge results in a smaller required search space for disparities. Global image correlation as defined in Eq. (11.21) has been used for vergence control, for example, by Ahuja and Abbott [24]. In human vergence movements, an averaging mechanism as described by Eq. (11.25) has been demonstrated by Mallot et al. [25]. Phase-based approaches to global disparity estimation have been discussed by Theimer and Mallot [26].

Inverse perspective mapping. As one example of a technical application of global stereopsis, we briefly discuss *obstacle avoidance* by *inverse perspective mapping* [27, 28]. Here, prior to disparity calculations, the images are transformed in a way that makes global disparity an even more interesting variable. The basic idea is illustrated in Fig. 11.9. Consider two stereoscopic views of a scene as depicted in Fig. 11.9a,b. If no obstacle were around, the right image could be predicted from the left by a perspective remapping technique. This remapping is a projective collineation that can be obtained by projecting the right image back to the ground plane and imaging the result with the left camera. Comparing the original and the predicted right image, one obtains deviations in those image regions where something is protruding or receding from the horizontal plane, that is, in obstacle regions. If both images are identical, no obstacle is present. An intuitive way to think of this is that inverse perspective mapping creates a zero-disparity plane (for comparisons of the right and the predicted right image) that coincides with the ground plane. Whenever a "disparity" occurs, an obstacle must be present.

The technique is not sensitive to cast shadows and other image structure as long as it is confined to the plane. Disparity is zero for points in the ground plane and increases with obstacle elevation. Inverse perspective mapping has been applied successfully in autonomous robots [22, 29] as well as to driver support systems on highways [30, 31].

Inverse perspective mapping is a projective collineation, most suitably formalized in terms of homogeneous coordinates. Let $\tilde{x}_l$ and $\tilde{x}_r$ denote the homogeneous representations of the left and right image points x_l and x_r. Intuitively, $\tilde{x}_l$ and $\tilde{x}_r$ are the rays passing through the respective image points. Inverse perspective mapping is then described by a 3×3 matrix Q with

$$\tilde{x}_r = Q\tilde{x}_l \qquad (11.26)$$

that depends on the rotation between the two cameras $M_l M_r^T$, the relative position of the camera nodal points, $n_l - n_r$, the normal of the assumed ground plane g, and the distance between the ground plane and the left camera nodal point d. The relation reads:

$$Q = M_l M_r^T + \frac{(n_l - n_r)g^\top}{d} \qquad (11.27)$$

For a proof, see Faugeras [32], proposition 6.1. Similar ideas can be applied to the monocular analysis of optical flow, in which case the inverse perspective mapping goes from the image plane to the assumed ground plane [27]. As compared to the stereoscopic case, optical flow has the disadvantage that it works only when the observer is moving, requiring faster motions when more reliable obstacle information is sought.

11.3 Depth-from-focus

Depth-from-focus addresses the reconstruction of the depth information by using the fact that images usually contain blur. A typical situation is well known from photographs taken with the lens focused to
a close distance. While the foreground is well focused, objects in the
background appear blurred. In general, the blur increases with increasing distance from the location of focus.

The basic idea of depth-from-focus is to correlate the grade of the
blurring with the distance and therefore estimate 3-D positions from
the defocus. Unfortunately, defocus is not the only source of blur,
which can also be disguised by smooth brightness changes in the scene.
Therefore, depth-from-focus either requires multiple views of the same
scene in order to distinguish defocus from blur, or making use of known
properties of the scene and the lens setup. Both approaches lead to
different realizations of depth recovery and will be discussed later in
this section.

11.3.1 Defocused imaging

Depth-of-field and -focus.   According to the basic lens equation (3.28)
only objects located at a fixed distance d_o are imaged well focused onto
the image plane at the fixed position d_i, whereas objects at other distances d'_o appear blurred. The distance range in which the blur does not
exceed a certain value is called the depth-of-field. Using the radius ϵ of
the blur circle in order to describe blur, the depth-of-field is determined
by the choice of a maximal radius of the blur circle, the so-called circle
of confusion ϵ_c. Expressed in terms of the magnification $M = d_i/d_o$,
the f-number $O = f/2R$, and the object distances, the depth-of-field is
given by

$$\Delta d_0 = \frac{2O}{Mf}d'_0\epsilon_c = \frac{d_0}{\frac{Mf}{2O\epsilon_c} - 1} \Rightarrow |\Delta d_0| = \frac{2O}{Mf}d'_0|\epsilon_c| = \frac{d_0}{1 \mp \frac{Mf}{2O\epsilon_c}} \quad (11.28)$$

In Eq. (11.28) we combined the two distinct cases of Δd_0 being positive or negative by understanding ϵ as having the same sign as Δd_0.
Distinguishing between positive and negative signs shows the inherent asymmetry for the depth-of-field, caused by the nonlinearity of
Eq. (3.28). Therefore it is a common practice to assume $MR \gg \epsilon_c$,
leading to the approximation of $d'_0 \approx d_0$ in Eq. (11.28) and removing
the asymmetry.

Moving the image plane instead of the object plane also causes a
defocused image. Equivalent to the depth-of-field in object space the
term depth-of-focus in image space denotes the maximal dislocation of
the image plane with respect to a given circle of confusion. The relation

between depth-of-focus and depth-of-field is given by the longitudinal magnification M^2

$$\Delta d_0 = M^2 \Delta d_i \qquad (11.29)$$

Point spread function. The point spread function is one of the central terms in depth-from-focus, because it describes the effect of image blur in a quantitative way. Because the image of a complex object is the superposition of the images of all object points, and the image of an object point is the *point spread function* (PSF) of the lens, the effect of blurring can be described as a convolution of the well-focused image, as it would be achieved by a pinhole camera, with the PSF

$$g(\boldsymbol{x}') = \int f(\boldsymbol{x}(\vec{\xi}'))\mathrm{PSF}(\vec{\xi}' - \boldsymbol{x}')\,\mathrm{d}^2\xi' = f(\boldsymbol{x}(\boldsymbol{x}')) * \mathrm{PSF}(\boldsymbol{x}') \qquad (11.30)$$

This is only true under certain assumptions, which are described in detail in Section 3.7.

In many cases, we can assume that the shape of the PSF is independent of its distance from the plane of best focus. Then, the PSF can be described by a shape function S and a scaling factor σ, which varies with the distance g'

$$\mathrm{PSF}_Z(\boldsymbol{x}) = \frac{1}{s} S\left(\frac{\boldsymbol{x}}{\sigma(Z)}\right) \qquad (11.31)$$

The denominator s normalizes the PSF to $\int \mathrm{PSF}_Z(\boldsymbol{x})\,\mathrm{d}^2 x = 1$, forcing gray-value preservation. In many cases it is sufficient to replace σ by the radius of the blur circle ϵ. The shape function can be completely different for different optical setups. Nevertheless, only a few shape functions are sufficient in order to describe the main properties of standard optics, namely, box functions, Gaussians and Airy disks. The details of the various point spread functions can be found in Section 3.7.1.

Defocus in the Fourier domain. In Fourier space, the convolution turns into a multiplication of the Fourier transform of the object function with the Fourier transform of the PSF. The latter is called the *optical transfer function (OTF)*. Its values give the transfer coefficient for spatial structures of different wavelength through the optical system. A value of zero indicates that this particular wavelength cannot be seen by the optics. A typical OTF will act as a low-pass filter, eliminating higher spatial frequencies, that is, high-resolution details.

11.3.2 Principles of depth-from-focus algorithms

As Eq. (3.35) shows, defocus appears as multiplication in Fourier space. Because of its commutativity, there is no distinction between the PSF and the object function. This has serious implications for depth-from-focus algorithms, because it means that the gray-value structure depends on both object properties as well as the PSF. A smooth gray-value transition may arise from either a massive defocus or merely reflects a nonuniform object surface. On the other hand, depth estimation from defocus requires the effect of blur caused by the PSF to be separated from other sources. Two different approaches to solve this problem are possible:

Multiple-view approaches. Using multiple cameras viewing the same scene with different focal or aperture settings results in a set of images with the same object function, but taken with different PSFs. Separation of the object properties from the PSF effects becomes possible. A variety of realization of these approaches is possible:

- **Focus series** A series of images is taken with a single camera while varying the focusing of the lens. Within the focus series, at each image point the image with the maximum sharpness is selected from the series, resulting in a depth map. Of course, this is only possible with static objects that are not moving during the image acquisition.

- **Dual focus view** Using two cameras with different object planes results in two images taken with different PSFs for every plane in between the two object planes. Only at the very center do the two PSFs become identical, thus leading to the same images at this position. Using cameras with different optics, for example, different focal length, eliminates this problem.

- **Multiple aperture view** Instead of using different focusing, two or more cameras can be focused at the same object while having different f-numbers, resulting in different blurring. As a special case, consider a combination of a pinhole camera with a camera of finite aperture. The image from the pinhole camera shows no blurring, thus giving the object function. With this information, the influence of the PSF can be calculated from the other image.

Single-view approaches. Solving the depth-from-focus problem by using a single image instead of multiple views allows the observation of fast-moving objects with little effort. To discriminate object function and PSF, *a priori* knowledge about the object function and the PSF is necessary. This class of algorithms therefore requires either the objects to be restricted to known shapes or the selection of regions, wherein the object features are known, for example, step edges or point objects.

Ambiguity of depth estimation. It is important to notice that there may be an ambiguity in depth estimation by depth-from-focus, due to the fact that the size of the PSF has its minimum at the plane of best focus, increasing in both directions: towards and farther away from the camera position. If no special arrangements are made, this results in an ambiguity of the depth estimation, because two positions of the object are possible and cannot be distinguished. This has to be taken into account especially with single-view methods, but also with multiple-view methods- because there is only a certain distance range in which no ambiguity occurs.

11.3.3 Multiple-view depth-from-focus

Multiple-view approaches use sets of views of the same scene, taken with different camera settings, and mainly with different focusing. Considering the changing camera parameter as an additional dimension of the image data, they start with an already 3-D data set. These data are transformed in order to achieve the desired depth information. These approaches are used most commonly with focus series.

Introduction to focus series. Focus series are a common approach for the investigation of motionless objects, and are often used in microscopy. The focus of a single camera is changed to a number of settings, resulting in a series of images taken with different planes of best focus (Fig. 11.10). The depth value of each pixel can be found directly from selecting the image showing the less blur from the series. This is done be calculating a sharpness measure on each image of the stack, and then for each pixel or small region of the image, finding the maximum of the sharpness measure along the depth axis. Unfortunately, usually the number of images is limited, resulting in a poor depth resolution. Interpolation of the sharpness measure between the images is therefore required in order to increase depth resolution.

The quality of the depth map is mainly given by the method used to located the image of best focus within the series, and the interpolation that is done in between these images.

Sharpness measure. As pointed out in Section 3.7.1, defocus causes suppression of higher spatial frequencies in the power spectrum of the image. Any filter sensitive to high spatial frequencies in a local neighborhood is therefore suitable as a sharpness filter. Obviously, a large variety of such filters exists, but most of the filters belong to the two main classes of contrast operators or bandpass filters. In the following, an example of each filter class is given.

Contrast filters allow a fast implementation of the sharpness measure. They measure the range of gray values available in a neighborhood N of the pixel. Because the lack of high spatial frequencies results in slower gray-value changes, the local contrast also decreases with increasing defocus. As contrast detector, either the local contrast

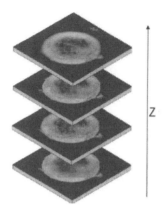

Z

Figure 11.10: *Focus series of a machine screw used for depth recovery.*

operator

$$C_l(\boldsymbol{x}) = \max_{\boldsymbol{x}' \in N} g(\boldsymbol{x}') - \min_{\boldsymbol{x}' \in N} g(\boldsymbol{x}') \tag{11.32}$$

or the normalized contrast

$$C_n(\boldsymbol{x}) = \frac{\max\limits_{\boldsymbol{x}' \in N} g(\boldsymbol{x}') - \min\limits_{\boldsymbol{x}' \in N} g(\boldsymbol{x}')}{\max\limits_{\boldsymbol{x}' \in N} g(\boldsymbol{x}') + \min\limits_{\boldsymbol{x}' \in N} g(\boldsymbol{x}')} \tag{11.33}$$

can be used. These filters are very sensitive to contrast changes, but also sensitive to isolated noise pixels. They can be improved by replacing the minimum and maximum operator by rank filters, for example, p-quantile filters. The p-quantile $Q(p)$ value in an neighborhood N is defined as the gray value at which the pth fraction of all gray values in N are below $Q(p)$ and the $1 - p$th fraction of gray values is above $Q(p)$. This can be expressed by the local gray-value histogram $H(g)$ of the neighborhood N as

$$Q(p) = F^{-1}(p) \quad \text{with} \quad F(g) = \sum_{-\infty}^{g} H(g) \tag{11.34}$$

$F(g)$ is the cumulative distribution function (CDF) [33] of the gray-value distribution. As the p-quantile is a generalization of minimum and maximum operators, it is used as a contrast filter by replacing $\max g(\boldsymbol{x})$ by $Q(1-p, Vx)$ and $\min g(\boldsymbol{x})$ by $Q(p, Vx)$ in Eq. (11.32) and Eq. (11.33), respectively.

In order to achieve high processing speed, a variance-based method has been implemented by one of the present authors. The results of

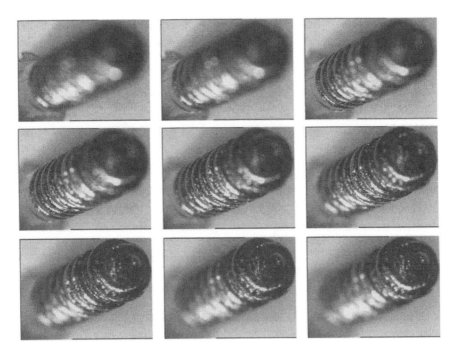

Figure 11.11: *Focus series of a metric screw taken with a telecentric optics with an object to image ratio of 20.*

this method, applied to a focus series of a screw (Fig. 11.11) are shown in Fig. 11.12a. To give a first estimate of the position, for each region of 16×16 pixel the image with the highest local contrast has been chosen. In addition, an overall sharp image is calculated by selecting each pixel from the image previously found to have the highest contrast at this position (see Fig. 11.12b).

In order to find image regions containing high spatial frequencies, high-pass and bandpass filters can be used. Although the high-pass filters seem to be optimal in selecting high frequencies, they tend to fail due to their noise sensitivity. Therefore, they are combined with a low-pass filter, which cuts the wavelength above the cut wavelength of the high-pass filter to form a bandpass. Bandpass filters select a range of spatial frequencies from the Fourier transform of the image. The center wave number and width of the filter can be optimized to meet the requirements of the image material. A bandpass filter can easily be constructed from the difference of two Gaussian filters, as the well-known Difference of Gaussian (DoG) filter

$$DoG_{\sigma_1,\sigma_2}(\boldsymbol{x}) = \frac{1}{\sqrt{2\pi}\sigma_1}e^{-\frac{x^2}{2\sigma_1^2}} - \frac{1}{\sqrt{2\pi}\sigma_2}e^{-\frac{x^2}{2\sigma_2^2}} \qquad (11.35)$$

a   b

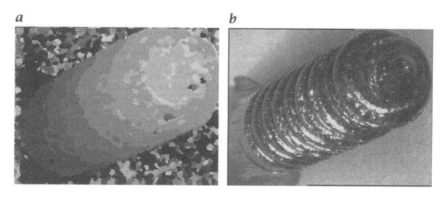

Figure 11.12: *a Depth map of a machine screw calculated by the variance method; b overall sharp image calculated from the original images using the depth map.*

As an effective implementation, pyramid decompositions of the images can preferably be used. Darell and Wohn [34] report an algorithm using first a bandpass decomposition of the image by a Laplacian pyramid, adequate for DoG filtering. In order to average the results over a larger area, a Gaussian pyramid is constructed on each level of the Laplacian pyramid, resulting in a dual pyramid structure $I^{k,l}$

$$I^{k,l} = \mathcal{E} G^{(k)} L^{(l)} I \qquad (11.36)$$

where I is the image, $G^{(k)}$ is the operator for the kth level of the Gaussian pyramid, $L^{(l)}$ is the operator for the lth level of the Laplacian pyramid, and $\mathcal{E}$ is the expansion operator suitable to interpolate the subsampled image back to the original image size. This is used as the final sharpness measure. Figure 11.13 shows the results of calculating the depth from the depth series in Fig. 11.11 using different levels for both the Gaussian as the Laplacian pyramid. For these images, the combination of the 0-th level of the Laplacian pyramid with the second level of the Gaussian pyramid selects the optimal wave-number range.

Three-dimensional reconstruction. So far, all methods result in a depth map, giving a distance value for each pixel in the image, also called a 2.5-D reconstruction. Therefore, only opaque surfaces can be surveyed with this method, as they appear in many technical applications. However, microscopic imaging typically deals with transparent or semitransparent objects. The question arises whether it is possible to perform a fully 3-D reconstruction of the object from depth series. This can be done by deconvolving the image stack with the inverse of the 3-D point spread function of the microscope.

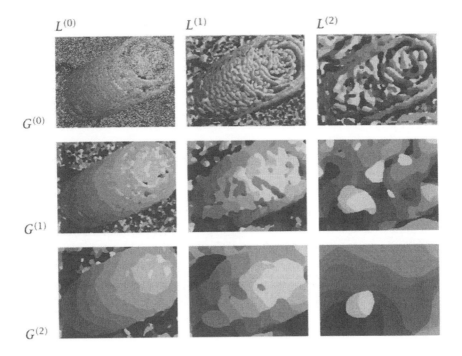

Figure 11.13: *Depth map calculated from different combinations of levels of the Laplacian and Gaussian pyramid. The best results are obtained from the combination of the 0-th level of the Laplacian pyramid with the first and second level of the Gaussian pyramid.*

11.3.4 Dual-view depth-from-focus

The basic idea of dual-view depth-from-focus techniques is to take two images of the same scene, but with different parameters of the optical setup to realize different point spread functions. To ensure that the image pair is taken at the same time, beamsplitters and folding mirrors are used as illustrated in Fig. 11.14.

Dual aperture. In order to achieve a depth estimate at a position x_0, a region centered at this point is considered. The choice of the size of this region determines the spatial resolution of the depth map. Pentland [35] developed a method based on the assumption of a Gaussian point spread function, which will be summarized here. Denoting the two images by g_i, the object function by O_i, and the variances of the two Gaussian PSFs by σ_i, the relation of the two images is given by

$$\frac{g_1(x)}{g_2(x)} = \frac{O_1(x) * G_{\sigma_1}(x)}{O_2(x) * G_{\sigma_2}(x)} \tag{11.37}$$

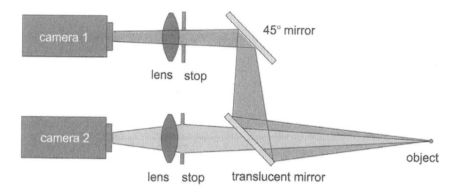

Figure 11.14: *Optical setup for a dual aperture camera system. One beamsplitter and a folding mirror are necessary to simultaneously acquire two images with different aperture of the same object.*

It is important to note that there is no matching problem, because the two camera setups are identical except for the f-number. Therefore the object functions are identical. In Fourier space, the convolution turns into a multiplication. By dividing the Fourier transforms instead of the images, the result becomes independent of the object functions

$$\frac{\hat{g}_1(\boldsymbol{k})}{\hat{g}_2(\boldsymbol{k})} = \frac{\hat{O}(\boldsymbol{k})\hat{G}_{\sigma_1}(\boldsymbol{k})}{\hat{O}(\boldsymbol{k})\hat{G}_{\sigma_1}(\boldsymbol{k})} = \frac{\sigma_2^2 G_{\sigma_1'}(\boldsymbol{k})}{\sigma_1^2 G_{\sigma_i'}(\boldsymbol{k})} \quad \text{with} \quad \sigma_i' = \frac{1}{\sigma_i} \tag{11.38}$$

or

$$\frac{\hat{g}_1(\boldsymbol{k})}{\hat{g}_2(\boldsymbol{k})} = \frac{\sigma_2^2}{\sigma_1^2} e^{-\frac{k^2}{2}(\sigma_1'^2 - \sigma_2'^2)} \sim G_\sigma(\boldsymbol{k}) \quad \text{with} \quad \sigma = \frac{1}{\sigma_1^2 - \sigma_2^2} \tag{11.39}$$

The ratio of the Fourier transforms of the two images therefore is a Gaussian with variance σ, which can be estimated with standard algorithms. From Eq. (3.29) the depth d_0' is known to be

$$\frac{\epsilon}{R} = \frac{d_i}{d_0} - \frac{d_i}{d_0'} \Rightarrow d_0' = \frac{d_i f}{d_i - f - 2O\epsilon} \tag{11.40}$$

Pentland [35] uses ϵ as a direct estimate for σ. If only two cameras are used, one has to be a pinhole camera in order to fix σ_1 to zero. Using three or more cameras with finite aperture results in a set of estimates of the differences of the σ-values

$$S_{ij} = \sigma_i^2 - \sigma_j^2 \tag{11.41}$$

and therefore allows for the solution of Eq. (11.40).

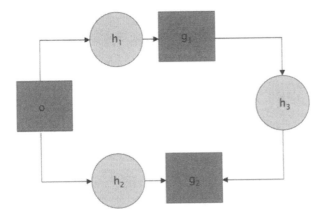

Figure 11.15: *Illustration of the convolution ratio of the two PSFs h_1 and h_2.*

Dual aperture and focus. In fact, it is possible to reconstruct depth information from only two cameras without the limitations to pinhole setups. Assuming again identical optics but for the aperture settings of the both cameras, two images are taken from the same scene O by the convolution with two different, now arbitrarily shaped point spread functions h_1 and h_2

$$g_1(x) = O(x) * h_1(x), \qquad g_2(x) = O(x) * h_2(x) \qquad (11.42)$$

Convolution ratio. As introduced by Ens and Lawrence [36], the *convolution ratio* h_3 of two defocus operators is defined as the convolution kernel that transforms the low aperture (and therefore less blurred) image g_1 into the high aperture image g_2, as indicated in Fig. 11.15

$$g_2(x) = g_1(x) * h_3(x) \qquad (11.43)$$

Now, g_2 can be expressed either in terms of h_2 or h_1 and h_3

$$g_2(x) = O(x) * h_1(x) * h_3(x) = O(x) * h_2(x) \qquad (11.44)$$

that is equivalent to

$$h_1(x) * h_3(x) = h_2(x) \qquad (11.45)$$

Depth recovery now requires two separate steps. First, the convolution ratio has to be computed from the image pair. Second, it has to be correlated with the true depth information. Ens and Lawrence [37] give a method based on inverse filtering to compute the convolution ratio. The windowed Fourier transform of the two images is given by

$$\begin{aligned} g_i(x)w_i(x) &= (O(x) * h_1(x))w_i(x) \quad \text{space domain} \\ \hat{g}_i(k) * \hat{w}_i(k) &= (\hat{O}(k)\hat{h}_1(k)) * \hat{w}_i(k) \quad \text{Fourier domain} \end{aligned} \qquad (11.46)$$

with the window functions $w_i(x)$. Windowing is necessary in order to calculate spatial resolved depth maps instead of a global depth estimate for the complete scene.

To isolate the convolution ratio, the ratio of the two Fourier transforms is taken

$$\frac{\hat{g}_2(k) * \hat{w}_2(k)}{\hat{g}_1(k) * \hat{w}_1(k)} = \frac{(\hat{O}(k)\hat{h}_2(k)) * \hat{w}_2(k)}{(\hat{O}(k)\hat{h}_1(k)) * \hat{w}_1(k)} \qquad (11.47)$$

The convolution ratio can be computed by means of Fourier transformation

$$h_3(x) = \mathcal{FT}^{-1}\left[\frac{\hat{w}_2(k) * \hat{h}_2(k)}{\hat{w}_1(k) * \hat{h}_1(k)}\right] \qquad (11.48)$$

The size of the window function is critical for the quality of the depth estimation, because larger sizes of the window improve the Fourier transformations, but, on the other hand, decrease the resolution of the depth maps. In addition, if the size of the window is large, only slow depth transitions can be detected. In the 1-D case, Ens and Lawrence [37] compute the correlation of accuracy and window size with a numerical simulation:

Window size	4	8	16	32
Error	66 %	24 %	6 %	1 %

For this calculation, a step edge scene $O = \{..., 0, 0, 1, 1, ...\}$ has been used with a defocus operator of a pinhole camera $h_1 = \{0, 1, 0\}$ and a defocus operator $h_2 = \{1, 1, 1\}$. Using a Gaussian window function, it can be seen that the error decreases as the size of the window function increases. To achieve smaller error, the window size has to be one order of magnitude larger than the PSF. If the size of w is small in order to guarantee a good spatial resolution of the depth map, its Fourier transform $\hat{w}$ can assumed to be constant. Thus Eq. (11.48) turns into the simpler representation

$$h_3(x) = \mathcal{FT}^{-1}\left[\frac{\hat{h}_2(k)}{\hat{h}_1(k)}\right] \qquad (11.49)$$

A common problem with inverse filtering are zero crossings of the Fourier transform, because these wave numbers cannot be reconstructed. The image functions $g_i = O * h_i$ have two kinds of zero crossings. The zero crossings of the object function O occur in both image functions, while the zero crossings of the defocus operators h_1 and h_2 differ. Unfortunately, the convolution of $\hat{O}$ with the Fourier transforms $\hat{h}_i$ can change the location of the zero crossings. The following sections introduce several algorithms suitable to solve the problems associated with zero crossing shifts.

Constraint inverse filtering. By using regularization, the problems with inverse filtering can be reduced. Therefore, the inverse filtering can be constrained by least squares fitting $\hat{h}_3(k)$ to a model. In this approach a quadratic model ($\hat{h}_3(k) = ak^2 + b$) is used, because it has been shown that the characteristic part of $\hat{h}_3(x)$ is a quadratic-type shape. Equation (11.49) can be written as

$$\hat{h}_1(k)\hat{h}_3(k) - \hat{h}_2(k) = 0 \qquad (11.50)$$

With H_1 is a matrix with $\hat{h}_1(k)$ stacked along its diagonal and $h_{2,3}$ stacked vectors formed from $\hat{h}_{2,3}(k)$; Eq. (11.50) can be denoted in matrix notation

$$H_1 h_3 - h_2 = 0 \qquad (11.51)$$

The regularized form of Eq. (11.51) minimized the functional

$$\|H_1 \cdot h_3 - h_2\|^2 + \lambda\|Ch_3\|^2 = \min \qquad (11.52)$$

where

- λ is a scalar parameter, which adjusts between fitting h_3 more to the data or to the quadratic shape; and
- C is a matrix that minimizes the second term if h_3 has quadratic shape.

To get the solution for this minimization problem and derive the best-fitted h_3, the Euler equation (Bertero and Poggio [38]) for Eq. (11.52) is solved for H_3

$$H_1^T H_1 h_3 - H_1^T h_2 + \lambda C^T C h_3 = 0 \qquad (11.53)$$

$$h_3 = \left(H_1^T H_1 + \lambda C^T C \right)^{-1} H_1^T h_2 \qquad (11.54)$$

From this the parameter to the best-fitted quadratic can be derived. By comparing the zero crossing of the quadratic and of the theoretically derived $\hat{h}_3$, that is, the Airy function mentioned in Section 11.3.1, the depth can be calculated.

11.3.5 Single-view depth-from-focus

Single-view depth-from-focus requires only one image of the scene to be taken. Therefore, it is necessary to know properties either of the object function or of the point spread function. Even if the shape of the PSF is completely known, restrictions to the object function are necessary in order to solve the depth-from-focus problem. A common

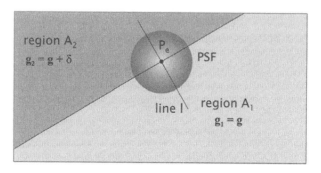

Figure 11.16: *Geometry at the step edge.*

approach is to calculate depth estimates only at image regions, whose properties can be estimated from the image itself, for example, line edges. This results in sparse depth maps, where values are given only at these positions. Often, the point spread function is approximated by box functions or Gaussians.

Sharp discontinuities.   Step edges in the gray value are ideal in order to separate the defocus from the image. For the implementation of such depth-from-focus algorithms, first, a detection of step edges has to be made. The actual depth estimation can only be performed in the neighborhood of these edges. This section will describe several approaches for the depth recovery near linear step edges. A step edge of height y along a straight line is defined by

$$O(x) = \begin{cases} g_0 + y & : \quad x \in A_2 \\ g_0 & : \quad x \in A_1 \end{cases} \tag{11.55}$$

An important prerequisite of the methods described here is that the point spread function is of known shape, and, in addition, has rotational symmetry. Furthermore, we assume the point spread function to be of Gaussian shape with variance $\sigma(z)^2$, where σ depends on the distance z of the object to the plane of best focus; σ is often denoted as the *spatial constant*. Because of the symmetry, images of objects located in front or behind this plane are indistinguishable. Therefore, the object position has to be limited to one side of the focal plane.

As the gray values in the neighborhood of a step edge are determined by the height of the steps g_1 and g_2 and the spatial constant σ, the analysis of the gray-value changes close to the edge provides a way to estimate σ. Algorithms of this kind have been introduced first by Pentland [39] and Grossman [40] who coined the term *depth-from-focus* to denote these methods.

The approach of Pentland [35] focuses on the estimation of σ from the gray value along a line l perpendicular to the edge, as indicated in Fig. 11.16.

Without loss of generality, the edge line may be in the y-direction at the position x_0 for the further computations. Therefore, instead of Eq. (11.55) we use $O_x(\boldsymbol{x})$ unless otherwise noted:

$$O_x(\boldsymbol{x}) = \begin{cases} g_0 + y & : \quad x > x_0 \\ g_0 & : \quad x < x_0 \end{cases} \tag{11.56}$$

We define the sharpness measure $C(\boldsymbol{x})$ as the Laplacian of the image, which itself is the convolution of the object function O with a Gaussian G_σ

$$\begin{aligned} C(\boldsymbol{x}) &= \Delta(G_\sigma * O_x) \\ &= \int \Delta G_\sigma(\sqrt{\boldsymbol{x} - \boldsymbol{x}'}) O_x(\boldsymbol{x}') \, d^2 x' \\ &= \delta\left[\frac{d}{dx} G_\sigma^1(x - x_0) \right] \end{aligned} \tag{11.57}$$

Herein G^1 denotes a 1-D Gaussian. The position of the step edge in the blurred image is defined as the zero crossing of the Laplacian of the image. At this very position, we obtain

$$C(\boldsymbol{x}) = \delta\left[\frac{d}{dx} G_\sigma^1(x) \right] = -\frac{\delta x}{\sqrt{2\pi}\sigma^3} e^{-\frac{x^2}{2\sigma^2}} \tag{11.58}$$

From

$$\ln\left| \frac{C(\boldsymbol{x})}{x} \right| = \ln \frac{\delta}{\sqrt{2\pi}\sigma^3} - \frac{x^2}{2\sigma^2} \tag{11.59}$$

we obtain an equation linear in x^2 as seen in Fig. 11.17

$$ax^2 + b = c \quad \text{with} \quad a = -\frac{1}{2\sigma^2} \quad b = \ln \frac{\delta}{\sqrt{2\pi}\sigma^3} \quad c = \ln\left| \frac{C(\boldsymbol{x})}{x} \right| \tag{11.60}$$

A standard linear regression then yields an estimate of σ, which is correlated to the depth.

Analyzing the gray values along lines perpendicular to the edges require precise edge finders. Especially, errors in the edge direction introduce deviations in the spatial constant and therefore lead to errors in the depth estimations. Lai et al. [41] extended Pentland's algorithms without requiring an exact determination of the line direction.

We start with a step edge

$$O(\boldsymbol{x}) = \begin{cases} g_0 + y & : \quad x < a + by \\ g_0 & : \quad x > a + by \end{cases} \tag{11.61}$$

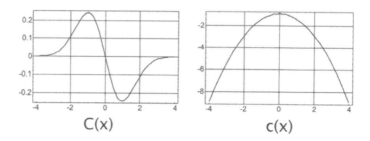

Figure 11.17: *Sharpness measures $C(x)$ and $c(x)$ along the line l.*

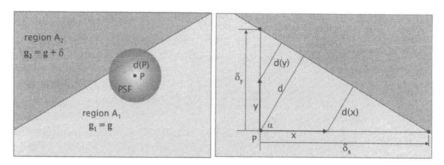

Figure 11.18: *Definitions of the horizontal and vertical edge distances.*

in an arbitrary direction, given by the line $x = a + by$. Again, assuming a Gaussian PSF, the gray value at a point P can be expressed by its distance d perpendicular to the edge

$$
\begin{aligned}
g(\boldsymbol{x}) = G_\sigma * O & = g_1 \int_{\boldsymbol{x} \in A_1} G_\sigma(\boldsymbol{x})\, \mathrm{d}^2 x + g_2 \int_{\boldsymbol{x} \in A_2} G_\sigma(\boldsymbol{x})\, \mathrm{d}^2 x \\
& = g_1 E\left(\frac{d(\boldsymbol{x})}{\sigma}\right) + g_2 E\left(-\frac{d(\boldsymbol{x})}{\sigma}\right)
\end{aligned} \tag{11.62}
$$

with

$$
E(x) = \int_{-\infty}^{x} G_1^1(x')\, \mathrm{d}x' \tag{11.63}
$$

The main idea of Lai et al. [41] is to decompose the spatial constant σ into two components σ_x and σ_y for the horizontal and vertical axis, and then derive equations for the horizontal and vertical gray-value changes. It is convenient to split the 2-D Equation (11.62) into two 1-D equations, using the horizontal and vertical edge distances δ_x and δ_y, as defined in Fig. 11.18.

To simplify matters, the origin of coordinate system shall be located at the currently investigated point P. Using $d = \cos\alpha(\delta_x - x)$ for solely horizontal movements and $d = \sin\alpha(\delta_y - y)$ for vertical ones, the gray value can be written as

$$g_{(x)}(x) = g(x, y = 0) = g_1 E\left(\frac{\delta_x - x}{\sigma_x}\right) + g_2 E\left(-\frac{\delta_x - x}{\sigma_x}\right)$$

$$g_{(y)}(y) = g(x = 0, y) = g_1 E\left(\frac{\delta_y - y}{\sigma_y}\right) + g_e E\left(-\frac{\delta_y - y}{\sigma_y}\right)$$

(11.64)

with $\sigma = \cos(\alpha)\sigma_x = \sin(\alpha)\sigma_y$.

Equation (11.64) can be rewritten as

$$g_{(x)} = g_2 + \Delta g N\left(\frac{\delta_x - x}{\sigma_x}\right)$$

$$g_{(y)} = g_2 + \Delta g N\left(\frac{\delta_y - y}{\sigma_y}\right)$$

(11.65)

According to Eq. (11.65), σ can be calculated by estimating the 1-D spatial constants σ_x and σ_y and combining them to

$$\sigma = \frac{\sigma_x \sigma_y}{\sqrt{\sigma_x^2 \sigma_y^2}}$$

(11.66)

To solve the depth-estimation problem, either the spatial constant σ or its decompositions σ_x and σ_y must be estimated from a suitable region of the image. First, this region has to be chosen in the neighborhood of step edges. The most general method is to formulate an optimization problem, either from Eq. (11.62) for direct estimation of σ or from Eq. (11.65) for the decomposed spatial constants. It can be formulated as

$$C(g_1, g_2, \sigma_i) = \sum\left(g(x) - g_2 - \Delta g E\left(\frac{\delta_x - x}{\sigma_x}\right)^2\right) \rightarrow \min \quad (11.67)$$

or, equivalently,

$$\frac{\partial C(g_1, g_2, \sigma_i)}{\partial g_1} = 0 \qquad \frac{\partial C(g_1, g_2, \sigma_i)}{\partial g_2} = 0 \qquad \frac{\partial C(g_1, g_2, \sigma_i)}{\partial \sigma_1} = 0$$

(11.68)

Lai et al. [41] use a standard Newton method to solve Eqs. (11.67) and (11.68).

Edge detection is a basic step in image processing for these algorithms (Chapter 9.7). Therefore, its accuracy should be as good as possible in order to eliminate errors in the depth estimation. Besides simple edge filters as first- and second-order derivatives, Lai et al. [41] prefer the *Laplace of Gaussian* (LoG) filter first proposed by Marr and Hildreth [42] and Hildreth [43] (see also Section 9.7.2). According to Haralick [44], it can be written as

$$\Delta g(\boldsymbol{x}) = \frac{1}{4\pi\sigma^4}\left(2 - \frac{|\boldsymbol{x}|^2}{\sigma^2}\right)\exp\left(-\frac{|\boldsymbol{x}|^2}{2\sigma^2}\right) \qquad (11.69)$$

Estimating depth. Depth estimation is carried out by correlating the spatial constant σ with the actual distance of the object. This is done by establishing an analytical relation between the spatial constant and depth, and by performing a calibration of the image-acquisition system. As a first-order approximation blurring is described by the blur circle, for example, a point spread function of uniform value (Subbarao and Gurumoorthy [45]). The radius of the blur circle is calculated assuming paraxial and aberration-free optics. As known from Eq. (3.29), the radius ϵ_c of the blur circle is given by

$$\frac{\epsilon_c}{R} = d_i\frac{\Delta d_o}{d_o d'_o} \qquad (11.70)$$

Therefore, the depth D is given by

$$D = d'_o = d_o + \Delta d_o = \frac{d_i f}{d_i - f - 2O\epsilon_c} \qquad (11.71)$$

with f being the focal length of the lens, O is its F-number, and d_i is the distance from the lens to the image plane. The assumption of a Gaussian point spread function instead of the blur circle can be expressed by replacing ϵ_c by the spatial constant σ and an adaptation factor k as $\epsilon_c = k\sigma$. According to Subbarao [46], k is in the range of $0 \le k \le 0.5$. Equation (11.71) can further be simplified to

$$D = \frac{A}{B - k\sigma} \quad \text{with} \quad A = k\frac{d_i f}{O} \quad \text{and} \quad B = k\frac{d_i - f}{O} \qquad (11.72)$$

where A and B can be seen as system constants, which are to be derived by the calibration procedure. This can be done easily be estimating σ for several points of known distance D and performing an optimization problem on Eq. (11.72).

Object-based depth-from-focus. Object-based algorithms represent a different approach for single-view depth-from-focus. These algorithms are of special interest when observing fast-moving objects. They assume that the images contain only a limited number of object classes, which can be clearly distinguished by image segmentation. Because the object properties are known, depth reconstruction becomes possible

with only one image. In fact, provided that an appropriate calibration
has been done, not even the shape of the point spread function has to
be known. Object-based algorithms have to be seen in clear contrast
to the algorithms described so far. These provide a depth map, which
may be dense or spare, on the image, while object-based approaches
first segment the image in order to find and classify objects, and result
in a depth estimate for each single object.

In this section, two different approaches of object-based depth-from-
focus will be discussed. Because of the different nature of the objects
the two methods use different object features in order to solve the
depth-recovery problem.

This algorithm has been developed by Jähne and Geißler [47] for objects of circular shape, but arbitrary size. In general, the algorithm can
be applied to any objects of given shape, which are distinguished only
in their size, that is, a scaling factor. Besides the depth the algorithm
results in a correct measurement of the size of the objects, even if they
undergo massive blur. The basic idea of the algorithm is to establish a
robust measure of both size and blur, and then correlate these parameters by means of a suitable calibration, thus giving correct size and
depth as the result.

As the first step of the algorithm, the shape of the objects has to
be parameterized. An object is represented by its shape function and
a scaling factor. For the application the algorithm has been developed,
and the shape function is a circular box function. Thus, an object of
radius r is described by

$$I(\boldsymbol{x}) = \Pi\left(\frac{|\boldsymbol{x} - \boldsymbol{x}_0|}{2r}\right) * \mathrm{PSF}(\boldsymbol{x})_z \quad \text{with} \quad \Pi(x) = \left\{ \begin{array}{ll} 1 & : \quad |x| \in [0, 1/2] \\ 0 & : \quad \text{otherwise} \end{array} \right.$$

$$(11.73)$$

By this means, the object is already blurred due to its defocused
position at the depth $z \neq 0$. As known from Section 11.3.1, the point
spread function can be described by a shape function, which remains
unchanged for every defocus, and a scaling parameter that describes
the amount of blur. In the following, we assume the image gray values to be normalized in such a manner that a well-focused object has a
minimum gray value of zero and a maximum gray value of 1.0. Furthermore, for the following calculations, we will assume the point spread
function is of rotational symmetry.

Besides the scaling due to the magnification of the imaging optics,
defocus itself changes the size of the objects, because there is no in-
escapable definition of the size of an object with blurred edges. Therefore, as the preliminary size of a blurred object, Jähne and Geißler [48]
chose the equivalent radius of the $1/q$-area of the object. The $1/q$-area

a   **b**

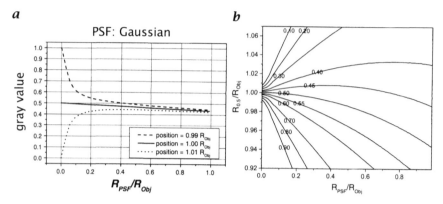

Figure 11.19: a *Gray value at the object edge for a Gaussian- and box-shaped point spread function.* **b** *Dependence of the 1/0.5 equivalent radius from the defocus.*

is hereby defined as the area over which the gray value of the object is larger than $1/q$ of the peak gray value.

Now, an optimal value of q has to be chosen. For a linear edge, the value $q = 0.5$ leads to a constant (normalized) gray value of 0.5 at the object boundary, as long as the scope of the PSF does not exceed the size of the object, because

$$g_{\text{object edge}} = \int\limits_{x \leq 0} \text{PSF}(x, y) \, \mathrm{d}x \, \mathrm{d}y \qquad (11.74)$$

due to the symmetry of the PSF.

Unfortunately, the objects are of circular shape. This leads to a smaller integration area than in Eq. (11.74), causing a slight decrease of the gray values at the object edges.

The change of the edge gray value with increasing defocus depends on the shape function of the PSF. The more the PSF is concentrated towards its center, the less distinct is the effect. Figure 11.19a illustrates this with a box-shaped and a Gaussian-shaped PSF, where the latter shows less variation.

Any value for q will therefore cause deviations in the size estimate of blurred objects. Therefore, there is no optimal value at all. In the following, we will choose 0.5, but this is for convenience only. This will cause the size shift as shown in Fig. 11.19b. In the depth-from-focus correlation of the input parameters, the correct size will be calculated.

As the measure of blur, the mean gray value g_m on the $1/q$-area is suitable. Due to the normalization of the gray values, g_m is also normalized and ranges from 0 to 1. Because the integral gray-value sum $\int g(x)d^2x$ is independent of defocus, the mean gray value decreases with increasing defocus. Thus, it provides a normalized and monotonic measure.

At this point, depth recovery could be done by establishing a calibration matrix, which correlates the $1/q$-area, and the mean gray value on it with the actual depth. However, it is possible to use the uniform shape of objects and PSF to reduce the calibration matrix to a 1-D calibration vector. This is explained in the next section.

For a better analysis of g_m we use the fact that the depth dependence of the PSF can be approximated by a scale factor $\eta(Z)$ and a shape function $\mathcal{P}$

$$\text{PSF}_Z(\boldsymbol{x}) = \frac{\mathcal{P}\left(\dfrac{\boldsymbol{x}}{\eta(Z)}\right)}{\displaystyle\int \mathcal{P}\left(\dfrac{\boldsymbol{x}}{\eta(Z)}\right) d^2x} \tag{11.75}$$

The $\boldsymbol{x}$ denotes coordinates on the image plane, while Z denotes the distance of the object point to the plane of focus. As already pointed out, all objects are of the same shape. Denoting the magnification of the optics by $V(Z)$, they are described by their shape function $\mathcal{O}$ and their radius R

$$G(\boldsymbol{x}) = \mathcal{O}\left(\frac{\boldsymbol{x}}{V(Z)R}\right) \tag{11.76}$$

The image of an object, which may be defocused, is therefore given by

$$n(\boldsymbol{x}) = G(\boldsymbol{x}) * \text{PSF}_Z(\boldsymbol{x}) \sim \mathcal{O}\left(\frac{\boldsymbol{x}}{V(Z)R}\right) * \mathcal{P}\left(\frac{\boldsymbol{x}}{\eta(Z)}\right) \tag{11.77}$$

Images of object with the same ratio between the scale factors $V(Z)R$ of the object function and the scale factor $\eta(Z)$ of the point spread function are distinguished only in scaling, but not in shape. In particular, the mean gray value remains unaffected. Therefore, the similarity condition Equation (11.78) holds as follows:

$$\frac{\eta(Z)}{V(Z)R} = \text{const} \quad \Leftrightarrow \quad g_m = \text{const} \tag{11.78}$$

In addition, g_m can be expressed as

$$g_m(Z, R) = g_m\left(\frac{\eta(Z)}{V(Z)R}\right) \tag{11.79}$$

With a telecentric optics, this can be further simplified. With this setup, explained in Section 3.6.3, the scaling of the PSF then becomes linear and symmetric in Z, and can be approximated as $\eta(Z) \sim |Z|$. In

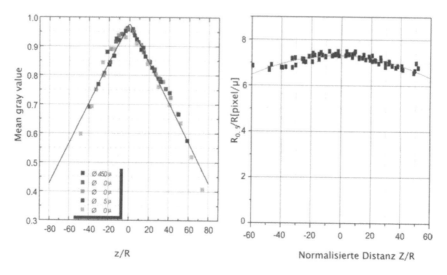

Figure 11.20: *Calibration data used for the depth-from-focus approach: left) calibration of mean gray value vs normalized depth; right) calibration of radius vs normalized depth.*

addition, $V(Z)$ remains constant over Z. Finally, the mean gray value depends only on the *normalized distance* $|Z|/R$

$$g_m(Z, R) = g_m\left(\frac{|Z|}{R}\right) \tag{11.80}$$

Similar considerations lead to the similarity condition for the equivalent radius. Images of objects with the same ratio Z/R are distinguished by a scale factor only, which has to be given by the object size. Therefore

$$R_{1/2} = R\rho\left(\frac{|Z|}{R}\right) \Leftrightarrow \frac{R_{1/2}}{R} = \rho\left(\frac{|Z|}{R}\right) \tag{11.81}$$

With Eqs. (11.79) and (11.81) the depth estimation is carried out by the following steps:

- **Segmentation.** The image is segmented in order to find the objects and to determine their $1/q$-area and respective mean gray value;
- **Normalized depth.** From the defocus measure g_m the normalized depth $|Z|/R$ is calculated according to the inversion of Eq. (11.80);
- **True radius.** From the $1/q$-equivalent radius $R_{1/q}$ and Eq. (11.81) the true radius R is obtained.
- **Depth estimation.** From the normalized depth $|Z|/R$ and the radius R the depth $|Z|$ can be calculated easily.

The relations between normalized depth, ratio of radii $R_{1/q}/R$ and mean gray value have to be obtained by a calibration procedure. Figure 11.20 shows the result of the calibration used for the depth-from-focus method. The application of the method to particle size and concentration measurements is described in detail in CVA3 [Chapter 29].

Pyramid-based depth-from-focus. As already pointed out, defocus can be measured by analyzing the suppression of high spatial frequencies. This has been used by Scholz et al. [49] and Suhr et al. [50] in order to solve the depth-from-focus problem for a biotechnological application. The application itself is described in detail in CVA3 [Chapter 29]. Here, we focus on the depth-from-focus algorithm.

Because the application deals with the detection of cells in a fluid medium, it concerns objects of similar shape and size. Due to the properties of the cells and the imaging technique used, all cells appear as approximately Gaussian-shaped objects of very similar size, but different brightness. The basic idea of the algorithm is to characterize the blurring of the cells by a feature vector. The feature vector is defined as the squared filter response on each level of the Laplacian pyramid (Section 8.10.3)

$$|L^{(k)}|^2 = \sum_{i=0}^{M-1} \sum_{j=0}^{N-1} (L_{i,j}^{(k)})^2 \tag{11.82}$$

whereby $L^{(k)}$ denotes the kth level of the Laplacian pyramid. The feature vector is then

$$F = (F_0, F_1, ..) = (|L^{(0)}|^2, |L^{(1)}|^2, |L^{(2)}|^2, ... |L^{(n)}|^2) \tag{11.83}$$

The orientation of F is independent of the brightness of the object, therefore the ratios of the components of the feature vector

$$O_{i,j} = \tan \phi_{i,j} = \frac{|L^{(j)}|^2}{|L^{(i)}|^2} \qquad i, j \in [0, 1, ..., n] \qquad \forall i \neq j \tag{11.84}$$

are normalized with respect to the brightness of the object. Each of the directional components $O_{i,j}$ is a measure of the defocus, and is sensitive to a certain wave-number range.

11.4   References

[1] Dhond, U. R. and Aggarwal, J. K., (1989). Structure from stereo—a review. *IEEE Trans. Sys. Man. and Cyb.*, **19**(6).

[2] Wheatstone, C., (1838). Some remarkable phenomena of vision. I. *Philosophical Trans. Royal Society*, **13**:371–395.

[3] Dhond, U. R. and Aggarwal, J. K., (1989). Structure from stereo—a review. *IEEE Trans. Systems, Man, and Cybernetics,* **19**:1489-1510.

[4] Jenkin, M. R. M., Jepson, A. D., and Tsotsos, J. K., (1991). Techniques for disparity measurement. *Computer Vision Graphics and Image Processing: Image Understanding,* **53**:14-30.

[5] Förstner, W., (1992). Image Matching. In *Computer and Robot Vision,* R. M. Haralick and L. G. Shapiro, eds., Vol. 2, Chapter 16. Reading, MA: Addison-Wesley.

[6] Julesz, B., (1971). *Foundations of Cyclopean Perception.* Chicago and London: Chicago University Press.

[7] Marr, D. and Poggio, T., (1979). A computational theory of human stereo vision. *Proc. Royal Society (London) B,* **204**:301-328.

[8] Anderson, B. L. and Nakayama, K., (1994). Toward a general theory of stereopsis: Binocular matching, occluding contours, and fusion. *Psychological Review,* **101**:414-445.

[9] Mallot, H. A., Arndt, P. A., and Bülthoff, H. H., (1996a). A psychophysical and computational analysis of intensity-based stereo. *Biological Cybernetics,* **75**:187-198.

[10] Arndt, P. A., Mallot, H. A., and Bülthoff, H. H., (1995). Human stereovision without localized image-features. *Biological Cybernetics,* **72**:279-293.

[11] Howard, I. P. and Rogers, B. J., (1995). *Bionocular Vision and Stereopsis.* Number 29 in Oxford Psychology Series. New York, Oxford: Oxford University Press.

[12] Blake, A. and Bülthoff, H. H., (1990). Does the brain know the physics of specular reflection? *Nature,* **343**:165-168.

[13] Helmholtz, H. v., (1909-1911). *Handbuch der physiologischen Optik,* 3rd edition. Hamburg: Voss.

[14] Burkhardt, D., Darnhofer-Demar, B., and Fischer, K., (1973). Zum binokularen Entfernungssehen der Insekten. I. Die Struktur des Sehraums von Synsekten. *Zeitschrift für vergleichende Physiologie,* **87**:165-188.

[15] Völpel, B. and Theimer, W. M., (1995). Localization uncertainty in area-based stereo algorithms. *IEEE Trans. Systems, Man, and Cybernetics,* **25**: 1628-1634.

[16] Caprile, B. and Torre, V., (1990). Using vanishing points for camera calibration. *International Journal of Computer Vision,* **4**:127-139.

[17] Solomons, H., (1975). Derivation of the space horopter. *British Jour. Physiological Optics,* **30**:56-90.

[18] Krotkov, E. P., (1989). *Active Computer Vision by Cooperative Focus and Stereo.* Berlin: Springer.

[19] Clark, J. J. and Ferrier, N. J., (1992). Attentive Visual Servoing. In *Active Vision,* A. Blake and A. Yuille, eds. Cambridge, MA: The MIT Press.

[20] Coombs, D. and Brown, C., (1993). Real-time binocular smooth pursuit. *International Journal of Computer Vision,* **11**:147-164.

[21] Pahlavan, K. and Eklundh, J.-O., (1992). A head-eye system—analysis and design. *Computer Vision Graphics and Image Processing: Image Under-*

standing, **56**:41–56.

[22] Seelen, W. v., Bohrer, S., Kopecz, J., and Theimer, W. M., (1995). A neural architecture for visual information processing. *International Journal of Computer Vision*, **16**:229–260.

[23] Murray, D. W., Du, F., McLauchlan, P. F., Reid, I. D., Sharkey, P. M., and Brady, M., (1992). Design of stereo heads. In *Active Vision*, A. Blake and A. Yuille, eds. Cambridge, MA: MIT Press.

[24] Ahuja, N. and Abbott, A. L., (1993). Active Stereo: Integrating disparity, vergence, focus, aperture, and calibration for surface estimation. *IEEE Trans. Pattern Analysis and Machine Intelligence*, **15**:1007–1029.

[25] Mallot, H. A., Roll, A., and Arndt, P. A., (1996b). Disparity-evoked vergence is driven by interocular correlation. *Vision Research*, **36**:2925–2937.

[26] Theimer, W. and Mallot, H. A., (1994). Phase-based binocular vergence control and depth reconstruction using active vision. *Computer Vision Graphics and Image Processing: Image Understanding*, **60**:343–358.

[27] Mallot, H. A., Bülthoff, H. H., Little, J. J., and Bohrer, S., (1991). Inverse perspective mapping simplifies optical flow computation and obstacle detection. *Biological Cybernetics*, **64**:177–185.

[28] Mallot, H. A., Schulze, E., and Storjohann, K., (1989). Neural network strategies for robot navigation. In *Neural Networks from Models to Applications*, L. Personnaz and G. Dreyfus, eds., pp. 560–569. Paris: I.D.S.E.T.

[29] Košecka, J., Christensen, H. I., and Bajcsy, R., (1995). Discrete event modeling of visually guided behaviors. *International Journal of Computer Vision*, **14**:179–191.

[30] Zielke, T., Storjohann, K., Mallot, H. A., and Seelen, W. v., (1990). Adapting computer vision systems to the visual environment: topographic mapping. In *Computer Vision—ECCV 90 (Lecture Notes in Computer Science 427)*, O. Faugeras, ed., INRIA. Berlin: Springer.

[31] Luong, Q.-T., Weber, J., Koller, D., and Malik, J., (1995). An integrated stereo-based approach to automatic vehicle guidance. In *5th International Conference on Computer Vision*, pp. 52–57. Los Alamitos, CA: IEEE Computer Society Press.

[32] Faugeras, O., (1993). *Three-Dimensional Computer Vision. A Geometric Viewpoint*. Cambridge, MA: MIT Press.

[33] Rice, J. A., (1988). *Mathematical statistics and data analysis*. Pacific Grove, California: Wadsworth & Brooks/Cole Advanced Books & Software.

[34] Darell, T. and Wohn, K., (1990). Depth from focus using a pyramid architecture. *Pattern Recognition Letters*, **11**:787 – 796.

[35] Pentland, A. P., (1987). A new sense for depth of field. *IEEE Trans. Pattern Analysis and Machine Intelligence*, **9**.

[36] Ens, J. and Lawrence, P., (1991). A matrix based method for determining depth from focus. In *Proceedings CVPR'91, Lahaina, Hawaii*, pp. 600–606, IEEE. Washington, DC: IEEE Computer Society Press.

[37] Ens, J. and Lawrence, P., (1993). An investigation of methods for determining depth from focus. *IEEE Trans. Pattern Analysis and Machine Intelligence*, **15**(2):97–108.

[38] Bertero, M. and Poggio, R. A., (1988). Ill-posed problems in early vision. *Proc. IEEE*, **76**(8):869–889.

[39] Pentland, A. P., (1985). A new sense for depth of field. In *Proceedings of International Joint Conference on Artificial Intelligence*, pp. 988–994.

[40] Grossman, P., (1987). Depth from focus. *Pattern Recognition Letters*, **5**: 63–69.

[41] Lai, S. H., Fu, C. W., and Chang, S. Y., (1992). A generalized depth estimation algorithm with a single image. *IEEE Trans. Pattern Analysis and Machine Intelligence*, **14**(6):405–411.

[42] Marr, D. and Hildreth, E. C., (1980). Theory of edge detection. *Proc. Royal Soc. London Ser. B*, **207**:187–217.

[43] Hildreth, E. C., (1983). The detection of intensity changes by computer and biological vision systems. *Comput. Vision Graphics Image Processing*, 22:1–27.

[44] Haralick, R. M., (1984). Digital step edges from zero crossings of second directional derivatives. *IEEE Trans. Patt. Anal. Machine Intell.*, **PAMI-6**: 58–68.

[45] Subbarao, M. and Gurumoorthy, N., (1998). Depth recovery from blurred edges. *IEEE Computer Society Conf. Comput. Vision Pattern Recognition*, pp. 498–503.

[46] Subbarao, M., (1997). Direct recovery of depth map I: differential methods. *Proc. IEEE Computer Society Workshop Comput. Vision*, pp. 58–65.

[47] Jähne, B. and Geißler, P., (1994). Depth from focus with One Image. In *Proceedings of the IEEE Conference on Computer Vision and Pattern Recognition 1994, Seattle*.

[48] Jähne, B. and Geißler, P., (1994). An imaging optical technique for bubble measurements. In *Sea Surface Sound '94 - Proceedings of the Third International Meeting on Natural Physical Related to Sea Surface Sound*, M. J. Buckingham and J. R. Potter, eds., pp. 290–303. Lake Arrowhead, California: World Scientific Publishing Co. Pte. Ltd., Singapore.

[49] Scholz, T., Jähne, B., Suhr, H., Wehnert, G., Geißler, P., and Schneider, K., (1994). A new depth-from-focus technique for in situ determination of cell concentration in bioreactors. In *Proceedings of the 16th DAGM Symposium, Wien*, pp. 145–154.

[50] Suhr, H., Bittner, C., Geißler, P., Jähne, B., Schneider, K., Scheper, T., Scholz, T., and Wehnert, G., (1995). In situ microscopy for on-line characterization of cell populations in bioreactors, including cell concentration measurements by depth from focus. *Biotechnology and Bioengineering*, 47:106–116.

12 Design of Nonlinear Diffusion Filters

Joachim Weickert

Lehrstuhl für Bildverarbeitung, Fakultät für Mathematik und Informatik
Universität Mannheim, Germany

12.1 Introduction

Starting with Perona and Malik's work in 1987 [1, 2], *nonlinear diffusion* filtering has become a popular tool in medical imaging [3, 4, 5, 6, 7, 8, 9] as well as many other areas; it has been used for improved subsampling algorithms [10], postprocessing of fluctuating numerical data [11], blind image restoration [12], computer-aided quality control [13, 14], segmentation of textures [15, 16] and remotely sensed data [17, 18]. In the meantime it has also entered commercial software packages such as the medical visualization tool Analyze[1].

Nonlinear diffusion filters regard the original image as the initial state of a diffusion process that adapts itself to the evolving image. Different adaptation strategies provide different ways to include *a priori*

---

[1]Analyze is a registered trademark of Mayo Medical Ventures, 200 First Street SW, Rochester, MN 55905.

knowledge into the evolution. The embedding of the original image into a family of gradually smoother, simplified versions of it allows nonlinear diffusion filtering to be considered as a *scale-space* technique. The fact that the nonlinear adaptation may also enhance interesting structures such as edges relates them to image enhancement and image-restoration methods.

The goal of the present chapter is to give an introduction to some selected key aspects of nonlinear diffusion filtering. We shall discuss some main ideas and study how they can be realized in practice by choosing adequate filter models and suitable parameters. Questions of this type are often posed by practitioners, but are hardly addressed in the literature. This chapter is not intended as a state-of-the art review of the relevant literature in this area because descriptions in this direction are already available elsewhere [19, 20]. For a unifying theoretical framework and algorithmic details we refer the reader to CVA2 [Chapter 15].

The chapter is organized as follows. Section 12.2 presents different nonlinear diffusion models. They comprise isotropic filters with a scalar-valued diffusivity as well as anisotropic ones with a diffusion matrix (diffusion tensor). The practically important question of how to select appropriate filter parameters is addressed in Section 12.3. In Section 12.4 extensions to higher-dimensional data sets and to multichannel images are sketched. Finally, Section 12.5 shows that variational image restoration can be regarded as an approximation to diffusion filtering. The chapter is concluded with a summary in Section 12.6.

12.2 Filter design

12.2.1 The physics behind diffusion

Most people have an intuitive impression of diffusion as a physical process that equilibrates concentration differences without creating or destroying mass. This physical observation can be easily cast in a mathematical formulation. The equilibration property is expressed by *Fick's law*

$$j = -D \, \nabla u \tag{12.1}$$

This equation states that a concentration gradient ∇u causes a flux j that aims to compensate for this gradient. The relation between ∇u and j is described by the *diffusion tensor* D, a positive-definite symmetric matrix. The case where j and ∇u are parallel is called *isotropic*. Then we may replace the diffusion tensor by a positive scalar-valued *diffusivity D*. In the general *anisotropic* case, j and ∇u are not parallel.

The observation that diffusion only transports mass without destroying it or creating new mass is expressed by the *continuity equation*

$$\partial_t u = -\operatorname{div} \boldsymbol{j} \tag{12.2}$$

where t denotes the time. If we plug in Fick's law, Eq. (12.1), into the continuity equation, we end up with the *diffusion equation*

$$\partial_t u = \operatorname{div}(\boldsymbol{D} \nabla u) \tag{12.3}$$

This equation appears in many physical *transport processes* [21]. In the context of heat transfer it is called *heat equation.*

In image processing we may identify the concentration with the gray value at a certain location. If the diffusion tensor is constant over the whole image domain, one speaks of *homogeneous diffusion*, and a space-dependent filtering is called *inhomogeneous*. Often the diffusion tensor is a function of the differential structure of the evolving image itself. Such a feedback leads to *nonlinear diffusion filters.*

Sometimes the computer vision literature deviates from the preceding notations: It can happen that homogeneous filtering is named isotropic, and inhomogeneous blurring is named anisotropic, even if it uses a scalar-valued diffusivity instead of a diffusion tensor.

12.2.2 Limitations of linear diffusion filtering

Let us consider a 2-D (scalar-valued) image that is given by a continuous bounded mapping $g : \mathbb{R}^2 \to \mathbb{R}$. One of the most widely used methods for smoothing g is to regard it as the initial state of a homogeneous linear diffusion process

$$\partial_t u = \partial_{xx} u + \partial_{yy} u \tag{12.4}$$
$$u(\boldsymbol{x}, 0) = g(\boldsymbol{x}) \tag{12.5}$$

From the literature on partial differential equations it is well known that its solution is given by the convolution integral

$$u(\boldsymbol{x}, t) = \begin{cases} g(\boldsymbol{x}) & (t = 0) \\ (K_{\sqrt{2t}} * g)(\boldsymbol{x}) & (t > 0) \end{cases} \tag{12.6}$$

where K_σ denotes a Gaussian with standard deviation σ

$$K_\sigma(\boldsymbol{x}) := \frac{1}{2\pi\sigma^2} \cdot \exp\left(-\frac{|\boldsymbol{x}|^2}{2\sigma^2}\right) \tag{12.7}$$

Linear diffusion filtering is the oldest and best-studied example of a scale-space. Usually, Witkin's 1983 work is regarded as the first reference to the linear scale-space idea [22], but linear scale-space had already been axiomatically derived by Iijima in 1962 [23, 24]. A detailed treatment of linear scale-space theory can be found in [25, 26, 27].

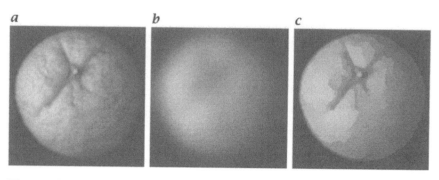

Figure 12.1: *a Orange,* 256 × 256 *pixels; b linear diffusion, t = 100; c Perona-Malik diffusion, λ = 3, t = 100.*

Figure 12.1a, b shows an example where an image depicting an orange is filtered by linear diffusion. In spite of its excellent smoothing properties, two disadvantages of linear diffusion filtering become apparent:

(a) Semantically useful information is eliminated in the same way as noise. Because linear diffusion filtering is designed to be uncommitted, one cannot incorporate image-driven information in order to bias the scale-space evolution towards a desired task, for instance, edge detection; and

(b) Linear diffusion filtering dislocates structures when moving from finer to coarser scales. Hence, structures that are identified at a coarse scale have to be traced back to the original image in order to get their correct location [22, 28]. In practice, this may be difficult to handle and give rise to instabilities.

12.2.3 Isotropic nonlinear diffusion

Basic Idea. In order to avoid the blurring and localization problems of linear diffusion filtering, Perona and Malik proposed a nonlinear diffusion method [1, 2]. Their nonuniform process (which they called anisotropic[2]) reduces the diffusivity at those locations that have a larger likelihood to be edges, that is, which have larger gradients (see Fig. 12.1c).

Let Ω denote a rectangular image domain and consider an image $g(\boldsymbol{x}) : \Omega \to \mathbb{R}$. Perona and Malik obtain a filtered image $u(\boldsymbol{x}, t)$ as the solution of the diffusion equation[3]

$$\partial_t u = \operatorname{div}(D(|\nabla u|^2)\,\nabla u) \qquad \text{on} \qquad \Omega \times (0, \infty) \qquad (12.8)$$

---

[2]In our terminology, the Perona–Malik filter is regarded as an isotropic model because it reveals a scalar-valued diffusivity and not a diffusion tensor.

[3]For smoothness reasons we write $|\nabla u|^2$ instead of $|\nabla u|$.

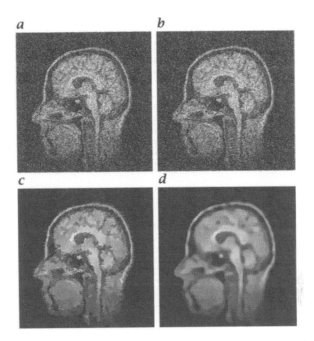

Figure 12.2: *a MR image degraded by additive Gaussian noise with zero mean, 256 × 256 pixels, signal-to-noise ratio: 1; **b** Perona–Malik diffusion, λ = 4, t = 25; **c** regularized isotropic nonlinear diffusion, λ = 4, σ = 2, t = 25; **d** edge enhancing anisotropic diffusion, λ = 4, σ = 2, t = 25.*

with the original image as initial condition

$$u(\boldsymbol{x}, 0) = g(\boldsymbol{x}) \qquad \text{on} \qquad \Omega \qquad (12.9)$$

and reflecting boundary conditions (∂_n denotes the derivative normal to the image boundary $\partial\Omega$)

$$\partial_n u = 0 \qquad \text{on} \qquad \partial\Omega \times (0, \infty) \qquad (12.10)$$

Among the *diffusivities* they propose is

$$D(|\nabla u|^2) = \frac{1}{1 + |\nabla u|^2/\lambda^2} \qquad (\lambda > 0) \qquad (12.11)$$

The experiments of Perona and Malik were visually impressive in that edges remained stable over a very long time. Edge detection based on this process clearly outperformed the linear Canny edge detector. This is due to the fact that diffusion and edge detection interact in one single process instead of being treated as two independent processes that are to be applied subsequently. However, the Perona-Malik approach reveals some problems that we shall discuss next.

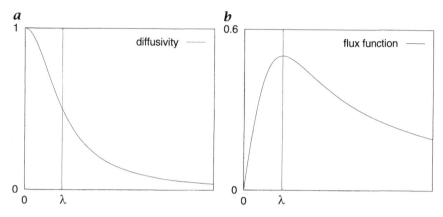

Figure 12.3: *a Diffusivity $D(s^2) = 1/(1 + s^2/\lambda^2)$; b Flux function $\Phi(s) = s/(1 + s^2/\lambda^2)$. From Weickert [19].*

Forward-backward diffusion. To study the theoretical behavior of the Perona-Malik filter, let us for simplicity of notation restrict ourselves to the 1-D case.

For the diffusivity Equation (12.11) it follows that the *flux function*[4] $\Phi(s) := sD(s^2)$ satisfies $\Phi'(s) \geq 0$ for $|s| \leq \lambda$, and $\Phi'(s) < 0$ for $|s| > \lambda$ (see Fig. 12.3). As Eq. (12.8) can be rewritten as

$$\partial_t u = \partial_x(\Phi(\partial_x u)) = \Phi'(\partial_x u)\, \partial_{xx} u \qquad (12.12)$$

we observe that (in spite of its nonnegative diffusivity) the Perona-Malik model resembles a *forward diffusion*

$$\partial_t u = \partial_{xx} u \qquad (12.13)$$

for $|\partial_x u| \leq \lambda$, and the *backward diffusion*

$$\partial_t u = -\partial_{xx} u \qquad (12.14)$$

for $|\partial_x u| > \lambda$. Hence, λ plays the role of a *contrast parameter* separating forward (low contrast) from backward (high contrast) diffusion areas. In the same way as the forward diffusion smoothes contrasts, the backward diffusion enhances them. Thus, the Perona–Malik model may enhance gradients whose absolute value is larger than λ; see Perona and Malik [2] for more details on *edge enhancement*.

The *forward-backward diffusion* behavior is explicitly intended in the Perona-Malik method, as it gives the desirable result of blurring small fluctuations and sharpening edges. Figure 12.1c shows an example. The edge-enhancing potential of the Perona-Malik approach is clearly visible at the contours of the orange.

---

[4]The mathematical flux function Ψ and the physical flux j differ by their sign.

An obvious practical problem of the Perona-Malik filter is that it misinterprets large gradients due to noise as semantically important edges that it should preserve. It is thus unsuited for denoising severely degraded images. This problem is illustrated in Fig. 12.2b.

Besides this practical problem, there is also a theoretical one. A reasonable requirement for an evolution process in image analysis is that of *well-posedness*, that is, the problem should have a unique solution that depends continuously on the initial image.

Unfortunately, forward-backward diffusion equations of Perona-Malik type reveal *ill-posedness* aspects; although there are some conjectures [29, 30] that they might have generalized solutions[5], until now no one else has been to prove their existence. If they exist, there is evidence that their steady states do not depend continuously on the original image [31].

However, the practical behavior of finite difference approximations is much better than one would expect from the forementioned theory: One can easily calculate a discrete solution for all times, and this solution converges to a flat image for $t \to \infty$. The mainly observable instability is the so-called *staircasing effect*, where a sigmoid edge evolves into piecewise-linear segments that are separated by jumps. A discrete explanation for this so-called *Perona-Malik paradox* [30] has been given in Weickert and Benhamouda [32]. They proved that a standard spatial finite difference discretization is sufficient to turn the Perona-Malik process into a well-posed system of nonlinear ordinary differential equations. If a simple explicit time discretization is applied, then the resulting scheme is *monotonicity preserving* in the 1-D case [33], that is, a monotone function remains monotone after filtering. Thus, oscillations cannot appear and artifacts are restricted to staircasing. In this sense, a naive implementation of the Perona-Malik filter often works reasonably well because of the regularizing[6] effect of the discretization. Different discretizations, however, may lead to strongly differing results. Thus, it seems to be more natural to introduce the regularization directly into the continuous Perona-Malik equation in order to become more independent of the numerical implementation [34, 35]. This shall be done next.

Regularized isotropic nonlinear diffusion. In 1992, Catté, Lions, Morel and Coll [34] proposed a regularization of the Perona-Malik process that has a unique solution, and which is even infinitely times differentiable. Besides this theoretical advantage, their modification is also more robust under noise.

---

[5]A generalized solution satisfies a generalized (integral) formulation of the diffusion equation. In particular, a generalized solution does not have to be twice differentiable in x.

[6]A regularization of an ill-posed problem is a well-posed approximation to it.

They propose to regularize the gradient within the diffusivity D by convolving it with a Gaussian K_σ with standard deviation $\sigma > 0$. Thus, their filter uses

$$\partial_t u = \text{div}(D(|\nabla u_\sigma|^2)\, \nabla u) \qquad (12.15)$$

where $u_\sigma := K_\sigma * u$. Experiments showed that this regularization leads to filters that can still *enhance* edges [33], produce less *staircasing* [35], and that are less sensitive to the discretization [36].

The regularizing effect of the modification by Catté et al. [34] is due to the fact that ∇u_σ remains bounded. Moreover, the convolution with a Gaussian K_σ makes the filter insensitive to structures at scales smaller than σ. Therefore, when regarding Eq. (12.15) as an image-restoration equation, it reveals (besides the contrast parameter λ) an additional *noise scale* σ. This avoids a shortcoming of the genuine Perona-Malik process that misinterprets strong oscillations due to noise as edges that should be preserved or even enhanced. This is illustrated in Fig. 12.2c. Noise within a region can be eliminated very well, but at edges, $|\nabla u_\sigma|$ is large and the diffusion is inhibited. Therefore, this regularization is not optimal in the vicinity of noisy edges.

To overcome this problem, a desirable method should prefer diffusion along edges to diffusion perpendicular to them. This cannot be done with a scalar-valued diffusivity, one has to use a diffusion matrix (diffusion tensor) instead. This leads us to anisotropic diffusion filters.

12.2.4   Edge-enhancing anisotropic diffusion

An anisotropic diffusion filter for edge-enhancing diffusion not only takes into account the contrast of an edge, but also its direction.

This can be achieved by constructing the orthonormal system of eigenvectors v_1, v_2 of the diffusion tensor D such that $v_1 \parallel \nabla u_\sigma$ and $v_2 \perp \nabla u_\sigma$. In order to prefer smoothing along the edge to smoothing across it, one can choose the corresponding eigenvalues λ_1 and λ_2 as [11]

$$\lambda_1 \quad := \quad D(|\nabla u_\sigma|^2) \qquad (12.16)$$
$$\lambda_2 \quad := \quad 1 \qquad (12.17)$$

In general, ∇u is not parallel to one of the eigenvectors of D as long as $\sigma > 0$. Hence, the behavior of this model is really anisotropic. If we let the regularization parameter σ tend to 0, we end up with the isotropic Perona–Malik process.

There is an interesting relation between the regularized isotropic diffusion in Eq. (12.15) and edge-enhancing anisotropic diffusion. While the former uses a scalar-valued diffusivity

$$D(|\nabla u_\sigma|^2) = D(\nabla u_\sigma^T \nabla u_\sigma) \qquad (12.18)$$

one can formally write the diffusion tensor of edge-enhancing diffusion as

$$D(\nabla u_\sigma) = D(\nabla u_\sigma \nabla u_\sigma^T) \qquad (12.19)$$

This can be seen as follows. If D can be represented as a globally convergent power series

$$D(s) = \sum_{k=0}^{\infty} \alpha_k s^k \qquad (12.20)$$

we can regard $D(\nabla u_\sigma \nabla u_\sigma^T)$ as the matrix-valued power series

$$D(\nabla u_\sigma \nabla u_\sigma^T) = \sum_{k=0}^{\infty} \alpha_k (\nabla u_\sigma \nabla u_\sigma^T)^k \qquad (12.21)$$

The matrix $(\nabla u_\sigma \nabla u_\sigma^T)^k$ has eigenvectors ∇u_σ and $\nabla u_\sigma^\perp$ with corresponding eigenvalues $|\nabla u_\sigma|^{2k}$ and 0. From this it follows that D has the eigenvectors ∇u_σ and $\nabla u_\sigma^\perp$ with corresponding eigenvalues $D(|\nabla u_\sigma|^2)$ and $D(0) = 1$.

   Figure 12.2d depicts a result of edge-enhancing anisotropic diffusion. We observe that it is capable of reducing noise at edges.

12.2.5 Coherence-enhancing anisotropic diffusion

A second motivation for introducing anisotropy into diffusion processes arises from the wish to process 1-D features such as line-like structures. We shall now investigate a modification of a model by Cottet and Germain [37], which is specifically designed for the enhancement of coherent flow-like structures [14].

   For this purpose one needs more sophisticated structure descriptors than ∇u_σ. A good descriptor for local orientation is the *structure tensor (second-moment matrix, scatter matrix, interest operator)* [38, 39] (see Section 9.8)

$$J_\rho(\nabla u_\sigma) := K_\rho * (\nabla u_\sigma \nabla u_\sigma^T) \qquad (12.22)$$

and its equivalent approaches [40, 41]. The componentwise convolution with the Gaussian K_ρ averages orientation information over an *integration scale* ρ. Because J_ρ is a symmetric positive-semidefinite matrix, there exists an orthonormal basis of eigenvectors v_1 and v_2 with corresponding eigenvalues $\mu_1 \geq \mu_2 \geq 0$. The eigenvalues measure the average contrast (gray-value variation) in the eigendirections within a scale ρ. Therefore, v_1 is the orientation with the highest gray-value fluctuations, and v_2 gives the preferred local orientation, the *coherence direction*. The expression $(\mu_1 - \mu_2)^2$ is a measure of the local coherence. If one wants to enhance coherent structures, one should smooth

a   b

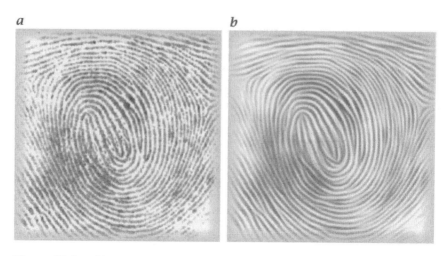

Figure 12.4: *a Fingerprint, 256×256 pixels; b coherence-enhancing anisotropic diffusion c = 1, σ = 0.5, ρ = 4, t = 20. From Weickert [14].*

mainly along the coherence direction v_2 with a diffusivity λ_2 that increases with respect to the coherence $(\mu_1 - \mu_2)^2$. This can be accomplished by designing D such that it possesses the same eigenvectors v_1, v_2 as J_ρ and choosing its corresponding eigenvalues as

$$\lambda_1 := \alpha \tag{12.23}$$

$$\lambda_2 := \begin{cases} \alpha & \text{if } \mu_1 = \mu_2, \\ \alpha + (1 - \alpha) \exp\left(\dfrac{-c}{(\mu_1 - \mu_2)^2}\right) & \text{else} \end{cases} \tag{12.24}$$

where $c > 0$. The small positive parameter $\alpha \in (0, 1)$ is mainly introduced for theoretical reasons; see CVA2 [Chapter 15] for more details.

Figure 12.4 shows the *restoration* properties of coherence-enhancing anisotropic diffusion when being applied to a fingerprint image. The diffusion filter encourages smoothing along the coherence orientation v_2 and is therefore well suited for closing interrupted lines. Due to its reduced diffusivity at noncoherent structures, the locations of the semantically important singularities in the fingerprint remain the same.

12.3 Parameter selection

Nonlinear diffusion filtering contains several parameters that have to be specified in practical situations. The goal of this section is to clarify their meaning and to present some empirical guidelines for their selection.

Because the time t is an inherent parameter in each continuous diffusion process, it has nothing to do with its discretization. The common practice in image analysis, however, is to assign unit length to a pixel. In this case, a different discretization has to be regarded as a rescaling of the image domain. The scaling behavior of diffusion processes implies that a spatial rescaling that replaces x by βx, has to replace t by $\beta^2 t$. This means, for instance, that a subsampling in each image direction by a factor 2 reduces the stopping time from t to $t/4$. Moreover, typical finite-difference implementations reveal a computational effort that is proportional to the pixel number. This gives another speed-up by a factor 4, such that the whole calculation becomes 16 times faster.

There remains another question to be addressed: what is a suitable *stopping time* t of the process? It should be observed that this question only appears when regarding the diffusion process as a *restoration method*. Considering it as a *scale-space* means that one is interested in the entire evolution. In a linear scale-space representation based on the diffusion process $\partial_t u = \Delta u$, the time t corresponds to a convolution with a Gaussian of standard deviation $\sigma = \sqrt{2t}$. Thus, specifying a spatial smoothing radius σ immediately determines the stopping time t.

In the nonlinear diffusion case, the smoothing is nonuniform and the time t is not directly related to a spatial scale. Other intuitive measures, such as counting the number of extrema, are also problematic for diffusion filters, as it is well known that for linear and nonlinear diffusion filters in dimensions ≥ 2, the number of local extrema does not necessarily decrease monotonically, that is, creation of extrema is not an exception but an event that happens generically [42].

However, there are other possibilities to define an average measure for the simplicity or globality of the representation. For instance, in [20] it is shown that the variance $v(t)$ of the evolving image $u(x,t)$ decreases monotonically from $v(0)$ to $v(\infty) = 0$. Prescribing a decay by a certain percentage provides us with an *a posteriori* criterion for the stopping time of the nonlinear diffusion process. Moreover, this strategy frees the users from any recalculations of the stopping time, if the image is resampled. Last but not least, the variance can also be used to synchronize different nonlinear diffusion scale-spaces in order to ease the comparison of results. Practical applications to the restoration of medical images have demonstrated the usefulness and simplicity of this criterion [43, 44].

For the Perona-Malik filter, it is evident that the "optimal" value for the *contrast parameter* λ has to depend on the problem. One possibility to determine a good practical value for λ is to calculate a cumulate histogram for $|\nabla g|^2$ and to set λ to a certain quantile of this histogram. Perona and Malik use the 90% quantile, that is, 90% of all gradients are smaller than λ. Often one can get better results by staying more in the backward diffusion region, for example, by choosing a 50 % quantile. The smaller the quantile, however, the slower the diffusion. Other proposals for choosing λ use statistical properties of a training set of regions that are considered as flat [45], or estimate it by means of the local image geometry [7].

Regularized isotropic nonlinear diffusion and edge-enhancing anisotropic diffusion use another parameter besides λ, namely the *noise scale* σ. Because these filters are insensitive to scales smaller than σ, one should adapt σ to the noise. Useful values range from less than one pixel size for "noiseless" images to several pixels for more degraded images.

Coherence-enhancing anisotropic diffusion uses three other parameters: α, c, and ρ.

We have already seen that the regularization parameter α was introduced to ensure a small amount of isotropic diffusion. This parameter is mainly important for theoretical reasons. In practice, it can be fixed to a small value (e.g., 0.001), and no adaptation to the actual image material is required.

The parameter c is a threshold parameter playing a role similar to that of the contrast parameter λ in the other processes. Structures with coherence measures $(\mu_1 - \mu_2)^2 \ll c$ are regarded as almost isotropic, and the diffusion along the coherence direction v_2 tends to α. For $(\mu_1 - \mu_2)^2 \gg c$, the diffusion along the coherence direction v_2 tends to its maximal value, which is limited by 1. Therefore, c can be estimated by calculating a cumulate $(\mu_1 - \mu_2)^2$ histogram for g, and by setting c to a certain quantile. If one estimates that 95 % of the image locations have strongly preferred 1-D structures, one may set c to the 95 % quantile of the process.

The *integration scale* ρ of the structure tensor should reflect the texture scale of the problem. For instance, for a fingerprint image, it should not be smaller than the distance between two neighboring lines. Because overestimations are by far less critical than underestimations [20], it is often not very difficult to find parameter estimates that work well over the whole image domain. For coherence-enhancing diffusion, it is important that the noise scale σ is significantly smaller than the integration scale ρ; too large values for σ results in a cancellation of opposite gradient, and the orientation information in the texture is destroyed.

The suggestions in this section are intended as first guidelines. It is often reported that people who start using nonlinear diffusion filters quickly develop a good intuition for selecting appropriate parameters.

12.4 Extensions

12.4.1 Higher dimensions

It is easily seen that many of the previous results can be generalized to higher dimensions. This may be useful when considering, for example, CT or MR image sequences arising from medical applications or when applying diffusion filters to the postprocessing of fluctuating higher-dimensional numerical data. Spatially regularized 3-D nonlinear diffusion filters have been investigated by Gerig et al. [4] in the isotropic case, and by Rambaux and Garçon [46] in the edge-enhancing anisotropic case. Experiments with 3-D coherence-enhancing diffusion are presented in Weickert [47].

12.4.2 Vector-valued models

Vector-valued images can arise either from devices measuring multiple physical properties or from a feature analysis of one single image. Examples for the first category are color images, multispectral Landsat exposures and multispin echo MR images, whereas representatives of the second class are given by statistical moments or the so-called *jet space* that is defined by the image itself combined with its partial derivatives up to a fixed order. Feature vectors play an important role for tasks such as texture segmentation.

The simplest idea of how to apply diffusion filtering to *multichannel images* would be to diffuse all channels separately and independently from each other. This leads to the undesirable effect that edges may be formed at different locations for each channel. In order to avoid this, one should use a common diffusivity that combines information from all channels. *Nonlinear isotropic vector-valued diffusion models* were studied by Gerig et al. [4] and Whitaker [15] in the context of medical imagery. They use filters of type

$$\partial_t u_i = \text{div}\left(D\left(\sum_{j=1}^{m} |\nabla u_{j,\sigma}|^2 \right) \nabla u_i \right) \qquad (i = 1, ..., m) \qquad (12.25)$$

where the vector $[u_1(x,t), \ldots, u_m(x,t)]^T$ describes the multichannel image. It is assumed that all channels are normalized such that they use a similar intensity range.

A corresponding *vector-valued edge-enhancing anisotropic diffusion* Process is given by Weickert [48]

$$\partial_t u_i = \text{div}\left(D\left(\sum_{j=1}^{m} \nabla u_{j,\sigma} \nabla u_{j,\sigma}^T \right) \nabla u_i \right) \qquad (i = 1, ..., m) \qquad (12.26)$$

Figure 12.5: *a Forest scene,* 226×323 *pixels; b regularized isotropic nonlinear diffusion* $\sigma = 2$, $\lambda = 10$, $t = 25$; *c coherence-enhancing anisotropic diffusion* $c = 1$, $\sigma = 0.5$, $\rho = 5$, $t = 10$. *From Weickert [49].*

Vector-valued coherence-enhancing diffusion uses a common structure tensor that results from the sum of the structure tensors in all channels [49]

$$\partial_t u_i = \text{div}\left(D\left(\sum_{j=1}^{m} J_\rho(\nabla u_{j,\sigma}) \right) \nabla u_i \right) \qquad (i = 1, ..., m) \qquad (12.27)$$

Figure 12.5 illustrates the effect of Eqs. (12.25) and (12.27) on a color image.

12.5 Relations to variational image restoration

Besides nonlinear diffusion filters, variational approaches also are popular techniques for image restoration. Interestingly, there is a close connection between these two paradigms.

Many variational methods calculate a restoration of some degraded image g as the minimizer of an energy functional

$$E_f(u) := \int_\Omega \left((u-g)^2 + \alpha T(|\nabla u|^2) \right) dx\, dy$$

where the potential T is an increasing function that should be convex in order to guarantee well-posedness. In Chapter 13 Schnörr gives a detailed analysis of approaches of this type.

The first summand encourages similarity between the restored image and the original one, while the second summand rewards smooth-

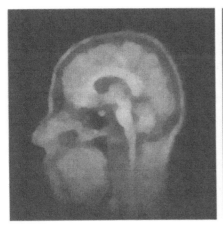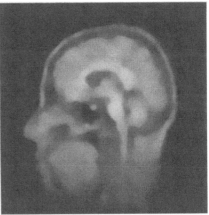

Figure 12.6: **a** *Denoising of Figure 12.2a with the variational approach Eq. (12.28),* $\lambda = 4$, $\alpha = 25$; **b** *the same experiment with the nonlinear diffusion filter Equation (12.29),* $\lambda = 4$, $t = 25$.

ness. The smoothness weight $\alpha > 0$ is called *regularization parameter*[7]. From variational calculus it follows that the minimizer of $E_f(u)$ satisfies the so-called Euler equation

$$\frac{u - g}{\alpha} = \text{div}(T'(|\nabla u|^2)\nabla u) \qquad (12.28)$$

This can be regarded as an approximation to the diffusion filter

$$\partial_t u = \text{div}(T'(|\nabla u|^2)\nabla u) \qquad (12.29)$$

with initial image g and stopping time α. This similarity is illustrated in Fig. 12.6 where the potential

$$T(|\nabla u|^2) = \lambda\sqrt{1 + |\nabla u|^2/\lambda^2} \qquad (12.30)$$

has been used. The corresponding diffusivity is given by

$$D(|\nabla u|^2) = T'(|\nabla u|^2) = \frac{1}{\sqrt{1 + |\nabla u|^2/\lambda^2}} \qquad (12.31)$$

From Fig. 12.6 we observe that the diffusion filter Equation (12.29) leads to slightly smoother results than the variational approach Equation (12.28). However, in both cases, edge-enhancement effects such as in Fig. 12.2d cannot be seen.

It should be noted that convex potentials create diffusivities $T'(|\nabla u|^2)$ that correspond to monotonically increasing flux functions. Hence,

---

[7]The parameter λ_h^2 in Chapter 13 plays a role similar to that of the regularization parameter α.

these approaches do not allow edge enhancement. In this sense they differ from the regularized forward-backward diffusion processes that we have studied before. However, they give valuable insights into the close relations between diffusion filtering and variational image restoration. More details about theoretical analogies can be found in [50], and numerical analogies are derived in [51].

12.6 Summary

In this chapter we have investigated several models for nonlinear diffusion filtering that serve as examples of how one can incorporate *a priori* knowledge in a scale-space evolution. These filters may also be regarded as enhancement methods for features such as edges or flow-like structures. They can be extended in a natural way to higher-dimensional image data as well as to multichannel images. We have presented guidelines for parameter selection, and we investigated a connection between diffusion filtering and variational image restoration.

This chapter is intended as an introduction to the topic. The area is very vivid, and much research is in progress with respect to theoretical foundations, highly efficient algorithms, relations between nonlinear diffusion and other image-processing methods such as curve evolutions, morphology, and snakes. For further studies of this and related areas, the reader is referred to Weickert [20], Caselles et al. [52], ter Haar Romeny [53], ter Haar Romeny et al. [54] and the references therein.

Acknowledgment

The forest image has been kindly provided by Dr. Martin Reißel.

12.7 References

[1] Perona, P. and Malik, J., (1987). Scale space and edge detection using anisotropic diffusion. In *Proc. IEEE Comp. Soc. Workshop on Computer Vision, Miami Beach, Nov. 30 – Dec. 2, 1987*, pp. 16–22. Washington DC: IEEE Computer Society Press.

[2] Perona, P. and Malik, J., (1990). Scale space and edge detection using anisotropic diffusion. *IEEE Trans. Pattern Anal. Mach. Intell.*, **12**:629–639.

[3] Bajla, I., Marušiak, M., and Šrámek, M., (1993). Anisotropic filtering of MRI data based upon image gradient histogram. In *Computer analysis of images and patterns*, D. Chetverikov and W. Kropatsch, eds., Vol. 719 of *Lecture Notes in Comp. Science*, pp. 90–97. Berlin: Springer.

[4] Gerig, G., Kübler, O., Kikinis, R., and Jolesz, F., (1992). Nonlinear anisotropic filtering of MRI data. *IEEE Trans. Medical Imaging*, **11**:221–232.

[5] Lamberti, C., Sitta, M., and Sgallari, F., (1992). Improvements to the anisotropic diffusion model for 2-D echo image processing. In *Proc. Annual Int. Conf. of the IEEE Engineering in Medicine and Biology Society*, Vol. 14, pp. 1872–1873.

[6] Loew, M., Rosenman, J., and Chen, J., (1994). A clinical tool for enhancement of portal images. In *Image processing, SPIE*, M. Loew, ed., Vol. 2167, pp. 543–550.

[7] Luo, D.-S., King, M., and Glick, S., (1994). Local geometry variable conductance diffusion for post-reconstruction filtering. *IEEE Trans. Nuclear Sci.*, **41**:2800–2806.

[8] Sijbers, J., Scheunders, P., Verhoye, M., Van der Linden, A., Van Dyck, D., and Raman, E., (1997). Watershed-based segmentation of 3D MR data for volume quantization. *Magnetic Resonance Imaging*, **15**:679–688.

[9] Steen, E. and Olstad, B., (1994). Scale-space and boundary detection in ultrasonic imaging using nonlinear signal-adaptive anisotropic diffusion. In *Image Processing, SPIE*, M. Loew, ed., Vol. 2167, pp. 116–127.

[10] Ford, G., Estes, R., and Chen, H., (1992). Scale-space analysis for image sampling and interpolation. In *ICASSP-92, Proc. IEEE Int. Conf. Acoustics, Speech and Signal Processing, San Francisco, March 23-26, 1992*, Vol. 3, pp. 165–168.

[11] Weickert, J., (1996). Theoretical foundations of anisotropic diffusion in image processing. In *Theoretical Foundations of Computer Vision, Computing Suppl. 11*, W. Kropatsch, R. Klette, and F. Solina, eds., pp. 221–236. Wien: Springer.

[12] You, Y.-L. and Kaveh, M., (1996). Anisotropic blind image restoration. In *Proc. IEEE Int. Conf. Image Processing, ICIP-96, Lausanne, Sept. 16-19, 1996*, Vol. 2, pp. 461–464.

[13] Weickert, J., (1994). Anisotropic diffusion filters for image processing based quality control. In *Proc. Seventh European Conf. on Mathematics in Industry*, A. Fasano and M. Primicerio, eds., pp. 355–362. Stuttgart: Teubner.

[14] Weickert, J., (1995). Multiscale texture enhancement. In *Computer Analysis of Images and Patterns*, V. Hlaváč and R. Šára, eds., Vol. 970 of *Lecture Notes in Comp. Science*, pp. 230–237. Berlin: Springer.

[15] Whitaker, R., (1993). Geometry limited diffusion in the characterization of geometric patches in images. *CVGIP: Image Understanding*, **57**:111–120.

[16] Whitaker, R. and Gerig, G., (1994). Vector-valued diffusion. In *Geometry-Driven Diffusion in Computer Vision*, B. ter Haar Romeny, ed., pp. 93–134. Dordrecht: Kluwer.

[17] Acton, S., Bovik, A., and Crawford, M., (1994). Anisotropic diffusion pyramids for image segmentation. In *IEEE Int. Conf. Image Processing, Austin, Nov. 13-16, 1994*, Vol. 3, pp. 478–482. Los Alamitos: IEEE Computer Society Press.

[18] Acton, S. and Crawford, M., (1992). A mean field solution to anisotropic edge detection of remotely sensed data. In *Proc. 12th Int. Geoscience and Remote Sensing Symposium, Houston, May 26–29, 1992*, Vol. 2, pp. 845–847.

[19] Weickert, J., (1997). A review of nonlinear diffusion filtering. In *Scale-Space Theory in Computer Vision*, B. ter Haar Romeny, L. Florack, J. Koenderink, and M. Viergever, eds., Vol. 1252 of *Lecture Notes in Computer Science*, pp. 3–28. Berlin: Springer.

[20] Weickert, J., (1998). *Anisotropic Diffusion in Image Processing.* Stuttgart: Teubner-Verlag.

[21] Crank, J., (1975). *The Mathematics of Diffusion.* 2nd edition. Oxford: Oxford University Press.

[22] Witkin, A., (1983). Scale-space filtering. In *Proc. Eight Int. Joint Conf. on Artificial Intelligence, IJCAI '83, Karlsruhe, Aug. 8–12, 1983*, Vol. 2, pp. 1019–1022.

[23] Iijima, T., (1962). Basic theory on normalization of pattern (in case of typical one-dimensional pattern). *Bulletin of the Electrotechnical Laboratory (in Japanese)*, **26**:368–388.

[24] Weickert, J., Ishikawa, S., and Imiya, A., (1997). On the history of Gaussian scale-space axiomatics. In *Gaussian Scale-Space Theory*, J. Sporring, M. Nielsen, L. Florack, and P. Johansen, eds., pp. 45–59. Dordrecht: Kluwer.

[25] Florack, L., (1997). *The Structure of Scalar Images.* Dordrecht: Kluwer.

[26] Lindeberg, T., (1994). *Scale-Space Theory in Computer Vision.* Boston: Kluwer.

[27] Sporring, J., Nielsen, M., Florack, L., and Johansen, P. (eds.), (1997). *Gaussian Scale-Space Theory.* Dordrecht: Kluwer.

[28] Bergholm, F., (1987). Edge focusing. *IEEE Trans. Pattern Anal. Mach. Intell.*, **9**:726–741.

[29] Kawohl, B. and Kutev, N., (1997). *Maximum and Comparison Principles for Anisotropic Diffusion (Preprint).* Cologne, Germany: Mathematical Institute, University of Cologne.

[30] Kichenassamy, S., (1997). The Perona-Malik paradox. *SIAM J. Appl. Math.*, **57**:1343–1372.

[31] You, Y.-L., Xu, W., Tannenbaum, A., and Kaveh, M., (1996). Behavioral analysis of anisotropic diffusion in image processing. *IEEE Trans. Image Proc.*, **5**:1539–1553.

[32] Weickert, J. and Benhamouda, B., (1997). A semidiscrete nonlinear scale-space theory and its relation to the Perona–Malik paradox. In *Advances in Computer Vision*, F. Solina, W. Kropatsch, R. Klette, and R. Bajcsy, eds., pp. 1–10. Wien: Springer.

[33] Benhamouda, B., (1994). *Parameter Adaptation for Nonlinear Diffusion in Image Processing.* Master's thesis, Dept. of Mathematics, University of Kaiserslautern, Germany.

[34] Catté, F., Lions, P.-L., Morel, J.-M., and Coll, T., (1992). Image selective smoothing and edge detection by nonlinear diffusion. *SIAM J. Numer.*

Anal., **29**:182–193.

[35] Nitzberg, M. and Shiota, T., (1992). Nonlinear image filtering with edge and corner enhancement. *IEEE Trans. Pattern Anal. Mach. Intell.*, **14**:826–833.

[36] Fröhlich, J. and Weickert, J., (1994). *Image Processing using a Wavelet Algorithm for Nonlinear Diffusion. Report No. 104, Laboratory of Technomathematics*. Kaiserslautern, Germany: University of Kaiserslautern.

[37] Cottet, G.-H. and Germain, L., (1993). Image processing through reaction combined with nonlinear diffusion. *Math. Comp.*, **61**:659–673.

[38] Förstner, M. and Gülch, E., (1987). A fast operator for detection and precise location of distinct points, corners and centres of circular features. In *Proc. ISPRS Intercommission Conf. on Fast Processing of Photogrammetric Data, Interlaken, 1987*.

[39] Rao, A. and Schunck, B., (1991). Computing oriented texture fields. *CVGIP: Graphical Models and Image Processing*, **53**:157–185.

[40] Bigün, J. and Granlund, G., (1987). Optimal orientation detection of linear symmetry. In *Proc. First Int. Conf. on Computer Vision (ICCV), London, June 8–11, 1987*, pp. 433–438. Washington: IEEE Computer Society Press.

[41] Kass, M. and Witkin, A., (1987). Analyzing oriented patterns. *Computer Vision, Graphics, and Image Processing*, **37**:362–385.

[42] Rieger, J., (1995). Generic evolution of edges on families of diffused gray value surfaces. *J. Math. Imag. Vision*, 5:207–217.

[43] Weickert, J., Zuiderveld, K., ter Haar Romeny, B., and Niessen, W., (1997). Parallel implementations of AOS schemes: a fast way of nonlinear diffusion filtering. In *Proc. 1997 IEEE International Conference on Image Processing, ICIP-97, Santa Barbara, Oct. 26–29, 1997*, Vol. 3, pp. 396–399. Piscataway, NJ: IEEE Signal Processing Society.

[44] Niessen, W., Vincken, K., Weickert, J., and Viergever, M., (1998). Three-dimensional MR brain segmentation. In *Proc. Sixth Int. Conf. on Computer Vision, ICCV '98, Bombay, Jan. 4–7, 1998*, pp. 53–58.

[45] Yoo, T. and Coggins, J., (1993). Using statistical pattern recognition techniques to control variable conductance diffusion. In *Information Processing in Medical Imaging*, H. Barrett and A. Gmitro, eds., Vol. 687 of *Lecture Notes in Computer Science*, pp. 459–471. Berlin: Springer.

[46] Rambaux, I. and Garçon, P., (1994). *Nonlinear Anisotropic Diffusion Filtering of 3-D Images*. Project work, Département Génie Mathématique, INSA de Rouen and Laboratory of Technomathematics, University of Kaiserslautern, Kaiserslautern, Germany.

[47] Weickert, J., (1999). Coherence-enhancing diffusion filtering. *To appear in Int. J. Comput. Vision*.

[48] Weickert, J., (1994). *Scale-Space Properties of Nonlinear Diffusion Filtering with a Diffusion Tensor*. Report No. 110, Laboratory of Technomathematics, University of Kaiserslautern, Kaiserslautern, Germany.

[49] Weickert, J., (1997). Coherence-enhancing diffusion of color images (Extended version to appear in Image and Vision Computing). In *Pattern Recognition and Image Analysis, VII NSPRIA, Barcelona, April 21–25, 1997*,

A. Sanfeliu, J. Villanueva, and J. Vitrià, eds., pp. 239–244. Barcelona: Centro de Visió per Computador.

[50] Scherzer, O. and Weickert, J., (1998). *Relations between regularization and diffusion filtering.* Technical Report DIKU 98/23, submitted, Dept. of Computer Science, University of Copenhagen, Universitetsparken 1, 2100 Copenhagen, Denmark.

[51] Weickert, J., Heers, J., Schnörr, C., Zuiderveld, K. J., Scherzer, O., and Stiehl, H. S., (1999). *Fast parallel algorithms for a broad class of nonlinear variational diffusion approaches.* Technical Report 5/1999, submitted, Computer Science Series, University of Mannheim, 68131 Mannheim, Germany.

[52] Caselles, V., Morel, J., Sapiro, G., and A. Tannenbaum (eds.), (1998). Partial differential equations and geometry-driven diffusion in image processing and analysis. *IEEE Trans. Image Proc.*, **7**(3).

[53] ter Haar Romeny, B. (ed.), (1994). *Geometry-Driven Diffusion in Computer Vision.* Dordrecht: Kluwer.

[54] ter Haar Romeny, B., Florack, L., Koenderink, J., and Viergever, M. (eds.), (1997). *Scale-space theory in computer vision*, Vol. 1252 of *Lecture Notes in Computer Science*, Berlin. Springer.

13 Variational Methods for Adaptive Smoothing and Segmentation

Christoph Schnörr

Lehrstuhl für Bildverarbeitung, Fakultät für Mathematik und Informatik
Universität Mannheim, Germany

13.1 Introduction

This chapter explains variational techniques for the adaptive processing of 2-D and 3-D images, vector-valued images, and image sequences for the purpose of nonlinear smoothing, segmentation, extraction of local image structure (homogeneous regions, edges, characteristic points), noise suppression and restoration, and computation of optical flow. For each category of image data, the exposition provides:

- a description of a variational approach,
- a consistent discretization of the approach,
- an iterative scheme to solve the resulting system of nonlinear equations numerically, and

459

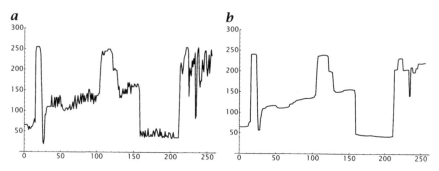

Figure 13.1: *a Data from a real image; b the data from a adaptively smoothed.*

- examples computed to indicate the range of applications.

The material presented introduces the reader to a specific research field of image processing and computer vision and should enable him or her to integrate these techniques into solution approaches to diverse application problems.

13.1.1 Motivation and general problem formulation

Consider the data in Fig. 13.1a and the result of applying a variational technique in Fig. 13.1b. Obviously, small signal variations have been smoothed out whereas the coarse signal structure in terms of more distinct signal variations has been preserved. Thus, the data have been processed by a smoothing process that is capable of adapting itself to the local signal structure. The need for this kind of unsupervised (pre)processing arises in numerous applications involving real data.

In a more general way, the following important issues underlie the design of variational techniques for adaptive image processing:

- Data reduction by adaptively suppressing image details (local signal variations), as illustrated in Fig. 13.1.
- Partitioning of the image domain into locations with significant signal variations and homogeneous regions (image segmentation). Localization of signal variations is important along with the robust contrast information of regions.
- Optimality of segmentations in terms of measures of "strength of local signal variation" and "homogeneity."
- Discretization and consistency. Many useful concepts and properties like "level lines of functions" or "rotational invariance" are meaningful only for continuous problem formulations. Approximate problem formulations that preserve such concepts and properties in the limit of increasingly fine discretizations are called *consistent*.

- Computational architecture and parallelism. As is obvious from Fig. 13.1, the result at a certain location cannot be computed by just taking two neighboring data points into consideration. Rather, a local context of several data points has to be considered. Nevertheless, all approaches described in this chapter can be realized on fine-grained parallel architectures with nearest-neighbor communication.

In general, a *variational approach* is formulated by considering input data $g \in S_1$ and the processed data $v_g \in S_2$ as elements of some spaces S_1, S_2 of functions defined over the given image domain A, and by defining v_g as a solution of a minimization problem:

$$v_g = \arg\min_{v \in S_2} J(v), \quad J(v) = \int_A L(g, v)\, d\boldsymbol{x} \tag{13.1}$$

where the function L depends on the problem at hand. In most cases, the right-hand side of Eq. (13.1) can be decomposed as follows:

$$J(v) = \int_A L_g(g, v)\, d\boldsymbol{x} + \int_{A_r} L_r(v)\, d\boldsymbol{x} + \int_{A_t} L_t(v)\, d\boldsymbol{x} \tag{13.2}$$

Here, the sets A_r and A_t define a partition of the image domain A into *regions* and *transitions* and are implicitly defined by local properties of the functions v, like the magnitude of the gradient, for example. As a consequence, the optimal segmentation of A is obtained by computing the minimum v_g of the functional J in Eq. (13.1).

13.1.2 Basic references to the literature

In this section, references are given to some important research papers as well as to other fields related to the contents of this chapter. No attempt, however, has been made to survey any aspect of variational modeling in image processing and early computer vision. The general references given here will be supplemented by more specific references in subsequent sections.

A clear-cut mathematical definition of the image segmentation problem has been given by [1]:

$$J_{MS}(v, K) = \alpha \int_A (v - g)^2\, d\boldsymbol{x} + \int_{A \setminus K} |\nabla v|^2\, d\boldsymbol{x} + \beta \mathcal{L}(K) \tag{13.3}$$

Given some image data g, a piecewise smooth function v_g, which may have jumps along a 1-D discontinuity set $K \subset A$, has to be determined such that the functional J in Eq. (13.3) attains a local minimum. According to the general form of Eq. (13.2), the functional Eq. (13.3) comprises three terms: The first term measures the distance between v and the data g with respect to the $L^2(A)$-norm, the second term measures the homogeneity of v in terms of the magnitude of the gradient of v:

$$|\nabla v| = \left\| \begin{bmatrix} v_x \\ v_y \end{bmatrix} \right\| = \left(v_x^2 + v_y^2 \right)^{1/2} , \quad \text{for} \quad \boldsymbol{x} = \begin{bmatrix} x \\ y \end{bmatrix} \in \mathcal{R}^2$$

and the third term measures the length of the discontinuity set K. The relative influence of these terms depends on two global parameters α and β that can be controlled by the user. The reader should note that dropping any term in Eq. (13.3) would lead to meaningless minimizers and segmentations, respectively.

The variational segmentation approach of Mumford and Shah provides a mathematically sound definition of what most conventional segmentation approaches (see, e.g., [2, 3]) try to achieve. This has been demonstrated in a recent review [4]. On the other hand, the approach of Eq. (13.3) turned out to be mathematically rather involved, and it is by no means straightforward to specify consistent discrete approximations of it (see [4, 5], and [6] for a simplified version of the approach of Eq. (13.3)). For these reasons, we confine ourselves in Section 13.2 to mathematically simpler yet practically useful variational problems that, in some sense, approximate the approach Eq. (13.3) of Mumford and Shah.

Rather influential results in the field of image segmentation and restoration have been presented by Geman and Geman [7]. Their approach can be seen as a discrete counterpart of the Mumford-Shah model given here. Furthermore, their seminal paper describes a probabilistic problem/solution formulation in terms of *Markov random fields*, *Gibbs distributions*, and Gibbs sampling, which turned out to be basic to much subsequent work. Gibbs distributions are nowadays widely used across several disciplines in order to model spatial context. This broader probabilistic viewpoint, touched upon in this chapter, is the subject of Chapter 15. In this chapter we merely point to the fact that all functionals J considered here induce Gibbs distributions over the space S_2 in Eq. (13.1) in a natural way by means of:

$$p(v) = \frac{1}{Z} \exp\left(-J(v) \right)$$

with a normalizing constant Z. For a recent review we refer to Li [8], and for a more mathematically oriented account to Geman [9] and Winkler [10].

Further important work has been reported by Blake and Zisserman [11]. In particular, their Graduated-Non-Convexity approach introduced the idea of homotopy-like deterministic minimization algorithms to the field of computer vision. The related concept of mean-field annealing has been presented by Geiger and Girosi [12]. See also Geiger and Yuille [13] for a review of variational segmentation approaches. Anticipating Section 13.2.3, let us mention that we do not pursue these concepts, which amount to solving sequences of *nonlinear* systems of equations, here. Rather, we explain a minimization algorithm in terms of sequences of *linear* systems of equations, which, from our point of view, is more compatible with current concepts of parallel computing.

Another important current research field is known under the keyword 'images and pde's' [14] (pde = partial differential equation). The connection to this field is given by the Euler-Lagrange equation, which corresponds to the functional Eq. (13.1) (see Section 13.2.1). This nonlinear diffusion equation may be used to describe how a starting point approaches a minimizer of the functional *J*. In the field 'images and pde's', however, more general types of nonlinear diffusion equations are investigated. Corresponding research topics include nonlinear smoothing schemes for edge-detection and image enhancement, extensions of the linear scale-space paradigm and invariance principles, and equations describing the evolution of active contours (so-called 'snakes'). For further details and surveys we refer to [15, 16, 17, 18].

Within this field, the nonlinear smoothing schemes described in this chapter form a special class. The distinguishing feature is that each approach obeys a global optimality criterion Eq. (13.1) that makes explicit how different criteria Eq. (13.2) are combined in order to compute an optimal segmentation of given image data. Note that Euler-Lagrange equations are not needed for implementing a variational technique. Furthermore, there are many well-posed variational approaches, like that of Eq. (13.3) for example, the functionals of which are not smooth enough to admit an equivalent description in terms of pde's.

13.2 Processing of two- and three-dimensional images

This section describes variational techniques for the processing of scalar-valued images. In Section 13.2.1, a variational principle is presented and related mathematical issues are discussed. In particular, we distinguish convex from nonconvex minimization approaches. Section 13.2.2 shows how these approaches are converted into nonlinear systems of equations. An algorithm to numerically compute a solution to these equations is described in Section 13.2.3. Finally, some representative numerical examples are presented in Section 13.2.4.

13.2.1 Variational principle

We consider a family of functionals Eq. (13.1) of the following form:

$$J(v) = \frac{1}{2} \int_A \left\{ (v - g)^2 + \lambda(|\nabla v|) \right\} \mathrm{d}\boldsymbol{x} \qquad (13.4)$$

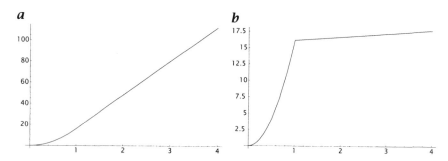

Figure 13.2: a *Graph of* λ_c, *which is a convex combination of a quadratic and a linear function* ($\lambda_h = 4, c_\rho = 1, \epsilon_c = 0.1$); **b** *graph of* λ_{nc}, *which quadratically combines a quadratic function with a linear function of slope* ϵ_{nc} ($\lambda_h = 4, c_\rho = 1, \delta t = 0.01, \epsilon_{nc} = 0.5$).

This formulation has been introduced by Nordström [19]. Among various possibilities, we choose two particular definitions of the function λ (see Fig. 13.2):

$$\lambda_c(t) = \begin{cases} \lambda_{c,\text{low}}(t) = \lambda_h^2 t^2 & , 0 \le t \le c_\rho \\ \lambda_{c,\text{high}}(t) = \epsilon_c^2 t^2 + (\lambda_h^2 - \epsilon_c^2)c_\rho(2t - c_\rho) & , 0 < c_\rho \le t \end{cases} \quad (13.5)$$

and

$$\lambda_{nc}(t) = \begin{cases} \lambda_{nc,\text{low}}(t) = \lambda_h^2 t^2 & , 0 \le t \le c_\rho \\ \lambda_{nc,\text{high}}(t) & , 0 < c_\rho \le t \end{cases} \quad (13.6)$$

where

$$\lambda_{nc,\text{high}}(t) = \begin{cases} \frac{1}{2\delta t}\Big[(\epsilon_{nc} - 2\lambda_h^2 c_\rho)t^2 \\ \quad + (2\lambda_h^2(c_\rho + \delta t) - \epsilon_{nc})c_\rho(2t - c_\rho)\Big] & , t \le c_\rho + \delta t \\ \epsilon_{nc}\left(t - c_\rho - \frac{\delta t}{2}\right) + c_\rho\lambda_h^2(c_\rho + \delta t) & , c_\rho + \delta t \le t \end{cases}$$

$0 < \epsilon_c, \delta t \ll 1$, and $\epsilon_{nc} < 2\lambda_h^2 c_\rho$. These functions are continuously differentiable, and the essential parameters to be specified by the user are λ_h and c_ρ. Definitions Eqs. (13.5) and (13.6) lead to representative examples of *convex* and *nonconvex* variational approaches, respectively, as they exhibit the essential features of other definitions that have been reported in the literature (see the list in [20], for example).

According to Eq. (13.2), the functional Eq. (13.4) takes the form:

$$J(v) = \frac{1}{2}\int_A (v - g)^2 \, d\boldsymbol{x} + \frac{1}{2}\int_{A_r} \lambda_{\text{low}}(|\nabla v|) \, d\boldsymbol{x} + \frac{1}{2}\int_{A_t} \lambda_{\text{high}}(|\nabla v|) \, d\boldsymbol{x} \tag{13.7}$$

where the region and transition sets A_r and A_t are defined by low and high magnitudes of the gradient of v, respectively:

$$A_r = \{x \in A \; : \; |\nabla v| \leq c_\rho\} \tag{13.8}$$

$$A_t = \{x \in A \; : \; |\nabla v| > c_\rho\} \tag{13.9}$$

Let us briefly discuss some major differences between the convex and nonconvex case of Eq. (13.4):

Convex case. In this case the continuous problem formulation Eq. (13.4) is well-posed for a certain choice of function spaces S_1, S_2 in Eq. (13.1), and for each given image data g there is a unique function v_g minimizing the functional J in Eq. (13.1) with $\lambda = \lambda_c$ from Eq. (13.5). With other words, the intrinsic properties of the approach are well-defined and do not depend on discrete concepts used for modeling sensors and computation. Furthermore, any discrete solution $v_{h,g}$ computed as shown in subsequent sections approximates the function v_g in the sense that, as the resolution of the sensor becomes increasingly better, we have:

$$\|v_g - v_{h,g}\|_{S_2} \to 0$$

Convex variational approaches have been advocated by several researchers (e.g., [21, 22, 23]), due mainly to uniqueness of the solution. Our definition Eq. (13.5) given in the preceding follows Schnörr [22]. We note, however, that in addition to uniqueness of the solution, convex variational approaches exhibit favorable properties like continuous dependence of the solution on the data and parameters, for example. Furthermore, a comparison of Eq. (13.7), regarded as an approximation of the Mumford-Shah model, with Eq. (13.3) reveals that using $\lambda_{c,\text{high}}$ for the transition measure in Eq. (13.7) does not intend to cause a poor compromise in order to achieve convexity. Rather, the length of the discontinuity set of v in Eq. (13.3) is replaced by length of level lines of v, which are summed up over the contrast at locations where v rapidly varies. This is a meaningful measure for real signals with bounded gradients [24].

Nonconvex case. In this case, to our knowledge, no continuous and well-posed problem formulation of Eq. (13.4) has been reported in the literature. This means that, strictly speaking, the variational approach of Eq. (13.4) with λ_{nc} from Eq. (13.6) makes sense mathematically only after having discretized the approach. In contrast to the convex case, the resulting approach depends on the particular discretization method used. Our definition Eq. (13.6) given here follows closely Blake and Zisserman [11], who thoroughly investigated a discrete version of the nonconvex approach of Eq. (13.4).

In general, there are multiple local minima $\{v_g\}$ for given image data g, making the approach dependent on the starting point and more sensitive against perturbations of the input image data and parameter values. A comparison of the nonconvex version of Eq. (13.4) with the Mumford-Shah model Eq. (13.3) shows that the 1-D discontinuity measure in Eq. (13.3) is approximated by the area of regions with a large gradient of v. In contrast to the convex case discussed here, however, further properties of v are not "measured" within these regions. A numerical example in Section 13.2.4 illustrates this point.

For the purpose of discretization in Section 13.2.2, we set the first variation of the functional Eq. (13.4) at the point v_g equal to zero, as a necessary condition for v_g to be a local minimizer of J. $\forall v \in S_2$:

$$\frac{\mathrm{d}}{\mathrm{d}\tau} J(v_g + \tau v)\big|_{\tau=0} = \int_A \left\{ (v_g - g)v + \rho(|\nabla v_g|)\nabla v_g^T \nabla v \right\} \mathrm{d}\boldsymbol{x} = 0$$

(13.10)

where we introduced the so-called diffusion coefficient:

$$\rho(t) = \frac{\lambda'(t)}{2t}, \quad t \geq 0$$

(13.11)

Note that in the convex case, Eq. (13.10) uniquely determines the global minimizer v_g of J in Eq. (13.4).

For the following it will be convenient to write Eq. (13.10) in a more compact form. To this end, we use the customary notation for the *linear* action of some functional q on a function v:

$$\langle q, v \rangle := q(v)$$

(13.12)

Equation (13.10) may then be written as follows:

$$\langle A(v_g), v \rangle = \langle f, v \rangle, \quad \forall v \in S_2$$

(13.13)

with a nonlinear operator A mapping v_g to the linear functional $A(v_g)$:

$$\langle A(v_g), v \rangle = \int_A \left\{ v_g v + \rho(|\nabla v_g|)\nabla v_g^T \nabla v \right\} \mathrm{d}\boldsymbol{x}$$

(13.14)

and the linear functional f:

$$\langle f, v \rangle = \int_A gv \, \mathrm{d}\boldsymbol{x}$$

(13.15)

Equation (13.13) is the starting point for the discretization with the finite element method (FEM) to be described in Section 13.2.2.

13.2.2 Finite element method discretization

In this section we explain the basic scheme that can be applied mechanically to obtain a proper discretization of all variational approaches described in this chapter. Detailed application examples of this scheme for the case of 1-D, 2-D and 3-D cases are illustrated in CVA2 [Chapter 16].

The material presented in this Section is fairly standard. A more general introduction and further details can be found in numerous textbooks on the *finite element method* (FEM).

Basic scheme. The first step is to triangulate the underlying domain A and to choose piecewise linear basis functions $\phi_i(x), i = 1, \ldots, N$. Examples will be given in the following sections. These basis functions define a linear subspace:

$$S_h := \text{span}\{\phi_1, \ldots, \phi_N\} \subset S_2$$

and we approximate problem Eq. (13.13) by restricting it to this subspace. Let $v_{h,g}, v_h \in S_h$ denote representatives of the functions $v_g, v \in S_2$ (h denotes the discretization parameter related to the mesh-width of the triangulation):

$$v_{h,g} = \sum_{i=1}^{N} v_{g,i}\phi_i(x), \qquad v_h = \sum_{i=1}^{N} v_i\phi_i(x) \tag{13.16}$$

Then our task is to solve the following equation for a minimizing function $v_{h,g}$:

$$\langle A(v_{h,g}), v_h \rangle = \langle f, v_h \rangle, \quad \forall v_h \in S_h \tag{13.17}$$

Inserting Eq. (13.16) yields (recall from Eq. (13.12) that the left-hand quantities in Eq. (13.17) act *linearly* on v_h):

$$\sum_{i=1}^{N} v_i \langle A(v_{h,g}), \phi_i \rangle = \sum_{i=1}^{N} v_i \langle f, \phi_i \rangle, \quad \forall v_h \in S_h$$

This equation has to be satisfied for *arbitrary* functions $v_h \in S_h$. Hence, we conclude that:

$$\langle A(v_{h,g}), \phi_i \rangle = \langle f, \phi_i \rangle, \quad i = 1, \ldots, N \tag{13.18}$$

Eq. (13.18) is a system of N nonlinear equations that has to be solved for the N real numbers $v_{g,j}, j = 1, \ldots, N$, that determine a minimizing function $v_{h,g}$ in Eq. (13.16). Again we note that in the convex case, this nonlinear vector equation has a unique solution v_g. Numerical schemes to compute v_g are the subject of Section 13.2.3.

13.2.3　Algorithm

This section describes a class of algorithms that can be used to solve the nonlinear system of Eq. (13.18) numerically. The design of such an algorithm is based on a technique that replaces the original nonlinear system by a sequence of linear systems of equations, which can be solved efficiently with various linear solvers. Only the linearization technique is described here. Algorithms for the solution of the resulting sparse linear systems can be found in numerous excellent textbooks (e.g., [25, 26]). For additional details, an investigation of alternative approaches and parallel implementations we refer to [27, 28].

In the following, it will be more convenient to specify modifications of Eq. (13.13) rather than Eq. (13.18). According to the discretization of Eq. (13.13) described in Section 13.2.2, the corresponding modifications of Eq. (13.18) are then immediate.

Minimization of convex functionals.　Consider Eq. (13.13). This nonlinear equation becomes linear if we "freeze" its nonlinear part by using the solution of the previous iteration step as its argument. With Eqs. (13.14) and (13.15), Eq. (13.13) thus becomes (k counts the iteration steps):

$$\int_A \left\{ v_g^{k+1} v + \rho(|\nabla v_g^k|)(\nabla v_g^k)^T \nabla v \right\} d\boldsymbol{x} = \int_A g v \, d\boldsymbol{x}, \quad \forall v \in S_2$$

(13.19)

To our knowledge, this approach was introduced as the so-called *Kačanov method* in the field of mathematical elasticity 25 yr ago (see [29, 30, 31]). In the case of convex functionals Eq. (13.4) with λ from Eq. (13.5), it can be shown that the sequence v_g^k according to Eq. (13.19) converges to the global minimizer v_g, that is, the unique solution of Eq. (13.13), irrespective of the starting point v_g^0 [28, 32].

Minimization of nonconvex functionals.　A linearization technique closely related to that of the previous section has been proposed by Geman and Reynolds [33] (see also Charbonnier et al. [34]). The idea is to rewrite the original functional Eq. (13.4) using an auxiliary function w:

$$J_{\text{aux}}(v, w) = \frac{1}{2} \int_A \left\{ (v - g)^2 + w|\nabla v|^2 + \psi(w) \right\} d\boldsymbol{x}$$

(13.20)

and to update, iteratively, v_g and w:

$$v_g^{k+1} = \arg \min_v J_{\text{aux}}(v, w^k)$$

(13.21)

and

$$w^{k+1} = \arg\min_{w} J_{\text{aux}}(v_g^{k+1}, w) \tag{13.22}$$

Note that w^k is fixed in Eq. (13.21), so that v_g^{k+1} is computed as the solution of the linear equation:

$$\int_A \left\{ v_g^{k+1} v + w^k (\nabla v_g^{k+1})^T \nabla v \right\} d\boldsymbol{x} = \int_A g v \, d\boldsymbol{x}, \quad \forall v \in S_2 \tag{13.23}$$

To make step Eq. (13.22) more explicit, we have to explain how the function ψ in Eq. (13.20) is chosen; ψ is chosen such that:

$$\lambda(t) = \inf_{w} \left(w t^2 + \psi(w) \right)$$

with λ from the original minimization problems Eqs. (13.4) and (13.6). If λ is such that ρ in Eq. (13.11) is strictly monotone and decreasing (as in Eq. (13.6)), then it is not difficult to show that step Eq. (13.22) reduces to:

$$w^{k+1} = \rho(|\nabla v_g^{k+1}|) \tag{13.24}$$

that is, ψ is not needed explicitly to carry out Eq. (13.22). As a result, we have the iteration Eq. (13.19) again, with ρ now defined by some non-convex function λ. As ρ defined by Eqs. (13.11) and (13.5) illustrates, it is possible to weaken the assumptions slightly and to consider functions ρ that are (not strictly) monotone decreasing, too.

According to nonconvexity, only a local minimum can be expected after convergence of the iteration from the preceding. Furthermore, this minimum generally depends on the starting point v_g^0.

13.2.4 Applications

In this section, we demonstrate various aspects of the variational approach Eq. (13.4) with a few numerical examples. In all experiments we used the convex case Eq. (13.5), with one exception (Fig. 13.8) to exhibit some differences to the nonconvex case. As a convergence criterion the following threshold with respect to the maximum residuum of the nonlinear Eq. (13.18) was used:

$$\max_{i \in \{1,\ldots,N\}} |\langle A(v_{h,g}) - f, \phi_i \rangle| \leq 0.1$$

Adaptive smoothing. We first illustrate the adaptive smoothing behavior with an academic example. Figure 13.3 shows an isocontour surface of a real 3-D data set in $\boldsymbol{a}$, superimposed with noise in $\boldsymbol{b}$, and $\boldsymbol{c}$ shows the corresponding isocontour surface of the minimizing function v_g by processing the noisy data g shown in $\boldsymbol{a}$. Two aspects can be seen here: First, noise can be eliminated without destroying significant signal structure in terms of large gradients. Second, whereas

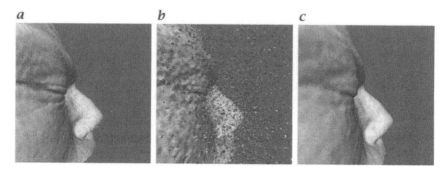

Figure 13.3: *a Isocontour surface of 3-D data set; b contaminated with noise; c after adaptive smoothing of the data shown in b (see text).*

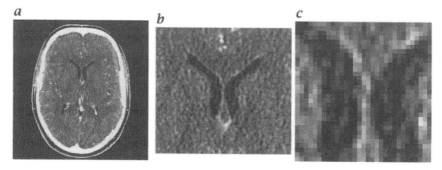

Figure 13.4: *a Slice of a 3-D CT image data set; b, c sections with an object of interest.*

smoothing stops locally along the gradient direction (i. e., normal to the surface), smoothing still occurs along the surface, as can be seen from the small ripples of the surface in Fig. 13.3b that have been eliminated in c. One main advantage of variational approaches is that such complex, locally adaptive smoothing behavior emerges from a global optimization principle and does not have to be encoded explicitly.

As a realistic application case, Fig. 13.4 shows a slice through a noisy 3-D CT data set *a* and sections with some object *b* and *c*. Figure 13.5 illustrates how adaptive variational smoothing of the 3-D image data eliminates noise without destroying the fairly complex signal structure. As a result, detection of the object by a simple threshold operation becomes robust.

Segmentation and feature extraction. In this section, we illustrate the segmentation of images into homogeneous regions Eq. (13.8) and transition regions Eq. (13.9). Figure 13.6 shows a Lab scene g in *a* and the processed image v_g in *b*. According to definitions Eqs. (13.8) and (13.9), v_g implicitly encodes a partition of the image plane as shown in

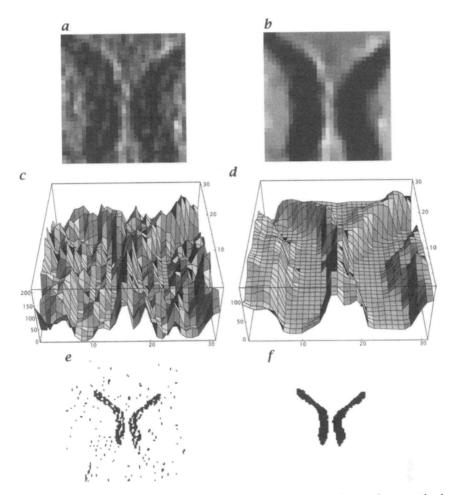

Figure 13.5: *Left column: Original data. Right column: Adaptively smoothed data:* ***a,b*** *section of Fig. 13.4;* ***c,d*** *3-D plot of* ***a*** *and* ***b****, respectively;* ***e,f*** *result of threshold operation.*

Fig. 13.6c. By choosing a smaller value for the scale parameter λ_h in Eq. (13.5), finer details can be resolved at the cost of less smoothing (i.e., noise suppression) within homogeneous regions (Fig. 13.6d). This latter aspect, that is feature detection through anisotropic locally adaptive processing while simultaneously smoothing within nonfeature regions, is a main property of variational approaches. Figure 13.7 illustrates this aspect in more detail. As a result, local contrast information around signal transitions becomes robust.

Finally, let us consider some differences between convex Eq. (13.5) and nonconvex Eq. (13.6) variational processing. Figure 13.8 shows the corresponding results for the image shown in Fig. 13.8a. Noise

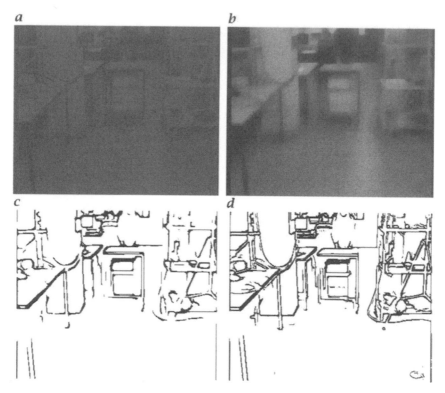

Figure 13.6: *a Lab scene g; b the unique minimizer v_g to Eq. (13.4); c the segmentation encoded by v_g according to Eqs. (13.8) and (13.9); d choosing a smaller scale parameter λ_h in Eq. (13.5) enables the computation of finer details.*

suppression along with region formation can be clearly seen for both approaches, whereas contrast is better preserved using the nonconvex version. However, as can be seen in Fig. 13.8d and e, the formation of transition regions is more susceptible to noise for the nonconvex than for the convex approach. This is due to the fact that smoothing almost completely stops in the nonconvex case, whereas in the convex case smoothing still continues in directions perpendicular to the gradient direction. From our viewpoint, this fact together with the existence of multiple local minima and the dependence on the starting point reduces the attraction of nonconvex approaches, in particular in the context of image sequence processing where gradual changes of the input image data may not lead to gradual changes of corresponding image segmentations.

Noise suppression and restoration. For large gradients $|\nabla v|$, the convex smoothness term of the functional Eqs. (13.4) and (13.5) is dominated by the so-called total variation measure, which for admissible

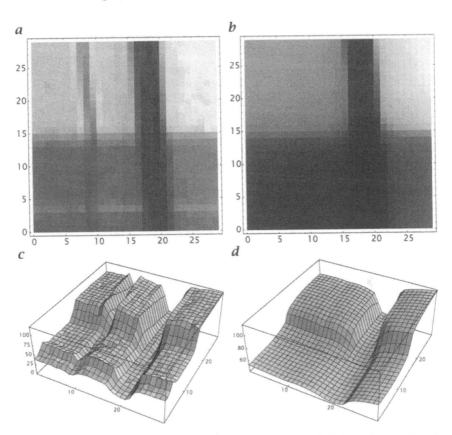

Figure 13.7: *a Section of the Lab scene shown in Fig. 13.6; b detection and localization of signal structure is not affected very much by elimination of smaller details. As a result, local contrast information around signal transitions becomes robust; c, d 3-D plots of a and b, respectively.*

functions with respect to problem Eq. (13.4) takes the simple form:

$$\int_{A_t} \lambda(|\nabla v|)\,\mathrm{d}x \sim \int_{A_t} |\nabla v|\,\mathrm{d}x$$

As an alternative to restoring signal transitions in the context of image segmentation, this measure can also be used to restore entire images by the variational approach [35, 36, 37]. This powerful approach can be simulated by choosing a small value for the parameter c_ρ in Eq. (13.5). Figure 13.9 shows as an example the restoration of a mammogram. We note, however, that a proper adaptation of the approach Eq. (13.4) to restoration tasks requires in general the inclusion of a blurring operator K into the first term of Eq. (13.4), which models the point-spread

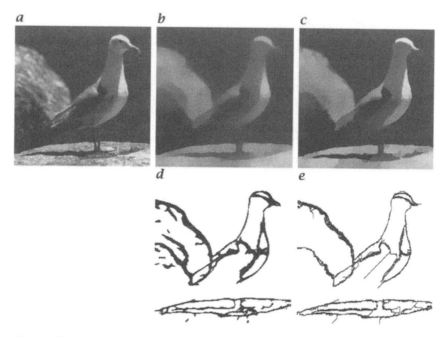

Figure 13.8: **a** *Real image;* **b** *unique minimum of the convex variational approach;* **c** *local minimizer of the nonconvex variational approach. Contrast is better preserved by the nonconvex approach;* **d**, **e** *segmentations according to* **b** *and* **c**, *respectively. Transitions detected by the convex approach are more robust against noise because smoothing does not stop completely.*

function of the imaging device:

$$\int_A (Kv - g)^2 \, \mathrm{d}x$$

13.3   Processing of vector-valued images

This section extends the variational approach of Eq. (13.4) to vector-valued images. We describe a straightforward extension appropriate for the processing of color images, for example. A variation of this approach that is useful for some image sequence processing tasks is presented in Section 13.4.

13.3.1   Variational principle

Let

$$\boldsymbol{g} : \boldsymbol{x} \in A \subset \mathcal{R}^d \to \mathcal{R}^n \tag{13.25}$$

a b

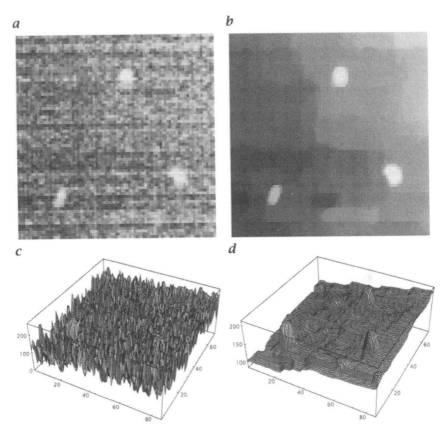

c d

Figure 13.9: *a Section of a mammogram; b restored image; c, d 3-D plots of a, b.*

denote a vector-valued image. For example, we have $d = 2$ and $n = 3$ for color images. For the gradient of vector-valued functions $\boldsymbol{v}$ we use the symbol:

$$Dv := \left[\ \nabla v_1, \ldots, \nabla v_n\ \right]$$

The corresponding inner product and norm are denoted as:

$$(D\boldsymbol{u}, D\boldsymbol{v}) = \text{trace}(D\boldsymbol{u}^T D\boldsymbol{v}), \qquad \|D\boldsymbol{v}\| = (D\boldsymbol{v}, D\boldsymbol{v})^{1/2}$$

The variational approach—analog to Eq. (13.4)—then reads ([38]):

$$J(\boldsymbol{v}) = \frac{1}{2} \int_A \left\{ |\boldsymbol{v} - \boldsymbol{g}|^2 + \lambda(\|D\boldsymbol{v}\|) \right\} d\boldsymbol{x} \qquad (13.26)$$

Computing the first variation, we again obtain a variational equation of the form Eq. (13.13) that, for λ defined by Eq. (13.5), uniquely determines the global minimizer $\boldsymbol{v}_g$ of the functional Eq. (13.26), where (see definitions Eqs. (13.14) and (13.15) in the scalar case):

$$\langle A(\boldsymbol{v_g}), \boldsymbol{v} \rangle = \int_A \left\{ \boldsymbol{v_g^T v} + \rho(\|D\boldsymbol{v_g}\|)(D\boldsymbol{v_g}, D\boldsymbol{v}) \right\} d\boldsymbol{x} \qquad (13.27)$$

and

$$\langle f, \boldsymbol{v} \rangle = \int_A \boldsymbol{g^T v}\, d\boldsymbol{x} \qquad (13.28)$$

Alternatively, one may use definition Eq. (13.6) in order to formulate a nonconvex variational approach. An alternative meaningful extension of the standard smoothness term in Eq. (13.4) to the case of vector-valued images is discussed in Sapiro and Ringach [39].

13.3.2 Numerical example: color images

Figure 13.10 shows a color image $\boldsymbol{g}$ and the minimizer $\boldsymbol{v_g}$ to Eq. (13.26) computed at a small ($\lambda_h = 2$) and a larger scale ($\lambda_h = 9$), respectively. The preservation of image structure as well as the formation of homogeneous regions is clearly visible.

13.4 Processing of image sequences

In this section, we describe a specific alternative to the smoothness term of the functional Eq. (13.26) adapted to the estimation of motion fields. A *motion field* is a vector field that describes the instantaneous velocity of projected scene points in the image plane. Estimates of the motion field for a fixed time point are referred to as *optical flow* fields f in the literature (see Chapter 10).

13.4.1 Preprocessing

To compute f, local constraints due to the spatiotemporal variation of the image data $g(\boldsymbol{x}, t)$ may be used:

$$\frac{dg}{dt} = \nabla g^T f + \frac{\partial g}{\partial t} = 0 \qquad (13.29)$$

Here, the assumption has been made that g behaves like a "conserved quantity." As this assumption is often severely violated under realistic illumination conditions, g is replaced by more robust quantities related to the output of bandpass filters. Furthermore, multiple constraint equations similar to Eq. (13.29) can be used (see, e.g., [40, 41, 42, 43]). For more information related to the topic "optical flow" the reader is referred to Chapter 10. A survey of current problems in the field of image sequence analysis has been presented by Mitiche and Bouthemy [44].

Figure 13.10: a *Color image;* **c,d** *the minimizer* $\boldsymbol{v}_g$ *computed at a small and a larger scale, respectively;* **b** *the segmentation corresponding to* **c**; *topologically connected regions are marked with the mean color, transitions are marked with black.*

13.4.2 Variational principle

In the following we focus on variational approaches to the computation of optical flow fields $\boldsymbol{f}$. The classical approach is due to [45] (see also Section 10.3.1, Eq. (10.33)):

$$J(\boldsymbol{f}) = \frac{1}{2} \int_A \left\{ (\boldsymbol{\nabla} g^T \boldsymbol{f} + g_t)^2 + \lambda^2 (|\boldsymbol{\nabla} f_1|^2 + |\boldsymbol{\nabla} f_2|^2) \right\} d\boldsymbol{x} , \ \lambda \in \mathcal{R}$$

$$(13.30)$$

which has been considerably generalized in the literature (see, e.g., [46] and references therein). Formally, $\boldsymbol{f}$ may be regarded as a vector-valued image, so the nonquadratic smoothness term in Eq. (13.26),

$$\frac{1}{2}\int_A \lambda(\|D\boldsymbol{f}\|)\,d\boldsymbol{x} \tag{13.31}$$

with λ from Eq. (13.5) or Eq. (13.6), can be used to replace the terms with derivatives of f_1, f_2 in Eq. (13.30). With this, the computation of $\boldsymbol{f}$ by minimizing the functional J becomes adaptive to so-called *motion boundaries*, that is, significant changes of the structure of the optical flow $\boldsymbol{f}$. An alternative to Eq. (13.31) that may be useful in some applications is given by [47]:

$$\frac{1}{4}\int_A \left\{\lambda_d(|\mathrm{div}(\boldsymbol{f})|) + \lambda_r(|\mathrm{rot}(\boldsymbol{f})|) + \lambda_s(|\mathrm{sh}(\boldsymbol{f})|)\right\}d\boldsymbol{x} \tag{13.32}$$

where:

$$\mathrm{div}(\boldsymbol{f}) = f_{1,x} + f_{2,y}\,,$$
$$\mathrm{rot}(\boldsymbol{f}) = f_{2,x} - f_{1,y}\,,$$
$$\mathrm{sh}(\boldsymbol{f}) = [f_{2,y} - f_{1,x}, f_{1,y} + f_{2,x}]^T$$

denote the component's divergence, vorticity, and shear of the vector-gradient $D\boldsymbol{f}$. The functions λ_d, λ_r and λ_s are defined by Eq. (13.5) (or Eq. (13.6)). Parameter values may differ for each function. Using definition Eq. (13.5) makes the functional Eq. (13.32) together with the first data term in Eq. (13.30) convex so that the minimizing $\boldsymbol{f}$ is unique [48]. For $c_\rho \to \infty$ in Eq. (13.5) the functional Eq. (13.32) becomes identical to the smoothness term in Eq. (13.30) due to the identity:

$$\|D\boldsymbol{f}\|^2 = \frac{1}{2}\left(\mathrm{div}^2(\boldsymbol{f}) + \mathrm{rot}^2(\boldsymbol{f}) + |\mathrm{sh}(\boldsymbol{f})|^2\right)$$

13.4.3 Numerical examples

Because the preprocessing step, that is, the evaluation of constraint equations like Eq. (13.29) is not the topic of this chapter, we restrict ourselves to illustrating the effect of using the smoothness term of Eq. (13.32). To this end, we generated noisy vector fields $\boldsymbol{f}_d$ and supplemented Eq. (13.32) with the data term:

$$\frac{1}{2}\int_A |\boldsymbol{f} - \boldsymbol{f}_d|^2\,d\boldsymbol{x}$$

The main difference between the standard smoothness measure of Eq. (13.31) and Eq. (13.32) is that the first term favors piecewise constant vector fields whereas the latter term admits vector fields with richer local structure. This is illustrated in Fig. 13.11, in which vector fields are nowhere constant.

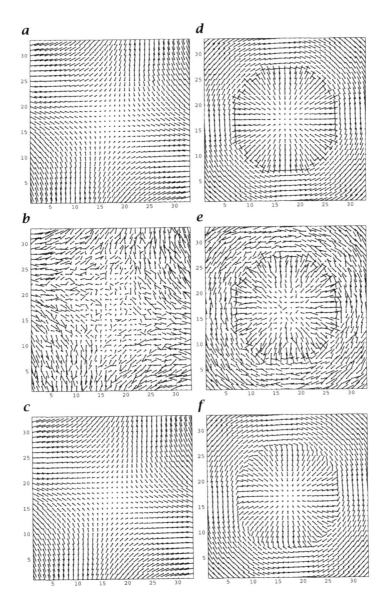

Figure 13.11: *Left column: Structure-selective smoothing:* **a** *computer-generated vector field; only the shear-term of the gradient is different from zero;* **b** *noisy input data;* **c** *reconstructed vector field by filtering divergent and rotational components. Right column: Structure-adaptive smoothing;* **d** *computer-generated vector field comprising a divergent and a rotational component;* **e** *noisy input data;* **f** *restored vector field. The smoothness term Eq. (13.32) automatically adapts to the local vector field structure.*

Acknowledgment. Image data depicted in Fig. 13.4 was kindly provided by ICS-AD from Philips Medical Systems, Best, and Philips Research Labs, Hamburg, courtesy of W.P.Th.M. Mali, L. Ramos, and C.W.M. van Veelen, Utrecht University Hospital. The author gratefully acknowledges comments by Josef Heers.

13.5 References

[1] Mumford, D. and Shah, J., (1989). Optimal approximations by piecewise smooth functions and associated variational problems. *Comm. Pure Appl. Math.*, **42**:577–685.

[2] Haralick, R. and Shapiro, L., (1985). Image segmentation techniques. *Comp. Vision, Graphics, and Image Proc.*, **29**:100–132.

[3] Pal, N. and Pal, S., (1993). A review on image segmentation techniques. *Patt. Recog.*, **9**:1277–1294.

[4] Morel, J.-M. and Solimini, S., (1995). *Variational Methods in Image Segmentation*. Boston: Birkhäuser.

[5] Richardson, T. and Mitter, S., (1994). Approximation, computation, and distortion in the variational formulation. In ter Haar Romeny [16], pp. 169–190.

[6] Koepfler, G., Lopez, C., and Morel, J., (1994). A multiscale algorithm for image segmentation by variational method. *SIAM J. Numer. Anal.*, **31**(1): 282–299.

[7] Geman, S. and Geman, D., (1984). Stochastic relaxation, Gibbs distributions, and the Bayesian restoration of images. *IEEE Trans. Patt. Anal. Mach. Intell.*, **6**(6):721–741.

[8] Li, S., (1995). *Markov Random Field Modeling in Computer Vision*. Tokyo: Springer.

[9] Geman, D., (1990). Random fields and inverse problems in imaging. In *École d'Été de Probabilités de Saint-Flour XVIII - 1988*, P. Hennequin, ed., Vol. 1427 of *Lect. Notes in Math.*, pp. 113–193. Berlin: Springer.

[10] Winkler, G., (1995). *Image Analysis, Random Fields and Dynamic Monte Carlo Methods*, Vol. 27 of *Appl. of Mathematics*. Heidelberg: Springer.

[11] Blake, A. and Zisserman, A., (1987). *Visual Reconstruction*. Cambridge, MA: MIT Press.

[12] Geiger, D. and Girosi, F., (1991). Parallel and deterministic algorithms from MRF's: surface reconstruction. *IEEE Trans. Patt. Anal. Mach. Intell.*, **13**(5):401–412.

[13] Geiger, D. and Yuille, A., (1991). A common framework for image segmentation. *Int. J. of Comp. Vision*, **6**(3):227–243.

[14] Alvarez, L., (1996). Images and PDE's. In Berger et al. [49], pp. 3–14.

[15] Sapiro, G. and Tannenbaum, A., (1993). Affine invariant scale-space. *Int. J. of Comp. Vision*, **11**(1):25–44.

[16] ter Haar Romeny, B. M. (ed.), (1994). *Geometry-Driven Diffusion in Computer Vision*, Dordrecht, The Netherlands. Kluwer Academic Publishers.

[17] Malladi, R., Sethian, S., and Vemuri, B., (1996). A fast level set based algorithm for topology-independent shape modeling. *Jour. Math. Imag. Vision*, 6(2/3):269-289.

[18] Caselles, V., Kimmel, R., Sapiro, G., and Sbert, C., (1997). Minimal surfaces based object segmentation. *IEEE Trans. Patt. Anal. Mach. Intell.*, 19(4): 394-398.

[19] Nordström, N., (1990). Biased anisotropic diffusion—a unified regularization and diffusion approach to edge detection. *Image and Vis. Comp.*, 8 (4):318-327.

[20] Black, M. and Rangarajan, A., (1996). On the unification of line processes, outlier rejection, and robust statistics with applications in early vision. *Int. J. of Comp. Vision*, 19(1):57-91.

[21] Stevenson, R., Schmitz, B., and Delp, E., (1994). Discontinuity preserving regularization of inverse visual problems. *IEEE Trans. Systems, Man and Cyb.*, 24(3):455-469.

[22] Schnörr, C., (1994). Unique reconstruction of piecewise smooth images by minimizing strictly convex non-quadratic functionals. *Jour. Math. Imag. Vision*, 4:189-198.

[23] Li, S., (1995). Convex energy functions in the DA model. In *Proc. Int. Conf. Image Proc.*

[24] Schnörr, C., (1998). A study of a convex variational diffusion approach for image segmentation and feature extraction. *Jour. of Math. Imag. and Vision*, 8(3):271-292.

[25] Hackbusch, W., (1993). *Iterative Solution of Large Sparse Systems of Equations*. Berlin: Springer.

[26] Kelley, C., (1995). *Iterative Methods for Linear and Nonlinear Equations*. Philadelphia: SIAM.

[27] Heers, J., Schnörr, C., and Stiehl, H., (1998). A class of parallel algorithms for nonlinear variational image segmentation. In *Proc. Noblesse Workshop on Non-Linear Model Based Image Analysis (NMBIA'98), Glasgow, Scotland.*

[28] Heers, J., Schnörr, C., and Stiehl, H., (1998). *Investigating a class of iterative schemes and their parallel implementation for nonlinear variational image smoothing and segmentation.* Technical report FBI-HH-M 283/98, Comp. Sci. Dept., AB KOGS, University of Hamburg, Hamburg, Germany.

[29] Fučik, S., Kratochvil, A., and Nečas, J., (1973). Kačanov-Galerkin method. *Comment. Math. Univ. Carolinae*, 14(4):651-659.

[30] Nečas, J. and Hlaváček, I., (1981). *Mathematical Theory of Elastic and Elasto-Plastic Bodies*. Amsterdam: Elsevier.

[31] Zeidler, E., (1985). *Nonlinear Functional Analysis and its Applications*, Vol. III. Berlin: Springer.

[32] Schnörr, C., (1998). *Variational approaches to image segmentation and feature extraction.* Habilitation thesis, University of Hamburg, Comp. Sci. Dept., Hamburg, Germany. In German.

[33] Geman, D. and Reynolds, G., (1992). Constrained restoration and the recovery of discontinuities. *IEEE Trans. Patt. Anal. Mach. Intell.*, **14**(3): 367–383.

[34] Charbonnier, P., Blanc-Féraud, L., Aubert, G., and Barlaud, M., (1997). Deterministic edge-preserving regularization in computed imaging. *IEEE Trans. in Image Proc.*, **6**(2):298–311.

[35] Rudin, L., Osher, S., and Fatemi, E., (1992). Nonlinear total variation based noise removal algorithms. *Physica D*, **60**:259–268.

[36] Rudin, L., Osher, S., and Fu, C., (1996). Total variation based restoration of noisy, blurred images. *SIAM J. Numer. Analysis.* submitted.

[37] Dobson, D. and Vogel, C., (1997). Convergence of an iterative method for total variation denoising. *SIAM J. Numer. Anal.*, **34**:1779–1791.

[38] Schnörr, C., (1996). Convex variational segmentation of multi-channel images. In Berger et al. [49], pp. 201–207.

[39] Sapiro, G. and Ringach, D., (1996). Anisotropic diffusion of multivalued images. In Berger et al. [49], pp. 134–140.

[40] Fleet, D. and Jepson, A., (1990). Computation of component image velocity from local phase information. *Int. J. of Comp. Vision*, **5**(1):77–104.

[41] Srinivasan, M., (1990). Generalized gradient schemes for the measurement of two-dimensional image motion. *Biol. Cybernetics*, **63**:421–431.

[42] Singh, A., (1992). *Optic Flow Computations: A Unified Perspective.* Los Alamitos, California: IEEE Comp. Soc. Press.

[43] Weber, J. and Malik, J., (1995). Robust computation of optical flow in a multi-scale differential framework. *Int. J. of Comp. Vision*, **14**(1):67–81.

[44] Mitiche, A. and Bouthemy, P., (1996). Computation and analysis of image motion: A synopsis of current problems and methods. *Int. J. of Comp. Vision*, **19**(1):29–55.

[45] Horn, B. and Schunck, B., (1981). Determining optical flow. *Artif. Intell.*, **17**:185–203.

[46] Black, M. and Anandan, P., (1996). The robust estimation of multiple motions: Parametric and Piecewise–Smooth Flow Fields. *Comp. Vis. Graph. Image Proc.: IU*, **63**(1):75–104.

[47] Schnörr, C., (1994). Segmentation of Visual Motion by Minimizing Convex Non-Quadratic Functionals. In *12th Int. Conf. on Pattern Recognition.* Jerusalem, Israel.

[48] Schnörr, C., Sprengel, R., and Neumann, B., (1996). A variational approach to the design of early vision algorithms. *Computing Suppl.*, **11**:149–165.

[49] Berger, M.-O., Deriche, R., Herlin, I., Jaffré, J., and Morel, J.-M. (eds.), (1996). *12th Int. Conf. on Analysis and Optim. of Systems: Images, Wavelets and PDEs*, Vol. 219 of *Lect. Notes in Control and Information Sciences*, Berlin. Springer.

14 Morphological Operators

Pierre Soille

Silsoe Research Institute, Silsoe, Bedfordshire, United Kingdom

14.1 Introduction

Mathematical morphology (*MM*) or simply *morphology* can be defined as a theory for the analysis of spatial structures [1]. It is called morphology because it aims at analyzing the shape and form of objects. Mathematical morphology is not only a *theory*, but also a powerful image analysis *technique*. The purpose of this chapter is to introduce the

Computer Vision and Applications

morphological operators used in practical applications[1]. The emphasis is therefore on the technique rather than the theory.

Morphological operators belong to the class of nonlinear neighborhood operators (Chapter 9). The neighborhood used for a given morphological operator is called *structuring element*. The operators are then defined by testing whether the structuring element does or does not fit the image objects considered as sets of an n-dimensional space. Set operators such as union and intersection can be directly generalized to gray-scale images of any dimension by considering the pointwise maximum and minimum operators.

Morphological operators are best suited to the selective extraction or suppression of image structures. The selection is based on their shape, size, and orientation. By combining elementary operators, important image processing tasks can also be achieved. For example, there exist combinations leading to the definition of morphological edge sharpening, contrast enhancement, and gradient operators.

Although most of the examples in this chapter deal with 2-D images, morphological operations directly apply to n-dimensional binary and gray-scale images. Their extension to multicomponent images requires the definition of a total ordering relationship between vectors. Alternatively, they can be handled by processing each component separately.

The chapter[2] is organized as follows. Background notions useful for defining and characterizing morphological operators are discussed in Section 14.2. A description of the fundamental and advanced morphological transformations including application examples follows in Section 14.3 and Section 14.4, respectively.

14.2 Preliminaries

14.2.1 Image transforms and cross sections

In mathematical terms, a gray-tone image f is a mapping of a subset $\mathcal{D}_f$ of $\mathbb{Z}^n$ called the definition domain of f into a finite chain of nonnegative integers:

$$f : \mathcal{D}_f \subset \mathbb{Z}^n \longrightarrow \{0, 1, \ldots, t_{\max}\}$$

where $t_{\max}$ is the maximum value of the data type used for storing the image (i. e., $2^n - 1$ for pixels coded on n bits). There is no need to consider negative values because usual morphological operators do preserve the dynamic range of the input image. Note that a binary image is nothing but a gray-scale image with only two gray-scale levels (0 for the background and 1 for the foreground).

---

[1]A comprehensive presentation of the principles and applications of morphological image analysis can be found in the treatise by Soille [2].

[2]An extended version of this chapter can be found in CVA2 [Chapter 21].

Morphological image transformations are image-to-image transformations, that is, the transformed image has the same definition domain as the input image and it is still a mapping of this definition domain into the set of nonnegative integers. We use the generic notation Ψ for such mappings. The *identity transform* I is a trivial example of image-to-image transformation.

A widely used image-to-image transformation is the threshold operator T, which sets all pixels x of the input image f whose values lie in the range $[t_i, t_j]$ to 1 and the other ones to 0:

$$[T_{[t_i,t_j]}(f)](x) = \begin{cases} 1, & \text{if } t_i \le f(x) \le t_j \\ 0, & \text{otherwise} \end{cases}$$

It follows that the threshold operator maps any gray-tone image into a binary image.

14.2.2 Set operators

The basic set operators are *union* $\cup$ and *intersection* $\cap$. For gray-tone images, the union becomes the *pointwise maximum* operator $\vee$ and the intersection is replaced by the *pointwise minimum* operator $\wedge$:

$$\begin{aligned} \text{union:} \quad & (f \vee g)(x) = \max[f(x), g(x)] \\ \text{intersection:} \quad & (f \wedge g)(x) = \min[f(x), g(x)] \end{aligned} \tag{14.1}$$

Another basic set operator is *complementation*. The complement of an image f, denoted by f^c, is defined for each pixel x as the maximum value of the data type used for storing the image minus the value of the image f at position x:

$$f^c(x) = t_{\max} - f(x) \tag{14.2}$$

The complementation operator is denoted by $\complement$: $\complement(f) = f^c$.

The *set difference* between two sets X and Y, denoted by $X \setminus Y$, is defined as the intersection between X and the complement of Y: $X \setminus Y = X \cap Y^c$.

The *transposition* of a set B corresponds to its symmetric set with respect to its origin:

$$\check{B} = \{-b \mid b \in B\}. \tag{14.3}$$

A set B with an origin O is symmetric if and only if $B = \check{B}$.

14.2.3 Order relationships

The set inclusion relationship allows us to determine whether two sets are ordered, that is, whether the first is included in the second or vice versa. Similarly, an image f is less than or equal to an image g if the value of f is less than or equal to the value of g at all pixels x:

$$f \leq g \iff \forall x, f(x) \leq g(x)$$

Order relationships for image transformations are defined by analogy: a transformation Ψ_1 is less than or equal to a transformation Ψ_2 if and only if, for all images f, $\Psi_1(f)$ is less than or equal to $\Psi_2(f)$:

$$\Psi_1 \leq \Psi_2 \iff \forall f, \Psi_1(f) \leq \Psi_2(f)$$

14.2.4   Discrete distances and distance functions

Definitions.   The concept of *distance* is widely used in image analysis and especially in mathematical morphology. There exist many discrete distances satisfying the three axioms of a metric (compare discussion in Section 8.3.3). The choice of a given *metric* depends on the application speed, memory load, and accuracy requirements.

The discrete distance d_G between two pixels p and q in a graph or grid G is the smallest length of the paths $\mathcal{P}$ linking p to q:

$$d_G(p, q) = \min\{L(\mathcal{P}) \mid \mathcal{P} \text{ path linking } p \text{ to } q \text{ in } G\} \qquad (14.4)$$

The path(s) corresponding to the smallest length is (are) called shortest path(s) or *geodesics*. If the underlying graph is 4-connected, the metric is known as the *city-block metric*, and denoted by d_b. The 8-connected graph defines the *chessboard metric* d_c. An alternative approach is to consider the points of the digitization network as if they were embedded into the Euclidean space $\mathbb{R}^n$. By doing so, the neighborhood relationships between points of the image definition domain are not taken into account and the actual *Euclidean distance* d_e is considered. In practice, Euclidean distances are often rounded to their nearest integer value.

The *distance function* D on a binary image f associates each pixel x of the definition domain $\mathcal{D}_f$ of f with its distance to the nearest zero-valued pixel:

$$[D(f)](x) = \min\{d(x, x') \mid f(x') = 0\} \qquad (14.5)$$

The distance function is sometimes referred to as the *distance transform*. Depending on whether d_e or d_G is used in Eq. (14.5), one defines a Euclidean or a discrete distance function. A distance function on a binary image of cells is shown in Fig. 14.1.

14.2.5   Image operator properties

The properties of linear shift-invariant image operators have already been described in Section 9.2. Morphological operators are nonlinear shift-invariant filters that may satisfy some other properties:

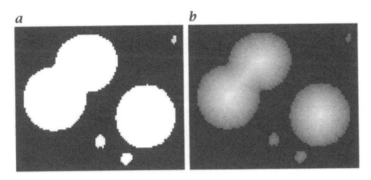

Figure 14.1: *Distance function on a binary image of cells. Note that the high values of the distance function correspond to the center of the cells: **a** binary image of cells; **b** rounded Euclidean distance function on (a).*

Idempotence. A transformation Ψ is idempotent if applying it twice to any image is equivalent to applying it only once:

$$\Psi, \text{ idempotent } \Leftrightarrow \Psi\Psi = \Psi$$

Extensivity. A transformation Ψ is extensive if it is greater than or equal to the identity transform I:

$$\Psi, \text{ extensive } \Leftrightarrow I \leq \Psi$$

Antiextensivity. A transformation Ψ is antiextensive if it is less than or equal to the identity transform I:

$$\Psi, \text{ antiextensive } \Leftrightarrow I \geq \Psi$$

Increasingness. A transformation Ψ is increasing if it preserves the order relationships (see Section 14.2.3) between images:

$$\Psi, \text{ increasing } \Leftrightarrow \forall f, g, \ f \leq g \Rightarrow \Psi(f) \leq \Psi(g) \qquad (14.6)$$

Duality. Two transformations Ψ and Φ are dual with respect to complementation if applying Ψ to an image is equivalent to applying Φ to the complement of the image and taking the complement of the result:

$$\Psi \text{ and } \Phi \text{ dual with respect to complementation } C \Leftrightarrow \Psi = C\Phi C \quad (14.7)$$

For example, setting to 0 all foreground-connected components whose surface area is less than a given threshold value λ is the dual transformation of setting to 1 all background-connected components whose surface area is less than λ.

Self-duality. A transformation Ψ is self-dual with respect to complementation if its dual transformation with respect to the complementation is Ψ itself:

$$\Psi, \text{ self-dual with respect to complementation } \complement \Leftrightarrow \Psi = \complement\Psi\complement$$

Linear shift-invariant filters (i.e., convolutions) are all self-dual operators. When a transformation is not self-dual, a symmetric processing can only be approximated by applying the transformation and then its dual (see Section 14.4.7).

14.2.6 Structuring element

An SE is nothing but a small set used to probe the image under study. An origin must also be defined for each SE so as to allow its positioning at a given point or pixel: an SE at point x means that its origin coincides with x. The elementary isotropic SE of an image is defined as a point and its neighbors, the origin being the central point. For instance, it is a centered 3×3 window for a 2-D image defined over an 8-connected grid. In practice, the shape and size of the SE must be adapted to the image patterns that are to be processed. Some frequently used SEs are discussed hereafter.

Digital approximations of line segments. Line segments are often used to remove or extract elongated image structures. There are two parameters associated with line SEs: length and orientation.

Digital approximations of the disk. Due to their isotropy, disks and spheres are very attractive SEs. Unfortunately, they can only be approximated in a digital grid. The larger the neighborhood size is, the better the approximation is.

Pair of points. In the case of binary images, an erosion with a pair of points can be used to estimate the probability that points separated by a vector v are both object pixels, that is, by measuring the number of object pixels remaining after the erosion. By varying the modulus of v, it is possible to highlight periodicities in the image. This principle applies to gray-scale images.

Composite structuring elements. A composite or two-phase SE contains two nonoverlapping SEs sharing the same origin. Composite SEs are considered for performing hit-or-miss transforms (Section 14.4.5).

Elementary structuring elements. Many morphological transformations consist in iterating fundamental operators with the elementary symmetric SE, that is, a pixel and its neighbors in the considered neighborhood. Elementary triangles are sometimes considered in the hexagonal grid and 2×2 squares in the square grid. In fact, the 2×2 square is the smallest isotropic SE of the square grid but it is not symmetric in the sense that its center is not a point of the digitization network.

14.3 Basic morphological operators

Morphological operators aim at extracting relevant structures of the image. This can be achieved by probing the image with another set of given shape called the *structuring element* (SE), see Section 14.2.6. Erosions and dilations are the two fundamental morphological operators because all other operators are based on their combinations.

14.3.1 Erosion and dilation

Erosion. The first question that may arise when we probe a set with a structuring element is *"Does the structuring element fit the set?"* The eroded set is the locus of points where the answer to this question is affirmative. In mathematical terms, the *erosion* of a set X by a structuring element B is denoted by $\varepsilon_B(X)$ and is defined as the locus of points x, such that B is included in X when its origin is placed at x:

$$\varepsilon_B(X) = \{x \mid B_x \subseteq X\} \tag{14.8}$$

Equation 14.8 can be rewritten in terms of an intersection of set translations, the translations being determined by the SE:

$$\varepsilon_B(X) = \bigcap_{b \in B} X_{-b}$$

This latter definition itself can be directly extended to binary and grayscale images: the erosion of an image f by a structuring element B is denoted by $\varepsilon_B(f)$ and is defined as the minimum of the translations of f by the vectors $-b$ of B:

$$\varepsilon_B(f) = \bigwedge_{b \in B} f_{-b} \tag{14.9}$$

Hence, the eroded value at a given pixel x is the minimum value of the image in the window defined by the structuring element when its origin is at x:

$$[\varepsilon_B(f)](x) = \min_{b \in B} f(x + b) \tag{14.10}$$

To avoid the erosion of the image structures from the border of the image, we assume that the image values outside the definition domain are set to t_{max}.

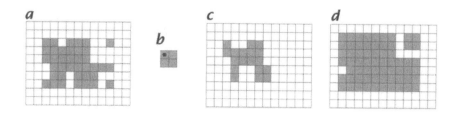

Figure 14.2: *Erosion ε and dilation δ of a set X by a 2 × 2 structuring element whose origin is the upper left pixel. **a** A binary image X. **b** A structuring element B. **c** Erosion of X by B. **d** Dilation of X by B.*

Dilation. The *dilation* is the dual operator of the erosion and is based on the following question: *"Does the structuring element hit the set?"* The dilated set is the locus of points where the answer to this question is affirmative.

The dilation of a set X by a structuring element B is denoted by $\delta_B(X)$ and is defined as the locus of points x such that B hits X when its origin coincides with x:

$$\delta_B(X) = \{x \mid B_x \cap X \neq \varnothing\} \tag{14.11}$$

The dilation and erosion of a discrete binary image are illustrated in Fig. 14.2.

Equation (14.11) can be rewritten in terms of a union of set translations, the translations being defined by the SE:

$$\delta_B(X) = \bigcup_{b \in B} X_{-b} \tag{14.12}$$

This latter definition can be directly extended to binary and gray-scale images: the dilation of an image f by a structuring element B is denoted by $\delta_B(f)$ and is defined as the maximum of the translation of f by the vectors $-b$ of B:

$$\delta_B(f) = \bigvee_{b \in B} f_{-b} \tag{14.13}$$

In other words, the dilated value at a given pixel x is the maximum value of the image in the window defined by the structuring element when its origin is at x:

$$[\delta_B(f)](x) = \max_{b \in B} f(x + b) \tag{14.14}$$

When dilating an image, border effects are handled by assuming a zero-extension of the image. Gray-scale erosion and dilation are illustrated in Fig. 14.3.

We denote by nB a structuring element of size n, that is, an SE B that has been dilated n times by its transposed $\check{B}$ (see Eq. (14.3)):

$$nB = \delta_{\check{B}}^n(B). \tag{14.15}$$

Notice that if $B = \check{B}$ then the following relationship holds: $\delta_B^n = \delta_{nB}$.

Properties. The dilation and the erosion are dual transformations with respect to complementation. This means that any erosion of an image is equivalent to a complementation of the dilation of the complemented image with the same structuring element (and vice versa). This duality property illustrates the fact that erosions and dilations do not process the objects and their background symmetrically: the erosion *shrinks* the objects but *expands* their background (and vice versa for the dilation).

Erosions and dilations are invariant to translations and preserve the order relationships between images, that is, they are increasing transformations.

The dilation distributes the pointwise maximum operator $\vee$ and the erosion distributes the pointwise minimum operator $\wedge$:

$$\delta(\bigvee_i f_i) = \bigvee_i \delta(f_i)$$

$$\varepsilon(\bigwedge_i f_i) = \bigwedge_i \varepsilon(f_i)$$

For example, the pointwise maximum of two images dilated with an identical structuring element can be obtained by a unique dilation of the pointwise maximum of the images. This results in a gain of speed.

The following two equations concern the composition of dilations and erosions:

$$\delta_{B_2}\delta_{B_1} = \delta_{(\delta_{\check{B}_2} B_1)} \tag{14.16}$$

$$\varepsilon_{B_2}\varepsilon_{B_1} = \varepsilon_{(\delta_{\check{B}_2} B_1)} \tag{14.17}$$

These two properties are very useful in practice as they allow us to decompose a morphological operation with a large SE into a sequence of operations with smaller SEs. For example, an erosion with a square SE of side n in pixels is equivalent to an erosion with a horizontal line of n pixels followed by an erosion with a vertical line of the same size. It follows that there are $2(n-1)$ min comparisons per pixel with decomposition and $n^2 - 1$ without, that is, $O(n)$ resp. $O(n^2)$ algorithm complexity.

The decomposition property is also important for hardware implementations where the neighborhood size is fixed (e.g., fast 3×3 neighborhood operations). By cascading elementary operations, larger neighborhood size can be obtained. For example, an erosion by a square of width $2n + 1$ pixels is equivalent to n successive erosions with a 3×3 square.

14.3.2 Morphological gradients

A common assumption in image analysis consists of considering image objects as regions of rather homogeneous graylevels. It follows that object boundaries or edges are located where there are high gray-level variations. Morphological gradients are operators enhancing intensity pixel variations within a neighborhood. The erosion/dilation outputs for each pixel the minimum/maximum value of the image in the neighborhood defined by the SE. Variations are therefore enhanced by combining these elementary operators.

The basic morphological gradient, also called *Beucher gradient* [3], is defined as the arithmetic difference between the dilation and the erosion with the elementary structuring element B of the considered grid. This morphological gradient is denoted by ρ:

$$\rho_B = \delta_B - \varepsilon_B. \tag{14.18}$$

From this latter equation, it can be seen that the morphological gradient outputs the maximum variation of the gray-level intensities within the neighborhood defined by the SE rather than a local slope.

The thickness of a step edge detected by a morphological gradient equals two pixels: one pixel on each side of the edge. Half-gradients can be used to detect either the internal or the external boundary of an edge. These gradients are one-pixel thick for a step edge.

The *half-gradient by erosion* or *internal gradient* ρ^- is defined as the difference between the identity transform and the erosion:

$$\rho_B^- = I - \varepsilon_B \tag{14.19}$$

The internal gradient enhances internal boundaries of objects brighter than their background and external boundaries of objects darker than their background. For binary images, the internal gradient will provide a mask of the internal boundaries of the objects of the image.

The *half-gradient by dilation* or *external gradient* ρ^+ is defined as the difference between the dilation and the identity:

$$\rho_B^+ = \delta_B - I \tag{14.20}$$

Note that the following relationships hold: $\rho^- = \rho^+ C$ and $\rho^+ + \rho^- = \rho$. The choice between internal or external gradient depends on the nature of the objects to be extracted. Morphological, external, and internal gradients are illustrated in Fig. 14.3.

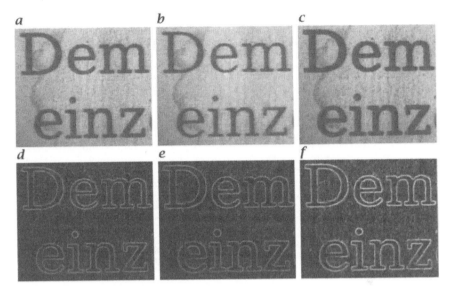

Figure 14.3: *Morphological gradients or how to combine erosion and dilation for enhancing object boundaries: **a** original image f; **b** dilated image $\delta(f)$; **c** eroded image $\varepsilon(f)$. Edge images: **d** $\rho^+(f) = \delta(f) - f$; **e** $\rho^-(f) = f - \varepsilon(f)$; **f** $\rho(f) = \delta(f) - \varepsilon(f)$. In this figure, the SE B is a 3×3 square.*

14.3.3 Opening and closing

Morphological opening. Once an image has been eroded, there exists in general no inverse transformation to get the original image back. The idea behind the morphological opening is to dilate the eroded image to recover as much as possible the original image.

The opening γ by a structuring element B is denoted by γ_B and is defined as the erosion by B followed by the dilation with the transposed SE $\check{B}$:

$$\gamma_B = \delta_{\check{B}} \varepsilon_B \qquad (14.21)$$

In Eq. (14.21), it is essential to consider the transposed SE for the dilation. Indeed, an erosion corresponds to an intersection of translations. It follows that a union of translations in the opposite direction (i.e., a dilation by the transposed SE) must be considered when attempting to recover the original image. Consequently, the opening of an image is independent from the origin of the SE.

Although the opening is defined in terms of erosions and dilations in Eq. (14.21), it possesses a geometric formulation in terms of SE fit using the question already introduced for the erosions: *"Does the structuring element fit the set?"* Each time the answer to this question is affirmative, the *whole* SE must be kept (for the erosion, it is the origin of the SE that

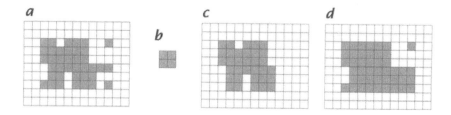

Figure 14.4: *Opening and closing of a 13×10 discrete binary image by a 2 × 2 square structuring element (the object pixels are the gray pixels): **a** a binary image X; **b** a structuring element B; **c** opening of X by B; **d** closing of X by B.*

is kept). Therefore, the opened set is the union of all SEs fitting the set:

$$\gamma_B(X) = \bigcup_x \{B_x \mid B_x \subseteq X\} \tag{14.22}$$

Morphological closing. The idea behind the morphological closing is to build an operator tending to recover the initial shape of the image structures that have been dilated. This is achieved by eroding the dilated image.

The closing by a structuring element B is denoted by ϕ_B and is defined as the dilation with a structuring element B followed by the erosion with the transposed structuring element $\check{B}$:

$$\phi_B = \varepsilon_{\check{B}} \delta_B \tag{14.23}$$

Contrary to the opening, the closing filters the set from the outside. The opening and closing of a discrete image by a 2×2 square SE is shown in Fig. 14.4.

Note that the opening removes all object pixels that cannot be covered by the structuring element when it fits the object pixels while the closing fills all background structures that cannot contain the structuring element. In Fig. 14.5, the closing of a gray-scale image is shown together with its opening.

Properties. Openings and closings are dual transformations with respect to set complementation. The fact that they are not self-dual transformations means that one or the other transformation should be used depending on the relative brightness of the image objects we would like to process. The relative brightness of an image region defines whether it is a background or foreground region. Background regions have a low intensity value compared to their surrounding regions and vice versa for the foreground regions. Openings filter the foreground regions from the inside. Closings have the same behavior on the background regions. For instance, if we want to filter noisy pixels with high intensity values an opening should be considered.

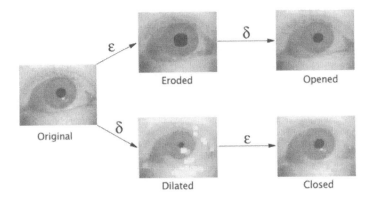

Figure 14.5: *Opening and closing of a gray-scale image with a* 5×5 *square SE.*

We have already stated that openings are antiextensive transformations (some pixels are removed) and closings are extensive transformations (some pixels are added). Therefore, the following ordering relationships always hold:

$$\gamma \leq I \leq \phi$$

Morphological openings γ and closings ϕ are both increasing transformations. This means that openings and closings preserve order relationships between images. Moreover, successive applications of openings or closings do not further modify the image. Indeed, they are both idempotent transformations: $\gamma\gamma = \gamma$ and $\phi\phi = \phi$. The idempotence property is often regarded as an important property for a filter because it ensures that the image will not be further modified by iterating the transformation.

14.4 Advanced morphological operators

14.4.1 Top-hats

The choice of a given morphological filter is driven by the available knowledge about the shape, size, and orientation of the structures we would like to filter. For example, we may choose an opening by a 2×2 square SE to remove impulse noise or a larger square to smooth the object boundaries. Morphological top-hats [4] proceed *a contrario*. Indeed, the approach undertaken with top-hats consists in using knowledge about the shape characteristics that are *not* shared by the relevant image structures. An opening or closing with an SE that does not fit the relevant image structures is then used to *remove* them from the image. These structures are recovered through the arithmetic difference between the image and its opening or between the closing and the image.

The success of this approach is due to the fact that there is not necessarily a one-to-one correspondence between the knowledge about what an image object is and what it is not. Moreover, it is sometimes easier to remove relevant image objects than to try to suppress the irrelevant ones.

The white top-hat or *top-hat by opening WTH* of an image f is the difference between the original image f and its opening γ:

$$WTH = I - \gamma \qquad (14.24)$$

As the opening is an anti extensive image transformation, the gray-scale values of the white top-hat are always greater or equal to zero.

The *black top-hat* or *top-hats by closing BTH* of an image f is defined as the difference between the closing ϕ of the original image and the original image:

$$BTH = \phi - I \qquad (14.25)$$

It follows that $BTH = WTH\,\complement$. Due to the extensivity property of the closing operator, the values of the black top-hat images are always greater or equal to zero.

If the image objects all have the same local contrast, that is, if they are either all darker or brighter than the background, *top-hat* transforms can be used for mitigating illumination gradients. Indeed, a top-hat with a large isotropic structuring element acts as a high-pass filter. As the illumination gradient lies within the low frequencies of the image, it is removed by the top-hat. White top-hats are used for dark backgrounds and black top-hats for bright backgrounds.

For example, Fig. 14.6a shows a badly illuminated image of seeds. A closing with a large structuring element removes the seeds but preserves the illumination function. The black top-hat or subtraction of the original image from the closing provides us with an evenly illuminated image (Fig. 14.6c). A more contrasted image can be obtained by dividing the original image with its closing (Fig. 14.6d).

14.4.2 Granulometries

Principle. The concept of a *granulometry* [5], or size distribution, may be likened to the sifting of rocks in a gravel heap. The rocks are sifted through screens of increasing size, leaving only the rocks that are too big to pass through the sieve. The process of sifting the rocks at a particular size is analogous to the opening of an image using a particular size of structuring element. The residue after each opening is often collated into a granulometric curve, revealing useful information about the distribution of object sizes in the image.

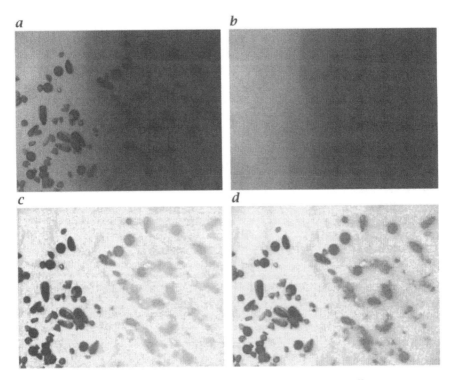

Figure 14.6: *Use of top-hat for mitigating inhomogeneous illumination:* ***a*** *Original image* f; ***b*** *Closing of* f *with a large square:* $\phi(f)$; ***c*** *Black top-hat:* $BTH(f) = \phi(f) - f$; ***d*** *Division of* f *by* $\phi(f)$.

In mathematical terms, a granulometry is defined by a transformation having a size parameter λ and satisfying the following three axioms:

- *Antiextensivity:* the rocks that remain in the sieve are a subset of the initial rocks.

- *Increasingness:* When sifting a subset of a heap of rocks, the rocks remaining in the sieve are a subset of those remaining after sifting the whole heap.

- *Absorption:* Let us consider a sifting transformation Φ at two different sizes λ and ν. Sifting with Φ_λ and then with Φ_ν will give the same result as sifting with Φ_ν prior to Φ_λ. It is only the size of the largest sieve that determines the result. This property is called *absorption*:

$$\Phi_\lambda \Phi_\nu = \Phi_\nu \Phi_\lambda = \Phi_{\max(\lambda,\nu)} \tag{14.26}$$

Note that for $\lambda = \nu$ the idempotence property is a particular case of the absorption property.

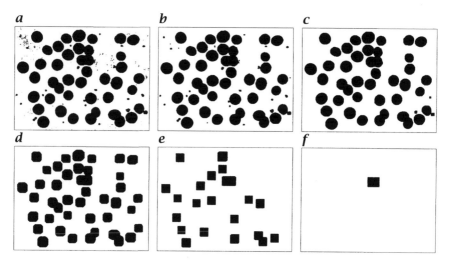

Figure 14.7: *Successive openings of a binary image of blood cells or granulometry (using square SEs of increasing size):* **a** *Original image* f; **b** *Opening of size 1:* $\gamma_B(f)$; **c** $\gamma_{3B}(f)$; **d** $\gamma_{9B}(f)$; **e** $\gamma_{13B}(f)$; **f** $\gamma_{15B}(f)$.

By definition, all openings satisfy the two first properties. However, not all openings with SEs of increasing size satisfy the absorption property. Disk-like SEs or line segments of increasing size are usually considered (families based on cascades of periodic lines are detailed in [6]). Figure 14.7 illustrates a granulometry with a family of square SEs of increasing size. Note that the size distribution does not require the particles to be disconnected.

Granulometries are interpreted through granulometric curves. Two kinds of granulometric curves are generally used:

1. Surface area of Φ_λ vs λ

2. Loss of surface area between Φ_λ and $\Phi_{\lambda+1}$ vs λ

The latter type of granulometric curve is often referred to as the *pattern spectrum* [7] of the image. A large impulse in the pattern spectrum at a given scale indicates the presence of many image structures at that scale. The granulometric curve associated with the granulometry presented in Fig. 14.7 is provided in Fig. 14.8 together with its pattern spectrum.

Granulometries also apply to gray-tone images. In this latter case, the surface area measurement should be replaced by the volume[3].

---

[3]The volume of an image equals the sum of the gray-level intensities of all its pixels.

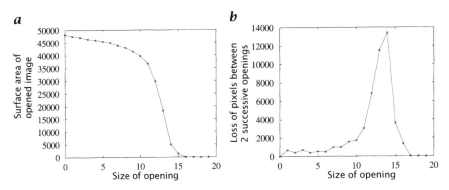

Figure 14.8: *Granulometric curves corresponding to Fig. 14.7.* **a** *Surface area of the opening vs size of the opening.* **b** *Derivative of* **a**. *The high peak observed in the pattern spectrum (b) indicates that most cells of Fig. 14.7a are at this size.*

14.4.3 Geodesic operators

All morphological operators discussed so far involved combinations of *one* input image with specific structuring elements. The approach taken with geodesic operators is to consider *two* input images. A morphological operator is applied to the first image and it is then forced to remain either greater or lower than the second image. Authorized morphological operators are restricted to elementary erosions and dilations. The choice of specific structuring elements is therefore eluded. In practice, geodesic transformations are iterated until stability, making the choice of a size unnecessary. It is the combination of appropriate pairs of input images that produces new morphological primitives. These primitives are at the basis of formal definitions of many important image structures for both binary and gray-scale images.

Geodesic dilation. A geodesic dilation involves two images: a marker image and a mask image. By definition, both images must have the same domain of definition and the mask image must be larger than or equal to the marker image. The marker image is first dilated by the elementary isotropic structuring element. The resulting dilated image is then forced to remain below the mask image. The mask image acts therefore as a limit to the propagation of the dilation of the marker image.

Let us denote by f the marker image and by g the mask image ($f \leq g$). The *geodesic dilation* of size 1 of the marker image f with respect to the mask image g is denoted by $\delta_g^{(1)}(f)$ and is defined as the pointwise minimum between the mask image and the elementary

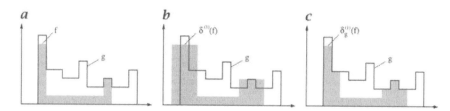

Figure 14.9: *Geodesic dilation of a 1-D marker signal f with respect to a mask signal g. Due to the pointwise minimum operator, all pixels of the elementary dilation of f having values greater than g are set to the value of g: **a** 1-D marker signal f and mask signal g, f ≤ g: **b** Elementary dilation $\delta^{(1)}(f)$; **c** Geodesic dilation $\delta_g^{(1)}(f)$.*

dilation $\delta^{(1)}$ of the marker image, as illustrated in Fig. 14.9:

$$\delta_g^{(1)}(f) = \delta^{(1)}(f) \wedge g \qquad (14.27)$$

The geodesic dilation of size n of a marker image f with respect to a mask image g is obtained by performing n successive geodesic dilations of f with respect to g:

$$\delta_g^{(n)}(f) = \delta_g^{(1)}[\delta_g^{(n-1)}(f)]$$

It is essential to proceed step-by-step and to apply the pointwise minimum operator after each elementary geodesic dilation in order to control the expansion of the marker image. Indeed, the geodesic dilation is lower or equal to the corresponding conditional dilation:

$$\delta_g^{(n)}(f) \leq \delta^{(n)}(f) \wedge g$$

Geodesic erosion. The *geodesic erosion* is the dual transformation of the geodesic dilation with respect to set complementation:

$$\varepsilon_g^{(1)}(f) = \varepsilon^{(1)}(f) \vee g \qquad (14.28)$$

where $f \geq g$ and $\varepsilon^{(1)}$ is the elementary erosion. Hence, the marker image is first eroded and second the pointwise maximum with the mask image is calculated.

The geodesic erosion of size n of a marker image f with respect to a mask image g is obtained by performing n successive geodesic erosions of f with respect to g:

$$\varepsilon_g^{(n)}(f) = \varepsilon_g^{(1)}[\varepsilon_g^{(n-1)}(f)]$$

Morphological reconstruction. Geodesic dilations and erosions of a given size are seldom used in practice. However, when iterated until stability, they allow the definition of powerful morphological reconstruction algorithms.

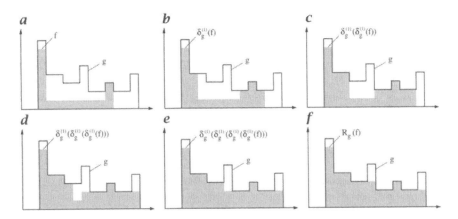

Figure 14.10: *Morphological reconstruction by dilation of a 1-D signal g from a marker signal f. The geodesic dilation of size 5 of the marker signal with respect to the mask signal g is equivalent to the reconstruction of g from f because further geodesic dilations no longer modify the result: a 1-D marker signal f and mask signal g; b geodesic dilation of size 1 of f with respect to g; c geodesic dilation of size 2 of f with respect to g; d geodesic dilation of size 3 of f with respect to g; e geodesic dilation of size 4 of f with respect to g; f geodesic dilation of size 5 of f with respect to g.*

Definition. The *reconstruction by dilation* of a mask image g from a marker image f ($f \le g$) is defined as the geodesic dilation of f with respect to g until stability and is denoted by $R_g(f)$:

$$R_g(f) = \delta_g^{(i)}(f)$$

where i is such that $\delta_g^{(i)}(f) = \delta_g^{(i+1)}(f)$.

The reconstruction by dilation on 1-D gray-tone signals is illustrated in Fig. 14.10. In this figure, stability is reached after the fifth geodesic dilation.

The *reconstruction by erosion* of a mask image g from a marker image f ($f \ge g$) is defined as the geodesic erosion of f with respect to g until stability is reached. It is denoted by $R_g^\star(f)$:

$$R_g^\star(f) = \varepsilon_g^{(i)}(f).$$

where i is such that $\varepsilon_g^{(i)}(f) = \varepsilon_g^{(i+1)}(f)$

On the choice of the mask and marker images. Morphological reconstruction algorithms are at the basis of numerous valuable image transformations. These algorithms do not require choosing an SE nor setting its size. The main issue consists of selecting an appropriate pair of mask/marker images. The image under study is usually used as a mask image. A suitable marker image is then determined using:

1. knowledge about the expected result;
2. known facts about the image or the physics of the object it represents;
3. some transformations of the mask image itself;
4. other image data if available (i. e., multispectral and multitemporal images); and
5. interaction with the user (i.e., markers are manually determined).

One or usually a combination of these approaches is considered. The third one is the most utilized in practice but it is also the most critical: one has to find an adequate transformation or even a sequence of transformations. As the marker image has to be greater (respectively, less) than the mask image, extensive (respectively, antiextensive) transformations are best suited for generating them.

14.4.4 Some reconstruction-based operators

Particles connected to the image border. In many applications it is necessary to remove all particles connected to the image border. Indeed, they may introduce some bias when performing statistics on particle measurements. Particles connected to the image border are extracted using the input image as a mask image and the intersection between the input image and its border as a marker image. The marker image contains therefore seeds for each particle connected to the image border and the reconstruction outputs the image of all these particles. Note that large blobs have a higher probability of intersecting the image border than small blobs. Statistical methods must be considered for compensating this bias.

The removal of objects connected to the image border can be extended to gray-scale images. In this latter case, the marker image equals zero everywhere except along its border where the values of the input image are considered.

Minima imposition. The minima imposition technique [8] concerns the filtering of the image minima[4]. It assumes that markers of relevant image features have been determined. The marker image f_m is then defined as follows for each pixel x:

$$f_m(x) = \begin{cases} 0, & \text{if } x \text{ belongs to a marker} \\ t_{\max}, & \text{otherwise} \end{cases}$$

The imposition of the minima of the input image g is performed in two steps. First, the pointwise minimum between the input image and the

---

[4]An image minimum is a connected component of pixels of identical intensity and whose external boundary pixels all have a greater intensity.

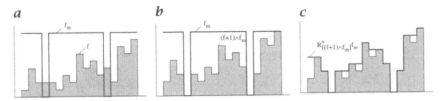

Figure 14.11: *Minima imposition technique. The input signal f contains seven minima. The two minima of the marker signal f_m are imposed to the input signal by using a morphological reconstruction by erosion: **a** Input signal f and marker signal f_m; **b** Pointwise minimum between f + 1 and f_m: $(f + 1) \wedge f_m$; **c** Reconstruction of $(f + 1) \wedge f_m$ from the marker function f_m.*

marker image is computed: $f \wedge f_m$. By doing so, minima are created at locations corresponding to the markers (if they do not already exist) and we make sure that the resulting image is lower or equal to the marker image. Moreover, two minima to impose may already belong to a minima of f at level 0. It is therefore necessary to consider $(f + 1) \wedge f_m$ rather than $f \wedge f_m$. The second step consists of a morphological reconstruction by erosion of $(f + 1) \wedge f_m$ from the marker image f:

$$R^{\star}_{[(f+1) \wedge f_m]}(f_m)$$

The imposition of minima is illustrated in Fig. 14.11 on a 1-D signal. The same developments apply for maxima imposition techniques.

Opening/closing by reconstruction. The opening by reconstruction of size n of an image f is defined as the reconstruction of f from the erosion of size n of f:

$$\gamma_R^{(n)}(f) = R_f[\varepsilon^{(n)}(f)] \qquad (14.29)$$

Contrary to the morphological opening, the opening by reconstruction preserves the shape of the components that are not removed by the erosion: All image features that cannot contain the structuring element are removed, the others being unaltered. This is illustrated in Fig. 14.12 for a binary image. The original image (Fig. 14.12a) is first eroded (Fig. 14.12b). The eroded sets are then used as seeds for a reconstruction of the original image. This leads to Fig. 14.12c.

Closings by reconstruction are defined by duality:

$$\phi_R^{(n)}(f) = R_f^{\star}[\delta^{(n)}(f)] \qquad (14.30)$$

The morphological closing and closing by reconstruction is shown in Fig. 14.13. The structuring element considered for both closings is a large square. The dark image structures that have been completely

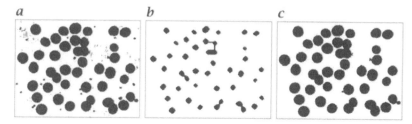

Figure 14.12: *Opening by reconstruction of a binary image: **c** the output image is the reconstruction of **a** the original image f using **b** the erosion as marker image (erosion of f by a square SE).*

Figure 14.13: *Morphological closing and (morphological) closing by reconstruction of an image of a container plate: **a** Image of a container plate f; **b** Closing of f by a 15×15 square; **c** Closing by reconstruction of f with the same square.*

filled by the morphological closing remain closed after the reconstruction. This happens for the 0 and the 2 surrounded by a rectangular box.

The following order relationships hold:

$$\gamma \le \gamma_R \le I \le \phi_R \le \phi.$$

Opening and closing by reconstruction are used for processing signals of at least two dimensions. Indeed, the opening (respectively closing) by reconstruction of 1-D signals is always equivalent to its morphological opening (respectively closing).

14.4.5 Hit-or-miss

The basic idea behind the hit-or-miss transform consists of extracting image pixels of a binary image having a given neighboring configuration such as a foreground pixel surrounded by background pixels (i. e., an isolated foreground pixel). The neighboring configuration is therefore defined by two disjoint sets, the first for the object pixels and the second for the background pixels. These two sets form what we call a composite SE that has a unique origin, that is, both sets share the same origin.

In order to perform a hit-or-miss transform, the SE is set to every possible position of the image. At each position, the following question is considered *"Does the first set fit the foreground while, simultaneously,*

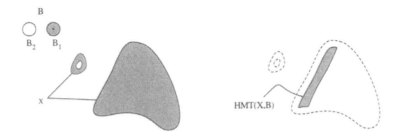

Figure 14.14: *Hit-or-miss transformation HMT of a set X by a composite struc-turing element B (B_1 is the gray disk and B_2 the white disk, the origin of both disks is located at the center of B_1).*

the second set misses it (i.e., fits the background)?". If the answer is affirmative, then the point defined by the origin of the SE is a point of the hit-or-miss transformation of the image. Let us now formalize this definition in terms of morphological transformations.

The hit-or-miss transformation HMT of a set X by a composite structuring element $B = (B_1, B_2)$ is the set of points x such that when the origin of B coincides with x, B_1 fits X and B_2 fits X^c:

$$HMT_B(X) = \{x \mid (B_1)_x \subseteq X, \ (B_2)_x \subseteq X^c\} \qquad (14.31)$$

The hit-or-miss transformation of a set X by a composite structuring element B is sometimes denoted by $X \circledast B$. Using the definition of the erosion Eq. (14.8), the HMT can be written in terms of an intersection of two erosions:

$$HMT_B(X) = \varepsilon_{B_1}(X) \cap \varepsilon_{B_2}(X^c) \qquad (14.32)$$

By definition, B_1 and B_2 have the *same* origin. They also need to be disjoint sets (i.e., $B_1 \cap B_2 = \varnothing$), otherwise the hit-or-miss would output the empty set whatever X.

An example is provided in Fig. 14.14. Both SEs of the composite SE B are disks but they have a common origin located at the center of the gray disk B_1.

It follows that B_2 does not contain its origin. Points of the hit-or-miss transform of the set X by the composite SE B (see right-hand side of the figure) are such that when the origin of B coincides with each of these points, the disk B_1 fits X and, simultaneously, the disk B_2 fits the background of X. Hence, the hit-or-miss transformation extracts all points of the image having a neighborhood configuration as defined by the composite SE B.

14.4.6 Thinning and thickening

Thinnings consist of removing the object pixels having a given config-uration. In other words, the hit-or-miss transform of the image is sub-tracted from the original image. Contrary to hit-or-miss transforms, there exists a definition of thinnings for gray-scale images.

Binary case. The thinning of a set or binary image X by a composite SE B is denoted[5] by $X \bigcirc B$ and defined as the set difference between X and the hit-or-miss transform of X by B:

$$X \bigcirc B = X \setminus HMT_B(X) \qquad (14.33)$$

The origin of the SE must belong to B_1 the set of object pixels, otherwise the operation comes down to the identity transform. By definition, thinnings are antiextensive and nonincreasing operators.

Gray-scale case. Due to their nonincreasingness, thinnings defined in Eq. (14.33) cannot be extended to gray-scale images using the threshold decomposition principle. However, there exists a definition for gray-scale image that comes down to Eq. (14.33) when applied to binary im-ages. The principle is the following. The gray-scale value of the image at position x is set to the largest value of the image within the neigh-borhood defined by the background pixels of the SE if and only if the smallest value of the image within the neighborhood defined by the ob-ject pixels of the SE equals the image value at position x, otherwise the gray-scale value of the image at position x is not modified (remember that, for a thinning, the origin of the SE must belong to the set B_1 of object pixels of the SE):

$$(f \bigcirc B)(x) = \begin{cases} [\delta_{B_2}(f)](x) & \text{if } [\delta_{B_2}(f)](x) < f(x) \text{ and} \\ & \quad f(x) = [\varepsilon_{B_1}(f)](x) \\ f(x) & \text{otherwise} \end{cases} \qquad (14.34)$$

In this equation, the dilated value can be smaller than the original value because the SE B_2 does not contain its origin. The definition for binary images is a particular case of this definition. Indeed, the dilation by B_2 equals zero if all points of B_2 fit the background of the set and the erosion by B_1 equals one if and only if all points of B_1 fit the foreground.

Binary case. The thickening of a binary image or set X by a composite SE B is denoted by $X \odot B$ and defined as the union of X and the hit-or-miss transform of X by B:

$$X \odot B = X \cup HMT_B(X)$$

---

[5]Beware that in the literature, the symbol ∘ is sometimes used for the morphological opening operator (and • for the morphological closing).

For a thickening, the origin of the SE must belong to the set B_2 of background pixels. Thickenings are extensive and nonincreasing transformations. Thinnings and thickenings are dual transformations:

$$X \odot B = (X^c \bigcirc B^c)^c \qquad (14.35)$$

where $B = (B_1, B_2)$ and $B^c = (B_2, B_1)$

Gray-scale case. The thickening of a gray-scale image by a composite SE B at a pixel x is defined as the eroded value of the image by B_2 if this value is larger than the original image value at x and if the dilated value by B_1 is equal to this original image value; otherwise the thickening remains at the original value:

$$(f \odot B)(x) =$$
$$\begin{cases} [\varepsilon_{B_2}(f)](x), & \text{if } [\delta_{B_1}(f)](x) = f(x) \text{ and } f(x) < [\varepsilon_{B_2}(f)](x), \\ f(x), & \text{otherwise} \end{cases}$$

14.4.7 Morphological filtering

Morphological filter definitions. The basic idea behind a morphological filter is to suppress image structures selectively. These structures are either noise or irrelevant image objects. It follows that the structures that are preserved should not be modified by further applications of the same filter. This illustrates a key property of a morphological filter: the idempotence. In this sense, a morphological filtering operation can be compared with the sifting of materials through a sieve: Once the materials have been sifted, they will not be further sifted by passing them through the same sieve. A morphological filter also shares the increasing property of a sifting process. This property ensures that the order relationships between images are preserved.

The idempotence and increasing properties are necessary and sufficient conditions for an image transformation to be a *morphological filter*:

$$\Psi, \text{ morphological filter} \Leftrightarrow \Psi \text{ is increasing and idempotent}$$

Consequently, closings are extensive morphological filters and openings are antiextensive morphological filters. They are the basic morphological filters.

Design of a morphological filter. New filters can be designed by combining elementary filters. However, all combinations are not allowed. For instance, the composition of two openings is generally not an opening nor a filter. In fact, the composition of two idempotent transformations is not necessarily an idempotent operation. In this section, we detail parallel and sequential combinations of existing filters leading to new filters.

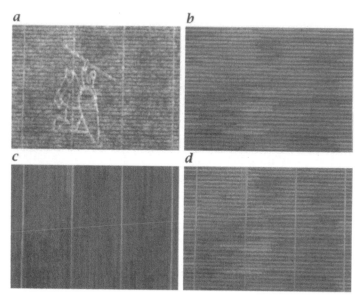

Figure 14.15: *Opening as a union of openings:* **a** *The input image represents a watermark on paper containing laid (horizontal) and chain (vertical) lines. The union of openings shown in* **d** *using* **b** *horizontal and* **c** *vertical structuring elements is an opening that can be used to extract laid and chain lines while suppressing the watermark.*

Parallel combinations. Let us consider for example the image of a watermark shown at the left of Fig. 14.15. Assume that we would like to design a filter extracting both laid and chain lines while removing the watermark. This can be simply achieved by calculating the union of two openings performed in parallel: the first with a horizontal SE and the second with a vertical SE.

It can be shown that this union of openings is extensive, idempotent, and increasing. It follows that it is still an opening (in the algebraic sense). This example illustrates an important way of building new openings from existing ones because any union of a series of openings is still an opening. The dual rule applies for closings:

1. Any union (or pointwise maximum) of openings is an opening: $(\bigvee_i \gamma_i)$ is an opening.

2. Any intersection (or pointwise minimum) of closings is a closing: $(\bigwedge_i \phi_i)$ is a closing.

Such parallel combinations are often used for filtering elongated image structures. In this case, openings (for bright objects) or closings (for dark objects) with line segments in several directions are considered (the longer the SE, the larger the number of directions).

Sequential combinations. We have already mentioned that the composition of two openings is not necessarily a filter. However, the composition of two ordered filters is always a filter. The pair of ordered filters considered is often an opening γ and the dual closing ϕ. An opening filters out bright image structures while a closing has the same filtering effect but on the dark image structures. If the image is corrupted by a symmetrical noise function, it is therefore interesting to use a sequential combination such as an opening followed by a closing or vice versa, the selection depending on the local contrast of the image objects that should be extracted.

Compositions of ordered filters leading to new filters are given hereafter:

$$\gamma\phi, \; \phi\gamma, \; \gamma\phi\gamma, \text{ and } \phi\gamma\phi \text{ are filters}$$

This rule is called the *structural theorem* [9]. Moreover, the following ordering relationships are always satisfied:

$$\gamma \leq \gamma\phi\gamma \leq \genfrac{}{}{0pt}{}{\gamma\phi}{\phi\gamma} \leq \phi\gamma\phi \leq \phi$$

The $\phi\gamma$ filter is often called an open-close filter as it consists of an opening followed by a closing. Close-open filters are defined by duality. Although open-close and close-open filters have almost the same filtering effect, they are not equivalent. Moreover, there exists no order relationship between $\gamma\phi$ and $\phi\gamma$ nor between $\gamma\phi$ and I or $\phi\gamma$ and I.

Consecutive applications of openings and closings are at the basis of the alternating sequential filters described in the next section.

Alternating sequential filters. As detailed in the previous section, the filtering of an image corrupted by dark and bright noisy structures can be achieved by a sequence of either close-open or open-close filters. When the level of noise is high in the sense that it contains noisy structures over a wide range of scales, a unique close-open or open-close filter with a large SE does not lead to acceptable results. For example, Fig. 14.16a shows a noisy interferogram that is filtered by open-close (Fig. 14.16b) and close-open (Fig. 14.16c) filters with 5×5 square. Due to the high level of noise, the opening of the open-close filter removes almost all structures, leading thereby to an almost dark image (Fig. 14.16b). The dual behavior is obtained with the close-open filter (Fig. 14.16c).

A solution to this problem is to alternate closings and openings, beginning with a small structuring element and then proceeding with ever increasing structuring elements until a given size is reached. This sequential application of open-close (or close-open) filters is called an *alternating sequential filter* [10, 11].

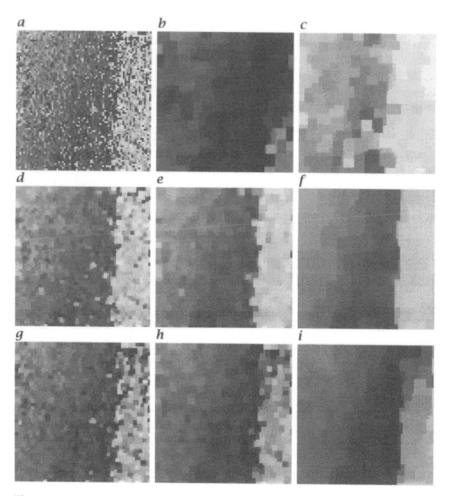

Figure 14.16: *Alternating sequential filters: **a** the original image is a subset of a noisy interferogram. The first row shows a direct application of **b** an open-close or **c** close-open filter with a 5 × 5 square; **d** to **f** display a series of ASFs of increasing size and starting with a closing; **g** to **i** show ASFs starting with an opening.*

Definition. Let y_i be an opening and ϕ_i be the dual closing of size i. Following the structural theorem the following combinations are all morphological filters:

$$m_i = y_i\phi_i, \quad r_i = \phi_i y_i \phi_i$$
$$n_i = \phi_i y_i, \quad s_i = y_i\phi_i y_i$$

An alternating sequential filter of size i is defined as the sequential combination of one of these filters, starting the sequence with the filter of size 1 and terminating it with the filter of size i:

$$
\begin{aligned}
M_i &= m_i \cdots m_2 m_1, & R_i &= r_i \cdots r_2 r_1 \\
N_i &= n_i \cdots n_2 n_1, & S_i &= s_i \cdots s_2 s_1
\end{aligned}
$$

It can be proved that alternating sequential filters (ASFs) are all morphological filters. Moreover, they satisfy the following absorption law:

$$
i \leq j \ \Rightarrow \ ASF_j ASF_i = ASF_j \text{ and } ASF_i ASF_j \leq ASF_j
$$

Note that M_i and N_i constitute a pair of dual filters that are not ordered. The final result depends therefore on whether an opening or the dual closing is used as the first filter in the sequence. Although ASFs are not self-dual, they act in a much more symmetrical way than closings and openings. The ASFs are particularly suited to noise reduction before applying other morphological operators like gradients and top-hats.

Example. Examples of ASFs are given in the last two rows of Fig. 14.16. The goal is to filter the noisy interferogram shown in Fig. 14.16a. The used structuring elements are squares of width equal to $2i + 1$ pixels where i denotes the size of the ASF. Figure 14.16d to f show ASF of type M. The ASF of type N are illustrated in Fig. 14.16g to i. Notice that both filters suppress noisy structures of the original image. The larger the size of the ASF, the larger the size of the structures that are removed.

14.4.8 Watershed segmentation

The morphological approach to image segmentation combines region growing and edge detection techniques: It groups the image pixels around the regional minima of the image and the boundaries of adjacent regions follow the crest lines dividing the influence zones of the minima. This is achieved by a transformation called the *watershed transformation*.

The watershed transformation. Let us consider the topographic representation of a gray-level scale image. Now, let a drop of water fall on such a topographic surface. According to the law of gravitation, it will flow down along the steepest slope path until it reaches a minimum. The whole set of points of the surface whose steepest slope paths reach a given minimum constitutes the *catchment basin* associated with this minimum. The *watersheds* are the zones dividing adjacent catchment basins. This is illustrated in Fig. 14.17a.

Definition in terms of flooding simulations. The definition of the watersheds in terms of water flows is not well-suited to an algorithmic

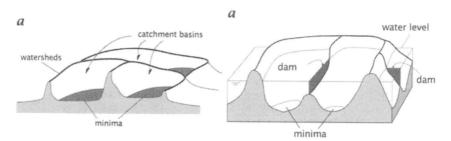

Figure 14.17: *a Minima, catchment basins, and watersheds on the topographic representation of a gray-scale image. **b** Building dams at the places where the water coming from two different minima would merge.*

implementation as there are many cases where the flow direction at a given point is not determined (e. g., flat regions or pixels having more than one neighbor pixel with the lowest gray-scale value). However, a definition in terms of flooding simulations alleviates all these problems. Consider again the gray tone image as a topographic surface and assume that holes have been punched in each regional minimum of the surface. The surface is then slowly immersed into a lake. Starting from the minima at the lowest altitude, the water will progressively flood the catchment basins of the image. In addition, dams are erected at the places where the waters coming from two different minima would merge (see Fig. 14.17b). At the end of this flooding procedure, each minimum is completely surrounded by dams, which delineate its associated catchment basin. The resulting dams correspond to the watersheds. They provide us with a partition of the input image into its different catchment basins. An efficient queue-based algorithm is detailed in [12, 13].

Marker-controlled segmentation. The basic idea behind the marker-controlled segmentation [8] is to transform the input image in such a way that the watersheds of the transformed image correspond to meaningful object boundaries. The transformed image is called the *segmentation function.* In practice, a direct computation of the watersheds of the segmentation function produces an over-segmentation, which is due to the presence of spurious minima. Consequently, the segmentation function must be filtered *before* computing its watersheds. Any filtering technique may be considered. However, the minima imposition technique described in Section 14.4.4 is the best filter in most applications. This technique requires the determination of a *marker function* marking the relevant image objects and their background. The corresponding markers are then used as the set of minima to impose to the segmentation function. The schematic of this approach is summarized in Fig. 14.18.

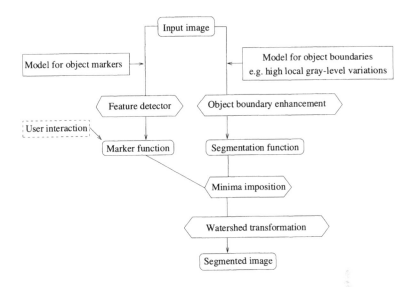

Figure 14.18: *Morphological paradigm for image segmentation. Image understanding is done at the very first stages of the process. The 'intelligent' part of the process is when it generates the marker and the segmentation functions. Then, the rest of the procedure is nonparametric.*

The object markers are extracted from the image using some feature detectors. The choice of appropriate feature detectors relies on some *a priori* knowledge or assumptions about the properties of an image object. Common features include image extrema, flat zones (i.e., connected components of pixels of constant gray-level value), zones of homogeneous texture, etc. In some applications, the markers may be defined manually. One marker per region is necessary as there will be a one-to-one correspondence between the markers and the segments of the final partition. However, if the class of object marked by each marker is known, several markers of the same class may be considered for each image object. The size of a marker can range from a unique pixel to a large connected component of pixels. When processing noisy images, large markers perform better than small ones.

The determination of the segmentation function is based on a model for the definition of an object boundary. For example, if the image objects are defined as regions of rather constant gray-scale values, a *morphological gradient* operator will enhance the object boundaries. If the image objects are regions of homogeneous texture, operators highlighting the transition between two textures should be considered.

The object markers are then used as the set of markers to impose to the segmentation function. Finally, the object boundaries are obtained by computing the watersheds of the filtered segmentation function.

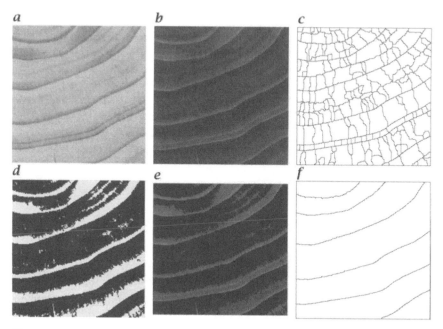

Figure 14.19: *Watershed segmentation of tree rings:* **a** *Original image* f; **b** *Complement of* f *as segmentation function;* **c** *Watersheds of* f^c; **d** *Filtered extended minima of* f^c *as marker function;* **e** *Filtered segmentation function;* **f** *Watersheds of filtered segmentation function.*

Example. A tree ring is the layer of wood cells produced by a tree in one year, usually consisting of thin-walled cells formed early in the growing season (called earlywood) and thicker-walled cells produced later in the growing season (called latewood). The beginning of earlywood formation and the end of the latewood formation form one annual ring, which usually extends around the entire circumference of the tree. Example Fig. 14.19a shows a sample of a cross-section of a tree. In this image, seven tree rings are visible. A watershed segmentation for extracting the boundaries of the tree rings requires determining a segmentation function transforming the input image in such a way that the tree ring boundaries will appear as crest lines. In this application, an appropriate segmentation function can be obtained by simply complementing the image of the tree rings (see Fig. 14.19b). A direct computation of the watersheds of this segmentation function leads to an oversegmentation (see Fig. 14.19c) because each tree ring contains many image minima. The solution is to a find an appropriate marker function containing one marker per tree ring. Here, the markers are defined as the extended minima[6] of the segmentation function having

---

[6]The extended minima of an image are defined as the minima of the reconstruction by dilation of the input image from the marker image obtained by adding a given constant value to the input image.

a surface area greater than a given threshold value. They are displayed in Fig. 14.19d. These markers are then used as the set of minima to impose to the segmentation function. The resulting filtered segmentation function is shown in Fig. 14.19e. The watersheds of the filtered segmentation function output a correct segmentation of the tree rings (see Fig. 14.19f).

This example illustrates the basis of the methodology described in [14]. References to additional applications of the watershed transformation are given in CVA3 [Chapter 12 and 19].

14.5 References

[1] Serra, J., (1982). *Image analysis and mathematical morphology.* London: Academic Press.

[2] Soille, P., (1999). *Morphological Image Analysis.* Berlin Heidelberg: Springer-Verlag.

[3] Rivest, J.-F., Soille, P., and Beucher, S., (1993). Morphological gradients. *Journal of Electronic Imaging,* **2**(4):326–336.

[4] Meyer, F., (1986). Automatic screening of cytological specimens. *Computer Vision, Graphics, and Image Processing,* **35**:356–369.

[5] Matheron, G., (1975). *Random sets and integral geometry.* Wiley.

[6] Jones, R. and Soille, P., (1996). Periodic lines: Definition, cascades, and application to granulometries. *Pattern Recognition Letters,* **17**(10):1057–1063.

[7] Maragos, P., (1989). Pattern spectrum and multiscale shape representation. *IEEE Transactions on Pattern Analysis and Machine Intelligence,* **11**(7):701–716.

[8] Meyer, F. and Beucher, S., (1990). Morphological segmentation. *Journal of Visual Communication and Image Representation,* **1**(1):21–46.

[9] Matheron, G., (1988). Filters and Lattices. In *Image analysis and mathematical morphology. Volume 2: theoretical advances,* J. Serra, ed., chapter 6, pp. 115–140. Academic Press.

[10] Sternberg, S., (1986). Grayscale morphology. *Computer Graphics and Image Processing,* **35**:333–355.

[11] Serra, J., (1988). Alternating sequential filters. In *Image analysis and mathematical morphology. Volume 2: theoretical advances,* J. Serra, ed., chapter 10, pp. 203–214. Academic Press.

[12] Soille, P. and Vincent, L., (1990). Determining watersheds in digital pictures via flooding simulations. In *Visual Communications and Image Processing'90,* M. Kunt, ed., Vol. SPIE-1360, pp. 240–250. Lausanne.

[13] Vincent, L. and Soille, P., (1991). Watersheds in digital spaces: an efficient algorithm based on immersion simulations. *IEEE Transactions on Pattern Analysis and Machine Intelligence,* **13**(6):583–598.

[14] Soille, P. and Misson, L., (1999). *Image analysis of tree rings.* In preparation, Silsoe Research Institute and Université catholique de Louvain.

15 Probabilistic Modeling in Computer Vision

Joachim Hornegger, Dietrich Paulus, and Heinrich Niemann
Lehrstuhl für Mustererkennung
Universität Erlangen-Nürnberg, Germany

15.1 Introduction

The mapping of real world objects to the image plane including the geometric and the radiometric parts of image formation is basically well understood [1, 2]. The image data and *prior knowledge* on the considered application are the major sources of information for various vision issues. Common examples are image restoration, filtering, segmentation, reconstruction, modeling, *detection*, *recognition* or *pose estimation* algorithms. The hardest problems in computer vision are related to object recognition [3]. Up to now, there have been no general algorithms that allow the automatic learning of arbitrary 3-D objects and their recognition and localization in complex scenes. State-of-the-art

Computer Vision and Applications

approaches dealing with high-level vision tasks are essentially dominated by model-based object recognition methods [4].

In the past, numerous applications have led to various types of representations for object models that allow the implementation of excellent recognition systems [5]. Many image processing and computer vision algorithms are characterized by prevailing *ad hoc* solutions. Most techniques apply intuitive ideas specified for the given application and neglect the exploration of precisely defined mathematical models. There exists no unified theoretical formalization that provides the framework for the analytical analysis of designed complete systems. For the most part, it is left to empirical studies to justify the usage of the chosen representation scheme.

It is beyond the scope of this chapter to provide an exhaustive overview and discussion of models successfully applied in computer vision. We also cannot introduce general models that fit all requirements of conceivable applications, but we do present some probabilistic modeling schemes and their basic features, which have been shown to be proper for a wide range of vision problems. The organization of the chapter is as follows: The next section summarizes arguments for a probabilistic formulation of computer vision modules and introduces the basic requirements for object models. The formal definitions of the considered vision problems that have to be solved using *probabilistic models* are summarized in Section 15.3.

Following the abstract framework, we introduce a family of probabilistic models. We start with a general modeling scheme and specialize this to various probabilistic models such as *histograms* (Section 15.4.1), *intensity-based models* (Section 15.4.2), mixtures of densities with incorporated feature transforms (Section 15.4.5), or *Markov random fields* (Section 15.4.6). For all models we give either references to applications or explicit examples. In Section 15.5 we will give several hints for solving problems that are usually related to probabilistic models, and how these can be solved in many cases—either heuristically or by means of theoretically well-understood techniques. The chapter concludes with a summary and a brief discussion.

15.2 Why probabilistic models?

An immediate question is why we should prefer a probabilistic setup to any other recognition algorithms. In fact, both from a pragmatic and a theoretical point of view, the advantages of a statistical framework are persuasive:

- Sensor signals and associated features show a probabilistic behavior due to sensor noise, varying illumination conditions or segmentation errors.

- Pattern recognition routines should use all available sources of information including *prior knowledge* and empirical data. A unified mathematical formulation incorporating all modules is given by probabilistic models.

- Decision theory guarantees the optimality of *Bayesian classifiers*, which maximize posterior probabilities (see also Section 15.3).

- The design of learning algorithms can utilize comprehensive results in statistics and statistical learning theory [6, 7].

- The success of probabilistic models in different areas of applied pattern recognition, such as speech recognition and handwritten character recognition, also motivate the use of statistical methods.

In addition to these general advantages, a probabilistic setting introduces some valuable tools for simplification and for the increase of computational tractability; the incorporation of independency assumptions regarding observed features leads to compromise solutions and paves the way to eliminate the trade-off between computational efficiency and models that are still rich enough to provide the required discriminating power. Marginalizations, that is the elimination of random variables by integration, reduce the complexity, allow the usage of probabilistic models, if the input data are incomplete, and provide techniques to define hierarchical modeling schemes.

In practice, the design and usage of probabilistic models should follow the general guideline: as much theory as necessary, and as simple as possible.

15.3 Object recognition as probabilistic modeling

Most computer vision problems correspond to standard pattern recognition problems such as *classification* and *regression*. A digital image f is mathematically considered as a matrix of discrete intensity values $f = [f_{m,n}]_{1 \leq m \leq M, 1 \leq n \leq N}$. For further processing, most high-level vision tasks require the labeling or segmentation of images. Based on these labels and segmentation results, recognition and the estimation of pose parameters have to be done. The following subsections will treat the recognition and pose estimation problems using a probabilistic framework. The important issue related to model generation and learning from observations is omitted and we refer to CVA2 [Chapter 26] for further details.

15.3.1 Recognition as classification

In a unified manner the solution of object identification problems can be considered as a labeling procedure [8]. A given image f (or the result of any preprocessing and segmentation steps) is assigned to a single class Ω_κ, which is an element of the set of considered classes $\Omega = \{\Omega_1, \Omega_2, \ldots, \Omega_K\}$.[1] If more objects are present, the classifier is expected to compute the set of corresponding classes. An image is thus mapped to a set of classes. Of course, there are different ways to associate pattern classes with objects. It usually depends on the given application and the features used, whether or not types of objects are considered to represent instances of the same class. For example, objects can share the same 3-D shape and differ in color. Whether the shape or the color are discriminating features depends on the given application. Another problem is caused by objects that are considered to be elements of different classes but share a common view, that is, there exist viewing directions where you cannot distinguish between these objects.

Including image segmentation, the task of object recognition, that is, the discrete mapping of images to pattern classes, is a composition of various classification processes. The mapping from the original image to discrete classes is mostly subdivided into the following stages (with variations [9]):

1. *Preprocessing*: in the preprocessing stage images are filtered. Domain and range of these image transforms are discrete intensity values;

2. *Segmentation*: the segmentation maps the image matrix to a matrix that defines, for instance, geometric primitives. In the most general case, segmentation algorithms transform images to parameters that define geometric features uniquely, for example, start and end points of straight-line segments. In this case a single image point can belong to different geometric primitives. Examples are points where lines intersect; and

3. *Classification*: the final classification stage maps segmentation results to classes.

The discussion so far reveals that the basic problem in object recognition can be stated as follows: We have to define and to provide a modeling scheme that allows one to compute a mapping δ from images to labels or classes, dependent on the given application. Without loss of generality, we restrict the description to classes and omit identical formulas for labels. The *classification* is defined by $\delta(f) = \kappa \in \{1, 2, \ldots, K\}$. This mapping δ characterizes the so-called *decision rule* of the classifier. It is not obvious for system design how to choose the decision rule and how to select an appropriate representation of objects that allow the comparison of models and observations. Due to our ultimate goal of implementing reliable object recognition systems, it is a natural consequence that we seek classifiers with minimum error rates.

---

[1]In the text the authors mostly prefer to denote a pattern class by Ω_κ instead of using the integer κ to reveal that classes are categorical variables without any ordering. Integers would imply the natural ordering, which is indeed not present.

For that purpose, let us define a *loss function* $L(\lambda, \kappa)$ that penalizes *classification* errors. The function $L(\lambda, \kappa)$ measures the price we pay for classifying an observation belonging to class Ω_λ to Ω_κ. Herein, we take for granted that correct decisions are cheaper than misclassifications. Now we choose the decision rule δ^* that minimizes the expected *classification* loss. With respect to this objective, the optimal classifier results from solving the minimization problem

$$\delta^*(f) = \mathrm{argmin}_{\delta(f)} \sum_{\lambda=1}^{K} L(\lambda, \delta(f)) \, p(\lambda | f) \qquad (15.1)$$

where $p(\lambda | f)$ is the *a posteriori* probability for observing class Ω_λ given the image f. Having especially a 0-1 loss function, where we charge classification errors by 1, the objective function in Eq. (15.1) takes its minimal value if we fade out the highest summand by correct decisions. Therefore, we determine that class of highest posterior probability, and the optimal decision rule minimizing the average loss is

$$\delta^*(f) = \mathrm{argmax}_\kappa \, p(\kappa | f) = \mathrm{argmax}_\kappa \, p(\kappa) p(f | \kappa) \qquad (15.2)$$

Classifiers applying this decision rule are called *Bayesian classifiers*. The observation that Bayesian classifiers minimize the expected loss and therefore the misclassification rate is the major reason for the introduction of probabilistic models in computer vision and other fields of pattern recognition [10, 11, 12]. We get an excellent classifier if we are able to characterize the statistical properties of objects appearing in sensor data. But usually this is a highly nontrivial task and represents the fundamental problem in probabilistic modeling: the definition and computation of posteriors based on empirical data. Without appropriate probabilistic models and accurate approximations of posteriors, there is no way to implement an optimal object recognition system.

15.3.2 Pose estimation as regression

Besides classification, the position and orientation of objects with respect to a reference coordinate system also are of potential interest. For instance, a robot that has to grasp objects requires pose parameters of high accuracy. Let us assume the intrinsic camera parameters are known. Thus *pose estimation* of objects is confined to the computation of rotation and translation. These transforms are referred to the world coordinate system. In the following we denote rotation by $R \in \mathbb{R}^{3\times3}$ and the translation by $t \in \mathbb{R}^3$. Details concerning the representation of the orthogonal rotation matrix are omitted, and we refer to [13]. For simplicity, the six degrees of freedom determining the pose are denoted by the vector θ. In contrast to the classification problem, the input data are no longer mapped to discrete variables such as class numbers, but to a real-valued vector θ. In terms of statistical decision theory, *pose estimation* thus corresponds to a *regression problem*. With regard to optimal regression, we introduce analogously to classification a penalty function for estimates. Pose parameters have to be determined such that the mean loss is observed. Here, the loss function $L(\boldsymbol{\theta}, \eta_\kappa(\boldsymbol{f}))$ charges the errors in pose estimates, where the *regression function* η_κ maps the observation to pose parameters. This function depends on the actual class Ω_κ of the shown object and is therefore indexed by κ, that is, $\eta_\kappa(\boldsymbol{f}) = \boldsymbol{\theta} \in \mathbb{R}^6$. The most commonly used loss function in *regression* is the square error, which is defined by $||\boldsymbol{\theta} - \eta_\kappa(\boldsymbol{f})||^2$. The regression problem associated with *pose estimation* is generally stated as the minimization task

$$\eta_\kappa^*(\boldsymbol{f}) = \mathrm{argmin}_{\eta_\kappa(\boldsymbol{f})} \int L(\boldsymbol{\theta}, \eta_\kappa(\boldsymbol{f}))\, p(\boldsymbol{\theta}|\boldsymbol{f}, \kappa)\, d\boldsymbol{\theta} \qquad (15.3)$$

where $p(\boldsymbol{\theta}|\boldsymbol{f}, \kappa)$ is the probability density function of $\boldsymbol{\theta}$ given the image $\boldsymbol{f}$ and the class Ω_λ. A similar argument to *Bayesian classifiers* shows that the optimal estimate regarding the square error loss function is given by the conditional expectation $\eta_\kappa^*(\boldsymbol{f}) = E[\boldsymbol{\theta}|\boldsymbol{f}, \kappa]$.

In practice, the major problem is the representation of the *regression* function, and many applications restrict the forementioned conditional expectation to a parametric family of functions. In these cases, the minimization Equation (15.3) reduces to *parameter estimation* problems. Commonly used parametric functions in statistics are, for example, linear functions [14]. In addition to parameterization, further constraints to regression functions can (and often should) be incorporated by regularization. For instance, we can also claim that the average curvature of the regression function in combination with the square error has to be minimized [6]. If the regression function is not restricted to a specific parametric family and regularization is not considered, the regression problem is generally ill-posed, and we observe an over-fitting to training data. Figure 15.1 illustrates the problem of over-fitting; the filled bullets represent the sample data and the solid and the dashed line indicate different approximations of the sampled function. In the case of over-fitting (solid line), the function values between sample data tend to be inaccurate and rough.

A general rule of thumb is to incorporate all available knowledge into the model and recognition process. Notably, the relation between the observation and pose parameters can be defined if the 3-D structure of objects and the projection properties of the chosen sensor are known. We suggest the *regression* of probability density functions for observations that are parameterized regarding the pose $\boldsymbol{\theta}$. From a theoretical point of view, we thus consider a generalization of the earlier-defined square error loss, and obviously the negative likelihood value of the parametric density function for given observations acts as the loss value of the estimated pose. Assuming a uniform distribution of pose

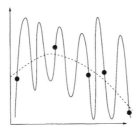

Figure 15.1: *An example of over-fitting (solid line: over-fitting with no errors regarding training samples; dashed line: smooth approximation with errors).*

parameters, the optimal pose parameters θ^* result from the maximum likelihood estimate

$$\theta^* = \text{argmax}_\theta \, p(f|\kappa; \theta) \qquad (15.4)$$

In this case, the pose estimation using probabilistic models corresponds to a standard *parameter estimation* problem.

15.3.3 Guidelines for probabilistic models

The discussion shows that *recognition* and *pose estimation* are finally a combination of two familiar problems in statistical decision theory—*classification* and *regression*. We conclude this section by summarizing the guidelines for the construction and usage of probabilistic models in object recognition and localization:

- We have to provide prior distributions $p(\kappa)$, $\kappa = 1, 2, \ldots, K$, which include all available knowledge regarding the given classes and their appearance in images; and
- The probabilities $p(f|\kappa; \theta)$, $\kappa = 1, 2, \ldots, K$, of observed images f (or features) have to be defined. Especially, if we are also interested in object localization, the probability density function has to be parameterized with respect to pose parameters denoted by θ. The specification of these probability density functions constitutes the hardest problem within the design of probabilistic models. In the following sections, the class density $p(f|\kappa; \theta)$ is also referenced by the term *model density*.

Related to the abstract mathematical structure of probabilistic models, there are several related computational aspects of practical importance:

- We have to provide learning algorithms that allow the automatic training of probability density functions from empirical data. From scratch, the training includes both the acquisition of the concrete model structure, for instance, the automatic decision for the required family of distributions, and the estimation of associated model parameters. Both theoretical and empirical results are necessary, which give hints on how to select the sample data for model acquisition, and which validation methods are advantageous to judge generated models; and

- In view of runtime efficiency it is very important to implement sophisticated (in terms of low complexity and high efficiency) *inference strategies*, which allow the fast evaluation of posteriors $p(\kappa|f;\theta)$ for given observations f and usually unknown pose parameters θ.

We begin the discussion of various probabilistic modeling schemes by a generic definition of model densities.

15.4 Model densities

The discrete image matrix $f = [f_{m,n}]_{1 \leq m \leq M, 1 \leq n \leq N}$ is formally considered as a random matrix. Each entry $f_{m,n}$ of the matrix f is characterized by three components: the position in the image defined by the 2-D grid coordinates $[m, n]^T$ and the associated pixel value $f_{m,n}$. For some reasons, which will become clear later, we take the image matrix f by a set of random vectors

$$\left\{ [m, n, f_{m,n}]^T \mid 1 \leq m \leq M, 1 \leq n \leq N \right\} \qquad (15.5)$$

and define both 2-D grid points and intensity values as potential random measures. Depending on the image type used, the intensity $f_{m,n}$ can be a color vector, a gray level or more generally a vector including any other label. Independent of the concrete dimension and interpretation of pixel values, the induced random vectors Equation (15.5) can be characterized by a conditional probability density function, which depends on the present pattern class Ω_κ. Because the appearance of objects in the image plane changes with the object pose, the density will also be parameterized regarding the pose θ.[2] Generally, we get for the whole image the probability density

$$p \left(\left\{ [m, n, f_{m,n}]^T \mid 1 \leq m \leq M, 1 \leq n \leq N \right\} | \kappa; \theta \right) \qquad (15.6)$$

which depends on the present object belonging to Ω_κ (or any other type of labels).

The model density (Eq. (15.6)) is far too general, not computationally feasible, and too abstract for any application. Nevertheless, it is the source of a broad class of model densities. The introduction of additional constraints, the consideration of dependencies of bounded order, the incorporation of specializations, and the usage of continuous instead of discrete random variables are basic tools that will induce reduced parameter sets and simpler models. Examples for well-

---

[2]We point out that θ is considered as a parameter and not as a random variable. This is also indicated in expressions by a separating semicolon.

studied continuous probability density functions are Gaussian densities and convex combinations of Gaussians [9]. Evident specializations are marginals, that is, integrating out random variables, and the introduction of independencies. The right combination of these techniques pushes the dimension of the final parameter space to mathematical feasibility and the curse-of-dimensionality can be beaten.

15.4.1 Histograms

An extreme case of marginalization and independency are *histograms* of intensity values. Relative frequencies of intensities represent a nontrivial probabilistic model of images given a pattern class Ω_κ. We compute the discrete probabilities of intensity values independently of their position in the image grid. To derive histograms or more precisely the product of histogram entries from Eq. (15.6), first, we decompose the probability density function according to the assumption that all intensity values are mutually independent; thus, we obtain the factorization

$$
\begin{aligned}
& p\left(\left\{[m,n,f_{m,n}]^T \mid 1 \le m \le M, 1 \le n \le N\right\} \mid \kappa; \boldsymbol{\theta}\right) \\
& = \prod_{m=1}^{M}\prod_{n=1}^{N} p\left([m,n,f_{m,n}]^T \mid \kappa; \boldsymbol{\theta}\right)
\end{aligned}
\tag{15.7}
$$

The marginal over the image coordinates leads to the demanded product discrete probabilities

$$
p\left(f \mid \kappa; \boldsymbol{\theta}\right) = \prod_{m=1}^{M}\prod_{n=1}^{N}\left(\sum_{m'=1}^{M}\sum_{n'=1}^{N} p\left([m',n',f_{m,n}] \mid \kappa; \boldsymbol{\theta}\right)\right)
\tag{15.8}
$$

Histograms show several obvious advantages: they are generated easily and these discrete probability mass functions exhibit some useful invariance properties. Assuming that we have normalized images, planar rotations and translations of objects will not (drastically) change the distribution of gray levels. Therefore, the pose parameters in the histogram can be reduced by these three degrees of freedom. The pose parameters include only out-of-plane rotations, denoted by φ_x and φ_y, and 1-D translations t_z along the optical axis. We gather from this example the important fact that clever marginals can reduce the dimension of pose parameters. Marginals provide a powerful technique for efficient *pose estimation* algorithms based on probabilistic models [15].

Histograms are accepted as simple and useful probabilistic models that are widely and successfully applied in computer vision [16]. However, discrete probabilities of intensities are also marginals that drastically simplify the real probability density function of object appearances in images. Marginalization is known to reduce the discriminatory power. Histograms only record the overall intensity composition of images. As a consequence, there is an increase in the rate of misclassifications. Histograms show tremendous invariances. Based on histograms, for instance, all images where we just permute pixels, lead to identical distributions of gray levels and thus the same classification results. Many applications defuse this property by restricting the computation of histograms to local window frames. But even in local histograms, the invariance to permutations is present. Remarkably, despite this extreme kind of invariance histograms have proven to be useful for a wide range of applications. Applications can be found, for instance, in [16].

15.4.2 Conditioned intensities

The major disadvantage of histograms for solving *classification* and *pose estimation* issues is due to invariance properties and the assumed independency of grid positions. A first step to generalize relative frequencies of intensity values is an isolated modeling of intensities dependent on grid points, that is, we do not consider the probability of observing a special intensity value in the image, but the probability of a certain intensity at a given grid point. Instead of eliminating grid points by marginalization, we thus compute the joint probability of the intensity value f at the randomly selected image point $[m, n]$. This probability density function is given by $p(m, n|\kappa)\, p(f|m, n, \kappa; \boldsymbol{\theta})$, where $\boldsymbol{\theta}$ denotes the pose parameter. Assuming mutually independent intensity values and image points, the density of the complete image f is obtained by the product

$$p(f|\kappa; \boldsymbol{\theta}) = \prod_{m=1}^{M} \prod_{n=1}^{N} p(m, n|\kappa)\, p(f_{m,n}|m, n, \kappa; \boldsymbol{\theta}) \qquad (15.9)$$

The priors of grid points are set equal if all image points are considered. Therefore, the probabilities $p(m, n|\kappa)$ in Eq. (15.9) include no additional information and can be omitted. Figure 15.2 illustrates the basic idea of the chosen model: all image points are separately modeled and mutually independent.

The introduced modeling scheme based on mutually independent image entries raises several questions:

- The first problem is the incorporation of pose parameters. Variations in position and orientation of objects have to be incorporated into this model. Because an object is modeled based on distributions where the intensities are included as continuous random variables and the grid points as discrete ones, even the simplest transforms in the image plane cause problems. Generally, planar rotations and translations define no discrete mapping of grid points. To

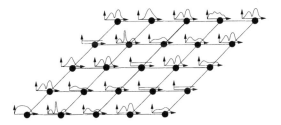

Figure 15.2: *Explicit modeling of intensity distribution in the image grid.*

deal with this problem, obviously resampling is required. In case of in-plane transforms, in [17] it is suggested to use linear interpolation between intensity values.

- Another fair criticism on this modeling scheme derives from the independency constraint of neighboring pixel values. Obviously, this independency assumption does not fit the real-world situation. Widely used constraints such as the smoothness criterion, which states that neighboring pixels share similar intensity values, require the explicit incorporation of dependencies.

An application of the modeling scheme introduced in the foregoing, to 3-D recognition and localization is described and experimentally evaluated in [17].

15.4.3 Conditioned image points

An alternative probabilistic model, which resolves some of the forementioned problems, results from a different factorization of the original probability $p([m, n, f_{m,n}]^T | \kappa; \boldsymbol{\theta})$ and a different interpretation of random variables: Now we consider the intensity values as discrete measures, the coordinates of grid points as continuous random variables. Instead of

$$p([m, n, f_{m,n}]^T | \kappa; \boldsymbol{\theta}) = p(m, n | \kappa)\, p(f | m, n, \kappa; \boldsymbol{\theta}) \qquad (15.10)$$

we use the decomposition

$$p([m, n, f_{m,n}]^T | \kappa; \boldsymbol{\theta}) = p(f_{m,n} | \kappa)\, p(m, n | f_{m,n}, \kappa; \boldsymbol{\theta}) \qquad (15.11)$$

Assuming again mutual independency of random vectors, the joint probability density function of the complete image showing class Ω_κ is now given by

$$p(\boldsymbol{f} | \kappa; \boldsymbol{\theta}) = \prod_{m=1}^{M} \prod_{n=1}^{N} p(f_{m,n} | \kappa)\, p(m, n | f_{m,n}, \kappa; \boldsymbol{\theta}) \qquad (15.12)$$

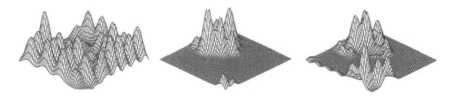

Figure 15.3: *Probability densities of image points conditioned on three different intensity values.*

Figure 15.3 shows three density functions. Each of these densities corresponds to a single intensity value, and visualizes the distribution of grid points showing a certain intensity value.

In the case of modeling distributions of intensities at image points, we were able to incorporate explicit knowledge on the sensor noise model. The density function $p(m, n | f, \kappa; \boldsymbol{\theta})$, however, is the probability measure that the image point $[m, n]$ appears showing the specific intensity value f. Therefore, this density characterizes the spatial distribution of a particular intensity in the image plane. For the parametric representation of grid-point distributions conditioned on an intensity value, a single Gaussian is obviously not an adequate approximation. The density associated with grid points is expected to be a multimodal and thus concave function. Therefore, we suggest the use of mixtures of densities [18]

$$p(m, n | f, \kappa; \boldsymbol{\theta}) = \sum_{i=1}^{l_f} p_i \, p(m, n | \boldsymbol{B}_{f,i,\kappa}; \boldsymbol{\theta}) \qquad (15.13)$$

where l_f denotes the order of the *mixture density*, the coefficients p_i sum up to 1, and the densities $p(m, n | \boldsymbol{B}_{f,i,\kappa}, \boldsymbol{\theta})$ are parameterized in $\boldsymbol{B}_{f,i,\kappa}$ and the pose vector $\boldsymbol{\theta}$. If, for instance, the mixture base densities are Gaussians, these parameters correspond to mean vectors and covariance matrices. Convex combinations of probability density functions are generally advantageous, because they show good approximation properties of multimodal functions, and they are not restricted to discrete values of $[m, n]^T$. This model obviously avoids interpolation for grid points if the object is rotated and translated in the image plane.

Example 15.1: Spatial distribution of intensities

The basic issue in defining an appropriate model using the representation suggested in Eq. (15.12) is the right choice of the density $p(m, n | f_{m,n}, \kappa; \boldsymbol{\theta})$ based on convex combinations. At first, we neglect the pose parameters and consider linear combinations of Gaussians [18] to model the spatial distribution of single intensity levels. Once the number l_f of mixture components associated with a certain inten-

Figure 15.4: *Toy car, cactus, candy box, block.*

sity value f is known, the multimodal density is represented by

$$p(m,n|f,\kappa) = \sum_{i=1}^{l_f} p_{i,f}\,\mathcal{N}([m,n]^T;\boldsymbol{\mu}_{\kappa,f,i},\Sigma_{\kappa,f,i}) \qquad (15.14)$$

where $p_{i,f} \geq 0$, $\sum_{i=1}^{l_f} p_{i,f} = 1$, and $\boldsymbol{\mu}_{\kappa,f,i} \in \mathbb{R}^2$ and $\Sigma_{\kappa,f,i} \in \mathbb{R}^{2\times2}$ denote the mean vector and covariance matrix of the ith mixture component associated with the gray level f.

The extension of this model based on Gaussian mixtures with respect to pose parameters is straightforward if pose parameters $\boldsymbol{\theta}$ define an affine mapping denoted by the matrix $\boldsymbol{R}$ and the vector $\boldsymbol{t}$. If an arbitrary normally distributed random variable with mean vector $\boldsymbol{\mu}$ and and covariance matrix Σ is transformed by this affine mapping, the resulting random variable is again Gaussian. The corresponding mean vector is defined by $\boldsymbol{R}\boldsymbol{\mu} + \boldsymbol{t}$ and the covariance matrix by $\boldsymbol{R}\Sigma\boldsymbol{R}^T$ [19]. Using this example, at least in-plane transformations are easily built in Eq. (15.14): For given 2-D rotations and translations we get the density

$$p(m,n|f,\kappa;\boldsymbol{R},\boldsymbol{t}) = \sum_{i=1}^{l_f} p_{i,f}\,\mathcal{N}([m,n]^T;\boldsymbol{R}\boldsymbol{\mu}_{\kappa,f,i} + \boldsymbol{t}, \boldsymbol{R}\Sigma_{\kappa,f,i}\boldsymbol{R}^T)$$

$$(15.15)$$

We have applied this modeling scheme to the recognition and localization of objects shown in Fig. 15.4. The intensity levels are automatically quantized to four different values minimizing the entropy. The hard problem of estimating the number of mixture components for each intensity value is solved by using a vector-quantization algorithm [12]; the remaining model parameters are estimated using the expectation-maximization algorithm [12]. Our experimental evaluation shows that the introduced modeling scheme allows the estimation of rotation angles with the variance less than 4° if only 64 uniformly chosen image points of 320×240 images are used for localization, that is, we use less than 1 % of the available image information and achieve reasonably good pose estimates. The same holds for recognition. The classification rate turns out to be 100 % if we use 512 sample points.

15.4.4 Appearance-based modeling

The probabilistic models so far are substantially restricted to 2-D images, and out-of-plane rotations and translations are still an open problem; the statistical characterization of 3-D objects and their appearance in the image plane including 6 degrees of freedom is not yet possible. The simplest way to extend these models is to quantize the pose and formally consider each 2-D view of an object as a separate class. This appearance-based strategy, however, shows the disadvantage that for each discrete set of pose parameters single probabilistic models have to be computed, and we have to deal with quantization errors in pose parameters. In [17], the authors suggest interpolating those density parameters that define the 2-D views and in-plane transformations dependent on pose parameters. Without additional geometric knowledge, regression (Section 15.3) provides the only way to generalize the given 2-D models to arbitrary pose parameters. The selection of an appropriate regression function, however, is a crucial and nontrivial issue.

The regression based on polynomials or arbitrarily selected parametric functions appears incidentally and without any geometric justification. A more obvious way would be to compute the distribution of the appearing object using the knowledge of the 3-D structure, the illumination model, and the mapping from the 3-D world to the image plane. An incorporation of the overall geometric relationships seems worthwhile. However, the major problem with respect to this issue is that the projection from 3-D to 2-D can be computed explicitly, not its inverse. But there is some hope: There exist first results towards the incorporation of geometry in probabilistic models if we use geometric features instead of intensities [15, 20, 21]. The next section considers segmentation results of images as random measures for pose estimation and summarizes existing probabilistic models using geometric features instead of intensity values or results of any preprocessing operations.

15.4.5 Model densities using geometric features

Let us assume that preprocessing and segmentation algorithms map the observed image to a set of 2-D points. The information provided by the whole image is thus reduced to a comparatively small set of features. We denote the set of points by $O = \{o_k | k = 1, 2, \ldots, m\}$, where $o_k \in \mathbb{R}^2$. Some examples for the segmentation of gray-level images into point features are shown in Fig. 15.5. Here the corners are features attached to the associated 3-D object. If we rotate and translate the corresponding 3-D points of the object in the 3-D space, this linear transform, the object geometry, and the projection to the image plane characterize the resulting 2-D features—apart from noise,

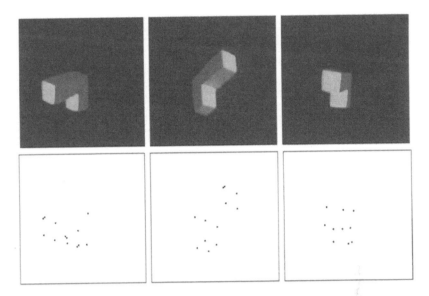

Figure 15.5: *Gray-level images and sparse sets of computed point features.*

occlusion, and segmentation errors. If the correspondences of 3-D and 2-D points are known, the transform can be written in a single equation. We denote the assignment of 2-D features o_k in the image to the index of the corresponding feature of the 3-D object by ζ_κ. The identifier ζ_κ in this context is not incidental. In fact, the assignment of 2-D and 3-D points can formally be considered as a *classification* or, in other words, all points get a label indicating the correspondence. If there are m observed features and n_κ 3-D points for class Ω_κ, the discrete mapping ζ_κ is defined by

$$\zeta_\kappa : \begin{cases} O & \to & \{1, 2, \ldots, n_\kappa\} \\ o_k & \mapsto & i_k \end{cases} \tag{15.16}$$

We get the probability observing a set of single points with a given assignment function ζ_κ by the following substitutions in our generic density Equation (15.6): The grid coordinates $[m, n]^T$ are now represented by the grid coordinates of segmented point features o_k, and instead of the intensity value $f_{m,n}$ characterizing each image point, we use $\zeta_\kappa(o_k)$ in the argument triple. Based on this substitution and considering the assignment as discrete random variables we obtain

$$p(\{(o_k, \zeta_\kappa(o_k)) | k = 1, 2, \ldots, m\} | \kappa; \boldsymbol{\theta}) = \prod_{k=1}^{m} p(\zeta_\kappa(o_k)) \, p(o_k | \zeta_\kappa, \kappa; \boldsymbol{\theta}) \tag{15.17}$$

if independent point features are assumed.

Unlike the intensity values f in the corresponding density Equation (15.12), the assignment $\zeta_\kappa(\boldsymbol{o}_k)$ of single-point features is unknown. We have *no information* on the correspondence between 3-D points and 2-D observations. Because the assignment is modeled as a random variable, we make use of the power of statistical framework and eliminate this random measure by marginalization. We sum Eq. (15.17) over all possible assignments. This yields the model density of the observed 2-D points without knowing the originally required correspondence defined by ζ_κ

$$p(\{\boldsymbol{o}_k|k = 1,2,\ldots,m\}|\kappa;\boldsymbol{\theta}) = \sum_{\zeta_\kappa} \prod_{k=1}^{m} p(\zeta_\kappa(\boldsymbol{o}_k))\, p(\boldsymbol{o}_k|\zeta_\kappa,\kappa;\boldsymbol{\theta}) \quad (15.18)$$

The probabilistic modeling of geometric modeling of features and the elimination of assignments by marginalization can be applied to various 2–D and 3–D object recognition and pose estimation problems. The interested reader will find more details in [15, 20], and [21].

The probabilistic models introduced so far use intensity images or segmentation results as input data, and in fact they represent extreme cases concerning independency assumptions; we have always used mutually independent random variables; either grid points, intensities, assignments or point features were independent and the corresponding densities properly factorized. In the following we will discuss statistical representations that also incorporate dependencies of higher (i.e., arbitrary) order.

15.4.6 Markov random fields

Very popular and widely used probabilistic models in image processing and computer vision are *Markov random fields* (MRFs) [8, 22, 23]; MRFs, in general, allow the use of locally bounded dependencies. We introduce the basic concepts of MRFs in an abstract manner, and illustrate these using concrete examples out of the field of computer vision.

Let $X = \{X_i | i = 1,2,\ldots,L\}$ define a set of random variables. We suppose that for each random variable X_i there exists a well-defined neighborhood. The set of neighbors of X_i is commonly denoted by [23]

$$\partial(X_i) = \{X_j|\ X_i \text{ and } X_j \text{ are neighbors}\} \quad (15.19)$$

In image-processing applications the random measures X_i are usually intensity values, and local *neighborhood* is based on the given structure of the image grid. For instance, we can consider each random measure associated with a pixel to be a neighbor of a certain random variable if the Euclidean distance of grid coordinates is one (*first-order neighborhood*) or lower or equal to $\sqrt{2}$ (*second-order neighborhood*). Figure 15.6 illustrates first- and second-order neighborhoods.

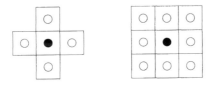

Figure 15.6: *Neighborhoods of first (left) and second (right) order.*

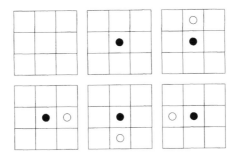

Figure 15.7: *Cliques corresponding to first-order neighborhoods.*

Mathematically, MRFs are defined by two basic properties:

1. *Positivity:* The probability of observing an arbitrary set of random variables X is nonzero, that is,

$$p(X) > 0 \qquad (15.20)$$

2. *Markov property:* The probability of observing a certain random variable $X_i \in X$ depends only on its neighbors $\partial(X_i)$, that is,

$$p(X_i | \{X_1, X_2, \ldots, X_{i-1}, X_{i+1}, \ldots, X_L\}) = p(X_i | \partial(X_i)) \qquad (15.21)$$

The Markov property introduces statistical dependencies of bounded order and defines the local characteristics of the MRF. The order of dependency is herein the cardinality of the set of neighbors. The preceding used neighborhood system induces a graph structure on the random variables, and therefore it enables us to use the language of graph theory in the context of Markov random fields; the vertices of the graph are defined by the random variables, and two vertices are connected by an edge if the corresponding random variables are neighbors. This analogy between neighborhoods, random variables and graphs also allows the notion of cliques. In graph theory a *clique* is defined as a set of vertices in which all pairs are mutual neighbors, that is, a clique defines a complete subgraph. Figure 15.7 shows the cliques to the graph associated with the first-order neighborhood. Note also that the empty graph is by definition a clique.

Equipped with the neighborhood systems and the concept of cliques, now we are able to compute the joint density of MRFs with the most current tools: The *equivalence theorem* for MRFs [23] states that the joint density $p(X)$ over all random variables X is proportional to a product of real-valued functions associated with cliques of the graph. The clique functions, however, have to be symmetric in their arguments, that is, whenever we change the order of input variables, the output is not affected. If $C = \{C_1, C_2, \ldots, C_P\}$ denotes the set of cliques and X_{C_i} the random variables belonging to clique C_i, then there exists a set of clique functions $\phi_{C_i}(X_{C_i})$, $i = 1, 2, \ldots, P$, such that

$$p(X) = \frac{1}{Z} \prod_{C_i \in C} \phi_{C_i}(X_{C_i}) \tag{15.22}$$

The denominator Z is a normalization factor, which guarantees that the integral over the complete domain of the density function turns out to be unity; Z is constant and due to its definition, is independent of the actual random variable X. Fortunately, the positivity constraint Equation (15.20) allows writing this product in *Gibbsian form*. For the set of random variables X, the overall density leads to the so-called *Gibbs field*

$$p(X) = \frac{1}{Z} \exp\left(-\sum_{C_i \in C} V_{C_i}(X_{C_i})\right) = \frac{1}{Z} \exp(-U(X)) \tag{15.23}$$

Gibbs distributions are well studied in statistical physics and according to physicists we call the function V_{C_i} *potential function*, which maps the set of random variables belonging to clique C_i to real values; the sum $U(X)$ of potentials is the *energy function*. In case of discrete random variables, here Z is defined by the marginal

$$Z = \sum_Y \exp(-U(Y)) \tag{15.24}$$

The computation of conditional densities using Gibbs distributions is surprisingly simple. If the Markov field is given in Gibbsian form, the conditional dependency for observing any random variable X_j satisfies

$$p(X_j | X_1, \ldots, X_{j-1}, X_{j+1}, X_L) = \frac{\exp\left(\sum_{C_i \in C} V_{C_i}(X_{C_i})\right)}{\sum_{X_j} \exp\left(\sum_{C_i \in C} V_{C_i}(X_{C_i})\right)}$$

$$= \frac{\exp\left(\sum_{C_i \in C(X_j)} V_{C_i}(X_{C_i})\right)}{\sum_{X_j} \exp\left(\sum_{C_i \in C(X_j)} V_{C_i}(X_{C_i})\right)} \tag{15.25}$$

where $C(X_j)$ is the set of all cliques including random variable X_j. All factors of the numerator and denominator cancel that do not contain an element of the clique C_j to which the random variable X_j belongs. This shows that the conditional density of random variable X_j depends on its local neighborhood—as required by the Markov property.

Most computer vision researchers are usually less familiar with statistical physics, and therefore the use of the Gibbs fields seems inconvenient and apparently not necessarily advantageous. However, we have seen in Eq. (15.25) that this notation is advantageous for the computation of conditional probabilities.

So far, we have seen that MRFs define a Gibbs field. The equivalence theorem states that this is also true in reverse order: each Gibbs field induces a Markov random field. This remarkable correspondence between Markov random and Gibbs fields was discovered by Hammersley and Clifford. The rather technical proof of the Gibbs-Markov equivalence is omitted and beyond the scope of this chapter. The interested reader will find a pretty elegant version in [23].

In practice, the knowledge of the equivalence theorem reveals two options to define priors and model densities based on MRF:

1. We ignore the result on Gibbs distributions and compute the joint density for a set of random variables by standard manipulations.

2. According to the given application we define a neighborhood system, consider the associated graph, and define the energy function in terms of clique potentials.

Both strategies—the explicit use of conditional densities and the application of Gibbsian densities—are in fact equivalent and useful in practice. It obviously depends on the concrete problem and the given model as to which representation is advantageous. Let us consider an example based on the Gibbsian form of Markov random fields that defines prior densities of images.

Example 15.2: The Ising model

One of the most referenced and nontrivial introductory examples of MRFs is the Ising model, which was invented by the physicist E. Ising. It is a statistical model to explain empirical observations on ferromagnetism theoretically. We state this model in terms of images and intensity values, as we are more familiar with this terminology. Let us consider images as a 2-D square lattice. We induce a graph structure according to neighbors of first order. The range of discrete intensity values $f_{m,n}$ is restricted to $\{\pm 1\}$. In the physical model these intensity values describe the *spin* at the considered lattice point. The energy of the complete random field is supposed to be minimal if all spins are identical. This is obviously valid for the energy function

$$U(f) = -\alpha \left(\sum_{m=1}^{M-1} \sum_{n=1}^{N} f_{m,n} f_{m+1,n} + \sum_{m=1}^{M} \sum_{n=1}^{N-1} f_{m,n} f_{m,n+1} \right) \qquad (15.26)$$

where $\alpha > 0$.

Figure 15.8: *Two images maximizing the prior defined by Eq. (15.27).*

Ising's model, however, does not weight singleton cliques (see also Fig. 15.6) by zero as suggested in Eq. (15.26), but incorporates these singleton potentials in the energy function as an additive term weighted by β

$$U(f) = -\alpha \left(\sum_{m=1}^{M-1} \sum_{n=1}^{N} f_{m,n} f_{m+1,n} + \sum_{m=1}^{M} \sum_{n=1}^{N-1} f_{m,n} f_{m,n+1} \right) + \beta \sum_{m=1}^{M} \sum_{n=1}^{N} f_{m,n}$$

$$(15.27)$$

We omit the physical interpretation of α and β, which basically depend on the temperature and the chosen material. For different choices of these parameters we get different binary images that maximize the density function of this Gibbs field. Figure 15.8 shows some examples.

Up to now we have considered MRFs in general and the given example has shown that MRFs can be used to define priors (Example 15.2); we can define a probability density for a given set of observations. The *Bayesian classifier*, however, requires the definition of posterior probabilities including priors and model densities.

Major applications of Markov random field models do not deal with object recognition and pose estimation, but with image labeling [8, 23]. Based on prior models and observations a labeled image is computed using Bayesian labeling: this can be a restored image [22], a transformation into line segments [24], or texture segmentation [25].

15.5 Practical issues

Before we conclude this chapter with a brief summary, we comment on some practical issues generally related to the usage of probabilistic models in computer vision.

The most critical decisions in probabilistic modeling are related to the dependency structure of considered random variables and the number of parameters in the chosen model. If probabilistic models do not result in satisfactory recognition rates, the most obvious problem might be caused by inaccurate independency assumptions and by the selection of inappropriate parametric distributions. The increase of dependencies and the related growth of free parameters suggest more accurate models. In fact, for many applications this is a totally false conclusion that is related to a fundamental problem in pattern recognition [26, 27]: the *curse-of-dimensionality*. Indeed it can be shown that:

- in high-dimensional spaces it is impossible to get large sample sets, that is, with increasing dimension an exponentially increasing number of data points is required to guarantee a densely sampled Euclidean space;
- all interpoint distances are large and rather equal;
- nearest neighborhoods are not local; and
- all data points are close to the boundary of the considered space.

The natural consequence of this principle is that a careless increase of model complexity will end in insufficient classification results. These are hard to understand if the engineer is not aware of the curse. The only way to avoid problems related to the curse-of-dimensionality is to restrict the considered functions to a special class of parametric functions. Reasonable high-dimensional models require some locally restricted structure or reduced parameters enforced by parameter tying; otherwise parametric models are not practical. But this strategy is two edged: Often probabilistic models are criticized because of incorporated independency assumptions—regardless of convincing experimental results. For a wide range of *classification* problems, however, even *naive Bayes* [11], which approximates class conditional densities of random vectors by the product of its marginals, is surprisingly successful. Theoretically, it is not yet completely solved and clear why these simple techniques often are superior to more sophisticated ones, but certainly one reason is the curse-of-dimensionality.

Another matter is based on the *bias variance trade-off* in parameter estimation. If a parameter set B has to be estimated using empirical data, the mean square error between the real value B_0 and its estimate $\hat{B}$ is a measure for the quality of the estimation procedure

$$E[(B_0 - \hat{B})^2] = (B_0 - E[\hat{B}])^2 + E[(\hat{B} - E[\hat{B}])^2] \tag{15.28}$$

The first term $(B_0 - E[\hat{B}])$ herein denotes the *bias* and $E[(\hat{B} - E[\hat{B}])^2]$ is the *variance* of the estimator. Typically, bias and variance interact: low bias induces high variance, low variance high bias. If the parametric model is correct, then the estimation is unbiased and even the variance will be low. However, if the chosen model does not exactly fit, we observe usually low bias but high variance, and minor changes in the training samples cause high variations in estimates. For that reason, restricted parametric models of lower variance are often preferred to more complex and highly parameterized density functions [28]. The high variance of these estimates also explains the success of the *bootstrap* [29], where the training set is sampled by replacement. Instead of using the training set as is, we randomly choose a subset of empirical data, estimate the parameters, and repeat this process several times. At the end the computed models are averaged and finally show a lower variance [30].

We assume implicitly that training data are sufficient for estimating the required parameters. The dimension of the chosen parameter space, the curse-of-dimensionality, the bootstrap, and the fact that we observe only samples of a subset of the real set of events are hints that this basic assumption is possibly wrong. Our models also have to consider and to predict random measures with a probability nonequal to zero, which are not part of the observation. At first glance, this seems awkward and most unrealistic. A simple example, however, shows its necessity: If we model objects by histograms it might happen that some intensity values are never observed. The histogram will include the probability 0 and whenever we observe this intensity value during runtime, the complete product of probabilities (Eq. (15.8)) will annihilate. This example shows that we also have to attend to methods that can deal with sparse training samples. Statistical models used for speech recognition have been used widely in this field. In many applications techniques such as *deleted interpolation* or *Good-Turing estimates* provide reliable estimates [12], and these methods will also support and improve probabilistic models in computer vision. Good estimates of parametric models are the crucial prerequisite for the successful use of probabilistic models.

15.6 Summary, conclusions, and discussion

This chapter provided an overview on probabilistic models in computer vision and related algorithms. The basic arguments that suggest a preference for probabilistic modeling schemes over others have been summarized. *Bayesian classifiers* allow the unified incorporation of prior knowledge and class-specific densities. However, it is a fundamental problem to define adequate statistical models that solve the trade-off between independency assumptions, the dimension of the parameter space, the curse-of-dimensionality, the size of available sample data, and the discriminatory power. The generic point of view starting with a general probabilistic model has proven to be advantageous: independencies and marginalization are powerful tools to switch between different levels of model densities. We have shown that *mixture density* models, *hidden Markov models*, Markov random fields, and others, have the same roots in the generic model of sensor data.

In the authors' opinion there is an immense potential for *probabilistic models* with regard to robust learning techniques, excellent classifiers, and a systematic and theoretically well-founded approach to active vision.

Acknowledgments

The authors gratefully acknowledge the fruitful discussions with William M. Wells (MIT, Harvard University) and Carlo Tomasi (Stanford University). This work was supported by the Deutsche Forschungsgemeinschaft (DFG), grants Ho 1791/2-1 and SFB 603.

15.7 References

[1] Xu, G. and Zhang, Z., (1996). *Epipolar Geometry in Stereo, Motion and Object Recognition—a Unified Approach*, Vol. 6 of *Computational Imaging and Vision*. Dordrecht: Kluwer Academic Press.

[2] Faugeras, O., (1993). *Three-Dimensional Computer Vision—a Geometric Viewpoint*. Cambridge, MA: MIT Press.

[3] Trucco, E. and Verri, A., (1998). *Introductory Techniques for 3-D Computer Vision*. Englewood Cliffs, NJ: Prentice Hall.

[4] Jain, A. K. and Flynn, P. J. (eds.), (1993). *Three-Dimensional Object Recognition Systems*. Amsterdam: Elsevier.

[5] Ponce, J., Zisserman, and Hebert, M. (eds.), (1996). *Object Representation in Computer Vision*, Vol. 1144 of *Lecture Notes in Computer Science*. Heidelberg: Springer.

[6] Vapnik, V. N., (1996). *The Nature of Statistical Learning Theory*. Heidelberg: Springer.

[7] Tanner, M. A., (1996). *Tools for Statistical Inference: Methods for the Exploration of Posterior Distributions and Likelihood Functions*, 3rd edition. Springer Series in Statistics. Heidelberg: Springer.

[8] Li, S. Z., (1996). *Markov Random Field Modeling in Computer Vision*. Heidelberg: Springer.

[9] Niemann, H., (1990). *Pattern Analysis and Understanding*, Vol. 4 of *Springer Series in Information Sciences*. Heidelberg: Springer.

[10] Devroye, L., Györfi, L., and Lugosi, G., (1996). *A Probabilistic Theory in Pattern Recognition*, Vol. 31 of *Applications of Mathematics, Stochastic Modeling and Applied Probability*. Heidelberg: Springer.

[11] Ripley, B. D., (1996). *Pattern Recognition and Neural Networks*. Cambridge: Cambridge University Press.

[12] Jelinek, F., (1998). *Statistical Methods for Speech Recognition*. Cambridge, MA: MIT Press.

[13] Altmann, S. L., (1986). *Rotations, Quaternions, and Double Groups*. Oxford: Oxford University Press.

[14] Green, P. and Silverman, B., (1994). *Nonparametric Regression and Generalized Linear Models: A Roughness Penalty Approach*, Vol. 58 of *Monographs on Statistics and Applied Probability*. New York: Chapman and Hall.

[15] Hornegger, J., (1996). *Statistische Modellierung, Klassifikation und Lokalisation von Objekten*. Aachen: Shaker.

[16] Schiele, B. and Crowley, J. L., (1998). Transinformation for active object recognition. In jh.ICCV:1998 jh. [31], pp. 249–254.

[17] Pösl, J. and Niemann, H., (1997). Wavelet features for statistical object localization without segmentation. In jh.ICIP 97 jh. [32], pp. 170-173.

[18] Redner, R. A. and Walker, H. F., (1984). Mixture densities, maximum likelihood and the EM algorithm. *Society for Industrial and Applied Mathematics Review*, **26**(2):195-239.

[19] Papoulis, A., (1991). *Probability, Random Variables, and Stochastic Processes*, 3rd edition. New York: McGraw-Hill.

[20] Hornegger, J. and Niemann, H., (1995). Statistical learning, localization, and identification of objects. In ICCV 95 ICC [33], pp. 914-919.

[21] Wells III, W. M., (1997). Statistical approaches to feature-based object recognition. *International Journal of Computer Vision*, **21**(2):63-98.

[22] Geman, S. and Geman, D., (1984). Stochastic relaxation, Gibbs distributions, and the Bayesian restoration of images. *IEEE Trans. Pattern Analysis and Machine Intelligence*, **6**(6):721-741.

[23] Winkler, G., (1995). *Image Analysis, Random Fields and Dynamic Monte Carlo Methods*, Vol. 27 of *Applications of Mathematics*. Heidelberg: Springer.

[24] Devijver, P. A. and Dekesel, M., (1987). Learning the parameters of a hidden Markov random field image model: A simple example. In Devijver and Kittler [34], pp. 141-163.

[25] Dubes, R. C. and Jain, A. K., (1993). Random field models in image analysis. In *Statistics and Images* Mardia and Kanji [35], pp. 121-154.

[26] Bellman, R. E., (1961). *Adaptive Control Process*. Princeton, NJ: Princeton University Press.

[27] Bishop, C. M., (1995). *Neural Networks for Pattern Recognition*. Oxford: Oxford University Press.

[28] Hastie, T. and Tibshirani, R., (1990). *Generalized Linear Models*, Vol. 43 of *Monographs on Statistics and Applied Probability*. New York: Chapman and Hall.

[29] Efron, B. and Tibshirani, R., (1994). *An Introduction to the Bootstrap*, Vol. 57 of *Monographs on Statistics and Applied Probability*. New York: Chapman and Hall.

[30] Shao, J. and Tu, D., (1995). *The Jackknife and Bootstrap*. Springer Series in Statistics. Heidelberg: Springer.

[31] (1998). *Proceedings of the 6th International Conference on Computer Vision (ICCV)*, Los Alamitos, CA. IEEE Computer Society Press.

[32] (1997). *Proceedings of the International Conference on Image Processing (ICIP)*, Los Alamitos, CA. IEEE Computer Society Press.

[33] (1995). *Proceedings of the 5th International Conference on Computer Vision (ICCV)*, Los Alamitos, CA. IEEE Computer Society Press.

[34] Devijver, P. A. and Kittler, J. (eds.), (1987). *Pattern Recognition Theory and Applications*, Vol. 30 of *NATO ASI Series F: Computer and System Sciences*, Heidelberg. Springer.

[35] Mardia, K. V. and Kanji, G. K., (1993). *Statistics and Images*, Vol. 1 of *Advances in Applied Statistics*. Abingdon: Carfax Publishing Company.

16   Fuzzy Image Processing

Horst Haußecker[1] and Hamid R. Tizhoosh[2]

[1]Xerox Palo Alto Research Center (PARC)
[2] Lehrstuhl für Technische Informatik, Universität Magdeburg, Germany

16.1   Introduction

Our world is *fuzzy*, and so are images, projections of the real world onto the image sensor. Fuzziness quantifies vagueness and ambiguity, as opposed to crisp memberships. The types of uncertainty in images are

541

Copyright © 2000 by Academic Press
All rights of reproduction in any form reserved.
ISBN 0-12-379777-2/$30.00

manifold, ranging over the entire chain of processing levels, from pixel-based grayness ambiguity over fuzziness in geometrical description up to uncertain knowledge in the highest processing level.

The human visual system has been perfectly adapted to handle uncertain information in both data and knowledge. It would be hard to define quantitatively how an object, such as a car, has to look in terms of geometrical primitives with exact shapes, dimensions, and colors. Instead, we are using a descriptive language to define features that eventually are subject to a wide range of variations. The interrelation of a few such "fuzzy" properties sufficiently characterizes the object of interest. Fuzzy image processing is an attempt to translate this ability of human reasoning into computer vision problems as it provides an intuitive tool for inference from imperfect data.

Where is the transition between a gray-value slope and an edge? What is the border of a blurred object? Exactly which gray values belong to the class of "bright" or "dark" pixels? These questions show that image features almost naturally have to be considered fuzzy. Usually these problems are just overruled by assigning thresholds—heuristic or computed—to the features in order to classify them. Fuzzy logic allows one to quantify appropriately and handle imperfect data. It also allows combining them for a final decision, even if we only know heuristic rules, and no analytic relations.

Fuzzy image processing is special in terms of its relation to other computer vision techniques. It is not a solution for a special task, but rather describes a new class of image processing techniques. It provides a new methodology, augmenting classical logic, a component of any computer vision tool. A new type of image understanding and treatment has to be developed. Fuzzy image processing can be a single image processing routine, or complement parts of a complex image processing chain.

During the past few decades, fuzzy logic has gained increasing importance in control theory, as well as in computer vision. At the same time, it has been continuously attacked for two main reasons: It has been considered to lack a sound mathematical foundation and to be nothing but just a clever disguise for probability theory. It was probably its name that contributed to the low reputation of fuzzy logic. Meanwhile, fuzzy logic definitely has matured and can be considered to be a mathematically sound extension of multivalued logic. Fuzzy logical reasoning and probability theory are closely related without doubt. They are, however, *not* the same but *complementary*, as we will show in Section 16.1.2.

This chapter gives a concise overview of the basic principles and potentials of state of the art fuzzy image processing, which can be applied to a variety of computer vision tasks.

16.1.1 Basics of fuzzy set theory

The two basic components of fuzzy systems are *fuzzy sets* and *operations on fuzzy sets*. *Fuzzy logic* defines rules, based on combinations of fuzzy sets by these operations. This section is based on the basic works of Zadeh [1, 2, 3, 4, 5].

Crisp sets. Given a universe of discourse $X = \{x\}$, a crisp (conventional) set A is defined by enumerating all elements $x \in X$

$$A = \{x_1, x_2, \ldots, x_n\} \tag{16.1}$$

that belong to A. The membership can be expressed by a function f_A, mapping X on a binary value:

$$f_A : X \longrightarrow \{0, 1\}, \quad f_A = \begin{cases} 1 & \text{if } x \in A \\ 0 & \text{if } x \notin A \end{cases} \tag{16.2}$$

Thus, an arbitrary x either belongs to A or it does not; partial membership is not allowed.

For two sets A and B, combinations can be defined by the following operations:

$$\begin{aligned} A \cup B &= \{x \mid x \in A \text{ or } x \in B\} \\ A \cap B &= \{x \mid x \in A \text{ and } x \in B\} \\ \bar{A} &= \{x \mid x \notin A, \; x \in X\} \end{aligned} \tag{16.3}$$

Additionally, the following rules have to be satisfied:

$$A \cap \bar{A} = \varnothing, \quad \text{and} \quad A \cup \bar{A} = X \tag{16.4}$$

Fuzzy sets. Fuzzy sets are a generalization of classical sets. A fuzzy set A is characterized by a *membership function* $\mu_A(x)$, which assigns each element $x \in X$ a real-valued number ranging from zero to unity:

$$A = \{(x, \mu_A(x)) \mid x \in X\} \tag{16.5}$$

where $\mu_A(x) : X \to [0, 1]$. The *membership function* $\mu_A(x)$ indicates to which extent the element x has the attribute A, as opposed to the binary membership value of the mapping function f_A for crisp sets Eq. (16.2). The choice of the shape of membership functions is somewhat arbitrary. It has to be adapted to the features of interest and to the final goal of the fuzzy technique. The most popular membership functions are given by piecewise-linear functions, second-order polynomials, or trigonometric functions.

Figure 16.1 illustrates an example of possible membership functions. Here, the distribution of an optical flow vector (Chapter 10),

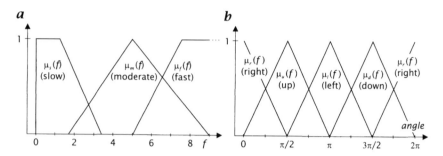

Figure 16.1: *Possible membership functions for **a** the magnitude and **b** the direction of an optical flow vector* f.

is characterized by fuzzy magnitude, $f = \|f\|$, and fuzzy orientation angle, given by two independent sets of membership functions.

Membership functions do not necessarily have to add up to unity:

$$\mu_A(x) + \mu_B(x) + \dots \neq 1 \tag{16.6}$$

as opposed to relative probabilities in stochastic processes.

A common notation for fuzzy sets, which is perfectly suited for fuzzy image processing, has been introduced by Zadeh [4]. Let X be a finite set $X = \{x_1, \dots, x_n\}$. A fuzzy set A can be represented as follows:

$$A = \frac{\mu_A(x_1)}{x_1} + \dots + \frac{\mu_A(x_n)}{x_n} = \sum_{i=1}^{n} \frac{\mu_A(x_i)}{x_i} \tag{16.7}$$

For infinite X we replace the sum in Eq. (16.7) by the following integral:

$$A = \int_X \frac{\mu_A(x)}{x} dx \tag{16.8}$$

The individual elements $\mu_A(x_i)/x_i$ represent fuzzy sets, which consist of one single element and are called *fuzzy singletons*. In Section 16.2.1 we will see how this definition is used in order to find a convenient fuzzy image definition.

Operations on fuzzy sets. In order to manipulate fuzzy sets, we need to have operations that enable us to combine them. As fuzzy sets are defined by membership functions, the classical set theoretic operations have to be replaced by function theoretic operations. Given two fuzzy sets A and B, we define the following pointwise operations ($\forall x \in X$):

$$
\begin{array}{lll}
\text{equality} & A = B & \Leftrightarrow \quad \mu_A(x) = \mu_B(x) \\
\text{containment} & A \subset B & \Leftrightarrow \quad \mu_A(x) \leq \mu_B(x) \\
\text{complement} & \bar{A}, & \mu_{\bar{A}}(x) = 1 - \mu_A(x) \\
\text{intersection} & A \cap B, & \mu_{A \cap B}(x) = \min\{\mu_A(x), \mu_B(x)\} \\
\text{union} & A \cup B, & \mu_{A \cup B}(x) = \max\{\mu_A(x), \mu_B(x)\}
\end{array}
\tag{16.9}
$$

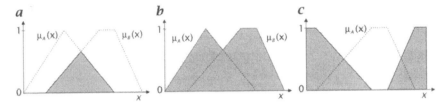

Figure 16.2: *Operations on fuzzy sets. The boundary of each of the shaded curves represents, respectively: the **a** intersection* $\mu_{A \cap B}$ *of the fuzzy sets* μ_A *and* μ_B; ***b** the union* $\mu_{A \cup B}$ *of the fuzzy sets* μ_A *and* μ_B; *and **c** complement* $\mu_{\bar{A}}$ *of the fuzzy set* μ_A.

It can be easily verified that the conditions of Eq. (16.4) are no longer satisfied

$$A \cap \bar{A} = \min\{\mu_A(x), 1 - \mu_A(x)\} \neq \emptyset$$
$$A \cup \bar{A} = \max\{\mu_A(x), 1 - \mu_A(x)\} \neq X \tag{16.10}$$

for $\mu(x) \neq 1$, due to the partial membership of fuzzy sets.

The results of the complement, intersection, and union operations on fuzzy sets are illustrated in Fig. 16.2. The operations defined in Eq. (16.9) can be easily extended for more than two fuzzy sets and combinations of different operations.

Linguistic variables. An important feature of fuzzy systems is the concept of *linguistic variables*, introduced by Zadeh [4]. To reduce the complexity of precise definitions, they make use of words or sentences in a natural or artificial language, in order to describe a vague property.

A linguistic variable can be defined by a discrete set of membership functions $\{\mu_{A_1}, \ldots, \mu_{A_N}\}$ over the set $\{x\} = U \subset X$. The membership functions quantify the variable x by assigning a partial membership of x with regard to the terms A_i. An example of a linguistic variable could be the property "velocity," composed of the terms "slow," "moderate," and "fast." The individual terms are numerically characterized by the membership functions μ_s, μ_m, and μ_f. A possible realization is shown in Fig. 16.1a.

Linguistic hedges. Given a linguistic variable x represented by the set of membership functions $\{\mu_{A_i}\}$, we can change the meaning of a linguistic variable by modifying the shape (i.e., the numerical representation) of the membership functions. The most important linguistic hedges are *intensity modification*, μ^i, *concentration*, μ^c, and *dilation*, μ^d:

$$\mu^i(x) = \begin{cases} 2\mu^2(x) & \text{if } 0 \leq \mu(x) \leq 0.5 \\ 1 - 2[1 - \mu(x)]^2 & \text{otherwise} \end{cases}$$
$$\mu^c(x) = \mu^2(x)$$
$$\mu^d(x) = \sqrt{\mu(x)} \tag{16.11}$$

An application example using dilation and concentration modification is shown later in Fig. 16.15.

Fuzzy logic. The concept of linguistic variables allows the definition of combinatorial relations between properties in terms of a language. *Fuzzy logic*—an extension of classical *Boolean logic*—is based on linguistic variables, a fact which has assigned fuzzy logic the attribute of *computing with words* [6]. Boolean logic uses *Boolean operators*, such as AND ($\wedge$), OR ($\vee$), NOT ($\neg$), and combinations of them. They are defined for binary values of the input variables and result in a binary output variable. If we want to extend the binary logic to a combinatorial logic of linguistic variables, we need to redefine the elementary logical operators. In fuzzy logic, the Boolean operators are replaced by the operations on the corresponding membership functions, as defined in Eq. (16.9).

Let $\{\mu_{A_i}(x_1)\}$ and $\{\mu_{B_i}(x_2)\}$ be two linguistic variables of two sets of input variables $\{x_1\}$ and $\{x_2\}$. The set of output variables $\{x_3\}$ is characterized by the linguistic variable $\{\mu_{C_i}(x_3)\}$. We define the following basic combinatorial rules:

if $(A_j \wedge B_k)$ then C_l:

$$\mu'_{C_l}(x_3) = \left(\min \left\{ \mu_{A_j}(x_1), \mu_{B_k}(x_2) \right\} \right) \mu_{C_l}(x_3) \qquad (16.12)$$

if $(A_j \vee B_k)$ then C_l:

$$\mu'_{C_l}(x_3) = \left(\max \left\{ \mu_{A_j}(x_1), \mu_{B_k}(x_2) \right\} \right) \mu_{C_l}(x_3) \qquad (16.13)$$

if $(\neg A_j)$ then C_l:

$$\mu'_{C_l}(x_3) = \left(1 - \mu_{A_j}(x_1) \right) \mu_{C_l}(x_3) \qquad (16.14)$$

Thus, the output membership function $\mu_{C_i}(x_3)$ is modified (weighted) according to the combination of A_i and B_j at a certain pair (x_1, x_2). These rules can easily be extended to more than two input variables. A fuzzy inference system consists of a number of if-then rules, one for any membership function μ_{C_i} of the output linguistic variable $\{\mu_{C_i}\}$.

Given the set of modified output membership functions $\{\mu'_{C_i}(x_3)\}$, we can derive a single output membership function $\mu_C(x_3)$ by *accumulating* all μ'_{C_i}. This can be done by combining the μ'_{C_i} by a logical OR, that is, the maximum operator:

$$\mu_C(x_3) = \max_i \left\{ \mu'_{C_i}(x_3) \right\} \qquad (16.15)$$

Defuzzification. The resulting output membership function $\mu_C(x_3)$ can be assigned a numerical value $x \in \{x\}$ by *defuzzification*, reversing the process of fuzzification. There are a variety of approaches to get a single number from a membership function reported in the literature. The most common techniques are computing the *center of area* (center of mass) or the *mean of maxima* of the corresponding membership function. Applications examples are shown in Section 16.3.3.

The step of defuzzification can be omitted if the final result of the fuzzy inference system is given by a membership function, rather than a crisp number.

16.1.2 Fuzzy logic versus probability theory

It has been a long-standing misconception that fuzzy logic is nothing but another representation of probability theory. We do not want to contribute to this dispute, but rather try to outline the basic difference.

Probability describes the uncertainty in the occurrence of an event. It allows predicting the event by knowledge about its relative frequency within a large number of experiments. After the experiment has been carried out, the event either has occurred or not. There is no uncertainty left. Even if the probability is very small, it might happen that the unlikely event occurs. To treat stochastic uncertainty, such as random processes (e. g., noise), probability theory is a powerful tool in computer vision (Chapter 15). There are, however, other uncertainties that can not be described by random processes. As opposed to probability, fuzzy logic represents the *imperfection* in the informational content of the event. Even after the measurement, it might not be clear whether the event has happened or not.

For illustration of this difference, consider an image to contain a single edge, which appears at a certain rate. Given the probability distribution, we can predict the likelihood of the edge to appear after a certain number of frames. It might happen, however, that it appears in every image or does not show up at all. Additionally, the edge may be corrupted by noise. A noisy edge can appropriately be detected with probabilistic approaches, computing the likelihood of the noisy measurement to belong to the class of edges. But how do we define the edge? How do we classify an image that shows a gray-value slope? A noisy slope stays a slope even if all noise is removed. If the slope is extended over the entire image we usually do not call it an edge. But if the slope is "high" enough and only extends over a "narrow" region, we tend to call it an edge. Immediately the question arises: How large is "high" and what do we mean by "narrow?"

In order to quantify the shape of an edge, we need to have a model. Then, the probabilistic approach allows us to extract the model parameters, which represent edges in various shapes. But how can we treat this problem, without having an appropriate model? Many real world applications are too complex to model all facets necessary to describe them quantitatively. Fuzzy logic does not need models. It can handle vague information and imperfect knowledge and combine them by heuristic rules—in a well-defined mathematical framework. This is the strength of fuzzy logic!

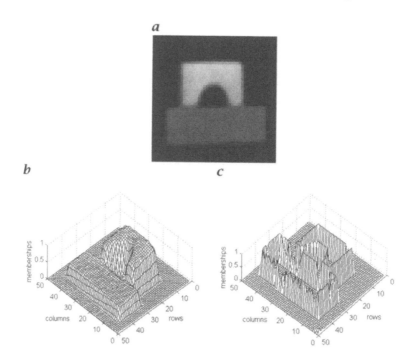

Figure 16.3: *Images as an array of fuzzy singletons. **a** Test image as a fuzzy set regarding **b** brightness (bright pixels have higher memberships), and **c** edginess (edge pixels have higher memberships).*

16.2   Fuzzy image understanding

To use fuzzy logic in image processing applications, we have to develop a new image understanding. A new image definition should be established, images and their components (pixels, histograms, segments, etc.) should be fuzzified (transformed in membership plane), and the fundamental topological relationships between image parts should be extended to fuzzy sets (fuzzy digital topology).

16.2.1   A new image definition: Images as fuzzy sets

An image G of size $M \times N$ with L gray levels can be defined as an array of fuzzy singletons (fuzzy sets with only one supporting point) indicating the membership value μ_{mn} of each image point x_{mn} regarding a predefined image property (e.g., brightness, homogeneity, noisiness, edginess, etc.) [7, 8, 9]:

$$G = \bigcup_{m=1}^{M} \bigcup_{n=1}^{N} \frac{\mu_{mn}}{x_{mn}} \qquad (16.16)$$

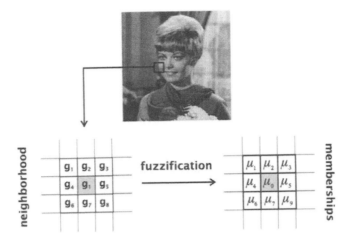

Figure 16.4: *On local neighborhood fuzzification [11].*

The definition of the membership values depends on the specific requirements of a particular application and on the corresponding expert knowledge. Figure 16.3 shows an example where brightness and edginess are used to define the membership degree of each pixel.

16.2.2 Image fuzzification: From images to memberships

Fuzzy image processing is a kind of nonlinear image processing. The difference to other well-known methodologies is that fuzzy techniques operate on membership values. The image fuzzification (generation of suitable membership values) is, therefore, the first processing step. Generally, three various types of image fuzzification can be distinguished: histogram-based gray-level fuzzification, local neighborhood fuzzification, and feature fuzzification [9].

As in other application areas of fuzzy set theory, the fuzzification step sometimes should be optimized. The number, form, and location of each membership function could/should be adapted to achieve better results. For instance, genetic algorithms are performed to optimize fuzzy rule-based systems [10].

Histogram-based gray-level fuzzification [9]. To develop any point operation (global histogram-based techniques), each gray level should be assigned one or more membership values (such as *dark, gray*, and *bright*) with respect to the corresponding requirements.

Local neighborhood fuzzification [9]. Intermediate techniques (e.g., segmentation, noise filtering etc.) operate on a predefined neighborhood of pixels. To use fuzzy approaches to such operations, the fuzzification step should also be done within the selected neighborhood (Fig. 16.4). The local neighborhood fuzzification can be carried out depending on the task to be done. Of course, local neighborhood fuzzification requires more computing time compared with the histogram-based approach. In many situations, we also need more thoroughness in designing membership functions to execute the local fuzzification because noise and outliers may falsify membership values.

Example 16.1: Edginess

Within 3×3-neighborhood U we are interested in the degree of membership of the center point to the fuzzy set *edge pixel*. Here, the edginess μ_e is a matter of grade. If the 9 pixels in U are assigned the numbers $0, \dots, 8$ and G_0 denotes the center pixel, a possible membership function can be the following [9]:

$$\mu_e = 1 - \left[1 + \frac{1}{\Delta} \sum_{i=0}^{8} \| G_0 - G_i \| \right]^{-1} \tag{16.17}$$

with $\Delta = \max_U (G_i)$.

Feature fuzzification [9]. For high-level tasks, image features usually should be extracted (e.g., length of objects, homogeneity of regions, entropy, mean value, etc.). These features will be used to analyze the results, recognize the objects, and interpret the scenes. Applying fuzzy techniques to these tasks, we need to fuzzify the extracted features. It is necessary not only because fuzzy techniques operate only on membership values but also because the extracted features are often incomplete and/or imprecise.

Example 16.2: Object length

If the length of an object was calculated in a previous processing step, the fuzzy subsets *very short, short, middle-long, long* and *very long* can be introduced as terms of the linguistic variable *length* in order to identify certain types of objects (Fig. 16.5).

16.2.3 Fuzzy topology: Noncrisp definitions of topological relationships

Image segmentation is a fundamental step in most image processing systems. However, the image regions can not always be defined crisply. It is sometimes more appropriate to consider the different image parts, regions, or objects as fuzzy subsets of the image. The topological relationships and properties, such as *connectedness* and *surroundedness*, can be extended to fuzzy sets. In image analysis and description, the digital topology plays an important role. The topological relationships between parts of an image are conventionally defined for (crisp) subsets of image. These subsets are usually extracted using different types

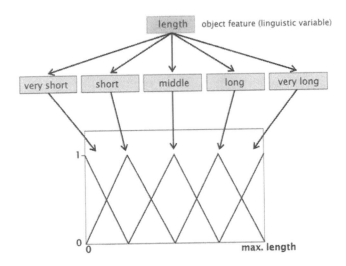

Figure 16.5: *Feature fuzzification using the concept of linguistic variables [9].*

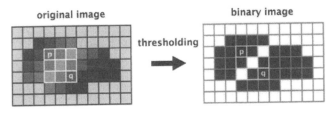

Figure 16.6: *On crisp and fuzzy connectedness. The pixels p and q are fuzzy connected in original image, and not connected in the binary image.*

of segmentation techniques (e. g., thresholding). Segmentation procedures, however, are often a strong commitment accompanied by loss of information. In many applications, it would be more appropriate to make soft decisions by considering the image parts as fuzzy subsets. In these cases, we need the extension of (binary) digital topology to fuzzy sets. The most important topological relationships are connectedness, surroundedness and adjacency. In the following, we consider an image g with a predefined neighborhood $U \subset g$ (e.g., 4- or 8-neighborhood).

Fuzzy connectedness [12]. Let p and $q \in U(\subset g)$ and let μ be a membership function modeling G or some regions of it. Further, let δ_{pq} be paths from p to q containing the points r. The degree of *connectedness* of p and q in U with respect to μ can be defined as follows (Fig. 16.6):

$$\text{connectedness}_\mu(p,q) \equiv \max_{\delta_{pq}} \left[\min_{r \in \delta_{pq}} \mu(r) \right] \qquad (16.18)$$

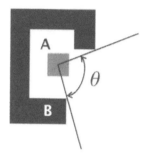

Figure 16.7: Example for calculation of fuzzy surroundedness.

Thus, if we are considering the image segments as fuzzy subsets of the image, the points p and q are connected regarding to the membership function μ if the following condition holds:

$$\text{connectedness}_\mu(p,q) \geq \min[\mu(p),\mu(q)] \qquad (16.19)$$

Fuzzy surroundedness [12, 13, 14]. Let μ_A, μ_B, and μ_C be the membership functions of fuzzy subsets A, B and C of image G. The fuzzy subset C separates A from B if, for all points p and r in $U \subset G$ and all paths δ from p to q, there exists a point $r \in \delta$ such that the following condition holds:

$$\mu(C)(r) \geq \min[\mu_A(p),\mu_B(q)] \qquad (16.20)$$

In other words, B surrounds A if it separates A from an unbounded region on which $\mu_A = 0$. Depending on the particular application, appropriate membership functions can be found to measure the surroundedness. Two possible definitions are given in Example 16.3, where $\mu_{B \odot A}$ defines the membership function of the linguistic variable 'B surrounds A' (Fig. 16.7) [9, 14].

Example 16.3: Surroundedness

$$\mu_{B \odot A}(\theta) = \begin{cases} \dfrac{\pi - \theta}{\pi} & 0 \leq \theta < \pi \\ 0 & \text{otherwise} \end{cases}, \quad \mu_{B \odot A}(\theta) = \begin{cases} \cos^2\left(\dfrac{\theta}{2}\right) & 0 \leq \theta < \pi \\ 0 & \text{otherwise} \end{cases}$$

Fuzzy adjacency [12, 13, 15]. The adjacency of two disjoint (crisp) sets is defined by the length of their common border. How can this definition be generalized to fuzzy sets?

Let μ_1 and μ_2 be piecewise-constant fuzzy sets of G. The image G can be partitioned in a finite number of bounded regions G_i, meeting

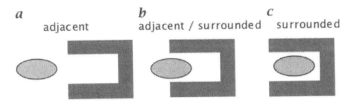

Figure 16.8: Relationship between adjacency and surroundedness.

pairwise along arcs, on each of which $\mu_1(i)$ and $\mu_2(j)$ are constant. If μ_1 and μ_2 are disjoint then in each region G_i either $\mu_1 = 0$ or $\mu_2 = 0$. Let $A(i,j,k)$ be the kth arc along which G_i and G_j meet. Then the adjacency of μ_1 and μ_2 can be defined as follows:

$$\text{adjacency}(\mu_1, \mu_2) = \sum_{i,j,k} \frac{\|A(i,j,k)\|}{1 + \|\mu_1(i)\mu_2(j)\|} \tag{16.21}$$

Now, to introduce a definition for degree of adjacency for fuzzy image subsets, let us consider two segments S_1 and S_2 of an image G. Further, let $B(S_1)$ be the set of border pixels of S_1, and p an arbitrary member of B. The degree of adjacency can be defined as follows:

$$\text{degree of adjacency}(\mu_1, \mu_2) = \sum_{p \in B(S_1)} \frac{1}{1 + \|\mu_1(i)\mu_2(j)\|} \frac{1}{1 + d(p)} \tag{16.22}$$

where $p \in S_1$ and $q \in S_2$ are border pixels, and $d(p)$ is the shortest distance between p and q. Here, it should be noted that there exists a close relationship between adjacency and surroundedness (Fig. 16.8a,b). Depending on the particular requirements, one may consider one or both of them to describe spatial relationships.

16.3 Fuzzy image processing systems

Fuzzy image processing consists (as all other fuzzy approaches) of three stages: fuzzification, suitable operations on membership values, and, if necessary, defuzzification (Fig. 16.9). The main difference to other methodologies in image processing is that input data (histograms, gray levels, features, ...) will be processed in the so-called membership plane where one can use the great diversity of fuzzy logic, fuzzy set theory, and fuzzy measure theory to modify/aggregate the membership values, classify data, or make decisions using fuzzy inference. The new membership values are retransformed in the gray-level plane to generate new histograms, modified gray levels, image segments, or classes of objects. In the following, we briefly describe each processing stage.

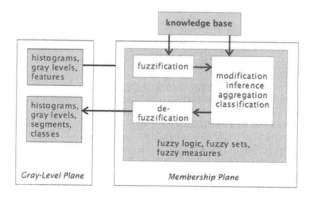

Figure 16.9: *General structure of fuzzy image processing systems [9].*

Table 16.1: *On relationships between imperfect knowledge and the type of image fuzzification [9].*

Problem	Fuzzification	Level	Examples
Brightness ambiguity/ vagueness	histogram	low	thresholding
Geometrical fuzziness	local	intermediate	edge detection, filtering
Complex/ill-defined data	feature	high	recognition, analysis

16.3.1 Fuzzification (coding of image information)

Fuzzification can be considered as input data coding. It means that membership values are assigned to each input (Section 16.2.2). Fuzzification does mean that we assign the image (its gray levels, features, segments, ...) one or more membership values with respect to the properties of interest (e. g., brightness, edginess, homogeneity). Depending on the problem we have (ambiguity, fuzziness, complexity), the suitable fuzzification method should be selected. Examples of properties and the corresponding type of fuzzification are given in Table 16.1.

16.3.2 Operations in membership plane

The generated membership values are modified by a suitable fuzzy approach. This can be a modification, aggregation, classification, or processing by some kind of if-then rules.

Aggregation. Many fuzzy techniques aggregate the membership values to produce new memberships. Examples are fuzzy hybrid connec-

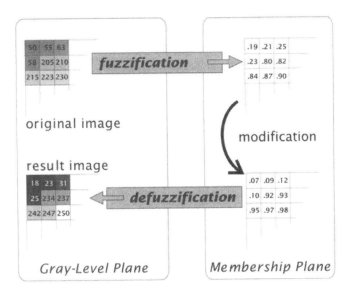

Figure 16.10: *Example for modification-based fuzzy image processing [9].*

tives, and fuzzy integrals, to mention only some of them. The result of aggregation is a global value that considers different criteria, such as features and hypothesis, to deliver a certainty factor for a specific decision (e. g., pixel classification).

Modification. Another class of fuzzy techniques directly modifies the membership values. The principal steps are illustrated in Fig. 16.10. Examples of such modifications are linguistic hedges, and distance-based modification in prototype-based fuzzy clustering. The result of the modification is a new membership value for each fuzzified feature (e. g., gray level, segment, object).

Classification. Fuzzy classification techniques can be used to classify input data. They can be numerical approaches (e. g., fuzzy clustering algorithms, fuzzy integrals, etc.) or syntactic approaches (e. g., fuzzy grammars, fuzzy if-then rules, etc.). Regarding the membership values, classification can be a kind of modification (e. g., distance-based adaptation of memberships in prototype-based clustering) or aggregation (e. g., evidence combination by fuzzy integrals).

Inference. Fuzzy if-then rules can be used to make soft decisions using expert knowledge. Indeed, fuzzy inference can also be regarded as a kind of membership aggregation because different fuzzy connectives are used to fuse the partial truth in premise and conclusion of if-then rules.

16.3.3 Defuzzification (decoding of the results)

In many applications we need a crisp value as output. Fuzzy algorithms, however, always deliver fuzzy answers (a membership function or a membership value). In order to reverse the process of fuzzification, we use defuzzification to produce a crisp answer from a fuzzy output feature. Depending on the selected fuzzy approach, there are different ways to defuzzify the results. The well-known defuzzification methods such as *center of area* and *mean of maxima* are used mainly in inference engines. One can also use the inverse membership function if point operations are applied. Figure 16.10 illustrates the three stages of fuzzy image processing for a modification-based approach.

16.4 Theoretical components of fuzzy image processing

Fuzzy image processing is knowledge-based and nonlinear. It is based on fuzzy logic and uses its logical, set-theoretical, relational and cognitive aspects. The most important theoretical frameworks that can be used to construct the foundations of fuzzy image processing are: fuzzy geometry, measures of fuzziness/image information, rule-based approaches, fuzzy clustering algorithms, fuzzy mathematical morphology, fuzzy measure theory, and fuzzy grammars. Any of these topics can be used either to develop new techniques, or to extend the existing algorithms [9]. Here, we give a brief description of each field. Soft computing techniques (e. g., neural fuzzy, fuzzy genetic) as well as combined approaches (e. g., neural fuzzy and fuzzy genetic techniques) are not mentioned due to space limitations.

16.4.1 Fuzzy geometry

Geometrical relationships between the image components play a key role in intermediate image processing. Many geometrical categories such as area, perimeter, and diameter, are already extended to fuzzy sets [12, 13, 15, 16, 17, 18, 19, 20, 21]. The geometrical fuzziness arising during segmentation tasks can be handled efficiently if we consider the image or its segments as fuzzy sets. The main application areas of fuzzy geometry are feature extraction (e. g., in image enhancement), image segmentation, and image representation ([9, 9, 15, 21, 22, 23], see also Table 16.2).

Fuzzy topology plays an important role in fuzzy image understanding, as already pointed out earlier in this chapter. In the following, we describe some fuzzy geometrical measures, such as compactness, index of area coverage, and elongatedness. A more detailed description of other aspects of fuzzy geometry can be found in the literature.

Table 16.2: *Theory of fuzzy geometry [9, 12, 13, 15, 16, 17, 18, 19, 20, 21]*

Aspects of fuzzy geometry	Examples of subjects and features
digital topology	connectedness, surroundedness, adjacency
metric	area, perimeter, diameter, distance between fuzzy sets
derived measures	compactness index of area coverage, elongatedness
convexity	convex/concave fuzzy image subsets
thinning/medial axes	shrinking, expanding, skeletonization
elementary shapes	fuzzy discs, fuzzy rectangles, fuzzy triangles

Fuzzy compactness [17]. Let G be an image of size MN, containing one object with the membership values $\mu_{m,n}$. The *area* of the object—interpreted as a fuzzy subset of the image—can be calculated as:

$$\text{area}(\mu) = \sum_{m=0}^{M} \sum_{n=0}^{N} \mu_{m,n} \tag{16.23}$$

The *perimeter* of the object can be determined as

$$\text{perimeter}(\mu) = \sum_{m=1}^{M} \sum_{n=1}^{N-1} \|\mu_{m,n} - \mu_{m,n+1}\| + \sum_{m=1}^{M-1} \sum_{n=1}^{N} \|\mu_{m,n} - \mu_{m+1,n}\| \tag{16.24}$$

The *fuzzy compactness*, introduced by Rosenfeld [17] can be defined as

$$\text{compactness}(\mu) = \frac{\text{area}(\mu)}{[\text{perimeter}(\mu)]^2} \tag{16.25}$$

In the crisp case, the compactness is maximum for a circle. It can be shown that the compactness of fuzzy sets is always more than a corresponding crisp case. Many fuzzy techniques are, therefore, developed for image segmentation, which minimizes the fuzzy compactness.

Index of area coverage [15, 21]. The *index of area coverage* of a fuzzy image subset μ, introduced by Pal and Ghosh [21], represents the fraction of the maximum image area actually covered by this subset. It is defined as follows:

$$\text{ioac}(\mu) = \frac{\text{area}(\mu)}{\text{length}(\mu)\text{breadth}(\mu)} \tag{16.26}$$

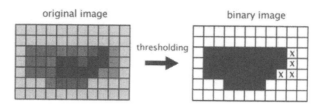

Figure 16.11: *Calculation of elongatedness of crisp image subsets is often accompanied by loss of information (pixels marked with "x" are lost during the thresholding task).*

Here, the length and breadth of the fuzzy image subset are calculated as follows:

$$\text{length}(\mu) = \max_m \left\{ \sum_n \mu_{m,n} \right\} \tag{16.27}$$

$$\text{breadth}(\mu) = \max_n \left\{ \sum_m \mu_{m,n} \right\} \tag{16.28}$$

The definition of the index of area coverage is very similar to compactness. For certain cases, it can be shown that there exists a relationship between the two definitions.

Fuzzy elongatedness [17]. As an example for cases that have no simple generalization to fuzzy sets, we briefly explain the *elongatedness* of an object. The elongatedness can serve as a feature to recognize a certain class of objects. Making strong commitments to calculate such geometrical features (e. g., thresholding), it can lead to loss of information and falsification of final results (Fig. 16.11).

Let μ be the characteristic function of a crisp image subset. The elongatedness can be defined as follows:

$$\text{elongatedness}(\mu) = \frac{\text{area}(\mu)}{[\text{thickness}(\mu)]^2} \tag{16.29}$$

Now, letting μ be the membership function of a fuzzy image subset, a closely related definition of fuzzy elongatedness is introduced by Rosenfeld [12]:

$$\text{fuzzy elongatedness}(\mu) = \max_{\delta>0} \frac{\text{area}(\mu - \mu_{-\delta})}{(2\delta)^2} \tag{16.30}$$

Here, μ_δ denotes the result of a shrinking operation in a given distance δ, where the local "min" operation can be used as a generalization of shrinking.

16.4.2 Measures of fuzziness and image information

Fuzzy sets can be used to represent a variety of image information. A central question dealing with uncertainty is to quantify the "fuzziness" or uncertainty of an image feature, given the corresponding membership function. A goal of fuzzy image processing might be to minimize the uncertainty in the image information.

Index of fuzziness. The intersection of a crisp set with its own complement always equals zero (Eq. (16.4)). This condition no longer holds for two fuzzy sets. The more fuzzy a fuzzy set is, the more it intersects with its own complement. This consideration leads to the definition of the *index of fuzziness* γ. Given a fuzzy set A with the membership function μ_A defined over an image of size $M \times N$, we define the *linear index of fuzziness* γ_l as follows:

$$\gamma_l(G) = \frac{2}{MN} \sum_{m,n} \min(\mu_{mn}, 1 - \mu_{mn}) \tag{16.31}$$

Another possible definition is given by the *quadratic index of fuzziness* γ_q defined by

$$\gamma_q(G) = \frac{1}{\sqrt{MN}} \left[\left(\sum_{m,n} \min(\mu_{mn}, 1 - \mu_{mn}) \right)^2 \right]^{1/2} \tag{16.32}$$

For binary-valued (crisp sets) both indices equal zero. For maximum fuzziness, that is, $\mu_{mn} = 0.5$, they reach the peak value of 1.

Fuzzy entropy. An information theoretic measure quantifying the information content of an image is *entropy*. The counterpart in fuzzy set theory is given by the *fuzzy entropy*, quantifying the uncertainty of the image content. The *logarithmic fuzzy entropy* H_{log} is defined by [24]

$$H_{log}(G) = \frac{1}{MN \ln 2} \sum_{m,n} S_n(\mu_{mn}) \tag{16.33}$$

where

$$S_n(\mu_{mn}) = -\mu_{mn} \ln(\mu_{mn}) - (1 - \mu_{mn}) \ln(1 - \mu_{mn}) \tag{16.34}$$

Another possible definition, called the *exponential fuzzy entropy*, has been proposed by Pal and Pal [25]:

$$H_{exp}(G) = \frac{1}{MN(\sqrt{e} - 1)} \sum_{m,n} \left\{ \mu_{mn} e^{(1-\mu_{mn})} + (1 - \mu_{mn}) e^{\mu_{mn}} - 1 \right\} \tag{16.35}$$

The fuzzy entropy also yields a measure of uncertainty ranging from zero to unity.

Fuzzy correlation. An important question in classical classification techniques is the *correlation* of two different image features. Similarly, the *fuzzy correlation* $K(\mu_1, \mu_2)$ quantifies the correlation of two fuzzy features, defined by the membership functions μ_1 and μ_2, respectively. It is defined by [7]

$$K(\mu_1, \mu_2) = 1 - \frac{4}{\Delta_1 + \Delta_2} \sum_{m,n} (\mu_{1,mn} - \mu_{2,mn})^2 \qquad (16.36)$$

where

$$\Delta_1 = \sum_{m,n} (2\mu_{1,mn} - 1)^2, \quad \text{and} \quad \Delta_2 = \sum_{m,n} (2\mu_{2,mn} - 1)^2 \qquad (16.37)$$

If $\Delta_1 = \Delta_2 = 0$, K is set to unity. Fuzzy correlation is used either to quantify the correlation of two features within the same image or, alternatively, the correlation of the same feature in two different images. Examples of features are brightness, edginess, texturedness, etc.

More detailed information about the theory on common measures of fuzziness can be found in [7, 25, 26, 27, 28, 29, 30]. A variety of practical applications are given by [9, 31, 32, 33, 34, 35, 36].

16.4.3 Rule-based systems

Rule-based systems are among the most powerful applications of fuzzy set theory. They have been of utmost importance in modern developments of fuzzy-controllers. Fuzzy logic usually implies dealing with some kind of rule-based inference, in terms of incorporating expert knowledge or heuristic relations. Whenever we have to deal with combining uncertain knowledge without having an analytical model, we can use a rule-based fuzzy inference system. Rule-based approaches incorporate these techniques into image processing tasks.

Rule-based systems are composed of the following three major parts: *fuzzification*, *fuzzy inference*, and *defuzzification*.

We outlined the components fuzzification and defuzzification earlier in this chapter. They are used to create fuzzy sets from input data and to compute a crisp number from the resulting output fuzzy set, respectively.

The main part of rule-based systems is the *inference engine*. It constitutes the brain of the fuzzy technique, containing the knowledge about the relations between the individual input fuzzy sets and the output fuzzy sets. The fuzzy inference system comprises a number of rules, in terms of if-then conditions, which are used to modify the membership functions of the corresponding output condition according to Eqs. (16.12) to (16.14). The individual output membership functions are accumulated to a single output fuzzy set using Eq. (16.15).

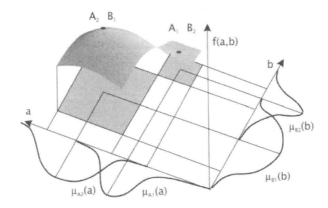

Figure 16.12: *The rules of a fuzzy-inference system create fuzzy patches in the product space A × B. These regions constitute the support of the function* $\mu_C(a, b)$.

An interesting aspect of rule-based systems is that they can be interpreted as a nonlinear interpolation technique approximating arbitrary functions from partial knowledge about relations between input and output variables. Consider $f(a, b)$ to be a function of the two variables a, and b. In case we do not know the analytical shape of f we need an infinite number of relations between a, b, and $f(a, b)$ in order to approximate f. If we quantify a and b by fuzzy sets A_i and B_i, it is sufficient to know the relations between the finite number of pairs (A_i, B_j). The continuous function f over the entire parameter space $A \times B$ can be interpolated, as illustrated in Fig. 16.12. In control theory, the function $f(a, b)$ is called the *control surface*. It is, however, necessary to carefully choose the shape of the membership functions μ_{A_i} and μ_{B_i}, as they determine the exact shape of the interpolation between the sparse support points, that is, the shape of the control surface.

More detailed information about the theory on rule-based systems can be found in [2, 3, 4, 5]. A variety of practical applications are given by [9, 37, 38, 39, 40, 41].

16.4.4 Fuzzy/possibilistic clustering

In many image processing applications, the final step is a classification of objects by their features, which have been detected by image processing tools. Assigning objects to certain classes is not specific to image processing but a very general type of technique, which has led to a variety of approaches searching for *clusters* in an n-dimensional *feature space*.

Figure 16.13a illustrates an example of feature points in a 2-D space. The data seem to belong to two clusters, which have to be separated.

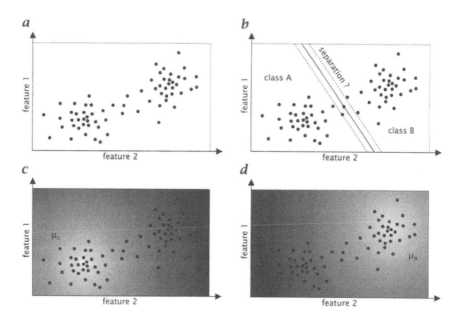

Figure 16.13: *Crisp vs fuzzy classification.* **a** *Set of feature points.* **b** *Crisp classification into two sets A and B. Features close to the separation line are subject to misclassification.* **c** *Fuzzy membership function μ_A and μ_B used for fuzzy clustering.*

The main problem of all clustering techniques is to find an appropriate partitioning of the feature space, which minimizes misclassifications of objects. The problem of a crisp clustering is illustrated in Fig. 16.13b. Due to a long tail of "outliers" it is not possible to unambiguously find a separation line, which avoids misclassifications. The basic idea of *fuzzy clustering* is not to classify the objects, but rather to quantify the partial membership of the same object to more than one class, as illustrated in Fig. 16.13. This accounts for the fact that a small transition in the feature of an object—eventually crossing the separation line—should only lead to a small change in the membership, rather than changing the final classification. The membership functions can be used in subsequent processing steps to combine feature properties until, eventually, a final classification has to be performed.

Within the scope of this handbook we are not able to detail all existing clustering techniques. More detailed information about the theory of fuzzy-clustering and the various algorithms and applications can be found in the following publications [9, 42, 43, 44, 45, 46, 47, 48, 49, 50, 51, 52].

16.4.5 Fuzzy morphology

Fuzzy morphology extends the concept of classical morphology (Chapter 14) to fuzzy sets. In the following we assume the image to be represented by a fuzzy membership function μ. In addition to the membership function at any pixel of the image of size $M \times N$, we need a "fuzzy" *structuring element* v. The structuring element can be thought of as the membership function. The shape of the structuring element, that is, the values of the membership function v_{mn}, determine the spatial area of influence as well as the magnitude of the morphological operation.

Without going into details regarding theoretical foundations, we show two possible realizations of the two basic morphological operations, *fuzzy dilation* and *fuzzy erosion*, respectively [9].

Example 16.4: Fuzzy erosion [53, 54]

$$E_v(x) = \inf \max \left[\mu(y), (1 - v(y - x))\right], \quad x, y \in X \qquad (16.38)$$

Example 16.5: Fuzzy dilation [53, 54]

$$E_v(x) = \sup \min \left[\mu(y), v(y - x)\right], \quad x, y \in X \qquad (16.39)$$

Other realizations and more detailed information about the theory of morphology can be found in the following publications [9, 55, 56, 57, 58, 59, 60, 61, 62, 63, 64].

16.4.6 Fuzzy measure theory

Fuzzy sets are useful to quantify the inherent vagueness of image data. Brightness, edginess, homogeneity, and many other categories are a matter of degree. The class boundaries in these cases are not crisp. Thus, reasoning should be performed with partial truth and incomplete knowledge. Fuzzy set theory and fuzzy logic offer the suitable framework to apply heuristic knowledge within complex processing tasks. Uncertainty arises in many other situations as well, even if we have crisp relationships. For instance, the problem of thresholding is not due to the vagueness because we have to extract two classes of pixels belonging to object and background, respectively. Here, the main problem is that the decision itself is uncertain—namely assigning each gray level with membership 1 for object pixels and membership 0 for background pixels. This uncertainty, however, is due to the ambiguity, rather than to vagueness. For this type of problems, one may take into account *fuzzy measures* and *fuzzy integrals*. Fuzzy measure theory—introduced by Sugeno [65]—can be considered as a generalization of classical measure theory [66]. Fuzzy integrals are nonlinear aggregation operators used to combine different sources of uncertain information [9, 67, 68, 69, 70, 71, 72, 73, 74, 75, 76, 77]. A detailed overview of the mathematical framework of fuzzy measures and fuzzy integrals can be found in CVA2 [Chapter 22].

16.4.7 Fuzzy grammars

Language is a powerful tool to describe patterns. The structural information can be qualitatively described without a precise numerical quantification of features. The theory of formal languages was used for speech recognition before it was considered to be relevant for pattern recognition. The main reason was that formal languages have been criticized for not being flexible enough for an application in pattern recognition, especially for dealing with disturbances such as noise or unpredictable events. *Fuzzy grammars*, introduced by Zadeh and Lee [78], are an extension of classical formal languages that are able to deal with uncertainties and vague information. Fu [79] uses the theory of fuzzy grammars for the first time in image processing. Theoretical and practical aspects of fuzzy languages are detailed in [80, 81, 82, 83]. Practical examples can be found in [84, 85, 86].

16.5 Selected application examples

16.5.1 Image enhancement: contrast adaptation

Image enhancement tries to suppress disturbances, such as noise, blurring, geometrical distortions, and illumination corrections, only to mention some examples. It may be the final goal of the image processing operation to produce an image, with a higher contrast or some other improved property according to a human observer. Whenever these properties can not be numerically quantified, fuzzy image enhancement techniques can be used. In this section we illustrate the example of *contrast adaptation* by three different algorithms.

In recent years, some researchers have applied the concept of fuzziness to develop new algorithms for contrast enhancement. Here, we briefly describe the following fuzzy algorithms: minimization of image fuzziness, fuzzy histogram hyperbolization, and a rule-based approach.

Example 16.6: Minimization of image fuzziness [8, 23, 87]

This method uses the intensification operator to reduce the fuzziness of the image that results in an increase of image contrast. The algorithm can be formulated as follows:

1. setting the parameters (F_e, F_d, g_{max}) in Eq. (16.40)

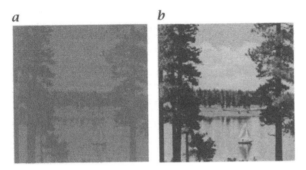

a   *b*

Figure 16.14: *Example of contrast enhancement based on minimization of fuzziness: **a** original image; and **b** contrast enhanced image.*

2. fuzzification of the gray levels by the transformation G:

$$\mu_{mn} = G(g_{mn}) = \left[1 + \frac{g_{max} - g_{mn}}{F_d}\right]^{-F_e} \tag{16.40}$$

3. recursive modification of the memberships ($\mu_{mn} \longrightarrow \mu'_{mn}$) by following transformation (intensification operator [2]):

$$\mu'_{mn} = \begin{cases} 2[\mu_{mn}]^2 & 0 \le \mu_{mn} \le 0.5 \\ 1 - 2[1 - \mu_{mn}]^2 & 0.5 \le \mu_{mn} \le 1 \end{cases} \tag{16.41}$$

4. generation of new gray levels by the inverse transformation G^{-1}:

$$g'_{mn} = G^{-1}(\mu'_{mn}) = g_{max} - F_d\left((\mu'_{mn})^{-1/F_e} - 1\right) \tag{16.42}$$

Figure 16.14 shows an example for this algorithm. The result was achieved after three iterations.

Example 16.7: Fuzzy histogram hyperbolization [9, 35]

Similar to the nonlinear human brightness perception, this approach modifies the membership values of an image by a logarithmic function. The algorithm can be formulated as follows (Fig. 16.15):

1. setting the shape of membership function
2. setting the value of fuzzifier β (Fig. 16.15)
3. calculating of membership values
4. modifying membership values by β
5. generating of new gray levels by following equation:

$$g'_{mn} = \left(\frac{L - 1}{\exp(-1) - 1}\right)\left(\exp\left(-\mu^\beta(g_{mn})\right) - 1\right) \tag{16.43}$$

Example 16.8: Fuzzy rule-based approach [9, 35]

The fuzzy rule-based approach is a powerful and universal method for many tasks in image processing. A simple rule-based approach to contrast enhancement can be formulated as follows (Fig. 16.16):

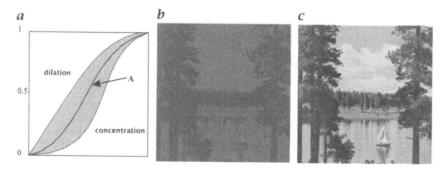

Figure 16.15: a *Application of dilation (β = 0.5) and concentration (β = 2) operators on a fuzzy set. The meaning of fuzzy sets may be modified applying such operators. To map the linguistic statements of observers in the numerical framework of image processing systems, linguistic hedges are very helpful.* **b** *and* **c** *are examples for contrast enhancement based on hyperbolization (β = 0.9).*

1. setting the parameter of inference system (input features, membership functions, ...)
2. fuzzification of the actual pixel (memberships to the dark, gray and bright sets of pixels, see Fig. 16.16a)
3. inference (if dark then darker, if gray then more gray, if bright then brighter)
4. defuzzification of the inference result by the use of three singletons

16.5.2 Edge detection

Edges are among the most important features of low-level image processing. They can be used for a variety of subsequent processing steps, such as object recognition and motion analysis. The concept of fuzziness has been applied to develop new algorithms for *edge detection*, which are perfectly suited to quantify the presence of edges in an intuitive way. The different algorithms make use of various aspects of fuzzy theory and can be classified into the following three principal approaches:

1. edge detection by optimal fuzzification [88];
2. rule-based edge detection [40, 41];
3. fuzzy-morphological edge detection [9].

Here, we briefly describe the rule-based technique, which is the most intuitive approach using fuzzy logic for edge detection. Other approaches to fuzzy-based edge detection can be found in [37, 38].

Example 16.9: Rule-based edge detection [40, 41]

A typical rule for edge extraction can be defined as follows:

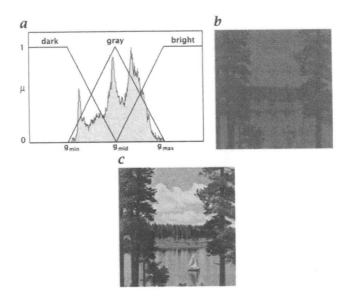

Figure 16.16: *a Input membership functions for rule-based enhancement based on the characteristic points of image histogram; **b** and **c** examples of contrast enhancement based on fuzzy if-then rules.*

> **if** a pixel belongs to an edge
>
> **then** it is assigned a dark gray value
>
> **else** it is assigned a bright gray value

This rule base is special in terms of using the "else" rule. In that way only one explicit logical relation is used and anything else is assigned the complement. It would be harder and more costly to specify all possible cases that can occur.

The input variables are differences between the central point P of a small 3×3 neighborhood U and all neighbors $P_i \in U$. Instead of computing all possible combinations of neighboring points, only eight different clusters of three neighboring points are used [9]. Each of the eight differences is fuzzified according to a membership function μ_i, $i = \{1, \ldots, 8\}$.

The output membership function μ_e corresponding to "edge" is taken as a single increasing wedge. The membership function μ_n of "no edge" is its complement, that is, $\mu_n = 1 - \mu_e$.

The fuzzy inference reduces to the following simple modification of the output membership functions:

$$\mu_e = \max\{\mu_i; i = 1, \ldots, 8\}, \quad \text{and} \quad \mu_n = 1 - \mu_e \qquad (16.44)$$

Figure 16.17 illustrates the result of this simple rule-based approach. The final mapping of edges onto gray values of an edge image can be changed by modifying the shape of the individual membership functions. If small differences are given less weight, the noise of the input

a   *b*

Figure 16.17: *Example for rule-based edge detection:* **a** *original image; and* **b** *fuzzy edge image.*

image will be suppressed. It is also very straightforward to construct directional selective edge detectors by using different rules according to the orientation of the neighboring point clusters.

16.5.3 Image segmentation

The different theoretical components of fuzzy image processing provide us with diverse possibilities for development of new segmentation techniques. The following description gives a brief overview of different fuzzy approaches to image segmentation [9].

Fuzzy rule-based approach. If we interpret the image features as linguistic variables, then we can use fuzzy if-then rules to segment the image into different regions. A simple fuzzy segmentation rule may be as follows: IF the pixel is dark AND its neighborhood is also dark AND homogeneous, THEN it belongs to the background.

Fuzzy clustering algorithms. Fuzzy clustering is the oldest fuzzy approach to image segmentation. Algorithms such as fuzzy c-means (FCM, [43]) and possibilistic c-means (PCM, [50]) can be used to build clusters (segments). The class membership of pixels can be interpreted as similarity or compatibility with an ideal object or a certain property.

Measures of fuzziness and image information. Measures of fuzziness (e. g., fuzzy entropy) and image information (e. g., fuzzy divergence) can also be used in segmentation and thresholding tasks (see the example that follows).

Fuzzy geometry. Fuzzy geometrical measures such as fuzzy compactness [12] and index of area coverage [21] can be used to measure the geometrical fuzziness of different regions of an image. Optimization of these measures (e. g., minimization of fuzzy compactness regarding the cross-over point of membership function) can be applied to make fuzzy and/or crisp pixel classifications.

Fuzzy integrals. Fuzzy integrals can be used in different forms:

1. segmentation by weighting the features (fuzzy measures represent the importance of particular features);

2. fusion of the results of different segmentation algorithms (optimal use of individual advantages); and

3. segmentation by fusion of different sensors (e. g., multispectral images, fuzzy measures represent the relevance/importance of each sensor).

Example 16.10: Fuzzy thresholding

In many image processing applications, we often have to threshold the gray-level images to generate binary images. In these cases, the image contains a background and one or more objects. The production of binary images serves generally the feature calculation and object recognition. Therefore, image thresholding can be regarded as the simplest form of segmentation, or more generally, as a two-class clustering procedure. To separate the object gray levels g_0 from the background gray levels g_B, we have to determine a threshold T. The thresholding can be carried out by the following decision:

$$g = \begin{cases} g_0 = 0 & \text{if } 0 \le g_i \le T \\ g_B = 1 & \text{if } T \le g_i \le L - 1 \end{cases} \tag{16.45}$$

The basic idea is to find a threshold T that minimizes/maximizes the amount of image fuzziness. To answer the question of how fuzzy the image G of size $M \times N$ and L gray levels $g = 0, 1, ..., L - 1$ is, measures of fuzziness-like fuzzy entropy [24]:

$$H = \frac{1}{MN \ln 2} \sum_{g=0}^{L-1} h(g) \left[-\mu(g) \ln(\mu(g)) - (1 - \mu(g)) \ln(1 - \mu(g)) \right] \tag{16.46}$$

or index of fuzziness [30]

$$\gamma = \frac{2}{MN} \sum_{g=0}^{L-1} h(g) \min(\mu(g), 1 - \mu(g)) \tag{16.47}$$

can be used, where $h(g)$ denotes the histogram value and $\mu(g)$ the membership value of the gray level g, respectively.

The general procedure for fuzzy thresholding can be summarized as follows:

1. Select the type of membership function (Fig. 16.18)
2. Calculate the image histogram

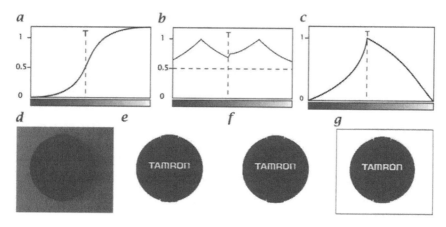

Figure 16.18: *Different membership functions for fuzzy thresholding applied by: **a** Pal and Murthy [32]; **b** Huang and Wang [33]; and **c** [9]; **d** original image; Results of thresholding: **e** Pal and Murthy [32]; **f** Huang and Wang [33]; and **g** Tizhoosh [36].*

3. Initialize the membership function
4. Move the threshold and calculate in each position the amount of fuzziness using fuzzy entropy or any other measure of fuzziness
5. Find out the position with minimum/maximum fuzziness
6. Threshold the image with the corresponding threshold

The main difference between fuzzy thresholding techniques is that each of them uses different membership functions and measures of fuzziness, respectively. Figure 16.18 illustrates three examples of fuzzy membership functions applied to thresholding together with the corresponding results on a test image. For the analytical form of the various membership functions, we would like to refer to the literature [23, 32, 33, 36].

16.6 Conclusions

Of the publications on fuzzy approaches to image processing, fuzzy clustering and rule-based approaches have the greatest share. Measures of fuzziness and fuzzy geometrical measures are usually used as features within the selected algorithms. Fuzzy measures and fuzzy integrals are becoming more and more an interesting research subject. The theoretical research on fuzzy mathematical morphology still seems to be more important than practical reports. Only a few applications of fuzzy morphology can be found in the literature. Finally, fuzzy grammars still seem to be as unpopular as the classical counterpart.

The topics detailed in Sections 16.3.1–16.4.7 can also be used to extend the existing image processing algorithms and improve their performance. Some examples are: *fuzzy Hough transform* [89], fuzzy mean filtering [90], and fuzzy median filtering [91].

Besides numerous publications on new fuzzy techniques, the literature on introduction to fuzzy image processing can be divided into overview papers [7, 26, 74, 92], collections of related papers [43], and textbooks [8, 9, 11, 51, 67].

Fuzzy clustering algorithms and rule-based approaches will certainly play an important role in developing new image processing algorithms. Here, the potential of fuzzy if-then rule techniques seem to be greater than already estimated. The disadvantage of the rule-based approach, however, is the costs involved in computation of local operations. Hardware developments presumably will be a subject of investigations. Fuzzy integrals will find more and more applications in image data fusion. The theoretical research on fuzzy morphology will be completed with regard to its fundamental questions, and more practical reports will be published in this area. Fuzzy geometry will be further investigated and play an indispensable part of fuzzy image processing.

It is not possible (and also not meaningful) to do everything in image processing with fuzzy techniques. Fuzzy image processing will play mostly a supplementary role in computer vision. Its part will probably be small in many applications; its role, nevertheless, will be pivotal and decisive.

16.7 References

[1] Zadeh, L. A., (1965). Fuzzy sets. *Information and Control*, **8**:338–353.

[2] Zadeh, L. A., (1972). A fuzzy-set-theoretic interpretation of linguistic hedges. *Jour. Cybernetics*, **2**:4–34.

[3] Zadeh, L. A., (1973). Outline of a new approach to the analysis of complex systems and decision processes. *IEEE Trans. System, Man and Cybernetics*, **3**(1):28–44.

[4] Zadeh, L. A., (1975). The concept of a linguistic variable and its applications to approximate reasoning. *Information Science*, **8**:199–249.

[5] Zadeh, L. A., (1975). The concept of a linguistic variable and its applications to approximate reasoning. *Information Science*, **9**:43–80.

[6] Zadeh, L. A., (1996). Fuzzy logic = computing with words. *IEEE Trans. Fuzzy Systems*, **4**(2):103–111.

[7] Pal, S. K., (1992). Fuzziness, image information and scene analysis. In *An introduction to Fuzzy Logic Applications in Intelligent Systems*, R. Yager and L. Zadeh, eds., pp. 147–184. Dordrecht: Kluwer Academic Publishers.

[8] Pal, S. K. and Dutta Majumder, D., (1986). *Fuzzy Mathematical Approach to Pattern Recognition*. New York: John Wiley & Sons.

[9] Tizhoosh, H. R., (1997). *Fuzzy Image Processing (in German)*. Berlin: Springer.

[10] Ishibuchi, H., Nozaki, K., and Yamamoto, N., (1993). Selecting fuzzy rules by genetic algorithms for classification. In *Proc. 2nd IEEE International Conference on Fuzzy Systems*, Vol. 2, pp. 1119-1124. San Francisco.

[11] Tizhoosh, H. R., (1997). A systematical introduction to fuzzy image processing (in German). In *AFN '97*, pp. 39-45. Magdeburg, Germany: University of Magdeburg.

[12] Rosenfeld, A., (1979). Fuzzy digital topology. *Information and Control*, **40**:76-87.

[13] Rosenfeld, A. and Klette, R., (1985). Degree of adjacency or surroundedness. *Pattern Recognition*, **18**(2):169-177.

[14] Wang, X. and Keller, J. M., (1997). Fuzzy surroundedness. In *Proc. FUZZ-IEEE'97, Barcelona, Spain*, Vol. 2, pp. 1173-1178.

[15] Pal, S. K. and Ghosh, A., (1992). Fuzzy geometry in image analysis. *Fuzzy Sets and Systems*, **48**:23-40.

[16] Rosenfeld, A., (1984). The diameter of a fuzzy set. *Fuzzy Sets and Systems*, **13**:241-246.

[17] Rosenfeld, A., (1984). The fuzzy geometry of image subsets. *Pattern Recognition Letters*, **2**:311-317.

[18] Rosenfeld, A., (1990). Fuzzy rectangles. *Pattern Recognition Letters*, **11**: 677-679.

[19] Rosenfeld, A. and Haber, S., (1985). The perimeter of a fuzzy set. *Pattern Recognition*, **18**:125-130.

[20] Rosenfeld, A. and Janos, L., (1982). Some results on fuzzy digital convexity. *Pattern Recognition*, **15**:379-382.

[21] Pal, S. K. and Ghosh, A., (1990). Index of area coverage of fuzzy image subsets and object extraction. *Pattern Recognition Letters*, **11**:831-841.

[22] Pal, S. K., (1989). Fuzzy skeletonization of an image. *Pattern Recognition Letters*, **10**:17-23.

[23] Rosenfeld, A. and Pal, S. K., (1988). Image enhancement and thresholding by optimization of fuzzy compactness. *Pattern Recognition Letters*, **7**: 77-86.

[24] De Luca, A. and Termini, S., (1972). A definition of a nonprobalistic entropy in the setting of fuzzy set theory. *Information and Control*, **20**: 301-312.

[25] Pal, S. K. and Pal, N. K., (1991). Entropy: a new definition and its applications. *IEEE Trans. System, Man and Cybernetics*, **21**(5):1260-1270.

[26] Pal, S. K., (1994). Fuzzy sets in image processing and recognition. In *Fuzzy Logic Technology and Applications*, R. J. Marks, ed., pp. 33-40. Piscataway: IEEE Technical Activities Board.

[27] Bhandari, D., Pal, N. R., and Majumder, D. D., (1992). Fuzzy divergence: a new measure for image segmentation. In *Proceedings 2nd International Conference on Fuzzy Logic & Neural Networks, Iizuka, Japan*, pp. 645-648.

[28] Bhandari, D., Pal, N. R., and Majumder, D. D., (1992). Fuzzy divergence, probability measure of fuzzy events and image threshold. *Pattern Recognition Letters*, **13**:857-867.

[29] Friedman, M., Kandel, A., and Schneider, M., (1989). The use of weighted fuzzy expected value (WFEV) in fuzzy expert systems. *Fuzzy Sets and Systems*, **31**:37-45.

[30] Kaufman, A., (1975). *Introduction to the Theory of Fuzzy Subsets - Fundamental Theoretical Elements*, Vol. 1. New York: Academic Press.

[31] Pal, S. K. and Kundu, M. K., (1990). Automatic selection of object enhancement operator with quantitative justification based on fuzzy set theoretic measures. *Pattern Recognition Letters*, **11**:811-829.

[32] Pal, S. K. and Murthy, C. A., (1990). Fuzzy thresholding: mathematical framework, bound functions and weighted moving average technique. *Pattern Recognition Letters*, **11**:197-206.

[33] Huang, L. K. and Wang, M. J., (1995). Image thresholding by minimizing the measure of fuzziness. *Pattern Recognition*, **28**:41-51.

[34] Kandel, A., Friedman, M., and Schneider, M., (1989). The use of weighted fuzzy expected value (WFEV) in fuzzy expert systems. *Fuzzy Sets and Systems*, **31**:37-45.

[35] Tizhoosh, H. R., Krell, G., and Michaelis, B., (1997). On fuzzy image enhancement of megavoltage images in radiation therapy. In *Proc. 6th IEEE International Conference on Fuzzy Systems*, Vol. 3, pp. 1399-1404. Barcelona, Spain.

[36] Tizhoosh, H., (1998). On image thresholding and potentials of fuzzy techniques *(in German)*. In *Informatik '98: Informatik zwischen Bild und Sprache*, R. Kruse and J. Dassow, eds., pp. 97-106. Berlin: Springer.

[37] Keller, J. M., (199). Fuzzy logic rules in low and mid level computer vision tasks. In *Proc. NAFIPS'96*, pp. 19-22.

[38] Law, T., Itoh, H., and Seki, H., (1996). Image filtering, edge detection, and edge tracing using fuzzy reasoning. *IEEE Trans. Pattern Analysis and Machine Intelligence*, **18**(5):481-491.

[39] Miyajima, K. and Norita, T., (1992). Region extraction for real image based on fuzzy reasoning. In *Proc. FUZZ-IEEE'92*, pp. 229-236. San Diego.

[40] Russo, F., (1992). A user-friendly research tool for image processing with fuzzy rules. In *Proc. 1st IEEE International Conference on Fuzzy Systems*, pp. 561-568. San Diego.

[41] Russo, F. and Ramponi, G., (1994). Edge extraction by FIRE operators. In *Proc. 3rd IEEE International Conference on Fuzzy Systems*, Vol. I, pp. 249-253.

[42] Bezdek, J. C., (1981). *Pattern Recognition with Fuzzy Objective Function Algorithms*. New York: Plenum Press.

[43] Bezdek, J. C. and Pal, S. K. (eds.), (1992). *Fuzzy Models For Pattern Recognition*. Piscataway, NJ: IEEE Press.

[44] Bezdek, J. C., Hall, L. O., Clark, M., Goldgof, D., and Clarke, L. P., (1996). Segmenting medical images with fuzzy methods: An update. In *Fuzzy Information Engineering: A Guided Tour of Applications*, R. Yager,

D. Dubois, and H. Prade, eds., pp. 69-92. New York: John Wiley & Sons.

[45] Dave, R. N., (1989). Use of the adaptive fuzzy clustering algorithms to detect lines in digital images. *Intelligent Robots and Computer Vision*, **1192**(2):600-611.

[46] Dave, R. N., (1992). Boundary detection through fuzzy clustering. In *Proceedings FUZZ-IEEE 1992, International Conference on Fuzzy Systems*, pp. 127-134.

[47] Dave, R. N., (1992). Generalized fuzzy c-shells clustering and detection of circular and elliptical boundaries. *Pattern Recognition*, **25**(7):127-134.

[48] Dave, R. and Krishnapuram, R., (1997). Robust clustering methods: A unified view. *IEEE Trans. Fuzzy Systems*, **5**(2):270-293.

[49] Krishnapuram, R. and Keller, J. M., (1993). A possibilistic approach to clustering. *IEEE Trans. Fuzzy Systems*, **1**(2):98-110.

[50] Krishnapuram, R. and Keller, J. M., (1996). The possibilistic c-means algorithm: insights and recommendations. *IEEE Trans. Fuzzy Systems*, **4**(3): 385-393.

[51] Kruse, R., Höppner, F., and F., K., (1997). *Fuzzy-Clusteranalyse*. Braunschweig: Vieweg.

[52] Pal, N. R., Pal, K., and Bezdek, J. C., (1997). A mixed c-means clustering model. In *Proc. FUZZ-IEEE'97*, pp. 11-21.

[53] Bloch, I., Pellot, C., Sureda, F., and Herment, A., (1996). Fuzzy modelling and fuzzy mathematical morphology applied to 3D reconstruction of blood vessels by multi-modality data fusion. In *Fuzzy Information Engineering*, D. Dubois, H. Prade, and R. Yager, eds., pp. 92-110. New York: John Wiley & Sons.

[54] De Baets, B., (1997). Fuzzy mathematical morphology: A logical approach. In *Uncertainty Analysis in Engineering and Science: Fuzzy Logic, Statistics, and Neural Network Approach*, B. Ayyub and M. Gupta, eds., pp. 53-67. Dordrecht: Kluwer Academic Publisher.

[55] Bloch, I. and Maitre, H., (1995). Fuzzy mathematical morphologies: A comparative study. *Pattern Recognition*, **28**(9):1341-1387.

[56] Bloch, I. and Maitre, H., (1993). Mathematical morphology on fuzzy sets. In *International Workshop on Mathematical Morphology and Its Applications to Signal Processing*, pp. 1303-1308. Barcelona.

[57] De Baets, B. and Kerre, E., (1993). An introduction to fuzzy mathematical morphology. In *Proc. NAFIPS 93*, pp. 129-133.

[58] Gader, P. D., (1997). Fuzzy spatial relations based on fuzzy morphology. In *Proc. FUZZ-IEEE 97*, Vol. 2, pp. 1179-1183. Barcelona.

[59] Goetcherian, V., (1980). From binary to gray tone image processing using fuzzy logic concepts. *Pattern Recognition*, **12**:7-15.

[60] Maccarone, M. C., (1994). Fuzzy mathematical morphology: concepts and applications. In *Vision Modeling and Information Coding, Vistas in Astronomy, Special issue*, A. Bijaoui, ed., Vol. 40, pp. 469-477.

[61] Nakatsuyama, M., (1993). Fuzzy mathematical morphology for image processing. In *Proc. ANZIIS*, pp. 75-78.

[62] Serra, J., (1982). *Image Analysis and Mathematical Morphology*, Vol. 1. London: Academic Press.

[63] Sinha, D. and Dougherty, E. R., (1992). Fuzzy mathematical morphology. *Jour. Visual Communication and Image Representation*, 3(3):286-302.

[64] Sinha, D. and Dougherty, E. R., (1993). Fuzzification of set inclusion. In *Proc. SPIE 93*. Orlando, USA.

[65] Sugeno, M., (1974). *Theory of Fuzzy Integrals and Its Applications*. PhD thesis, Tokyo Institute of Technology, Japan.

[66] Wang, Z. and Klir, G. J., (1992). *Fuzzy Measure Theory*. New York: Plenum Press.

[67] Chi, Z., Yan, H., and Pham, T., (1996). *Fuzzy Algorithms with Applications to Image Processing and Pattern Recognition*. Singapore: World Scientific Publishing.

[68] Gader, P. D., Mohamed, M. A., and Keller, J. M., (1996). Fusion of handwritten word classifiers. *Pattern Recognition Letters*, 17:577-584.

[69] Grabisch, M. and Nicolas, J. M., (1994). Classification by fuzzy integral: performance and tests. *Fuzzy Sets and Systems*, 65:255-271.

[70] Grabisch, M., Nguyen, H. T., and Walker, E. A., (1995). *Fundamentals of Uncertainty Calculi with Applications to Fuzzy Inference*. Dordrecht: Kluwer Academic Publishers.

[71] Grabisch, M., (1996). Fuzzy measures and integrals: A survey of applications and recent issues. In *Fuzzy Information Engineering: A Guided Tour of Applications*, R. Yager, D. Dubois, and H. Prade, eds., pp. 507-530. New York: John Wiley & Sons.

[72] Keller, J. M., Gader, P., Tahani, H., Chiang, J. H., and Mohamed, M., (1994). Advances in fuzzy integration for pattern recognition. *Fuzzy Sets and Systems*, 65:273-283.

[73] Keller, J. M., Qiu, H., and Tahani, H., (1986). Fuzzy logic rules in low and mid level computer vision tasks. In *Proc. NAFIPS'96*, pp. 324-338.

[74] Keller, J. and Krishnapuram, R., (1994). Fuzzy decision models in computer vision. In *Fuzzy Sets, Neural Networks and Soft Computing*, R. Yager and L. Zadeh, eds., pp. 213-232. New York: Van Nostrand Reinhold.

[75] Pham, T. D. and Yan, H., (1996). Color image segmentation: a fuzzy integral mountain-clustering approach. In *Proc. Image Segmentation Workshop 1996, The Australian Pattern Recognition Society*, pp. 27-32. Sydney.

[76] Tahani, H. and Keller, J. C., (1992). The fusion of information via fuzzy integration. In *Proc. NAFIPS'92*, pp. 468-477. Puerto Vallarta, Mexico.

[77] Tizhoosh, H. and Michaelis, B., (1998). Improvement of image quality based on subjective evaluation and Fuzzy aggregation techniques. In *EUFIT'98, Aachen, Germany*, Vol. 2, pp. 1325-1329.

[78] Zadeh, L. A. and Lee, E. T., (1969). Note on fuzzy languages. *Information Science*, 1:421-434.

[79] Fu, S., (1982). *Syntactic Pattern Recognition and Application*. Englewood Cliffs, NJ: Prentice-Hall.

[80] DePalma, G. F. and Yau, S. S., (1975). Fractionally fuzzy grammars with application to pattern recognition. In *Fuzzy Sets and Their Applications to Cognitive and Decision Processes*, L. A. Zadeh, K. S. Fu, K. Tanaka, and M. Shimura, eds., pp. 329–351. London: Academic Press.

[81] Majumder, A. K., Ray, A. K., and Chatterjee, B., (1982). Inference of fuzzy regular language using formal power series representation. In *Proc. Indian Statistical Institute Golden Jubilee Conference on Advances in Information Science and Technology*, pp. 155–165. Calcutta.

[82] Majumder, D. D. and Pal, S. K., (1977). On fuzzification, fuzzy languages and pattern recognition. In *Proc. 7th IEEE Int. Conf. on Cybern. and Soc.*, pp. 591–595. Washington.

[83] Tamura, S. and Tanaka, K., (1973). Learning of fuzzy formal language. *IEEE Trans. System, Man and Cybernetics*, **3**.

[84] Pal, S. K. and Pathak, A., (1991). Fuzzy grammars in syntactic recognition of skeletal maturity from x-rays. *IEEE Trans. System, Man and Cybernetics*, **16**(5):657–667.

[85] Kickert, W. J. M. and Koppelaar, H., (1976). Application of fuzzy set theory to syntactic pattern recognition of handwritten capitals. *IEEE Trans. System, Man and Cybernetics*, **6**:148–151.

[86] Parizeau, M. and Plamondon, R., (1995). A fuzzy-syntactic approach to allograph modeling for cursive script recognition. *IEEE Trans. Pattern Analysis and Machine Intelligence*, **17**(7):702–712.

[87] Pal, S. K. and King, R. A., (1981). Histogram equalization with S and p functions in detecting x-ray edges. *Electronics Letters*, **17**(8):302–304.

[88] Gupta, M. M., Knopf, G. K., and Nikiforuk, P. N., (1988). Edge perception using fuzzy logic. In *Fuzzy Computing—Theory, Hardware and Applications*, M. M. Gupta and T. Yamakawa, eds., pp. 35–51. Amsterdam: Elsevier Science Publishers.

[89] Han, J., Koczy, L., and Poston, T., (1994). Fuzzy Hough transforms. *Pattern Recognition Letters*, **15**:649–658.

[90] Lee, C.-S., Y.-H., K., and Yau, P.-T., (1997). Weighted fuzzy mean filter for image processing. *Fuzzy Sets and Systems*, **89**(2):157–180.

[91] Taguchi, A., (1996). A design method of fuzzy weighted median filters. In *Proc. ICIP'96*.

[92] Krishnapuram, R. and Keller, J. M., (1992). Fuzzy set theoretic approach to computer vision: an overview. In *Proc. FUZZ-IEEE'92*, pp. 135–142. San Diego.

17 Neural Net Computing for Image Processing

Anke Meyer-Bäse

Department of Electrical Engineering and Computer Science
University of Florida

17.1 Introduction

Artificial neural networks are an attempt to emulate the processing capabilities of biological neural systems. The basic idea is to realize systems capable of performing complex processing tasks by interconnecting a high number of very simple processing elements that might even work in parallel. They solve cumbersome and intractable problems by learning directly from data. An artificially neural network usually consists of a large amount of simple processing units, namely, neurons, via mutual interconnection. It learns to solve problems by adequately

577

adjusting the strength of the interconnections according to input data. Moreover, it can be easily adapted to new environments by learning. At the same time, it can deal with information that is noisy, inconsistent, vague, or probabilistic. These features motivate extensive researches and developments in artificial neural networks.

The main features of artificial neural networks are their massive parallel processing architectures and the capabilities of *learning* from the presented inputs. They can be utilized to perform a specific task only by means of adequately adjusting the connection weights, that is, by *training* them with the presented data. For each type of artificial neural network, there exists a corresponding *learning algorithm* by which we can train the network in an iterative updating manner. Those learning algorithms fit into two main categories: *supervised learning* and *unsupervised learning*.

For supervised learning, not only the input data but also the corresponding target answers are presented to the network. Learning is done in accordance with the direct comparison of the actual output of the network with known correct answers. It is also referred to as *learning with a teacher*. By contrast, if only input data without the corresponding target answers are presented to the network for unsupervised learning. In fact, the learning goal is not defined at all in terms of specific correct examples. The available information is in the correlations of the input data. The network is expected to create categories from these correlations, and to produce output signals corresponding to the input category.

Neural networks have been successfully employed to solve a variety of computer vision problems. They are systems of interconnected simple processing elements. There exist many types of neural networks that solve a wide range of problems in the area of image processing. There are also many types of neural networks and they are determined by the type of connectivity between the processing elements, the weights (*synapses*) of the connecting links, the processing elements characteristics, and training or learning rules. These rules specify an initial set of weights and indicate how weights should be modified during the learning process to improve network performance.

The theory and representation of the various network types is motivated by the functionality and representation of biological neural networks. In this sense, processing units are usually referred to as *neurons*, while interconnections are called synaptic connections. Although different neural models are known, all have the following basic components in common [1]:

1. A finite set of *neurons* $a(1), a(2), \ldots, a(n)$ with each neuron having a specific neural value at time t, which will be denoted by $a_t(i)$.

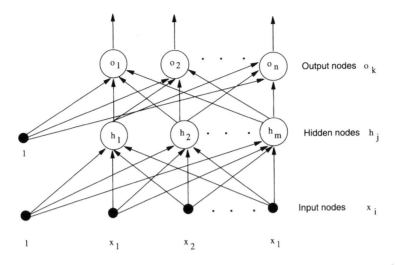

Figure 17.1: *Two-layer perceptron.*

2. A finite set of *neural connections* $W = (w_{ij})$, where w_{ij} denotes the strength of the connection of neuron $a(i)$ with neuron $a(j)$.

3. A *propagation rule* $\tau_t(i) = \sum_{j=1}^{n} a_t(j) w_{ij}$.

4. An *activation function* f, which takes τ as an input and produces the next state of the neuron $a_{t+1}(i) = f(\tau_t(i) - \theta)$, where θ is a threshold and f a hard limiter, threshold logic, or sigmoidal function, which introduces a nonlinearity into the network.

17.2 Multilayer perceptron (MLP)

Multilayer perceptrons (MLP) are one of the most important types of neural nets because many applications are successful implementations of MLPs. Typically the network consists of a set of processing units that constitute the *input layer*, one or more *hidden layers*, and an *output layer*. The input signal propagates through the network in a forward direction, on a layer-by-layer basis. Figure 17.1 illustrates the configuration of the MLP.

A node in a hidden layer is connected to every node in the layer above and below it. In Fig. 17.1 weight w_{ij} connects input node x_i to hidden node h_j and weight v_{jk} connects h_j to output node o_k. Classification begins by presenting a pattern to the input nodes x_i, $1 \le i \le l$. From there data flow in one direction through the perceptron until the output nodes o_k, $1 \le k \le n$, are reached. Output nodes will have a value of either 0 or 1. Thus, the perceptron is capable of partitioning its pattern space into 2^n classes.

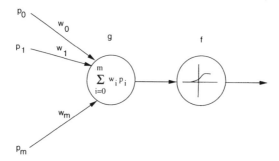

Figure 17.2: *Propagation rule and activation function for the MLP network.*

In a typical pattern-recognition system, the first step is the acquisition of data. These raw data are preprocessed to suppress noise and to normalize input. Features are those parts of the signal that carry information salient to its identity and their extraction is an abstraction operation where the important is extracted and the irrelevant is discarded. Classification is the assignment of the input as an element of one of a set of predefined classes. The rules of classification are generally not known exactly and thus estimated. Neural networks estimate the discriminant functions directly without needing a statistical model. From a statistical perspective, a multilayer network is a linear sum of nonlinear basis functions. Those are the hidden units and the parameter are called connection weights. In a training process, given a training example, the weights that minimize the difference between network outputs and required outputs are computed.

The steps that govern the data flow through the perceptron during *classification* are [1]:

1. Present the pattern $\boldsymbol{p} = [p_1, p_2, \ldots, p_l] \in \mathcal{R}^l$ to the perceptron, that is, set $x_i = p_i$ for $1 \le i \le l$.

2. Compute the values of the hidden-layer nodes as it is illustrated in Fig. 17.2.

$$h_j = \frac{1}{1 + \exp\left[-\left(w_{0j} + \sum_{i=1}^{l} w_{ij}x_i\right)\right]} \qquad 1 \le j \le m \qquad (17.1)$$

The activation function of all units in the MLP is the sigmoid function $f(x) = 1/(1 + \exp -x)$ and it is also the most common form of activation function in feedforward neural networks. It is defined as a strictly increasing function that exhibits a graceful balance between nonlinear and linear behavior.

3. Calculate the values of the output nodes according to

$$o_k = \frac{1}{1 + \exp\left(v_{0k} + \sum_{j=1}^{m} v_{jk}h_j\right)} \qquad 1 \le k \le n \qquad (17.2)$$

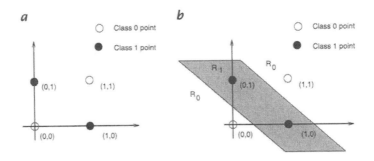

Figure 17.3: *XOR-problem and solution strategy using the MLP.*

4. The class $c = [c_1, c_2, \ldots, c_n]$ that the perceptron assigns p must be a binary vector. So o_k must be the threshold of a certain class at some level τ and depends on the application.

5. Repeat steps 1,2,3, and 4 for each pattern that is to be classified.

Multilayer perceptrons (MLPs) are highly nonlinear interconnected structures and are, therefore, ideal candidates for both nonlinear function approximation and *nonlinear classification* tasks. A classical problem that can be solved only by the MLP is the *XOR-problem*. While a linear classifier is able to partition $\mathcal{R}^m$ into regions separated by a hyperplane, the MLP is able to construct very complex decision boundaries as illustrated in Fig. 17.3.

Applied to image processing the MLP has as an input features extracted from images or from regions from these images. Such features can be shape, size, and texture measures, and attempt to capture the key aspects of an image.

Multilayer perceptrons have been applied to a variety of problems in image processing, including *optical character recognition* [2] and *medical diagnosis* [3, 4].

17.2.1 Backpropagation-type neural networks

Multilayer perceptrons (MLPs) have been applied successfully to solve some difficult and diverse problems by training them in a supervised manner with a highly popular algorithm known as the error backpropagation algorithm. This process consists of two passes through the different layers of the network: a forward and a backward pass. During the forward pass a training pattern is presented to the *perceptron* and classified.

The backward pass recursively, level by level, determines error terms used to adjust to the perceptron weights. The error terms at the first level of the recursions are a function of c^t and output of the perceptron $(o_1, o_2, \ldots, o_n)$. After all the errors have been computed, weights are adjusted using the error terms that correspond to their level. The algorithmic description of the *backpropagation* is given here [1]:

1. **Initialization:** Initialize the weights of the perceptron randomly with numbers between -0.1 and 0.1; that is,

$$w_{ij} = \text{random}([-0.1, 0.1]) \quad 0 \le i \le l, 1 \le j \le m$$
$$v_{jk} = \text{random}([-0.1, 0.1]) \quad 0 \le j \le m, 1 \le k \le n \tag{17.3}$$

2. **Presentation of training examples:** Present $\boldsymbol{p}^t = \left[p_1^t, p_2^t, \ldots, p_l^t \right]$ from the training pair $(\boldsymbol{p}^t, \boldsymbol{c}^t)$ to the perceptron and apply steps 1, 2, and 3 from the perceptron classification algorithm described earlier.

3. **Forward computation:** Compute the errors $\delta_{ok}, 1 \le k \le n$ in the output layer using

$$\delta_{ok} = o_k(1 - o_k)(c_k^t - o_k) \tag{17.4}$$

where $\boldsymbol{c}^t = \left[c_1^t, c_2^t, \ldots, c_n^t \right]$ represents the correct class of $\boldsymbol{p}^t$. The vector $(o_1, o_2, \ldots, o_n)$ represents the output of the perceptron.

4. **Forward computation:** Compute the errors δ_{hj}, $1 \le j \le m$, in the hidden-layers nodes using

$$\delta_{hj} = h_j(1 - h_j) \sum_{k=1}^{n} \delta_{ok} v_{jk} \tag{17.5}$$

5. **Backward computation:** Let v_{jk} denote the value of weight v_{jk} after the tth training pattern has been presented to the perceptron. Adjust the weights between the output layer and the hidden layer using

$$v_{jk}(t) = v_{jk}(t-1) + \eta \delta_{ok} h_j \tag{17.6}$$

The parameter $0 \le \eta \le 1$ represents the learning rate.

6. **Backward computation:** Adjust the weights between the hidden layer and the input layer according to

$$w_{ij}(t) = w_{ij}(t-1) + \eta \delta_{hj} p_i^t \tag{17.7}$$

7. **Iteration:** Repeat steps 2 through 6 for each element of the training set. One cycle through the training set is called an iteration.

Design considerations. The MLPs construct global approximations to nonlinear input-output mapping. Consequently, they are capable of generalization in regions of the input space where little or no data are available.

The size of a network is an important consideration from both the performance and computational points of view. It has been shown [5] that one hidden layer is sufficient to approximate the mapping of any continuous function.

The number of neurons in the input layer is equal to the length of the feature vector. Likewise, the number of nodes in the output layer is usually the same as the number of classes. The number of subsequent hidden layers and the number of neurons in each layer are design choices. In most applications, the latter number is a small fraction of the number of neurons in the input layer. It is usually desirable to keep this number small to reduce the danger of overtraining. On the other hand, too few neurons in the hidden layer may make it difficult for the network to converge to a suitable partitioning of a complex feature space. Once a network has converged, it can be shrunk in size and retrained, often with an improvement in overall performance.

Data used for training must be representative of the population over the entire feature space and training patterns should be presented randomly. The network must be able to generalize to the entire training set as a whole, not to individual classes one at a time.

17.2.2 Convolution neural networks (CNN)

Convolution neural networks (CNN) represent a well-established method in medical image processing [6, 7]. The difference between a CNN and an MLP applied to image classification is that a CNN works directly with images and not with extracted features. The basic structure of a CNN is shown in Fig. 17.4, which represents a four-layer CNN with two input images, three image groups in the first hidden layer, two groups in the second hidden layer, and a real-valued output [6]. The number of layers and the number of groups in each layer are implementation-oriented. The image propagates from input to output by means of convolution with trainable weight kernels.

Forward Propagation. Let $H_{l,g}$ denote the gth image group at layer l, and let $N(l)$ be the number of such groups. Image propagation from the input layer ($l = 1$) to the output layer ($l = L$) proceeds as follows [6]. The image $H_{l,g}(l \geq 2)$ is obtained by applying a pointwise *sigmoid nonlinearity* to an intermediate image $I_{l,g}$, that is,

$$H_{l,g}(i,j) = \frac{1}{1 + \exp(-I_{l,g}(i,j))}, \quad g = 1,\ldots,N(l) \tag{17.8}$$

The intermediate image $I_{l,g}$ is equal to the sum of the images obtained from the convolution of $H_{l-1,g'}$ at layer $l - 1$ with trainable *kernel of*

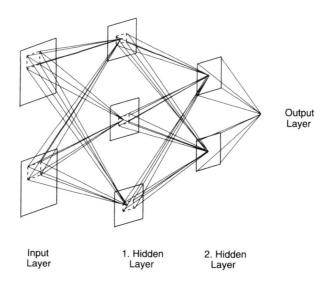

Output
Layer

Input   1. Hidden   2. Hidden
Layer   Layer   Layer

Figure 17.4: *Convolution neural network.*

weights $w_{l-1,g,g'}$. More precisely,

$$I_{l,g} = \sum_{g'=1}^{N(l-1)} H_{l-1,g'} * w_{l-1,g,g'}$$ (17.9)

where $*$ denotes a 2-D convolution with the 2-D kernel $w_{l-1,g,g'}$ of weights connecting the g'th group in the $(l-1)$th layer of the gth group in the lth layer.

The *spatial width* $S_w(l-1)$ of the *weight kernel* $w_{l-1,g,g'}$ defines the *receptive field* for the layer l. The spatial width $S_H(l)$ of an image at layer l is related to the image width at the layer $l-1$ by

$$S_H(l) = S_H(l-1) - S_w(l-1) + 1$$ (17.10)

Consequently, the image width becomes smaller as the layer number increases. The edge effect in convolution is avoided by using this definition. The width of the receptive field of a given node in the lth layer is equal to the sum of the kernel widths of the proceeding layers minus $(l-2)$. The spatial width of the image at the output layer $(l = L)$ is one. The output of the CNN, defined as $O(g) \equiv H_{L,g}(0,0)$, is thus a real number.

Note that an MLP is a special case of a CNN. If for the weight kernels and image groups in a CNN we substitute real numbers, then we get ordinary MLP weights for the weight kernels and nodes for the images. The underlying equations in both networks are the same.

Backpropagation. Like the MLP the CNN learns through backpropagation. For each training image p (or set p of training images in case the input layer processes more than one image) we can define the desired output value $O_d^{(p)}(g)$, where $g = 1, \ldots, N(L)$ denotes the output node number. At each training epoch t, training images are applied to the CNN and the actual CNN outputs $O_a^{(p)}[t]$ are computed using Eqs. (17.8) and (17.9). The CNN output error for training image p at training epoch t is defined as

$$E^p[t] = \frac{1}{2} \sum_{g=1}^{N(L)} (O_d^{(p)}(g) - O_a^{(p)}(g)[t])^2 \qquad (17.11)$$

and the cumulative CNN error during training epoch t is defined as

$$E[t] = \sum_{p=1}^{P} E^{(p)}[t] \qquad (17.12)$$

where p is the total number of training samples.

It can be shown that for a CNN, the computation for the weights updating can be carried out as a backpropagation process. The derivation of the backpropagation algorithm is given in Sahiner et al. [6].

17.3   Self-organizing neural networks

In a *self-organizing map*, the neurons are placed at the nodes of a lattice that is usually 1-D or 2-D. The neurons become selectively tuned to various input patterns or classes of input patterns in the course of a competitive learning process. The location of the neurons so tuned (i. e., the winning neurons) tend to become ordered with respect to each other in such a way that a meaningful coordinate system for different input features is created over the lattice [8]. A self-organizing *feature map* is therefore characterized by the formation of a topographic map of the input patterns, in which the spatial locations (i. e., coordinates) of the neurons in the lattice correspond to intrinsic features of the input patterns, hence the name "self-organizing feature map" [9].

17.3.1   Kohonen maps

The principal goal of a Kohonen self-organizing map is to transform an incoming signal pattern of arbitrary dimension into a 1-D or 2-D discrete map, and to perform this transformation adaptively in a topological ordered fashion. Many activation patterns are presented to the network, one at a time. Typically, each input presentation consists simply of a localized region of activity against a quiet background. Each

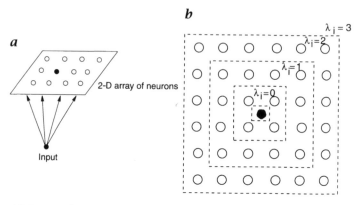

Figure 17.5: *a Kohonen neural network; and b neighborhood* Λ_i, *of varying size, around "winning" neuron i, identified as a black circle.*

such presentation causes a corresponding localized group of neurons in the output layer of the network to be active.

The essential components of such a network are [9]:

1. A 1-D or 2-D *lattice of neurons* that computes simple discriminant functions of inputs received from an input of arbitrary dimension as shown in Fig. 17.5a.

2. A procedure that compares these discriminant functions and selects the neuron with the largest discriminant function value ("winner neuron").

3. An interactive network that activates the selected neuron and its neighbors simultaneously. The neighborhood $\Lambda_{i(x)}(n)$ of the winning neuron is chosen to be a function of the discrete time n. Figure 17.5b illustrates such a neighborhood, which usually first includes all neurons in the network and then shrinks gradually with time. Because it is a symmetric lattice it will shrink to only one "winning neuron", which is marked in the figure as a black circle.

4. An adaptive process that enables the activated neurons to increase their discriminant function values in relation to the input signals.

The learning algorithm of the self-organized map is simple and is outlined here:

1. **Initialization**: Choose random values for the initial *weight vectors* $w_j(0)$ to be different for $j = 1, 2, \ldots, N$, where N is the number of neurons in the lattice. The magnitude of the weights should be small.

2. **Sampling**: Draw a sample x from the input distribution with a certain probability; the vector x represents the activation pattern that is presented to the lattice.

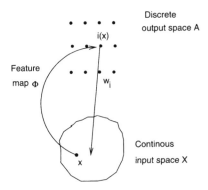

Figure 17.6: *Mapping between input space X and output space A.*

3. **Similarity Matching:** Find the best matching *(winning) neuron* $i(\boldsymbol{x})$ at time n, using the minimum-distance Euclidean criterion:

$$i(\boldsymbol{x}) = \arg\min_{j} ||\boldsymbol{x}(n) - \boldsymbol{w}_j(n)||, \quad j = 1, 2, \dots, N \qquad (17.13)$$

4. **Updating:** Adjust the synaptic weight vectors of all neurons, using the update formula

$$\boldsymbol{w}_j(n+1) = \begin{cases} \boldsymbol{w}_j(n) + \eta(n)[\boldsymbol{x}(n) - \boldsymbol{w}_j(n)], & j \in \Lambda_{i(\boldsymbol{x})}(n) \\ \boldsymbol{w}_j(n) & \text{otherwise} \end{cases}$$

$$(17.14)$$

where $\eta(n)$ is the learning-rate parameter, and $\Lambda_{i(\boldsymbol{x})}(n)$ is the *neighborhood function* centered around the winning neuron $i(\boldsymbol{x})$; both $\eta(n)$ and $\Lambda_{i(\boldsymbol{x})}$ are varied dynamically during learning for best results.

5. **Continuation:** Continue with Step 2 until no noticeable changes in the feature map are observed.

The presented learning algorithm has some interesting properties, which are explained based on Fig. 17.6. To begin with, let X denote a spatially continuous input (sensory) space, the topology of which is defined by the metric relationship of the vectors $\boldsymbol{x} \in X$. Let A denote a spatially discrete output space, the topology of which is endowed by arranging a set of neurons as the computation nodes of a lattice. Let Φ denote a nonlinear transformation called a feature map, which maps the input space X onto the output space A, as shown by

$$\Phi : X \to A \qquad (17.15)$$

Property 1: Approximation of the input space: The self-organizing feature map Φ, represented by the set of synaptic weight vectors $\{\boldsymbol{w}_j | j =$

$1, 2, \ldots, N\}$, in the input space $\mathcal{A}$, provides a good approximation to the input space X.

Property 2: Topological ordering: The feature map Φ computed by the learning algorithm is topologically ordered in the sense that the spatial location of a neuron in the lattice corresponds to a particular domain or feature of input patterns.

Kohonen maps have been applied to a variety of problems in image processing, including texture segmentation [10] and medical diagnosis [11].

Design considerations. The success of the map formation is critically dependent on how the main parameters of the algorithm, namely, the *learning-rate parameter* η and the *neighborhood function* Λ_i, are selected. Unfortunately, there is no theoretical basis for the selection of these parameters. But there are some practical hints [12]:

The learning-rate parameter $\eta(n)$ used to update the *synaptic vector* $w_j(n)$ should be time-varying. For the first 100 iterations $\eta(n)$ should begin with a value close to unity and decrease thereafter gradually, but stay above 0.1.

For topological ordering of the weight vectors w_j to take place, careful consideration has to be given to the neighborhood function Λ_i. Λ_i can take many geometrical forms but should include always the winning neuron in the middle. The neighborhood function Λ_i usually begins such that all neurons in the network are included and then it gradually shrinks with time. During the first 1000 iterations the radius of the neighborhood function Λ_i shrinks linearly with time n to a small value of only a couple of neighboring neurons.

17.3.2 Learning vector quantization

Vector quantization [9] is a technique that exploits the underlying structure of input vectors for the purpose of data compression. Specifically, an input space is split into a number of distinct regions, and for each region a reconstruction vector is defined. When the quantizer is presented a new input vector, the region in which the vector lays is first determined, and it is represented by the reproduction vector of that region. Thus, by using an encoded version of this reproduction vector for storage in place of the original input vector, considerable savings can be realized. The collection of possible reconstruction vectors is called a reconstruction *codebook* and its members are called *codewords*.

A vector quantizer with minimum encoding distortion is called a *Voronoi quantizer*. An input space is divided into four Voronoi cells with associated Voronoi vectors as shown in Fig. 17.7. Each Voronoi cell contains those points of the input space that are the closest to the Voronoi vector among the totality of such points.

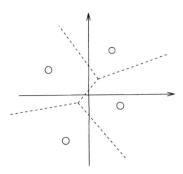

Figure 17.7: *Voronoi diagram involving four cells. The small circles indicate the Voronoi vectors and are the different region (class) representatives.*

Learning vector quantization (LVQ) is a supervised learning technique that uses class information to move the Voronoi vectors slightly, so as to improve the quality of the classifier decision regions. An input vector x is picked at random from the input space. If the class labels of the input vector x and a Voronoi vector w agree, then the Voronoi vector is moved in the direction of the input vector x. If, on the other hand, the class labels of the input vector x and the Voronoi vector w disagree, the Voronoi vector w is moved away from the input vector x.

Let $\{w_j | j = 1, 2, \ldots, N\}$ denote the set of Voronoi vectors, and $\{x_i | 1, 2, \ldots, L\}$ denote the set of input vectors. We assume that there are more input vectors than Voronoi vectors. The learning vector quantization (LVQ) algorithm proceeds as follows [9]:

1. Suppose that the Voronoi vector w_c is the closest to the input vector x_i. Let C_{w_c} denote the class associated with the Voronoi vector w_c, and C_{x_i} denote the class label of the input vector x_i. The Voronoi vector w_c is adjusted as follows:

$$w_c(n + 1) = \begin{cases} w_c(n) + \alpha_n [x_i - w_c(n)] & C_{w_c} = C_{x_i} \\ w_c(n) - \alpha_n [x_i - w_c(n)] & \text{otherwise} \end{cases} \quad (17.16)$$

   where $0 < \alpha_n < 1$.

2. The other Voronoi vectors are not modified.

The learning constant α_n should decrease monotonically with the number of iterations n. The relative simplicity of the LVQ, and its ability to work in *unsupervised mode*, has made it a useful tool for image-segmentation problems [11].

17.4   Radial-basis neural networks (RBNN)

17.4.1   Regularization networks

The design of a *supervised network* may be accomplished in many different ways. The backpropagation algorithm for the design of a multilayer perceptron can be viewed as an application of an *optimization method* known in statistics as *stochastic approximation*. In this section we present a different approach by viewing the design of a neural network as an approximation problem in a high-dimensional space. In the context of a neural network, the hidden units provide a set of "functions" that constitute an arbitrary "basis" for the input patterns (vectors) when they are expanded into the hidden-unit space; these functions are called *radial-basis functions*. Major contributions to the theory, design, and application of radial-basis function networks include papers by Moody and Darken [13] and Poggio and Girosi [14].

The construction of a radial-basis function (RBF) network in its most basic form involves three different layers. For a network with N hidden neurons, the output of the ith output node $f_i(\boldsymbol{x})$ when the n-dimensional input vector $\boldsymbol{x}$ is presented, is given by

$$f_i(\boldsymbol{x}) = \sum_{j=1}^{N} w_{ij} \Psi_j(\boldsymbol{x}) \tag{17.17}$$

where $\Psi_j(\boldsymbol{x}) = \Psi(||\boldsymbol{x}-\boldsymbol{m}_j||/\sigma_j)$ is a suitable *radially symmetric function* that defines the output of the jth hidden node. Often $\Psi(.)$ is chosen to be the *Gaussian function* where the width parameter σ_j is the standard deviation; $\boldsymbol{m}_j$ is the location of the jth centroid, where each centroid is represented by a kernel/hidden node, and w_{ij} is the weight connecting the jth kernel/hidden node to the ith output node. Figure 17.8a illustrates the configuration of the network.

The steps that govern the data flow through the radial-basis function network during classification are:

1. Present the pattern $\boldsymbol{p} = [p_1, p_2, \dots, p_n] \in \mathcal{R}^l$ to the RBF network, that is, set $x_i = p_i$ for $1 \leq i \leq n$.

2. Compute the values of the hidden-layer nodes as it is illustrated in Fig. 17.8b.

$$\psi_i = \exp\left(-d(\boldsymbol{x}, \boldsymbol{m}^i, K^i)/2\right) \tag{17.18}$$

$d(\boldsymbol{x}, \boldsymbol{m}_i) = (\boldsymbol{x} - \boldsymbol{m}_i)^T K_i (\boldsymbol{x} - \boldsymbol{m}_i)$ is a metric norm and is known as the *Mahalanobis distance*. The *shape matrix* K^i is positive definite and its elements k_{jk}^i

$$k_{jk}^i = \frac{h_{jk}^i}{\sigma_j^i * \sigma_k^i} \qquad (17.19)$$

represent the correlation coefficients h_{jk}^i, and σ_j^i the standard deviation.

We have for h_{jk}^i: $h_{jk}^i = 1$ for $j = k$ and $|h_{jk}^i| \leq 1$ otherwise.

3. Calculate the values of the output nodes according to

$$f_{oj} = \phi_j = \sum_i w_{ji} \psi_i \qquad (17.20)$$

4. The class $c = [c_1, c_2, \ldots, c_n]$ that the RBF network assigns p must be a binary vector.

5. Repeat Steps 1,2,3, and 4 for each pattern that is to be classified.

The learning process undertaken by an RBF network may be viewed as follows. The linear weights associated with the output units of the network tend to evolve on a different "time scale" compared to the nonlinear activation functions of the hidden units. The weight-adaptation process is a linear process compared to the nonlinear parameter adaptation of the hidden-layer neurons. As the different layers of an RBF network are performing different tasks, it is reasonable to separate the optimization of the hidden and output layers by using different techniques. The output layer weights are adjusted according to a simple delta rule as shown in the MLP case.

There are different strategies we can follow in the design of an RBF network, depending on how the centers of the RBF network are specified [9]:

1. Fixed centers selected at random: It is the simplest approach to assume fixed radial-basis functions defining the activation functions of the hidden units. Specifically, the locations of the centers may be chosen randomly from the training set.

2. Self-organized selection of centers: The locations of the centers of the hidden units are permitted to move in a self-organized fashion, whereas the linear weights of the output layer are computed using a supervised learning rule. The self-organized component of the learning process serves to allocate network resources in a meaningful way by placing the centers of the radial-basis functions in only those regions of the input space where significant data are present.

3. Supervised selection of centers: The centers and all other free parameters of the network undergo a supervised learning process; in other words, the RBF network takes on its most generalized form.

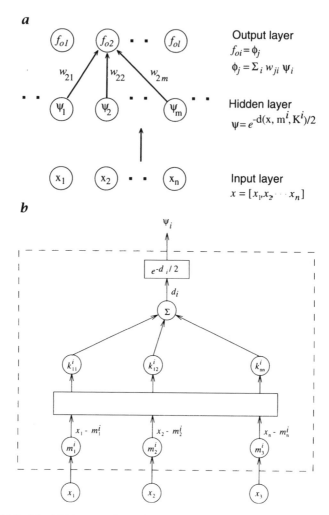

Figure 17.8: *The RBF network: **a** three-layer model; and **b** the connection between input layer and hidden-layer neuron.*

A natural candidate for such a process is *error-correction learning*, which is most conveniently implemented using a *gradient-descent procedure* that represents a generalization of the *LMS algorithm*.

The RBF networks have been applied to a variety of problems in image processing, such as *image coding* and analysis [15], and also in medical diagnosis [16].

Design considerations. The RBF networks construct local approximations to nonlinear input-output mapping, with the result that these networks are capable of fast learning and reduced sensitivity to the order of presentation of training data. In many cases, however, we find that in order to represent a mapping to some desired degree of smoothness, the number of radial-basis functions required to span the input space adequately may have to be very large. This fact can be very inappropriate in many practical applications.

The RBF network has only one hidden layer and the number of basis functions and their shape is problem-oriented and can be determined online during the learning process [17, 18]. The number of neurons in the input layer is equal to the length of the feature vector. Likewise, the number of nodes in the output layer is usually the same as the number of classes.

17.5 Transformation radial-basis networks (TRBNN)

The selection of appropriate features is an important precursor to most statistical pattern recognition methods. A good feature-selection mechanism helps to facilitate classification by eliminating noisy or nonrepresentative features that can impede recognition. Even features that provide some useful information can reduce the accuracy of a classifier when the amount of training data is limited. This so-called "curse of dimensionality," along with the expense of measuring and including features, demonstrates the utility of obtaining a minimum-sized set of features that allow a classifier to discern pattern classes well. Well-known methods in literature applied to feature selection are the floating search methods [19] and genetic algorithms [20].

Radial-basis neural networks are excellent candidates for feature selection. It is necessary to add an additional layer to the traditional architecture (see, e. g., Moody and Darken [13]) to obtain a representation of relevant features. The new paradigm is based on an explicit definition of the relevance of a feature and realizes a linear transformation of the feature space.

Figure 17.9 shows the structure of a radial-basis neural network with the additional layer 2, which transforms the feature space linearly by multiplying the input vector and the center of the nodes by the matrix B. The covariance matrices of the input vector remain unmodified:

$$x' = Bx, \quad m' = Bm, \quad C' = C \qquad (17.21)$$

The neurons in layer 3 evaluate a kernel function for the incoming input while the neurons in the output layer perform a weighted linear summation of the kernel functions:

$$y(x) = \sum_{i=1}^{N} w_i \exp\left(-d(x', m'_i)/2\right) \qquad (17.22)$$

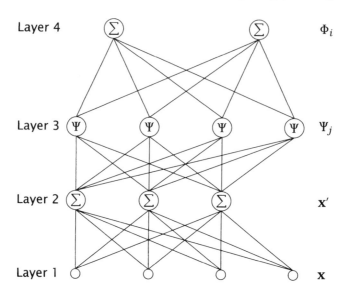

Figure 17.9: *Linear transformation radial basis neural network.*

with

$$d(x', m_i') = (x' - m_i')^T C_i^{-1} (x' - m_i') \qquad (17.23)$$

Here, N is the number of neurons in the second hidden layer, x is the n-dimensional input pattern vector, x' is the transformed input pattern vector, m_i' is the center of a node, w_i are the output weights, and y represents the m-dimensional output of the network. The $n \times n$ covariance matrix C_i is of the form

$$C_{jk}^i = \begin{cases} \dfrac{1}{\sigma_{jk}^2} & \text{if } m = n \\ 0 & \text{otherwise} \end{cases} \qquad (17.24)$$

where σ^{jk} is the standard deviation. Because the centers of the *Gaussian potential function units* (GPFU) are defined in the feature space, they will be subject to transformation by B as well. Therefore, the exponent of a GPFU can be rewritten as:

$$d(x, m_i') = (x - m_i)^T B^T C_i^{-1} B (x - m_i) \qquad (17.25)$$

and is in this form similar to Eq. (17.23).

For the moment, we will regard B as the identity matrix. The network models the distribution of input vectors in the feature space by the weighted summation of Gaussian normal distributions, which are provided by the Gaussian Potential Function Units (GPFU) Ψ_j. To measure the difference between these distributions, we define the relevance ρ_n for each feature x_n:

$$\rho_n = \frac{1}{PJ} \sum_p \sum_j \frac{(x_{pn} - m_{jn})^2}{2\sigma_{jn}^2} \tag{17.26}$$

where P is the size of the training set and J is the number of the GPFUs. If ρ_n falls below the threshold ρ_{th}, we will discard feature x_n. This criterion will not identify every irrelevant feature: If two features are correlated, one of them will be irrelevant, but this cannot be indicated by the criterion.

Learning paradigm for the transformation radial-basis neural network. We follow the idea of Lee and Kil [17] for the implementation of the neuron allocation and learning rules for the TRBNN. The network-generation process starts initially without any neuron.

The mutual dependency of correlated features can often be approximated by a linear function, which means that a linear transformation of the input space can render features irrelevant.

First, we assume that layers 3 and 4 have been trained so that they comprise a model of the pattern-generating process while B is the identity matrix. Then the coefficients B_{nr} can be adapted by gradient descent with the relevance ρ'_n of the transformed feature x'_n as the target function. Modifying B_{nr} means changing the relevance of x_n by adding x_r to it with some weight B_{nr}. This can be done online, that is, for every training vector x_p without storing the whole training set. The diagonal elements B_{nn} constrained to be constant 1, because a feature must not be rendered irrelevant by scaling itself. This in turn guarantees that no information will be lost; B_{nr} will only be adapted under the condition that $\rho_n < \rho_p$, so that the relevance of a feature can be decreased only by some more relevant feature. The coefficients are adapted by the learning rule:

$$B_{nr}^{new} = B_{nr}^{old} - \mu \frac{\partial \rho_n}{\partial B_{nr}} \tag{17.27}$$

with the learning rate μ and the partial derivative:

$$\frac{\partial \rho_n}{\partial B_{nr}} = \frac{1}{PJ} \sum_p \sum_j \frac{(x'_{pn} - m'_{jn})}{\sigma_{jn}^2} (x'_{pr} - m'_{jr}) \tag{17.28}$$

In the learning procedure, which is based on, for example, Lee and Kil [17], we minimize according to the LMS criterion the target function:

$$E = \frac{1}{2} \sum_{p=0}^{P} |y(x) - \Phi(x)|^2 \tag{17.29}$$

where P is the size of the training set. The neural network has some useful features as *automatic allocation of neurons*, discarding of degenerated and inactive neurons and variation of the learning rate depending on the number of allocated neurons.

The relevance of a feature is optimized by gradient descent:

$$\rho_i^{new} = \rho_i^{old} - \eta \frac{\partial E}{\partial \rho_i} \tag{17.30}$$

Based on the new introduced relevance measure and the change in the architecture we get the following correction equations for the neural network:

$$\frac{\partial E}{\partial w_{ij}} = -(y_i - \Phi_i)\Psi_j$$

$$\frac{\partial E}{\partial m_{jn}} = -\sum_i (y_i - \Phi_i)w_{ij}\Psi_j \sum_k (x'_k - m'_{jk})\frac{B_{kn}}{\sigma_{jk}^2} \tag{17.31}$$

$$\frac{\partial E}{\partial \sigma_{jn}} = -\sum_i (y_i - \Phi_i)w_{ij}\Psi_j \frac{(x'_n - m'_{jn})^2}{\sigma_{jn}^3}$$

In the transformed space the hyperellipses have the same orientation as in the original feature space. Hence they do not represent the same distribution as before. To overcome this problem, layers 3 and 4 will be adapted at the same time as B. Converge these layers fast enough and they can be adapted to represent the transformed training data, providing a model on which the adaptation of B can be based. The adaptation with two different target functions (E and ρ) may become unstable if B is adapted too fast, because layers 3 and 4 must follow the transformation of the input space. Thus μ must be chosen $\ll \eta$. A large gradient has been observed causing instability when a feature of extreme high relevance is added to another. This effect can be avoided by dividing the learning rate by the relevance, that is, $\mu = \mu_0/\rho_r$.

17.6 Hopfield neural networks

17.6.1 Basic architecture considerations

A pattern, in parlance of an N node *Hopfield neural network*, is an N-dimensional vector $\boldsymbol{p} = [p_1, p_2, \ldots, p_N]$ from the space $\mathbf{P} = \{-1, 1\}^N$. A special subset of $\mathbf{P}$ is the set of patterns $\mathbf{E} = \{\boldsymbol{e}^k : 1 \leq k \leq K\}$, where $\boldsymbol{e}^k = [e_1^k, e_2^k, \ldots, e_N^k]$. The Hopfield net associates a vector from $\mathbf{P}$ with an exemplar pattern in $\mathbf{E}$. The neural net partitions $\mathbf{P}$ into classes whose members are in some way similar to the exemplar pattern that represents the class. The Hopfield network finds a broad application area in image restoration and segmentation.

As already stated in the Introduction, neural networks have four common components. For the Hopfield net we have the following:

Neurons: The Hopfield network has a finite set of neurons $x(i), 1 \leq i \leq N$, which serve as processing units. Each neuron has a value (or state) at time t denoted by $x_t(i)$. A neuron in the Hopfield net has one of the two states, either -1 or +1; that is, $x_t(i) \in \{-1, +1\}$.

Synaptic Connections: The cognition of a neural net resides within the interconnections between its neurons. For each pair of neurons $x(i)$ and $x(j)$, there is a connection w_{ij} called the synapse between $x(i)$ and $x(j)$. The design of the Hopfield net requires that $w_{ij} = w_{ji}$ and $w_{ii} = 0$. Figure 17.10a illustrates a 3-node network.

Propagation Rule: It defines how states and connections influence the input of a neuron. The propagation rule $\tau_t(i)$ is defined by

$$\tau_t(i) = \sum_{j=1}^{N} x_t(j) w_{ij} + b_i \tag{17.32}$$

b_i is the externally applied bias to the neuron.

Activation Function: The activation function f determines the next state of the neuron $x_{t+1}(i)$ based on the value $\tau_t(i)$ calculated by the propagation rule and the current value $x_t(i)$. Figure 17.10b illustrates this fact. The activation function for the Hopfield net is the hard limiter defined here:

$$x_{t+1}(i) = f(\tau_t(i), x_t(i)) = \begin{cases} 1, & \text{if} \quad \tau_t(i) > 0 \\ -1, & \text{if} \quad \tau_t(i) < 0 \end{cases} \tag{17.33}$$

The network learns patterns that are N-dimensional vectors from the space $\mathbf{P} = \{-1, 1\}^N$. Let $e^k = [e_1^k, e_2^k, \ldots, e_n^k]$ denote the kth exemplar pattern where $1 \leq k \leq K$. The dimensionality of the pattern space determines the number of nodes in the net, such that the net will have N nodes $x(1), x(2), \ldots, x(N)$.

The training algorithm of the Hopfield neural network.

1. Assign weights w_{ij} to the synaptic connections:

$$w_{ij} = \begin{cases} \sum_{k=1}^{K} e_i^k e_j^k, & \text{if} \quad i \neq j \\ 0, & \text{if} \quad i = j \end{cases} \tag{17.34}$$

Keep in mind that $w_{ij} = w_{ji}$, thus it is necessary to perform the preceding computation only for $i < j$.

2. Initialize the net with the unknown pattern. The pattern to be learned is now presented to the net. If $p = [p_1, p_2, \ldots, p_N]$ is the unknown pattern, put

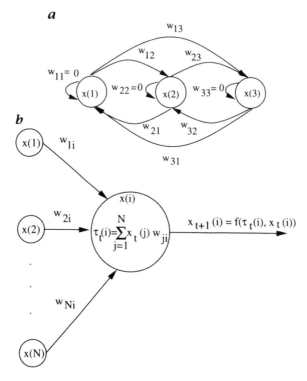

Figure 17.10: a *Hopfield neural network; and* **b** *propagation rule and activation function for the Hopfield network.*

$$x_0(i) = p_i, \quad 1 \le i \le N \tag{17.35}$$

3. Iterate until convergence. Using the propagation rule and the activation function we get for the next state

$$x_{t+1}(i) = f\left(\sum_{j=1}^{N} x_t(j)w_{ij}, x_t(i) \right) \tag{17.36}$$

This process should be continued until any further iteration will produce no state change at any node.

4. Continue the classification process. For learning another pattern, repeat steps 2 and 3.

The convergence property of Hopfield's network depends on the structure of W (the matrix with elements w_{ij}) and the updating mode. An important property of the Hopfield model is that if it operates in a sequential mode and W is symmetric with nonnegative diagonal elements, then the energy function

$$
\begin{aligned}
E_{hs}(t) &= \frac{1}{2}\sum_{i=1}^{n}\sum_{j=1}^{n} w_{ij}x_i(t)x_j(t) - \sum_{i=1}^{n} b_i x_i(t) \\
&= -\frac{1}{2}\boldsymbol{x}^T(t)\boldsymbol{W}\boldsymbol{x}(t) - \boldsymbol{b}^T\boldsymbol{x}(t)
\end{aligned}
\tag{17.37}
$$

is nonincreasing [21]. The network always converges to a fixed point.

17.6.2 Modified Hopfield network

The problem of restoring *noisy-blurred images* is important for many applications ([22, 23, 24]; see also Chapter 13). Often, the image degradation can be adequately modeled by a linear blur and an additive white Gaussian process. Then the degradation model is given by

$$
\boldsymbol{z} = \boldsymbol{D}\boldsymbol{x} + \eta
\tag{17.38}
$$

where $\boldsymbol{x}, \boldsymbol{z}$ and η represent the ordered original and degraded images and the additive noise. The matrix $\boldsymbol{D}$ represents the linear spatially invariant or spatially varying distortion.

The purpose of *digital image restoration* is to operate on the degraded image $\boldsymbol{z}$ to obtain an improved image that is as close to the original image $\boldsymbol{x}$ as possible, subject to a suitable optimality criterion. A common optimization problem is:

$$
\text{minimize} \quad f(\boldsymbol{x}) = \frac{1}{2}\boldsymbol{x}^T\boldsymbol{T}\boldsymbol{x} - \boldsymbol{b}^T\boldsymbol{x} \quad \text{subject to} \quad 0 \le x_i \le 255
\tag{17.39}
$$

where x_i denotes the ith element of the vector $\boldsymbol{x}$, $\boldsymbol{b} = \boldsymbol{D}^T\boldsymbol{z}$ and $\boldsymbol{T}$ is a symmetric, positive semidefinite matrix equal to

$$
\boldsymbol{T} = \boldsymbol{D}^T\boldsymbol{D} + \lambda\boldsymbol{C}^T\boldsymbol{C}
\tag{17.40}
$$

In Eq. (17.40), $\boldsymbol{C}$ is a high-pass filter and λ, the regularization parameter, controls the trade-off between deconvolution and noise smoothing. Comparing Eq. (17.39) and Eq. (17.37) it is clear that the function $f(\boldsymbol{x})$ to be minimized for the restoration problem equals E_{hs} for $\boldsymbol{W} = -\boldsymbol{T}$ and $\boldsymbol{x} = \boldsymbol{v}$.

Updating rule. The modified Hopfield network for image restoration that was proposed in [21] is shown in Fig. 17.11 and is given by the following equations:

$$
x_i(t+1) = g(x_i(t) + \Delta x_i), \quad i = 1,\dots,n
\tag{17.41}
$$

where

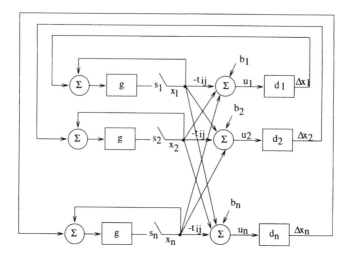

Figure 17.11: *Block diagram of the modified Hopfield network model applied to image restoration.*

$$g(v) = \begin{cases} 0, & v < 0 \\ v, & 0 \le v \le 255 \\ 255, & v > 255 \end{cases} \tag{17.42}$$

$$\Delta x_i = d_i(u_i) = \begin{cases} -1, & u_i < -\theta_i \\ 0, & -\theta_i \le u_i \le \theta_i \quad \text{with} \\ 1, & u_i > \theta_i \end{cases} \tag{17.43}$$

$$\theta_i = \tfrac{1}{2} t_{ii} > 0 \quad \text{and} \quad u_i = b_i - \textstyle\sum_{j=1}^{n} t_{ij} x_j(t)$$

The degraded image z is used as the initial condition for x; x_i are the states of neuron, which take discrete values between 0 and 255, instead of binary values. This consideration is possible because the interconnections are determined in terms of pixel locations and not gray-level values, as can be seen from Fig. 17.11.

In the following, an algorithm is presented that sequentially updates each pixel value according to the updating rule. For the analysis to be followed let $l(t)$ denote a partition of the set $\{1,\dots,n\}$. The algorithm has the following form:

1. $x(0) = D^T z; t := 0$ and $i := 1$.

2. Check termination.

3. Choose $l(t) = \{i\}$.

4. temp $= g(x(t) + \Delta x_i e_i)$ where Δx_i is given by Eq. (17.43).

5. If temp $\neq x(t)$ then $x(t+1) := $ temp and $t := t + 1$.

Table 17.1: Recognition rate.

Iterations	Number of discarded features	Recognition rate
800	–	100%
801 – 1200	13	92.6 – 97%
1201 – 1500	17	93.5 – 99.5%

Table 17.2: Comparison of the proposed method with other techniques.

Feature select. method	Min. error	Best subset
TRBNN	0.07	110001110110001010110100001000
Seq. backward select.	0.123	011001110010011010100000000110
Genetic algorithm	0.23	110001110011001011010000100110

6. $i; = i + 1$ (if $i > n, i = i - n$) and go to step 1.

In step 3 of the preceding algorithm, the function $g(.)$ is used with a vector as an input. In this case $g(x) = [g(x_1), \ldots, g(x_n)]$, where $g(x_i)$ is defined by Eq. (17.42).

17.7 Application examples of neural networks

17.7.1 Relevant feature selection

The performance of the transformation radial basis network is compared in terms of the best feature subset with very well–known methods such as the floating-search method and genetic algorithms. In the search for subsets of features each subset can be coded as a d–element bit string or binary–valued vector (d is the initial number of features), $a = \{x_1, \cdots, x_d\}$, where x_i assumes value 0 if the ith feature is excluded from the subset and 1 if it is present in the subset.

The feature-selection methods were tested on a set from infrared–image data of two normally distributed classes in a 30-D space and equal covariance matrix. For the TRBNN we set $\mu = 0.05$ and $\eta = 0.9$.

For each class a set of 60 training and 60 test vectors is available.

The proposed network TRBNN is discarding the irrelevant features during the learning phase, without deteriorating the recognition rate. This aspect is shown in Table Table 17.1.

A comparison between different feature-selection methods shows the best feature subset that could be achieved based on each method. Table 17.2 shows the best subset and minimum error that was obtained with each method. The TRBNN has the lowest minimum error and the

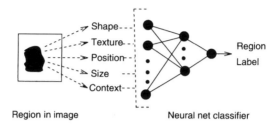

Figure 17.12: *Classification of a region based upon a feature set.*

best recognition rate. The genetic algorithm was implemented similar to the technique outlined in [20] and we obtained the best subset at level 15 while the sequential backward selection was implemented as described in [19] and has the best subset at level 18. The mutation rate for the GA was $p_m = 0.1$, the crossover rate $p_c = 0.6$ and the population size was 40.

17.7.2 Region-based classification

There are two types of classification known in image processing: region-based and pixel-based classification. An object is classified in region-based classification based on features that are usually computed to describe the entire object. Those are mostly geometric features as various size and shape measurements. Figure 17.12 illustrates this fact. Other features, such as texture, are computed at pixel level. This means that in pixel-level classification a feature value is computed for each pixel and so each pixel is classified individually as shown in Fig. 17.13.

Once an image has been segmented, the individual regions detected need to be identified in terms of certain structures. This is attempted, in a bottom–up approach, by extracting a set of features from each region under consideration, and then classifying the regions based on the feature vectors generated.

Feature extraction can be very expensive computationally if features become quite sophisticated. Examples of features measurable from regions are shape, texture, intensity, size, position within the image, contextual features, fractal characteristics, and frequency-domain characteristics. This approach can be used to determine the types of tumors detected, by neural net contextual pixel labeling, from ultrasonic images of the eye. The first stage detects tumors in ultrasonic images of the human eye by the use of contextual pixel labeling and neural nets. The second stage classifies the type of tumor detected as belonging to one of three types. In the second stage a set of five features were measured from tumors detected. Two features represented the size of the tumor, and three measured the characteristics of the normalized power

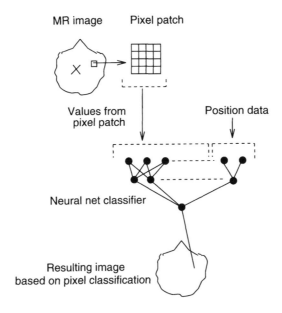

MR image **Pixel patch**

Values from
pixel patch

Position data

Neural net classifier

Resulting image
based on pixel classification

Figure 17.13: *Classification at pixel-level.*

spectra from the Fourier analysis of tumor tissue backscatter. These five features formed vectors that were used to classify the tumors detected. A comparison was made of the performance of a neural net classifier and discriminant analysis. On unseen cases the neural net achieved an accuracy of 91% and the discriminant analysis achieved 84.5%.

17.7.3 Pixel-based classification and image segmentation

This section presents an approach for image segmentation using suboctave wavelet representation and a radial-basis neural network. The algorithm is applied to identify regions of masses in mammographic images with varied degrees of difficulty. In the process of image segmentation, each mammographic image having a mass is first decomposed into wavelet representations of suboctave frequency bands. A feature vector for each pixel through the scale space is constructed based on this representation from fine to coarse scales. The feature vectors are used to drive a radial-basis neural network classifier for segmentation.

The neural network is used for segmentation of regions in masses in mammographic images with varied degrees of difficulty. Fig. 17.14 shows four experimental results of mass segmentation within cropped regions.

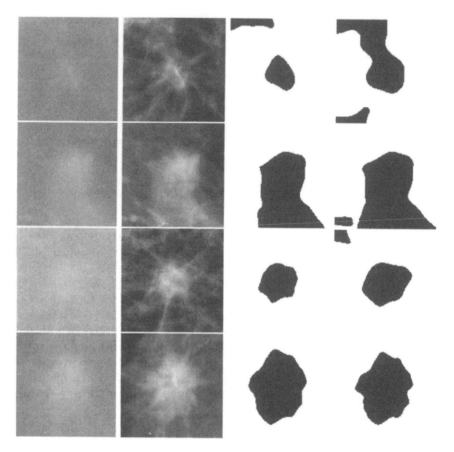

Figure 17.14: *Test Images. First row: original images; Second row: smoothed and enhanced images; Third row: ideal segmentation results.*

The network is trained with 25 images and achieves a recognition rate of 92.7% compared to Bayes classifier that achieves only 91% for the same data.

17.8 Concluding remarks

In this chapter we have presented the most important architectures of neural networks and their training algorithms. Several architectures are specially designed for image-processing tasks and try to emulate aspects derived from our visual system.

Neural networks can be applied to different topics such as feature extraction and selection as well as to classification, compression, segmentation and restoration.

There are two main categories of learning algorithms: supervised and unsupervised. The supervised methods provide (based on their powerful training algorithms) a highly efficient model-free method to design nonlinear mappings between inputs and outputs using a data base of training samples. Those methods are mostly applied in classification and segmentation. A limitation of this method is the collecting of training samples, which is very expensive. On the other hand, unsupervised methods do not require that the target class for each object be specified. Those methods are extremely efficient in image compression. In summary, the algorithm selection must be tailored to the application being considered.

17.9 References

[1] Ritter, G. X. and Wilson, J. N., (1996). *Handbook of Computer Vision Algorithms in Image Algebra*. Boca Raton: CRC Press.

[2] Säckinger, E., Boser, B. E., Bromley, J., LeCun, Y., and Jackel, L. D., (1992). Application of an ANNA neural network chip to high-speed character recognition. *IEEE Trans. Neural Networks*, 3:498–505.

[3] Dhawan, A. P., Chitre, Y., Kaiser, C., and Moskowitz, M., (1996). Analysis of mammographic microcalcifications using gray-level image structure features. *IEEE Trans. Medical Imaging*, 15:246–259.

[4] Dhawan, A. P. and LeRoyer, E., (1988). Mammographic feature enhancement by computerized image processing. *Computer Methods and Programs in Biomedicine*, 7:23–25.

[5] Hartman, E. J., Keeler, J. D., and Kowalski, J. M., (1990). Layered neural networks with Gaussian hidden units as universal approximations. *Neural Computation*, 2:210–215.

[6] Sahiner, B., Chan, H. P., Petrick, N., Wei, D., Helvie, M. A., Adler, D., and Goodsitt, M. M., (1996). Classification of mass and normal breast tissue: A convolution neural network classifier with spatial domain and texture images. *IEEE Trans. Medical Imaging*, 15:598–610.

[7] Lo, S. B., Chan, H. P., Lin, J., Freedman, M. T., and Mun, S. K., (1995). Artificial convolution neural network for medical image pattern recognition. *Neural Networks*, 8:1201–1214.

[8] Kohonen, T., (1988). *Self-Organization and Associative Memory*. New York: Springer.

[9] Haykin, S., (1994). *Neural Networks*. New York: Maxwell Macmillan Publishing Company.

[10] Oja, E., (1992). Self-organizing maps and computer vision. *Neural Networks for Perception*, 1:368–385.

[11] Kotropoulos, C., Magnisalis, X., Pitas, I., and Strintzis, M. G., (1994). Nonlinear Ultrasonic Image Processing Based on Signal-Adaptive Filters and Self-Organizing Neural Networks. *IEEE Trans. Image Processing*, 3:65–77.

[12] Kohonen, T., (1982). Self-organized formation of topologically correct feature maps. *Biological Cybernetics,* **43**:59–69.

[13] Moody, J. and Darken, C., (1989). Fast learning in networks of locally-tuned processing units. *Neural Computation,* **1**:281–295.

[14] Poggio, T. and Girosi, F., (1990). Networks for approximation and learning. *Proc. IEEE,* **78**:1481–1497.

[15] Saha, A., Christian, D. S., Tang, D. S., and Wu, C. L., (1991). Oriented non-radial basis functions for image coding and analysis. *Touretky's Connectionist Summer School,* **2**:728–734.

[16] Zong, X., Meyer-Bäse, A., and Laine, A., (1997). Multiscale segmentation through a radial basis neural network. *IEEE Int. Conf. on Image Processing,* I:400–403.

[17] Lee, S. and Kil, R. M., (1991). A Gaussian potential function network with hierarchically self-organizing learning. *Neural Networks,* **4**:207–224.

[18] Platt, J., (1991). A resource-allocating network for function interpolation. *Neural Computation,* **3**:213–225.

[19] Pudil, P., Novovicova, J., and Kittler, J., (1994). Floating search methods in feature selection. *Pattern Recognition Letters,* **15**:1119–1125.

[20] Siedlecki, W. and Sklansky, J., (1989). A note on genetic algorithms for large-scale feature selection. *Pattern Recognition Letters,* **10**:335–347.

[21] Hopfield, J. J., (1982). Neural networks and physical systems with emergent collective computational abilities. *Proc. National Academy of Science,* **79**:2554–2558.

[22] Katsaggelos, A. G., (1991). *Digital Image Processing.* Berlin: Springer.

[23] Sun, Y., Li, J. G., and Wu, S. Y., (1995). Improvement on performance of modified Hopfield neural network for image restoration. *IEEE Trans. Image Processing,* **4**:688–692.

[24] Figueiredo, M. A. T. and Leitao, J. M. N., (1994). Sequential and parallel image restoration: neural network implementations. *IEEE Trans. Neural Networks,* **3**:789–801.

Part III

Application Gallery

A Application Gallery

Computer Vision and Applications

A1   Object Recognition with Intelligent Cameras

Thomas Wagner, and Peter Plankensteiner

Intego GmbH, Erlangen, Germany

Problem statement.   Object-recognition problems are widespread on industrial production floors. In many situations, the customer will decide to use automatic inspection methods only if robust low-cost solutions are available. Today, solutions for object recognition tasks are either PC-based or they consist of special hardware. An example of a system that is compact and cost-efficient is a so-called intelligent camera (Fig. A.1 a, based on the VC-series from Vision Components www.vision-components.de). The idea behind intelligent cameras is to develop a stand-alone product containing camera and processor. An intelligent camera integrates a sensor and a processing unit within the camera chassis and therefore requires a minimum of space (Fig. A.1 b). Furthermore, due to the direct processing in the camera, potential bottlenecks such as the PC bus are avoided. Intelligent cameras can communicate directly with the production line by the use of dedicated interfaces.

Used algorithms.   To adapt the Intelli-Cam System to a special image processing problem, only a few steps have to be performed (Fig. A.2 b). The training is done by a PC-based application providing a graphical user interface (Fig. A.1 b) for a straightforward parameterization of the system. After marking the relevant regions in an image, the internal training via the synergetic MELT algorithm [1] is started. This algorithm has shown itself to be very robust in industrial applications. High recognition rates, short classification times, and especially short training periods are its most prominent features. Finally, the user has to define a rejection threshold. From that moment, the camera works in a stand-alone mode, and the PC may be disconnected.

Results.   Two applications for Intelli-Cam are given in Fig. A.3.   In Fig. A.3 a, contacts on relays must be correctly covered in order to protect users from electric shocks. At the end of the production process, some of these plastic plates are distorted or completely damaged. To avoid risks for users, the defect contactors must be detected and removed. The figure gives an example of a correct plate and some typical defects. The total time for the examination of one contactor is about 320 ms, including time for frame grabbing and positioning. Classification alone takes about 60 ms. The training procedure took about 90 s on a Pentium with 90 MHz. In Fig. A.3 b, an intelligent camera is used to identify different types of empties on a conveyor belt. Further details on the described application can be found in CVA3 [Chapter 13].

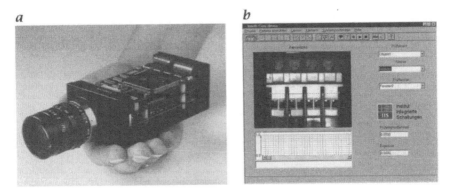

Figure A.1: The platform: **a** the interior of an intelligent camera; and **b** graphical user interface for the parameterization of Intelli-Cam.

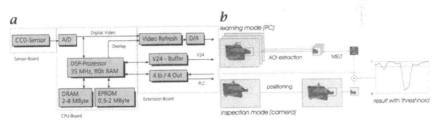

Figure A.2: Evaluation concept: **a** schematic hardware setup of the intelligent camera; **b** the training and the inspection process in Intelli-Cam.

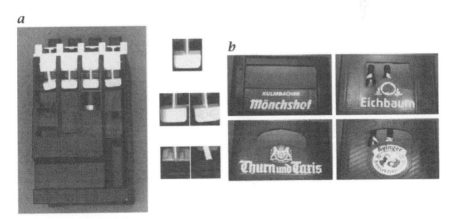

Figure A.3: Example images: **a** a contactor: one correct plate, two typical minor faults and two major defects; **b** different types of empties on a conveyor belt have to be identified automatically.

A2   3-D Image Metrology of Wing Roots

Horst A. Beyer

Imetric SA, Technopole, Porrentruy, Switzerland

Problem statement.   British Aerospace manufactures wings for the Airbus line of planes. The interfaces of a wing with the fuselage are areas where large forces must be transmitted. The positions and angles of interface surfaces between wing and fuselage are geometrically inspected before the wings are shipped to the integration sites. Traditional techniques required that each wing be impaired for approximately 5 h.

Used algorithms.   A three-dimensional image metrology system using special adapters (mechanical constructions with targets where the geometric relation of targets to mechanical references is precisely known, see Fig. A.5) was selected. The adapters are placed and removed during production. Figure A.4 shows a wing root with an operator posing with a camera. The camera has the typical circular flash to illuminate the targets.

The system uses "coded" targets and fully automated processing. After reduction of the image data and the computation of the 3-D coordinates, scaling, and transformation into the coordinate system, the measurement results are compared to the nominal values and protocols are produced.

Results.   The system reduces production interruptions to the acquisition of images, which is in the order of 5 to 10 min. The production personnel inspect two or more wings per day. The system has a repeatability of 0.015 mm in all three coordinate axes on a wing root spanning $2.8 \times 1.0 \times 0.5$ m. The typical measurement accuracy in the images approaches 0.01 pixel.

The next major improvement will be that of replacing the Kodak DCS420s with the metrology cameras ICam (see Fig. A.6). These cameras use CCD-sensors with 3000×2000 and 7000×4000 pixels and are specifically designed for high accuracy 3-D measurements. They have an integrated computer with Windows NT. Thus all computations and the analysis can be performed on site. The introduction of these cameras is expected to improve throughput by a factor of two and more.

References.   [2, 3], [CVA3, Chapter 16]

Figure A.4: *Operator and wing root showing camera with flash, target adapters on wing and scale bar to the right (Photograph courtesy of British Aerospace Airbus).*

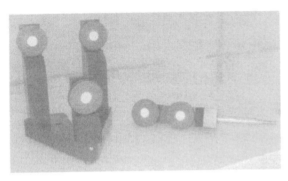

Figure A.5: *Adapters used for the measurement of the wing interfaces.*

Figure A.6: *Metrology camera ICam with integrated computer showing 3000 × 2000 and 7000 × 4000 CCD-sensors.*

A3   Quality Control in a Shipyard

Hans-Gerd Maas
Faculty of Civil Engineering and Geosciences
Delft University of Technology, The Netherlands

Problem statement. Larger ships are usually assembled on a building dock from sections, which have been built up and equipped as far as possible in a factory hall. A typical section of a ship may have dimensions of 25 m × 25 m × 12 m and a weight of several hundred tons. Figure A.7 shows the face of a section of a ship in a factory hall; Fig. A.8 shows the face of the ship under construction, where the section has to be integrated. Obviously, quality control has to assure an accurate fit of the section. While traditional geodetic techniques such as theodolite or tape measurements are rather time and cost expensive, image-based techniques may depict an efficient and accurate measurement tool for this task.

Data acquisition and processing. Critical points on the section and the hull were signalized by retroreflective targets, which are clearly visible in Fig. A.8. A high-resolution digital still-video camera was used to capture sets of 9 to 12 images of both facades from different viewpoints. Imaged using a ring-light flash and suitable exposure settings, the retroreflective targets reproduce very well in the images (Fig. A.9), and their image coordinates can be determined with subpixel accuracy by centroid operators or least squares template matching. Processing the data by photogrammetric bundle adjustment of images taken from different viewpoints and under different viewing directions, this subpixel accuracy can be translated into object space. Using self-calibration techniques [4] in combination with highly redundant information obtained from multiple images, camera parameters such as interior orientation and lens distortion can be determined simultaneously.

Results. Using proper illumination and exposure settings, a precision in the order of $1/20 - 1/50$ of a pixel can be obtained in image space. Using a high-resolution still-video camera with an image format of 3000×2000 pixels and self-calibrating bundle adjustment techniques, this translates into an accuracy potential in the order of a few tenths of a millimeter in object space. Processing is often performed semiautomatically with the user pointing to approximate locations interactively. Based on an available CAD-model of the ship or the use of coded targets [5], a full automation of the measurement procedure can be obtained.

Figure A.7: Section of a ship under construction inside factory hall.

Figure A.8: Location on building dock for above section to be integrated.

Figure A.9: Retroreflective target in a digital image.

A4   Topographical Maps of Microstructures

Torsten Scheuermann[1], Georg Wiora[2] (née Pfundt), and Matthias Graf[3]

[1]Fraunhofer USA Inc., Ann Arbor (MI), USA
[2]Forschungszentrum DaimlerChrysler AG Ulm, Germany
[3]Institut für Kunststoffprüfung und Kunststoffkunde (IKP), Stuttgart, Germany

Problem statement. Measuring surface topography in the submicron range has become increasingly important as *microsystems* have become more market relevant. Microparts are used, for example, in ink jet printer or as accelerometers for airbags. The production requires high geometric accuracy. Quality control includes the shape measurement of *microstructures*. The depth-from-focus method provides an efficient way to measure the topography of microstructures with standard components and simple algorithms [CVA3, Chapter 18]; [6].

System setup and algorithm. The system consists of an ordinary reflection microscope with a computer-controlled stage and a structured grating at the location of the bright field aperture (Fig. A.10). During the measurement process, the object stage is moved incrementaly along the z-axis. For each position, an image is acquired by the CCD-camera. For each pixel in each image a local contrast value is computed (Fig. A.11 a). This is basically the gray value difference of neighboring pixels. Generally the local image contrast is low if the object is out of focus and high if the object is in focus, assuming the object has a visible surface texture. A lack of texture can be compensated by projecting an optical texture onto the object. This is done with a grating in the bright field aperture (Fig. A.11 b). Next for a certain pixel the maximum contrast value in all images is searched. The image containing the maximum is related to a z-position of the object stage during its acquisition. This position can be assigned to that pixel as height value. When this is done for all pixels the result is a topographic map of the object surface. To avoid keeping all images in memory during evaluation, this task can be done with a sequential algorithm. If, in addition to the absolute maximum of contrast the next smaller one is also detected, the thickness of transparent layers can be measured with this method as well [7].

Results. This method has been applied to a large variety of microstructures. The lateral resolution is given by the optical theory of a microscope : $h = 0.61\lambda/A$. The accuracy in depth depends nearly linearly on the objective aperture. For high-aperture objectives ($A = [0.7..1.0]$) an accuracy of 100 nm is possible under real conditions. For low apertures 1 μm accuracy is typical. Figure A.12 a and b show some results. For further examples see `columns.tif`, `hole.tif`, `cross.tif`, and `ditches.tif` in `/images/a04/`.

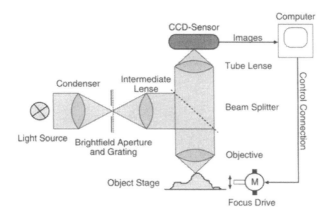

Figure A.10: *The main components of the surface measurement system: reflection microscope, structured grating, CCD-Camera, focus drive and computer.*

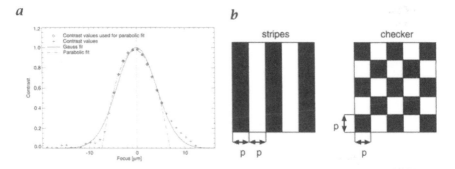

Figure A.11: *a Contrast curve over z with fit parabola and maximum location. b Possible patterns for the illumination grating. Pattern size p is about two camera pixels. The stripe pattern has a higher dynamic range than the checker pattern.*

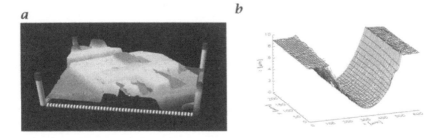

Figure A.12: *a Topographical map of a silicon structure. Total height of the structure is about 5 μm, lateral size is about 80×60 μm. b Surface of a standard groove produced by the Physikalisch Technische Bundesanstalt (PTB), Braunschweig, Germany.*

A5 Fast 3-D Full Body Scanning for Humans and Other Objects

Norbert Stein and Bernhard Minge

VITRONIC Dr.-Ing. Stein Bildverarbeitungssysteme, Wiesbaden, Germany

Problem statement. To perform fast and complete 3-D scans on humans or other living objects is a challenge. The development of multi-sensor systems operating on the basis of the laser light stripe method has proved to be an effective means to fulfill this task. Within seconds the 3-D shape of human beings and other objects can be measured.

System realization. Within this process we use a laser in combination with a cylinder lens . A video camera is positioned at a defined angle to the light source. The measured data obtained in this way encode the spatial coordinates x, y, z of the laser's line of incidence on the object for a complete profile section over the entire width of the image field. As the sensor is moved over the object a 3-D image of the outer contour of the object is produced. To generate the whole measuring volume at a time several sensors have to be connected in parallel to the evaluation unit (multisensor system). For this purpose, high-performance processors are combined with realtime image processing chips that were specially designed for VIRO 3D systems. These image processing chips allow to record the image data from practically any number of sensors and to evaluate it synchronously in video realtime. They supply 3-D raw data for each sensor, which is stored in the main memory of the computer and processed by the processor. The 3-D raw data is then converted from pixel to a metric unit and undergoes a mathematical regression analysis of object-dependent order, so that a smooth signal form can be generated. The measured data from all section planes are combined to form a 3-D model (Fig. A.13).

Results. For humans the system actually will be used for studies in the clothing industry and ergonomical products field. These applications need 3-D information of parts or complete human bodies for creating made-to-measure products on an actual data basis. Most of the industrial scanning systems basically follow the same design and measuring principles, but offer a range of different measuring volumes and resolutions by using different numbers of lasers and cameras with different focal lengths. Depending on the set-up in different industrial applications the resolutions displayed in Table A.1 are achieved. New impulses will be given to made-to-measure products, rapid prototyping processes, quality inspection, film, art, and photography. In movies actors are already emulated and animated in virtual reality.

References. [8], [CVA3, Chapter 21]

Figure A.13: *a - b Full-body scanner; c scanning result; d CNC milling result.*

Table A.1: *Examples for ranges of resolution in applications*

Resolution range	Application
≥ 1 mm	Measurement of complete human beings and wooden surface profiles
0.1 mm - 1 mm	Measurement of parts of human beings and aluminum ingots; welding seam inspection of steel wheels; piston assembly
0.01 mm - 0.1 mm	Welding seam Inspection of laser-welded products; inspection of tubes for the tightening of seat belts; visual inspection of applied solder paste

A6   Reverse Engineering Using Optical Range Sensors

Stefan Karbacher and Gerd Häusler

Lehrstuhl für Optik, Universität Erlangen-Nürnberg, Germany

Problem statement.   Optical 3-D sensors are used as tools for *reverse engineering* to digitize the surface of real 3-D objects. Multiple range images from different points of view are necessary to capture the whole surface of an object and to reduce data loss due to reflexes and shadowing. The raw data are not directly suitable for import in CAD/CAM systems. The images usually consist of millions of single points, given in the sensor coordinate system, and are distorted by outliers, noise, and aliasing. Thus, three problems need to be solved: the transformation of the raw data into metrical coordinates (*calibration*); the *registration* of the single range images into one common coordinate system; and the *surface reconstruction* from the point cloud data to regain object topology, so as to eliminate measurement errors and reduce the amount of data.

Used Methods.   We work on building up a nearly automatic procedure covering the complex task from gathering data with an optical 3-D sensor to generating meshes of triangles [CVA3, Chapter 17]:

Data acquisition: Usually multiple range images of one object are taken to acquire the whole object surface [CVA1, Chapter 19].

Calibration: Measuring a standard with an exactly known shape, a polynomial for transforming the pixel coordinates into metrical coordinates is computed. This method calibrates each measurement individually. As a result each view has its own coordinate system.

Registration: The various views are transformed into a common coordinate system and are adjusted to each other. First the surfaces are coarsely aligned one to another with a feature-based Hough method. Then a fine-tuning algorithm (ICP) minimizes the deviations between the surfaces [9].

Surface reconstruction: The views are merged into one single object model resulting in a mesh of curved triangles with curvature dependent density. Measurement errors, such as sensor noise, aliasing, calibration, and registration, can be eliminated without damaging the object edges.

Results.   We have tested our reverse engineering method by digitizing many different objects, technical as well as natural. Calibration, registration and smoothing errors are usually less than the sensor noise. The following examples (Figs. A.14–A.16, `movies/a06/helmet.mov`) were digitized by our sensors and reconstructed with our SLIM$^{3\text{-}D}$ software.

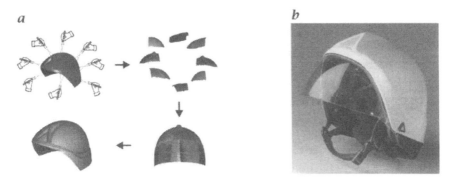

Figure A.14: *a Data acquisition, registration and mesh reconstruction of a firefighter's helmet(/movies/17/helmet.mov); b a mesh of Bézier triangles was used to produce the helmet; mesh reconstruction took 7 min on an Intel Pentium® II 300 CPU.*

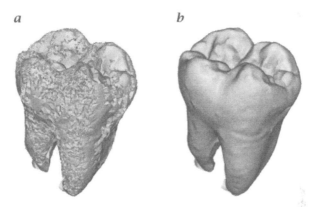

Figure A.15: *a Distorted mesh of a human tooth, reconstructed from seven badly matched range images; b result of our new smoothing method for triangle meshes.*

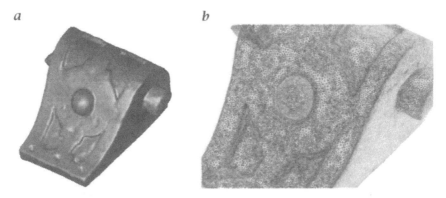

Figure A.16: *Console of an altar: a rendered surface; b zoom into wire frame.*

A7   3-D Surface Reconstruction from Uncalibrated Image Sequences

Reinhard Koch[1,2], Marc Pollefeys[1], and Luc Van Gool[1]

[1]Center for Processing of Speech and Images, K.U. Leuven, Belgium
[2]now at Institut für Informatik und Praktische Mathematik, Univ. Kiel, Germany

Problem statement.   The demand for realistic 3-D modeling of environments and objects is increasing steadily. Of specific interest is the 3-D scanning of objects for *reverse engineering*, documentation, preservation and display. We describe a system to reconstruct 3-D scenes from a sequence of images taken with a single handheld camera. The scene is observed from multiple viewpoints by freely moving the camera around the object (Fig. A.17). No restrictions on camera movement and internal camera parameters like zoom are imposed, as the camera pose and intrinsic parameters are automatically calibrated from the sequence. The system is easy to use and requires no specialized equipment other than a standard consumer photo- or video camera.

Approach.   The approach is divided into three steps:

Camera calibration: Salient image features such as intensity corner points are tracked robustly throughout the sequence and a projective reconstruction of the camera poses and 3-D corner points is obtained (Fig. A.18 a). The tracking utilizes the concept of the Fundamental matrix, which relates corresponding image points in different images by the epipolar constraint. The projective ambiguity is then removed by *camera self-calibration*, which exploits additional constraints [10].

Depth estimation: The sparse scene structure lacks surface detail and is updated to dense surface geometry (Fig. A.18 b). Pairs of the now calibrated sequence are treated as stereoscopic image pairs from which dense and precise depth maps are estimated pairwise by correlation-based correspondence search. All depth maps from different viewpoints are then fused together for highest accuracy [11].

3-D surface modeling: The depth estimates are converted to 3-D triangulated surface meshes. The surface mesh approximates the 3-D structure and stores the visible surface texture of the real object by projecting the image color texture onto the model surface (Fig. A.18 c) [CVA3, Chapter 20].

Results.   The approach was successfully applied to reconstruct outdoor scenes like old buildings (Fig. A.18) and to obtain reconstructions of an archaeological excavation site (Fig. A.19); movies: bath.mov, baths.mov, castle.mov, head.mov, site.mov,and temple.mov. Because it is independent of object scale it can model complete environments and landscapes as well as small objects. Due to the dense surface modeling even small geometric details can be reconstructed.

a   b   c

Figure A.17: *Three of the 22 input images for the reconstruction of a building.*

a   b   c

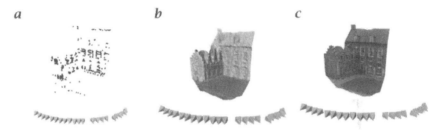

Figure A.18: *Results of the building reconstruction: **a** calibration of cameras (little pyramids) and structure of 3-D tracking points; **b** surface geometry after dense depth estimation; **c** view of 3-D surface model with texture mapping.*

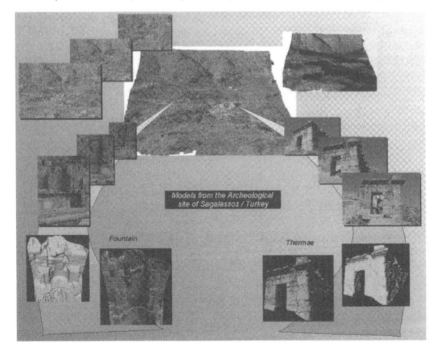

Figure A.19: *Reconstruction examples of parts of the Sagalassos Archaeological excavation site in Sagalassos, Turkey.*

A8 Motion Tracking

Robert Frischholz

Mikromak GmbH, Erlangen, Germany

Problem statement. The quantitative acquisition of the movement of certain objects in a video sequence, motion analysis, is required in many fields such as sports, medicine, and industry. Conventional motion analysis systems usually consist of a video camera, a digitizing unit, and a PC with a certain software to acquire object locations for each image. Even nowadays, those locations often have to be set manually by a human operator.

The task of a motion tracking algorithm is the automatic recognition of certain objects within the image, the determination of their locations, and the tracking of those objects along the complete sequence (Fig. A.20). Typical approaches to this task use special markers applied to the moving objects. In this contribution, an automatic motion analysis system is presented, which overcomes the restrictions of using special markers.

Used algorithms. Instead of using markers, the flexible technique of template matching [12] is used. This procedure is basically as follows: A small area surrounding the point to be tracked is used as the template. This template is then searched for in the next image frame by use of correlation techniques. The location with the highest correlation result is the best match between template and image (Fig. A.21 a).

Template matching is a very flexible and powerful method for tracking objects with small distortions from one frame to the next. By adapting the templates along the image sequence, even larger deformations can be tracked (Fig. A.21 b).

A new subpixel precision method was developed for the matching process, thus enhancing the accuracy of the detected locations [13]. Other enhancements include the use of neural net approximation and camera calibration [CVA3, Chapter 15].

Results. In the presented system, object detection was automated by use of adaptive template matching. The user selects the objects of interest in the first image of the sequence, all further images are tracked automatically. Therefore it is much faster than manual tracking, and, by use of subpixel precision techniques, even more accurate. The system is used in many fields, such as the automotive (Fig. A.22 a) and sports industries (Fig. A.22 b).

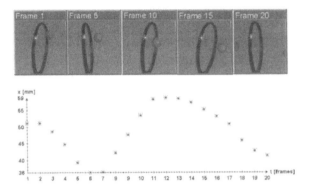

Figure A.20: Example of an image sequence of a tennis ball hitting a racket. The horizontal position of the marked point on the racket over time defines the trajectory.

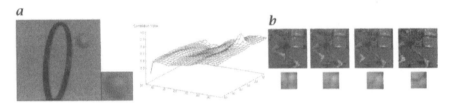

Figure A.21: Basic algorithms: *a* original image (left) showing a ball and a racket; template (middle) used for correlation; correlation surface (right) — highest value indicates best matching position; *b* example sequence with the corresponding adapted templates, showing the ability of tracking objects even under rotation.

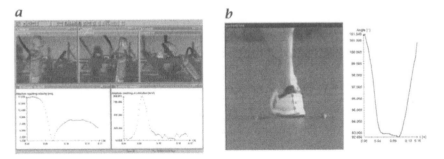

Figure A.22: Results: *a* Impact of a test dummy onto a steering wheel in a car crash test. Three images of the overall sequence, the head's velocity, and the acceleration along time are shown; *b* shoe stability test. Two points on the shoe and two objects on the ground define the angle shown in the diagram.

A9   Tracking "Fuzzy" Storms in Doppler Radar Images

J. L. Barron[1], R. E. Mercer[1], D. Cheng[1], and P. Joe[2]

[1] Dept. of Computer Science, University of Western Ontario, Canada
[2] King City Radar Station, Atmospheric Environmental Services, AES, Canada

Problem statement.   Because of the devastation inflicted by severe storms, the forecasting of storm movement is an important task facing meteorologists.   To help with this task we have developed an automatic storm tracking system for storms in Doppler radar images. Since 1985, the Cloud Physics Research Division of AES, Canada, has been developing a Doppler radar system to detect severe storms including thunderstorms and tornadoes. It generates intensity and radial velocity images, examples of which are shown in Fig. A.23a and b.

The algorithm.   The recognition and tracking of storms in these radar images is currently performed manually by human experts and the task is time consuming.   To improve the efficiency and quality of weather forecasting, AES is interested in developing an automatic storm tracking system for use in their operations. We have developed a tracking program with visualization capabilities that uses a *hypothesize and verify* model to detect storms in radar images and construct storm tracks. We first hypothesize storm masses in the Doppler radar intensity images.   Then we verify the correctness of these hypothesized storms by tracking them over time. If an hypothesized storm can be tracked over a desired number of frames, we conclude that the storm is a valid storm and we record its track. When all potential storms are verified, a set of valid storm tracks is given as output. We use a spatiotemporal relaxation labeling algorithm [CVA3, Chapter 38]; [14] to realize storm tracking over multiple consecutive images. To diminish the effect of the arbitrariness of storm location of the storm tracks, we have modified the representation of the center of a storm from a Euclidean point to a *fuzzy point* [14]. A *fuzzy point* is a circle whose inner region represents the uncertainty of the location of a targeted point.

Results.   The series-18 Doppler radar sequence has 30 images consisting of complex storm movements: Storms are moving from the northeast to the southeast and from west to east. In the end both storm movements merge into one large storm moving southeast. This can be seen from the verified storm tracks shown in Fig. A.24a-d, which show the verified storms tracks for storm in images 5, 12, 19 and 30. By using fuzzy storm centers and relaxation labeling we are able to obtain storm tracks that are both long and smooth and which closely match human perception of a "motion picture" of the storm image sequence.

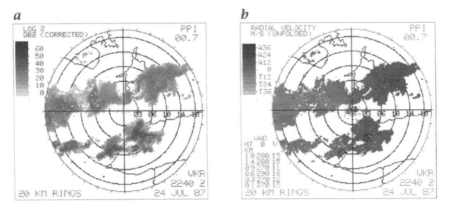

Figure A.23: *Example Doppler radar radial and velocity image.*

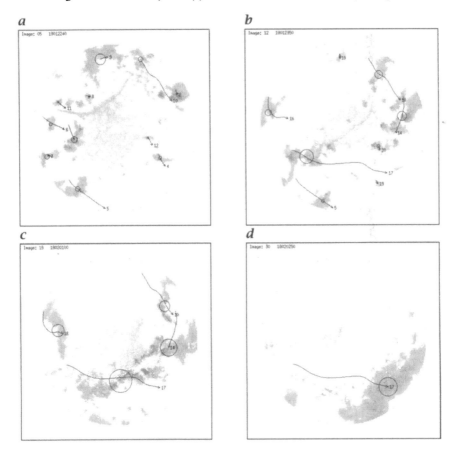

Figure A.24: *The storm tracks for the (a) 5th, (b) 12nd, (c) 19th and (d) 30th images of the 18-series; $T_d = 5.0$ and $T_{sc} = 0.6$. Circles are used to represent the fuzzy storms.*

A10   3-D Model-Driven Person Detection

Christof Ridder, Olaf Munkelt, and David Hansel
Bayerisches Forschungszentrum für Wissensbasierte Systeme (FORWISS)
München, Germany

Introduction. Automatically obtaining and describing human body motion and postures in digital video images can be used in several applications, that is, in the fields that range from motion analysis in sports or medicine tasks up to man-machine interfaces in virtual reality tasks. The presented approach is a *model-driven system* for *detecting* and *tracking persons* and their 3-D posture in image sequences. The used model is a hierarchical composition of *object model parts* (OMP); it enfolds a description of the internal structure (Fig. A.25 a), the geometric outlook (Fig. A.25 b), as well as sets of image operations to extract relevant features of the OMPs. As the system works in 3-D space, the setup of the camera(s) has to be calibrated in advance.

Interpretation process. The interpretation process is controlled by the object model (Fig. A.26). The 2-D image features lead to the 3-D scene features by using a stereo or a monocular approach. All determined 3-D scene features have to be matched to the 3-D features of the object model. The matching process is performed by an interpretation tree [15]. Constraints are used to restrict the search by using the rigid bone structure of the human body. The results of the matching process are associations of model features to scene features. This can be seen as the applied inner structure (Fig. A.27 a). Afterwards the angles between the OMPs have to be determined. The geometric model can be applied with the calculated angles (Fig. A.27 b) and further geometric restrictions can be used. Hereafter several hypotheses for the detected objects are generated. These hypotheses have to be evaluated by using a history based on a prediction of motion.

Applications. Currently there are two main applications of the system. One of them uses only one feature: the skin-colored ellipsoid of the head. By the use of an adaptive color classifier [16], the system determines the appropriate image feature. In this application the system estimates the 3-D position of monitored persons for surveillance tasks. This 3-D position of the person can be handed over to further cameras as well as to a pan/tilt camera for tracking. In the second application all joints of the human body are marked, so that their positions in the pair of stereo images can be segmented easily. The determined 3-D posture of the detected person is used for the configuration of a CAD-model. These models are used, for example, in the automobile industry for ergonomic analysis. For more details see CVA3 [Chapter 22].

Figure A.25: *Object model:* **a** *the internal model, which represents the inner structure of an object and the connection between the object model parts; and* **b** *the geometric model, which extends the internal model by a geometric description.*

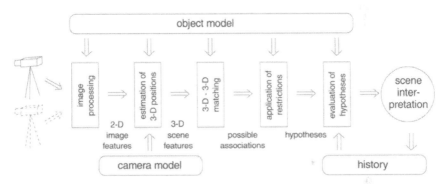

Figure A.26: *Processing steps: The object model serves all of the processing steps needed for scene interpretation.*

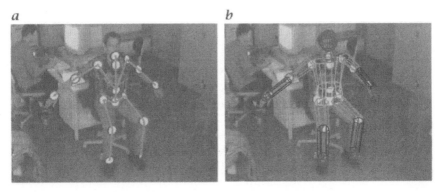

Figure A.27: *Results:* **a** *matching of the detected image features to the joints of the object model; and* **b** *according to the matching, the geometric model is superimposed on the image; in this laboratory environment the stereo approach is used and round plates are used to mark the joints of the human body.*

A11   Knowledge-Based Image Retrieval

Thorsten Hermes[1,2] and Otthein Herzog[1]

[1] TZI – Center for Computing Technologies, Universität Bremen, Germany
[2] TC TrustCenter for Security in Data Networks GmbH, Hamburg, Germany

Problem statement.   In order to retrieve images from an archive, human beings tend to think of special contents of searched scene, such as rural land features or a technical drawing. The necessity of a semantics-based retrieval language leads to content-based analysis and retrieval of images. We developed in the Image Retrieval for Information Systems (IRIS) project a new way to automatically generate textual content descriptions of images, using a combination of computer vision and knowledge representation [17]. The image retrieval process has two stages: automatically generating the image annotations and afterwards retrieving images. An obvious idea for image annotation is a textual description generated by users, for example, the title and caption of the images as well as some additional descriptors [18, 19, 20]. This approach is restricted by the effort needed for manual annotations and the user-dependent differences in the annotations themselves, which leads very soon to inconsistencies in the annotations.

Used algorithms.   The IRIS system consists of two main modules: the image analysis module and the retrieval module (Fig. A.28). The image analysis module consists of four submodules: three modules extract the low-level features of color, texture, and contour. The fourth module implements object recognition. The color module, the texture module, and the contour module extract image segments, which are represented as structured texts. These features are extracted independently of each other, thus providing three independent information sources. These descriptions offer a low-level annotation of an analyzed image. The object recognition module combines these low-level descriptions, which fit together according to a description in a knowledge base, thus identifying objects on a symbolic level. The methods used for the three segmentation modules and the object recognition module are described in CVA3 [Chapter 25]. An extension of IRIS to video retrieval can be found in [21].

Results.   The original image (Fig. A.29a) is a RGB model with 728×472 pixels. Figure A.29b gives the result of color segmentation. The corresponding texture segmentation is shown in Fig. A.29c. For the contour-based shape analysis the contours are extracted as a contour map. To determine the dominant regions, a region or shape analysis is then carried out (Fig. A.29d). The result of the object recognition step is displayed in Fig. A.30.

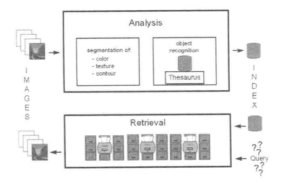

Figure A.28: *Architecture of the IRIS system.*

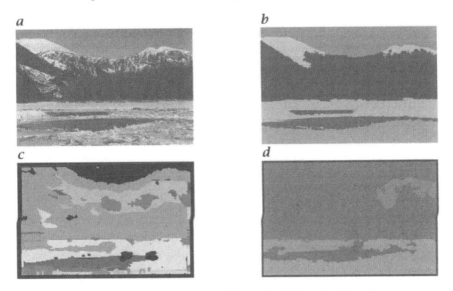

Figure A.29: *a Original landscape image; b result of the color-based segmentation; c result of the texture-based segmentation; d result of the contour-based segmentation.*

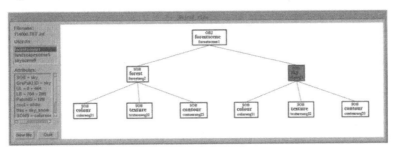

Figure A.30: *Results of the object recognition step.*

A12   Monitoring Living Biomass with in situ Microscopy

Peter Geißler[1,2] and Thomas Scholz[1]

[1]Interdisziplinäres Zentrum für Wissenschaftliches Rechnen (IWR)
Universität Heidelberg, Germany
[2]Now at München, Germany

Problem statement. Bioreactors are widely used in biotechnical industries to obtain products by the enzymatic activity of microorganisms (Fig. A.31 a). Consequently, the cell concentration and biological state are of greatest importance. In a cooperation between the research center of ABB Heidelberg, the University of Hannover, and the University of Heidelberg, an in situ probe (Fig. A.31 b) was developed that is able to monitor the living biomass during a fermentation cycle [22]. Living cells can be separated from dead cells and other objects by using the fluorescence of the NAD(P)H, an intermediate protein of the metabolic chain. It is therefore present only in living cells. Fluorescence is excited by a nitrogen laser pulse of 2 ns duration. The weak fluorescence signatures of the cells are imaged by means of a light amplifying camera.

Used algorithms. The ambient light of extremely defocused cells contributes to an uneven background (Fig. A.32 a). As a first step, images are normalized using a recursive background tracking filter. Due to the necessity of using a light amplifying camera, the signal-to-noise ratio of the images is unacceptable poor. Hence an adaptive filter is applied that suppresses noise but preserves the edge steepness of the objects (Fig. A.32 c) by smoothing along contour lines only. These are obtained from the orientation vector, which is calculated from the local variance in different directions (Fig. A.32 b). Depth estimation is performed by first separating individual cells from the images and constructing the Laplacian pyramid on each cell image. This bandpass decomposition detects the suppression of high spatial frequencies with increasing blur. To be independent of the brightness of the cell, the ratios of the squared signal amplitudes on consecutive levels of the pyramid are interpreted as the components of a feature vector (Fig. A.33 a). As it encodes the blur of each cell, which increases with its distance from the ISM lens, it can be correlated with this distance and therefore the measuring volume is obtained [CVA3, Chapter 29].

Results. Despite bad image quality, segmentation and robust depth-from-focus could be applied to the images, allowing reliable estimation of living biomass concentration and the monitoring of the progress of fermentations. A comparison with standard off-line cell counting methods shows an excellent agreement within the precision limits of the off-line method [23]. Figure A.33 b and c show the development of the cell concentration under different environmental conditions.

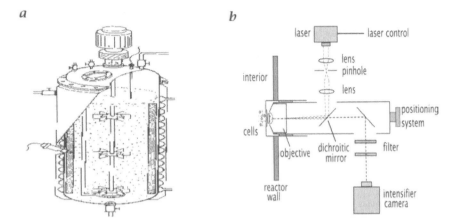

Figure A.31: *Experimental setup:* **a** *sketch of a typical bioreactor; and* **b** *components of the ISM probe.*

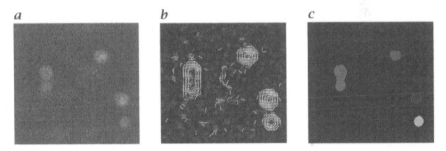

Figure A.32: *Intermediate processing steps:* **a** *raw image with uneven illumination and high noise level;* **b** *orientation field (color coded) and contour lines (white) along which the smoothing filter kernel is deformed;* **c** *result of segmentation of the image. Cells that border each other and appear as a single cell cluster will be recognized by the form of their border.*

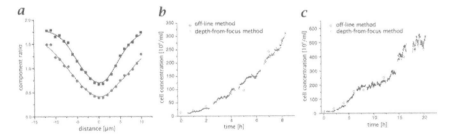

Figure A.33: *Results:* **a** *two components of the feature vector, clearly showing the strong correlation with depth;* **b** *cell concentration during a batch fermentation;* **c** *cell concentration during a fed-batch fermentation; and comparison with off-line data.*

A13   Analyzing Size Spectra of Oceanic Air Bubbles

Peter Geißler[1,2] and Bernd Jähne[1]

[1]Interdisziplinäres Zentrum für Wissenschaftliches Rechnen (IWR)
Universität Heidelberg, Germany
[2]Now at München, Germany

Problem statement. Counting and measuring size statistics of free-floating particles is a common problem in technical, biological and other applications. Close-range imaging used to observe small or even microscopic particles shows a small depth of field, typically much smaller than the volume the particles float in. Therefore, the measuring volume is determined by the optics and the image processing method, and not *a priori* known. An instrument has been developed for the measurement of size distributions of oceanic air bubbles. They are entrained by breaking waves, where they contribute to air-sea exchange processes. In order to monitor bubble populations, an optical sensor based on controlling the measuring volume by depth-from-focus (DFF) is used. As natural bubble populations typically range from $10\,\mu m$ up to more than $1000\,\mu m$ radius, a multicamera setup has been chosen with each camera having a different magnification factor (Fig. A.34 a). For measurements in the ocean (Fig. A.34 c), the instrument was integrated into a floating buoy [24] (Fig. A.34 b).

Used algorithms. First, the images are normalized with respect to the possibly uneven background of the back-lit illumination (Fig. A.35 a). Most of the bubbles are blurred due to defocusing. By quantifying the defocus, we are able to correlate it with the distance of the bubble from the plane of best focus. Thus the 3-D world coordinates of all bubbles observed during the measurement are known. Hence it is possible to calculate the true measuring volume from the image sequences. This is done within the DFF step, which first needs the exact boundaries of the bubbles. A fast region growing algorithm, adopted for the special needs of images showing heavily blurred object, is used (Fig. A.35 c). The DFF itself uses a measure of blur and a measure of size, both calculated on the segmented object area, together with a suitable calibration (Fig. A.36 a) to reconstruct depth and true size of each individual object. Further details of the applied algorithms can be found in [CVA3, Chapter 29].

Results. Despite the additional constraint to use only a single image, the DFF technique allows to reliable estimate the 3-D position of the particles, independently of the point spread function of the particular optics. Control of a virtual measuring volume by an algorithmic method is therefore a proven and robust technique. Comparisons with independent methods [25] show an excellent agreement of the size spectra (Fig. A.36b).

Figure A.34: *Experimental setup:* **a** *schematic of the three-camera optics;* **b** *instrument mounted on a floating buoy; and* **c** *deployment of the instrument in the ocean.*

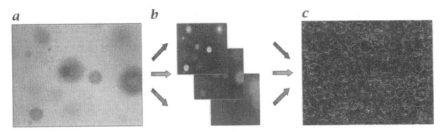

Figure A.35: *Intermediate processing steps:* **a** *raw image, with the images from the three cameras packed into a single RGB image;* **b** *unpacking, normalization, and processing of the three data streams; and* **c** *combining the results of the segmentation of an image sequence.*

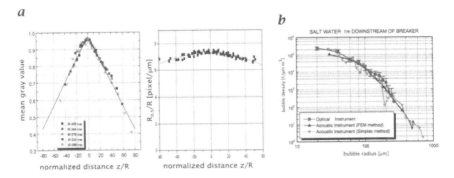

Figure A.36: *Results:* **a** *measured calibration data used by the depth-from-focus method. These fields are used for the decoupling of size and distance of the images of blurred objects.* **b** *Seawater size spectra for air bubbles, and comparison with acoustic measurements.*

A14 Thermography to Measure Water Relations of Plant Leaves

Bernd Kümmerlen[1,2], Stefan Dauwe[1,2], Dominik Schmundt[1,2], and Ulrich Schurr[1]

[1] Botanisches Institut, Universität Heidelberg, Germany
[2] Interdisziplinäres Zentrum für Wissenschaftliches Rechnen (IWR) Universität Heidelberg, Germany

Problem statement. Transpiration of water from plant leaves is very important for a wide range of physiological functions in the plant, such as photosynthesis and nutrient transport [26]. As it also has a strong impact on leaf temperature, water relations can be studied using thermographic methods. Thermography matches several requirements for botanical research: It shows little interference with the plant and its environment, and has high temporal and spatial resolution. Two different techniques were evaluated: a passive method to measure transpiration and an active method to determine local heat capacites on the leaf.

Experiments. A thorough theoretical analysis of the leaf energy budget shows that in equilibrium, the temperature difference between leaf and nontranspiring object is linearly dependent on transpiration rate. To verify this relationship, transpiration rates of *ricinus* leaves were measured using a standard gas exchange cuvette system (Figure A.37 a). Simultaneously, infrared (IR) image sequences (Fig. A.38 a) were acquired with a thermographic camera. In each image, temperature differences between the leaf and a reference body were calculated. In another setup (Fig. A.37 b), the leaf was subject to a periodically changing IR radiation flux. The resulting temperature changes of the leaf were again imaged with the IR camera and recorded together with other parameters, such as air temperature and humidity. The periodical changes of leaf temperature in these experiments were analyzed with a digital Fourier transform in the time direction. The phase shift of the temperature signal with respect to the input signal is shown in Fig. A.38 b and is directly related to the local heat capacity of the leaf.

Results. The simultaneous measurement of leaf temperature and transpiration rate allowed verification of the linear relationship (Fig. A.39), which is directly related to the heat transfer velocity over the leaf-air boundary layer. This quantity is very important for further spatially resolved determination of heat capacities and mapping of transpiration rates, which has already been carried out [27]. It has been shown that IR-imaging techniques have a high potential benefit for the analysis of dynamic processes in water relations of plants.

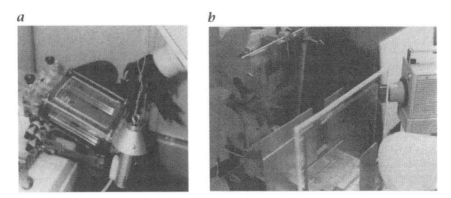

Figure A.37: **a** *Passive thermography setup, the IR camera is in the upper right corner, the plant in the back has one leaf fixed inside the cuvette.* **b** *Active thermography setup, the IR radiator illuminates the leaf through a set of screens and filters.*

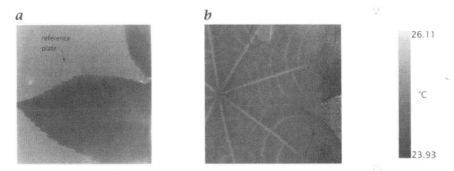

Figure A.38: **a** *IR image of a transpiring plant leaf, transpiration is high, therefore the leaf is cool. The reference body is indicated above the leaf.* **b** *Parameter image depicting the phase shift of the leaf-temperature signal with respect to the input radiation.*

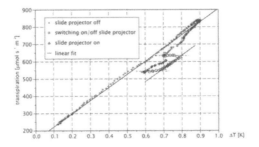

Figure A.39: Transpiration rate plotted against temperature difference. For the unperturbed phases of the experiment, the linear relationship is obvious. During fast temperature changes (circles) the relationship is not valid due to differences in heat capacity.

A15   Small-Scale Air-Sea Interaction with Thermography

Uwe Schimpf[1,2], Horst Haussecker[1,3], and Bernd Jähne[1,2]
[1]Interdisziplinäres Zentrum für Wissenschaftliches Rechnen (IWR)
Universität Heidelberg, Germany
[2]Scripps Institution of Oceanography, La Jolla, CA, USA
[3]Xerox Palo Alto Research Center (PARC)

Problem statement. The development of climatological models requires an understanding of the various parameters that influence the transfer of heat and gases across the air-sea interface.The knowledge of the underlying transport processes is quite incomplete because the transfer across the air-sea interface is very difficult to observe and is dominated by complex interaction of molecular diffusion and microturbulence within the first millimeter of the ocean surface [28]. In recent years, new technology and image-processing techniques have been developed to obtain an insight into these processes. (For an example of an experimental setup, see Fig. A.40.)

Used algorithms. Two different techniques, an active and a passive method, are used for in situ measurements of the transfer rate for heat [CVA3, Chapter 35]. Using active thermography, small patches at the water surface are heated up periodically by an infrared laser (Fig. A.41 a). In the recorded image sequences the heat spots are tracked (Fig. A.41 b) with a tensor approach for low-level motion estimation. The obtained decay curves (Fig. A.41 c) of the temperature distribution yield the time constant t_* of the heat transfer process. Applying the passive method, the temperature difference ΔT across the interface is directly estimated from statistical properties of the natural sea surface temperature (SST) obtained from the infrared image sequences (Fig. A.41 b). An accurate calibration technique is necessary to obtain reliable temperature information from the infrared imaging system. Furthermore, a scale analysis by means of pyramids (Fig. A.42 a) reveals the spatial structure of the microturbulence [29].

Results. By using novel visualization and image-processing techniques, it is for the first time possible to get an insight into the mechanism of dynamic transport processes within the microscopic boundary layer right at the ocean surface. The CFT [30] is the only field technique available so far that not only measures the transfer rate at high spatial and temporal resolution (Fig. A.41 c) but also gives a direct insight into the spatiotemporal structure of the microturbulence at the ocean surface and thus the mechanisms of air-water gas transfer.

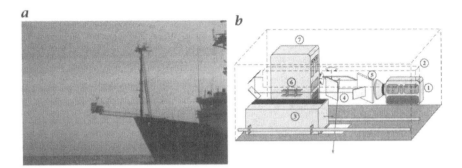

Figure A.40: Experimental setup: **a** CFT instrument mounted on a 7-m long boom at the bow of the Research Vessel Oceanus during the cruise in the North Atlantic, July 1997; and **b** schematic setup of the CFT. 1: Infrared camera, 2: CO_2-Laser, 3: calibration device, 4: x/y-Scanner, 5: beam splitter, 6: laser optic, 7: PC.

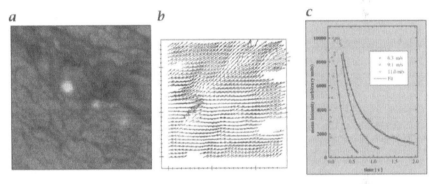

Figure A.41: Active thermography: **a** small patches at the water surface are heated up by an infrared laser; **b** the displacement vector field is calculated and the heat spot is tracked; **c** the obtained decay curves of the temperature distribution yield the time constant t_* of the heat transfer.

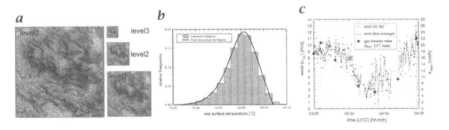

Figure A.42: Scale analysis of microturbulence: **a** Gaussian pyramid of an infrared image; **b** the temperature distribution at different levels of the pyramid is calculated and compared with the theoretical prediction; **c** the gas transfer velocity is calculated from the statistical properties of the sea surface temperature distribution.

A16 Optical Leaf Growth Analysis

Dominik Schmundt[1,2] and Uli Schurr[2]

[1] Interdisziplinäres Zentrum für Wissenschaftliches Rechnen (IWR),
Universität Heidelberg, Germany
[2] Botanisches Institut, Universität Heidelberg, Germany

Problem statement. Growth is one of the principle characteristics of living organisms. In plants, growth is organized in a modular fashion that allows the adaptation of the plant´s architecture and function to the environmental constraints, while meeting the intrinsic requirements for coordination of function between the different parts of the plants—for example, leaves gain carbon and energy, while roots acquire nutrients. Growth studies are thus the basis for evaluation of plant function and its interaction with the environment. As both environmental conditions and growing tissues change dynamically, growth analysis must consider spatial and temporal aspects simultaneously.

Used algorithms. In a setup of heavy stands (Fig. A.43 a) time lapse sequences of growing leaves are captured (Fig. A.43 b). These are analyzed using the structure tensor technique [CVA2, Chapter 13]. The obtained displacement vector field (DVF) of the leaf surface (Fig. A.44 a) is then regularized and interpolated by normalized convolution [31] (Fig. A.44 b). The divergence of the DVF is a map of the leaf growth (Fig. A.45 a). With an error of the velocity estimation of 0.01 pixel per frame error propagation provides a temporal resolution of 5 min with a simultaneous spatial resolution of 5×5 mm over a field of view of 100×80 mm [32]. The simultaneous high spatial and temporal resolution provides for the first time an adequate tool to analyze the dynamics of the regulation of growth.

Results. During the development of this system that included a standard tool it was possible to obtain relevant botanical results: Speculations that plant leaves only grow at the leaf base for a limited period of the day could be verified. Maps of the growth distribution reveal the basipetal gradient (Fig. A.45 a and b)—a gradient from the leaf base to the leaf tip—of growth also described by Maksymowych [33]. They can also be used for comparison with other physiological data from other channels in the future, for example, biomolecular techniques allow the expression of certain proteins to be visualized using luminescent markers. And entirely new insights—which could not be obtained by classical growth analysis—about the behavior in root pressure experiments could be gained. Meanwhile the new technique is currently used in laboratory experiments for systematic investigations.

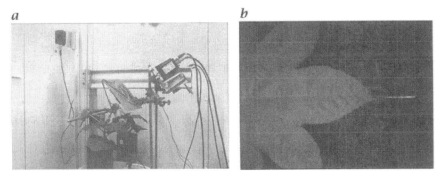

Figure A.43: Setup: **a** two tobacco plants in a setup for growth analysis. A cross-beam from heavy stands holds the camera and a panel of IR LED in the center of the image. **b** raw image of a ricinus leaf—the grid spacing is 10 × 10 mm.

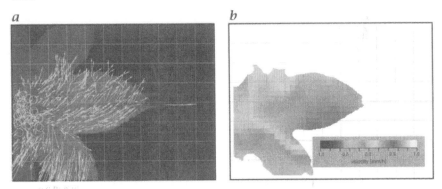

Figure A.44: Intermediate processing steps: **a** the DVF in a vector representation as an overlay on the original leaf image; **b** the interpolated displacement vector field (DVF, x-component) obtained by normalized convolution.

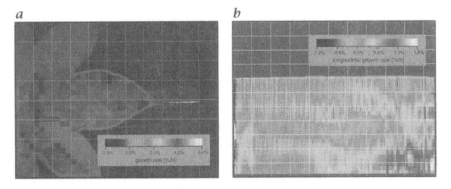

Figure A.45: Results: **a** the divergence of the DVF as an overlay. The high growth rates at the lower lobe are due to a motion of this lobe out of plane; **b** nocturnal longitudinal growth rate of the middle lobe of a ricinus leaf, depicted as xt-image—the grid spacing is 10 × 60 min.

A17   Analysis of Motility Assay Data

Dietmar Uttenweiler and Rainer H. A. Fink

II. Physiologisches Institut, Universität Heidelberg, Germany

Problem statement. The ability of heart and skeletal muscle to contract is based on the fundamental interaction of the two contractile proteins actin and myosin. This basic interaction can be studied in the *in vitro* motility assay originally devised by Kron and Spudich [34]. It consists of a myosin-decorated surface over which fluorescently labeled actin filaments move in the presence of adenosine triphosphate (ATP) (Fig. A.46). The kinetic parameters of this motion, as, for example, the filament velocities or the fraction of moving filaments, have been shown to be an important measure for the molecular interaction of the two proteins involved. Therefore an accurate automated analysis of the motion of actin filaments is essential in using this assay as a quantitative standardized experimental tool.

Methods and materials. The isolated actin filaments in the flow chamber are labeled with the fluorescent indicator rhodamine-phalloidin and visualized with a very sensitive fluorescence imaging setup. The time series shown in Fig. A.47 is recorded with a frequency of 25 Hz and 8-bit resolution. With an image size of 768×576 pixel, a typical 4-s data set has a size of 43 MB. The fluorescence originates from single actin molecules with a diameter much less than the microscopic resolution and therefore the S/N ratio is very weak. Due to this fact and the large amount of data the analysis of actin filament motion poses very high demands on automated algorithms. The automated determination of actin filament motion is achieved with an algorithm using the structure tensor approach (see Chapter 10). The method is adopted to the noisy fluorescence images and calculates the displacement vector field on a higher level of a Gaussian pyramid to reduce the influence of the noise. The displacement vector field is calculated with subpixel accuracy and due to the fast pyramidal implementation a 43 MB dataset is processed in less than 30 s on a standard PC.

Results. With our new approach using the structure tensor method it is possible to automatically determine the velocity of actin filament movement in the *in vitro* motility assay. The displacement vector field as shown in Fig. A.48a is computed with subpixel accuracy. From the displacement vector field all other quantities can be derived, as, for example, the histogram of filament velocities shown in Fig. A.48b. This approach is also very valuable for other applications, where fluorescence imaging techniques are used to monitor cellular or molecular processes.

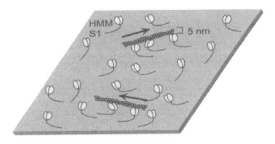

Figure A.46: *Schematic experimental setup for an* in vitro *motility assay. Isolated fluorescently labeled actin filaments move over a myosin (S1 or HMM) decorated surface. The flow chamber is mounted on an inverted fluorescence microscope (see Section A25). The motion of the fluorescently labeled actin filaments is recorded with an intensified CCD-camera.*

Figure A.47: *Time series of fluorescence images, where the actin filament motion is visible as the displacement of fluorescent rod-like structures. The S/N ratio is very weak in these images, as the fluorescence signal originates from single actin molecules labeled with the fluorescence indicator rhodamine-phalloidin.*

 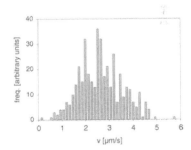

Figure A.48: *Results: **a** displacement vector field obtained with the structure tensor method calculated on the second level of a Gaussian pyramid. **b** From the displacement vector field the histogram of velocity distribution can be derived. The histogram represents a good measure of filament motility and hence of the underlying molecular interactions.*

A18   Fluorescence Imaging of Air-Water Gas Exchange

Sven Eichkorn[1,2], Thomas Münsterer[1,3], Ulrike Lode[1], and Bernd Jähne[1,4]

[1] Institut für Umweltphysik, Universität Heidelberg, Germany
[2] now at Max-Planck-Institut für Kerphysik, Heidelberg, Germany
[3] now at Vitronic Bildverarbeitung GmbH, Wiesbaden, Germany
[4] Interdisziplinäres Zentrum für Wissenschaftliches Rechnen (IWR)
Universität Heidelberg, Germany

Problem statement.   The research field air-water gas exchange is dedicated to the question, of whether the ocean can act as a reservoir for CO_2 and thus dampen the greenhouse effect caused by increasing CO_2 emissions. To quantify the amount of gas absorbed by the ocean, one has to know the transfer coefficient k. It takes several hours to measure k in wind-wave tunnels by classical methods. The laser induced fluorescence (LIF) technique described here makes it possible to measure k instantaneously. The technique uses an acid-base reaction of a fluorescence indicator to visualize 2-D concentration profiles of gases in the aqueous mass boundary layer [CVA3, Chapter 30].

Used algorithms.   A scanned laser beam pierces the water surface perpendicular from the topside. The resulting light sheet is imaged by a CCD camera. Each measurement run (each corresponding to a certain wind speed) provides a sequence of 1800 images. A raw image is shown at Fig. A.49a. The dark line (highest gas concentration) represents the water surface. The upper part of the image pictures the reflection of the light sheet at the water surface and the lower part pictures the 2-D concentration profile of invading CO_2. The dark dots are the consequence of dirt on the CCD chip. Those were removed by a high-pass filter [35]. Such a cleaned and smoothed image can be seen in Fig. A.49b. In the following the water surface was found by a minimum operator and moved to the top of the image. An averaging over each sequence was performed with the images processed this way. The absorption of fluorescence intensity in the water was corrected and finally the extracted mean profile allowed for calculating the transfer coefficient k. Image processing steps are summarized in Fig. A.50.

Results.   Figure A.51 shows the gas transfer coefficient k of CO_2 plotted vs the wind speed measured by [35] with LIF compared to a theoretical curve and to classical gas exchange measurements. They correspond well. The image sequences provide a deep insight into the processes that control air-water gas exchange in the aqueous mass boundary layer. The most breathtaking result of the analysis was the first direct observation of surface renewal events [36]. Those statistically occurring events are turbulence eddies that reach the water surface.

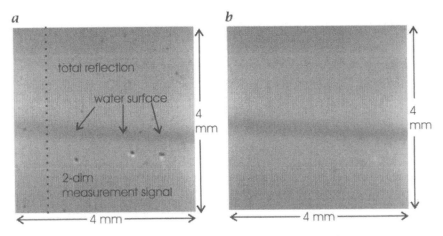

Figure A.49: *a Raw image; and b clean, smoothed image.*

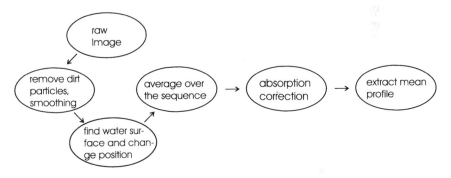

Figure A.50: *Image processing steps.*

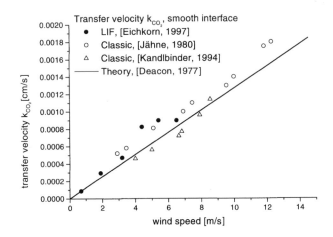

Figure A.51: *Dependence of k (CO₂) on the wind speed.*

A19   Particle-Tracking Velocimetry

Dirk Engelmann, Michael Stöhr, Christoph Garbe, and Frank Hering[1]
Interdisziplinäres Zentrum für Wissenschaftliches Rechnen (IWR)
Universität Heidelberg, Germany
[1] now at SAP AG, Walldorf, Germany

Problem statement. One important aspect in fluid mechanics is to study the dynamics of the fluid flow field. The particle-tracking velocimetry (PTV) algorithm was developed and applied to obtain the Lagrangian representation of the flow field. It allows to track the movement of individual seeding particles (or air bubbles Fig. A.52)—which are added to a liquid—in time and space (2- or 3-D) and to obtain their trajectories.

Used algorithms. The PTV algorithm has to identify the distinct seeding particles in each image frame and track these identified particles in the subsequent images of the image sequence. A segmentation procedure identifies the individual particles from the background.Then the correspondence problem has to be solved for finding each particle in the subsequent image frames. In this way the particles are tracked through the sequence of images [37]. The stereo PTV additionally needs a stereoscopic correspondence search (comparing images taken from different camera perspectives). Using a geometric camera model consisting of an extended pinhole camera, which includes lens distortion and multiple media geometry, the stereoscopic correspondence is solved [38]. To gain quantitative data the calibration procedure is crucial. The calibration for each camera is done with subpixel precision by using a transparent grid. The stereoscopic calibration is performed by numerically minimizing the optical path with the usage of the geometric camera model [39].

Results. The particle-tracking velocimetry is a powerful method for studying dynamic processes. Investigations in a wind-wave flume and in a gas-liquid reactor (Fig. A.52) show the strength of the method; the Lagrangian representation is an important advantage compared to other methods that obtain a Eulerian representation of the flow field. The extension to stereo PTV for spatial flow fields allows to obtain the complete physical information of the particle movement with sub(volume-) pixel precise spatial resolution (Fig. A.53). The method is also applicable for many other purposes, not only in flow visualization applications (Fig. A.54). For practical purposes the simple experimental setup is of advantage. Therefore the described (stereo) PTV is a good choice to study dynamic processes in the 2- or 3-D space.

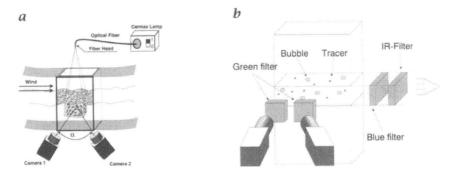

Figure A.52: *Experimental setup: **a** flow visualization in a wind-wave flume; and **b** in a gas-liquid reactor.*

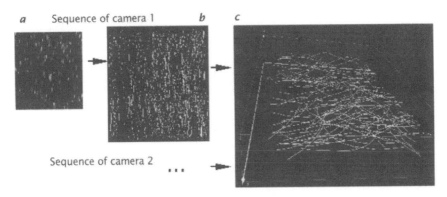

Figure A.53: *Streak image as imaged by the CCD camera **a** and the trajectories gained by PTV **b** . Out of the two sequences the stereoscopic trajectories representing the flow are calculated as in **c** .*

Figure A.54: *Trajectories of air bubbles in a gas-liquid reactor.*

A20   Analyzing Particle Movements at Soil Interfaces

Hagen Spies[1], Hermann Gröning[1,2], and Horst Haußecker[1]

[1] Interdisziplinäres Zentrum für Wissenschaftliches Rechnen (IWR)
Universität Heidelberg, Germany
[2]Xerox Palo Alto Research Center (PARC)

Problem statement.   The German Federal Waterways Engineering and Research Institute (BAW), Karlsruhe, seeks to protect river embankments from erosion and destabilization. In a cooperation with Heidelberg University, the influence of hydraulic load changes on sediment instability is investigated [40]. In order to visualize the transport processes within the sediment, a large pressure tank was built that allows for simulation of realistic pressure gradients acting on subsurface soil layers in a laboratory environment (Fig. A.55 a) [41]. Using endoscopic optics (Fig. A.55 b) with attached CCD cameras, image sequences of vertical cross sections of sediment layers are acquired. The task of image sequence processing is to reliably detect moving sediment particles and to get quantitative estimates of the temporal course of particle motions.

Used Algorithms.   Due to vignetting effects in the endoscopic optics and uneven illumination from the internal fiber glass light conductor, the images show an extremely uneven brightness (Fig. A.56 a). The first step is to normalize the images using a highly smoothed image as a correction factor. Figure A.56 b shows the result using the fifth level of a *Gaussian pyramid* as *illumination correction. Motion analysis* is carried out by the *structure tensor* technique, that is, a local spatiotemporal TLS estimator. The output displacement vector field (DVF) can only be computed reliably in regions with sufficient image structure (Fig. A.56 c). In order to get a dense DVF (Fig. A.57 a), the sparse information is interpolated using the *normalized convolution* in conjunction with the *confidence measure* of the structure tensor technique. From the dense DVF, higher-order properties of the motion field, such as divergence (Fig. A.57 b) or vorticity can be computed. Further details of the applied algorithms can be found in CVA3 [Chapter 32].

Results.   Despite the bad image quality of endoscopic image sequences, this technique allows for reliably estimating motion fields of sediment particles and extracting the relevant physical parameters, such as divergence, rotation, and mixing. A comparison of the theoretically expected and the measured sediment motion with respect to the temporal pressure changes shows an excellent agreement for stable sediment layers (Fig. A.57 c). It has been shown that unstable sediment structures exhibit a much higher velocity with irreversible structural changes [41], [CVA3, Chapter 32].

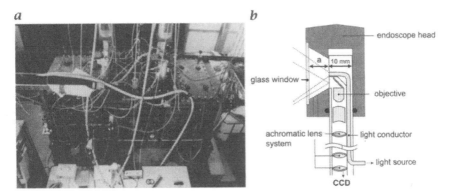

Figure A.55: *Experimental setup:* **a** *pressure tank; and* **b** *schematic vertical cross section through the endoscope.*

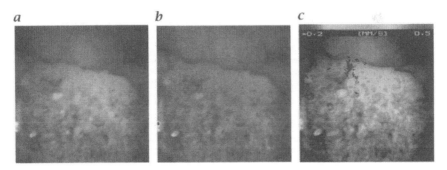

Figure A.56: *Intermediate processing steps:* **a** *raw image with uneven illumination;* **b** *image after illumination correction;* **c** *sparse displacement vector field as output of the structure tensor technique for motion analysis.*

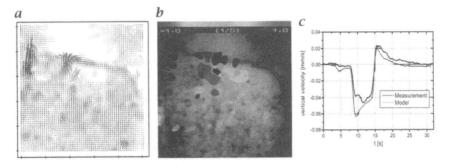

Figure A.57: *Results:* **a** *displacement vector field of the sediment right after the pressure decrease; the sand grains show a net upward motion with local disturbances;* **b** *divergence of the displacement vector field after interpolation by normalized convolution;* **c** *temporal course of measured and theoretically calculated velocities.*

A21 3-D Velocity Fields from Flow Tomography Data

Hans-Gerd Maas

Faculty of Civil Engineering and Geosciences, Delft University of Technology, The Netherlands

Problem statement. For the examination of mixing processes in turbulent flows a system based on a high-speed solid state camera has been implemented, which allows for the quasi-simultaneous acquisition of sequences of flow tomography data. Mixing processes can be visualized by marking one of two fluids to be mixed by fluorescein at a rather low concentration. The fluorescein becomes clearly visible when animated by laser light of a certain wavelength (LIF - laser-induced fluorescence). By scanning an observation volume of typically $15 \times 15 \times 3\,\mathrm{mm}^3$ by a laser light sheet in 50 layers within $1/10\,\mathrm{s}$ and recording images with a 256×256 pixel highspeed camera at an imaging rate of 500 frames per second, 10 consecutive voxel data sets of $256 \times 256 \times 50$ voxels each can be recorded within one s (Fig. A.58).

Data processing. The 3-D Least-Squares-Matching (3-D LSM, [42]) is being used for tracking cuboids of typically $15 \times 15 \times 15$ voxels in consecutive data sets. It tries to determine the 12 coefficients of a 3-D affine transformation for a cuboid in one data set to its transformed counterpart in the next data set by minimizing the sum of the squares of gray-value differences. Formulated as a least-squares adjustment problem, the technique converges after a few iterations, provided sufficient contrast and good approximate values. The 3 shift parameters of the 3-D affine transformation represent the local velocity vector; the 9 remaining parameters represent the deformation of fluid elements. Additionally, 3-D LSM also delivers the full covariance matrix, allowing for an analysis of the quality of the results. To improve the convergence behavior in regions with poor contrast, additional constraints have been implemented: Based on the incompressibility of the fluids, the volume covered by each cuboid must remain constant; based on the assumption of a sufficient sampling rate, transformation parameters must show some local and temporal correlation.

Results. Figure A.59 shows a cuboid at one time instant and the convergence of 3-D LSM to the correct solution in the next time instant. Figure A.60 shows the resulting velocity field overlaid on the concentration data of one data layer, with red and blue tips indicating negative and positive depth components of the velocity vector. Under good contrast conditions, a precision in the order of $1/50$ voxel can be achieved for the three components of the velocity vector, corresponding to 1-2 μm in object space.

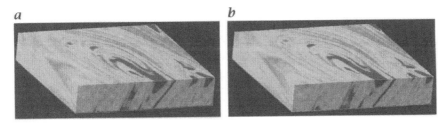

Figure A.58: *Color-coded display of two consecutive 3-D LIF datasets in an experiment on mixing of fluids.*

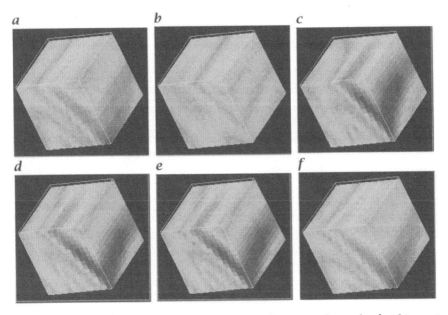

Figure A.59: *a* 15^3 *voxel cuboid; b–f corresponding transformed cuboid in next dataset after 0, 1, 2, 5 and 8 iterations of 3-D LSM.*

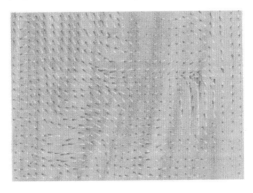

Figure A.60: *Sample velocity field.*

A22   Cloud Classification Analyzing Image Sequences

Mark Wenig[1,2], Carsten Leue[1,2], and Ulrich Platt[1]

[1] Institut für Umweltphysik, Universität Heidelberg, Germany
[2] Interdisziplinäres Zentrum für Wissenschaftliches Rechnen (IWR)
Universität Heidelberg, Germany

Problem statement.   The Global Ozone Monitoring Experiment (GOME) aboard the European Space Agency's Earth Resources Satellite (ERS-2) measures concentrations of several trace gases using Differential Absorption Spectroscopy (DOAS) [CVA3, Chapter 37]. For further processing of this data, information about clouds is very important. Therefore, a cloud-detecting algorithm is needed.

Used algorithms.   The cloud-detection algorithm presented here relies on information from the spatially high resolution PMD data coming from the GOME instrument. These data yield an integral of the light intensity over three wavelength intervals in the UV and visual spectral range and will thus be regarded as RGB values for further image processing. The basic idea for the cloud-detecting algorithms is to concentrate on two characteristics of clouds, their degree of whiteness (see Fig. A.61 a) and the fact that they form a moving layer in front of a static background. The appropriate color model to measure whiteness is the HSV (**H**ue, **S**aturation and brightness **V**alue) color model. In this space we can define a subset that characterizes the clouds (see Fig. A.61 b and c). Hence efficient detection can be achieved by applying a threshold in the S-V color space. The results of the HSV method can be improved by considering that clouds are moving, forming, and dissolving. Therefore, those SV values nearly constant with time are likely to belong to the background whereas those that change should belong to cloudy pixels. That approach is successful, if the majority of days are cloud-free. Apparently, that condition is fulfilled through the HSV-preclassification. The implementation of this idea is realized in the employed iterative algorithm (see Fig. A.62).

Results.   The result of the algorithm is global maps of cloud cover. The resulting cloud cover for the PMD values shown in Fig. A.61 a can be seen in Fig. A.63 c. It is also possible to use the background image to determine the ground albedo, which can be seen in Fig. A.63 d. The algorithm is very robust and can simply be extended. Once reference images for different seasons are generated, annual changes, such as variations due to vegetation cycles, are also considered. For a more detailed description see [43].

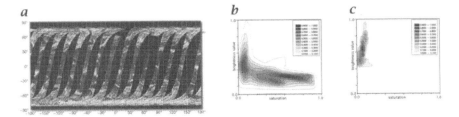

Figure A.61: *Visualization of the PMD data:* **a** *global map of the PMD values interpreted as RGB values;* **b** *histogram plot of the PMD values transformed into HSV color space;* **c** *histogram plot of PMD images in which the clouds were classified manually.*

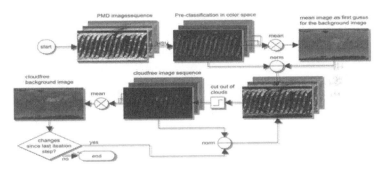

Figure A.62: *Flowchart of the cloud-detecting method. In the first step the clouds are removed with the HSV method. Then each image is compared with the mean over all images and pixels with high deviation are removed. This step is iterated until the mean image remains constant.*

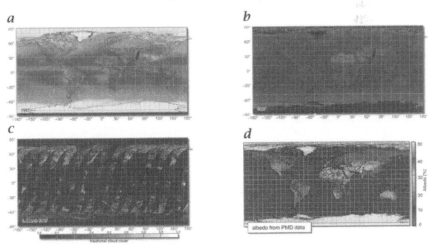

Figure A.63: *The results of the algorithm:* **a** *for comparison the mean image of the image sequence;* **b** *the background image;* **c** *global map of the HSV-Cloud Cover;* **d** *Global albedo (vis.) map calculated from the background image.*

A23 NO_X Emissions Retrieved from Satellite Images

Carsten Leue[1,2], Mark Wenig[1,2], and Ulrich Platt[1]

[1] Institut für Umweltphysik, Universität Heidelberg, Germany
[2] Interdisziplinäres Zentrum für Wissenschaftliches Rechnen (IWR)
Universität Heidelberg, Germany

Problem statement. Nitric oxides (NO_X) play a very important role among the anthropogenic trace gases produced globally. Besides affecting human health they also have an impact on ozone chemistry and influence climatic changes. Since 1995 the Global Ozone Monitoring Experiment (GOME) onboard the ERS-2 satellite has provided the possibility of monitoring the global NO_2 distribution. The GOME spectrometer measures the earthshine absorption spectra in the wavelength range between 240 nm and 790 nm, which contain the spectral 'fingerprints' of the trace gases in the light path. The goal of this application is the calculation of the global NO_X budget; this requires two main steps (Fig. A.64),: spectral retrieval of the trace gases from the GOME spectra by numerical inversion algorithms (DOAS) [44] and the formation of global trace gas maps from the spectral results by image processing.

Used algorithms. The spectral retrieval is based on the Differential Optical Absorption Spectroscopy (DOAS) approach. It relies on a numerical inversion algorithm that models the measured absorption spectra from the superposition of reference spectra. Using an interpolation algorithm based on B-splines and an implicit fitting technique, it has become possible to develop a retrieval algorithm that allows evaluation of the GOME data in realtime [CVA3, Chapter 37]. The GOME instrument scans the earth in orbits and achieves global coverage of the earth's surface every three days. To compensate for this effect spatiotemporal interpolation by normalized convolution has been applied. As the spectral retrieval results in vertical column densities (concentrations integrated along the vertical light path) the maps contain both stratospheric and tropospheric contributions. The separation of both is performed by the combination of a low-pass filtering step and a normalized convolution (Fig. A.65). Further details can be found in CVA3 [Chapter 37].

Results. This application made it possible to calculate the tropospheric source strengths of NO_X from GOME spectra with the combination of improved spectral retrieval and image processing. The procedure is totally independent of previous methods and results in a global source strength of $(48 \pm 19)\,\mathrm{Tg\,N\,yr^{-1}}$ (Fig. A.66). The accuracy of this method is at least as good as that of established statistical approaches.

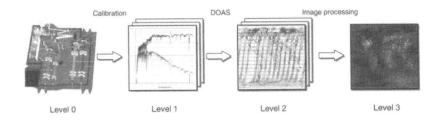

Level 0   Level 1   Level 2   Level 3

Figure A.64: *Main processing steps: level 0: acquisition of earthshine spectra by the GOME instrument; level 1: spectral and radiometric calibration; level 2: retrieval of slant column densities; level 3: calculation of the global NO$_X$ budget*

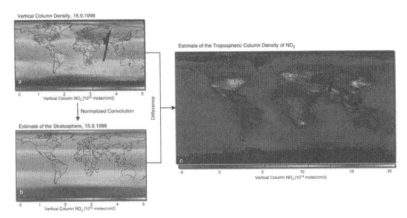

Figure A.65: a *Image of the vertical column densities of NO$_2$ containing both a stratospheric and tropospheric contribution;* **b** *estimate of the stratospheric contribution using normalized convolution;* **c** *the tropospheric contribution can be estimated calculating the difference of **a** and **b** .*

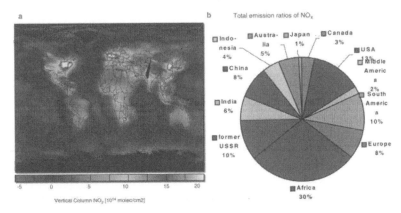

Figure A.66: a *Albedo corrected total NO$_X$ emissions for 1997;* **b** *ratios of the NO$_X$ source strengths for selected regions derived from the global NO$_X$ maps.*

A24   Multicolor Classification of Astronomical Objects

Christian Wolf, Klaus Meisenheimer, and Hermann-Josef Roeser

Max-Planck Institut für Astronomie, Heidelberg, Germany

Problem statement.   The Max-Planck-Institute for Astronomy (MPIA), Heidelberg, conducts a sky survey to study the evolution of galaxies in the universe (Calar Alto Deep Imaging Survey = CADIS). It aims at obtaining a complete sample of stars, galaxies and quasars from 10 fields on the sky of $0°.17 \times 0°.17$ area each. The object database will contain brightness, type, and redshift (=distance, age) information of several 10,000 objects [45, 46, 47]. The CCD images taken with 3-m-class telescopes are processed with standard procedures of flat-fielding, removing cosmic ray hits and co-adding dithered exposures. The following steps include object detection, morphological analysis, and photometry. Atmospheric conditions cause image sharpness to change and require blurring to a common PSF for accurate photometry. Usually, the most decisive analytic tool in astronomy is spectroscopy, but it is not feasible to collect spectra of many thousand faint objects. On the other hand, imaging the sky through a sequence of color filters provides spectral photometry with low resolution for all objects in the field simultaneously. This crude color information can replace a slit spectrum for rough analysis. Important ingredients for the analysis are accurate color measurements, a library of colors for all expected kinds of objects, and a suitable classification algorithm.

Used algorithms.   The color libraries were taken from the literature and cover all observable redshifts. The library objects resemble a statistical ensemble generating the measurement, each with its own probability being calculated from the measurement errors. We use Parzen's kernel estimator to determine the likelihood of an object to be either a star, a galaxy, or a quasar. For galaxies and quasars we estimate mean redshifts from the probability distribution of the library objects.

Results.   The classification outperforms earlier photometric approaches in astronomy due to its many accurately measured colors and the proper statistical classification method. Among the 200 brightest objects per field only 2% are misclassified and spectroscopic confirmation is indeed not required. Especially, quasars are found with much higher completeness and efficiency than was previously the case. An exciting new result is that we find many more quasars at high redshift (i. e., large distances and look-back times into the young universe) than in previous studies. We challenge the established picture of quasar evolution, now pointing to earlier formation times for these structures in the universe. These data provide important and accurate input for models of galaxy formation.

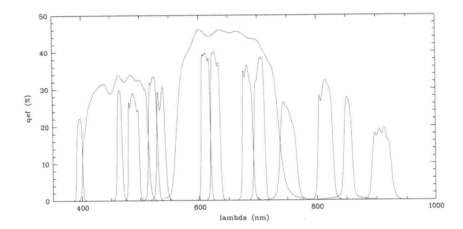

Figure A.67: *Optical filterset used in CADIS to obtain photometric spectra of astronomical objects ranging from the violett to the near-infrared.*

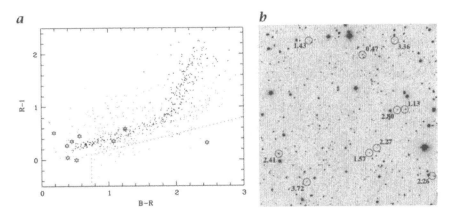

Figure A.68: *Classification results:* **a** *Based on a color library objects are statistically classified into stars (black dots), galaxies (gray dots) and quasars (asterisks). Their location is shown in a color diagram with the flux ratios blue/red and red/infrared. Most quasars found show colors quite similar to stars and galaxies. Common search techniques use only broadband filters and have to select quasars from a region of unusual colors (area below dashed line) to avoid strong contamination by abundant stars and galaxies.* **b** *Detected quasars marked by a circle and annotated with the observed redshift.*

A25 Model-Based Fluorescence Imaging

Dietmar Uttenweiler and Rainer H. A. Fink

II. Physiologisches Institut, Universität Heidelberg, Germany

Problem statement. Fluorescence imaging techniques have evolved to a central tool in many fields of scientific applications. Especially the various disciplines in life sciences have profited from these techniques for studying cellular and molecular processes and medically relevant pathogenic diseases. In particular the possibility of monitoring intracellular ion concentrations with high spatial and temporal resolution has led to a much deeper understanding of many basic processes, as, for example, the function of the brain, or the molecular basis of muscular contraction and its regulation. The accurate interpretation of the image series obtained by the various techniques has to include a detailed knowledge of the process of image acquisition, the intermediate steps of digital image processing, and a comprehensive mathematical analysis as described in detail in CVA1 [Chapter 12] and CVA3 [Chapter 34].

Methods and materials. Figure A.69 summarizes a typical experimental setup used for intracellular ion concentration measurements using fluorescent indicators. A monochromator is used for fast changes in excitation wavelength for ratiometric fluorescence measurements. The fluorescence signal is detected by an intensified CCD-camera. Confocal laser scanning microscopy and multiphoton microscopy offer in addition high axial resolution and the latter also provides a deep penetration in thick and highly scattering preparations. A N_2 UV-laser in the microscope can be used for the very precise microdissection of specimens (cutting diameter < 500 nm). A typical Ca^{2+}-release in permeable muscle fibers recorded with the ratiometric Ca^{2+}-indicator Fura-2 is shown in Fig. A.70. The analysis of the image sequence has to be done with sophisticated mathematical models as shown in Fig. A.71 (see Uttenweiler et al. [48]).

Results. The many fluorescence imaging techniques have significantly improved the choice of a suitable technique for chemical, biophysical and physiological investigations in the various life sciences fields. Although temporal and spatial resolution has dramatically increased, the unbiased information about the underlying processes can only be gained with powerful mathematical models that take into account experimental inaccuracies, fluorescence indicator properties, and the complex nature of molecular and cellular processes.

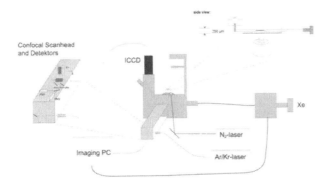

Figure A.69: *Experimental setup: confocal fluorescence microscope with additional epi-fluorescence illumination using a monochromating device and an ICCD camera for detection. The N₂ UV-laser in the microscope is used for microdissection of specimens.*

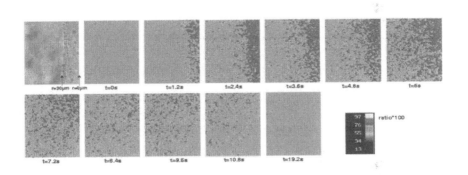

Figure A.70: *Time series of a caffeine-induced Ca^{2+}-transient, recorded with the Ca^{2+}-sensitive dye Fura-2 using the wavelength pair 340nm/380nm (Uttenweiler et al. [48]).*

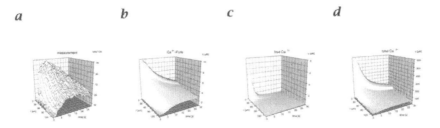

Figure A.71: *a Experimentally determined spatiotemporal distribution of Ca^{2+}-ions; b – d the simulated spatiotemporal ion-distributions as obtained by the model calculations.*

A26　Analyzing the 3-D Genome Topology

Harald Bornfleth, Peter Edelmann, and Christoph Cremer

Institut für Angewandte Physik, and Interdisziplinäres Zentrum für Wissenschaftliches Rechnen (IWR), Universität Heidelberg, Germany

Problem statement. The quantitative analysis of 3-D confocal microscopic images of biological specimens can contribute greatly to the understanding of genome topology and function. However, the resolution of a confocal microscope as given by its point spread function (PSF) is limited mainly in the axial direction to about 750 nm. It is highly desirable to analyze biological objects below this resolution limit, for example, replication foci (diameter 400-800 nm). Furthermore, the algorithms and quantitative parameters used should be insensitive to photon noise.

Used algorithms. For the morphological analysis of whole chromosome territories several parameters were computed: volume, surface area and two shape parameters, the roundness factor and the recently introduced *smoothness factor*. For details and definitions see [CVA3, Chapter 41]. The influence of the number of detected photons on the result of the image analysis was tested by means of simulated model images. For the topological analysis of objects with volumes smaller or comparable to the observation volume of the microscopic PSF a *model-based* algorithm for *volume-conserving segmentation* was used [49]: First local intensity maxima were found by a specially adapted *top-hat filter*. Starting from these spot centers, an *iterative conditional region-growing process* was performed. Comparisons with model-calculations allowed individually stopping the region-growing process when the true spot volume was obtained. As intensity signals of closely neighboring spots overlap after the imaging process, the algorithm was expanded by a procedure [CVA3, Chapter 41], which transferred each spot into a subvolume and sequentially eliminated the intensity contributions of neighboring spots.

Results. The test of the morphology analysis revealed that in contrast to the parameter's surface area and (consequently) roundness factor, the parameter's volume and *smoothness factor* did not depend on the number of detected photons. This allowed significant differences in the morphology of chromosomes in different stages of the cell cycle to be analyzed [CVA3, Chapter 41]. The excellent performance of the volume-conserving algorithm and its capability to reduce signal contributions from neighboring spots is demonstrated in Fig. A.72a-d. For more details and successful application to the analysis of the clustering of early and late replicating DNA see [CVA3, Chapter 41] and Zink et al. [50].

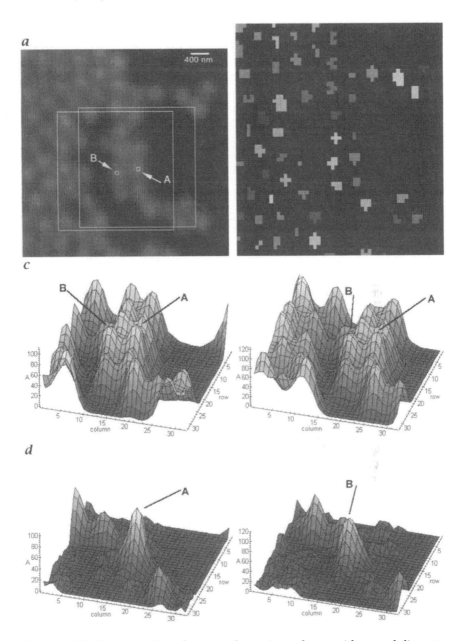

Figure A.72: *Segmentation of quartz glass microspheres with a total diameter of 416 nm and fluorescent core of 200 nm. **a** A central section from a 3-D confocal data stack is shown. **b** Result after segmentation; different objects are denoted by different gray shades. Subtraction of neighboring intensities: Each spot is transfered into a subvolume, the situation at the beginning **c** and at the end (after 7 iterations) **d** of the subtraction procedure is shown.*

A27 References

[1] Dieckmann, U., Plankensteiner, P., and Wagner, T., (1995). Multi-sensory pattern analysis for person identification with synergetic computers. In *Proceedings of the International Workshop on Automatic Face and Gesture Recognition*, pp. 368-371. Zurich/Switzerland.

[2] Beyer, H., (1992). *Geometric and Radiometric Analysis of a CCD-camera based Photogrammetric Close-Range System*. Diss. No. 9701, ETH Zürich, Aachen: Shaker Verlag.

[3] Gruen, A. and Beyer, H., (1986). Real-time photogrammetry at the digital photogrammetric station (DIPS) of ETH Zurich. *Canadian Surveyor*, **41**(2): 181-199.

[4] Brown, D., (1971). Close-range camera calibration. *Photogrammetric Engineering*, **37**(8):855-866.

[5] van den Heuvel, F. and Kroon, R., (1992). Digital close range photogrammetry using artificial targets. *International Archives of Photogrammetry and Remote Sensing*, **37**(B5):222-229.

[6] Scheuermann, T., (1997). *Berührungslose Gestaltvermessung von Mikrostrukturen durch Fokussuche*. Dissertation, Universität Stuttgart and Fraunhofer Institut für Chemische Technologie, Pfinztal, Germany.

[7] Graf, M., (1997). *Schichtdickenmessung durch Strukturprojektion und Fokussuche*. Master's thesis, Universität Karlsruhe and Fraunhofer Institut für Chemische Technologie, Pfinztal, Germany.

[8] Ellson, R. N. and Nurre, J. H. (eds.), (1997). *Three-dimensional image capture*, Vol. 3023 of *Conf. Proc. of the SPIE*, Bellingham, WA. SPIE.

[9] Häusler, G. and Ritter, D., (1999). Feature-Based Object Recognition and Localization in 3D-Space Using a Single Video Image. *Computer Vision and Image Understanding*, **73**(1):64-81.

[10] Pollefeys, M., Koch, R., and VanGool, L., (1998). Self-Calibration and Metric Reconstruction in spite of Varying and Unknown Internal Camera Parameters. In *Proc. 6th ICCV'98, Bombay*, pp. 90-95. New York: IEEE.

[11] Koch, R., Pollefeys, M., and VanGool, L., (1998). Multi viewpoint stereo from uncalibrated video sequences. In *Computer Vision - ECCV'98*, H. Burkhardt and B. Neumann, eds., Vol. 1406/1 of *Lecture Notes in Computer Science*, pp. 55-71. Heidelberg: Springer.

[12] Barnea, D. and Silverman, F., (1972). A class of algorithms for fast digital image registration. *IEEE Transactions on Computers*, **C-21**:179-186.

[13] Frischholz, R., (1998). *Beiträge zur automatischen dreidimensionalen Bewegungsanalyse*. Diss., Universität Erlangen, Aachen: Shaker Verlag.

[14] Cheng, D., Mercer, R., Barron, J., and P.Joe, (1998). Tracking severe weather storms in Doppler radar images. *Intl. Journal of Imaging Systems and Technology*, **9**:201-213.

[15] Grimson, W. E. L., (1989). The combinatorics of object recognition in cluttered environments using constrained search. *AI*, **11**(6):632-643.

[16] Hafner, W. and Munkelt, O., (1996). Using color for detecting persons in image sequences. *Pattern Recognition and Image Analysis*, **7**(1):47-52.

[17] Hermes, T., Klauck, C., Kreyß, J., and Zhang, J., (1995). Image Retrieval for Information Systems. In *Proc. of SPIE - The Inter. Soc. for Optical Engineering, Storage and Retrieval for Image and Video Databases*, pp. 394–403.

[18] Leung, C. H. C., (1990). Architecture on an image database system. *Information Services & Use*, 10:391–397.

[19] Bordogna, G., (1990). Pictorial indexing for an integrated picturial and textual information retrieval environment. *Information Services & Use*, 16:165–173.

[20] Chakravarthy, A., (1994). Toward semantic retrieval of pictures and video. In *Proc. Riao'94, Intelligent Multimedia Information Retrieval Systems and Management*, pp. 676–686. New York.

[21] Alshuth, P., Hermes, T., Voigt, L., and Herzog, O., (1998). On video retrieval: Content analysis by ImageMiner. In *IS&T/SPIE Symposium on Electronical Imaging Sciene & Technology (Storage and Retrieval for Images and Video Databases)*, Vol. 3312, pp. 236–247. San Jose, CA.

[22] Suhr, H., Bittner, C., Geißler, P., Jähne, B., Schneider, K., Scheper, T., Scholz, T., and Wehnert, G., (1995). In situ microscopy for on-line characterization of cell populations in bioreactors, including cell concentration measurements by depth from focus. *Biotechnology and Bioengineering*, 47:106–116.

[23] Scholz, T., Jähne, B., Suhr, H., Wehnert, G., Geißler, P., and Schneider, K., (1995). In situ determination of cell concentration in bioreactors with a new cepth from focus technique. In *Computer Analysis of Images and Patterns—Proceedings of the 6th International Conference , CAIP '95*, V. Hlaváč and R. Šára, eds., Lecture Notes in Computer Science, pp. 392–399. Prague, Czech Republic: Springer, Berlin,... ISBN 3-540-60268-2.

[24] Geißler, P. and Jähne, B., (1996). A 3D-sensor for the measurement of particle concentration from image sequences. In *Proc. of the 18th ISPRS Congress, Vienna. In Int'l Arch. of Photog. and Rem. Sens.*, Vol. 31, Part B5.

[25] Melville, W. K., Terrill, E., and Veron, F., (1997). Bubbles and turbulence under breaking waves. In *Sea Surface Sound '97 - Proceedings of the Fourth International Conference on Natural Physical Processes Associated with Sea Surface Sound*, T. G. Leighton, ed., pp. 135–146. Chilworth Manor, Hampshire, UK: CBC Print and Media Resources, Fordingbridge, Hampshire, UK. ISBN 0-85-432636-7.

[26] Nobel, P. S., (1991). *Physicochemical and Environmental Plant Physiology*. Boston: Academic Press.

[27] Kümmerlen, B., (1998). *Infrarot-Thermographie zum Studium physiologischer Parameter von Pflanzenblättern*. Diploma thesis, University of Heidelberg.

[28] Jähne, B., Münnich, K., Bösinger, R., Dutzi, A., Huber, W., and Libner, P., (1987). On the parameters influencing air-water gas exchange. *Journal of Geophysical Research*, 92(C2):1937–1949.

[29] Schimpf, U., Haußecker, H., and Jähne, B., (1999). Studies of air-sea gas transfer and micro turbulence at the ocean surface using passive thermography. In *Proc. Air-Sea Interface Symp. '99, in press*. Sydney.

[30] Jähne, B., Libner, P., Fischer, R., Billen, T., and Plate, E., (1989). Investigating the transfer process across the free aqueous viscous boundary layer by the controlled flux method. *Tellus*, **41B**:177–195.

[31] Knutson, H. and Westin, C.-F., (1993). Normalized and differential convolution. In *IEEE Conference on Computer Vision and Pattern Recognition*, pp. 515–523. IEEE.

[32] Schmundt, D., (1999). *Development of an Optical Flow Based System for the Precise Measurement of Plant Growth*. Dissertation, University of Heidelberg.

[33] Maksymowych, R., (1990). *Analysis of Growth and Development of* Xanthium. Cambridge University Press.

[34] Kron, S. and Spudich, J., (1987). Fluorescent actin filaments move on myosin fixed to a glass surface. *P.N.A.S.*, **83**:6272–6276.

[35] Eichkorn, S., (1997). *Visualisierung und Quantifizierung des CO_2 Gasaustausches mittels laserinduzierter Fluoreszenz (LIF)*. Diploma thesis, Institut für Umweltphysik, Universität Heidelberg.

[36] Münsterer, T., (1996). *LIF investigation of the mechanisms controlling airwater mass transfer at a free interface*. Dissertation, Institut für Umweltphysik, Universität Heidelberg.

[37] Hering, F., (1996). *Lagrangesche Untersuchungen des Strömungsfeldes unterhalb der wellenbewegten Wasseroberfläche mittels Bildfolgenanalyse*. Dissertation, Institute for Environmental Physics, University of Heidelberg.

[38] Engelmann, D., Garbe, C., Stöhr, M., Geißler, P., Hering, F., and Jähne, B., (1998). Stereo particle tracking. In *Proc. 8th International Symposium on Flow Visualization*. Sorrento, Italy. ISBN 0-9533991-0-9.

[39] Lenz, R., (1988). Zur Genauigkeit der Videometrie mit CCD-Sensoren. In *Proc. 10. DAGM. Symposium on Pattern Recognition 1988, Informatik-Fachberichte 180*, pp. 179–189. Berlin: Springer.

[40] Köhler, H. J., (1993). The influence of hydraulic head and hydraulic gradient on the filtration process. In *Filters in Geotechnical and Hydraulic Engineering*, Brauns, Heibaum, and Schuler, eds. Balkema: Rotterdam.

[41] Köhler, H. J., Haußecker, H., and Jähne, B., (1996). Detection of particle movements at soil interfaces due to changing hydraulic load conditions, localised by a digital image processing technique. In *2nd International Conference on Geofilters*, J. Lafleur and A. L. Rollin, eds., pp. 215–226. Montreal.

[42] Maas, H.-G., Stefanidis, A., and Grün, A., (1994). From pixels to voxels - Tracking volume elements in sequences of 3-D digital images. *International Archives of Photogrammetry and Remote Sensing*, **30**(3/2).

[43] Wenig, M., (1998). *Wolkenklassifizierung mittels Bildsequenzanalyse auf GOME-Satellitendaten*. Master's thesis, University of Heidelberg.

[44] Stutz, J. and Platt, U., (1996). Numerical analysis and error estimation of differential optical absorption spectroscopy measurements with least-squares methods. *Applied Optics*, **35**:6041–6053.

[45] Meisenheimer, K., Beckwith, S., Fockenbrock, R., Fried, J., Hippelein, H., Huang, J., Leinert, C., Phleps, S., Röser, H.-J., Thommes, E., Thompson, D., Wolf, C., and Chaffee, F., (1998). The Calar Alto deep imaging survey for galaxies and quasars at $z > 5$. In *The Young Universe*, S. D'Odorico, A. Fontana, and E. Giallongo, eds., Vol. 146 of *ASP Conf. Ser.*, p. 134.

[46] Wolf, C., Meisenheimer, K., Röser, H. J., Beckwith, S. V. W., Fockenbrock, R., Hippelein, H., Von Kuhlmann, B., Phleps, S., and Thommes, E., (1999). Did most high-redshift quasars escape detection? *Astronomy & Astrophysics*, **343**:399–406.

[47] Wolf, C., (1999). *Vielfarben-Klassifikation in CADIS und die Suche nach Quasaren*. Dissertation, Universität Heidelberg.

[48] Uttenweiler, D., Weber, C., and Fink, R. H. A., (1998). Mathematical modeling and fluorescence imaging to study the Ca^{2+}-turnover in skinned muscle fibers. *Biophys. J.*, **74**:1640–1653.

[49] Bornfleth, H., Sätzler, K., Eils, R., and Cremer, C., (1998). High-precision distance measurements and volume-conserving segmentation of objects near and below the resolution limit in three-dimensional confocal microscopy. *J. Microsc.*, **189**:118–136.

[50] Zink, D., Bornfleth, H., Visser, A., Cremer, C., and Cremer, T., (1999). Organization of early and late replicating DNA in human chromosome territories. *Exp. Cell Res.*, **247**:176–188.

Index